Canadian NURSING FACES THE FUTURE

SECOND EDITION

EDITORS
Alice J. Baumgart, RN, PhD
Vice-Principal, Human Services
Queen's University, Kingston, Ontario

AND
Jenniece Larsen, RN, PhD
Professor and Dean, Faculty of Nursing
University of Manitoba, Winnipeg, Manitoba

illustrated

 Mosby
Year Book

St. Louis Baltimore Boston Chicago London Philadelphia Sydney Toronto

Mosby
Year Book
Dedicated to Publishing Excellence

Executive Editor: Linda L. Duncan
Developmental Editor: Glennis Zilm
Associate Developmental Editor: Kathy Sartori
Project Manager: Carol Sullivan Wiseman
Production Editor: Florence Achenbach
Designer: Elizabeth Fett

SECOND EDITION

Printed in Canada

Mosby-Year Book, Inc.
11830 Westline Industrial Drive
St. Louis, Missouri 63146

Times Mirror Professional Publishing
130 Flaska Drive
Markham, Ontario L6G 1B8

Canadian Cataloging in Publication Data

Canadian nursing faces the future
2nd ed.
Includes bibliographical references and index.
ISBN 0-8016-6330-X

1. Nursing—Canada.   I. Baumgart, Alice J.
II. Larsen, Jenniece.

RT6.A1C36   1992   362.1'73'0971   C92-094056-0

93 94 95 96   GW/BR   9 8 7 6 5 4 3 2

Contributors

Carolyn B. Attridge, RN, PhD
Associate Professor and Former Director
School of Nursing, University of Victoria
Victoria, British Columbia

Irmajean Bajnok, RN, MScN
Education Advisor, The Gerald P. Turner
Department of Nursing
Mount Sinai Hospital
Toronto, Ontario

Alice J. Baumgart, RN, PhD
Vice-principal, Human Services
Queen's University
Kingston, Ontario

Joy D. Calkin, RN, PhD
Vice President (Academic) and Provost
The University of Calgary
Calgary, Alberta

Karen I. Chalmers, RN, PhD
Assistant Professor
School of Nursing, University of
Manitoba
Winnipeg, Manitoba

Kathleen M. Clark, RN, PhD
Research Coordinator (McMaster)
Quality of Nursing Worklife Research
Unit
McMaster University School of Nursing/
University of Toronto Faculty of Nursing
Toronto, Ontario

Kathleen A. Dier, RN, MScN
Professor Emeritus (Nursing)
University of Alberta
Edmonton, Alberta

Gail J. Donner, RN, PhD
Director of Nursing Education
Hospital for Sick Children, Toronto;
Associate Professor (part-time)
School of Nursing, University of Toronto
Toronto, Ontario

Peggy Anne Field, RN, PhD
Professor, Faculty of Nursing
University of Alberta
Edmonton, Alberta

Theresa George, RN, PhD
Associate Professor, School of Nursing
University of Manitoba
Winnipeg, Manitoba

Jean Cuthand Goodwill, RN, LLD
President, Canadian Society for
Circumpolar Health
Fort Qu'Appelle, Saskatchewan

David M. Gregory, RN, MN
Assistant Professor
School of Nursing, University of
Manitoba;
Doctoral Candidate, University of
Arizona
Tucson, Arizona

Judith M. Hibberd, RN, PhD
Associate Professor, Faculty of Nursing
University of Alberta
Edmonton, Alberta

Phyllis Marie Jensen, RN, PhD
Consultant, Research on Health and
Justice;
Private Practice "Smokefree"
Toronto, Ontario

Linda J. Kristjanson, RN, PhD
Assistant Professor, School of Nursing
University of Manitoba
Winnipeg, Manitoba

Louise Lemieux-Charles, RN, PhD
Assistant Professor, Department of
Health Administration;
Program Director, Hospital Management
Research Unit
University of Toronto
Toronto, Ontario

Jenniece Larsen, RN, PhD
Dean, Faculty of Nursing
University of Manitoba
Winnipeg, Manitoba

Rita Maloney, RN, PhD
Dean, Faculty of Nursing
Queen's University
Kingston, Ontario

Jessie Mantle, RN, MSN
Professor, School of Nursing
University of Victoria;
Clinical Nurse Specialist (Gerontology)
Juan de Fuca Hospitals
Victoria, British Columbia

Dorothy Meilicke, RN, MEd
Manager, Operational Commissioning
Cross Cancer Institute;
Assistant Professor, Faculty of Nursing
University of Alberta
Edmonton, Alberta

Helen K. Mussallem, OC, RN, EdD
Consultant;
President VON Canada
Ottawa, Ontario

Dorothy M. Pringle, RN, PhD
Dean, Faculty of Nursing
University of Toronto
Toronto, Ontario

Margaret Risk, RN, MScN
Executive Director
College of Nurses of Ontario
Toronto, Ontario

Judith Anne Ritchie, RN, PhD
Professor, School of Nursing and Faculty
of Graduate Studies
Dalhousie University;
Director of Nursing Research
Izaak Walton Killam Hospital for Children
Halifax, Nova Scotia

Donna J. Roe, RN, MScN
National Executive Director
Victorian Order of Nurses for Canada
Ottawa, Ontario

Donna Lynn Smith, RN, MEd
Manager of Program Development, Long
Term Care Branch
Acute and Long Term Care Division
Alberta Health
Edmonton, Alberta

Shirley M. Stinson, RN, EdD, LLD
Professor, Faculty of Nursing;
Professor, Department of Health Services
Administration and Community Medicine
University of Alberta
Edmonton, Alberta

Janet L. Storch, RN, PhD
Dean, Faculty of Nursing
University of Calgary
Calgary, Alberta

Marie-France Thibaudeau, RN, MScN
Doyenne, Faculté des sciences infirmières
l'Université de Montréal
Montréal, Quebec

Sherry Wiebe, RN, LLB
Nurse and Lawyer
Consulting Practice in Health Law
Winnipeg, Manitoba

Dorothy Wylie, RN, MSc (HRD)
Principal, Dorothy M. Wylie Associates;
Associate Professor, Faculty of Nursing
University of Toronto
Toronto, Ontario

Reviewers

Darlene Steven, RN, BScN, BA, MHSA, PhD
Associate Professor School of Nursing
Lakehead University
Thunder Bay, Ontario

Miriam J. Stewart, PhD
Professor School of Nursing
Dalhousie University
Halifax, Nova Scotia

Foreword

The challenge for Canadian nurses, as they prepare for a new century, is directed by the inevitable changes that will occur as our health care system moves toward the goal of universal well-being for all. Canada's nurses are competent professionals, committed to world health and the promotion of community-based, preventive care measures. The size of the task only makes the profession more determined to prepare to meet these challenges. Nurses will be ready, not only for professional and personal reasons but also because as knowledgable, key participants they can create a better future for Canada and its citizens.

As Executive Directors of two major national nursing associations, we are often called upon to provide Canadian perspectives on current issues, to share impressions, and to verify perceived trends generated within the discipline of nursing. The advent of this new edition of *Canadian Nursing Faces the Future* facilitates our task, as well as fills obvious gaps in Canadian nursing literature.

We congratulate the authors for their foresight in creating a book that captures and analyses key issues facing nursing as it enters the twenty-first century. The book succeeds in identifying nursing's place in the ever-changing health care context through examination of the complex issues that encompass national unity, professional responsibility, and constitutional reform. As well, these issues are placed within an evolutionary framework, thus contributing to an historical understanding of the major roles played by such factors as education and power in the development of nursing options for the future.

The importance of this book to the nursing scene is already well acknowledged. Since the first edition appeared in 1988, this book has been widely quoted by nurses, educators, students, other health care leaders, and politicians. The strength of the book lies in its Canadian orientation, its analytical approach to the issues, and the quality of its contributors. The fact that a new, much revised edition is already necessary is testament to the ever-changing face of nursing and to the need for nurses to be abreast of issues that will shape the future of the profession and of health care in Canada.

Shaping the future has long been a key activity of both Alice Baumgart and Jenniece Larsen, and they have contributed to some of nursing's key changes in the past. These author-editors are to be commended for their foresight in selecting other nursing leaders-contributors who bring a broad Canadian vision and an acknowledged expertise to nursing issues. In this latest endeavor, all contributors skillfully provide and articulate overview of current trends and issues and create a cohesive vantage point for viewing the future so that nursing can take further action.

Jeannette Bouchard, Executive Director
Canadian Association for University
Schools of Nursing
and
Judith Oulton, Executive Director
Canadian Nurses Association

Preface

E ach generation of nurses faces its own challenges and, by its response to them, puts its distinctive stamp on the profession's covenant with society. The traditional covenant between nursing and society has been rooted in nineteenth century Nightingale ethics of caring as a moral duty. Although the imprint of this ethic is still felt, its force has waned. Today, the clarion call is for an enlarged and refurbished convenant, a covenant that has a healthier balance between the public duties nurses are expected to discharge and their rights to attend to their own needs and aspirations.

Striking such a balance is complex and often elusive. Yet there are encouraging signs of change. As Canadian nurses move toward a new century, they are seeking changes in how they live and work. This book focuses on how Canadian nursing is changing and on the paths being taken to make it more responsive to emerging needs and circumstances. Change is normal to the human condition. To help shape the process an appreciation of historical antecedents of contemporary developments is important, as is an adequate mapping and analysis of current trends and issues.

Until the publication in 1988 of the first edition of *Canadian Nursing Faces the Future* and the publication in the same year of a companion text, *Canadian Nursing: Issues and Perspectives*, edited by Drs. Jannetta McPhail and Janet Kerr, Canadian nurses, nursing students, and others interested in the future of Canadian nursing had difficulty finding written analyses of many of the pertinent themes. Admittedly, Canadian nurses had available to them a voluminous English language literature on nursing and, to a lesser extent, a French language literature. However, little of this literature incoporated a Canadian perspective that took into account the unique history of Canadian nursing and characteristic features of Canadian society. Nor did this literature give much recognition to the complex interplay between Canadian nursing, the Canadian health care system, provincial and federal health care programs, and social and economic policies.

Our students' increasing reluctance to purchase American texts, together with our personal frustrations in trying to piece together reading lists on the unique aspects of Canadian nursing and its rich historical legacy, led us to write the first edition. That a second edition is needed is a source of satisfaction to authors no less than to publishers.

The original purposes of the book remain the same for the second edition:

1. To enable the reader to obtain, in one volume, information on dominant trends and issues affecting contemporary Canadian nursing.
2. To demonstrate how the impact of these trends and issues is shaped and affected by the particular history, structure, and values of Canadian society.
3. To identify Canadian nurses, past and present, who have participated in creating a distinctive profession whose lists of accomplishments, nationally and internationally, can be a source of pride to all Canadians.

As in the first edition, the perspectives we adopted in choosing topics for inclusion in the second edition are both theoretical and practical. From a theoretical standpoint, we believe that the book should highlight issues and trends in practice and education that reflect the uniqueness of nursing in Canada. The book should also describe the environments in which nurses in Canada practice, and the support systems, regulatory framework, and research bases that aid Canadian nurses in fulfilling their mandate to society.

In keeping the list of topics for this edition to a manageable size, we are indebted to our anonymous reviewers and our publisher, Mosby–Year Book, Inc. We are also indebted to the many nurses across Canada who expressed their enthusiasm for the first volume, offered their feedback on the topics covered, and underlined that an updated edition would be welcomed.

The second edition resembles the first in purpose, character, and scope, but it is, in important respects, a new book. Three things are responsible for these changes. First, much has happened in Canadian nursing since 1988. Second, we have been heirs to helpful comments from many readers. Third, the lapse of time and the widening knowledge and interpretations now possible in regard to selected issues gave us an opportunity to alter the treatment and placement of selected chapters.

Among the many changes are new chapters on technology, regulation, and international nursing, three areas receiving renewed attention and re-evaluation in the 1990s. In the first edition of this book, consideration of technology was confined to the use of computers in nursing. Heightened concerns about costs and about humane applications of a wide variety of health care technologies have generated a need for nurses to have a broader understanding of technology design and use, including its social impact on the workplace. In regard to regulation, legislation governing professional practice and the operation of health care facilities and services often embodies a restricted view of the contributions nursing can make to health care. Removal of these legal barriers is once again coming under the microscope in Canada and elsewhere as adaptability and cost-effective use of health workers becomes a more urgent consideration in health care reform. The addition of a chapter on international nursing underlines the impressive contributions of Canadain nurses to the international scene and the growing importance of globalization of economic activity and international cooperation as forces affecting the health agenda of the 1990s.

This second edition also provides new or expanded treatment of social change processes and the involvement of nurses in health care innovation and reform. For example, the emphasis in the chapter on the Victorian Order of Nurses has shifted from the provision of home care services to the influential role that all voluntary agencies play in pioneering new health care programs and services. An enlarged overview chapter on nursing power reflects the evolution now underway in public policy processes in Canada and how this influences the public dialogues on many of the critical issues of the day. Although these are the most apparent changes, new authors, deletion of certain chapters, and extensive rewriting and updating of every section of the book has been undertaken. The changes reflect new forces that have come into play in health care decision making, including strong pressures for nurses to find ways of maintaining excellent care in the face of economic constraints.

The selection of contributors to the second edition was guided by many of the same considerations as the first edition: to have knowledgeable and competent authors; to enhance the visibility of Canadian nurses who are helping to shape the future of the profession, nationally and internationally; to have contributors who represented a wealth of knowledge, technical expertise, and first-hand experience with trends and issues they discuss. It was also our desire to include a broad mix of practitioners, administrators, educators, researchers, thinkers, and doers. We asked each of them to write a chapter, grounded in the history of nursing in Canada, that identified prominent Canadian leaders and events that have shaped the present. They were to identify current issues, problems, and pressure points. In response to reviews of the first edition, we also asked them to bring into sharper focus future directions and to present a vision of where Canadian nursing should go from here. In addition, they were asked to include new Canadian source materials in their references and bibliographies.

Our intellectual support, material resources, and emotional sustenance for the second edition, as for the first, came from many sources. Our students at the University of Manitoba and Queen's University continue to test and sharpen our ideas. We have also had the privilege of serving as Executive Officers of two national nursing associations: the Canadian Association of University Schools of Nursing (CAUSN) and the Canadian Nurses Association (CNA). These opportunities have enriched our understanding of Canadian nurses in the nursing profession in Canada immeasurably. Many colleagues and friends have also helped by their suggestions and criticisms, and by their continuing support of our work at every stage.

There are a number of people, institutions, and organizations we especially want to thank for their part in helping us to revise the book. The Canadian Nurses Association, the Canadian Association of University Schools of Nursing, the National Federation of Nurses' Unions, the provincial and territorial nurses' associations and unions, and the College of Nurses in Ontario all provided us with valuable assistance in compiling information about their organizations and keeping us in touch with the merging trends.

Joan Gilchrist, a former CNA President, and Pat Cutshall, Executive Director of the Registered Nurses Association of British Columbia, gave us the benefit of their valuable knowledge and insight regarding professional associations by their reading of selected sections of the book.

The pictures that accompany each chapter were culled from many sources. We are grateful for the assistance of our chapter authors, their colleagues, and friends for making this pictorial material available to us and for giving us permission to reproduce it. We continue to applaud the special efforts of Elizabeth Hawkins Brady and Martha Ippersiel, reference librarians at the Hellen K. Mussallem Library, Canadian Nurses Association. They continued to be valuable resources to us in locating appropriate materials for the book. The reference librarians at the Woodward Biomedical Library in Vancouver also helped us greatly by verifying countless bits of information.

Our research assistants made the task of locating source materials less onerous. Katherine Kilpatrick, a graduate in Classics and now a nursing undergraduate at Queen's University, was a continuing source of help in obtaining up-to-date references on Canadian nursing and compiling statistics for the chapter on the nursing work force. We would also like to acknowledge the assistance of Major Beverley Anderson, an officer with the Canadian Armed Forces and a graduate student in nursing from the University of Manitoba. Her support, cheer, and assistance were much appreciated. Nursing colleagues Bonnie Hoffer and Brenda Snider from Manitoba and Judith Haines of Ontario deserve special thanks for their research and scholarly work on selected chapters.

As senior university administrators, our schedules were often filled to overflowing with meetings and appointments. The help and support of our associates has been important to complete the revisions. They are Dr. Janet Beaton, Associate Director, Graduate Program, and Dr. Ina Bramadat, Associate Director, Undergraduate Programs, School of Nursing, University of Manitoba. We are also grateful to our administrative staff, Doreen McGuff in Winnipeg and Kenneth Brodie and Deborah Shea in Kingston, for attending to a myriad of administrative duties as we toiled away.

Our publisher, Mosby–Year Book, Inc., continues to be extraordinarily helpful and patient. Rick Perry was always supportive and ready to provide cheers from the bleachers. Linda Duncan had the responsibility for keeping up the appropriate degree of pressure to ensure that our writing continued, and Kathy Sartori handled many details of production; they deserve a resounding vote of thanks. In the first edition we gave special thanks to Jeff Snook, formerly with Mosby–Year Book, Inc. Toronto, who encouraged us to pursue our ideas for a book, and to John Hirst, International Manager, Mosby–Year Book, Inc. Toronto, who understood the importance of having a Canadian nursing text and supported us in the process of preparing our first manuscript. We continue to appreciate the important role they played in our writing efforts.

Three persons without whose assistance this revision could not have been completed are our secretaries, Mary Edwardsson, Shirley Dick, and Barbara Paquette. Until September 1991, Mary Edwardsson carried the burden of responsibility for coordinating our efforts, handling correspondence, and following up on the many details that go into the preparation of a multi-authored manuscript. Her common sense, conscientiousness, and effectiveness are gratefully acknowledged. Following her retirement, Shirley Dick continued these sterling efforts. Barbara Paquette bore responsibility for keeping the channels of communication between Winnipeg and Kingston flowing smoothly and seeing that files were complete and in their proper place. She did this with her usual extraordinary grace and efficiency. Joyce Boyechko of the University of Manitoba and Maureen Fagan of Queen's typed many of our manuscripts to meet our editors' exacting requirements. All five contributed essential expertise.

Our families and friends will once again be glad to know that our book-writing labors are once again ended. A special group of people include Mawney, Christopher, and David Larsen, Jack Scharf, Dr. Arlene Crowe, and Dr. Wesley McDonald. We also owe a debt of gratitude to Dora Scharf, at whose cottage in Northern Saskatchewan we initially drafted the outline for the book and where we later put our hearts and minds into preparing the second edition.

Finally, we continue to be grateful to Glennis Zilm, a nursing colleague and our developmental editor. She continued to supply her extraordinary technical and editorial skills to each chapter of the book. Her dual expertise in nursing and in preparation of publications contributed immeasurably to the overall design and contents of the book. We continue to be thankful for her friendship and expertise and for helping us to reap the intellectual rewards of collaborative efforts.

Alice J. Baumgart
Jenniece Larsen

Contents

SECTION I

NURSING IN CANADA

Student nurses entering the profession today, as in the past, will face a challenging, dynamic, and exciting future, one filled with development and change. (Photograph of nursing students, School of Nursing, taken 1987 by Annette Borger and supplied courtesy of Queen's University School of Nursing.)

CHAPTER ONE

Introduction to Nursing in Canada

JENNIECE LARSEN, RN, PhD
ALICE J. BAUMGART, RN, PhD

Jenniece Larsen, RN, BScN, MEd, PhD (Alberta), is Professor and Director, School of Nursing, University of Manitoba.

Alice J. Baumgart, RN, BSN (British Columbia), MSc (McGill), PhD (Toronto), is Vice Principal, Human Services, Queen's University.

Both are well-known nursing leaders who speak and write nationally and internationally on issues and trends in nursing and health care, and both teach issues and trends in nursing and health care courses in their respective universities. They have collaborated on the planning and writing of this text and selected the authors, all experts in their various areas, to highlight the various issues that Canadian nurses will face during the next decade.

O ften called a sleeping giant, the nursing profession in Canada is awakening to the unique skills and insights it contributes to the delivery of health services and the quest for an economically sustainable health care future. This newfound sense of self-worth and political efficacy owes much to broadly based changes in the surrounding society—changes in economic and political realities, alterations in the age composition of the population, and shifts in social attitudes regarding how women and other equality seeking groups should be involved in work and education.

These societal trends, in interaction with the dramatic transformations of health care now underway in Canada, have deeply touched the personal and working lives of nurses. They have also reshaped nursing practice roles and responsibilities. Nursing's supporting infrastructures, including its educational, administrative, and research activities and its array of professional associations and unions, have grown and diversified accordingly.

Altogether, this complex set of personal and professional changes in Canadian nursing has redefined what nurses are and how they fulfill their societal mission. In the process, new opportunites inviting creativity and innovation have opened up and heightened nurses' career expectations and ambitions. At the same time, a widening gap between the rapidly changing real world of nursing and prevailing public perceptions and stereotypes results in serious stresses and strains in the workplace and undermines public understanding of the services nurses provide.

To redress these problems and capitalize on nursing's traditional strengths and emerging potential requires, among other things, investment by society and by nurses themselves in new visions of the future of nursing. These visions must attract and retain able practitioners and develop their capacities for leadership. Such capacities should enable nurses to be effective spokespersons, well informed on key issues, able to command the support of the nursing community, and also able to articulate the issues for the public and for policymakers.

Securing new investments for nursing is, of course, a highly political and often painful process. As a female-dominated profession, nursing is the subject of extraordinary public ambivalence. This ambivalence is tied into broader problems of gender and class in our society (Reverby, 1987) and is reflected in the disparity between nursing's central role in health care and its meager powers in influencing health policy.

The challenge for Canadian nurses, as they prepare for the emerging world of the twenty-first century, will be to strike a new balance or workable equilibrium between the accrued skills of the work force and the quality of the social and material supports available to it. This is not a simple task. Given the pace of societal change and the growing complexity of nurses' work and personal lives, the agenda for professional action must attend to several levels or dimensions of nursing work, including the links between nursing and the surrounding society.

A framework adapted from Friss (1982) provides a useful model for charting a manageable course through this complexity. Building from Friss' framework, we believe a mutual fit or workable equilibrium must be sought between six facets of professional activity. These facets are:

1. *Knowledge* fit: the extent to which nurses' knowledge and skills are used, developed, and recognized
2. *Task* fit: the extent to which the design or organization of nursing work is meaningful and challenging, making possible the use of discretion and judgment
3. *Ethical* fit: the extent to which individual and professional values of nurses are congruent with those of employing agencies and institutions
4. *Psychological* fit: the opportunities available to nurses for achievement, recognition, responsibility, and status

5. *Economic rewards* fit: the extent to which nurses receive financial rewards and benefits deemed appropriate
6. *Political* fit: the capacity of nurses to communicate effectively with the public and the opportunities available to them for involvement and participation in policy development and decision making

To the extent that one dimension is neglected or out of balance, the balance in the others is altered. The growing maturity and stature of the nursing profession in Canada is reflected in the greater number of these dimensions now receiving concerted attention by the profession and by the public. The six dimensions in our model also serve as indicators of nursing requirements in the future.

This book looks at these dimensions in relation to five broad aspects of nursing in Canada. They are:

1. The social milieu in which nursing in Canada enacts its commitments to society
2. Major domains of nursing practice
3. Characteristic features and variables affecting nursing workplaces
4. Systems of nursing education
5. Power and use of political processes by the organized profession and its members

For each topic, a diverse set of analyses is offered so that readers may gain an appreciation of the historical and contemporary forces that contributed to the current ferment in Canadian nursing. Situations calling for reform, as well as gaps in knowledge, are identified, and problems and issues needing resolution are highlighted.

Although each aspect of nursing in the book is analyzed in its own right, certain broad features, or universal characteristics, are considered in this introductory chapter. Three features—professionalism, operational structures or bureaucracies, and gender—may be looked upon as basic determinants or organizers of what Canadian nurses do and how they do it, regardless of the nursing pursuits or settings in question. A fourth feature—change—affects all the others and is a common thread. The chapter concludes with comments on the Canadian context into which all these factors and dimensions must fit.

PROFESSIONALISM

The first of these broad features is the concept of professionalism and what is meant when an occupation claims to be a profession. Nurses tend to describe themselves as professionals, as do many members of the public. Moreover, organized nursing bodies such as the Canadian Nurses Association, provincial nurses' associations, and nurses' unions draw on conceptions of professional roles and responsibilities as they seek to influence nursing's destiny. Generally, however, professionalism has been regarded as a mixed blessing (Noddings, 1990).

The struggle of Canadian nurses for professional stature began in the early 1900s in the efforts to obtain provincial legislation to regulate who practiced nursing. Today the struggle is evidenced in the endeavors to obtain university-based education for entrance to the profession and the work for a research-based nursing practice. The legacy of the early efforts is that the nursing profession in Canada is among a handful of self-regulating professions; others include medicine, law, engineering, dentistry, and architecture. Provincial professional practice acts granting self-regulation usually outline the scope of professional practice, criteria for registration and discipline of members, standards of practice and education, and codes of ethical conduct.

Nursing legislation, like other professional legislation in Canada, embodies many of the classic characteristics that distinguish professional work. These characteristics were originally formulated by Flexner during his study of medical education in Canada and the United States in 1910. Later descriptions of professions (e.g., Goode, 1960; Greenwood, 1957; Taylor, 1968) include remarkably similar attributes. These attributes include:

1. Possessing specialized knowledge and skills, which are usually acquired in universities, and which are reflected in the approach to professional practice
2. Accepting an ongoing intellectual commitment to improving and updating one's knowledge and skills
3. Having professional autonomy in decision making concerning client needs and services
4. Sharing a set of values about work with clients and colleagues
5. Having collegial responsibility for setting standards and for discipline and ethical conduct

At the core of these attributes is the nature of the relationship that professionals have with clients. Professionals declare publicly that they will meet distinctive standards of conduct when serving clients (Curtin, 1990). This conception of how professions may be distinguished from other occupations has been criticized on many grounds, including inadequate recognition of the power dimensions of client and work relationships (Friedson, 1970; Johnson, 1972) and neglect of class and gender issues (Stacey, 1988).

Historically, occupations that successfully claimed to be professions and thus gained autonomy and became dominant are male-dominated occupations; occupations that have had difficulties in becoming professions have been female dominated (Stacey, 1988). This gender order, which reflects the differential valuing of knowledge and tasks and the establishment of authority relationships betweeen the sexes, is clearly evident in the claims of medicine and nursing for recognition as professional occupations. Historically, the myths, symbols, and values associated with professionalism have been used by members of the dominant coalition (organized medicine, hospital administrators, and government officials) to control nursing through manipulation of the "good nurse–good woman" connection and by the co-option of nursing leaders and nursing organizations. The current unrest by nurse practitioners and nursing leaders alike suggests that the ideology of professionalism as a control strategy has run its course. Nurses now expect the privileges and benefits, as well as the obligations and duties, of being a professional.

A further criticism of professionalism concerns the breakdown of mechanisms for accountability to the public, such as failure of self-disciplinary procedures and the suppression of alternative approaches to attending to client needs. As a consequence, professionals have lost some degree of public trust. In response, provincial governments have revised the professional practice acts of most self-regulatory professions, including nursing, to limit their statutory powers. Actions taken include appointment of consumers to professional governing bodies, requirements that decision making be more open to the public, more rigorous scrutiny of misconduct and incompetencies, and governmental approval of changes to professional regulations and bylaws.

As knowledge becomes more specialized and technology more complex, the power and control of professionals is enhanced. This is true not only of power over clients but also power in major government and corporate institutions. Jennings, Callahan, and Wolf (1987) argue that growth of professional power must carry a stronger sense of ethical responsibility to clients and to society as a whole. In addition to expert service to individual clients, human service professionals must inform and enrich the society by providing their distinctive perspective on public policy issues. Professionals, through associations such as the national and provincial nurses' associations, perform this societal role indirectly through the development of standards and codes of professional practice and directly through political action to influence public opinion and shape legislation. In this way, professions serve the common good by enhancing the quality of discourse about society's goals and by contributing to what Jennings, Callahan, and Wolf call "the collective and cooperative search for a reasonable and workable deliberative process that respects the diverse ethical perspectives and traditions of our pluralistic society" (1987, p. 10).

PROFESSIONAL BUREAUCRACIES

A more far-reaching challenge to professionalism comes from the organization of the contemporary work world, often referred to as "the system." Most professionals now practice as members of large-scale bureaucracies. Indeed, it is estimated that two thirds of all professionals in Canada work in public sector institutions (Ponak, 1982). The professional paradigm for organizing work has its roots in an earlier era when professionals were mainly independent agents or self-employed workers in the marketplace. Difficulties arise when professionals are employees acting both in a corporate capacity and as agents for their clients. Equally problematic are rigid hierarchies that limit decision-making options and cloud professional accountability to clients. The design of organizational forms suitable to the complexities of simultaneous practice of various groups of professionals needs considerable theoretical and practical attention. The need for the attention is acute in professional bureaucracies where nurses work side by side with myriad other professional practitioners.

Any attempt to understand present trends and issues in professional nursing practice must include a second broad feature or organizer, namely, the structures and modes of operation of the large professional bureaucracies in which most nurses in Canada are employed. Drucker (1988) describes such work environments as knowledge-based or information-based organizations. Examples include hospitals, public health agencies, and universities and colleges.

The primary work in a professional bureaucracy is performed by an operating core composed largely of professionals from a variety of specialties (or disciplines) who direct and evaluate their own work based on feedback from peers, clients, and central administration. Each professional group has its own training, knowledge, skills, and language. Individual professionals work relatively independently of colleagues, but closely with clients. For example, a staff nurse works alone in a patient's room or home when providing nursing care, somewhat isolated from other nurses and supervisors. Each professional also has fairly broad decision-making authority regarding work with clients.

Given the complexity of the work of professionals, the usual command and control approaches to standardization and coordination of work found in other bureaucratic organizations such as factories or the military are dysfunctional in a professional bureaucracy. The standards of professional work originate largely outside the organization, usually with self-governing professional associations to which the professionals belong. Professional associations rely on educational organizations to train and socialize neophytes into professional roles. As a result, most of the necessary coordination between professionals occurs as a function of the standardization of skills and knowledge. Each professional group learns what to expect of others in the work situation.

Professional bureaucracies are highly decentralized, and professionals exercise a great deal of influence over services to clients. In health care organizations, the influence of the various professionals is distributed unevenly on the basis of knowledge and skills. The resulting status differences among various groups of professionals may produce considerable conflict over resource acquisition, territorial prerogatives, and quality of client services. The potential for conflict has escalated in recent years as governments search for cost control and increased efficiency.

A major part of the work of administrative staff in professional bureaucracies concerns the inevitable conflict that arises from the operating core of the organization. Administrators have key roles at the boundary of the organization with governmental, professional, and consumer groups, to name just a few. Administrators buffer professionals from external pressures and encourage groups outside the organization to support the work of the professionals inside. An example is the work that nursing administrators do with community-based service clubs, which raise money for special needs such as equipment for burn units. Another aspect of this buffer role involves responding to the demands of professional associations and unions on behalf of their members inside the organization. For example, the Registered Nurses Association of Ontario (1988) and the Manitoba Organization of Nursing Associations (1989) commissioned highly publicized studies on the quality of work life of nurses. These studies were used by nursing administrators in Manitoba and Ontario hospitals to provide advice to their governing boards and executive officers on improving working conditions for their nursing employees.

The work of nurses in large bureaucracies is also significantly affected by the introduction of new programs and activities through the work of "professional entrepreneurs" (Mintzberg, 1983, p. 201) who are able to amass the necessary financial and political support from inside and outside the organization (e.g., establishment of a heart transplant program affects not only the skills and knowledge required by the individual nurses involved but also the allocation of human and financial resources within the nursing department as a whole).

The many tensions and difficulties experienced by professionals who work in large bureaucracies is the subject of a voluminous body of writings by organizational theorists. However, with the notable exception of early studies by Corwin and Taves (1962) and Kramer (1974) and a handful of recent writings on women's work (Game and Pringle, 1984; Oakley, 1986; Stacey, 1988), nursing has received scant attention.

The size and cost of the professional nursing labor force in most professional bureaucracies is vast in terms of the organization's overall budget and total work force. Yet most nursing issues are invisible to everyone except nurses, and nurses themselves often fail to understand their workplace issues within the broader organizational and social context. The resultant "mutual myopia" ensures the marginalization of nursing practice during organizational and public policy debates (Robinson, 1989).

Drucker (1988) recommends that fundamental reform in professional bureaucracies must address the following four special organizational problems:

1. Developing rewards, recognition, and career opportunities for professionals
2. Creating a common vision in an organization of professionals
3. Devising a structure to administer an organization of professionals
4. Ensuring the supply, preparation, and testing of organization leaders

Specific recommendations to address these special problems have been made repeatedly in numerous reports, past and present, by various professional nurses' associations and nurses' unions and more recently in documents from employers' associations and governments. Recent labor disputes and nursing shortages catapulted the need for fundamental reform of nursing workplaces to the front pages of the nation's press. Yet nothing much has changed. The sense of powerlessness of nurses to control their practice and the quality of their work experience continues.

Deficiencies in nursing workplaces historically receive scant attention. In a zeal to enhance the quality of clinical nursing, the significance of the organizational context to the performance of professional nurses has been virtually ignored. The predominant strategy has been simply to recruit a new supply of nurses. That strategy has run its course despite changing expectations by nurses and the demand for nurses. The decline in applications to schools of nursing as a result of declining birth rates and new career opportunities for women makes the need for creative thinking and action an urgent one. Morgan (1986) reminds us that "there is a close relationship between the way we think and the way we act, and that many organizational problems are embedded in our thinking" (p. 335). Current approaches to thinking about organizations and organizational problems rarely match the complexity, ambiguity, and paradoxes of organizational life.

GENDER AND NURSING WORK

As a major force for change, social movements represent conscious, collective activities to "protest against the established power structure and against the dominant norms and values" (Dahlerup, 1986, p. 2). The women's movement has sharply criticized the enormous social, physical, and emotional costs that conventional bureaucracies impose on front-line workers. Nursing as a largely female occupation must be seen within the context of broad social changes in gender roles and in women's conceptions of themselves. Nursing exemplifies many of the limitations of

so-called women's occupations or women's ghettos. The dynamics involved constitute the third strand or broad feature of nursing that is important to take into account
in considering contemporary nursing trends and issues in Canada.

The history of the development of nursing work is ideal for studying the social
construction of gender in Western societies. In recent years, nurses have begun to
examine their history with a more critical lens, resulting in re-interpretation and
fresh analysis. Any analysis of the gendered nature of nursing work requires the
recognition that in all societies where social institutions have developed outside of
the home, there is a division of labor into public and domestic domains (Stacey and
Price, 1981).

Until the latter part of the nineteenth century, most nursing, like other aspects
of health and illness care, took place in the home or was provided by members of
religious orders who cared for the poor and a few travellers in their monastaries and
hospices. The sick were cared for by female members of households or, if the family
were financially able, by women who were hired to come into the home. These
nursing tasks, like the tasks performed by housewives and household servants, were
part of the domestic division of labor. As Stacey (1988) observes, "the nurses were
domestic servants" (p. 91).

Women were employed in the hospitals of the nineteenth century as nurses to
care for the sick while performing domestic work. While these women have been
portrayed as unskilled, untrustworthy "Sairey Gamps," the harshness of their work
and living conditions is slowly being documented (Abel-Smith, 1960; Davis, 1980).
Successive reforms in training, cleanliness, and effectiveness weaned nursing away
from the cruder aspects of domestic labor. Led by the efforts in England of Elizabeth
Fry and, later, Florence Nightingale, nursing was slowly transformed from domestic
service into a respectable occupation (Williams, 1980). However restricted and controlled, modern nursing offered Victorian women acceptable, even praiseworthy,
work in the public domain. At the same time, nursing committed them to a "great
deal of drudgery, long hours, low pay and subservience to medical men" (Stacey,
1988, p. 96).

Two classes of women were recruited to be nurses: upper class, often spinster,
women seeking an escape from oppressive domestic situations, who often became
leaders; and working class women, who were the ordinary ward probationers (Abel-
Smith, 1960). The higher social class of many of the women was a "constant source
of annoyance to medical and surgical officers" who feared that training of nurses
would undermine male authority (Abel-Smith, 1960, p. 65). Probationers were to be
Christian ladies displaying womanly qualities of attractiveness, patience, and virtue.
The probationer's training, haphazard at best, consisted of practical instruction at
the hand of the ward sister concerning treatments for various types of illness and
hard, often unpleasant, physical labor. Brockbank (1970) quotes one English probationer as writing in 1893 that the training:

> in the sense that nurses require it, embraces habits of order, cleanliness, gentleness and
> quietness: without these, the theoretical training would be worth nothing, and no true
> woman would object to scouring provided it was for the good of the patient. (p. 65)

This situation began to change dramatically when Florence Nightingale outlined
the foundational principles on which nursing was to be conducted and described

how relationships between nurses and the other members of hospital staff should be carried out. Nightingale envisioned nursing as a highly disciplined occupation with its own code of conduct and ethical standards. However, as Garmarnikow (1978) observes, one of the long-term consequences was that the organization of the modern hospital mirrored the bourgeois Victorian household: doctor-father, nurse-mother, and patient-child. The focus of nursing work was the care of the patient's personal hygiene and the supervision and often cleaning of the patient's environment. The nurse had her own sphere of influence, but, as Stacey (1988) notes, "it was to be one in which she was subordinate to the doctor and bound to take his orders" (p. 64).

Nursing emerged from Victorian England encased in two forms of the division of labor: (1) the division of labor between domestic and public and (2) the sexual division of labor in health care. Translated from the domestic domain, nursing is still stereotyped as the natural work of women relying on knowledge either intuitive in nature or experientially learned and therefore requiring little special education, research, reward, or recognition. This situation is compounded by the blatant sexual division of labor in health care where world-wide cultural values have embedded masculine and feminine prescriptions into what nurses and physicians are able to do for their patients and for themselves (Delamothe, 1988; Game and Pringle, 1984). Physicians cure and nurses care! These divisions are sharply drawn by the authority structures of present day hospitals and further accentuated by the gatekeeper role assigned to medicine in the Canadian health care system.

Reverby (1987) encapsulates many of these issues with the assertion that nursing is a form of labor shaped by "the order to care in a society that refuses to value caring" (p. 1). The history and ultimately the identity of nursing is bonded to the cultural meanings and values attached to caring as women's work. Despite its ubiquity, caring, like most aspects of women's household work, is not counted as productive work in the market place. In her book, *If Women Counted*, Waring's (1988) trenchant analysis shows how current economic structures render women's work invisible by failing to factor a value for the myriad of things that women do every day. Much of women's work lies outside current economic definitions of production.

Instead, the duty to care is a learned part of women's socialization and embedded in the patterns of gender relationships; as Graham (1985) notes, "caring touches simultaneously on who you are and what you do" (p. 13). Caring is work, as well as identity. The slogan "Nurses Care" reinforces the iron link between nursing and womanhood, prescribing who we as nurses are and what we do. Reverby (1987) underscores the importance of the context in which caring work is practiced:

> Particular circumstances, ideologies, and power relations . . .create the conditions under which caring can occur, the forms it will take and the consequences it will have for those who do it. (p. 202)

Doing caring work extracts a high emotional and social price from the caregiver in that caring serves the needs of the broader society but provides few rewards to the individual. As Jean Baker Miller (1976) observes in her classic work, *Toward a New Psychology of Women*, women know serving others is important work, but the message received from the dominant culture is that caring is unimportant "low level stuff" (p. 60). Women are trapped: doing good but feeling bad. The costs of doing good and feeling bad are clearly visible in the anger and frustration of staff nurses as they wage a constant battle to achieve social and financial recognition for nursing work. A further and long-lasting cost is to the nurses' self-esteem, hindering the articulation of personal needs for support and retarding the development of group solidarity. The situation is compounded when the service provided to the patient is subverted by understaffing, by inadequate supplies and equipment, and by according priority to the execution of medical treatments over other aspects of nursing care (Harding, 1980).

With few exceptions, the majority of white- and blue-collar women continue to be employed in jobs segregated by sex. This segregation persists despite two decades of efforts for change. A variety of explanations include: demands of family life, lower levels of education and skill development, differing commitment to work, individual preferences, and hiring biases. Whatever the causes, segregation remains a significant barrier to genuine workplace equality. Although nursing bears the same burdens as other occupations in which women predominate, it constitutes, in Melosh's words (1982), a kind of "labor aristocracy" (p. 218) or elite among women's occupations. As such, nursing possesses an extensive storehouse of resources to apply in pressing for change.

These resources include nursing's recognition as an essential service, its considerable degree of prestige, and its long history of providing services to people in every corner of the globe. Nurses also have well-functioning, permanent associations, organized on regional, national, and international bases, that are acknowledged and respected by members of political establishments. An extensive array of journals adds to nurses' sense of purpose and gives them a forum for discussing shared concerns. Burke (1987) notes also that, with the trend to decentralization in organizational management, more nurses than ever before are in positions of power and are able to influence administrative decision making. Augmenting their power base is the size of annual operating budgets that executive nurses now manage. In large teaching hospitals, these budgets may run as high as $100 million and comprise more than half the operating budget. As a predominantly female group, nurses have an enormous human and organizational capacity to create change.

CHANGE

Change pervades all our endeavors and, as Goodman and Kurke (1982) observe, "we need to think about change and to change our thinking about change" (p. 2). There are many shades of meaning for change: to transform, to substitute, to remove, to shift, to replace. Common to all is the idea of making something different. In the context of nursing, the object of the change process might be the attitudes, beliefs, and behavior of nurses, doctors, and patients, or changes in the structure and processes of health care organizations, or change in governmental policies about health and illness care.

In understanding and responding to change, it is crucial to distinguish between structural and cyclical change. Structural change is irreversible. People must learn to live with it. The invention and use of the fax machine to accelerate communication is an example. Wars and economic recessions, and perhaps the march of democracy in various parts of the world, are examples of cyclical change. The pendulum of cyclical change swings back and forth. The complexity of these changes is likely to increase as technological, social, and information revolutions combine to challenge the fundamental assumptions on which nurses and their employing organizations have learned to rely. Adapting to change, whether structural or cyclical, requires new knowledge, new attitudes, and new skills.

Individual learning is at the core of any change process. In his theory of change, Argyris (1982) distinguished between two kinds of learning, single loop and double loop, both of which are important in a change process. Single loop learning involves behavior changes that do not require change in values or other governing premises (e.g., learning to use the computer or fax machine). Double loop learning includes behavior change that requires alteration of values (e.g., learning a new attitude toward the health care practices of a recent immigrant). Almost without exception, single loop learning is easily accomplished, but individuals experience extreme difficulties with double loop learning. In fact, these difficulties persist even when the individual knows that their actions and verbalizations and insights are clearly inconsistent. Argyris describes this problem as a discontinuity between espoused theories and actual theories-in-use. Theories-in-use consist of values and cognitive premises laid down in early socialization; these remain important, unquestioned, and resistant to change.

Theories-in-use continue to shape behavior without the individual being aware of their influence. Argyris (1982) asserts that "individuals are walking social structures who cannot undergo double loop learning without reflecting on their actions" (p. 84). Such reflection requires individuals to examine the validity of their reasoning processes. Theories-in-use are often reinforced by the social structures of the broader society. Fundamental behavior change usually requires change in the theories that people use and in the structures of the society that reinforce the theories. For example, in studying diffusion of participatory work structures in several countries, Cole (1982) demonstrated that slower rates of diffusion are related to insufficient support from the broader society. Without such support, organizational changes do not take root.

These are sobering observations for people concerned with organizational change. Although a good deal of organizational change requires only single loop learning, more fundamental change will not easily occur without structures and processes that help organizational members challenge accepted values. Many of the changes in health care organization demanded by nurses, such as valuing nursing work or participation in organizational decision making, require double loop learning by members of the organization's dominant coalition of senior administrators, physicians, government officials, and nurse leaders, if change is to occur.

Even when organizations plan carefully to alter established ways of doing things, the success rate for both the induction and long-term maintenance of a change is very low. Beer, Eisenstat, and Spector (1990) found that the prospects for success are enhanced when the organizational context requires new role behavior as a result of new responsibilities and new relationships and when instrinsic, as well as extrinsic, rewards are clearly contingent on the maintenance of the changed behavior. This observation reflects much of the current thinking about change in organizations. The institutionalization of change requires a multidimensional approach involving re-socialization and the adaptation of work structures and processes to anchor and reinforce new behavior. Process interventions, such as attending management train-ing workshops, in the absence of genuine changes in the workplace have limited impact.

Language has a unique significance in a change process. The use of language, metaphors, and rituals to create and maintain shared meanings is a crucial organi-zational leadership responsibility, albeit at the symbolic level. Adaptation to change requires the use of different language and new rituals to modify these shared mean-ings. As Kahn (1982) observes, an organization's leaders who attempt change "must provide a new language: the old language maintains the old ways" (p. 414). In redesigning nursing workplaces, the label *staff nurses* could be replaced with a new language, such as nurse clinicians or managers of patient care, contributing to learn-ing new behavior and values toward nursing practice by nurses and members of other groups.

The conventional image of organization change is based on orderly and rational thinking, systematic analysis, and formulation of courses of action to be implemented as scheduled. This image distorts the process by which effective change strategies are developed. Mintzberg (1987) argues that a "crafting image" more accurately describes change strategies that work. Crafting evokes images of traditional skills, dedication, and mastery of detail. The potter or silversmith learns as the process goes on, incorporating feedback and changing circumstances. This result is what Mintzberg calls *emergent strategies,* dynamic and open to new information and based on continual learning. Mintzberg compares emergent strategies to weeds, because they pop up all over, but cautions against automatically rooting them out because today's weeds sometimes turn out to be tomorrow's orchids. To elicit emergent strategies, organizational leaders must create a culture in which a variety of strategies can grow. In complex organizations such as hospitals or universities, this means building flexible structures, hiring creative people, outlining broad umbrella strat-egies, and "watching for the patterns that emerge" (p. 75).

The management of emergent strategies requires the changemaster to see prob-lems as wholes and, as Kanter (1984) observes, "the willingness to move beyond received wisdom, to combine ideas from unconnected sources, to embrace change as an opportunity to test limits" (p. 55). Changemasters use the "power tools" of information, hierarchial and peer support, and financial and human resources to turn vague ideas into successful innovations.

THE CANADIAN CONTEXT

The four broad characteristics or organizers identified in this chapter have a per-vasive influence on the structure of nursing in Canada and the way in which its problems are perceived and managed. The four—the concept of professionalism, the structure and operational modes of the large professional bureaucracies in which most Canadian nurses are employed, gender as a central organizing principle in the work and social standing of nurses, and social change—are, of course, common to nurses in many countries. With the availability of almost instant worldwide mass communication, there is a sense in which the experience of these conditions is also international. However, as Robert Evans (1986), a Canadian health care economist, observes with respect to Canada's health care system, nations do not borrow other nations' institutions; they do not fit their value systems. Nor do they fit the history, geography, political systems, or economic conditions.

An understanding of contemporary trends and issues in Canadian nursing must, therefore, include a fifth factor, namely, the Canadian context that surrounds and is reflected in nursing in this country. Clearly, nursing in Canada has much in common with nursing in other countries, a commonality that is growing with globalized communication, transportation, and information networks and the emergence of a new world economy. However, there is also a distinctiveness to Canadian nursing. Canadian nurses do not always address or attend to the same key issues as nurses in other countries. Even when working with the same questions and concerns, their approaches may differ as a result of differing histories and the particular socioeconomic and political arrangements and conditions prevailing in Canada. An illustration of these differences may be seen in responses of the American and Canadian Nurses Associations to the issue of access to health care and efforts to stem the rise of health care expenditures. In Canada, where government traditionally has a larger role in provision of services and where most medical care is tax-financed, the Canadian Nurses Association has actively lobbied for preservation of a publicly funded health care system incorporating the principle of universality under uniform terms and conditions (CNA, 1988). This emphasis on the role of government as the key funding source is largely absent in the American Nurses Association (ANA) position on securing equitable access to basic health care benefits (ANA, 1991). In keeping with a political ethos of anti-establishment populism or distrust of concentrations of power, whether in business, government, or labor (Lipset, 1990), the American Nurses Association affirms the position that access should be extended through a mix of public and private sources (ANA, 1991).

Beyond this specific example, an appreciation of the imprint of Canadian society on Canadian nursing may be gained by looking at certain enduring features of national life. For instance, no discussion of Canadian society can ignore the vast expanse of the country, its climate and topography, its rich but uneven distribution of natural resources, and its thinly spread rural and northern populations. Nor can one overlook the duality of French and English, the two major founding European cultures in Canada. This duality has dominated political life since the nation's beginning and continues to do so today.

Less visible, but nonetheless an indisputable aspect of Canada's social fabric, are the approximately one million persons who make up Canada's native populations. The native people, the first people of Canada, now constitute about 3% of the population and include approximately 25,000 Inuit in the Arctic and 300,000 status Indians living on reserves. Drawn from diverse linguistic and cultural traditions, the first people of Canada reside mainly in Ontario, the four Western provinces, the Yukon, and the Northwest Territories. Now the focus of an important native rights movement centered on land claims and the powers of self-government according to their traditional ways, Canada's first people have also been trying to revive their distinct cultures.

Another frequently noted characteristic of Canadian society is the centrality to the Canadian consciousness of the presence of the United States to the south. George Woodcock, the noted Canadian social historian and man of letters, suggests that it is the presence of the United States as much as any other factor that has maintained what he calls "Canada's precarious unity" (1979, p. 53).

Other aspects of Canada's distinctiveness include the substantial flow of immigrants to Canada over the course of the twentieth century. Early in the century, immigration was concentrated in the West and by 1921 almost half of the Western Canadian population was foreign born. These immigrants came mostly from Europe and the United States. The period of immigration commencing in 1945 saw a broadening of source countries, and, by the 1980s, immigration had become far more diverse in terms of national, religious, and racial backgrounds. Now included on the list of top 10 source countries are the Asian, Caribbean, and Latin American regions of the world. The impact of this immigration is largely an urban phenomenon, with heavy flows to Montreal, Toronto, and Vancouver (Health and Welfare Canada, 1989). Canada's diverse ethnocultural makeup is underscored in the entrenchment of multiculturalism in the 1982 Canadian constitution and the widely shared belief that cultural pluralism rather than the American melting-pot philosophy is a defining characteristic of the country. Despite Canada's reputation as a humanitarian nation and its official policy of multiculturism however, recent studies reveal increasing racist and ethnic tensions within Canada's population (Berry, Kalin, and Taylor, 1977). Other frequently cited characteristics include the acceptance of the need for a strong state and respect for authority and a lack of a controlling set of values or national creed, such as the American one that was forged out of the legacy of Puritanism and the experiences of the American Revolution (Clark, 1973; Lipset, 1990; Wardhaugh, 1983; Woodcock, 1979).

Observers of Canadian society (Clement, 1975; Lipset, 1990; Newman, 1975; Olsen, 1980; Porter, 1965) have also documented the degree to which the levers in power in Canada are controlled by a small elite of about 2000 individuals whose controls extend to the business world, the media, and the patronage of the arts. They also constitute Canada's political elite.

Another distinguishing feature of Canadian life is the strength of regional interests and the growing insistence of the provinces and territories on preserving and extending their autonomy (Simeon, 1988). A more decentralized federation than any other federal state, Canada has conditions that promote a unique set of relationships and tensions between the federal government and the provinces and territories, and these have become an abiding hallmark of Canadian political life (Wardhaugh, 1983).

The conflict is compounded by disparate views of Canada's political framework (Pepin, 1968; Smiley, 1968), views that have fuelled numerous constitutional debates for the past 30 years. In broad terms, these views cluster around four models. One sees Canada as a federation of autonomous provinces in which the federal government should do only those things the provinces cannot do. A second view, labelled *cooperative federalism,* recognizes that the federal and provincial governments have overlapping interests and emphasizes the mechanisms that facilitate cooperation and accommodation. A third view, historically the position taken by Quebec, is that Canada is a federation of two charter groups, the French and the English, with Quebec being a distinct society and having special constitutional status. A fourth model has a division of powers that assigns to the federal government a smaller set of powers than it now has and gives all other powers uniquely or concurrently to the regions.

These constitutional debates took on a new urgency after the failure of the Meech Lake Accord in 1990, confrontations with native Canadians of Oka later that summer, rising support for the Reform party in Western Canada, and, in early 1991, proposals by Quebec forcing the issue of the province's sovereignty and separation from Canada. These series of constitutional crises rocked the foundations of confederation and led to a deep-seated pessimism about the survival of Canada as a nation-state.

Complicating the task of finding a solution and getting Canada working again are new crosscurrents emanating from the way the world is changing. The globalization of business and industry has led to a greater role for the market and a lesser role for national governments in managing economies. This process is illustrated by the curtailing effect of the Free Trade Agreement on interventions by the federal government. These changes in the political landscape are intensified by a growing public disenchantment with the political process and create a set of forces that taken together are hastening the consensus for radical change in Canada's constitutional framework.

The convergence of factors shaping Canadian society and the characteristics of the Canadian health care system and the nursing profession in Canada may be experienced at many levels—from the unique role in the Canadian health care system of northern nursing stations to the tensions and conflicts that dominate federal-provincial negotiation of financial arrangements for health services. Another example may be found in how the dual French and Anglophone heritage is reflected and reinforced in Canadian health care by the prominent role of the French religious sisterhoods, such as the Grey Nuns, in Canadian nursing history and in the establishment of hospitals nationwide (Kerr, 1990; Petitat, 1989). Founded in 1738 by Marguerite d'Youville, the Grey Nuns also served as Canada's first visiting nurses. The intertwining of English and French is evident as well in the inspiration Canadian nurses draw from the legendary Jeanne Mance, a lay women from a wealthy French family, who was a co-founder of Montreal and also the founder of the Hotel Dieu Hospital there in 1642 (Desjardin, Giroux, and Flanagan, 1970). Predating the work of Florence Nightingale by two centuries, her formative influence on Canadian nursing has yet to be adequately probed.

The distinctiveness of Canadian nursing also owes much to its grounding in the Canadian health care system and the unique structure of the national health insurance program whose evolution is described in Chapter 2. Launched with the introduction of hospital insurance in 1957 and expanded to include medical insurance in 1958, the health insurance program was born out of protracted bargaining between the federal and provincial governments over financial arrangements and the preservation of provincial autonomy and flexibility. Its guiding principle—that need, rather than ability to pay, should govern access to services—has been described as "a pledge that Canadians hold dear and politicians ignore at their peril" (Gruending, 1985, p. 81). However, its emphasis on acute care and the continuing pressures to reduce the proportion of government spending on health care has been characterized as a "pressure cooker that is building up steam on a hot stove" (Iglehart, 1986, p. 203).

LOOKING AHEAD

These conditions provide a volatile and often confusing environment for both consumers and health care professionals. However, they also encourage creativity and so enhance the opportunities for change and adaptation. The effectiveness of the adaptation and change will depend, in turn, on how well the problems are analyzed and the issues understood.

It is against this background that the changing structure and dynamics of Canadian nursing as it faces the future are examined in succeeding sections of the book. The remaining chapters in Section I build up a picture of the social environment in which the day-to-day activities of Canadian nurses take place. Chapter 2 describes the evolution of the Canadian health care system. Chapter 3 presents a statistical profile of the Canadian nursing work force. The section concludes with some of the distinctive features of nursing culture and how it relates to professional effectiveness and empowerment.

Section II considers the content of nursing practice in various institutional and community settings and how it is being reshaped by changes such as the aging of the Canadian population, shifts in government spending and health care priorities, and developments in knowledge and technology. The section also contains a chapter on the services provided by Canadian nurses who have lived and worked in the international arena. Canadian involvement in international nursing has a long and illustrious history, and recent trends to globalization reinforce the importance of the cross-national links between nurses.

Section III considers several factors affecting the work and life of nurses: administrative patterns and trends, ethical questions, regulating legislation, the impact of technology in the workplace, legal issues, nursing research, specialization, and changing career patterns.

Section IV examines the patterns of initial, graduate, and continuing education for nurses in Canada and describes the ferment now evident in the educational field.

Having laid the groundwork for formulation of nursing goals and priorities in the upcoming twenty-first century, Section V looks at nursing power, political activity, and leadership. All three processes are important aspects of professional activity and provide the means whereby nurses participate in influencing and shaping the future. To illustrate their importance, the changing roles of professional associations and unions are considered, and three instruments for change in Canadian nursing are examined. They are the formation of the Indian and Inuit Nurses Association of Canada, strikes by Canadian nurses, and the role of a voluntary nursing service, the Victorian Order of Nurses, in shaping health care practice and policy.

The final section of the book, Facing the Future, identifies the necessary ingredients in planning for the future of Canadian nursing in the decades ahead.

REFERENCES

Abel-Smith, B. (1960). *A history of the nursing profession*. London: Heinemann.

American Nurses Association. (February 1991). Nursing proposes health care system. *The American Nurse, 23*(2), 1.

Argyris, C. (1982). "How learning and reasoning processes affect organizational change." In P. Goodman & Associates (Eds.), *Change in organizations* (pp. 47-86). San Francisco: Jossey-Bass.

Baker Miller, J. (1976). *Toward a new psychology of women*. Boston: Beacon Press.

Beer, M., Eisenstat, R., & Spector, B. (1990). Why change programs don't produce change. *Harvard Business Review, 68*(6), 158-166.

Berry, J.W., Kalin, R., & Taylor, D.M. (1977). *Multiculturalism and ethnic attitudes in Canada*. Ottawa: Department of Supply & Services.

Brockbank, W. (1970). *History of nursing at the Manchester Royal Infirmary*. Manchester: Manchester University Press.

Burke, B. (1987). Strategy for nurses to improve the quality of work life: "Strengthening the weakest link." In C. Attridge & M. Callahan (Eds.), *Women in women's work: Nurses' perspectives of quality work environments* (Research Report #1), (pp. 87-89). Victoria: University of Victoria, Faculty of Human and Social Development.

Canadian Nurses Association. (1988). *Health for all Canadians: A call for health care reform*. Ottawa: Author.

Clarke, S. D. (1973). Canada and the American value system. In O. Kruhla, R. Schultz, & S. Pobilhushchy (Eds.), *The Canadian political process: A reader* (Rev. Ed.), (pp. 61-68). Toronto: Holt, Rinehart & Winston.

Clement, W. (1975). *The Canadian corporate elite: An analysis of economic power*. Toronto: McClelland and Stewart.

Cole, R. (1982). Diffusion of participatory work structures in Japan, Sweden and the United States. In P. Goodman & Associates (Eds.), *Change in organizations* (pp. 166-255). San Francisco: Jossey-Bass.

Corwin, R., & Taves, M. (1962). Some concomitants of bureaucratic and professional conceptions of the nursing role. *Nursing Research, 11*(4), 223-227.

Curtin, L. (1990). The commitment of nursing. In T. Pence & J. Cantrall (Eds.), *Ethics in nursing: An anthology*, (Pub. No. 20-2294) (pp. 283-286). New York: National League for Nursing.

Dahlerup, D. (1986). Introduction. In D. Dahlerup (Ed.), *The new women's movement: Feminism and political power in Europe and the USA* (pp. 1-25). Beverly Hills, CA: Sage Publications.

Davies, C. (Eds.). (1980). *Rewriting nursing history*. London: Croom Helm.

Delamothe, T. (1988). Nursing grievances. *British Medical Journal, 292*, 25-28.

Desjardins, E., Giroux, S., & Flanagan, E. (1970). *Histoire de la profession infirmière au Québec*. Montreal: L'Association des Infirmières et Infirmiers de la Province de Québec.

Drucker, P.F. (1988). The coming of the new organization. *Harvard Business Review, 66*(1), 45-53.

Evans, R. (1986). The spurious dilemma: Reconciling medical progress and cost. *Health Matrix 1986, 1*(4), 25-34.

Flexner, A. (1910). *Medical education in the United States and Canada: A report of the Carnegie Foundation for the Advancement of Teaching*. Boston: The Merrymount Press.

Friedson, E. (1970). *Profession of medicine*. New York: Harper and Row.

Friss, L. (1982). Hospital nurse staffing: An urgent need for management reappraisal. *Health Care Management Review, 7*(1), 21-27.

Game, A., & Pringle, R. (1984). *Gender at work*. London: Pluto Press.

Gamarnikow, E. (1978). Sexual division of labour: The case of nursing. In A. Kahn & W. Walpe (Eds.), *Feminism and materialism: Women and modes of production* (pp. 96-123). London: Routledge and Kegan Paul.

Goode, W. J. (1960). The profession: Reports and opinion. *American Sociological Review, 25*, 902-914.

Goodman, P., & Kurke, L. (1982). Studies of change in organizations: A status report. In P. Goodman & Associates (Eds.), *Change in Organizations* (pp. 1-46). San Francisco: Jossey-Bass.

Graham, H. (1985). Providers, negotiators and mediators: Women as the hidden carers. In E. Lewin & V. Olesen (Eds.), *Women, health and healing: Toward a new perspective* (pp. 25-52). London: Tavistock.

Greenwood, E. (1957). Attitudes of a profession. *Social Work, 2*(4), 45-55.

Gruending, D. (1985). *Emmett Hall: Establishment radical.* Toronto: Macmillan.

Harding, S. (1980). Value-laden technologies and the politics of nursing. In S. Spicker & S. Gadow (Eds.), *Nursing images and ideals* (pp. 49-75). New York: Springer.

Health and Welfare Canada. (1989). *Charting Canada's future: A report of the demographic review.* Ottawa: Author.

Iglehart, J. (1986). Canada's health care system: (first of three parts). *New England Journal of Medicine, 315*(3), 203-208.

Jennings, B., Callahan, D., & Wolf, S. (1987). *The professions: Public interest and common good.* A Hastings Centre Report, *17*(1), 3-10, Special Supplement/February, 1987.

Johnson, T. (1972). *Professions and power.* London: Macmillan.

Kahn, R. (1982). Critical themes in the study of change. In P. Goodman & Associates (Eds.), *Change in Organization* (pp. 409-429). San Francisco: Jossey-Bass.

Kanter, R. (1984). Innovation—the only hope for time ahead. *Sloan Management Review,* Summer, pp. 51-55.

Kerr, J. (1990, June). The work of the Grey Nuns in Alberta 1859-1899: A feminist perspective. In *Proceedings of the Canadian Association for the History of Nursing Third Annual Conference.* Calgary: p. 49-72.

Kramer, M. (1974). *Reality shock: Why nurses leave nursing.* St. Louis: Mosby—Year Book, Inc.

Lipset, S. (1990). *Continental divide: The values & institutions of the United States & Canada.* New York: Routledge.

Manitoba Organization of Nurses Associations. (1989). *The Nurse's perspective on their role and health care in Manitoba.* Winnipeg: Author.

Melosh, B. (1982). *"The physician's hand": Work—culture and conflict in American Nursing.* Philadelphia: Temple University Press.

Mintzberg, H. (1983). *Structure in fives: Designing effective organizations.* Englewood Cliffs, NJ: Prentice-Hall.

Mintzberg, H. (1987). Crafting Strategy. *Harvard Business Review,* 4 (July-August), pp. 66-77.

Morgan, G. (1986). *Images of organization.* Beverly Hills, CA: Sage Publications.

Newman, P. (1975). *The Canadian establishment.* Toronto: McClelland and Stewart.

Noddings, N. (1990). Feminist critiques in the professions. In C.B. Cazden (Ed.): *Review of research in education* (pp. 393-424). Washington, DC: American Educational Research Assn.

Oakley, A. (1986). On the importance of being a nurse. *Telling the truth about Jerusalem: A collection of essays and poems* (pp. 180-274). Oxford: Basil Blackwell.

Olsen, D. (1980). *The state elite.* Toronto: McClelland and Stewart.

Pepin, J. L. (1968). Co-operative federalism. In J. P. Meekison (Ed.). *Canadian federalism: Myth or reality?* (pp. 320-329). Toronto: Methuen.

Petitat, A. (1989). *Les infirmières: De la Profession à la vocation.* Montreal: Boreal.

Ponak, A. (1982). Public sector collective bargaining. In J. Anderson & M. Gunderson (Eds.), *Union-management relations in Canada* (pp. 343-378). Don Mills, ON: Addison-Wesley.

Porter, J. (1965). *The vertical mosaic: An analysis of social class and power in Canada.* Toronto: University of Toronto Press.

Registered Nurses' Association of Ontario. (1988). *Sorry, no care available due to nursing shortage. A prescription for reforming human resources planning in health care.* Toronto: Author.

Reverby, S. (1987). *Ordered to care: The dilemma of American nursing* (1850-1945). Cambridge: Cambridge University Press.

Robinson, J. (1989). Nursing in the future: A cause for concern. In M. Jolley and P. Allan (Eds.), *Current issues in nursing* (pp. 151-178). London: Chapman and Hall.

Simeon, R. (1988). Meech Lake and shifting conceptions of Canadian federalism. *Canadian public policy.* 14 (Supplement), pp. S7-S24.

Smiley, D. (1968). The Rowell-Sirois report: Provincial autonomy and post-war Canadian federalism. In P. Meekison (Ed.), *Canadian federalism: Myth or reality* (pp. 65-81). Toronto: Methuen.

Stacey, M. (1988). *The sociology of health and healing.* London: Unwin Hyman.

Stacey, M., & Price, M. (1981). *Women, power and politics,* London: Tavistock.

Stein, L. (1967). The doctor-nurse game. *Archives of General Psychiatry, 16,* 699-703.

Taylor, L. (1968). *Occupational sociology.* New York: Oxford University Press.

Wardhaugh, R. (1983). *Language and nationhood: The Canadian experience.* Vancouver: New Star Books.

Waring, M. (1988). *If women counted.* San Francisco: Harper.

Williams, K. (1980). From Sarah Gamp to Florence Nightingale: A critical study of hospital nursing systems from 1840 to 1897. In C. Davies (Ed.), *Rewriting Nursing History* (pp. 41-75), London: Croom Helm.

Woodcock, G. (1979). *The Canadians.* Don Mills, Ont: Fitzhenry and Whiteside.

Portrait doll showing a Knight of the Order of St. John, during the Crusades, circa 1099, when nursing was dominated by male nursing orders. The doll is from the historical nursing dolls collection of Sheila Rankin Zerr, visiting assistant professor, School of Nursing, University of Victoria. (Photograph courtesy of the Registered Nurses Association of British Columbia. Used with permission.)

CHAPTER TWO

Evolution of the Canadian Health Care System

ALICE J. BAUMGART, RN, PhD

Alice J. Baumgart, RN, BSN (British Columbia), MSc (McGill), PhD (Toronto), is Vice-Principal, Human Services, Queen's University. She has an extensive background in nursing as a clinician, researcher, and teacher and has served on many international, national, and provincial nursing committees and boards. She is President of the Canadian Nurses Association for 1991-1992. Her experience includes liaison with federal government departments and with provincial ministries of health in British Columbia and Ontario.

C anada's health care system enjoys broad popular support and is widely admired internationally as one of the finest in the world. Through it, Canadians have access to a rich mix of facilities and services directed toward restoring and maintaining health and ameliorating suffering. These resources are complemented by a large and diverse health care work force. A publicly financed insurance program, now in place for more than 25 years, provides universal coverage for hospital and medical costs. Consequently, Canadians, regardless of age, health status, or ability to pay, are protected against devastating financial losses from ill health and disability.

Yet, the affordability and effectiveness of the system, in company with health care systems worldwide, have increasingly been questioned. The precipitating factors are many-sided and are related to wider societal changes such as harsher economic conditions, a shifting political landscape, and the aging of Canada's population. Other challenges come from rising health care costs, the pressures of health care technology, and accumulating evidence showing that, although health care services can have a significant part in advancing and protecting the health status of a population, social and environmental conditions, material standards of living, and lifestyle factors are of even greater importance (Mustard, 1987; Evans and Stoddart, 1990; Wilkins, Adams, and Brancker, 1990).

Together, these factors force a critical and continuing re-examination of the future of Canada's health services and policy framework. This chapter traces the history of these developments and examines major themes informing current debates about health care in Canada.

HISTORICAL OVERVIEW

Evans (1981) describes the evolution of modern health care systems as passing through three distinctive stages: the heyday of infectious diseases, the age of chronic illness, and the era of social and environmental pathology. Each stage brought different challenges to public health and medical services and reshaped thinking about appropriate approaches to health and healing. In the Canadian context, recorded history of the first stage dates mainly from seventeenth century French settlement and extends to the early years of the twentieth century. This period saw the emergence of modern public health and laid the foundations for medicine as a scientific discipline and developing political force.

Early Health Care Patterns

Life in the New World for those who explored its shores and hinterlands and settled beside its waterways was often one of considerable privation and hardship. Infectious diseases such as smallpox and typhus, long the scourge of Europe, became one of the most visible effects of early colonization. Lacking previous exposure, the ranks of aboriginal peoples were decimated by the periodic epidemics. The first French settlers often fared little better. Although their isolated settlements offered them some protection from the spread of epidemic diseases, their resistance was often weakened by malnutrition and inadequate clothing and shelter for the harsh winter climate.

Records of the French regime show early attempts to prevent the entry and spread of epidemic diseases within the colony through various public health measures. Public ordinances were enacted, for example, to prevent sale of meat from diseased animals, and to allow civil authorities to inspect dwellings for their state of cleanliness. Almost from the time of the first settlers, local priests kept records of births, marriages, and deaths. By the early 1700s, physicians were boarding vessels to examine passengers and crew before they landed at Quebec. By 1721, the first formal quarantine regulations were promulgated (Heagerty, 1980).

Expanded trade and commerce, larger settlements, and a steady increase in the number of immigrants led to widespread new epidemics on the shores of the St.

Lawrence and Great Lakes in the period of British rule. The growth of towns, with a lack of clean water supplies and inadequate sewage disposal, exacerbated the problems of disease spread. In response to massive outbreaks of cholera and typhus in the period from 1832 to 1854, the legislatures of Upper Canada, Lower Canada, Nova Scotia, New Brunswick, and Newfoundland passed legislation setting up local boards of health. They also authorized various public health measures, including establishment of quarantine facilities, inspection of premises, and recording of mortality statistics. The measures were regarded as emergency ones, however, and lapsed when an outbreak subsided (Hastings and Mosely, 1980).

The cruel mortality statistics—20,000 deaths in a population of 900,000 during the 1847 typhus epidemic (Heagerty, 1980)—attest to the negligible success of these public health measures. Only after the persuasive work of Koch, Pasteur, and others, and the triumph of the germ theory of disease causation in the late nineteenth century, would contagion and sanitation be understood and modern ideas of disease control become possible.

The limited capabilities of mid-nineteenth century medicine and prevailing laissez-faire ideas about individual initiative and social provision would directly affect constitutional arrangements embodied in the British North America Act of 1867. This act, establishing Canada as a formal political entity, made few explicit references to health; nor did it set out appropriate roles for the central and provincial governments in health matters (Splane, 1965). Sections 91 and 92 of this Act, now known as the Constitution Act, 1867, assigned to the federal government responsibilities for taxation, census and statistics, criminal law, quarantine, and establishment and maintenance of marine hospitals. The provinces were assigned jurisdiction over the establishment, maintenance, and management of hospitals, asylums, charities, and eleemosynary institutions in and for the provinces, other than marine hospitals, and all matters of a local or private nature. Subsequent constitutional interpretations have led to a legal framework in which the federal government has the tax authority, but the provinces exercise the primary constitutional prerogative in health matters. More will be said later in the chapter about the contemporary significance of this division of powers.

Post-Confederation Era

From Confederation until the end of World War I in 1918, Canada embarked on a period of economic transformation and scientific change that made possible the transition to modern health care patterns. Beginning in the 1850s in Southern Ontario and Quebec, industry, through the factory system, began to progress rapidly. The expansion of communications and transport, together with industrialization, fostered the migration of people from rural to urban industrial centers. The population of cities such as Toronto, Montreal, and Hamilton expanded quickly. Winnipeg, serving as the conduit for massive immigration from Britain and Europe into the West, grew even more rapidly (Phillips and Phillips, 1983).

The concentration of factory workers and their families in cities, their rampant poverty, and their overcrowded and unsanitary living conditions brought new infectious diseases to prominence. Tuberculosis, typhus, and typhoid now accounted for most of the mortality and morbidity among adults, whereas children increasingly succumbed to communicable diseases such as scarlet fever, whooping cough, and diphtheria. However, by the late 1800s, a discernible decline in mortality and morbidity rates was evident, first among adults, and somewhat later among infants and children. For a long time, it was assumed that this could be attributed to the successes of scientific medicine and better aseptic conditions in hospitals and clinics. However, the demonstration that the declines in mortality and morbidity preceded rather than followed the isolation of specific etiologic agents and the use of immunization and specific antimicrobial drugs has discredited this explanation. It is now generally conceded that the decline was mainly due to a combination of the effects of public health legislation imposing sanitary reforms and the improved nutritional and general living standards accompanying greater prosperity (Grob, 1983; McKeown, 1979).

Supported by the new industrial economic order, these two developments were also nourished by the intellectual ferment and social movements of mid-nineteenth century Britain and Western Europe. No single medical orthodoxy about epidemic disease had yet emerged. However, public attention was focused on the links between disease, poverty, and environmental conditions by social reformers such as Edwin Chadwick, Florence Nightingale, and Friederick Engels (Baly, 1989; Chadwick, 1965; Engels, 1958). It was Chadwick's monumental *Report on the Sanitary Condition of the Labouring Class in Great Britain*, of 1842, and his constant advocacy of sanitary reform that led to the passage of the Public Health Act of 1848. A major milestone in the history of public health, this Act established the principles of modern public health organization and sanitary codes. It also represented a major advance of social policy. As Flinn (1965) points out, an environmental approach to the sanitation question was no less than a complete reversal of prevailing nineteenth century social thinking ascribing poverty to shortcomings of character. Economic thinking was also changing and reflected mounting concern about the interaction of health and industrial productivity. A healthier, more reliable work force became a more pressing issue as complex, heavy machinery became an increasingly important part of factory production processes. In Europe, the links between health and the need for a sound working class found expression in the passage of sickness insurance laws, the first one being enacted in Germany in 1883.

Thus by the 1880s, there was considerable public support in Canada to bring comprehensive public health programs within the scope of government action (Wallace, 1980). All provinces, beginning with Ontario in 1884, passed legislation based on the English consolidated Public Health Act of 1875. These acts required every municipality or region in a province to appoint a permanent Board of Health and impose sanitary regulations (Hastings and Mosley, 1980). Other public welfare measures enacted at this time included provisions for the sick poor, custodial care for the mentally ill, and protection of victims of industrial accident through Worker's Compensation (Splane, 1965).

Birth of Scientific Medicine

The changes in living conditions and family structure that accompanied the influx of workers to urban settings during the rise of industrialism also brought significant changes to the patterns of personal health care. Dispersed in a rural society, most

Canadians prior to Confederation had limited access to physicians or hospitals. The women of a family were expected to tend the sick in the home and to provide a store of appropriate herbs and home remedies. Untrained but skilled residents in the communities were often asked to serve as midwives, lay healers, and bone setters. Although by the mid-1800s hospitals run by religious orders and charitable groups existed in most larger towns, until the twentieth century their main role was providing social support for the poor rather than medical attention (Heagerty, 1980).

On migration to the cities, the self-sufficiency of the pioneer family broke down. Crowded conditions and the necessity for more than one wage earner to support a family made care of the sick in the home difficult, if not impossible. At the same time, the application of science to medical practice began to improve the treatment efficacy and the prestige of the healing arts. Reforms in hospital hygiene, improved surgical techniques, and the introduction of anesthetics also helped to shift care previously rendered by physicians in the home or office to the hospital. As a result, the balance of attention was diverted from public health and prevention to diagnosis and treatment of disease (Evans, 1981; Starr, 1982). The increasing alliance of medicine with science also helped to solidify the medical profession's dominance over competing healing occupations such as apothecaries and midwives and gave modern health care systems their heavy emphasis on curative medicine and acute hospital care (Torrance, 1987; Waitzkin, 1983).

In North America, the shift in the focal point of health care was heavily influenced by the publication in 1910 of Flexner's classic report, *Medical Education in the United States and Canada*. The report had an underlying assumption that scientific medicine, oriented to teaching the biologic basis of disease, produced a higher quality and more effective medical practice (Waitzkin, 1983). This thinking quickly became the norm for medical education, as well as practice and research, and widened the split between preventive and curative approaches to health care. Reinforcing the process was the popular belief that emerged in the early part of the twentieth century that complete conquest of disease was possible. Together, these developments helped to account for the phenomenal growth of public support for curative medicine some years before it had many powerful tools in its therapeutic arsenal.

The major breakthroughs and expansion of diagnostic and therapeutic capabilities came in the period from 1920 to 1950. The advent of highly effective, mass produced pharmaceuticals such as antibiotics and continuing improvements in surgical technique gave physicians increased control over the mastery of disease. Improvements in technology for blood transfusions, x-rays, and laboratory analysis of biological specimens, along with devices such as the electrocardiograph, added to the advance of scientific medicine. These developments were reflected in an increasing proportion of the population escaping infection and surviving any given episode of illness. As a result, infant mortality and life expectancy began to take on modern dimensions and brought about a shift in the prevailing patterns of disease from acute to chronic illness. These changes ushered in a second stage in the evolution of modern health care systems—making medical care more accessible to wider segments of the population (Torrance, 1987). The key sequence of events here is the emergence of hospital and medical insurance programs and the increase in importance of government involvement in health services.

DEVELOPMENT OF GOVERNMENT HEALTH INSURANCE

As more and more Canadians began to accept the claims of scientific medicine and the benefits of hospitalization for serious illness, barriers of access related mainly to ability to pay for services and, in some regions, to a shortage of practitioners and hospitals. Since free care had been provided to the poor through charitable clinics and hospital services and the wealthy could afford to pay, it was the more prosperous working and middle classes for whom the idea of health insurance had strong appeal (Torrance, 1987).

The origins of such insurance in Canada go back to 1665 when Etienne Bouchard, a physician in Montreal, offered a form of prepaid coverage to 26 families in that city (Health and Welfare Canada, 1974). In the early 1900s, various friendly societies, employers, and commercial insurance firms introduced voluntary plans to prepay part or all of medical and hospitalization costs. The province of Saskatchewan has been the modern pioneer in widening access to medical and hospital services through publicly-financed insurance. Its Union Hospital Act of 1916 enabled municipalities to pool resources to build and maintain hospitals. In the same year, the Rural Municipality Act allowed Saskatchewan municipalities to levy property taxes for purposes of paying a retaining fee to doctors providing general practitioner and public health services in an area, a step that encouraged doctors to settle in the province. Similar, although less extensive, plans were introduced in Manitoba in 1921 and Alberta in 1926. In Newfoundland, then not part of Canada, a cottage hospital plan was initiated in 1934 to provide hospital services and to retain physicians for outpost communities, a scheme supplementing the network of hospitals and nursing stations established by Sir Wilfred Grenfell and the International Grenfell Association. However, such plans covered less than one third of the population (Soderstrom, 1978).

The ravages of the Great Depression of the 1930s accelerated the search for more universal methods of health care financing. Economic hardship was widespread. Unemployment rose to nearly 25%, and wages fell. These conditions were reflected in the rising rates of disease as poverty and malnutrition took their toll. As people increasingly defaulted on payment of medical and hospital bills or simply avoided using health services, physicians' incomes declined and hospital deficits grew. Some medical societies introduced insurance plans to provide coverage for the costs of medical care and to provide physicians with some income. Local authorities, unable to cope with the burden of care for large numbers of unemployed, turned increasingly to provincial governments and to the federal government for financial help.

Path to National Health Insurance

It was against this background that the first significant political steps toward government insurance at the national level were taken. In 1935, the federal government placed the Employment and Social Insurance Act on the statute book. This Act would have allowed the federal government to directly administer a health and welfare program financed by premium payments. The provinces challenged the legislation on the basis of the British North America Act of 1867, and the Supreme Court of Canada in 1937 declared the legislation *ultra vires* or beyond its scope, thus reconfirming provincial jurisdiction over most health matters.

However, the federal government maintained a continuing interest in a national health program and in 1942 established an advisory committee. Its proposals, including a draft health insurance bill, formed the basis of federal proposals placed before the provinces in 1945. Despite a favorable climate of public opinion and support from various national labor and consumer groups and from the Canadian Medical Association, the Canadian Hospital Association, and the Canadian Nurses Association, the proposals foundered because of disagreements over fiscal arrangements (Health and Welfare Canada, 1974; Taylor, 1980).

Meanwhile, the province of Saskatchewan decided to proceed independently and in 1947 launched the first universal program in North America providing hospital care to all residents of the province regardless of means. British Columbia followed with a universal plan of its own in 1949. In the same year, Alberta introduced a plan providing partial coverage, and Newfoundland entered Confederation with such a plan already in operation.

At the federal level, the first formal steps in the transfer of hospital and medical services from the private to the public sector was the enactment of the National Health Grant Program in 1948. These grants provided financial assistance to the provinces to build hospitals, to strengthen public health services, and to improve services pertaining to specific diseases such as cancer, tuberculosis, and sexually transmitted disease (LeClair, 1976; Soderstrom, 1978).

By the mid-1950s, public pressure for a nationwide program of health insurance was growing. The provinces also began to press the federal government for further action to help pay for the escalating costs of providing hospital services.

In January, 1956, the federal government placed before the provinces a proposal to share the costs of a hospital insurance program on condition that a majority of the provinces took part and a majority of the population was covered. The federal enabling legislation, the Hospital and Diagnostic Services Act, was passed in 1957. When it took effect on July 1, 1958, the federal government had signed agreements with five provinces—British Columbia, Alberta, Saskatchewan, Manitoba, and Newfoundland. By 1961, all of the provinces and territories were participating in the program and providing federally assisted hospital insurance to 99% of Canadian residents.

Insured services varied somewhat from province to province, but all were required to provide certain standard benefits, including the basic cost of acute treatment and convalescent and chronic care in approved hospital facilities; laboratory, radiological, and other diagnostic procedures; and a range of emergency and outpatient services. Additional benefits such as extended or home care could be provided without affecting the federal-provincial agreement. In conformity with provincial constitutional prerogatives, organization and administration of hospital services remained in the hands of the provinces and local authorities. As a result, most hospitals in Canada are still owned and governed by local voluntary boards.

The second step in the implementation of the national insurance program, the introduction of medical insurance, proved a more controversial one. Saskatchewan was the vanguard once again, introducing a government-sponsored plan in 1962. Although it had much popular support, the plan was strongly opposed by the medical profession, which saw it as encroaching on clinical freedom. When it went into effect on July 1, 1962, about 90% of the province's doctors went on strike. As public opinion began to move against the striking physicians, the Saskatchewan College of Physicians and Surgeons renewed negotiations and, on July 23, the parties signed a document known as the Saskatoon agreement. This allowed doctors the right to bill patients directly and to charge patients more than would be reimbursed under the government plan, provisions that were later included in several provincial medical insurance agreements to gain the cooperation of the medical profession (Badgley and Wolfe, 1967; LeClair, 1976).

Following the lead of Saskatchewan, Alberta in 1963, British Columbia in 1965, and Ontario in 1966 implemented voluntary medical insurance plans, but none covered all residents. The Alberta plan used commercial insurance carriers. The British Columbia and Ontario plans co-existed with other nongovernmental plans. Newfoundland had been financing physicians' services for hospitalized children under 16 years of age since 1958. All provinces subsidized medical coverage for low income people (Soderstrom, 1978).

A year before the Saskatchewan doctors' strike, Prime Minister John Diefenbaker named Emmett Hall, then Chief Justice of Saskatchewan, as chair of a Royal Commission on Health Services. That Commission, commonly known as the Hall Commission, was appointed in part because of pressure from the Canadian Medical Association (LeClair, 1976).

The report of the Hall Commission (Government of Canada, 1964), based on the most thorough and comprehensive study of health care ever undertaken in Canada, was released in June 1964. It completely rejected the medical association's proposal that any government steps should attempt to subsidize low income persons so as to allow them to purchase policies from insurance companies or physician-sponsored plans. Instead, the report strongly recommended a universal program by the provinces, subsidized by matching federal funds. The approach recommended by the medical profession would have required means testing of half or more of Canadians, an administrative task not considered worth the effort. In Taylor's words (1980, p. 188), "It was clearly much simpler to subsidize the ten [provincial] insurance funds than millions of individuals."

The responsibility for acting on the proposed legislation fell to the recently elected government of Prime Minister Lester Pearson, whose Liberal Party reaffirmed its commitment to health insurance during the 1962 election campaign. There was considerable opposition from Alberta and Quebec, the primary objection being that the federal government was interfering with provincial priorities. Despite this opposition, the Medical Care Bill was enacted in 1966 and implemented in 1968. Saskatchewan and British Columbia entered the plan at its inception. Newfoundland, Nova Scotia, Manitoba, Alberta, and Ontario joined in 1969, Quebec and Prince Edward Island in 1970, New Brunswick and the Northwest Territories in 1971, and the Yukon Territory in 1972 (Health and Welfare Canada, 1974; Shah, 1987).

To be eligible for cost-sharing under the Medical Care Act, provinces were required to meet four criteria, the so-called "Four Points." The coverage had to be **comprehensive;** that is, it had to provide all services rendered by a physician without dollar limits or other restrictions provided there was medical need. The plan had to be **universally available** to all residents of a province and cover at least 95% of the

eligible population. The plan also had to be **portable between provinces** for beneficiaries temporarily absent from their own province or moving to another one.
Finally, the plan had to be **operated on a nonprofit basis and publicly administered**
by an agency accountable to the provincial government for its financial transactions.

Until 1977, the federal government reimbursed the provinces for approximately
50% of the costs of approved hospital and medical services. In response to rising
health care expenditures and mounting concerns that federal matching of provincial
spending on hospitals and medical care was leading to an over-reliance on the most
expensive forms of health care, a new block funding system was introduced in 1977
under the terms of the Federal-Provincial Fiscal Arrangements and Established Programs Financing Act. Federal contributions were based on the average rate of growth
of the gross national product. They took the form of cash transfers plus a transfer
of tax and associated equalization payments to the provinces. Per capita cash contributions were also made to the provinces for the cost of certain extended services,
such as nursing home, ambulatory, and home care services.

Further revisions to the block funding formula were made in 1982 and again in
1984 as part of the Canada Health Act. This legislation responded to growing complaints of erosion of medicare and curbs on access because of user charges. The Act
consolidated the Hospital Insurance and Diagnostic Services and Medical Care Acts
and reaffirmed and clarified the basic principles of the insurance program. It also
gave the federal government power to levy financial penalties against provinces and
territories failing to comply with these principles. The most controversial provision
was the loss of federal cash contributions, on a dollar for dollar basis, to any province
or territory passing on costs to consumers through hospital user charges or extra-
billing by physicians (the collection of fees in excess of those allowed by the provincial
medical fee schedule). The heated controversy was strongest in the province of
Ontario, where the introduction of government legislation banning extra-billing pro-
voked the longest strike by physicians in Canada's history. By 1987, all provinces
passed legislation eliminating the user charges unacceptable to the federal government.

The ability of the federal government to require certain performance from the
provinces and territories, so that the principles embodied in the Canada Health Act
are protected, continues to be severely tested. Since 1984, as part of its deficit reduction program, the federal government imposed a series of reductions in the rate
of growth of transfer payments under the Established Programs Financing Act formula. The most massive of these changes were introduced in 1990 and reinforced
in 1991 with passage of Bill C-69, the Expenditures Restraint Act. Combined with
previous freezes, Bill C-69 will result in cash transfer entitlements disappearing earlier
than expected. The first province to feel the effect will be Quebec in 1994-1995.
Overall, the annual losses in transfer payments sustained by the provinces and
territories will amount to an estimated $6.6 billion by the end of the 1995-1996 fiscal
year. The total accumulated losses from 1986-1987 to 1995-1996 are expected to reach
$30 billion. Few provinces will find it easy to cope with this scale of reduction in
federal support (Thomson, 1991). The issues surrounding the reductions in federal
financing are being closely examined by the provinces and are likely to be of major
importance in the coming years.

CURRENT HEALTH CARE SYSTEM

Prevailing health care arrangements in Canada bear the imprint of the foregoing history and political dynamics and give the country's health care system its unique character. The limited legislative powers of the federal government in relation to health matters restrict Ottawa's role, in large part, to regulatory functions, international relations, and use of the spending powers of the federal parliament to make payments to provinces and individuals in fields in which it has no constitutional authority. This economic power enables the federal government to share the costs of the national health insurance program, fund health care research, and provide various information, advocacy, coordinating, and consultative services. The federal government is also responsible for service delivery to specific populations identified in the British North America Act of 1867, which includes Canada's aboriginal people, residents of the Yukon, members of the armed forces, and certain groups of immigrants and refugees.

Federal Health Organization

The principal agency governing health matters on the federal level is Health and Welfare Canada. Its objective of maintaining and improving the quality of health and well-being of Canadians is pursued in conjunction with other federal departments and agencies and with provincial and local governments. A formal structure has also been developed to facilitate federal/provincial/territorial cooperation and coordination. It includes conferences of ministers and deputy ministers, and federal/provincial/territorial advisory committees on institutional health and medical services, community care, mental health services, international health, health promotion, health human resources, environmental and occupational health, AIDS, alcohol and other drug problems, and women's health (Health and Welfare Canada, 1990a).

Within Health and Welfare Canada, health activities are organized into four main branches: Health Protection, Medical Services, Health Services and Promotion, and Fitness and Amateur Sport. A fifth branch, the Policy, Planning and Information Branch, is responsible for monitoring health issues, undertaking analyses, and providing policy support and advice to government officials and the Department's program branches.

The Health Protection Branch has responsibility for identifying, assessing, and managing risks to human health. To achieve this goal, the Branch administers various activities associated with food standards and safety, regulation of drugs, cosmetics, medical and radiation-emitting devices, and environmental health. This branch is also responsible for the Laboratory Centre for Disease Control and the Federal Centre for AIDS.

The Medical Services Branch provides health care to a number of client groups including registered Indians and Inuit, international travellers, civil aviation personnel, and prospective immigrants. As part of its services to Canada's aboriginal people, the Medical Services Branch operates a large network of health centers, nursing stations, and small hospitals across Canada. Transfer of administrative responsibility for these services is now being negotiated with various First Nations communities. (See also Chapter 9 and 29.)

The Health Services and Promotion Branch administers the Canada Health Act and facilitates information exchange on the operation of provincial health insurance programs. Other major programs within the branch include the National Health Research and Development Program, preventive health services, community and mental health, health facilities design, and health human resources. The newest and one of the most active programs within the branch is health promotion, established in 1978, to help Canadians achieve healthy lifestyles.

The Fitness and Amateur Sport Branch was established by an act of Parliament in 1961 and seeks to raise the level of fitness of Canadians and encourage lifelong participation in sport and recreation.

Health and Welfare Canada also has a number of advisory councils, such as the National Advisory Council on Aging, and individuals with special roles. These include the Senior Advisor—Status of Women and the Principal Nursing Officer; the latter position provides the Department with policy advice on matters pertaining to nursing and health (Shah, 1990; Health and Welfare Canada, 1990a).

Provincial/Territorial and Local Health Services

All provinces and, to an increasing extent, the Yukon and Northwest Territories play major roles in health care financing and the organization of services, including hospitals, physicians' services, public health, home care, long-term care, mental health, and ambulance services. The provinces and territories also provide a variety of administrative support services such as vital statistics, standard setting for health services, and health services and human resources planning and regulation.

Methods of organizing, financing, and administering health insurance plans vary across the provinces and the two territories. In some provinces, the plans are administered directly by provincial health ministries. In others, the plans are under separate public authorities reporting directly to the responsible minister.

Each province or territory is free to determine how its share of hospital and medical costs will be financed. Most provinces finance these services through general revenues, although British Columbia and Alberta impose premiums, and Ontario has an employer levy. Premium assistance is available in these jurisdictions for persons with limited income. Premium exemption is provided in Alberta and Ontario for most persons over 65 years of age.

Medical care for Canadians is provided by subsidizing private medical practitioners rather than through public clinics. Arrangements for payment of physicians and delivery of medical services vary. About 95% of Canada's physicians are paid on a fee-for-service basis. Rates are negotiated between provincial governments and medical associations, and increases are generally granted on an aggregate basis with medical associations deciding how the increases will be divided according to specialty. Individual practitioners in most provinces may choose whether to bill the insurance plan directly or bill the patient, the patient being eligible for reimbursement up to the provincial benefit level.

Most general and allied hospitals in Canada receive the largest part of their revenues from provincial or territorial insurance plans. These institutions are governed by provincial Hospital Acts, but responsibility for administration and provision of services is delegated to local authorities. Each institution is subject to provincial budget review, and operating budgets are negotiated annually on a global basis. For capital spending on hospital construction or renovation, or acquisition of new technology and equipment, hospitals must receive provincial government approval. This provides provincial governments with a strong lever to control the growth of hospital services and expenditures (Iglehart, 1986).

Basic to the operation of both hospital and medical insurance plans is the principle that patients may consult the physician of their choice and select the hospital in which they wish to be treated, provided that the attending physician has admitting privileges.

In Canada, as in many developed countries, the delivery of curative services is separated from that of preventive and public health services. Public health departments and community health agencies administer services such as communicable disease control and environmental sanitation and offer a range of programs related to maternal and child health, nutrition, school health services, health promotion, accident prevention, and dental hygiene. Health departments are also responsible for collection of vital statistics. In addition, most provinces maintain public health laboratories to ensure safety of milk, water, and food supplies and to assist local health agencies and health professionals in control of infectious diseases. In some provinces, such as British Columbia and Ontario, provincial health departments also finance and administer home care services. Most public health and community health activities are supported by a combination of provincial and local revenues.

Provincial governments have also played a major role in the provision of mental health services, with mental hospitals being directly financed and administered by them. Transfer of many treatment services to psychiatric units in general hospitals and the trend to de-institutionalize the mentally ill has resulted in a corresponding emphasis on community care and the development of community health services either through community outreach programs of hospitals or through official and voluntary community health agencies (Statistics Canada, 1989).

Hospital services are provided through a network of more than 1200 general, teaching, pediatric, and allied specialty hospitals with a bed capacity of about 188,000 beds, or approximately 7 beds per 1000 population. This capacity is higher than that of the United States (6/1000), but lower than countries such as Sweden (14/1000) and Australia (11/1000) (OECD, 1987). Of the total number of beds available, two thirds are listed as general acute care and one quarter as extended care. Over half of Canada's hospitals have under 100 beds. At the other end of the spectrum, mergers during the 1980s in cities such as Victoria, Vancouver, Edmonton, Winnipeg, London, and Toronto created megahospitals with more than 1000 beds each. There are also 42 provincial psychiatric hospitals throughout Canada (Health and Welfare Canada, 1990b). The nearly 3000 long-term care centers, made up of special care and nursing homes, homes for the aged, and community care facilities, have a total bed capacity of about 185,000, or 7.2 beds per 1000 population.

A broad array of voluntary agencies and associations is also involved in health care in Canada. Examples include the Canadian Red Cross, VON, and the Canadian Heart Foundation. Historically, voluntary agencies have played a major role in pioneering new services and promoting public awareness and action in relation to specific health problems (see also Chapter 30). With the rising prevalence of chronic illness, there has been a significant growth in voluntary mutual aid and self-help groups (Stewart, 1990). The annual value of services in the voluntary health and social services sector is estimated at about $1 billion (Statistics Canada, 1989).

Physicians are the major health professionals concerned with diagnosis and therapy. Their numbers have risen about 40% in the last 20 years and now total about 58,000. The increase can be attributed to two factors: an increasing number of graduates of Canadian medical schools and, prior to 1975, the addition of almost as many immigrant physicians per year as Canadian medical graduates. About half of the active physicians in Canada are general practitioners or family physicians. This compares with about 20% in the United States. Physicians comprise about 14% of the health work force in Canada; nursing personnel account for nearly 70%, health care technologists, 9%; and licensed pharmacists, 4%.

EXPENDITURES AND USE OF HEALTH SERVICES

The overall costs of health care in Canada, including expenditures by the private sector and all levels of government, reached $50 billion by 1990. Of this total, government contributions amounted to nearly 80%, with one third coming from Ottawa and two thirds from the provinces and territories. The distribution of these expenditures by type of service has remained relatively unchanged for more than a decade. Hospitals are quantitatively the most important, accounting for about 40% of expenditures, and other institutional services such as nursing homes another 13%. Physicians' services took roughly 16%; drugs and appliances accounted for 12%, dental care for about 6%, and other services, including public health, research, and capital expenditures, 13%. The $50 billion total amounted to nearly $2000 per person annually and represents an increase in health spending in constant dollars per capita since the completion of universal medicare coverage in 1971 of 1.6% per year (Evans et al., 1989). Health care expenditures now comprise about one third of the annual budget of most provinces and territories and nearly 9% of Canada's Gross National Product (GNP). This is up from the fairly stable figures of between 7.4% and 7.5% of the GNP in the 1970s and the rise to 8.6% in the 1982 recession but is still well below recent figures of 11% to 12% in the United States (Evans et al., 1989; Statistics Canada, 1990). The single largest health care expenditure growth factor since the mid-1970s is the increase in use and intensity of services per person (OECD, 1987).

The major users of health care facilities are the elderly, who now constitute about 10% of the population but use 40% of patient days in hospital. The major causes of hospitalization in terms of patient days per 100,000 population are, in rank order, heart disease, complications of pregnancy and childbirth, mental disorders, neoplasms, and respiratory disorders. On average, physician consultations per 1000 Canadians have been increasing at the rate of about 3% per year since the mid-1970s and now total 280. During this same period, hospital admissions dropped from 170 per 1000 population to 146 (Statistics Canada, 1985, 1990; Sutherland and Fulton, 1988).

Future Directions and Dilemmas in Canadian Health Care

Governments have been revamping Canada's health care system since it became publicly-administered in the 1960s. The lapse of time has demonstrated the complexity and political sensitivity of the process. The expansionist era of the 1960s, which saw the implementation of the national health insurance program and rapid growth in the size of the hospital sector and health care work force, quickly led to concern about high health care costs. These pressures prompted a series of federal government reports and commissions in the late 1960s and early 1970s, drawing attention to the cost trends and urging consideration of various options to achieve more effective and efficient health care delivery.

The transformation of the health care agenda took a new turn with the publication in 1974 of the Lalonde report, *A New Perspective on the Health of Canadians*. This report caught public imagination worldwide and set in motion a shift in focus from guaranteeing access to medical care to improving the health of the population. Of the required changes, a much higher priority was to be given to health promotion and disease prevention (Siler-Wells, 1988). This reorientation received substantial support from the World Health Organization's commitment to work toward the goal of "Health for All by the Year 2000" through the provision of primary health care services. The focus on safeguarding health was reaffirmed in 1986 with Health Minister Jake Epp's report, *Achieving Health for All*. This report recommended that, in the promotion of health, priority be given to fostering public participation, strengthening community services, and coordinating healthy public policy. Also in 1986, a similar set of strategies were emphasized in the Ottawa Charter for Health Promotion, a product of the First International Conference on Health Promotion held in Ottawa under the joint sponsorship of the World Health Organization, Health and Welfare Canada, and the Canadian Public Health Association. These and similar initiatives give the transformed health policy agenda political visibility and practical meaning (O'Neill, 1989). However, as Crichton (1986) observes, they have done little to change prevailing health care arrangements in Canada. Pressures to increase resources for high technology medicine and curative services remain high, as the newsworthiness of wait-lists for cardiac surgery and attendant tragedies illustrates. Nonetheless, countervailing pressures to recast the mission and goals of the health care system and to respond to the changing nature of health problems continue to accumulate.

The current disease burden consists largely of the chronic degenerative diseases such as cancer, heart disease, and chronic respiratory problems. Mental illness also remains a major problem. The demographic changes associated with the aging of the population mean that many more people will be living with these chronic conditions for longer periods in their lives than people did in the past. As McKeown (1979), Evans (1981), and others point out, the causal factors in these health problems come from complex combinations of behavioral and genetic factors, environmental exposure, and changes in social conditions associated with problems such as poverty, violence, drugs, and industrial pollutants. The personal health care system with its emphasis on disorders of bodily structure and function deals only with the consequences of such problems. According to Evans (1981), the health care systems have come through the phases in which emphasis was on infectious diseases and then on chronic illness; the new techniques needed to encourage healthy behavior and to recognize and treat social and environmental pathology are beginning to move modern health care systems into a third phase of their development. However, the precise shape of this new phase is far from clear. The remainder of the chapter examines some of the major themes in the debate about future directions in Canadian health care services.

Two overarching concerns have been driving health care reform in Canada during the last few years. As noted earlier, these are finding a pathway to an economically sustainable health care future and modifying the present system and policy framework in a manner that yields greater improvements in the health status of the population. These challenges are fundamental. They are also interrelated. Both have been brought to the forefront again by another round of health care task forces and commissions appointed during the 1980s (see Table 2-1) to help provinces accelerate their efforts to stem the rise in health care costs. The recommended strategies, many of which are now being tested, cover a wide spectrum of policy options. They include freezes on hospital budgets, wage restrictions, capping of physicians' fees, and adoption of new hospital funding formulae that consider factors such as case severity and efficient case management. Policies to restrain hospital use have also received wide attention. Measures range from closure of hospital beds, either temporarily or permanently, to use of deterrent fees such as the one approved in Quebec in 1991 to curb use of hospital emergency rooms. There is still much debate on whether such charges to the consumer are effective.

There also continues to be considerable interest in the question of what services should be covered by medical insurance plans and whether there should be an infusion of private funding. As a matter of policy, Canada has largely discouraged health care alternatives in the private sector, making it an exception in the Western world (Iglehart, 1990). Several provinces have looked at de-insuring or removing certain physician services from the list of items covered by the insurance plan. Of concern to critics of this move is the identification of exactly what services are to be de-insured. To preserve the principles of the Canada Health Act, they would have to fall in the "elective" or "frivolous" category. But what services are these? Who will decide? Is cosmetic surgery a personal luxury or psychiatric necessity? Who should pay for experimental surgery? The idea of a two-tier system raises fears of compromising the principle of universal access that Canadians have long held dear.

Another policy option attracting increasing attention is adding economic efficiency criteria to establish which items will be paid for by an insurance plan. This poses a significant challenge to the medical profession, which would face more rigorous evaluation of the appropriateness and efficacy of the clinical care rendered by physicians.

Another challenge to the medical profession comes from attempts in Canada to control the number of physicians. Research shows that the highly stable character of physician income in Canada is related to the ability of physicians to influence demands for patient care, a practice that contributes to the escalation of costs. The options under consideration or being tested in various provinces include restrictions on immigration of physicians into Canada, reductions in enrollment in Canadian

TABLE 2-1 **Selected Provincial and Federal Health Care Commissions and Task Forces 1983-1992**

Province	Year	Type of Task Force
Newfoundland	1983-1984	Royal Commission on Hospital and Nursing Home Costs
	1987-1988	Advisory Committee on Nursing Workforce
New Brunswick	1989	Commission on Selected Health Care Programs
	1988	Nursing Resources Advisory Committee
	1990-1992	Premier's Council on Health Strategy
Nova Scotia	1988-1989	Royal Commission on Health Care
Quebec	1983-1984	Comité d'étude sur la promotion de la santé
	1986-1987	Commission d'enquête sur les services de santé et les services sociaux
	1986-1987	Comité de la politique de santé mentale
	1986-1987	Comité d'étude sur la main-d'oeuvre en soins infirmiers
	1986-1989	Comité de travail sur les nouvelles technologies de reproduction humaine
Ontario	1982-1992	Health Professions Legislation Review
	1984-1987	Minister's Advisory Group on Health Promotion
	1986-1987	Health Review Panel
	1986-1987	Panel on Health Goals for Ontario
	1986	Task Force on Implementation of Midwifery in Ontario
	1989	Premier's Council on Health Strategy
	1989	Task Force on the Use and Provision of Medical Services
Manitoba	1988	Health Advisory Network Steering Committee
Saskatchewan	1988-1990	Commission on Directions in Health Care
Alberta	1987-1989	Advisory Committee on the Utilization of Medical Services
	1988-1989	Premier's Commission on Future Health Care for Albertans
British Columbia	1990-1991	Royal Commission on Health Care and Costs
Canada	1983-1984	Task Force on the Allocation of Health Care Resources
	1984-1987	Committee on the Health Care of the Elderly
	1985	Commission of Inquiry on the Pharmaceutical Industry
	1989-1992	Royal Commission on New Reproductive Technologies

Compiled from Angus DE (1991). *Review of significant health care commissions and task forces in Canada since 1983-1984*, Ottawa: Canadian Hospital Association, Canadian Medical Association, and Canadian Nurses Association.

medical schools, and incentives to move from fee-for-service to salary reimbursement arrangements.

A major emphasis of cost containment in hospitals has been management training and organizational reform. A great deal of this interest focuses on medical and nursing services, but little data exist on whether the adoption of new organizational models and management strategies are having the desired effect on resource use (Meilicke, 1990) (see also Chapter 6).

Since the hospital sector consumes more than 40% of health care funds, it is natural that this sector should receive special scrutiny in regard to cost containment. Much of the growth of hospital cost is attributed to the volume of hospital services or intensity of care rather than an increase in the number of persons being treated. Studies over the past decade show that significant variations in intensity of services and in the use of diagnostic and surgical procedures cannot be justified on the basis of quality or outcomes. It has been estimated that while operational efficiency measures could lower costs by 10% to 15%, potential savings of 20% to 25% could be achieved by bringing utilization rates of selected therapies and procedures within an average target range (Auer, 1991).

In combining resource-based cost containment strategies with outcome measures, however, the availability of good data is critical. Computerized management information systems have become essential to provide information on resource use. Unfortunately, quality control sytems are still in a rudimentary stage of development. To begin to address broader information needs, a National Health Information Council was formed in 1988 to develop some consensus on information requirements pertaining to costs and outcomes and to develop appropriate data standards to facilitate inter-institutional comparisons.

Despite its preoccupation with controlling health care costs, on the whole, Canada has a good record relative to other countries. Through keeping administrative overhead low, controlling payments to physicians and hospitals, and restraining diffusion of new technology, Canada continues to be successful in combining universal coverage with substantially lower expenditure for health services (Detsky et al., 1990; Evans et al., 1989; Rachlis and Kushner, 1989).

However, strains on the system are building, due in part to a slowing economy, the size of the federal deficit, and decreased fiscal transfers from the federal government. Adding to the strains are the increased scrutiny the government faces from the public, the media, and professional interest groups as they focus attention on several areas of perceived inadequate funding (Detsky et al., 1990). Other often-cited threats to the affordability of universal health care in Canada include the introduction of a wider range of high cost technology and the future impact of an aging population on health care expenditures. Canada does not have a well-developed system of technology assessment, but assessment capabilities will be enhanced by the creation of the Canadian Coordinating Office for Health Technology Assessment. A paucity of data on the linkages between technology use, intensity of services, health outcomes, and costs make it difficult to judge the degree to which technology threatens affordability (OECD, 1987).

Other than direct costs, technological advances have also changed the moral landscape of health care and constitute one of the most important social choices involving the health care system of the future. We can maintain life at a much earlier stage of infant prematurity while also prolonging life at the other end of the age spectrum with a vast array of machinery and medications. Existing technology in genetic screening, transplants, life support, and genetic manipulation force society to examine questions it never had to face openly before. These questions range from "How important is the quality of life?" to "What kinds of genetic characteristics does one want to include or exclude from future generations?"

The above moral and ethical questions assume special meaning in addressing some of the priority health care problems of an aging population. Together with the very young, it is the very old who generate the highest health care costs. One estimate suggests that Canada could face overall cost increases of 30% over the next 25 years or so as a result of changing demographics (OECD, 1987). Such estimates do not go unchallenged. However, they serve as an important catalyst for governments to encourage development of community-based care alternatives. Community health care centers, home care, and community support services have all experienced substantial growth over the last decade. There have also been significant strides in improving coordination of services and achieving better linkages between hospital and community-based care. For example, the Extra-Mural hospital program in New Brunswick (Ferguson, 1991) and the Greater Victoria Health project in British Columbia (Peck, 1991) both demonstrate an impressive ability to keep elderly people in the home through a well-integrated set of services.

The provincial health care system that has probably advanced farthest in reorganizing services for the future is Quebec's. Beginning in 1972, health and social services were amalgamated, and a regional planning and service network established. This network involved consumers in health care decision making and fostered the development of multidisciplinary approaches. The most important service innovation was the local community service center (centres locaux des services communautaires, or CLSCs). The services they provide include medical care, home care, health education, and general social services. They also operate various community outreach programs. Compared with most community health centers in other provinces, CLSCs are demedicalized institutions (Desrosiers, 1986; Sutherland and Fulton, 1988).

Nursing associations throughout Canada have been advocating that Canada move more aggressively to adopt the World Health Organization concept of primary health care as a central organizing principle in a reformed health care system. This model is seen as being more compatible with the priority health issues of today and the social and political values that underlie the shift in emphasis from curative medicine to health promotion and disease prevention. It has also drawn increased attention to the social determinants of health and the role that health care providers working with consumers must play in this arena (CNA, 1988; RNABC, 1990).

CONCLUSION

This chapter reviews the principal developments that shaped the Canadian health care system and outlines some of the issues that are central to debates about its future. Many of these themes will be discussed in subsequent chapters. The changes we are now witnessing have important implications for many stakeholders, including consumers and members of the health professions. The challenge will be to change the culture of health care into one of innovation and quality while preserving the best of the system and including the successes of cost containment. The fact that Canada's system of universally accessible health care has not eradicated social inequalities in the health status of the population also suggests an urgent need for health professionals to look beyond disciplinary and health care boundaries in thinking about how to improve the health of Canadians. One of the most significant needs in moving ahead will be the development of national health goals to guide action and encourage collaborative efforts. A number of provinces have taken this important step. It is now time for national action. In this light and in view of nurses' significant contributions to the health care system, it is a necessary professional and political task for both individual nurses and organized nursing interest groups to look to a new future for health in Canada and to participate in the ongoing public debates that surround health issues in Canada.

REFERENCES

Angus, D.E. (1991). *Review of significant health care commissions and task forces in Canada since 1983-84.* Ottawa: Canadian Hospital Association, Canadian Medical Association, and Canadian Nurses Association.

Auer, L. (1991). *Proposal for a council document on health care.* Ottawa: Economic Council of Canada.

Badgley, R., & Wolfe, S. (1967). *Doctors' strike: Medical care and conflict in Saskatchewan.* Toronto: Macmillan.

Baly, M.E. (1989, Autumn). Florence Nightingale and the development of public health nursing. *Humane Medicine, 5,* 37-45.

Canadian Nurses Association. (1988). *Health for all Canadians: A call for health care reform.* Ottawa: Author.

Chadwick, E. (1965). *Report on the sanitary condition of the labouring popultaion of Gt. Britain* (Edited, with an introduction by M.W. Flinn). Edinburgh: University Press. (Original work published in 1842)

Crichton, A. (1986). The shift from entrepreneurial to political power in the Canadian health system. *Social Science and Medicine, 10,* 59-66.

Desrosiers, G. (1986). The Quebec health care system. *Journal of Public Health Policy, 7*(2), 211-217.

Detsky, A.S., O'Rourke, K., Naylor, C.D., Stacey, S.R., & Kitchens, J.M. (1990). Containing Ontario's hospital costs under universal insurance in the 1980's: What was the record? *Canadian Medical Association Journal, 142*(6), 565-572.

Engels, F. (1958). *The condition of the working class in England* (W.O. Henderson & W.H. Chaloner, Trans.). Oxford: Basil Blackwell. (Original work published in 1845)

Epp, J. (1986). *Achieving health for all.* Ottawa: Charter for Health Promotion.

Evans, J. (1981). *Measurement and management in medicine and health services.* New York: The Rockefeller Foundation.

Evans, R.G., Lomas, J., Barer, M.L., Labelle, R.J., Fooks, C., Stoddart, G.L., Anderson, G.M., Feeny, D., Gafni, A., Torrance, G.W., & Tholl, W.G. (1989). Controlling health expenditures—the Canadian reality. *New England Journal of Medicine, 320*(9), 571-577.

Evans, R.G., & Stoddart, G.L. (1990). Producing health, consuming health care. *Social Science and Medicine, 31*(12), 1347-1363.

Ferguson, G. (1991). Extra-Mural: The hospital without walls. *Dimensions in Health Service, 68*(5), 16-19.

Flexner, A. (1910). *Medical education in the United States and Canada: A report to the Carnegie Foundation for the Advancement of Teaching.* New York: Carnegie Foundation (Bulletin #4).

Flinn, M.W. (1965). Introduction. In E. Chadwick, *Report on the sanitary conditions of the labouring population of Gt. Britain.* Edinburgh: University Press.

Government of Canada. (1964). *Royal Commission on Health Services.* Ottawa: Queen's Printer.

Grob, G. (1983). Disease and environment in American history. In D. Mechanic (Ed.), *Handbook of health, health care, and the health professions* (pp.3-22). New York: The Free Press.

Hastings, J., & Mosley, W. (1980). Introduction: The evolution of organized community health services in Canada. In C. Meilicke & J. Storch (Eds.), *Perspectives on Canadian health and social services policy: History and emerging trends* (pp.145-155). Ann Arbor, MI: Health Administration Press.

Heagerty, J. (1980). The development of public health in Canada. In C. Meilicke & J. Storch (Eds.), *Perspectives on Canadian health and social services policy: History and emerging trends* (pp.137-144). Ann Arbor, MI: Health Administration Press.

Health and Welfare Canada. (1974). *Social security in Canada.* Ottawa: Information Canada.

Health and Welfare Canada. (1990a). *Annual report 1989-1990* (Cat. No. H1-3/1990). Ottawa: Supply and Services Canada.

Health and Welfare Canada. (1990b). *Mental health services in Canada 1990* (Cat. No. H39-182/1990E). Ottawa: Supply and Services Canada.

Iglehart, J.K. (1986). Canada's health care system. *New England Journal of Medicine, 315,* 778-784.

Iglehart, J.K. (1990). Health policy report: Canada's health care system faces its problems. *New England Journal of Medicine, 322* (8), 562-568.

Lalonde, M. (1974). *A new perspective on the health of Canadians*. Ottawa: National Health and Welfare.

LeClair, M. (1976). The Canadian health care system. In S. Andreopoulos (Ed.), *National health insurance: The Canadian experience* (pp.11-93). New York: John Wiley and Sons.

McKeown, T. (1979). *The role of medicine: Dream, mirage or nemesis* (2nd ed). Oxford: Blackwell.

Meilicke, C. (1990). Nurses and physicians in the modern hospital: Watering the garden. *Canadian Health Care Management Vol. 1, OD, 11*, 1-6.

Mustard, J.F. (1987). Health in a post industrial society. In J.N. Clarke, L. Demers, M. Kelly, D. McCreary, & B. Noble (Eds.), *Health care in Canada: Looking ahead*. Ottawa: Canadian Public Health Association.

Organization for Economic Co-operation and Development (OECD). (1987). *Financing and delivering health care: A comparative analysis of OECD countries*. Paris: Author.

O'Neill, M. (1989/90, Winter). Healthy public policy: The WHO perspective. *Health Promotion, 28*(3), 6-8.

Peck, S.H.S. (1991). Meeting needs through integrated care. *Dimensions in Health Service, 68*(5), 2-27.

Phillips, P., & Phillips, E. (1983). *Women and workd: Inequality in the labour market*. Toronto: Lorimer.

Rachlis, M., & Kushner, C. (1989). *Second opinion: What's wrong with Canada's health care system and how to fix it*. Toronto: Collins.

Registered Nurses Association of British Columbia (RNABC). (1990). *Submission to the Royal Commission on Health Care and Costs*. Vancouver: Author.

Shah, C. (1987). *An introduction to Canadian health and the health care system* (2nd ed.). Toronto: University of Toronto Department of Preventative Medicine and Biostatistics.

Shah, C.P. (1990). *Public health and preventative medicine in Canada* (2nd ed.). Toronto: University of Toronto Press.

Siler-Wells, G.L. (1988). *Directing change and changing direction: A new health policy agenda for Canada*. Ottawa: Canadian Public Health Association.

Soderstrom, L. (1978). *The Canadian health care system*. London: Croom Helm.

Splane, R.B. (1965). *Social welfare in Ontario 1791-1893*. Toronto: University of Toronto Press.

Starr, P. (1982). *The transformation of American medicine*. New York: Basic Books.

Statistics Canada (1985). *The Canada year book 1985*. Ottawa: Author.

Statistics Canada (1989). *The Canada year book 1990: A review of economic, social and political developments in Canada*. Ottawa: Author.

Statistics Canada (1990). *Health reports 1989* (Vol. 1, No. 2). Ottawa: Author.

Stewart, M.J. (1990). Professional interface with mutual-aid self-help groups: A review. *Social Science and Medicine, 31*(10), 1143-1158.

Sutherland, R.W., & Fulton, M.J. (1988). *Health care in Canada: A description and analysis of Canadian health services*. Ottawa: The Health Group: Ralph W. Sutherland and M. Jane Fulton.

Taylor, M. (1980). The Canadian health insurance program. In C. Meilicke & J. Storch (Eds.), *Perspectives on Canadian health and social services policy: History and emerging trends* (pp.183-197). Ann Arbor, MI: Health Administration Press.

Thomson, A. (1991). *Federal support for health care: A background paper*. Ottawa: Alistair Thomson Policy Inc.

Torrance, G. (1987). Socio-historical overview: The development of the Canadian health system. In D. Coburn, C. D'Arcy, G. Torrance, & P. New (Eds.), *Health and Canadian society* (2nd ed.) (pp. 6-32). Markham, ON: Fitzhenry & Whiteside.

Waitzkin, H. (1983). A Marxist view of health and health care. In D. Mechanic (Ed.), *Handbook of health, health care, and the health professions* (pp.657-682). New York: The Free Press.

Wallace, E. (1980). The origin of the social welfare state in Canada, 1867-1900. In C. Meilicke & J. Storch (Eds.), *Perspectives on Canadian health and social services policy: History and emerging trends* (pp.25-37). Ann Arbor, MI: Health Administration Press.

Wilkins, R., Adams, O., & Brancker, A. (1990). Changes in mortality by income in urban Canada from 1971 to 1986. *Health reports 1989* (Vol. 1, No. 2). Ottawa: Author.

Graduates from hospital schools of nursing formed the principal supply of registered nurses until these schools began closing during the 1960s and 1970s. This photograph shows the last graduating class from St. Paul's Hospital, Vancouver, in 1974. (Photograph courtesy of *RNABC News*, Registered Nurses Association of British Columbia. Used with permission.)

CHAPTER THREE

The Nursing Work Force in Canada

ALICE J. BAUMGART, RN, PhD
MARY M. WHEELER, RN, MEd

Alice J. Baumgart, RN, BSN *(British Columbia), MSc (McGill), PhD (Toronto), is Vice-Principal, Human Services, Queen's University. She has held numerous leadership posts on international, national, and provincial nursing committees and boards and is President of the Canadian Nurses Association for 1991-1992. Her professional and scholarly interests include the use of nursing's human resources, the role and status of women in health care, and the history of nursing.*

Mary M. Wheeler, RN, BN *(Dalhousie), MEd (Toronto), has a consulting practice focusing on Transition Management. Her previous position was Interim Executive Director for the Registered Nurses' Association of Ontario. At RNAO, she also managed the Health Human Resources Planning portfolio, which included overseeing the development and publication of* Sorry No Care Available Due to the Nursing Shortage.

In Canada, nursing personnel account for nearly two thirds of the health sector labor force. They are made up of four broad occupational groups. The largest category, registered nurses (RNs), numbers some 250,000 and forms the single largest professional occupation in Canada. The other major categories in the field are: registered nursing assistants (RNAs), known in some regions as licensed practical nurses (LPNs); various types of aides, attendants, and orderlies; and, in the four Western provinces, separately trained and regulated psychiatric nurses (RPNs).

Since the mid-1980s, this work force has encountered a more complex, volatile, and uncertain employment landscape. The transformation is the product of a broad mix of forces ranging from Canada's weak economic growth and high public debt to new priorities for health service provision. These trends affect both the supply and demand sides of the nursing labor market. On the supply side, notable changes include large gains in participation by married women and rising educational levels, yielding a more experienced and flexible work force but one less willing to sacrifice personal fulfillment for organizational goals. On the demand side, ongoing technological innovations continue to serve as a catalyst for more varied and specialized roles and responsibilities, making it difficult for nurses to shift from job to job without additional training. Other new practice demands, such as the move toward community-oriented forms of treatment and care for the elderly, have appreciably altered skill requirements and patterns of career choice.

In the 1990s, the centrality of these trends in determining the character and conditions of nursing work is being overshadowed by powerful pressures to contain health care spending. The resulting cost cutting measures and structural changes in health care are serving up a difficult and unsettling blend of new opportunities and wrenching adjustments for many nursing personnel. The rebound effects are especially severe in hospitals, which account for 40% of health care expenditures, and where the largest proportion of the nursing work force is employed. The painful costs range from exhausting workloads to recurrent job losses but are perhaps most obvious in the widespread dissatisfaction of nurses with hospital employment and its rewards. One consequence is an increasing number of nursing labor disputes in which unsafe patient care and a deteriorating work environment are central issues.

These developments come at a time when future health care requirements are expected to be heavily dependent on nursing personnel (Employment and Immigration Canada, 1988; World Health Organization, 1989). In the face of these challenges, the dynamics of nursing employment and related human resource issues have assumed a much higher priority on public policy agendas across Canada. An important event in this regard was the National Nursing Symposium, convened in Winnipeg in November, 1990, under the auspices of the ministers of health of the territories and provinces (National Nursing Symposium Steering Committee, 1991). The symposium provided a national forum to examine issues facing Canadian nursing from the perspective of employers, government, and key nursing provider groups. Similar exercises have been carried out in a number of provincial jurisdictions. Although a consensus on future directions is still a long way off, these events have helped to move discussions an important step forward by bringing into sharper focus nursing resource planning and development issues needing policy attention.

This chapter looks at these issues from the perspective of registered nurses. The first part of the chapter examines the rapid growth in the aggregate supply of registered nurses since the 1960s and the gradual remoulding of the RN work force to reflect new societal and workplace demands. This is followed by an examination of recent employment trends and the factors contributing to problems of supply and demand. The final section considers some of the key issues associated with human resource planning and development for registered nurses in the 1990s. Before proceeding, however, a word of explanation is in order on the availability of statistical data on registered nurses in Canada.

DATA ON REGISTERED NURSES IN CANADA

Compared to most countries, Canada has a well-developed system for compiling, analyzing, and disseminating information on health personnel, including registered nurses. Nationwide statistics on the supply of health workers are compiled annually by Statistics Canada from various sources, including educational institutions, provincial licensing and registering bodies, and professional association membership lists. Supplementary data are available from Statistics Canada labor force surveys carried out monthly and from census information collected every 5 years. Since 1972, selected information from these data bases has been published by Health and Welfare Canada in the annual *Canada Health Manpower Inventory*, which was renamed *Health Personnel in Canada* in 1987. Recent editions have included data on 30 health occupations.

In terms of registered nurses, annual statistics have been compiled and published since 1965 when the Research Unit of the Canadian Nurses Association was established and a standardized form adopted by regulatory authorities for registration purposes. These statistics have been available in various reports: initially in a CNA publication called *Countdown;* then, starting in 1972, as part of the *Canada Health Manpower Inventory* and its successor, *Health Personnel in Canada;* from 1986 to 1988 in a separate monograph entitled *Nursing in Canada;* and, since 1989, as a supplement to the Statistics Canada publication, *Health Reports.* These publications provide information on the personal and professional profile of nurses currently registered in Canada plus basic statistics on nursing education.

Although these data systems are useful in formulating public policy and analyzing the nursing labor market, they are blunt instruments for work force planning. A major deficiency is the absence of adequate data on demands for nursing personnel. Currently, such data are difficult to assemble or may not exist. In part, this stems from the fact that most health sector statistics in Canada are gathered and analyzed by the provincial and federal authorities to assist in program planning and fiscal control and so do not routinely include separate breakdowns on human resource requirements and utilization. Compounding the problem is the dearth of applied health services research on human resource questions, such as contemporary patterns of nurse utilization.

In response to increasing calls in recent years to improve health human resources information systems, a number of provinces and and various nursing organizations across Canada have started routinely to track RN employment trends using various job vacancy and employment opportunity surveys (Ontario Hospital Association/ Ontario Ministry of Health, 1987; Registered Nurses Association of British Columbia, 1990). There is also increasing activity in Canada and the United States to identify components of automated record systems necessary to assist in describing the quality, costs, and outcomes of nursing care (Hannah, 1988; McCormick, 1991; Werley, Devine, and Zorn, 1990).

The data on the registered nurse work force drawn together for this chapter reflect the foregoing gaps, inconsistencies, and limitations in nursing data bases in Canada. Also, because of incomplete provincial returns to Statistics Canada for 1990 (the latest year for which detailed data on nursing in Canada have been published), descriptive information on registered nurses is taken from the Statistics Canada publication, *Registered Nurses Management Data 1989*, unless otherwise noted.

INCREASES IN RN SUPPLY

One of the most striking changes in the RN work force over the last 30 years is the unprecedented increase in the number of registered nurses. This pattern of growth is a worldwide phenomenon in which almost every country has seen its health care labor force grow at a faster rate than its population. In many cases, increases in supply have also outpaced growth in the national economy, adding substantially to health care costs (World Health Organization, 1988).

Expansion in the supply of registered nurses in Canada gained momentum with the economic prosperity and growth of hospitals in the 1960s. It has continued at a rate exceeding population growth ever since. By 1989, the number of registered nurses stood at an all time high of 252,189. Peak growth was in the 1970s when it averaged 5% per year. However, even in the volatile economic climate of the 1980s, increases averaged 2% annually, about double the growth rate experienced by Canada's population. In contrast, between 1980 and 1988, the supply of registered nursing assistants increased only slightly, from 82,297 to 82,826, then fell to 82,281 in 1989. The RN:RNA ratio now stands at about 3 RNs for every RNA (Table 3-1).

TABLE 3-1 **Increases in Supply: Registered Nurses, Registered Nursing Assistants, Canada, (1965-1989)**

	1965	1970	1980	1985	1989
Registered nurses					
Number living and/or working in Canada*	104,349	135,047	177,182	203,849	252,189
Increase (%)	—	29.4	31.2	15.1	9.8
RNs/100,000 population	551	634	781	848	962
Registered nursing assistants					
Number living and/or working in Canada	30,172	46,184	69,475	80,297	82,281
Increase (%)	—	53.1	50.4	15.6	−0.9
RNAs/100,000 population	154	217	306	334	313

Sources: Canadian Nurses Association, 1968, 1971.
Health and Welfare Canada, 1976, 1986, 1990.
Statistics Canada, 1974, 1981a, 1981b, 1983b, 1989a, 1989b, 1990a, 1990b.
*Some nurses register in more than one province; these data refer to registered nurses, resident in Canada, after inter-provincial duplicates have been removed.

A comparison with other health occupations in Canada puts the current supply of registered nurses in Canada into broader perspective. After registered nurses, the next three largest occupational groups consist of some 58,000 physicians, 21,000 medical laboratory technologists, and an almost equal number of pharmacists (20,000) (Health and Welfare Canada, 1990).

Although international comparisons are difficult to make because of limited comparability of data, 1984 statistics indicate that, with 884 registered nurses per 100,000 population, Canada ranked with Australia (934/100,000), the United States (830/100,000), and New Zealand 1238/100,000) in having among the highest nurse to population ratios in the world (World Health Organization, 1988; Health and Welfare Canada, 1986).

All geographical regions within Canada have shared in the growth of registered nurses, with most areas of the country having ratios per 100,000 population close to or above the national average (806). The exceptions are Newfoundland, where the concentration is lower relative to other provinces (757), and the Northwest Territories and the Yukon, where nursing resources are much more thinly spread (568 and 476 respectively).

Not surprisingly, the majority of registered nurses in Canada are found in Ontario (82,935) and Quebec (55,027), the most densely populated provinces. Together, these provinces account for 62% of Canada's RN supply.

These gains in supply have been matched by important changes in the personal and professional profile of the RN work force, changes that flow from both societal trends and workplace demands.

CHANGING PROFILE OF THE RN WORK FORCE

In terms of personal characteristics, Canada's RN work force remains female dominated. The proportion of men employed in nursing has risen only marginally since the 1970s and, for the past decade, has remained stable at around 3%. However, this figure masks the substantial increase in the number of men entering the profession. The 1980s saw the largest growth in the number of male nurses, from 3936 to 7316 (Okrainec, 1991; Statistics Canada, 1989c). Of this total, more than one half are employed in the province of Quebec, where they account for nearly 7% of the active RN population.

A more conspicuous change is the steady increase in the representation of married women; in 1990 they made up more than 70% of the RN work force. This contrasts with 30 years ago when only one in four practicing nurses was married. One result of the influx of married nurses into the work force is a significant change in the age structure of the RN population. Prior to the 1960s, an estimated one third of nurses left the work force within 10 years of graduation, and only about 50% remained employed, either continuously or intermittently, until pensionable age (International Labor Office, 1960). This meant that the vast majority of nurses were under 30 years of age. In 1990, the RN population in Canada was older. The median age has increased to 38 years, and the proportion 40 years of age and older is approaching 45%. The biggest change is the decrease in the size of the cohort aged 29 and under, down from 39.2% in 1970 to 17.8% in 1989 (Table 3-2).

TABLE 3-2 Employed Registered Nurses by Age Group, Canada, 1970, 1980, 1989

Age group (years)	1970 (%)	1980 (%)	1989 (%)
Less than 25	15.2	4.7	4.2
25-29	24.0	21.8	13.6
30-34	14.2	21.3	16.2
35-39	10.5	16.2	18.9
40-44	8.8	11.6	16.3
45-49	7.1	8.9	8.4
50-54	6.2	7.0	8.4
55 and over	9.6	8.8	9.3
Not stated	4.4	0.6	0.2
TOTAL	107,284	155,178	220,999

Sources: Canadian Nurses Association, 1971.
Statistics Canada, 1980, 1989c.

TABLE 3-3 Registered Nurses Employed Part-time by Field of Employment, Canada, 1970, 1980, 1989

Field of employment	1970 Part-time (%)	1980 Part-time (%)	1989 Part-time (%)
Hospital	28.9	33.3	32.3
Nursing home, home for the aged	—*	45.2	45.0
Community Health	19.0	27.3	32.0
Physician's office, family practice unit	43.3	47.0	54.4
Educational institution	13.0	20.3	23.8
Other	45.7	38.4	33.6
Not stated	25.0	42.0	20.0
TOTAL	29.3	33.8	33.6
TOTAL NUMBER EMPLOYED	107,284	155,178	220,999

Sources: Canadian Nurses Association, 1971.
Statistics Canada, 1980, 1990b.
*Not available.

In terms of activity status, nearly 90% of the 252,189 registered nurses in Canada are employed in a nursing capacity. Even in the 10% of nurses out of the work force or employed elsewhere, one third report that they are seeking a position in nursing. This is a remarkably high labor force participation rate in a predominantly female occupation and represents a 10% increase over 1980 participation rates. It is also 10% above 1988 U.S. rates (Moses, 1991).

About one third of employed registered nurses work part-time (Table 3-3), up only slightly since 1970 (from 29.3% to 33.6%) and about 8% above the rate for women in the labor force as a whole (Statistics Canada, 1990c). By far the largest share of registered nurses who work part-time is drawn from the ranks of married women (87%). Also of interest is the wide variation in the rates of part-time employment in different provinces, the figure ranging from a high of 52% in Prince Edward Island to a low of 16% in Newfoundland. Differences in rates also exist across the various employment sectors, with the highest rates of part-time employment being among nurses working in physicians' offices or family practice units (52.2%), followed by nursing homes and homes for the aged (44.5%). What portion of these variances is due to employee preference or because it is the only work available is not known.

Information on the current distribution and growth of registered nurses by employment field is displayed in Tables 3-4 and 3-5. Despite the increasing diversity of health care settings in which registered nurses work, nearly three quarters (72%) continue to be employed by hospitals, followed by community health (10.4%) and nursing homes and homes for the aged (7.0%). This may be partly explained by the increasing use of nurse-intensive technology in hospitals and the greater acuity of care required by contemporary hospital patients. As Table 3-4 shows, the major new field of employment for nurses is in the care of the elderly and chronically ill in

TABLE 3-4 **Percentage of Registered Nurses by Field of Employment, Canada, 1970, 1980, 1989**

Field of employment	1970	1980	1989
Hospital	81.9	73.6	72.0
Nursing home, home for the aged	—*	6.2	7.0
Community Health	5.8	8.9	10.4
Physician's office, family practice unit	3.0	2.8	2.5
Educational institution	3.2	3.0	2.6
Other	6.1	3.3	4.2
TOTAL NUMBER EMPLOYED	107,284	155,178	220,999

Sources: Canadian Nurses Association, 1971.
Statistics Canada, 1980, 1989c.
*Not available.

TABLE 3-5 **Growth in Size of Registered Nurses Work Force by Field of Employment, Canada, 1980-1989**

Field	Number of RNs 1989	Size of increase or decrease from 1980-1989	Change (%)
Hospital	159,062	44,832	39.2
Nursing home, home for the aged	15,572	5905	61.1
Community Health	22,907	9168	66.7
Physician's office, family practice unit	5601	1255	28.9
Educational institution	5844	1198	25.8
Other	9253	4085	79.0
Not stated	2760	− 622	− 18.4
TOTAL	220,999	65,821	42.4

Sources: Statistics Canada, 1980, 1989c.

TABLE 3-6 **Registered Nurses by Type of Positions Held, Canada, 1980, 1989**

Position	1980 N	Work force (%)	1989 N	Work force (%)	Change in number employed (%)
Director, assistant/ associate director	3792	2.4	5,321	2.4	40.3
Supervisor/coordinator, assistant supervisor/ coordinator	7672	4.9	10,923	4.9	42.4
Clinical specialist	2676	1.7	1532*	0.7	− 42.8
Head nurse	16,263	10.5	16,295	7.4	0.2
General duty/staff nurse	103,179	66.5	157,977	71.5	53.1
Instructor/professor	4360	2.8	5683	2.6	30.3
Other	9881	6.4	13,940	6.3	41.0
Not stated	7355	4.8	9328	4.2	26.8
TOTAL NUMBER EMPLOYED	155,178	100.0	220,999	100.0	42.4

Sources: Statistics Canada, 1980, 1989c.
*Some differences in definition between 1980 and 1989 make these data difficult to compare.

TABLE 3-7 **Registered Nurses by Age Group and Highest Level of Education in Nursing, Canada, 1989**

Age group (years)	Total (%)	Basic RN (%)	Post-basic diploma (%)	Baccalaureate (%)	Master's and higher (%)
Under 30	17.8	76.6	7.0	16.2	0.2
30-39	35.1	69.5	15.2	14.3	0.9
40-49	29.2	67.9	18.5	12.3	1.3
Over 50	17.6	67.2	22.0	9.1	1.7
TOTAL	220,999	69.9	16.0	13.1	1.0

Source: Statistics Canada, 1989c.

nursing homes and homes for the aged, a category not even included in the array of published statistics on nursing in 1970.

Table 3-6 shows that the most common jobs filled by registered nurses were general duty or staff nursing positions (71.5%) and lower and middle management roles such as head nurse or supervisor (12.3%). The major growth area since 1980 has been in the general duty or staff category, with the number up 53.1%. In keeping with the growth in numbers of general duty/staff nurses, management categories have also seen substantial growth (40.3% for directors, assistant/associate directors; 42.4% for supervisory personnel). Regardless of job title, nearly 90% of registered nurses reported their principal area of responsibility as direct patient care. These data certainly do not support the claims made from time to time that fewer registered nurses are providing "hands on" patient care.

Another characteristic of the RN work force showing signs of change is educational levels (Table 3-7). Nearly one third of registered nurses hold educational qualifications beyond basic diploma training. Of this total, 16% have additional nursing-related education in the form of a certificate or diploma, another 13% hold a baccalaureate degree as their highest level of education, and 1% have completed a master's or doctoral degree. This is roughly double the proportion holding additional qualifications in 1970 (Canadian Nurses Association, 1971), and 10% above 1980 levels. Table 3-7 also demonstrates the strong correlation between the age of nurses and type of educational attainment, with the highest proportion of university educated nurses in the under 30 age group and falling progressively in older age cohorts. However, the older the nurse, the greater the likelihood of completion of a post-basic nursing diploma or certificate program.

With regard to income, salaries of registered nurses vary by region, with starting salaries for full-time general duty/staff nurses in hospitals in 1990 ranging from a high in British Columbia of $35,676 to a low in Prince Edward Island of $27,475 (Table 3-8). Generally, starting wage rates in Ontario and the Western provinces are

TABLE 3-8 **Annual Salaries Registered Nurses Working as General Duty/Staff**
Nurses in Hospitals July, 1991

Province	Annual salary		Hourly rate		Number of steps	Maximum/ minimum difference
	Minimum*	Maximum†	Minimum	Maximum		
British Columbia	$35,676.00	$41,268.00	$18.23	$21.08	6	$ 5592.00
Alberta	35,430.36	43,507.95	18.51	22.73	8	8077.59
Saskatchewan	35,422.40	44,449.60	17.03	21.37	10	9027.20
Manitoba	33,643.00	39,824.00	16.69	19.76	5	6181.00
Ontario	32,779.50	52,006.50	16.81	26.67	9	19,227.00
Quebec	28,162.16	40,942.20	14.94	21.72	12	12,780.04
New Brunswick	31,804.50	39,897.00	17.56	22.06	6	8092.50
Nova Scotia	27,800.00	36,824.00	14.21	18.82	6	9024.00
Prince Edward Island	27,475.00	34,205.00	14.04	17.47	5	6730.00
Newfoundland	31,108.45	40,248.60	13.78	17.40	8	9140.15

Sources: Canadian Nurses Association, 1991a.
*Average starting salary is $31,930.13.
†Average maximum salary is $41,317.28.

at or above the national average, while those in Atlantic Canada are 5% to 10% below average. A comparison of maximum full-time nurses' salaries yields a picture fairly similar to starting rates. Ontario has the highest maximum salaries ($52,000), followed by Saskatchewan ($44,449) and Alberta ($43,507). Nurses in Atlantic Canada have maximum salaries ranging from 17% below the national average in Prince Edward Island to 2.5% below the national average in Newfoundland.

Adjusted for price increases, these salary levels show little or no gains in real income for registered nurses over the course of the 1980s, a pattern also applying to most family income levels in Canada during this period (Statistics Canada, 1990c). A comparison with other health care occupations (using 1986 Census data), shows average full-time annual salaries of registered nurses at about one third that of physicians, 10% below pharmacists, and hovering within 5% of physiotherapists, occupational therapists, and medical laboratory technologists. Registered nursing assistants had average annual incomes about 25% below those of registered nurses (Statistics Canada, 1989b).

TRENDS IN EMPLOYMENT

In broad terms, three main processes facilitated and moulded the employment patterns and makeup of the RN work force. First, labor market demands changed. Second, increased educational spending during the 1960s and 1970s made it possible for an unprecedented number of young adults from the baby-boom generation, born during the high fertility years of 1946 to 1966, to obtain a postsecondary education.

Third, changes in the life patterns and values of Canadian women since the 1960s encouraged, and sometimes forced, women to seek paid employment and develop stronger career commitments (Jones, Marsden, and Tepperman, 1990).

The Changing Demand for Nurses

Until the 1980s, the demand side of the labor market for nurses received little analytic attention and was often overlooked by policymakers. Cyclic fluctuations in the number of nurses required by the health care system were commonly attributed to problems such as inability to recruit staff with desired qualifications, high turnover rates, and enrollment shortfalls in basic education programs. It took the prolonged and persistent nursing shortages of the 1980s in many countries to bring attention to demand-driven work force issues (Aiken, 1990a; Hancock, 1990; McKibbin, 1990).

The most common explanations (McKibbin, 1990; Meltz, 1988) offered for the sharp rise in demand for registered nurses include:

- Expansion of hospital services
- Increased intensity of care required by hospital patients
- Aging of the population
- Greater prevalence of chronic disease
- Substitution of registered nurses for other health care personnel such as RNAs
- The high proportion of the nurses working part-time, thus requiring more individuals to provide the same amount of service

Examination of three of these changes illustrates the dynamics of recent demand pressures.

What dominated the demand picture until the early 1970s was the imposing scale of public investment in health services in Canada. This began with the introduction of publicly-financed hospital construction programs in 1948 and continued through to the implementation of hospital and medical insurance programs throughout the country. The most immediate impact was an increase in hospital beds, with more than 80,000 being added during this period, raising the ratio of beds per 1000 population from 5 to 7 (Taylor, 1987). Most of these beds were in acute care.

Following the introduction of hospital insurance in 1957, per capita hospital admission rates also increased but, as Taylor (1987) points out, the 7% rise was surprisingly low given that the proportion of the insured population had more than doubled. The more specific impact was a massive change in staffing patterns. Torrance (1987) calls World War II the transition point in hospitals' evolution from relatively simple, quasi-charitable organizations to large modern industries. He notes, however, that resources devoted to training and paying staff lagged behind investments in physical plant and new technology. It took until the 1970s for the transition to modern staffing to be relatively complete. Some of the more important dimensions of the process were the replacement of unpaid student nurse trainees with salaried graduate nurses, and a pronounced increase in the number of personnel needed to staff the same 100 beds, the number almost tripling from the 1930s to the 1980s (from 67 employees per 100 beds in 1934 to 184 per 100 beds by 1983) (Torrance, 1987, p. 402).

This had the effect not only of creating more jobs for nurses but also of drawing an increasing proportion of them into hospital employment. Contrary to popular belief, it was only after World War II, with the transfer to hospitals of much medical care previously rendered in doctors' private offices or patients' homes, that the balance of nursing employment shifted to hospital work. Private duty nursing, or the employment of nurses by families to provide nursing services in the home, was the primary field of employment for 60% of registered nurses in the 1930s and continued as a prominent choice of work until the late 1940s.

Expansion of the health and social service sector labor force continues to be a significant contributor to the growing importance of service-based industries in the Canadian economy. According to Statistics Canada (1981a, 1983b), the period between 1971 and 1981 saw the number of health workers nearly double. Although increases in registered nurses and physicians contributed less to this growth than increases of other health occupations, they were still impressive. The number of registered nurses rose by 73%, well over the percentage increase from 1965 to 1970 (29%), and considerably higher than the growth rate of the overall labor force (43.5%). Hospitals continued to pick up the largest portion of these increases, a trend that shows up clearly in the recent employment statistics for registered nurses (Table 3-5). The growth in concentration of employment in health and social services continues to the present day with 9.4% of all employment in Canada now found in this sector (Economic Council of Canada, 1991).

A second and closely related spur to nurse demand came from the widespread introduction of medical advances such as renal dialysis, open heart surgery, and cardiac monitoring devices. This technology reflects the increase in the number of treatable acute and chronic illnesses. Whereas much industrial technology has reduced the need for labor, most of the new hospital technology has been labor intensive, expanding the need for nursing personnel and often requiring new skills. For example, in intensive care units, use of life support systems with the recommended standard of one nurse per patient has greatly accelerated nurse staffing requirements. In addition, shorter patient stays in hospital since the 1970s have increased the amount and intensity of work for registered nurses. Auer (1987), in a study of Canadian hospital costs and productivity prepared for the Economic Council of Canada, estimated that from 1961 to 1980 nursing hours per inpatient day rose from 3 to 5; nursing hours per surgical procedure from 9 to 11; and nursing hours per obstetrical delivery from 11 to 21 (an increase associated with greater numbers of Caesarean births). Auer concludes that almost 90% of the rise in hospital costs since the 1960s have resulted not from increased hospital admissions but from greater service intensity.

A third demand pressure that has added to the amount and diversity of work undertaken by nurses has arisen from the search for means to control health care costs. Because of their numbers, the many settings in which they practice, and the broad scope of their responsibilities, nurses are versatile employees. In hospitals, they can provide all the services for which hospitals sometimes employ nursing assistants or practical nurses. They also perform a wide range of clinical support functions, including those assigned to laboratory technicians, pharmacists, and physical therapists. In addition, nurses substitute for physicians. Aiken and Mullinix (1987) argue that the lower salaries received by nurses provide an incentive to use nurses in lieu of other kinds of workers, a process bearing the technical labels of substitution or task delegation. It was this reasoning that led to the training of nurse practitioners in Canada in the early 1970s and the many demonstrations that they could substitute for expensive physician services. Registered nurses have also been called upon to meet the heightened demands for complex home care services resulting from the earlier discharge of patients from hospitals. Another example is the replacement of nursing assistants in acute care hospitals by registered nurses, a trend documented in studies conducted in the 1980s in several provinces, including Alberta, Saskatchewan, Manitoba, Ontario, and New Brunswick (College of Nurses of Ontario, 1987; Meltz, 1988).

The changed care environment in hospitals has also redirected the work of nurses into roles such as discharge planners, case managers, and quality improvement staff (Donley and Flaherty, 1989). Moreover, hospital downsizing in support services such as patient transport, housekeeping, and clerical services has added substantially to the nonclinical work carried out by registered nurses (Aiken, 1990b). A 1988 U.S. study (International Council of Nurses, 1990) estimated that only 26% of a hospital RN's time was spent on direct care activities. The largest proportion of time (52%) was consumed in housekeeping details, answering telephones, and ordering supplies.

The combined effects on RN supply in hospitals of increasing intensity of hospital services and reductions in support staff, including RNAs, may be seen in data compiled by Meltz (1988). He found that, for Ontario hospitals, had the ratio of beds to full-time equivalent RNs in 1988 (1:1.45) remained at the 1977 level of 1:1.88, the number of registered nurses needed would have been 26,241 instead of the actual 33,981, a difference of 7740.

Sources of RN Supply

How have the scale and complexity of these demand processes been supported by changes on the supply side? Two main factors illustrate this: expansion of post-secondary education in Canada and the increasing participation of women in the work force. A brief examination of these trends follows.

The number of graduates of initial diploma and baccalaureate nursing programs in Canada rose sharply from the late 1960s to mid-1970s, peaked at just over 10,000 in 1972, then tapered to a low of 7396 in 1981, and has averaged just over 8000 since. These graduates have been the principal source of supply of registered nurses in Canada in recent years, with over 93,000 qualifying for practice between 1970 and 1980 and another 80,000 qualifying between 1980 and 1990.

Today, more than 90% of all registered nurses working in nursing in this country received their initial preparation in Canadian schools of nursing. In the past, when Canada was receiving large inflows of immigrants, and when many Canadian-trained nurses were emigrating to the United States, nurses educated in other countries constituted a slightly more important source of supply (Table 3-9). However, net gains from immigration have always been much smaller in nursing than in medicine, where, by the early 1970s, foreign physicians made up over one quarter of Canada's physician manpower (Hacon, 1973).

The surge in nursing graduates in the late 1960s reflected, among other factors,

TABLE 3-9 **Percentage of Employed Nurses Graduating From Canadian and Foreign Schools of Nursing, Selected Years, 1971-1988**

Year	Total employed in nursing	Canada (%)	Graduates of other countries (%)	Not stated (%)
1971	108,630	79.0	13.0	8.0
1974	125,475	80.9	11.3	7.8
1977	139,989	86.9	11.9	1.2
1980	155,309	86.7	10.6	2.7
1983	176,768	87.6	9.7	2.7
1986	204,723	87.5	9.1	3.4
1988	210,628	90.6	8.4	1.0

Sources: Health and Welfare Canada, 1976, 1986, 1990.
Statistics Canada, 1986.

the entry into adulthood of the baby-boom generation and the higher proportion of this age cohort seeking advanced education and training. These resulted in a 75% jump in the size of the 18-24 age group and a growth in postsecondary enrollment between 1962 and 1976 of over 200% (von Zur-Muehlen, 1978). This significantly increased the number of persons who were likely to pursue nursing education. The federal and provincial governments also played a critical role by providing funds to increase the enrollment capacity of schools of nursing. This strategic role bore the imprint of the social environment of the time, with broader access to social services such as education being seen as essential to social progress (Commission on Post-Secondary Education, 1972). Similar assumptions led the Royal Commission on Health Services in 1964 to urge the federal government to introduce a comprehensive, tax-supported system of health insurance, in the Commission's words, "to make all the fruits of the health sciences available to all our residents without hindrance of any kind" (p. 10).

As a first requirement for implementation of the program, the Royal Commission recommended a rapid acceleration in the number of nurses, physicians, dentists, and other health care personnel, the basic postulate being that health manpower was in short supply and inadequate for the flood in demand that was expected with the introduction of universal health insurance (Hatcher, 1981). In response, the federal government launched the Health Resources Fund in 1965, an allocation of $500 million to assist in expansion of training facilities. A large number of projects supported by these funds were devoted to training facilities for nursing assistants and diploma- and university-prepared registered nurses (LeClair, 1975). The need to train more nursing personnel was also a leading premise of most provincial health work force policies at the time and helped to spur the changes in nursing education described in Section V.

As important as the sizeable output of new graduates has been in ensuring adequate nursing resources in Canada, it is only part of the picture. Like other predominantly female occupations, the supply of nurses has also been profoundly influenced by the more permanent participation of Canadian women in the paid labor force and the social and economic forces underpinning this participation (Laing and Rademaker, 1990). If these trends continue, by the year 2000 one in two persons in paid employment will be women, compared to one in five in 1950. The most dramatic change has been in the labor force participation rate of women with preschool and school-aged children. Thirty years ago, the predominant pattern was for women to forsake paid employment for marriage or for the arrival of their first child. In the 1990s, an overwhelming majority of married women, including almost 50% of women with preschool children and more than 60% of women with school-aged children, are employed outside the home. These women are expected to continue to participate in the work force, sending sharply upward the number of actively employed women over 35 years of age (Economic Council of Canada, 1985; Labour Canada, 1986; Statistics Canada, 1990c).

HUMAN RESOURCE ISSUES AND CHALLENGES

The response to the scale of demand for registered nurses over the last 2 decades has been impressive. Yet signs indicate that the period of relatively easy expansion of supply, made possible by increases in educational output and the influx of married women into the work force, is rapidly coming to a close. In part, this reflects the greater range of career opportunities open to women. A more critical factor is demographics. Most of the baby-boom cohort is already in the work force, and, since 1961, Canadian fertility rates have declined significantly (Stone and Fletcher, 1986). This means that fewer young adults will enter the work force in the foreseeable future, and returning workers will become more plentiful as the baby-boom generation moves into the ranks of the middle-aged and older population. These trends are serious both in terms of nurse recruitment and retention and projected increases in demands for nursing services. When coupled with current fiscal pressures in health care, they make questions of productivity and efficiency of the nursing work force matters of steadily increasing urgency. Two spheres of action have generally been regarded as being most critical to realigning nursing work force policies and employment practices to these new realities: the mix of qualifications and skills and the conditions of nursing work.

The Mix of Qualifications and Skills

The call for a richer mix of knowledge and skills among registered nurses reflects the need to satisfy different health care requirements, such as the blend of generalist and specialty services, educational and administrative leadership, and the generation and application of new knowledge to improve patient care. Contemporary health care organizations also need an innovative and adaptable nursing work force to cope with an increased pace of change. Until recently, a majority of employers relied on a model of nurse hiring and staffing that was based on the expectation that nurses should be able to function equally adeptly in almost any setting and role without any education beyond diploma training. Since the late 1970s, complex technology, changes in the organization and patterns of health care in Canada, and a general increase in the level of education of Canadians have led to greater acknowledgement of the need for nurses who are educationally and experientially qualified for advanced positions in nursing.

With an increase in the number of elderly persons in the next decade, there is also greater support for re-directing professional competencies toward certain specialty requirements. Special health care professionals such as gerontological nurses, audiologists, physiotherapists and occupational therapists, all of whom are already in short supply, will continue to be required. There will also be a continued need for support workers, not only to assist in providing care, but also to take on tasks presently done by health care professionals but which do not require advanced preparation.

Current patterns of care, whether formal or informal, depend on the work of women. Much of the work of caring for the sick has shifted to self-care and family members; families, usually the women, are doing the work once done for pay in clinics and hospitals (Corbin and Strauss, 1988). But where will the supply of caregivers come from to meet the health care needs of the future? Health professions have tended to focus specifically on meeting their own human resource needs without regard to the health care system as a whole or the overall mix of health occupations and potential pool of family caregivers. For example, until recently there has been an obsession in government policy circles with the supply of physicians to the exclusion of concern about the supply of other health care providers or the involvement of relatives, friends, and volunteers in caring tasks. In the future, other providers of service, consumers of those services, and the limited dollars that will be available to finance such services must be considered.

This means that, as well as attempting to define the right mix of skills and knowledge among nurses, key stakeholders in the health care system (consumers, providers, employers, and government) must be concerned about the appropriate mix of health occupations and informal caregivers. As a result, coordinated health human resource planning (CHHRP) has once again become a consideration in answering questions of who, where, and how to deliver health care and is increasingly viewed as an essential component of a rational and well-managed system (World Health Organization, 1990). However, governments have been slow to consider coordinated planning approaches and development of relevant information systems.

Who should be involved in setting health human resource policies? Which models should be used to define need? Because of the pivotal role of nursing personnel in Canadian health care, these are questions that nursing should take part in answering. Indeed, all health care professionals need to examine their roles, now and in the future. Power bases are beginning to shift. In Ontario, for example, two important initiatives are underway and will affect CHHRP. The first is a new regulatory framework for the health professions approved in 1991. This legislation, the Regulated Health Professions Act, governs more than 20 health disciplines, providing each with a scope of practice, and allowing consumers to approach the health care professional of their choice. A second initiative is the formation in 1989 of an umbrella association, Interhealth, which serves as a forum for discussion of professional issues, including health human resource planning. Consisting of all the groups coming in under the above regulatory legislation, Interhealth was initiated by the Registered

Nurses Association of Ontario in response to its 1988 report on the nursing shortage, which recommended an independent Institute for Coordinated Health Manpower Planning (Meltz, 1988). Similarly, the Canadian Nurses Association has advocated formation of a Canada health forum or council, which would represent consumers and providers and advise government on matters relating to health care on a national basis. More recently, the Barer and Stoddart report on physician resources in Canada (1991) and a report on health care by the National Council of Welfare (1990) recommended that governments at all levels work more closely with each other and with the health care professions on Canada's health human resource needs.

In its report, *Healthy Americans: Practitioners for 2005*, the Pew Health Professions Commission (Shugars, O'Neil, and Bader, 1991) argues that if such coordinated planning efforts are to reach their potential, they must be accompanied by fundamental alterations in who delivers care to whom, when, and where. This includes less reliance on the physician as the primary point of entry to the health care system. Other requirements include developing mechanisms to obtain better information on what programs and care activities work and standardizing patterns of practice to reflect these evaluations.

In regard to future organization, deployment, and utilization of nursing personnel, there is ample evidence that nursing care is a critical variable in the life chances and improved well-being of patients in hospitals and community settings. However, this research is not well known. Nor does it contain much precise information on the impact of various kinds of staffing patterns or methods of organizing the delivery of nursing services. The natural tendency, in the face of fiscal constraints or a shortage of registered nurses, is to employ more nursing assistants and aides. The value-added potential of well qualified, clinical nursing specialists is rarely considered. The report of a major field test of clinical specialization by Georgopoulos and Christman (1990) is enlightening in this context. Their data show that where graduate-prepared clinical specialists were added to hospital units, there were both clinical and economic gains. The economic benefits included less staff turnover and absenteeism, savings in supply budgets, and lower dietetic, housekeeping, and administrative costs. These savings more than offset the higher salaries of the specialists. One of the major variables contributing to enhanced clinical efficacy was the improved communication milieu in patient units, especially enhanced nurse-physician relations. Such evidence strongly supports the need for a richer appreciation of nursing skill requirements and the tradeoffs in employing various levels of nursing personnel.

Where will our future nursing work force come from? Societal demographic trends are reflected in the composition of the work force. Canadian society is becoming older, more multicultural, and more reliant on women working for pay. These trends have implications for how we recruit, educate, and manage the future nursing work force. Challenges that will face educators include providing relevant curricula to meet current and future practice requirements, offering remedial programs for students with lower admission qualifications, integrating minority and immigrant students into the programs, implementing flexible programming for older part-time students and second careerists, and providing educators qualified in adult education techniques.

TABLE 3-10 Registered Nurses by Type of Position Held and Highest Level of Education, Canada, 1989

Position	Number	Work force (%)	Diploma* (%)	Baccalaureate (%)	Master's and higher (%)
Director, assistant/associate director	5321	2.4	66.3	27.2	6.5
Supervisor/coordinator, assistant supervisor/coordinator	10,923	4.9	77.3	21.0	1.7
Clinical specialist	1532	0.7	59.0	24.9	16.1
Head nurse	16,295	7.4	86.2	12.9	0.9
General duty/staff nurse	157,977	71.5	89.8	9.9	0.3
Instructor/professor	5683	2.6	33.6	55.3	11.1
Other	13,840	6.3	75.3	22.6	2.1
Not Stated	8328	4.2	90.1	9.4	0.5
TOTAL NUMBER EMPLOYED	220,999	100.0	85.9	13.1	1.0

Sources: Statistics Canada, 1980, 1986, 1989c.
*Includes RNs with post-basic diploma/certificate.

TABLE 3-11 Percentage of Nursing Directors, Associate and Assistant Nursing Directors Who Have Baccalaureate or Graduate Degrees in Nursing

| | Level of educational preparation | | | |
| | 1980 | | 1989 | |
Field of employment	Baccalaureate (%)	Master's or higher (%)	Baccalaureate (%)	Master's or higher (%)
Hospital	24.3	5.1	32.4	8.9
Nursing home, home for the aged	7.3	0.6	13.8	1.5
Community health	19.5	3.4	35.2	6.2
Educational institution	44.1	24.5	52.2	28.6
TOTAL	19.6	4.3	27.2	6.4

Sources: Statistics Canada, 1980, 1989c.

Managers will be faced with an older work force that will demand more input into decision making, be autonomous, and bring varied life-experiences to the workplace while continuing to balance home and work lives. Managers will need to enrich the place of employment, thereby recognizing the needs of a changed society (Archer and Lea, 1989; Chaykowski and Verma, in press 1992; Kent, 1990; Young, 1989). Currently, there is a dearth of well qualified persons in nursing to assume these senior management responsibilities. Tables 3-10 and 3-11 highlight the problem. The data in Table 3-10 show, for example, that only 33.7% of persons holding positions of director or associate/assistant director have a baccalaureate or graduate degree in nursing. This is about the same proportion as in 1970 (Canadian Nurses Association, 1971). The proportion declined to 23.9% in 1980, a drop reflecting the difficulties of keeping pace with increases in the number employed in such positions. Table 3-11 reveals that even in work settings such as educational institutions and community health, where a baccalaureate degree is either mandatory or strongly preferred, a relatively high proportion of persons employed in the director category do not possess degree qualifications. In community health, the figure is a surprisingly high 58.6% and in education, 19.1%.

Conditions of Work

A second pressure for modernization of nursing work force policies and employment practices arises from the conditions of nursing work. Much has been written recently about the job stresses and strains of nurses, especially in hospitals, a problem exacerbated by government fiscal policies aimed at curbing hospital costs. Many of the pertinent issues will be considered more fully in Section III, Nursing Workplaces, and Section V, Nursing Power. Here it is sufficient to look at a few salient points and the relevant Canadian data.

The dynamics of nursing employment are a crucial component of the secondary status accorded to women in the paid labor force. They are characterized by what has been called an "easy entrance-early exit" system (Friss, 1981, p. 699). Few social support structures or incentives have been laid down to encourage sustained or durable careers, promotion opportunities are limited, the differential in pay for additional education or expertise is small or non-existent, and maximum salaries are reached in a few steps and after a few years in the work force.

Some of these problems are illustrated by data in Table 3-8 on 1991 salaries for general duty/staff nurses, head nurses, and first-line supervisors covered by major hospital collective agreements throughout Canada. As noted earlier, starting salaries range from a low in Prince Edward Island of $27,475 a year to a high of $35,676 in British Columbia, the average being $31,930.13. These are respectable figures, comparing favorably with salaries reported by full-time employed graduates of Canadian universities. However, the relatively small differences between minimum and maximum salaries should be noted. Although the number of steps in the salary scale is an improvement over the three or four steps that were common in collective agreements in the 1970s, the dollar differences in all provinces except Ontario and Quebec are small, ranging from a low of $5592 in British Columbia to a high of $19,024 in Nova Scotia. This means that someone likely to work 20 years faces the prospect of a salary increment of less than $280 per year if working in British Columbia or, at best, an increment of just over $960 per year if working in Ontario. In other words, the existing wage structure in most provinces offers few rewards for continuous service. Also out of the question with such a wage structure is any sort of significant pay differential for the type of nursing work done, for added expertise and education, or for working unpopular shifts. As well, nurses who wish to maximize their incomes are put in the position of having to forsake clinical nursing careers for administrative posts where the salaries offered are generally higher.

Can the health care system afford to lose experienced clinical nurses to other careers? Is it possible to reward these nurses for advanced clinical knowledge, skills, and responsibilities? As in any market-driven environment, inadequate compensation affects the supply of workers. Adequate compensation is a key strategy that should be used to recruit and retain nurses. Historically, unions have tended to support egalitarian distribution of wages. This position is beginning to be challenged by a chronic shortage of nurses in certain geographic and specialty areas. An interesting experiment in this regard is the Hospital for Sick Children in Toronto, which gave wage increases and bonuses up to $9000 a year in 1990 to counter staff shortages that had closed intensive care unit beds ("Hospital to offer bonuses . . . ," 1990).

Another variable that is influencing working conditions of nurses is legislation encoding fair employment practices. For example, pay equity legislation, which has been introduced in several provinces, including Ontario, Manitoba, and Nova Scotia, supports the principle of equal pay for work of equal value. Although the methods for assessing comparable worth have flaws, pay equity does have the potential to assist in recruitment and retention of nurses by making the profession financially attractive.

Probably the major human resources challenge to nurses and employers alike in the next few years is how to bear the burden of continued restructuring and rationalization of health services. These conditions will ensure sustained pressures to raise productivity while revitalizing the world of work and working relationships. Such a balance will not be easily achieved. Management needs work force cooperation to allow jobs to evolve to fit new organizational structures and streamline work processes. However, as a 1991 Conference Board of Canada Report (Wright, 1991) points out, among labor ranks there is some disagreement about the appropriate response to management pleas for cooperation. Many translate it as a demand for concessions and feel that the interests of working people and the basic tenets of distributive justice are being denied, as is a meaningful role for participation of employees in the decision making process.

These tensions are as evident in nursing as elsewhere in the labor force (Attridge and Callahan, 1990; Goddard, 1989; Wright, McGill, and Collins, 1990). To aid and abet understanding of concerns about quality of work-life in Canadian nursing, numerous studies of the nursing work force have been completed in the last 10 years. In 1989, the Canadian Nurses Association and the Canadian Hospital Association undertook a macro analysis of 23 of these studies. The report, entitled *Nurse*

Retention and Quality of Worklife: A National Perspective (1990), identified the most frequently cited factors causing dissatisfaction as:

- Too many non-nursing tasks
- Lack of input into organizational decision making
- Lack of recognition
- Poor communications
- Lack of support for training and education
- Inadequate compensation for the level of responsibility
- Lack of adequate staffing
- Inflexible work schedules

In response to work-life concerns among nurses, a number of initiatives have been undertaken throughout Canada. Most provinces have set up government nursing advisory committees or are in the process of doing so. Senior nurse advisors, reporting at the deputy minister level, have also been put in place in several provinces, including Ontario, Alberta, and British Columbia. Nursing innovation funds in these same three provinces assist in improving working conditions and encouraging new models of practice and education, and are an important advance. Projects funded to date include support for increasing access to postdiploma baccalaureate programs, a rural nursing consultation service, an orientation program for foreign-trained nurses, and the creation of nursing work force data bases and research centers (Canadian Nurses Association, 1991b).

Despite these tangible steps, there is concern that progress may come to an abrupt halt because of health care funding cutbacks. The economic recession in the opening years of the 1990s, coupled with the reduction of federal transfer payments to the provinces for health and education, have added to the anxiety about the fate of work-life initiatives. These same conditions have led to a heightened anxiety about the potential erosion of standards of care, a problem that is beginning to present itself in all areas of nursing. At this stage, nursing also lacks knowledge of where and when to use various kinds of skill mix. An understanding of appropriate and safe staffing patterns and organizational models to deliver nursing services is seriously incomplete.

A FUTURE AGENDA

The changed profile of the work force in Canada since the early 1970s has brought into sharp focus the gaps and limitations of traditional human resource management practices in nursing. Such limitations include: preoccupation with finding enough staff; use of ad hoc and uncoordinated approaches to training for the new tasks and responsibilities undertaken; and lack of attention to how the composition of the work force and the workplace environment affect the costs and quality of nursing services. The cost pressures in Canadian health services in the 1990s, together with new workplace values and demands, have forced a change of perspective and driven health care organizations to re-examine the priority given to human resources planning and management. However, it would be wrong to suggest that any dramatic breakthrough is likely to occur. While there is every indication that the future health care system will continue to place enormous reliance on the skills and training of highly qualified registered nurses, the long history of low societal investment in the active nursing work force, inherited from generations of thinking of women as temporary workers, makes the re-adjustment process a vast undertaking (Fagin, 1987). Moreover, in the face of cost constraints, health care services have become heavily dependent on the flexibility of nurses to adjust to new demands and pressures. Under such conditions, welfare of patients often recedes into the distance. If the Canadian nursing work force is to keep quality of work-life issues alive, nurses have a responsibility to Canadians to ensure that standards of care are not jeopardized. At the same time, they must be thoughtful in identifying workplace conditions and work force requirements that provide nurses with challenging and rewarding work while they deliver care in the least expensive, most appropriate manner.

This is not a modest agenda but it is widely agreed that it is a feasible one. In an insightful article entitled "The new productivity challenge," Drucker (1991) says raising the productivity of service work is the most pressing social challenge developed countries face today. In his prescriptions, drawn together from a broad span of occupations, including nursing, he asserts that the easiest and perhaps greatest gains in productivity are by being clear about the goals that must be accomplished. He observes that:

> The great majority of engineers, teachers, salespeople, nurses, middle managers, and the like must carry a steadily growing load of busywork, activities that contribute little if any value and that have little if anything to do with what these professionals are qualified and paid for.
>
> The worst case may be that of nurses in U.S. hospitals. We hear a great deal about the shortage of nurses. But how could it possibly be true? The number of graduates entering the profession has gone up steadily for a good many years. At the same time, the number of bed patients has been dropping sharply. The explanation of the paradox: nurses now spend only half their time doing what they have learned and are paid to do—nursing. The other half is eaten up by activities that do not require their skill and knowledge, add neither health-care nor economic value, and have little or nothing to do with patient care and patient well-being. (Drucker, 1991, pp. 74)

According to Drucker, the cure is fairly easy. It is to concentrate the work on the task. Nurses' task is caring for patients. Drucker's remaining prescriptions focus on "working smarter": defining quality and efficiency standards and building them into work processes; making employees partners in productivity improvement and the first source of ideas for it; and building continuous learning and teaching opportunities into the job of every employee and work team (on the assumption that service workers learn most when they teach others the secrets of their success).

Many of these human resources challenges are under the control of management. There is also an essential role for public policy and for nursing associations and unions. Ultimately, traditional perspectives on nursing work and the quantity and quality of nursing care available to Canadians must be reshaped by employers, government, and nurses acting in concert to build a better tomorrow for Canada's health care system and its one-quarter million registered nurses.

REFERENCES

Aiken, L.H. (1990a). An analysis of the U.S. experience. In C. Fagin. (Ed.), *Nursing leadership: Global strategies* (pp. 3-14). New York: National League for Nursing.

Aiken, L.H. (1990b). Charting the future of hospital nursing. *Image: Journal of Nursing Scholarship, 22* (2), 72-78.

Aiken, L., & Mullinix, C. (1987). The nurse shortage: Myth or reality? *The New England Journal of Medicine, 317* (10), 641-651.

Archer, M.A., & Lea, B. (1989). Surmounting plateauing: How one company handled employee career slowdown. *Human Resources Professional, 7(9)*, 8-10, 29.

Attridge, C., & Callahan, M. (1990). Nurses' perspectives of quality work environments. *Canadian Journal of Nursing Administration, 3* (3), 18-24.

Auer, L. (1987). *Canadian hospital costs and productivity* (A study prepared for the Economic Council of Canada). Ottawa: Canadian Government Publishing Centre.

Barer, M., & Stoddart, G. (1991). Toward integrated medical resource policies for Canada. Winnipeg: Conference of Deputy Ministers of Health. National Library Database.

Canadian Nurses Association. (1968). *Countdown 1968*. Ottawa: Author.

Canadian Nurses Association. (1971). *Countdown 1971*. Ottawa: Author.

Canadian Nurses Association. (1974). *Countdown 1974*. Ottawa: Author.

Canadian Nurses Association. (1991a). *Annual salaries, major hospital agreements, Canada, July, 1991*. Ottawa: Author.

Canadian Nurses Association. (1991b). *Briefing note: Work life issues* (File 560-9). Ottawa: Author.

Canadian Nurses Association/Canadian Hospital Association. (1990). *Nurse retention and quality of worklife: A national perspective*. Ottawa: Author.

Chaykowski, R.P., & Verma, A. (Eds.). (In press, 1992). *Industrial relations in Canadian industry*. Toronto: Holt, Rinehart & Winston.

College of Nurses of Ontario. (1987). *Briefing paper on issues concerning the registered nursing assistant and the health care aide*. Toronto: Author.

Commission on Post-Secondary Education in Ontario. (1972). *The learning society*. Toronto: Ministry of Government Services.

Corbin, J.M., & Strauss, A. (1988). *Unending work and care: Managing chronic illness at home*. San Francisco: Jossey-Bass.

Donley, Sr. R., & Flaherty, Sr. M.J. (1989). Analysis of the market driven nursing shortage. *Nursing and Health Care, 10* (4), 183-187.

Drucker, P. (1991). The new productivity challenge. *Harvard Business Review, 69* (6), 69-79.

Economic Council of Canada. (1985). *Towards equity: Proceedings of a colloquium on the economic status of women in the labour market, November 1984*. Ottawa: Canadian Government Publishing Centre.

Economic Council of Canada. (1991). *Employment in the service economy*. Ottawa: Minister of Supply and Services Canada.

Employment & Immigration Canada. (1988). *The labour market for nurses in Canada*. Ottawa: Author.

Fagin, C. (1987). The visible problems of an "invisible" profession: Crisis and challenge for nursing. *Inquiry, 24*, 119-126.

Friss, L. (1981). Work force policy perspectives: Registered nurses. *Journal of Health Politics, Policy and Law, 5(4)*, 696-719.

Georgopoulos, B., & Christman, L. (1990). *Effects of clinical nursing specialization: A controlled organizational experiment*. Queenston, ON: Edwin Mellen Press.

Goddard, R. (1989). Workforce 2000. *Personnel Journal, 68(2)*, 65-71.

Hacon, W. (1973). *The health manpower situation in Canada* (Report Number 5-73). Ottawa: Department of National Health and Welfare.

Hancock, C. (1990). Manpower needs: Womenpower demands. In C. Fagin (Ed.), *Nursing leadership: Global strategies* (pp. 29-37). New York: National League for Nursing.

Hannah, K. (1988). Computers in nursing practice. In A. Baumgart & J. Larsen (Eds.), *Canadian nursing faces the future* (pp. 263-277). Toronto: Mosby.

Hatcher, G. (1981). *Universal free health care in Canada, 1947-77* (NIH Publication No. 81-2052). Washington: U.S. Government Printing Office.

Health and Welfare Canada. (1976). *Canada health manpower inventory 1976*. Ottawa: Author.

Health and Welfare Canada. (1979). *Canada health manpower inventory 1978*. Ottawa: Minister of National Health and Welfare.

Health and Welfare Canada. (1986). *Canada health manpower inventory 1986*. Ottawa: Author.

Health and Welfare Canada. (1990). *Health personnel in Canada 1988* (Catalogue H 1-9/1-1988). Ottawa: Author.

Hospital to offer bonuses, lure staff. (1990, July 5). *Globe & Mail*, p. 2.

International Council of Nurses. (1990). Misuse of nurses: USA. *Socio-Economic News No. 86*. Geneva: Author.

International Labour Office. (1960). *Employment and conditions of work of nurses* (Studies and Reports New Series, No. 55). Geneva: La Tribune de Genève.

Jones, C., Marsden, L., & Tepperman, L. (1990). *Lives of their own: The individualization of women's lives*. Toronto: Oxford University Press.

Kent, D. (1990, September). Beyond thirtysomething. *Working Woman*. pp. 150-153.

Labour Canada. (1986). *Women in the labour force* (1985-86 edition) (Labour Canada Catalogue Number L24-1468/86B). Ottawa: Author.

Laing, G., & Rademaker, A. (1990). Married registered nurses' labour force participation. *The Canadian Journal of Nursing Research, 22*(1), 21-38.

LeClair, M. (1975). The Canadian health care system. In S. Andreopoulos (Ed.), *National health insurance: Can we learn from Canada?* (pp. 11-96). New York: John Wiley & Sons.

McCormick, K.A. (1991). Future data needs for quality of care monitoring, DRG considerations, reimbursement and outcome measurement. *Image: Journal of Nursing Scholarship, 23*(1), 29-32.

McKibbin, R.C. (1990). *The nursing shortage and the 1990's: Realities and remedies*. Kansas City, MI: American Nurses Association.

Meltz, N.M. (1988). *Sorry no care available due to nursing shortage. The shortage of registered nurses: An analysis in a labour market context*. Toronto: Registered Nurses' Association of Ontario.

Moses, E. (1991). Profile of the contemporary nursing population: Findings from 1988 sample survey of registered nurses. In National League for Nursing, *Perspectives in Nursing, 1989-1991* (pp. 33-43). New York: National League for Nursing.

National Council of Welfare. (1990). *Health, health care and medicare*. Ottawa: Author.

National Nursing Symposium Steering Committee. (1991). National nursing symposium: Report to the provincial and territorial Ministers of Health. Winnipeg: Author.

Okrainec, G. (1991). Men and nursing: A growing trend. *Nursing BC, 23*(4), 14-15.

Ontario Hospital Association/Ontario Ministry of Health. (1987). *Hospital nurse staffing survey*. Toronto: Author.

Registered Nurses Association of British Columbia. (1990). *Submission to the Royal Commission on Health Care and Costs. New directions for health care*. Vancouver: Author.

Royal Commission on Health Services. (1964). *Report*. Ottawa: Queen's Printer.

Shugars, D., O'Neil, E., & Bader, J. (1991) *Healthy America: Practitioners for 2005, an agenda for action for U.S. health professional schools*. Durham, NC: The Pew Health Professions Commission.

Statistics Canada. (1974). *1971 Census of Canada. Occupations. Occupations by sex, for Canada and provinces* (Catalogue 94-717, volume 3, part 2). Ottawa: Minister of Industry, Trade and Commerce.

Statistics Canada. (1980). *Revised registered nurses data series*. Ottawa: Author.

Statistics Canada. (1981a). *1981 Census: Labour force-Occupation by cultural characteristics* (Catalogue 92-918, Volume 1, National Series). Ottawa: Author.

Statistics Canada. (1981b). *Standard occupational classification 1980* (Catalogue 12-565E). Ottawa: Minister of Supply and Services Canada.

Statistics Canada. (1983a). *Historical labour force statistics-Actual data, seasonal factors, seasonally adjusted data* (Catalogue 71-201). Ottawa: Author.

Statistics Canada. (1983b). *1981 Census of Canada. Population. Labour force—occupation by demographic and educational characteristics: Canada, provinces, urban, rural non-farm and rural farm* (Catalogue 92-917, Volume 1—National Series). Ottawa: Minister of Supply and Services Canada.

Statistics Canada. (1986). *Registered nurses management data*. Ottawa: Author.

Statistics Canada. (1989a). *Census of Canada 1986. The Nation: Occupation, population and dwelling characteristics* (Catalogue 930112). Ottawa: Minister Regional Industrial Expansion and the Minister of State for Science and Technology.

Statistics Canada. (1989b). *Registered nurses management data 1989*. Ottawa: Canadian Centre for Health Information.

Statistics Canada. (1990a). *Health Reports 1989, Volume 1, Number 2: Hospital Annual Statistics, Volume 4—Personnel* (Catalogue 82-003S). Ottawa: Minister of Supply and Services Canada.

Statistics Canada. (1990b). *Nursing in Canada 1988* (Catalogue 83-226). Ottawa: Minister of Supply and Services Canada.

Statistics Canada. (1990c). *Women in Canada: A statistical report* (2nd ed.) (Catalogue 89-503E). Ottawa: Minister of Supply and Services Canada.

Stone, L., & Fletcher, S. (1986). *The seniors boom* (Catalogue 89-515). Ottawa: Statistics Canada.

Taylor, M. (1987). The Canadian health-care system: After medicare. In D. Coburn, C. D'Arcy, G. Torrance, & P. New (Eds.), *Health and Canadian society* (2nd ed.)(pp. 73-101). Markham, ON: Fitzhenry and Whiteside.

Torrance, G. (1987). Hospitals as health factories. In D. Coburn, C. D'Arcy, G. Torrance, & P. New (Eds.), *Health and Canadian society* (2nd ed.)(pp. 73-101). Markham, ON: Fitzhenry and Whiteside.

von Zur-Muehlen, M. (1978). *From the sixties to the eighties: A statistical portrait of Canadian higher education*. Ottawa: Statistics Canada.

Werley, H., Devine, E., & Zorn, C. (1990). The nursing minimum data set (NMDS). In J. McClosky & H. Grace (Eds.), *Current issues in nursing* (3rd ed.) (pp. 64-76). St. Louis: Mosby.

World Health Organization. (1988). *World health statistics annual/Annuaire de statistiques sanitaires mondiales 1988*. Geneva: Author.

World Health Organization. (1989). *Forty-second World Health assembly. Provisional agenda item 18.2. The role of nursing and midwifery personnel in the strategy for health for all: Report by the director-general*. Geneva: Author.

World Health Organization. (1990). *Coordinated health and human resources development: Report of a WHO study group*. Geneva: Author.

Wright, R. (1991). *1991 industrial relations outlook*. Ottawa: Conference Board of Canada.

Wright, V., McGill, J., & Collins, J. (1990). Are nurses less satisfied than other workers? *Nursing Economics, 8*(5), 308-313.

Young, W.B. (1989). Taking advantage of the older age profile of today's registered nurses. *Nursing and Health Care, 10*(4), 189-191.

Canadian nurses have always been active when Canada has been involved in wars. This photo shows Nursing Sisters of No. 5 Canadian General Hospital marching to the train in Victoria, British Columbia, in August 1915, as they began the trek that would take them to Salonika, Greece, one of the fierce battle areas of World War I. (Photograph from *Canada's Nursing Sisters,* by G.W.L. Nicholson (Toronto: Samuel Stevens, 1975) and courtesy of the Canadian War Museum. Used with permission.)

CHAPTER FOUR

Nursing: A Culture in Transition

JENNIECE LARSEN, RN, PhD
THERESA GEORGE, RN, PhD

Jenniece Larsen, RN, BScN, MEd, PhD (Alberta), is Professor and Director, School of Nursing, University of Manitoba. She has held numerous leadership posts and was President of the Canadian Association of University Schools of Nursing and past Board Member of the Manitoba Association of Registered Nurses and the Alberta Association of Registered Nurses. Her research interests include the career development of nurses, and she is especially interested in the relationships between the women's movement and nursing.

Theresa George, RN, BS (Kerala, India), MS (Boston), PhD (Utah), is Associate Professor, School of Nursing, University of Manitoba. She has had varied experiences as a nursing educator in Africa, India, and the United States before coming to Canada. She introduced the first feminist course on "Women and Health" through the Women's Studies program in the Faculty of Arts, University of Manitoba. She is a member of various international, national, and local societies.

W hen people work, they not only produce goods and services or earn a living, they also produce a culture—the work culture of the group (Cockburn, 1985). Work culture refers to the basic values and patterns of behavior that are shared by members of an occupation and that help to define who they are, what they do, and how they see the world in which they work (Morgan, 1986). As Edgar Schein (1985) explains in his book, *Organizational Culture and Leadership*, these basic assumptions and beliefs tend to operate unconsciously and define, in a "take it for granted" fashion, the group's view of itself and its environment; these are learned responses ensuring the group's status quo, its homogeneity, and, finally, its survival. Work culture is a learned product of an occupation's history, shared experiences, and social environment leading, over time, to a set behavior of prescriptions and understandings that are taught to new members as normal, correct, and appropriate ways to act and think. Through the use and the teaching of these assumptions and beliefs to new members of the group, the continuity of the group is ensured.

What are the attitudes and assumptions underlying the nursing culture? How do nurses learn these attitudes and assumptions?

Many aspects of a culture are embedded in everyday practice and are easily identifiable. In nursing, these include the ways that care is given to patients, the particular theoretical ideas used to guide patient care, and the styles of communication among nurses and with other professionals. Aspects that help define the work culture also include seemingly unimportant matters such as modes of dress (e.g., the operating room gown or the wearing of a stethoscope around the neck). Language is another significant factor of culture. For example, when a nurse describes a patient's status by saying "the patient is stable," this has a specific meaning to other nurses.

The meanings behind the message—or the underlying assumptions that create the prevailing ideology of the group and infuse cultural objects with meaning—are more difficult to recognize. The assumptions made by individuals within the culture, even unconsciously, help determine their place in the world. The positioning of a specific work culture relative to other groups that may share all or part of its working space is referred to as the *power dimension*. Like many other aspects of nursing culture, the power dimension is currently undergoing change.

This chapter about the culture of nursing focuses on ways in which nurses are culturized or taught the social behavior expected of them as nurses. To analyze the nursing culture in more detail, terms and tools of analysis from economics, sociology, and anthropology will be used. The literature that analyzes nursing culture from this perspective is still small, and empirical study a rare event. In seeking to further illuminate the culture of nursing, the chapter will attempt to synthesize selected aspects of what is known about work culture, as well as about nurses' role in health care and illness, both historically and in the present day.

FEMALE WORLD

Ninety percent of all nurses worldwide are women; this percentage is significant enough not to be discounted. The internal workings, as well as the external perceptions of the nursing culture, have been described as being similar to those of a female world. Jessie Bernard (1981, 1987), a prominent social scientist in the field of women's studies, identified some characteristics of the female world. As yet there is insufficient research from which to draw a more comprehensive portrait of the female world but, as Bernard (1981) explains, "recognition of the female culture as part of the female world, independent from the male culture and world, will have considerable benefits for female understanding" (p. 22). Like men in the dominant culture, women do not respond to circumstances in an identical manner.

According to Bernard, the female world is bound by kinship and familial relationships and encompasses women's female friendships from which support and sustenance critical to women's emotional survival are derived. Females often embrace an ethos or fundamental belief of love and duty, particularly in relation to reproduction and motherhood. The nonegalitarian nature of this ethos prescribes a constant "stroking" of others by "showing solidarity, raising the status of others, giving help, rewarding, agreeing, concurring, complying, understanding, [and] passively accepting" that the needs of others are often more important than one's own needs (Bernard, 1981, p. 502). Out of this concern and involvement with nurturing, females are expected to espouse humanitarian concerns.

In this female world, inequality between women is rarely directly challenged through overt aggression; this lack of direct, open confrontation often creates complex, unspoken power struggles. As Bernard (1981) says, "equality as a general principle has not been a salient feature in female culture" (p. 484). Conflict resolution through compromise, the use of cooking and food as social mediators, and private discussions reflect a world in which interpersonal relationships are highly valued. Females are expected to learn behavior characteristics that reflect a more dependent, passive, sensitive, emotional, noncompetitive, and intuitive approach to people and circumstances.

Caring for the sick has for a long time been considered the duty, role, and responsibility of women. As Welter (1966) describes, "the sickroom called for the exercise of higher qualities of patience, mercy and gentleness as well as . . . housewifely arts" (p. 163). The central role women play in the family resulted in women being charged with the social responsibility of keeping family ties and passing on tradition. The emphasis on self-sacrifice and duty to husband and children has led to an unspoken presumption that women are morally superior, and that part of their responsibility is improvement of society's moral standards.

Another aspect of the female world has been the socialization of girls to be wives, mothers, and family nurturers and to remain at home, primarily performing helpmate work for men. Until recent years, women's work outside the home was not seen as a lifelong commitment but as a brief interlude before the women assumed their adult places as mothers and homemakers. Many women still continue to wrestle with their internalized feelings of responsibility about child care and household management while they work full-time or part-time outside the home. Rather than feeling liberated to pursue a career and to share the responsibility for child care and housework with men, they struggle to maintain both. Since the majority of practicing nurses are women of child-bearing age, the reality of juggling two major roles is a prominent feature in nursing culture.

As a result of being a constant presence in the home, women serve an integrating and coordinating role pivotal to family functioning. Nurses have a similar role in the hospital culture. They are the professionals who are constantly available to patients remaining on the nursing unit while other caregivers move freely about the hospital (Valentine and and McIntosh, 1990).

Competition as such is often a difficult situation for women, especially competition with other women. Most women seem ill-prepared for the competition experience and have difficulty in coping with it. Keller and Moglen's (1987) study of academic women suggests that, where tenured positions are rare commodities, the resulting competition between women for jobs causes difficulties, especially when the presence of competition conflicts with the ideals of sisterhood and cooperation. This study corroborated previous observations that a certain uneasiness with competition and conflict is characteristic of the female world. Recognition of these difficulties is essential before resolution is possible because "denial . . . delimits not the conflict but the possibilities of a creative solution to that conflict" (Keller and Moglen, 1987, p. 508).

Conflict and competition have been problematic in nursing workplaces and in schools of nursing, where, for example, individual competition that occurs for high grades often mediates against the development of effective team work. Valentine's (1988) study of the instructors in a diploma school of nursing reveals that conflict resolution was difficult in this female-dominated world in which the nursing teachers tend to avoid conflict. Competition was covert except in relation to clothing or cooking. This suggests another observable feature of the female world: the importance imparted to personal appearance. Food was used as an element of cohesion and, in difficult situations, social events involving food were often used as a way to work at solving problems. The importance of interpersonal support and the need to structure opportunities for the maintenance of group cohesion were other significant parts of this work culture. Although conflict and competition may pose difficulties for some women, there is other evidence that women are more participatory in their approach to decision making and helping others feel important, included, and energized (Rosener, 1990).

One benefit of describing and analyzing the evolving female world has been to change:

> the way the world was seen and [to tackle] . . . the very way the mind worked, the way gender relationships were conceptualized, the language that defined them. It was attitudes, feelings, thinking itself that the female world was seeking to change. (Bernard, 1987, p. 106)

Because these attitudes and feelings have been internalized throughout generations of social behavior, alteration in women's day-to-day life may take generations, although many prevalent attitudes are already undergoing significant change.

The close association between the female world and the world of nursing is explained by the observation that "femaleness has traditionally been built into the very definition of nursing" (Doyal, 1979, p. 202). The characteristics of the female world influence the way in which nurses are "culturized" or taught the social behaviors expected of them. Since nurses' work is often considered to be "doing what comes naturally for women," the assumption is made that nursing work is neither special nor even especially skilled and certainly does not require a long period of advanced education. One consequence is that nursing is stereotyped as a culture inhospitable to individuals of high intelligence, creativity, or entrepreneurial bent. Nurses, when compared with people in other professions, have been described as "people who rank low on self-esteem and initiative and higher on submissiveness and need for structure" (Marriner, 1978, p. 13). These societal prescriptions are reflected in the difficulties that nurses have had controlling their practice, their education, their workplaces, or their special destiny (Larsen, 1988).

CONTROL MYTHS IN NURSING

Socialization occurs not only through processes that affect the individual but also through the more pervasive social context. Lipman-Blumen (1984) argues that this social context is enriched by ancient images handed down through tradition, art, literature, and folk tales. These ancient images form "the nucleus of full-blown control myths that shape behavior, values and attitudes" (p. 69). Control myths permeate our culture and, within this social context, both women and men learn appropriate gender role behavior. Enculturation for these roles is carried out both overtly and covertly in social institutions such as family, school, and religious organizations, and by friends, peers, and professional colleagues. Control myths are powerful vehicles that hold groups together over time and carry group values from one generation to the next.

Lipman-Blumen (1984) identifies several control myths, which, when internalized, act as self-fulfilling or taken-for-granted mechanisms, controlling and limiting the behavior and attitudes of both men and women. Included is the myth about women being weak, passive, dependent, and fearful, whereas men are strong, aggressive, independent, and fearless. Another control myth characterizes females as intuitive, holistic, and contextual and males as analytical, abstract, field-independent—and therefore smarter than females. The belief that women are more altruistic, more nurturant, and more moral than men is a third control myth. The Biblical story of Eve is a powerful example of a control myth—a potent reminder to the curious woman that stepping out of line invites rejection and disapproval. A similar myth about women's lack of academic ability contributed to the exclusion of women from institutions of higher learning for hundreds of years. Aspects of other myths are used by numerous religious groups and reinforced in the general society to control the behavior and the social opportunities of females. Many of these control myths had and continue to have an impact on nursing by influencing who nurses are and what nurses do.

The nature of the social relationships embedded in these myths traditionally assign more power, status, and resources to males. The unequal power balance promoted by these potent mechanisms of social control is only beginning to be challenged. In the process of societal change, old myths are often replaced with new myths of similar nature, or myths may reappear at various times. As Lipman-Blumen (1984) states, ancient images "bleed through even the most contemporary gender role portraits" (p. 69).

The influence of control myths is often hidden, creating and mythologizing heroes and heroines, and developing ideals toward which males and females aspire. Even heroines such as Florence Nightingale have been used to reinforce control myths and to create sex-gender role models. By highlighting certain aspects of Nightingale's character such as her insistence on obedience and downplaying other characteristics such as her equal vehemence about sanitation, she has been portrayed as a hand-maiden to the medical profession. Her fierce crusading spirit, her scientific zeal, and other more predominant tough characteristics, which so often are assigned to males, are frequently overlooked. In this way, a heroine like Florence Nightingale can be belittled and used as an effective control myth rather than as a role model to inspire confidence in crusaders for change.

The nursing culture is continuously affected by many of these control myths, creating a dissonance between the culturally prescribed female roles and the work-life realities of nursing practice. In addition, the culture of nursing has its own control myths to perpetuate specific behaviors in nurses such as the idea that nurses must always put the needs and care of their patients before their own needs. When striking for decent salaries and safe working conditions, many nurses experienced severe distress when they did not care for sick patients. Jenny (1990) asserts that the professional socialization of nurses is the most crucial problem facing nurses today. She suggests that careful examination is required of the processes through which nurses are culturized and are forced "to reconcile . . . second-class image with . . . important high-risk and demanding work" (p. 19).

Historically, nurses have been inculcated to be obedient. In fact, Canada's first training hospital for nurses had as its motto "I see and am silent." In her article outlining a history of nursing in Ontario, Coburn (1981) recounts how nurses were socialized to be subservient through a combination of social class expectations and gender-role prescriptions. Student nurses, often working class, unemployed, un-married women, were controlled through the imposition of upper and middle class values. As an unpaid labor force charged with a mission to serve both their patients and their hospital, these students worked long hours and performed heavy physical work. This work, combined with an irregular series of lectures, was deemed to be nurses' training. Subservience to doctors and to senior nurses at the bedside— stressed throughout the period of hospital training—was translated into subservi-ence in the broader organizational and political arena as well. Nurses were to be subordinate, subservient, and silent. The power of this socialization is still apparent today in the education of many nurses in settings isolated from other major profes-sional and academic groups. Nursing education is still too often characterized by demands for "good girl" behavior, which rewards passivity and is intolerant of assertiveness; the consequences are students who are "less trouble" and who have a high survival rate in bureaucracies, but who are denied intellectually challenging learning experiences. This form of education is "anachronistic in view of the com-petencies and competitiveness required by nurses to gain recognition for their worth" (Remick, 1984, p. 93).

Inculcating student nurses with notions of professionalism has been used as a form of control to develop and perpetuate acceptable behavior and attitudes. But, as Allen (1986) observes, the reality of the workplace has not allowed nurses to benefit from true professional autonomy in terms of patient accountability and decision making. Historically, the medical profession has had significant influence in nursing workplaces and, currently, administrative control of nursing practice is pervasive. Although the rhetoric calls for nurses to be advocates for their patients, to assert their values, and to challenge the system, the realities of most nursing practice and education are at odds with this dictate.

Despite the continuing press for change, educational institutions and the family have been among society's most potent indoctrinators of gender-role attribution. One of the first messages communicated to girls at school has been that they are less important than boys. Instructional materials purvey a limited image of women's roles and achievements. The portrayal is most extreme in the presentation of science as a prototypical masculine endeavor. The fact is that girls consistently do better than boys in reading, mathematics, and speaking until they reach high school, when their performance in school and on some ability tests begins to drop (Fennema, 1985). The decline in girls' performance, particularly in mathematics and science, is believed to be a function of the strong male bias in the content of courses and in measures used to evaluate performance, as well as in the prevailing idea that young women's success is due to effort more than to ability. Both parents and teachers assume female students have less potential in science and mathematics and succeed more because of effort than ability and may not do as well in the future (Mura, Kimball, and Cloutier, 1987). This lack of confidence in the intellectual ability of girls may be related to the popularly held, but inaccurate, control myth that women are less able to be analytical, abstract, or field-independent in their learning patterns. As a result, young women were and are channelled into the more feminine subjects of the arts and social sciences, whereas boys were and are encouraged to tackle the "hard sciences." This type of tracking not only channelled the two sexes into two different occupational directions, but further served to keep both boys and girls from learning skills useful in later life. In recent years, the overall participation rate by young women in mathematics and sciences has not changed significantly and has become a subject of national concern. The participation of young men in the social sciences has not received similar attention.

Families have traditionally expected less aggression from female children, providing passive toys and fewer opportunities for competitive behavior. Daughters were overprotected and endowed with the manipulative tools of tears instead of the independent skills learned in team sports or other more direct ways of obtaining goals. Fathers and male authority figures were represented as the ones who knew best, and men are still assigned work responsibilities with more power and prestige in the affairs of state, in the marketplace, in health care, and in education. Women were taught to aspire toward subordinate roles, and failure to comply resulted in stigmatization. This unequal power balance was further complicated by the fact that many women gained power, especially power over other women, through partnership with a powerful man. Elements of this type of power are still evident in some nurse-physician and nurse-administrator relationships.

Although the so-called feminine traits are usually considered less valuable and natural only to women, many are qualities needed by both sexes to "humanize" society (Heide, 1973). The contradiction between perception and reality directly affects the nursing culture. Nurses are expected to be compassionate, kind, and caring, and those nurses who are perceived to be political, bright, and visible have been roundly criticized. In this way, control myths reinforce sex-stereotyped behavior by rewarding compliant behavior and by criticizing any behavior deemed unacceptable. With society constantly changing, what is said and what appears to be the reality of daily life is often at odds, creating stressful dichotomies. Women socialized for a more traditional role may find real-world workplaces competitive, uncooperative, and selfish. Severe internal conflict, which contributes to a lowering of self-esteem, anguish, and anger, may result.

Just as females raised in a paternalistic society learn to act in ways that make males feel superior, nurses have been taught to make doctors look knowledgeable and feel powerful and in control. Nurses have been taught to be silent and obedient and not to challenge the control myth that identifies women as weak, passive, dependent, and fearful. This interaction has become so ingrained as part of the nursing culture that it has been labelled the "doctor-nurse game." Nurses and physicians now acknowledge the need for change in the traditional nurse-physician relationship because the traditional relationship lessens nurses' self-esteem and results in their extreme dissatisfaction, and it neither acknowledges nurses' expertise nor validates their vital contributions to patient care. As Stein, Watts, and Howell (1990) observe, nursing shortages and strikes today are clear proof of the need for change.

Flannelly and Flannelly (1984) conclude that:

> both the masculine and feminine sides of an individual are critical to providing adequate nursing care; and while this challenge may be new for men entering the profession, it is the identical demand that has been made on women throughout the history of nursing. (p. 167)

As a first step to achieve needed changes in the nursing culture, a reassessment of the socialization processes to outline a pro-nurse agenda is required.

CONFLICTS IN NURSING

For decades, nursing was one of the few legitimate avenues in which women could fulfill personal work goals and obtain higher education. Once immersed in the day-to-day reality of nursing work, little opportunity to challenge societal and organizational barriers to advancement or recognition existed. Roberts (1983) states that oppression of a group is maintained through the co-option of its leaders by the dominant society, with the consequences that nurses have encountered barriers from within their own group as well as from without. Roberts further argues that, until recent years, nurses in leadership positions internalized the values of hospital administrators and physicians to such an extent that the practice of nursing has been marginalized. The seeming incompatibility of goals and values between nursing leaders and staff nurses has resulted in intraprofessional disagreement, as well as public criticism. These difficulties are aggravated by the disparities in professional and career opportunities attached to different types of nursing work and education and by the adversarial nature of management-worker relationships that are often a reality of highly unionized workplaces. Sadly, these struggles consume an inordinate amount of time with little apparent reward.

Difficulties within the nursing profession have been labelled and treated as conflicts and have led to a culture in which nurses may not develop strong bonds to one another and in which change is often resisted by various factions within the profession. Before oppression can be overcome, recognition of the existence and consequence of being an oppressive group must first take place. As Roberts (1983) states, "this includes the understanding that nurses are not inherently inferior but have been placed in a culture that does not value their attributes" (p. 29). Further, intraprofessional conflict serves the interest of powerful outsiders wishing to maintain the status quo and is an effective form of social control.

The size and complexity of the nursing profession are rarely considered when the issues of conflict and oppression are discussed. White (1988) states that, because nursing is a large pluralist occupation with multiple realities, differences in objectives and strategies should be expected and not confused with disunity. In her words:

> A tension permits growth and change by allowing new groups and ideas to emerge. In a healthy pluralist society, there should always be a tension between the prevailing group and the countervailing groups. In nursing, we have been slow to recognize this as we have almost universally, it seems, been socialized into the concepts of a unitary occupational society. (White, 1988, p. xxi)

Labelling legitimate differences as disunity is usually a strategy to maintain the status quo. The challenge and responsibility for the leaders of the diverse groups within the nursing profession is to create (recreate) visible common values that bond nurses together while working to achieve specific objectives.

MEN IN NURSING

What effect has gender-specificity and lack of power had on men who practice nursing? In Canada, the percentage of men in nursing changed only marginally in the last 20 years; only 3% of nurses were men in 1988 (Statistics Canada, 1990) compared to 1% in 1969 (Canadian Nurses Association, 1969). However, the percentage of male students in diploma schools of nursing was 9.5% in 1985 (Canadian Nurses Association, 1986) compared to 1% in 1966 (Canadian Nurses Association, 1967), reflecting a gradual change in both nursing and societal values. Similar data concerning the enrollment of male students in university programs are not available.

Although the nursing profession has had difficulties recruiting men since the early 1900s, men have a long but often ignored history of caring for the sick dating back at least to the Middle Ages. Between the eleventh and thirteenth centuries, nursing orders of military knights, such as the Knight Hospitallers, cared for the wounded from battlefields or for people with dreaded infectious diseases such as leprosy (Kelly, 1975). In the early 1800s, Canadian hospitals employed male attendants to give physical care to male patients and protected female caregivers from violent patients (Mussallem, 1964). The suitability of males providing direct and highly personal patient care was seriously questioned when the morality of the Victorian era swept around the Western world. This legacy was apparent as late as 1958 in Quebec, when provincial legislation did not permit nursing to be practiced by male nurses (Canadian Nurses Association, 1960). Today, male nurses frequently work in nursing education or administration, where they often are promoted to leadership roles, or are concentrated in specialized fields of practice such as psychiatry or the military where the need to touch and the need to wear nursing uniforms may be less apparent (Streubert and O'Toole, 1991).

Nursing practice and nursing education have not been particularly hospitable to male nurses. During the 1960s, only 15% of diploma nursing schools in Canada accepted male applicants; the reported reason for not accepting these applicants was the lack of suitable residential accommodation (Robson, 1964). Once admitted, men were often not permitted to provide intimate care to female patients, particularly in obstetrical and gynecological nursing services; instead they were assigned care of male patients in urology but were accountable for obstetrical and gynecological theory on examinations (Okrainec, 1990b). Despite these past discriminatory practices within the nursing profession toward men, the most significant barrier to men entering the field of nursing is the societal perception of nursing as traditional women's work. The effect of this gender bias is apparent in that neither nurses' salaries nor funding of educational programs for nurses has achieved parity with those of male-dominated professions.

Now that traditionally male-dominated fields such as medicine and engineering are more hospitable to women, nursing has experienced a decline in applications to schools of nursing from the traditionally female population from which recruits were drawn. This places the field of nursing in double jeopardy: unable to attract men, while its attractiveness to women declines. Equally problematic are difficulties experienced in securing financial support for nursing education programs. When faced with shortages of engineers or business administration graduates, governments seem more receptive to funding requests for these university programs than for programs to allay significant shortages of nurses, even when hospital beds must be closed because of lack of nurses. The seemingly low societal value attached to nursing work is further emphasized when one reflects on the availability in Canada of national fellowships to attract women to engineering and the absence of similar fellowships to attract men to nursing. These factors, compounded by the inequity of salary and working conditions, contribute to the profession's continued difficulty to attract men, and recently women, to its ranks.

Okrainec (1990a) argues that males must be reintegrated into nursing by various strategies, including the provision of supportive role models (especially males in faculty positions in schools of nursing) and by positive reinforcement for the importance of their career choice. Many of the strategies suggested by Okrainec (1990a, 1990b) are similar to strategies advocated for the acceptance of women in male-dominated fields.

The establishment of support groups such as Manitoba's Men in Nursing Group (MING) raises awareness of the societal restrictions imposed on men who are nurses.

In addition to individual support, the objectives of these groups include developing strategies for societal, as well as professional, recognition of the valuable contributions made by male nurses. As Halloran (1990) concludes, male nurses "are not the answer to all the problems of the nursing profession, but their presence in greater numbers may well be a barometer of the economic value society affords nurses" (p. 553). Men in nursing can be viewed as harbingers of societal change but will face issues and problems similar to those of women in male-dominated fields.

POWER OF LANGUAGE

Language is an insidious and powerful tool for both political and social control. Specifically, in the use of certain words and phrases, assumptions are made that perpetuate the imbalance of power between the sexes. The language of powerful groups expresses control over not-so-powerful others. Common examples illustrate: physicians give orders, nurses carry them out; medical knowledge is "scientific," nursing knowledge is "practical"; physicians' work is "clinical," nurses' work is "supportive and caring."

Nursing has taken language from the female world and embedded it within the ideology of nursing practice. Prominent examples are the use of the word "caring" or the labelling of the practice of nursing as "the nursing process." These labels may contribute to nursing's expertise being dismissed as something that comes naturally to women, something more akin to intuition than to science. While the centrality of expert nursing care to patient survival and well-being is slowly being documented in many patient care settings (Flood and Diers, 1988; Hartz et al., 1989), caring work with a primary focus on human comfort has long been viewed as secondary to curing work, which has its emphasis on disease elimination.

Continued use of these descriptors of medicine and nursing illustrates the use of language to control and perpetuate myths about nursing and medical culture and keeps the two professions—one male-dominated and the other female-dominated—in unequal places, just as men and women have been kept in unequal places in society at large. A more consistent and substantiated language to describe and label previously hidden aspects of nursing work is required. One such attempt is the use of "nursing diagnosis," now a familiar concept in nursing practice and education. There is, however, considerable conceptual and theoretical ambiguity about the application of this term. Turkoski's (1988) survey of 35 years of literature concerning nursing diagnoses found scant evidence of research directed at validating the use of specific nursing diagnosis. She argues for a language to describe nursing practice that represents the depth of current nursing knowledge and lends itself to worldwide research to verify the congruence between nursing theory and practice. A key but controversial step in this direction is the North American Nursing Diagnosis Association's project to standardize nursing terminology (Hurley, 1986). From a broader societal perspective, the ideology of feminism may provide nursing with a sharper political language to press for equality of opportunity. The demand by nurses for the right to determine how to "care" for patients challenges deeply held beliefs about gender relations.

FEMINISM AND NURSING

Feminism as an ideology re-emerged in the 1960s and advocated female independence and equality. With the expanding access to postsecondary education and the availability of oral contraception, women began to spend a much greater proportion of their adult lives in the paid work force. Their freedom to act as individuals was enhanced. Since then, the reality of the social, economic, and political constraints in women's lives has been the subject of relentless public debate.

Historical and present attempts to define feminism imply that the world is genderized (i.e., is socially and intellectually differentiated by sex). Feminist approaches provide a framework for analyzing the consequences of being a woman in a patriarchal world and emphasize such issues as the changing and variable patterns of women's lives, the invisibility of women in Canadian history, and the overt mother-blaming in many psychiatric theories. This critique touches many disciplines, including history, biology, sociology, physiology, and medicine.

Although the relationship between nursing and feminism has to be fully studied, the conventional wisdom is that feminist thinking is not an integral part of the culture of nursing. A variety of analyses have been offered. Ashley (1976), in her study of the role of the nurse in American hospitals, argues that sexism by physicians and paternalistic hospital structures inhibit the development of a nursing culture with a shared understanding of women's oppression or feminist ideas. The legacy of these structural constraints is blocked opportunity, powerlessness, tokenism, and, as Baumgart (1980) stresses, limited development of collective responses to common problems.

After extensive study of the history of American nursing during the period from 1850 to 1945, Reverby (1987) concludes that nursing was an "example of a group of women so divided by class that their common oppression based on gender could not unite them" (p. 6). During these years, nursing became an occupation of women who had diverse training, experience, skills, social backgrounds, and work opportunities, and who were forced to compete with each other for work in a changing labor market. Bound in an ideology based on woman's duty (and not in women's rights), nursing created a professional purpose but lacked sufficient means to defend its occupational role or to control its practice effectively. A rigid hierarchical structure was established within agencies to control the work of nurses with varied training and experience. This female hierarchy served to further restrict the growth of gender bonds between the women who practiced nursing in different levels in the hierarchy. The creation of a common work culture for nursing was fractured by patriarchal constraints from above and differences among women from within (Reverby, 1987).

Melosh's (1982) analysis of the work culture of American nursing from 1920 to 1970 identifies similar themes concerning gender and social class; these themes were expressed in the context of tensions between the leadership's quest for professional autonomy and the rank and file's efforts to maintain control of nursing practice. Rooted in the apprenticeship tradition of hospital schools of nursing, the work culture of nurses on the job valued direct involvement with the sick, respect for experience and manual skills, and, often, a mistrust of theory, carefully crafted methods, and self-control (Melosh 1982, p. 5). The shared experience of daily work shaped the aspirations and ideology of the staff nurses, and they did not share the hope of professionalization espoused by the leadership of the day. Although distant from the leaders, nurses on the job were often threatened by the strategies adopted by the leaders to raise the standards of education and practice. Melosh (1982) stresses that, although the leaders strove for the advancement of the nursing profession as a whole, they often overlooked the pressing realities of the women who practiced nursing on a daily basis. The efforts of nursing's leaders to gain greater professional credibility merely escalated the conflicts. Bound by its ideology and constrained by limited resources, nursing had difficulties making a collective transition out of a culture of obligation to challenge oppressive workplace structures and beliefs about nursing practice. The tension between these two cultures still underlies and informs much of the effort to control nursing practice and education.

McPherson's (1990) research concerning the work of Canadian nurses during the 1920s and 1930s also reveals the segmented nature of the nursing labor market. Like their American sisters, the leaders of Canadian nursing invested tremendous effort to upgrade the practice of nursing with improved training and provincial registration of trained nurses. And, as with their American counterparts, the practice of staff nurses was shaped by an apprenticeship short on theory and long on experience. From these experiences, the staff nurses forged a strong identity and took pride in their nursing work. However, Canadian staff nurses did appear to be less alienated than their American counterparts from the leadership of the day. Various factors may account for this difference, including a more extensive network of student, alumni, and professional associations; fewer hospitals and schools of nursing; the prominence of religious sisterhoods; and the influence of voluntary organizations such as the Victorian Order of Nurses and the Canadian Red Cross (McPherson, 1990).

Although more historical research is essential, a better understanding of the influences of these and related factors should occur from the analysis underway (see Bramadat, 1990; Keddy et al., 1984; Kerr and Paul, 1990; Kirkwood, 1989; Stuart, 1989). A more current analysis of the relationship between the nursing elite and the rank and file may reveal deeper cleavages. Unlike the American situation, the rank and file of Canadian nursing is highly unionized with an extensive network inside nursing workplaces; this network affords frequent opportunity to challenge traditional administrative control of nursing practice. At the same time, the rank and file are openly dissatisfied and impatient with the elite agenda and organizational style of their professional associations. The history of nursing work experience challenges the usual assumption that paid work merely reinforces women's societal subordination. Paid work, at least in nursing, seems to heighten "the contradictions that women confront as social actors who are both participants and outsiders in their own culture," disrupting existing notions about the proper place of women in the workplaces (Melosh, 1982, p. 219).

The revisionist analyses of McPherson (1990), Melosh (1982), and Reverby (1987) highlight three basic tenets of the feminist critique: marginality, invisibility, and the so-called "personal as political." Marginality occurs when individuals or groups live in two worlds simultaneously, one of which has traditionally been regarded as superior (Klein, 1972). Marginal individuals or groups have the potential to threaten more dominant groups but usually exist at the edge of what is considered culturally acceptable. Women's place in society is frequently described as a marginal one. Similarly, nurses have been described as marginal by virtue of their work as well as gender. As a result of having a marginal status, many aspects of nursing practice are unspoken, unrecognized, and unappreciated (Miller, 1991). For example, interruptions are characteristic of the work that nurses do. Nurses are socialized to expect interruptions from patients, physicians, adminstrators, and other caregivers and to develop strategies for coping. Doing three or four things at the same time requires tremendous skill in rapid decision making, priority setting, and communication— most of which is unrecognized.

From the feminist perspective, invisibility refers to the virtual absence of women's words, experiences, and activities from historical and present day accounts of events. Invisibility often accompanies marginality. Some early conclusions of an ongoing study of invisibility in nursing work by Stelling and her colleagues (1990) reveals that normal requirements of nursing work such as reprioritizing patient needs during a busy shift or interactional activities with patients and their families may be examples of invisible aspects of nursing work. Significantly, this work was often invisible even to the nurses in the study, who were reluctant to label activities that nurses do "because we are human" as work; examples include managing personal emotions or providing emotional comfort to patients and colleagues (Stelling, Olijnek, and Graham, 1990, p. 10). However, in a precedent-setting ruling in June 1991, an Ontario Pay Equity Tribunal directed employers to ensure that pay equity evaluation systems recognize the "invisible" work that nurses do ("Pay equity ruling . . .," 1991).

Since a predominant feature of good nursing practice is ensuring patient safety and preventing things from going wrong, nursing practice becomes highly visible when problems or mistakes occur. Unlike medical practice in which mistakes or problems are viewed as inevitable by-products of high-risk work, mistakes in nursing are treated as characteristic of the perpetrator and not characteristic of the work itself (Stelling, 1989). Elaborate rituals have been developed around many nursing tasks to ensure patient safety and to prevent mistakes. The use of the "five rights" of giving medications is an example. The concern with mistakes is also reflected in the patterns of close supervision of nursing work and organizational practices such as incident forms. Although the purpose of these mechanisms may be to ensure patient safety, they also serve to connect mistakes to individual nurses. A better understanding of invisibility in nursing work elucidates the difficulties experienced by individual nurses when their work is rendered visible.

Although much of nursing's history is preserved in documents of hospitals and other public health agencies, as well as in books and journals, the limited analysis of this social history renders the achievements and experiences of nurses invisible. This situation is accentuated by the minimal teaching of nursing history throughout the country. A small but active group of nursing scholars has begun to study nursing history, often using archival and oral history approaches. The Canadian Association for the History of Nursing was formed in 1987, and nursing history interest groups are now organized in many provinces. The aims of these associations are to stimulate interest in and to promote the study of nursing history by providing forums for discussion, assisting in the preservation of historical materials, encouraging the teaching of nursing history, and facilitating historical research in nursing.

A third tenet of the feminist critique—"the personal as political"—asserts that the personal and intimate experiences of women are not isolated and specific, but are social, political, and systemic. This tenet holds that the individual and collective experiences of nurses are representative of the broader societal struggles of all women. Nurses have been relatively isolated from the mainstream of the women's movement (Heide, 1985). Ironically, part of the isolation derives from the misogynistic application of key aspects of the feminist ideology. For example, nurses have been upbraided by more strident feminists for being nurses and not doctors. The uneasy alliance between feminism and nursing began to strengthen in the 1980s as an awareness grew within the nursing profession of the gender bias built into many of nursing's perpetual workplace and educational problems. Nurses are now discussing their oppression and are becoming advocates for others. The Manitoba Association of Registered Nurses' study of nurse abuse (1989) is an important example. However, mainstream feminist groups are slow to accept nurses as role models and leaders even when nurses have considerable if often untapped human and organizational resources to contribute to the struggle.

The implicit assumption of some feminist ideology that all women share common interests and concerns has been subjected to serious challenge. In the effort to promote the well-being of women in general, the practice of stereotyping has not been destroyed, but instead new stereotypes such as Super Mom and the Caring Sex have been created. Crittenden (1990) explains:

> . . . what has been left intact and unchallenged is the old (misogynistic) doctrine that women are a group of people whose interests, opinions, talents and desires can be categorized; that women, unlike men, should hold identical values, that they should think and behave in the same way, toward the same end. (p. A14)

Although they share fundamental rights and obligations, nurses as individuals hold differing opinions and have diversified interests. It would be a great tragedy if nurses, who for so long have been the victims of stereotyping, should fall into the trap of enforcing new stereotypes as they work to change the culture of nursing progresses.

RIGHTFUL KNOWLEDGE

The witch-hunts of the late 1500s and early 1600s were a concerted effort by the Church and the emerging medical profession to invalidate the knowledge and skills of lay healers who were primarily women. The 1983 Grange Royal Commission of Inquiry into the deaths at the Hospital for Sick Children in Toronto can be viewed as a modern day witch-hunt. In her study of this Inquiry, Day (1987) documents a consistent practice of the nurses being threatened, ridiculed, and harassed, along with having their knowledge and experience discounted or simply ignored, while the testimony of physicians and hospital administrators was treated with respect and accepted as credible. One of the reasons the nurses became scapegoats for events that have not yet been fully explained is the lack of social recognition for nurses as "rightful knowers" (Day, 1987, p. 31).

Rightful knowledge is portrayed as objective and context free. It is a type of "separate knowing" that has been enshrined in Western notions of logic, legal precepts, and scientific method (Harding, 1987, p. 7). Knowledge of a more subjective and context-dependent nature is judged less meritorious. It is knowing "connected" to understanding of the circumstances of others (Belenky, Clinchy, Goldberger, and Tarule, 1986, p. 113). This type of knowledge is generally assumed to be of a more primitive nature than so-called objective modes of knowing. The different ways of knowing are not limited by gender, but "separate knowing" has been characteristically associated with the intellectual development of men and "connected knowing" with that of women. Similarly, nursing's ways of knowing about patients, derived from interaction and observation, have many features of "connected knowing," whereas medical knowledge derived from the accepted scientific method and based in a technological orientation to patient care is seen as "separate" or more rightful knowing.

The practice of equating knowledge, reason, and objectivity with "maleness" lies deep in the philosophic traditions of Western thought. Lloyd (1984) argues that, in the quest for rational knowledge, philosophers from Plato to Sartre associated male characteristics "with a clear, determined mode of thought, femaleness with the vague and indeterminate" (p. 3). In the last century, theories in the social and basic sciences offered numerous explanations of how and why sex is "a variable in the distribution of rationality" (Harding, 1983, p. 43). Examples of the biological arguments advanced to deny women access to knowledge were that women's brains were smaller than men's or that studying would cause women's uteruses to deteriorate (Clarke, 1972). In recent years, the universality of these philosophic cannons have been severely challenged over their relevance to time and culture as well as gender. Still, relatively little scholarly attention has been paid to modes of knowing, valuing, and learning that may be specific to, or at least common in, women.

An exception is the work of Gilligan (1982), who traced the development of morality in girls and women, observing patterns of development organized around premises of responsibility and care of oneself and others. This "ethic of care" encompassed a recognition of differences in need among individuals and contrasted sharply with the morality of abstract rights described by Kohlberg (1981) in his study of the evolution of moral reasoning in boys and men. However, Gilligan (1982) argues that while "the different voice" in her study has been associated with women, it is in reality characterized not by gender but by theme (p. 2).

Building on Gilligan's work, Belenky, Clinchy, Goldberger, and Tarule (1986) examined women's ways of knowing and described five different perspectives from which women view reality: silence, received knowledge, subjective knowledge, procedural knowledge, and constructed knowledge. These five perspectives have similarities with, and differences from, the established forms of epistemological development described by Perry (1970) in his influential study of male college students.

This extraordinary study of women's struggles to find their own voices has already begun to influence the understanding of nurses' ways of knowing. For example, Knowlden (1991) shows that nurses use knowledge constructed from their educational and practice experiences to understand what is happening with their patients.

The "world of silence" described by Belenky and her colleagues is a way of knowing common to the lived experience of many women. It is a world of being seen but never heard; a world occupied by women in powerless circumstances. Working in a "world of silence" is an accepted part of the experience of frontline caregivers in nursing. Being silenced and excluded from the circle of "rightful knowers" exacts a high toll on nurses' self-esteem. Strategies that overtly recognize worth and reconfirm ability are often prerequisites before previously excluded individuals can meet new learning demands at work and particularly in higher education. Belenky and her colleagues (1986) point out that some of the conditions most beneficial to men's learning (e.g., competition) may actually "act more as impediments than as goads to independent thinking" in women (p. 216).

The past decade witnessed a deliberate effort to define nursing as an applied science and to ground nursing practice in research based knowledge. Yet much of the repertoire of knowledge and skills used in daily nursing practice has to be organized and validated in a scientific manner. This includes the need to examine the contextual nature of many nursing phenomena, which are combined with more abstract knowledge during the delivery of nursing care. The use of a more descriptive language to label nursing phenomena is an essential part of the validation process. Further, the intellectual processes of nursing practice have been subject to limited analysis. The most prominent example of this type of analysis is Benner's (1984) study of the characteristics of novice and experts in nursing practice. More recently, theorists have questioned the adequacy of the traditional scientific paradigm to deal with nursing's most substantive problems, arguing instead for a paradigm that allows the personal meanings attached to human responses to health and illness to emerge (Beaton and Tinkle, 1983; Hagell, 1989).

While acknowledging the pressing need to understand the contextual nature of nursing knowledge, the basic science foundation on which much of illness care and biomedical technology is based cannot be ignored. Mathematics and science are essential components of the intellectual armory of nurses working in complex technological environments, and urgent action is required to ensure that nurses have opportunities to learn basic and more advanced "hard science" knowledge essential to patient care in these high-tech settings. The idea that nursing work requires few skills grounded in science contributes to the economic evaluation of nursing as essential but not very complex work.

ECONOMIC VALUE OF NURSES' WORK

Nurses are in a peculiarly difficult economic situation in that their work at home as wives and mothers and their work as professionals on the job have many similarities. The unpaid work of women to maintain their homes and support their families has been so taken for granted that it is often not even seen as work. The low value attached to much of this work extends to other work that women do outside the home, whether paid or unpaid.

Mainstream economic theory ignores much of the traditional work of women in estimations of productivity such as gross national product (GNP). As Waring (1988) declares, this work is excluded from definitions of production and has no assigned economic value:

> the skewed definitions of work and labor that are used by economists result in an equally skewed concept of production . . . [and] economists usually use labor to mean only those activities that produce surplus value (that is, profit in the market place). (p. 27)

Consequently, work that does not produce profit is not considered production. Excluded from the category of work are all activities within the informal economy: mutual aid, subsistence agriculture, do-it-yourself construction and maintenance, housework, raising children, and volunteering, as well as the global use of barter, which Henderson (1990) estimates now accounts for 25% of all world trade. Waring (1988) documents how the same work, when performed by women, becomes categorized as "uneconomic" and how women are designated as "not employed" even when they grow most of the world's food and take care of most of the world's households and children.

As a consequence of the close association with the unpaid work of women, nursing work suffers similar problems of economic invisibility and devaluation. Within the block grants allocated to hospitals and community agencies by governments for patient services, nurses are regarded as a unit of care, undifferentiated by time, place, or expertise. Although nursing is usually the largest single item of expenditure in these budgets, the study of nursing economics has not been a research priority among health care economists. In the first comprehensive review of literature concerning the economics of nursing, Gray (1987) postulates that the reasons for this comparative neglect include the failure to appreciate the economic importance of nursing as an autonomous category of labor and concern that the low status of nursing would reflect on the status of the researcher. Although economists have paid little attention to nursing as a field of study, research by nurses has burgeoned (there is now a journal, *Nursing Economics*, published in the United States). However, Gray (1987) cautions, as Aydelotte did in 1973, that much research by nurses concerning economics issues has been of poor quality.

Most studies of nursing economics concentrate on labor market issues of supply and demand and work force planning, with much less attention given to issues of efficiency and effectiveness of nursing work. There is a notable absence of studies examining the effect of nursing care on patient outcomes, a subject that is critical to understanding issues associated with nursing productivity. Given the widespread attention to the cost of health care in Canada, the urgency for research concerning the economic aspects of nursing work cannot be over-emphasized.

The economic factors associated with nursing salaries and working conditions capture political attention episodically in response to severe shortages or during contract negotiations. Although comprehensive studies have not been undertaken, two distinct explanations are offered for the wage compression and conditions characteristic of nursing workplaces. From the supply-side perspective, the heavy concentration of women in few occupations has the result of "too many women chasing too few jobs" and driving the price down (Anselm, 1990, p. 21). The situation is aggravated by the inelastic nature of female labor compared to male labor. Women's choice of employment is often restricted by the geographic location of the husband's work and to jobs compatible with family responsibilities. The availability of child care is also a mitigating factor. Market forces are further restrained by the predominance of government as the major buyer of nursing labor in a highly unionized environment. Supply-side solutions to wage discrimination in nursing involve concerted efforts to mobilize nursing labor skills to better match the needs of future workplaces. A related approach is to expand the occupational choices of men into female-dominated sectors of the economy in a manner similar to the expanded choices now available to women in traditional male-dominated workplaces.

From the demand-side perspective, nursing salaries are low in part as a function of the historic undervaluing of women's work and women's abilities and in part to the idea that nursing salaries were nonessential, second family incomes. Pay equity is one mechanism now available to redress these historic injustices. By focusing on the content of the job, previously overlooked aspects of women's work, including the skills and efforts required to do the job and the responsibilities embedded in the work tasks, are assigned values for monetary purposes. Implementation of pay equity, at least in nursing, is fraught with problems. Without an obvious male comparison group, nurses' work has been compared to that of pastry chefs, maintenance supervisors, technicians, and policemen. Treating nurses as a homogeneous group in large agencies has resulted in a failure to recognize the diversity of nursing expertise, training, and skills across different work groups. Legislation concerning pay equity created different categories of inclusion and exclusion across the provinces. For example, Ontario is the only province to include the private sector in the legislation, whereas in Nova Scotia agencies with fewer than 10 nurses are excluded. The benefits of pay equity for nursing remain an open question.

Economic issues associated with increasing rates of part-time employment in nursing workplaces have not been carefully analyzed. Although the reasons for part-time work seem clear—multiple roles, shift work, stress management—the economic costs in terms of patient care and the consequence for individual nurses are unknown. The effects of flexible work schedules and other strategies to help nurses balance work and family responsibilities may resemble "an organizational menstrual hut," which Ward (1991) describes as

> a confine for women wherein they can work hard and enjoy each other's company but from which they do not get the major promotions nor the benefits from full equality in the workplace. (p. 104)

A long and critical view of this and other economic issues such as the aging of the nursing work force is essential to help determine the economic value of caregiving work in nursing.

MEDIA IMAGES OF NURSING CULTURE

Images in the mass media, including print, radio, and television, act as subtle models that shape sensibilities as to what is considered acceptable behavior. The media emanate "cultural notions" so indigenous as to be taken for granted (Pollner, 1982, p. 28). After an intensive content analysis of several mass media sources, Kalisch and Kalisch (1987) trace the images of American nursing through several historical phases. These phases are described as Angels of Mercy (1854-1919), Girl Friday (1920-1929), Heroine (1930-1945), Mother (1946-1966), and Sex Object (1966-1982). The conflicting images of nurses that emerge from this analysis—"intimacy and eroticism, Madonna and whore, angel and bawd, spirituality and earthiness"— reflect the historical and contemporary cultural confusion about the role of women (Jones, 1988, p. xxi).

Images of female nurses in the media seem always to be symbolic of Women writ large (Hunter, 1988). Nursing imagery often reflects the subtle but powerful myth that beauty and sexuality are women's most valuable assets. As late as 1986, this myth was exploited in Canadian government promotional material, which used a chorus line in nurses' uniforms performing a cancan to publicize Expo in Vancouver. The Canadian Nurses Association lodged a complaint and the chorus line was eventually withdrawn. Another recurrent theme in nursing imagery, which both attracts and repels, reflects the societal struggle with female power. The power of the nurse in media portrayals is derived from the intimate nature of nursing work, which violates the usual social taboos about seeing and touching patient's bodies, as well as from patient dependency during illness and death, and from the evil power women often are perceived to possess in male sexual fantasies. No matter how highly technical and skilled, nurses are, in Anne Hudson Jones' (1988) words, "the quintessential female profession having its etymological and cultural origins in the biological aspects of femaleness" (p. xix).

The Kalisches' research further indicates that nurses today are depicted in the public media as humanistic, committed to their work, technically competent, usually submissive, sometimes intelligent, but rarely autonomous or scholarly. Much of this portrayal was confirmed in a recent public opinion survey commissioned by the Alberta Association of Registered Nurses. While identifying deep respect for nurses as health care professionals, Albertans viewed nurses as playing a supportive role to physicians in patient care and as not having independent influence on health care systems issues (Turner, 1990). Such images harm the profession's ability to shape public opinion and to influence choices of decision makers. In this way, popular images have a powerful and oppressive effect.

What can or should be done about these negative images is a question central to the future health of the nursing profession. Understanding why negative images exist is an important first step. The next and much more difficult steps necessitate the use of social marketing and mass communication strategies to shape public opinion. Influencing the agenda setting function of the mass media must be a priority strategy. Often the media provide a major share of the public's information about selected topics and, as a consequence, shape perceptions of what is important and unimportant (McCombs and Shaw, 1978). Gaining access to reporters, producers, and related media personnel who serve as gatekeepers of the agenda is essential. The media awards presented by the Canadian Nurses Association for positive and accurate portrayal of nursing and health care issues is an excellent strategy to influence this agenda subtly and gain visibility with media decision makers. Another approach used by many provincial nursing associations is establishment of media watch committees to evaluate and, if necessary, protest negative portrayals of nurses.

An important finding in the Alberta survey is that public opinion about nursing was formulated in some measure through direct contact with the health care system and not solely by exposure to mass media. Successful strategies to educate the public (and the media) about the changing role of nurses must direct a major focus at nurses themselves; nurses must show increasing sensitivity to the enormous potential of shaping public opinion about nursing by using the daily opportunities nurses have to communicate to the public (Turner, 1990).

The image of Florence Nightingale carrying her lamp at Scutari is a worldwide symbol of professional nursing. This symbol, together with the nursing uniform, cap, and pin, now is often rejected as archaic. However, as Smith (1979) points out, one consequence of breaking away from traditional ideology is that no images, symbols, or vocabularies exist to express the new experience. Since symbols and myths are powerful vehicles that hold groups together, old symbols must be replaced with new ones to ensure bonding within nursing as a group and to form symbolic connections with the public. The important work of creating and anchoring new symbols in a culture is usually undertaken by group leaders. How leaders of nursing could be more effective in creating and transmitting new cultural values requires intensive study. A final set of strategies would commit nurses to join in the broader societal work to elevate the status of women and all female labor to which the image of nursing is inextricably bound.

CONCLUSION

The chapter offers brief glimpses of selected historical and contemporary dimensions that shaped the culture of nursing. These dimensions highlight critical economic, demographic, institutional, and political conditions that must be put in place to enable nurses to fulfill their societal mandate. Ways must be found to overcome the indignities suffered as a consequence of being a female profession doing traditional women's work. Cultural change of this magnitude will be an uncertain, fragile, and controversial undertaking. For nurses to have their words and voices heard, it is also essential.

REFERENCES

Allen, D. (1986). Professionalism, occupational segregation by gender and control of nursing. *Women and Politics*, 6(3), 1-24.

Anselm, M. (1990). Why women's wages stay low. *Policy Options*, 11(4), 19-22.

Ashley, J. (1976). *Hospitals, paternalism and the role of the nurse*. New York: Teachers College Press.

Aydelotte, M. (1973). *Nurse staffing methodology: A review and critique of selected literature* (DHSS Publication No. (HRA) 80-14028). Washington, DC: U.S. Government Printing Office.

Baumgart, A. (1980). Nurses and political action: The legacy of sexism. *Nursing Papers*, 12(4), 6-15.

Beaton, J., & Tinkle, M. (1983). Toward a new view of science. *Advances in Nursing Science*, 5(3), 27-36.

Belenky, M., Clinchy, B., Goldberger, N., & Tarule, J. (1986). *Women's ways of knowing*. New York: Basic Books.

Benner, P. (1984). *From novice to expert*. Menlo Park, CA: Addison-Wesley.

Bernard, J. (1981). *The female world*. New York: The Free Press.

Bernard, J. (1987). *The female world from a global perspective*. Indianapolis: Indiana University Press.

Bramadat, I. (1990, September). *Nursing in the Canadian West 1900-1930: Impact of European immigration*. Paper presented at the 5th Biennial (open) Conference of the Work Group of European Nurse Researchers, Budapest, Hungary.

Campbell-Heider, N., & Pollack, D. (1987). Barriers to physician-nurse collegiality: An anthropological perspective. *Social Science Medicine*, 25,(5), 421-425.

Canadian Nurses Association. (1960). *Facts and figures about nursing in Canada*. Ottawa: Author.

Canadian Nurses Association (1967). *Countdown 1966 Canadian nursing statistics*. Ottawa: Author.

Canadian Nurses Association. (1969). *Countdown 1969 Canadian Nursing Statistics*, Ottawa: Author.

Canadian Nurses Association. (1986). *Nursing in Canada—1985*. Ottawa: Author.

Clarke, E. (1972). *Sex in education; or, a fair chance for the girls* (originally published in 1873). New York: Arno Press and the New York Times.

Coburn J. (1981). "I see and am silent": A short history of nursing in Ontario. In D. Coburn, C. D'Arcy, P. New, & G. Torrance (Eds.), *Health and Canadian society* (pp. 182-201). Toronto: Fitzhenry & Whiteside.

Cockburn, C. (1985). *Machinery of dominance: Women, men and technical know-how*. London: Pluto Press.

Crittenden, D. (1990, December 27). New stereotypes replace the old. *Globe and Mail*, p. A14.

Day, E. (1987). A 20th century witch hunt: A feminist critique of the Grange Royal Commission into death at the Hospital for Sick Children. *Studies in Political Economy*, 24(Autumn), 13-39.

Doyal, L. (1979). *The political economy of health*. London: Pluto Press.

Fennema, E. (1985). Explaining sex-related differences in mathematics: Theoretical models. *Educational Studies in Mathematics*, 16(3), 303-320.

Flannelly, L., & Flannelly, K. (1984). The masculine and feminine in nursing. *Nursing Papers*, 21(4), 162-165.

Flood, S., & Diers, D. (1988). Nurse staffing, patient outcome and cost. *Nursing Management*, 19(5), 34-43.

Gilligan, C. (1982). *In a different voice: Psychological theory and women's development*. Cambridge, MA: Harvard University Press.

Gray, A. (1987). *The economics of nursing: A literature review*. Nursing Policy Studies 2, Nursing Policy Studies Centre, Coventry, England: University of Warwick.

Hagell, E. (1989). Nursing knowledge: Women's knowledge; a sociological perspective. *Journal of Advanced Nursing*, 14(3), 226-233.

Halloran, E. (1990). Men in nursing. In J. C. McCloskey & H. K. Grace (Eds.), *Current issues in nursing*, (3rd ed.) (pp. 547-553). St. Louis: C.V. Mosby.

Harding, S. (1983). Is gender a variable in conceptions of rationality: A survey of issues. In C. Gould (Ed.), *Beyond domination: New perspectives on women and philosophy* (pp. 43-63). Totowa, NJ: Rowman and Allanheld.

Harding, S. (1987). Struggling for self definition (Review of *Women's ways of knowing: The development of self, voice and mind* by M. F. Belenky, B. M. Clinchy, N. R. Goldberger, & J. Tarule (Eds.)). *The Women's Review of Books,* 4(6), 6-7.

Hartz, A., Krahauer, H., Kuhn, E., Young, M., Jacobsen, S., Gay, G., Muenz, L., Katzoff, M., Bailey, R., & Rimm, A. (1989). Hospital characteristics and mortality rates. *New England Journal of Medicine, 321*(25), 1720-1725.

Heide, W. S. (1973). Nursing and women's liberation: A parallel. *American Journal of Nursing, 73*(5), 824-27.

Heide, W. S. (1985). *Feminism for the health of it.* Buffalo, NY: Margaret Daughters Inc.

Henderson, H. (1990). Economics demolition and reconstruction: Review of *If women counted: A new feminist economics* by M. Waring, *Futures, 22*(5), 530-532.

Hunter, K. (1988). Nurses: The satiric image and the translocated ideal. In A. H. Jones (Ed.), *Images of nurses' perspectives from history, art and literature* (pp. 113-127). Philadelphia: University of Pennsylvania Press.

Hurley, M. (Ed.) (1986). *Classification of nursing diagnosis: Proceedings of the sixth conference.* St. Louis: Mosby.

Jenny, J. (1990). Self-esteem: A problem for nurses. *The Canadian Nurse, 86*(10), 19-21.

Jones, A.H. (1988). Introduction. In A.H. Jones (Ed.), *Images of nurses' perspectives from history, art and literature* (xix-xxii). Philadelphia: University of Pennsylvania Press.

Kalisch, P., & Kalisch, B. (1987). *The changing image of the nurse.* Menlo Park, CA: Addison-Wesley.

Keddy, B., LeDrew, M., Thompson, B., Nowarzek, L., Stewart, M., & Englehart, R. (1984). The nurse as mother surrogate: Oral histories of Nova Scotia nurses from the 1920s and 1930s. *Health Care for Women International,* 5(4), 181-193.

Keller, E., & Moglen, H. (1987). Competition and feminism: Conflicts for academic women. *Signs: Journal of Women in Culture and Society,* 12(3), 493-511.

Kelly, L. (1975). *Dimensions of professional nursing* (3rd ed.). New York: Macmillan.

Kerr, J., & Paul, P. (1990). *The work of the Grey Nuns in Alberta-1859-1899: A feminist perspective.* In Canadian Association for the History of Nursing, *Proceedings of the Third Annual Conference* (pp. 49-63). Calgary: Author.

Kirkwood, R. (1988). *The development of university nursing education in Canada, 1920-1975: Two case studies.* Unpublished doctoral dissertation, University of Toronto.

Klein, V. (1972). *The feminine character: A history of an ideology.* Urbana, IL: University of Illinois Press.

Knowlden, V. (1991). Nurse caring as constructed knowledge. In R. Neil & R. Watts (Eds.), *Caring and nursing: Explorations in feminist perspectives* (pp. 201-208). New York: National League for Nursing.

Kohlberg, L. (1981). *The philosophy of moral development.* New York: Harper and Row.

Larsen, J. (1988). Being powerful: From talk into action. In R. White (Ed.), *Political issues in nursing: Past, present and future* (pp. 1-13). London: John Wiley and Sons.

Lipman-Blumen, J. (1984) *Gender roles and power,* Englewood Cliffs, NJ: Prentice-Hall.

Lloyd, G. (1984). *The man of reason: "male" and "female" in Western philosophy.* Minneapolis: University of Minnesota Press.

Manitoba Association of Registered Nurses (1989). *Nurse abuse report.* Winnipeg: Author.

Marriner, A. (1978). Theories of leadership. *Nursing Leadership, 1*(3), 13-17.

McCombs, M., & Shaw, D. (1978). The agenda setting function of the mass media. In E. Daniels, A. Ismach, & D. Gillmore (Eds.), *Enduring issues in mass communication* (pp. 95-103). St. Paul, MN: West Publishing Company.

McPherson, K. (1990). *Skilled service and women's work: Canadian nursing 1920-1939.* Unpublished doctoral dissertation, Simon Fraser University, Vancouver.

Melosh, B. (1982). *The physicians' hand.* Philadelphia: Temple University Press.

Miller, K. (1991). A study of nursing's feminist ideology. In R. Neil & R. Watts (Eds.), *Caring and nursing: Exploration in feminist perspectives* (pp. 43-56). New York: National League for Nursing.

Morgan, G. (1986). *Images of organization.* London: Sage Publications.

Mura, R., Kimball, M., & Cloutier, R. (1987). Girls and science programs: Two steps forward, one step back. In J. Gaskell & A. McLaren (Eds.), *Women and education, a Canadian perspective* (pp. 133-150). Calgary: Detselig Enterprises.

Mussallem, H. (1964). *Nursing education in Canada*. Ottawa: Queen's Printer.

Okrainec, G. (1990a). Males in nursing: Historical perspectives and analyses. *AARN Newsletter, 46*(2), 6-8.

Okrainec, G. (1990b). Male nursing students' satisfaction with nursing education. *AARN Newsletter, 46*(11), 20-22.

Pay equity ruling sets precedent. (1991, September). *The Nursing Report, 41,* 16.

Perry, W. (1970). *Forms of intellectual and ethical development in the college years.* New York: Holt, Rinehart and Winston.

Pollner, M. (1982). Better dead than wed. *Social Policy, 13*(1), 28-31.

Remick, H. (1984). Dilemmas of implementation: The case of nursing. In H. Remick (Ed.), *Comparable worth and wages discrimination: Technical possibilities and political realities* (pp. 90-98). Philadelphia: Temple University Press.

Reverby, S. (1987). *Ordered to care: The dilemma of American nursing 1850-1945.* Cambridge: Cambridge University Press.

Roberts, S.J. (1983). Oppressed group behavior: Implications for nursing. *Advances in Nursing Science, 5*(4), 21-30.

Robson, R. (1964). *Sociological factors affecting recruitment in the nursing profession.* Ottawa: Queen's Printer.

Rosener, J. (1990). Ways women lead. *Harvard Business Review, 68*(6), 119-125.

Schein, E. (1985). *Organizational culture and leadership.* San Francisco: Jossey-Bass.

Smith, D. (1979). A sociology for women. In J. Sherman & J. Beck (Eds.), *The prism of sex* (pp. 135-137). Madison: University of Wisconsin Press.

Statistics Canada. (1990). *Nursing in Canada 1988.* Ottawa: Canadian Government Publishing Centre.

Stein, L. I., Watts, D. T., & Howell, T. (1990). Sounding board: The doctor-nurse game revisited. *New England Journal of Medicine, 322*(8), 546-549.

Stelling, J. (1989, September). *Sources of stress for staff nurses: A sociological perspective on nursing work.* Unpublished paper presented at the Nursing Explorations Conference, McGill University, Montreal.

Stelling, J., Olijnek, D., & Graham, I. (1990, May). *Researching women's work: A question of methodology.* Unpublished paper presented at the Annual Meetings of the Canadian Sociology and Anthropology Association, University of Victoria.

Streubert, H., & O'Toole, M. (1991). Review of research on male nursing students. In P. Baj & G. Clayton (Eds.), *Review of research in nursing education* (Vol 4) (pp. 31-50). New York: National League for Nursing.

Stuart, M. (1989). Ideology and experience: Public health nursing and the Ontario rural child welfare project 1920-25. *Canadian Bulletin of Medical History, 6,* 111-131.

Turkoski, B. (1988). Nursing diagnoses in print 1950-1985. *Nursing Outlook, 36*(3), 142-144.

Turner, A. (1990). Public opinion survey: A special report to the AARN Newsletter, *AARN Newsletter, 46*(1), 5-6.

Valentine, P. (1988). *A hospital school of nursing: A case study of a predominantly female organization.* Unpublished doctoral dissertation, University of Alberta, Edmonton.

Valentine, P., & McIntosh, G. (1990). Food for thought: Realities of a women-dominated organization. *The Alberta Journal of Educational Research, 34*(4), 353-369.

Ward, D. (1991). Gender and cost in caring. In R. Neil & R. Watts (Eds.), *Caring and Nursing: Explorations in Feminist Perspectives* (pp. 97-104). New York: National League for Nursing.

Wardaugh, R. (1983). *Language and nationhood: The Canadian experience.* Vancouver: New Star Books.

Waring, M. (1988). *If women counted: A new feminist economics.* San Francisco: Harper and Row.

Welter, B. (1966). The cult of true womanhood. *American Quarterly, 18*(2), 51-174.

White, R. (Ed.). (1988). *Political issues in nursing: Past, present and future* (Vol. 3, pp. xiii-xxi). New York: J. Wiley.

NURSING PRACTICE

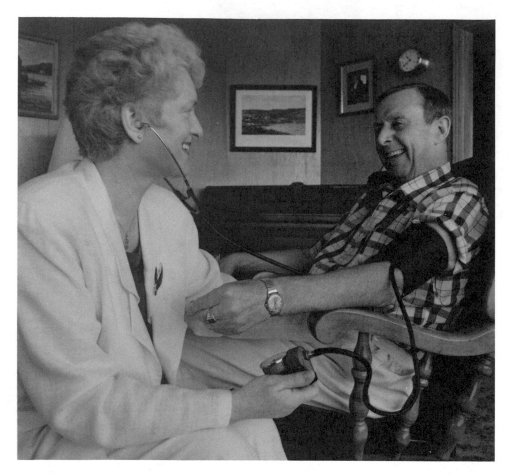

Nursing practice takes place in many different locales. In 1991, the Association of Registered Nurses of Newfoundland produced a poster to show the many facets of nursing today. This photo from the poster shows a nurse from the Primary Health Care Project in Bay Bulls, Newfoundland, checking the blood pressure of a local resident. (Photograph courtesy Prime Communications Consultants, St. John's, Lane Photographics Ltd., St. John's, and the Association of Registered Nurses of Newfoundland. Used with permission.)

CHAPTER FIVE

Overview: Nursing Practice in Canada

ALICE J. BAUMGART, RN, PhD
JENNIECE LARSEN, RN, PhD

Nursing practice in Canada is changing in complicated ways and reflects new health care problems and priorities and a corresponding shift in perspectives about appropriate societal responses to health and illness. Some of the emerging trends that will have the greatest effect on nursing practice during the 1990s include public policy that emphasizes wellness and health promotion; increasing pressure from governments to control health care costs, as well as to demonstrate positive outcomes of nursing interventions; and proliferation of new technical devices.

Increasingly, technology will allow people requiring such mechanical supports as dialysers, respirators, or sophisticated pain control systems to be cared for in long-term facilities or their own homes. This dynamic environment will continue to place new demands on nurses working in all health care settings and to accelerate the development of specialty nursing roles. Nurses, in turn, will need education and training that will prepare them for these evolving roles. Moreover, because of the complexity of nursing and because of nursing's considerable importance to the health care system, nurses are demanding greater involvement in decision making and greater recognition of expertise acquired during lifelong careers. Such changes do not proceed in a neat and orderly way. They evoke anger, frustration, and anxiety. They yield costs and gains in relation to the intellectual, emotional, and physical requirements of nursing work. Alterations in nursing practice roles also inevitably alter the work of other health professionals, thus adding to the stresses and strains nurses and others experience.

The resulting continuities and discontinuities between past and present practice in various health care settings are discussed in the next five chapters. The settings include acute care hospitals, long-term care institutions, community health agencies, northern nursing stations serving Canada's native people, and international organizations that provide health care assistance in countries around the world. Change to prepare for practice in such diverse settings is not a simple linear process; it requires new models of practice and major adjustments in the current health care system. Strategies to induce change are not yet fully developed, as the succeeding chapters on nursing practice show. What is certain is the need for strategies to address three important areas:

- Changing demographic and morbidity trends and health care needs
- Contributions of nursing in the provision of health services
- Education of nurses for contributions of nursing in the provision of health services

DEMOGRAPHY, MORBIDITY, AND CHANGING HEALTH CARE NEEDS

A widely recognized and far-reaching factor affecting the future of nursing practice in Canada is the changing social structure of the Canadian population. Three aspects bear special notice. The first is that there are more old people and fewer young people. Advances in health care contribute to increased longevity, and fertility rates decline because of more effective birth control, changing patterns of female employment, and other cultural shifts. Mantle notes in Chapter 7, on nursing practice in long-term care agencies, that Canada became a "greying" country in the early 1970s, and that the percentage of Canadians over age 65 accelerated more quickly during the 1980s (Stone and Frenken, 1988). Experts predict that, by the opening of the twenty-first century, in excess of 12% of the population will be more than age 65, with the largest percentage increases in this age cohort being persons 85 years and older. This long-term trend is exacerbated by effects related to the baby boom of the 1940s and the 1950s. The baby-boom group, as it ages, will constitute a large body of senior citizens requiring health care services and other special requirements for the elderly. Another dimension of the changing age structure of Canada's population that pertains to nursing practice is the preponderance of women among the elderly, a result of the widening gap between female and male longevity. Since 1981, women outnumber men in the 85+ group by more than 2:1 (Stone and Frenken, 1988), and a substantial proportion of these elderly women are in the low income category and live alone.

This leads to a second change of consequence in the social structure of the population, namely the decreasing number of households occupied by the protypical husband/wife family group. Between the 1976 census and the 1986 census, the number of one-person households in Canada rose by 40%. An increasing number of persons living alone, especially among the elderly, and a decreasing number of children in Canadian families resulted in an overall decline in the average size of the Canadian household from 3.5 persons in 1976 to 2.8 in 1986. The same period saw a rise in the proportion of single-parent families from 9.8% to 12.7%.

A third characteristic of Canada's population with implications for nursing practice is its cultural diversity. In terms of mother tongue, the two principal language groups are English (61%) and French (26%), with Italian and German ranking third and fourth. A small percentage (2.8%) of the population, but significant from a health care perspective, are aboriginal Canadians; Cree, the mother tongue of about 13% of the native peoples, is the most common of the native languages. Nearly 16% of Canada's population is foreign born. More than one half of the immigrant population arrived since 1945. The 1986 census shows that most immigrants came from Europe (7%), Britain (3.7%), and Asia (1.7%) (Statistics Canada, 1985; 1986a; 1986b). During the 1980s, immigration patterns differed significantly from those before the 1960s. Throughout the 1980s, almost half of the people immigrating to Canada were from Asia. For instance, in 1989, 50% of immigrants originated in Asia and 26% originated in Europe. This is in contrast to the early 1960s when the majority of immigrants were from Europe or North America (Logan, 1991).

Health care policymakers in Canada have been particularly sensitive to the increasing number of elderly persons and the economic implications for a health care system heavily weighted toward hospital care. Currently, for example, the 10% of the population who are seniors account for about 40% of hospital use. About one third of the so-called frail elderly or "old-old" (over 85 years) also need extensive nursing care at home or in long-term institutions (Bergman, 1986). As a response to these demographic trends, attention is being focused on strategies such as health promotion and disease prevention for the well elderly and on provision of services in the home and community, or what Walker (1987) aptly calls "enlarging the caring capacity of the community" (p. 369).

However, not all of these strategies may prove widely applicable over the long run. They must be based on a responsible assessment of needs and resources (Walker, 1987). For example, the current enthusiasm for using informal social support networks of family, friends, and neighbors to provide care in the home must be tempered by the fact that many Canadians live alone and hundreds of miles from family members. Also, the number of potential caregivers in a family is reduced by the smaller size of Canadian households, greater participation of women in the paid work force, and higher divorce rates. Moreover, among the "old-old," the caregivers themselves may be seniors who are physically unable to cope with the arduous physical demands that care of the disabled often entails. The aging of Canada's immigrant population suggests the need to direct attention to the special requirements arising from language barriers and cultural differences in caregiving attitudes and practices.

Political and professional responses to the increase of elderly in Canada have been shaped by broader trends, which Fox (1986) calls "the crisis of authority" (p. 7) in health care (i.e., a shifting of power between consumers, providers, and funders of health services). The crisis, to a large degree, stems from changing morbidity patterns and changed thinking about how a community should organize its responses to health and illness. For the better part of the twentieth century, priority has been accorded to preventing, diagnosing, and treating acute illness, with most health care resources spent on episodic medical care and acute care hospitals.

Because people are living longer, the incidence of chronic degenerative conditions such as heart disease, arthritis, cancer, and diabetes is increasing. Also increasing are the rates of drug abuse, accidents, and certain infectious diseases such as AIDS and sexually-transmitted diseases. These changes in morbidity patterns put considerable new demands on the health care system and force health caregivers and policymakers to question the appropriateness of current practice. In many cases, major health problems today are linked to individual behavior and environmental factors. These behavioral and environmental factors are expensive to study and treat, and, moreover, the resulting health problems involve long-term management and require a coordinated array of community and personal health services.

An equally deeply rooted facet of the change in thinking about health care is the eclipse of professional power by the rise of consumerism and the erosion of public confidence in the claims of medical science. These trends put pressures on health care organizations and on professionals to become more responsive to various new concerns. For example, the bioethics movement is a major force in the introduction of revised practices for informed consent and for the protection of patients and other research subjects from harm arising out of scientific experimentation. The effect of contending forces on health care institutions is also evident in the struggles in Canada and elsewhere between providers and consumers over reproductive technology and birth practices. The Royal Commission on Reproductive Technology provides an illuminating example of such conflicts over priorities given to high technology versus primary prevention in reproductive care (Canadian Nurses Association, 1990).

The most obvious and sweeping manifestation of the crisis caused by changed priorities is the unremitting pressure on the health care system to control costs. This is combined with a far greater degree of consumer and political participation in determining health care priorities and in scrutinizing health care activities.

However, insistent as the accumulation of these demands and pressures for change may be, the broad shape of the health care system's responses still needs definition. Health care resources in Canada remain heavily invested in curative medicine rather than health promotion and disease prevention. Moreover, the powerful central position of acute care hospitals all but obscures long-term care needs and community-based health care services. This reflects entrenched professional and bureaucratic interests within the health care system and also public ambivalence, as the media's elevation of heart transplant patients to the status of folk heroes suggests. Nevertheless, there are many signs that a shift in the prevailing concept of health is occurring and inevitably affecting how health problems are approached (Evans and Stoddart, 1990; Mustard, 1987).

SHIFTING REQUIREMENTS AND NEW PRACTICE OPPORTUNITIES

These crosscurrents and their effects on nurses and nursing practice in Canada are evident in many of the following chapters. New practice opportunities are opening for nurses and will continue to do so throughout the 1990s. In general, the impact of these forces is fivefold:

- Content of nursing practice is being markedly altered by factors such as new technology, the aging of the population, and the "wellness" revolution
- Nursing practice roles are becoming more differentiated with the trend toward clinical specialization now well established
- Definition of the traditional nurse/patient relationship is undergoing revision as a partial response to changed public expectations and new ethical and legal imperatives; emerging is a clearer delineation of the nurse's accountability to patients and the attendant duties and obligations
- Increasing prominence of chronic, degenerative diseases and the search for more cost-effective methods of care are creating opportunities for nurses to develop more independent and autonomous clinical roles
- Nurses in practice are experiencing stresses and strains of endemic conflicts and dilemmas that arise out of the squeeze on health care resources and the expectations that they should continue to do all their traditional jobs while taking on new roles and responsibilities

These personal and professional dislocations are compounded by pressures from the increase of physicians and other health care professionals in Canada whose greater power and longer education could make nurses into what Christman (1987) calls "the baby-sitters" (p. 3) of the health care system. Unless the disparity between the levels of education of nurses and other health professionals is corrected, nurses may, in Christman's words, "find themselves in the position of making other professions look good instead of directly serving patients and improving the practice of nursing" (p. 3).

The shifting interface between the role of nurses and that of other health professionals and its impact on patient care is most conspicuous in hospitals. In Chapter 6, on nursing practice in acute care hospitals, Smith states that nursing is one of three groups of stakeholders with an interest in the quality of nursing services. The other two groups are community stakeholders, with patients and families being of paramount importance, and stakeholders for other professions. She argues that fulfillment of the professional mandate of nursing requires flexible, responsive, and cooperative relationships among all three groups.

Many observers of current nursing practice assert that such relationships are increasingly difficult to achieve in the complex hospital bureaucracies in which a majority of nurses work. The main sources of difficulty are generally thought to lie in three areas. The first is the cultural ambience from which nursing emerged. Despite changing societal attitudes toward women's roles, it remains extraordinarily difficult for nurses to escape perceptions that expect them to behave subordinately and dependently toward physicians and hospital officials. The problem has been compounded in recent years by the fact that many clinical activities formerly regarded as solely those of physicians are now commonly shared by nurses. Yet the authority of nurses to make necessary and timely decisions remains ambiguous, thus contributing to inconvenience and discomfort for patients and diminished productivity for nurses and other health professionals. Adding to the stresses and strains experienced by hospital nurses is a second factor, the increased complexity and diversity of hospital work. This is attributable, in large measure, to a greater acuity of patient populations, rapid introduction of new technology and modalities of treatment, and implementation of policies to make health care services more efficient. Third, the nature and diversity of clinical responsibilities in hospitals today frequently require knowledge and skills beyond the current repertoire of many nurses (Canadian Nurses Association & Canadian Hospital Association, 1990).

As Cox (1982) states, proposals to deal with such problems "must be evaluated using criteria of optimization of the quality care provided and the rational use of resources" (p. 4). In Chapter 6, Smith identifies many tools and techniques that have been developed in recent years to help nurses balance these two considerations in their day-to-day activities. The tools include patient classification and workload indices and quality assurance and risk management programs. However, as hospitals become more oriented to business practices and the measurement and recording of hospital performance, concerns for efficiency and the rationing of nursing services may far outweigh those for quality. Nursing is particularly vulnerable to these risks. With nursing labor costs constituting a significant proportion of hospital budgets, nursing services become targets for making hospitals more efficient. Adding to nursing's vulnerability is the rudimentary research for measuring the effect of nursing activities on patient welfare.

The importance of nurses working effectively with new technology and being prepared to see themselves as essential and contributing members of the health care team is underscored by many authors (e.g., Campbell, 1988; McConnell and Murphy, 1990; Quivey, 1990). The charge to nurses by Smith, and in Section III by Maloney, is to undertake an aggressive advocacy of patient care to ensure that the risks of new tools and technologies do not at any time outweigh the benefits. More specifically, Smith urges nurses to become involved "in the development and evaluation of new devices, products, and treatment modalities." Furthermore, she recommends nurses take responsibility for introducing new functions into nursing practice and monitoring their impact.

A fundamental question in balancing quality and cost factors is how to structure nursing services so that nurses can be accountable for the services that they provide. In Smith's view, achieving accountability in nurse/patient relationships is the single most significant ethical challenge facing nurses working in hospitals. Unless the obstacles to fully accountable nurse/patient relationships are removed, the unique contribution of nurses to patient care will become meaningless.

A detailed discussion of the problems of accountability is provided in Section III. In this overview chapter, it is sufficient to highlight a few steps taken by Canadian nurses to create practice environments in which nurses can adequately fulfill their clinical obligations to patients. In many of these settings the intense preoccupation with adequate numbers of nurses is gradually being replaced by a concern for quality and competence. One important change is to provide social supports and rewards for more professional approaches to nursing care. In response to changing funding formulas, many acute care hospitals have introduced case management systems and managed care. Smith notes that nurses can have an important role in defining case management systems to ensure that a client's care is coordinated efficiently within a specific facility and also across various agencies over time. She suggests case management can result in greater job satisfaction for nurses and make them more accountable for the outcomes of the care they provide.

To free up expensive hospital beds, new funding arrangements encourage a shift to more services in ambulatory settings, more home care services, and more community-based health care programs. Such changes in care delivery have had a significant effect on acute care facilities, as well as community agencies. Consequently, new nursing roles have emerged and old ones are dramatically altered.

The mental health field, specifically the community psychiatry movement and deinstitutionalization of mental patients in the 1960s and 1970s, has provided another venue for role restructuring in nursing. As a part of the reorientation of psychiatric care, nurses have become key professionals in providing counseling and life skills training and in developing community support networks and psychiatric services in the community (Yonge and Osborne, 1991). Also, the interface between hospital care and care in the community has become blurred; individuals, especially the elderly, the mentally ill, and the chronically ill, now alternate between acute care, chronic care, and community care. Some hospitals have teams of nurses and other professionals who provide care in the homes to delay admissions or facilitate early discharge. Day surgery is increasingly common. Such movement between kinds of care places increased pressures on nurses and other health professionals to develop ways to communicate better and to work as partners in delivering services.

These pressures have increased significance in light of current shortfalls in mental health services. These shortfalls, highlighted in a 1991 report by the Canadian Nurses Association, include the need to address disparities in access to required services for several populations: children and adolescents, the poor and homeless, seniors, members of the First Nations in remote and urban centers, the chronically mentally disabled, those incarcerated by the Canadian criminal justice system, and people with multiple diagnoses.

Probably the most politically sensitive emerging practice role for nurses in Canada is midwifery. Although an accepted occupational role in many parts of the world, the question of legalizing midwifery practice continues to be a heavily debated topic in Canada. However, because of growing consumer pressure for alternatives to medicalized childbirth in hospital settings, several provinces, including Ontario and Quebec, have taken steps in the last few years to grant legal recognition to independent midwifery practice and to establish formal training and regulatory mechanisms. For the most part, this legislation approves nurse midwives and midwives trained through direct entry programs (Burtch, 1988).

Another practice development is the growing number of settings experimenting with theory-based practice systems. The most extensively documented and tested theoretical model for new roles in nursing in Canada was developed by the School of Nursing at McGill (Gottlieb and Rowat, 1987). Former Director Dr. Moyra Allen, who spearheaded the theoretical development and practical testing of the McGill model for new roles for nurses for many years, states that what is needed in Canadian health care is not so much nurse practitioners to perform tasks previously assumed by physicians but nurses who may develop unique and independent roles for nurses as primary promoters and facilitators of family health (Gottlieb and Rowat, 1987). The McGill model has been tested in various practice sites, including ambulatory care, pediatric and intensive care units, and communities. Its effect on patients' well-being is an important component of the research that underpins it (Frasure-Smith, Allen, and Gottlieb, 1980; Gottlieb and Rowat, 1987).

The significance of the role restructuring experiments undertaken during the 1970s and 1980s and the continuing development and testing of the McGill model lies in the delineation of nursing's unique contribution to health care and its centrality to emerging health concerns and problems. Through this work, nurses are offered a glimpse of more independent and creative roles and have opportunities to develop their professional aspirations in partnership roles with medicine or as autonomous practitioners contributing to a broad spectrum of community health services.

Chapters 7 to 10 describe nursing practice settings in which nurses can experiment with new approaches to nursing services and create a vision for the future that includes nurses as the predominant primary caregivers. Also, individual nurses are establishing independent practice to provide new ways of giving care. For example, some nurses now offer support and counseling on breast-feeding to new mothers. Others are health promotion consultants to employee health services in industry.

In Chapter 7, Mantle discusses the development of nursing services for the institutionalized elderly. Long-term care, in the community and in institutions, is the most rapidly growing segment of health care. The Canada Health Survey in 1978/ 1979 estimated that about 12% of the population, or 3.7 million Canadians, had activity limitations due to ill health (Statistics Canada, 1985). Mantle notes, only a small proportion of this total requires institutional care. However, improved survival of the frail elderly and functionally impaired chronically ill has resulted in an apparent explosion in needs for long-term care facilities, including day care services and residential facilities.

Mantle emphasizes the immense potential for nurses to provide leadership in improving long-term care and to develop innovative primary and specialty care roles. However, the long-term care sector is faced with many problems arising out of its rapid growth and the history of long-term institutional care as a low status and minimally funded service. As Vladeck (1982) observes about nursing homes: no one seems to like them very much, but we probably cannot do without them. Like any rapidly growing field in which the needs of clients are slowly becoming better appreciated and understood, nursing practice in long-term care suffers from a dearth of persons with adequate training to facilitate the development of appropriate systems for delivery of nursing care. Most long-term care institutions have a high proportion of staff who are trained on the job or in short-term health care aide programs. Among registered nurse staff, a majority have no added training in long-term care. Thus they often bring to this work a model of care and understanding appropriate for the acute care setting but inadequate for practice in which the mix of care includes preventive health, life enrichment, health promotion, and physical and emotional care of persons with varying degrees of physical and mental frailty. The small but growing cadre of clinical nurse specialists in gerontological nursing in Canada have a vital role in redefining optimal nursing practice and devising clinical protocols to improve nursing services for the elderly. The clinical investigative ability of gerontology nurse clinicians is also critical in expanding knowledge of client needs and how nurses can contribute to meeting them.

In Chapter 8, Chalmers and Kristjanson trace the evolution in Canada, from the 1600s to the present, of community nurses' roles in preventing disease and promoting health. As primary health care providers, community health nurses are concerned with maximizing client independence and responsibility; as public health practitioners, their interest is the health of the population. Individual nurses face role conflicts as these new roles develop, but new theoretical perspectives can provide some guidelines.

The World Health Organization's widely proclaimed goal of Health for All by the year 2000 forms the basis for the primary health care model and the health promotion movement in many settings. In Canada, the Canadian Nurses Association, with provincial and territorial nursing associations, advocates using the primary health care model rather than the illness model to guide development of the health care system. These associations have also been active in encouraging demonstration projects incorporating primary health care principles. Such projects are underway or being developed in several provinces, including Alberta, Newfoundland, and Saskatchewan. Probably the best known is the joint Association of Registered Nurses of Newfoundland (ARNN) and the Danish Nurses Organization project to provide primary health care services, the Newfoundland project site being the Southern Shore of the Avalon Peninsula (ARNN, 1990).

Primary health care represents a philosophy that is basic to all nursing. With this approach, health is considered a resource for everday living. Basic requirements for health include income, shelter, and food. Improvement in health also requires information and life skills, a supportive environment providing opportunities for making healthy choices, and conditions in the environment that enhance health. Therefore it represents a mediating strategy between people and their environments, combining personal choice with social responsibility for health (Berland, 1991; Nutbeam, 1986).

These perspectives also provide foundations for the health promotion movement. Central to this concept is effective public participation in the definition of problems and decision making and action to change and improve the determinants of health. For this reason, health promotion represents a strategy that is both political and directed toward policy, and an enabling approach to health directed at life-styles (Nutbeam, 1986; O'Neill, 1989/90).

Health promotion programs benefitted by the WHO initiative and by an explosion of research since the 1970s on life-style modification and determinants of health behavior. These studies include many major community-based research projects that test the effectiveness of mass communication technology in changing at-risk behavior. Such projects introduce an entirely new approach to program development in acute care facilities, as well as the community. For instance, the Canadian Hospital Association (Baskerville, 1988) released a report reaffirming its commitment to involve health care facilities in health promotion initiatives. The report suggests ways in which a health care facility may introduce programs to promote health. In addition, the report recommends strategies health care facilities may use to advance the goal of health promotion at the national level.

Chapters 9 and 10 illustrate how fundamental the concepts of primary health care and health promotion are by describing how nurses apply them in the Canadian North and throughout the world. In Chapter 9, Gregory examines provision of health care in isolated and semi-isolated communities; these rely heavily on services of registered nurses and primarily serve the native peoples of Canada's North. In these settings, nurses often serve as primary care professionals and also attend to various public health and social needs. Although such communities could benefit from the primary health care perspective described in Chapters 9 and 10, the quality of services available is often compromised by two sets of interrelated factors. First, the policy framework within which nurses work continues to emphasize individual health care while slighting the critical influence of environment and social conditions on the prevalent health problems. For example, conditions in many communities require long-term efforts to achieve acceptable standards for sanitary water supplies, housing, and sewage disposal. The poverty of many communities also poses critical threats to the health potential of individuals and families. The problem is compounded by an age structure very different from that of Canada as a whole: 40% of the population in native communities is under 14 years of age. The second compromising factor is the highly varied educational background of nurses in rural and northern services. As Gregory observes, nurses may be placed in difficult ethical and legal situations when they are required to provide services beyond those they are capable of performing. More importantly, clients may be in jeopardy when they do not receive the care they require. Aside from inadequate basic education, many nurses do not have sufficient specialized training to cope with the unique climatic, geographic, and cultural situations in which they find themselves. Gregory also states that there is an urgent need for native nurses recruited from rural and northern communities who possess an intimate link with native culture, a command of local language, and awareness of the socioeconomic and cultural realities of native communities.

In Chapter 10, Dier briefly describes the valuable contributions made worldwide by Canadian nurses in recent years. She describes how the role of the international nurse has evolved from one of caregiver to one of advisor, consultant, and advocate. She predicts this role will become more and more a collaborative relationship involving nurses from all countries with the purpose to promote the concept of primary care through education and research.

ADAPTING TO NEW ROLES FOR NURSES

Thus far, two sets of factors important in establishing an appropriate future for nursing practice have been examined. They are the significance for nursing practice of changing demographic and morbidity trends and health care needs, and the goals, aspirations, opportunities, and constraints that are influencing opportunities for nursing practice in hospitals and community settings today. A third set of factors critical in establishing an appropriate future for nursing practice is how nurses will adapt to the new roles that are evolving. As Mantle indicates in Chapter 7, the provision of quality services in any setting is based on the premise that caregivers have the requisite knowledge, skills, and attitudes to meet client needs.

The veritable revolution in content and design of nursing practice roles in the last 10 years has, in many instances, overwhelmed the resources of educational and training programs. Increasing shortages of nurses with specialty training that equips them for work in high technology settings such as critical care units is a prime example. Factors that contribute to the difficulties include lack of financial resources, shortages of qualified teachers, and the difficulties experienced in attempting to graft new requirements onto educational patterns devised for another, earlier era. The search for effective solutions has also been compromised by what McIntosh (1985) calls the improvisation, or "make do," problem in nursing. Short-term and expedient solutions to educational problems are frequently employed. Nurses are expected to assume responsibilities for which they are ill-prepared. McIntosh makes clear, "Improvisation has its place, but if it is allowed to persist indefinitely in a time of cutbacks, then ultimately standards will fall to an unacceptable level" (p. 63). She continues: "Deficiencies of service provision must be regarded as issues worthy of public debate and representation, not treated merely as problems to be resolved by reorganizing resources that are already inadequate." (p. 63).

To become the "advocates of quality" (p. 63) such as McIntosh recommends involves, among other things, helping expert nurse clinicians describe their practice so that standards of excellence can be set. It also involves helping nurses become more conscious of the adequate conditions to perform their work (Benner, 1984). Both perspectives are important in helping to conceptualize the educational problems that massive expansion and change in nursing practice have brought (Canadian Nurses Association & Canadian Hospital Association, 1990).

In terms of practical policy, the nursing profession must also become more active in the policy community in pressing its claims for better educational resources and a rationalization of the system of basic and graduate education and specialty training. A more appropriate educational framework must be established to consider the diversity and degree of specialization that now characterize nursing work. (This issue is discussed more fully in Section IV on Nursing Education.)

Another set of factors that affects all areas of nursing practice concerns job satisfaction and nurse retention. In recent years, all practice areas have had to deal with more and more registered nurses leaving their jobs, and even leaving nursing, because they are dissatisfied with working conditions. Acute care and long-term care hospitals experience the greatest problems with rapid nurse turnover, but community health agencies and other facilities may also find it increasingly difficult to keep nursing staff. (These issues are discussed more fully in Chapters 3 and 11, which deal with the nursing work force and the nursing workplace.)

CONCLUSION

It is almost certain that for the foreseeable future Canadian health policy will be designed to support health promotion activities and the delivery of primary health care. At the same time, governments will expect health care institutions and care-givers to contain costs and to demonstrate that patient-related interventions have positive outcomes.

Within this context, the many changes in nursing practice identified by the authors in the next set of chapters on nursing practice suggest a long agenda for nursing in the decades ahead. However, four issues of immediate consequence are:

- The need to become advocates of quality care
- The need to turn social and technological trends to advantage in restructuring nursing roles
- The need to become aggressive advocates for nursing in the competition for shrinking resources
- The need to reconceptualize the kinds of educational and environmental supports required to establish an appropriate future for nursing practice throughout the 1990s and beyond

Although this may be a complex and difficult agenda, nursing practice is a field under rapid change, animated and moved in novel ways by changes in health care demands. This fluid environment offers nurses unparalleled challenges as practitioners and as negotiators of important changes on behalf of patients.

REFERENCES

AARN. (1990). World-wide first in health care. *AARN Access, 10*(4), 1-2.

Baskerville, B. (1988). *Health care facilities' role in improving health through health promotion: Report of the National Focus Group on Health Promotion in Health Care Facilities.* Ottawa: Canadian Hospital Association.

Benner, P. (1984). *From novice to expert. Excellence and power in clinical nursing practice.* Menlo Park, CA: Addison-Wesley.

Bergman, R. (1986). Nursing in a changing world. *International Nursing Review, 33*(4), 110-116.

Berland, A. (1991). Primary health care: What does it mean for nurses? *Canadian Nurse, 87*(9), 25-26

Burtch, B. (1988). Promoting midwifery, prosecuting midwives: The state and the midwifery movement in Canada. In. B. Bolaria & H. Dickinson. (Eds.). *Sociology of health care in Canada.* (pp. 313-327). Toronto: Harcourt Brace Jovanovich.

Campbell, M. (1988). The structure of stress in nurses' work. In B. Bolaria & H. Dickinson (Eds.), *Sociology of health care in Canada* (pp. 393-405). Toronto: Harcourt Brace Jovanovich.

Canadian Nurses' Association, & Canadian Hospital Association. (1990, November). *Nurse retention and quality of work life: A national perspective.* Ottawa: Canadian Nurses' Association.

Canadian Nurses Association. (1990). *New reproductive technologies: Accessible, appropriate, participative.* (A brief to the Royal Commission on Reproductive Technologies). Ottawa: Canadian Nurses Association.

Canadian Nurses Association. (1991). *Mental health care reform: A priority for nurses.* Ottawa: Author.

Christman, L. (1987). The future of the nursing profession. *Nursing Administration Quarterly, 11*(2), 1-8.

Cox, C. (1982). Frontiers of nursing in the 21st century: Lessons from the past and present for the future directions in nursing education. *International Journal of Nursing Studies, 19*(1), 1-9.

Evans, R.G., & Stoddart, G.L. (1990). Producing health consuming health care. *Social Science in Medicine, 31*(12), 1347-1363.

Fox, D. (1986). AIDS and the American health policy: The history and prospects of a crisis of authority. *The Milbank Quarterly, 64*(Supplement 1), 7-33.

Frasure-Smith, N., Allen, M., & Gottlieb, L. (1980). Models of nursing practice in a changing health care system: Overview of a comparative study in three ambulatory care settings. In R.C. MacKay & G. Zilm (Eds.), *Research for practice: Proceedings of the National Nursing Research Conference* (pp. 90-138). Halifax: School of Nursing, Dalhousie University.

Gottlieb, L., & Rowat, K. (1987). The McGill model of nursing: A practice-derived model. *The Journal of Advances in Nursing Science, 9*(4), 51-61.

Logan, R. (1991). Immigration during the 1980s. *Canadian Social Trends, 20*(2), 10-13.

McConnell, E.A., & Murphy, E.K. (1990). Nurses' use of technology: An international concern. *International Nursing Review, 37*(5), 331-334.

McIntosh, J. (1985). District nursing: A case of political marginality. In R. White (Ed.), *Political issues in nursing: Past, present and future* (Vol. 1) (pp. 45-66). New York: John Wiley & Sons.

Mustard, F. (1987). Achieving health for all: Implications for Canadian health and social policies. *Canadian Medical Association Journal, 136,* 471-473.

Nutbeam, D. (1986). Health promotion glossary. *Health Promotion, 1*(1), 113-118.

O'Neill, M. (1989/90, Winter). Healthy public policy: The WHO perspective. *Health Promotion. 28*(3), 6-8, 24.

Quivey, M. (1990). Advanced medical technology: Finding the answers. *International Nursing Review, 37*(5), 329-330 & 344.

Statistics Canada. (1985). *The Canada year book: 1985.* Ottawa: Author.

Statistics Canada. (1986a). *Age, sex and marital status: 1986 Census* (Catalogue 92-901). Ottawa: Author.

Statistics Canada. (1986b). *Manitoba profile: 1986 Census (Part 1).* Ottawa: Author.

Stone, L., & Frenken, H. (1988). *Canada's seniors: 1986 Census of Canada.* Ottawa: Minister of Supply and Services Canada.

Vladeck, B. (1982). Nursing homes: A national problem. In L. Aiken (Ed.), *Nursing in the 1980s: Crisis, opportunities, challenges* (pp. 183-194). Toronto: Lippincott.

Walker, A. (1987). Enlarging the caring capacity of the community: Informal support networks and the welfare state. *International Journal of Health Services, 17*(3), 369-385.

Yonge, O., & Osborne, M. (1991). Opening doors and keys to the future: History of psychiatric nursing in the province of Alberta. *AARN Newsletter, 47*(10), 8-10.

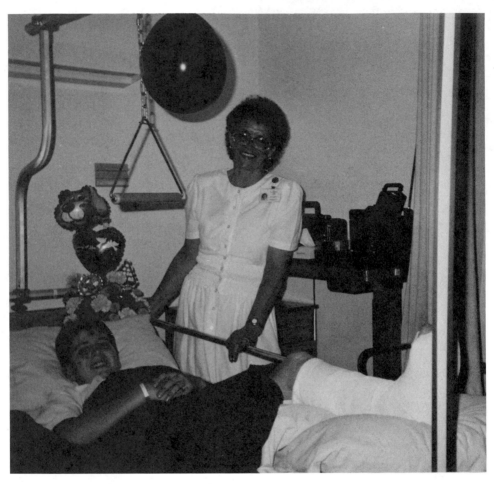

Most registered nurses work in hospitals, whether large or small. This photograph is one of a collection of more than 1000 photographs showing "nurses at work" that were submitted by members to the Alberta Association of Registered Nurses for a commemorative book to celebrate its 75th Anniversary. The photo shows Kathreen Shirey, RN, with patient Christopher Gillot at the Hinton (Alberta) Hospital. (Photograph courtesy of the Alberta Association of Registered Nurses. Photographer was Carrie Rogalsky, RN. Used with permission.)

CHAPTER SIX

Nursing Practice in Acute Care Hospitals

DONNA LYNN SMITH, RN, MEd

Donna Lynn Smith, RN, BScN, MEd (Alberta), has had experience in clinical nursing, in nursing education, and in leadership roles in acute and long-term care. Throughout her career, she has initiated and supported innovative clinical, administrative, and nursing research projects. She holds associate faculty appointments in the Faculty of Nursing and in the Division of Biomedical Ethics and Humanities in the Faculty of Medicine at the University of Alberta. She was a founding director of the Joint Faculties Bioethics Project on the University of Alberta campus. Currently she is the Manager of Program Development in the Long Term Care Branch of the Acute and Long Term Care Division of Alberta Health.

I n the public's imagination and in the minds of some professionals, acute care hospitals are the center stage of the health care system, where the most important dramas of life and death unfold. This perspective is revealed in the use of the naive term "active treatment" to describe acute care hospitals, implying (one hopes inadvertently) that within other components of the health care system treatment is "inactive." In fact, nurses and other professionals can and do provide active health care in a variety of settings. The aura of high drama surrounding acute care results from the complexities and uncertainties that occur as members of interdependent professions work together in an environment often perceived as a last resort in the search for a cure for catastrophic illness or the preservation of life.

Much has been written about acute care hospitals from the perspective and experiences of nurses and patients (Anderson, 1979; deCrosta, 1987; Gino, 1982; O'Malley, 1986). Numerous studies document the diffusion, differentiation, and tensions within the nursing role, which contribute to problems of burnout and high turnover often associated with acute care nursing (Chaska, 1983, 1990; Growe, 1991; Kramer and Schmalenberg, 1977; McConnell, 1982). The focus in this chapter is on the characteristics of the acute care environment and the implications for nurses who work within it. An understanding of the nature of these workplaces, in which a majority of nurses are still employed, can contribute to the development of realistic expectations and necessary skills. Such an understanding is essential if nurses are to achieve the full potential of their role as caregivers, coordinators, and advocates within this setting.

The chapter begins with a discussion of several perspectives from which acute care can be defined. The process by which scientific and technical advances led to the development of special care units, which in turn resulted in shortages of specialized nursing personnel, educational challenges, and associated costs, is then discussed. Several other current developments in acute care are highlighted, including the emergence of ambulatory care, the elderly in acute care, and case management.

Rationing, new funding systems, and demands for reallocation of health care resources are among the factors that are creating instability in the acute care sector. A description of these developments, and of three stakeholder groups that have an interest in the outcomes and milieu of acute care hospitals, illustrates the diversity and complexity that characterize this environment. The preservation of an accountable nurse-to-patient relationship is identified as a pressing professional and ethical necessity that has become difficult to achieve as acute care hospitals become more complex.

DILEMMA OF DEFINING ACUTE CARE

Acute care hospitals are generally assumed to be specialized health facilities in which persons with severe episodic or clinically unstable conditions receive diagnosis and short-term treatment. When acute care hospitals are contrasted with other health facilities or services such as rehabilitation or extended care hospitals, nursing homes, community health centers, or home care programs, the distinctions can be misleading. The condition of an individual in any health care setting can vary from day to day in response to many factors. For example, patients with a diagnosed chronic illness may primarily require rehabilitation and continuing care for this chronic condition but may also require diagnosis and treatment for a recently acquired acute illness. Palliative, preventive care, and health promotion are important dimensions of some acute care programs, but they are also offered in other settings.

The assumption that complex health care technologies can only be managed in acute care hospitals clearly is no longer valid. Many people are now cared for in the home or on an ambulatory basis while receiving continuous ventilation, renal dialysis, total parenteral nutrition, or intravenous medication. Ironically, these same individuals may be considered too "acutely" ill to be cared for in smaller acute care hospitals or extended care facilities.

Not all patients in so-called acute care hospitals have acute illnesses or unstable conditions. Until recently, funding to hospitals has been based on their historical utilization, creating an incentive to use acute care facilities instead of less costly and perhaps more appropriate alternatives. The continued operation (and, in some provinces, the proliferation) of small rural hospitals may reflect political exigencies more than actual health needs of the population. In many communities, hospitals have been the major employing agencies, and an acute care hospital is still viewed by members of the public and by many professionals as the most prestigious type of health facility for a community to have, even though it may be consistently operating at low occupancy or caring for people who could and would be cared for at home or in continuing care facilities elsewhere. A number of factors are prompting re-examination of the roles of rural acute care hospitals.

Another approach to defining acute care is that of assessing the resources or services that are used in caring for individuals and groups of patients. Two such operational approaches to defining acute care are nursing workload measurement and case-mix measurement.

Defining Acute Care in Terms of Nursing Resource Requirements

The need for nursing care can arise from permanent or temporary physical or psychological deficits such as immobility, confusion, unconsciousness, dehydration, or agitation; it can also arise from, or be associated with, instability in an individual's condition. In some cases, clinical instability is created or increased by medical interventions. Treatment such as surgery, dialysis, or the administration of certain drugs creates increased acuity, as do some diagnostic procedures. For example, when an arterial line is inserted for the purpose of monitoring blood gas levels, the patient is at risk of severe hemorrhage if the line becomes dislodged. For this reason, patients with arterial lines in place are usually cared for in special care units where constant nursing observation is possible. The earlier method of assessing blood gas levels by means of periodic arterial puncture did not require the same amount of nursing observation to ensure patient safety. However, continuous monitoring through the use of an indwelling arterial line is now considered to be clinically superior to the former method for critically ill patients. This is only one of many examples of the way in which technological capability and medical knowledge have increased the amount of nursing care required, and the knowledge and skills required for state-of-the-art nursing practice.

Patient classification and workload measurement systems provide a quantitative means of describing the patients within a hospital in terms of their requirements for nursing care (Giovannetti and Thiessen, 1983). Four or five standard patient "types" can be identified through the use of objective indicators that describe patients' conditions. The need for nursing resources and the types of resources required (i.e., professional or auxiliary nursing personnel, or nurses with skills in a specialized area such as psychiatry or critical care) can then be determined.

Patient classification systems were developed in the late 1960s and early 1970s using work sampling techniques derived from operations research. These systems are used to measure the nursing time required by patients with similar characteristics. Within such systems, the concepts of acuity or severity of illness are used to describe patient needs that give rise to requirements for nursing care. The use of patient classification systems has been supported by the U.S. Joint Commission for Hospital Accreditation and the Canadian Council on Hospital Accreditation, and most North American hospitals are now using such systems for staffing, budgeting, decision making, and, more recently, costing (Fryer, 1990).

Patient classification and nursing workload measurement systems have sometimes been criticized, particularly by some authors writing from the perspective of nurses' unions. Although it has certain limitations, this approach to the assessment of nursing resource needs represents an improvement on earlier approaches that involved simple multiplication of the number of patients by an arbitrarily determined number of nursing care hours. When properly implemented and maintained, such systems also provide a means of assuring equity in the allocation of staff resources among the nursing units in larger hospitals.

Defining Acute Care by Case-Mix Measurement

Acute care hospitals can be distinguished from one another and from other types of health care settings by measuring their case-mix. The term "case-mix" is used to describe the types of patients treated by a hospital. Case types have been distinguished from one another on the basis of variables such as disease, length of stay, cost, or resource consumption (Fryer, 1990, pp. 21-22).

Case-mix may be measured for a number of reasons, the most common being reimbursement. As Wright (1990) points out, hospital costs are perceived to be "spiralling," and pressure is now being placed on Canadian hospitals to follow the American example of establishing systems that relate hospital costs (inputs) to hospital products (outputs). Case-mix groups are being viewed by governments and administrators as the means of identifying the total hospital product.

As a result of legislation passed in 1983, American hospitals were reimbursed on the basis of the case-mix groups as documented in their medical records the preceding year. This system is known as prospective payment. The majority of literature on case-mix classification schemes focuses on the Diagnosis Related Groups (DRGs) of the United States (Fryer, 1990, p. 27). In Canada, the Hospital Medical Records Institute, a voluntary, nonprofit organization, developed a DRG-type case-mix classification called Case-Mix Groups (CMGs).

The relationship between case-mix groups and the nursing resources required to provide care is of particular interest to nurses and health care consumers. Fryer (1990) discusses the limitations of patient classification, DRGs, and case-mix groupings as management tools. There continues to be considerable uncertainty whether DRGs or case-mix groups adequately reflect nursing resource needs, and a number of American studies have found significant variation of nursing resource need within and between DRGs. Fryer's own recent research concludes that if DRGs were used to reimburse the Canadian hospitals in her study, the hospitals would not receive appropriate funds for nursing resource need as measured by the patient classification system most widely used in Canada and the United States. She recommends further study into the hospital and patient-specific factors that influence nursing resource need (pp. 82-84). A similar conclusion was drawn by Wright (1990, p. 90), who found variability of nursing resource consumption within and between case-mix groups derived from data obtained in a Canadian hospital in 1988/1989. As prospective payment based on case-mix groupings becomes more common in Canada, the approach to defining acute care may change to reflect factors relevant to the acute care funding system, such as diagnosis, length of stay, co-morbidity, and severity of illness.

Health care needs and services form a continuum. Although the vertical separations defining boundaries between acute care and other types of care can serve useful administrative purposes, they may create artificial, costly, and bewildering fragmentation when experienced from the consumer's point of view. The need to eliminate this costly fragmentation, to facilitate horizontal movement of patients along the health care continuum, and to fill the gaps between health care services is now being recognized. This challenge will be discussed later in this chapter.

TYPES OF ACUTE CARE HOSPITALS

Relationships with schools of medicine, the presence of various levels of medical students, and the existence of medical research programs are sources of complexity in acute care hospitals. They also influence the nature and organization of hospital nursing services. Three main types of acute care hospitals can be distinguished by the nature of their relationship to schools of medicine. These are:
1. Community general hospitals
2. Teaching hospitals
3. University hospitals or health sciences centers

Community general hospitals exist in both large and small communities and usually are not affiliated with medical schools. In small communities, the general hospital is usually the only health care institution, although it sometimes includes extended-care beds or is associated with an extended-care facility. The medical staff of a community hospital is usually (although not exclusively) composed of general medical practitioners. There is no medical house staff. The community hospital is designed to offer primary and secondary health care; patients requiring tertiary care are, or usually should be, referred to regional centers of specialization. In some parts of Canada, the development of regional hospitals or programs has been encouraged as a means of making specialized health services available to a defined geographic area, which may include isolated and remote parts of the country. More formal definition of regional roles for hospitals will occur over the next decade as the need to avoid duplication and identify gaps in service becomes more pressing in response to financial constraints.

Teaching hospitals are community hospitals associated with medical schools. Some members of the medical staff may be general practitioners; many will have specialty or subspecialty qualifications. Not all teaching hospitals have provision for graduate level medical students (residents), but most offer internships. Medical research programs may or may not be present.

University hospitals are usually located on or near a university campus, and members of the medical staff are required to have the qualifications necessary for a university appointment. Therefore the medical staff is composed primarily, and sometimes exclusively, of specialists and subspecialists, some of whom receive full-time university salaries. There is an emphasis on research and graduate level medical education; therefore several levels of house staff will be present. State-of-the-art treatment is generally available, and new forms of treatment are constantly emerging from research programs or as a result of the availability of new technology and drugs.

Health sciences centers are a type of university hospital in which physical facilities and, in some cases, personnel are shared between university-based health sciences faculties and one or more hospitals that have a common administration. The school of medicine has traditionally been the most senior partner, but other health sciences faculties, such as nursing, pharmacy, physical medicine and rehabilitation, and dentistry, may also be members of the partnership. These partners have vested interests in the use of space, development of program priorities, and appointment of senior staff within the hospital. The unique funding and administrative arrangements in health sciences centers have led some organizational theorists to identify these as the most complex of all organizational structures.

Impact of Scientific and Technical Advances

For the first several decades of this century, infectious diseases such as tuberculosis, poliomyelitis, and pneumonia were responsible for much of the morbidity and mortality in Canada and other Western countries. Most life-saving treatment in hospitals consisted of basic nursing interventions. The tepid sponge was the treatment of choice for fever; turpentine stupes were used to treat distension; and the mustard plaster constituted the primary treatment for pneumonia. The Wangensteen suction, gavage feeding, early forms of intravenous therapy, sulfa drugs, penicillin, and the iron lung were major advances in medical care that began to change nursing practice in the 1930s and 1940s. In the late 1950s, technology for extracorporeal circulation fostered the development of cardiovascular surgery; ventilators and antibiotics were beginning to be widely used. At this time, research in nursing was primarily concerned with educational issues; it was not until the 1970s that clinical nursing research became a widely recognized endeavor.

New medical treatments that became available in the 1960s included cardiopulmonary resuscitation, cardiac monitoring, and hemodialysis. The 1970s were characterized by the proliferation of advances in invasive diagnostic and monitoring procedures, total parenteral nutrition, and cancer chemotherapies, to name only a few. In the 1980s, scientific and technical advances in a number of disciplines resulted in exponential changes affecting all health care disciplines. These are exemplified in care of critically ill neonates, in patients undergoing organ transplantation, and in persons being treated for multiple traumas.

Ironically, in the 1980s and 1990s infectious diseases re-emerged as an area of major concern. Resistant organisms have evolved in response to widespread use of antibiotics. Tuberculosis, which is often a clinically "silent" disease, faded from general awareness after effective forms of treatment were discovered, and sanatoria were closed. Nevertheless, this disease is currently recognized as a growing problem in some indigenous and immigrant populations, among the poor, and particularly among the elderly (Canadian Lung Association, 1988; Bentley, 1990). As with tuberculosis and poliomyelitis earlier, acute care hospitals are experiencing the initial clinical impact arising from the spread of blood-borne viruses (Hepatitis B and HIV).

Nurses who practice in acute care hospitals face challenges, risks, and stresses, as well as unique satisfactions that arise from new knowledge and technology and emerging health care concerns. As technology and specialization have developed, the acute care setting has become a "showcase" for nursing's potential, as well as a stage for ideological and ethical conflicts (Dracup and Marsden, 1990).

It is this rapid rate of change in health care that dictates the necessity of university-based preparation for nursing in the next century. A broad education in the basic sciences is essential as a basis for assessing, implementing, and evaluating the nursing care required for patients as new technologies are developed and employed. The idea that the nursing role in such instances is "merely technical" reflects a limited understanding of what patients and families experience and need in these circumstances.

Fortunately, within the Canadian nursing context, there has been resistance to the arbitrary distinction between "technical" and "professional" nursing that arose in the United States in the 1960s and 1970s (Richardson, 1986; Schumacher, 1977; Smith, 1983). As a new concept or intervention is introduced into the patient care environment, there is a period during which its application is highly discretionary, and during that time the assessment and evaluation components of the nursing process are of utmost importance. In some hospitals, technicians, not nurses, are employed in cardiac catheterization laboratories, and wider use of technicians in the operating room and intensive care units is being advocated as a safeguard against rising labor costs and shortages in nursing. Ironically, this trend is supported by some ideological nursing literature, which equates achieving clinical competence in critical care nursing with the "medicalization" of nursing. Such a perspective fails to recognize the need for nursing assessment and intervention while "technical" procedures, particularly those of an invasive nature, are being performed.

Although it is simplistic to assume that all new technologies are beneficial, it is equally simplistic to view them as inherently undesirable (Feeny, Guyatt, and Tugwell, 1986; Sanford, 1986). There is a pressing need for nursing educators and administrators to be able to anticipate, rather than to catch up to, the clinical applications of science and technology and to become actively involved in the development and clinical evaluation of new devices, products, and treatment modalities. It is equally important that the nursing profession monitor and control the introduction of new functions into nursing, the transfer of medical functions to nursing, and the transfer of functions from the professional to the technical realms of practice. Unless this can be accomplished, it will remain difficult to differentiate and interpret unique nursing functions, models, and concerns to the public and within the health care context.

The initial effect of new advances is usually experienced within acute care hospitals and creates unique challenges for nurses as they cope with development, testing, and application of new health care knowledge. These advances lead to changes in hospitals, such as the emergence of new specialty programs and alternative ways of organizing and delivering care. They also raise issues for nursing, including personnel shortages in special areas, demands for inservice education, and need for new educational approaches.

Development of Special Care Units

In research and teaching centers, it is not uncommon for new drugs and devices to be used in clinical treatment before they have "official" status in the hospital. The evolution of special care units (SCUs) in hospitals is described by Myers and colleagues (1984) as a slow process of equipment acquisition, piecemeal remodelling, and incremental increases in nurse staffing that may span several years. These authors note:

> It may not be clear that a new SCU is evolving until it is a fait accompli. Decisions are incremental, and SCU development is not considered to be a formal project. The impetus comes from physicians and nurses as they respond to gradual changes in patient severity of illness, technological, and surgical innovations, and perceptions of competition with other specialties or hospitals. (p. 116)

In one respect, this may seem to be at odds with good administrative practice. Alternatively, it can be viewed as a necessary ability of a leading-edge health care facility to use newly developing scientific knowledge to make adaptive responses to the needs of patients.

SCUs evolved in a relatively short period of time. Dracup and Marsden (1990, p. 305) describe the evolution of critical care nursing in the United States, beginning with cardiac surgery units and postoperative recovery rooms in the 1950s. The new knowledge base required for intensive care nursing had a professionalizing effect as nurses needed and assumed new levels of autonomy and responsibility. The American Association of Critical Care Nurses grew from a "handful" of members in 1969 to almost 57,000 in 1988 (Hartshorn, 1988).

A similar pattern was evident in Canada. A Western Canadian example illustrates the exponential growth and effect of intensive care units (ICUs) in Canadian hospitals. The first formally designated ICU was established in a renovated sun parlor at the University of Alberta Hospital in 1966. At that time, the specialty of neonatal intensive care nursing was nonexistent. Nurses in the premature nursery had to master the skills involved in caring for babies who had been given exchange transfusions for Rh incompatibility and in gavage feeding of babies who were too frail to suck. In 1987, the 843-bed Walter C. Mackenzie Health Services Centre included a total of 104 ICU and intermediate care beds. Approximately 140 nurses were employed in the neonatal intensive care unit of 40 beds. The overall percentage of nurses working in critical care areas in this hospital increased from less than 5% of the nursing staff to nearly 30% during two decades. This trend is evident in most major tertiary care centers and has given rise to a staffing crisis in critical care nursing. As Growe (1990) points out, the number of full-time equivalent RNs needed for every hospital bed in Canada rose by 36% from 1981 to 1986. What used to be a 33% proportion of severely ill patients in hospitals is now close to 90%, and health care policy analysts are predicting that every general hospital in Canada in the year 2000 will resemble "one big intensive care unit" (Growe, 1990. p. 68).

Data on use of intensive care units and their overall effect on health care costs are becoming available in Canada. Noseworthy and Jacobs (1990) point out that, since 1969, ICU days, as a proportion of all inpatient days, have grown at a rate of approximately 5% a year. These authors note that ICU costs increased from 5% to over 13% of all general hospital inpatient costs between 1969 and 1986, accounting for 0.2% to 0.3% of the gross national product. Since intensive care (including cardiopulmonary resuscitation) has risks, costs, and contraindications as well as benefits, these authors believe that resource-based decisions for patients entering or in the ICU should not be handled on a first-come, first-served basis. Rather, they suggest physicians must individualize patient care and try to allocate resources, if they are limited, "to all those eligible and for whom maximum benefit is foreseen" (p. 7). They propose a model for allocating ICU resources that takes clinical, economic, and ethical factors into account. The medical facts, including the likelihood of ICU treatment to increase length and quality of life or relieve suffering, as well as the perceived will and best interests of the patient and other external factors, must be considered for each individual patient.

Nursing care must also be rationed in the ICU, and between the ICU and other areas of the hospital. Stress arising from nurse-physician conflicts, heavy workloads related to inadequate staffing, and moral distress have been documented in studies of ICU nurses (Dracup and Marsden, 1990, p. 304). Therefore many nurses would welcome a more formal and ethically based approach to decision making in ICUs, such as that advocated by Noseworthy and Jacobs.

Nursing Shortages, Educational Issues, and Costs

There is a relatively constant difficulty in recruiting nurses to certain hospitals and communities, particularly in some rural and remote parts of Canada. However, nursing shortages in acute care hospitals exhibit a cyclical pattern that can be shown to be closely associated with the exponential growth in certain specialized units and with the ebb and flow of health care funding. These cyclical shortages, followed by the now familiar studies of nursing job satisfaction, can be expected to continue as long as the health care system is allowed to develop in an ad hoc and reactive fashion in response to the availability of technology and medical expertise.

Acute care hospitals have had to absorb significant costs of on-the-job education for nurses who work in developing specialties. Such education usually has been provided through orientation or hospital-sponsored inservice or clinical postgraduate programs. Orientation to major ICUs typically takes from 1 to 3 months, depending on the previous clinical experience of the nurse. During most of this time, nurses are supernumerary. Direct costs and labor replacement costs for specialty unit orientation have gone largely unrecognized by external funding agencies.

Unlike their medical counterparts, academic nursing faculty are rarely involved in assessing or introducing new health care technologies and are therefore at a disadvantage in determining where and when to introduce emerging knowledge and skills into the nursing curriculum. The dilemma is further complicated by the fact that the nurses who first become knowledgeable in these evolving areas tend not to be those who write and publish.

Not all technological change results from direct care requirements. Introduction and automation of various clinical and administrative support processes will also result in a need for related inservice education. McCormick predicted in an article published in 1986 that, by 1990, hospitals would no longer be able to afford the costs of teaching nurses to work with new technologies. As an example, she estimated that, if a nursing department maintains a turnover rate of nearly 20%, and if orienting new nursing personnel to computer literacy continues to take 20 to 40 hours for each, it would cost a hospital an additional $20,000 per month to keep a 500-member nursing staff capable of documenting nursing practice.

At one time it was common for major teaching hospitals to offer clinical post-graduate courses to nurses in specialty areas such as cardiology, operating room, and neurosurgical nursing. Such programs developed in an ad hoc fashion, and although they often required a significant commitment of time and money from nurses, the "credentials" tended to be nontransferable between hospitals and not eligible for credit in postsecondary institutions. In 1980, the Division of Nursing at the University of Alberta Hospital and the Faculty of Nursing at the University of Alberta collaborated in the development of a clinical postgraduate program in neonatal intensive care nursing for which university credit could be earned. Since then, many such programs have been developed, including critical care programs at the universities of Manitoba and Alberta. This approach has gained a growing acceptance as a bridge between diploma and baccalaureate education, which enables nurses to gain recognized and transferable credentials in developing areas of practice.

A benchmark paper, released in 1989 by the Alberta Hospital Association and widely endorsed by nurses' organizations and other health care and educational stakeholders, outlines the differences between orientation, inservice education, and education for specialty practice, and the responsibilities of employers, educational institutions, and nursing professionals in relation to the various types of education. Formal preparation of nurse clinicians is advocated, with a major premise for program development being that all such programs should provide nurses the opportunity to earn university credit (Alberta Hospital Association, 1989). For the immediate future, such programs offer a means of designing and educating for expanding nursing responsibilities within both established and developing areas of clinical specialization.

CURRENT DEVELOPMENTS IN ACUTE CARE

In addition to the development of knowledge, technology, and specialization, which are the central features of acute care, other developments are having an effect on this sector of the health care system. These include the emergence of ambulatory care, a recognition of the need for specialized acute care services for the elderly, a focus on case management, and rationing and reallocation of resources. These and other factors create a climate of organizational instability in acute care hospitals. Each of these developments will now be discussed in more detail.

Emergence of Ambulatory Care

A shift from traditional acute inpatient care began in the 1980s as a result of several factors, including the effects of technological advances, limited and often decreased resources, new approaches to health care reimbursement by governments, and third party and more knowledgeable health care consumers (Hartigan, 1990). Development of ambulatory care (sometimes called "day care") has had and is having several effects on the health care system, but two of particular relevance to nurses will be discussed here. The first effect involves the impact of ambulatory care on the inpatient units of acute care hospitals. The second effect arises from the nature of the ambulatory care setting and the professional challenges it affords to nurses.

Within the ambulatory care setting, a wide range of diagnostic and therapeutic procedures are now employed. These include myleograms, angiograms, bronchoscopies, and various examinations of the gastrointestinal tract. Biopsies and the administration of intravenous medications are other frequent interventions. A majority of eye, ear, nose, and throat surgery now is done in ambulatory care, as well as many gynecological procedures, hernia repairs, and even cholecystectomies. It has been estimated that 40% to 45% of all surgery performed in hospitals will eventually take place in ambulatory care (Skene, 1990).

When acute care services are delivered in an ambulatory setting, hospitals experience a number of spin-off effects. Many of the nonemergency or elective services that once required hospital admission are now provided in the ambulatory setting. When unexpected complications arise during the course of ambulatory care, the client may become an emergency hospital admission. As more of the elective and predictable acute care services are performed in ambulatory care departments, a corresponding increase in the acuity of the inpatient population is to be expected, as hospitals deal with people whose conditions are unstable or who are experiencing health care and personal emergencies. This change in the acuity of the inpatient population places new demands on nurses and medical house staff as general medical and surgical units in major hospitals begin to resemble the intensive care units of 10 years ago.

Emergence of ambulatory care provides an alternative work setting and a potentially rewarding professional role for nurses. People receiving health care in an ambulatory setting must be screened and assessed to ensure that they are appropriate candidates for ambulatory care, and also to ensure that they, or their significant others, are capable of following the regimen of preparation and after-care they require. Since only limited opportunity is available to observe the client before the intervention, the observation and assessment skills of nurses become the key factor in identifying unexpected or untoward responses to treatment. If recovery proceeds within the expected time frame, there will be a need to teach the client or the support person how to manage follow-up care. Liaison with community caregivers may be necessary to ensure that follow-up care is available and appropriate.

When the nursing role in ambulatory care is designed with an awareness of clients' needs and an appreciation of the full range of nurses' knowledge and skills, a positive effect on health outcomes for clients should be the result. If the role is allowed to devolve into a series of functional tasks, the benefit of the nurse's holistic perspective may be lost, and ambulatory care is more likely to become a haphazard and costly series of contacts with various segments of the health care system. The increasing complexity and intensity of ambulatory care dictates the need for highly skilled nursing professionals in this expanding sector of acute care.

Elderly in Acute Care

As in other western countries, the Canadian population is aging. A majority of elderly Canadians live independently in their own homes. However, senior citizens account for 49% of the bed days in Canadian acute care hospitals, and a small number of elderly persons account for the most lengthy hospital stays (Government of Canada, 1988). With the obvious exception of pediatric and obstetrical services, acute care hospitals are designed for the care of "generic" adults temporarily incapacitated by an acute illness. The elderly frequently have multiple and interactive health problems, which may include sensory and/or cognitive deficits. They are therefore particularly susceptible to the many iatrogenic effects of the acute care environment, including development of dependency and disorientation induced by the institutional nature of most hospital environments and routines. Illness often presents differently in older people, making diagnosis and treatment more complex. Physical frailty or incapacity, difficulties in communication, and complex or fragile personal support networks add challenging dimensions to the nursing care of the elderly.

An elderly person entering the acute care system is in double jeopardy. Treatable or reversible illness is often attributed to old age and goes unrecognized by the elderly and their health care providers. Conversely, when elderly persons are admitted to hospital, they may be subjected to the full barrage of acute care interventions by well-meaning health professionals without an informed opportunity to reflect on the effect such interventions may have on their quality of life and prognosis in the short or longer term. Concern about this possibility has led senior citizens' groups and others to lobby for legislation providing for advanced treatment directives (living wills and enduring power of attorney) as means to guarantee that the older person's own wishes regarding the application of acute care interventions and life support measures are communicated to and respected by caregivers. It is particularly challenging to find practical means of ensuring that the voices of the "decisionally incapacitated" can be heard within the acute care setting.

Although age-based discrimination has not been a predominant feature in the Canadian health care system, escalating health care costs have seen a re-emergence of the idea that it may be appropriate to ration health care based on the criterion of age (Callahan, 1987). An alternative to such arbitrary approaches can be found in the development of acute care services targeted for the elderly in which they can receive expert assessment and diagnosis and become active participants in decision making regarding their own care.

As the specialties of geriatric medicine and gerontological nursing developed in Canada (see also Chapter 7), many acute care hospitals established geriatric assessment and rehabilitation units, often in association with specialty geriatric clinics that address commonly occurring problems such as incontinence, memory failure, foot disorders, and so on. Acute geriatric services are provided by an expert interdisciplinary team that includes a geriatrician, nurses with current knowledge in both gerontological and acute care nursing, social workers, and rehabilitation professionals.

Hospital stays for some elderly persons can be avoided or shortened if a day hospital is available. Similar to other forms of ambulatory care, a day hospital offers preventive and diagnostic services and rehabilitative or therapeutic services. Obviously, appropriate transportation to and from the day hospital must be available if this approach to care is to be effective. Clients attend regularly one or more days a week until they achieve their potential for rehabilitation. At that time, they may be discharged or transferred to a day program or other services with a continuing care focus. The Health Services and Promotion Branch of Health and Welfare Canada published Guidelines for Geriatric Services in Acute Care Hospitals (1990). These guidelines clearly outline the goals and program elements for geriatric assessment and treatment units and geriatric day hospitals.

Although it is widely assumed that the elderly over use health care services, a number of studies show that many elderly people do not recognize illness or report their symptoms to health professionals. Elderly persons who are particularly at risk include the very old, especially those living alone; the recently widowed; persons with chronic disabling conditions such as stroke, arthritis, dementia, depression, and diabetes; and persons recently relocated. Elderly persons recently discharged from hospital are also at risk, and 30% of them will be readmitted within a 6-month period (Health and Welfare Canada, 1990). A quick-response team based in the emergency department of an acute care hospital often can provide expert assessment, screening, and referral to intensified community support services for older persons who are not acutely ill but who have come to hospital as a last resort. The purpose of such teams is to provide substitute services where appropriate, not to restrict access by the elderly to acute care.

Elderly persons who cease to be "interesting" or remunerative to professionals in the acute care environment are sometimes disparagingly referred to as "bed blockers." If such persons have no further need or potential to benefit from acute care, they should be referred to alternative services that can more appropriately meet their ongoing needs. This does not necessarily imply that they will be transferred to an extended care facility. Unfortunately, many health professionals are poorly informed about the differences between geriatric assessment and rehabilitation (an acute care service) and long-term care services for the elderly. They may also be unaware of the growing number of community-based services for the elderly, such as day care or respite care, home care, sheltered housing, and transportation. Whether or not they intend to work in units or programs for the elderly, nurses in acute care settings need to be familiar with resources available for the elderly in their own hospitals and communities. A formal approach to case management and discharge planning is required to assure that appropriate alternatives are explored with the active involvement of the elderly person in the decision-making process.

At the level of the health care system, it has become obvious that acute care hospitals cannot "opt out" of elder care, and that dominant or competitive behavior in relation to other health care sectors and agencies is highly dysfunctional. In the Toronto area, a coordinated approach to the provision of services for the elderly is reflected in a unique, regional program. The Victoria Health Project in British Columbia's capital offers another current Canadian example of how acute care hospitals can work in partnership with large and small community agencies and the long-term care sector to create the continuum of care that is needed for appropriate care of the elderly. In this project, it is possible to overcome some of the barriers that traditionally divided various sectors of the health care system from one another by means of a collaborative focus on meeting clients' needs over time.

Health professionals who have chosen to exclude the elderly from their sphere of professional interest and concern should be aware that there is a growing social consensus that resources must be reallocated from the acute care sector to achieve the development of a continuum of health services, many of which can be provided at lower cost and with greater quality of life than hospital care. In the future, increasing professional opportunities for nurses will be found in the areas of geriatrics and continuing care. This area of practice offers many opportunities for expanded nursing roles, with an emphasis on the independent and interdependent domains of nursing practice.

Case Management

Case management and managed care have been implemented during the past decade as acute care hospitals, faced with prospective pricing for Diagnosis Related Groups, search for ways to minimize patients' length of stay and maximize hospital outcomes of specific case-mix groups. In such systems, the expertise of nurses in comprehensive assessment, care planning, problem solving, decision making, negotiation, advocacy, and coordination has been recognized as having the value-added benefit of being able to assist the hospital in fiscal management.

Case management is defined as "a system of health assessment, planning, service procurement/delivery/coordination, and monitoring to meet the multiple needs of clients" (Fuszard et al., 1988, p. 1). Managed care, sometimes called care mapping, involves the use of standard critical paths that reflect the usual patterns or standards of care for a typical patient in a case-mix group, including an established time frame for achieving them. Variances from the critical path are noted and analyzed, and various consultative and communications strategies are used to deal with the variances (Zander, 1990, p. 39).

Case management systems can help solve some of the problems of job design that lead to reduced job satisfaction among nurses who have high levels of professionalism and autonomy. Clients benefit by knowing that someone is assuming the role of advocate on their behalf and accepting personal accountability for the outcomes of their care. Case management can be implemented, or its goals achieved, by means of various organizational strategies and models (Mayer, Madden, and Lawrenz, 1990). When introduced to the case management concept, most nurses will recognize that it incorporates elements of the traditional roles of clinical nurse specialists or other nurses who have been given organizational opportunities to develop and use their expertise to work with particular groups of patients in a relatively autonomous fashion. The care of children with chronic illnesses such as cystic fibrosis or the management of specific modalities of treatment such as total parenteral nutrition have evolved in this way. Diabetic and home dialysis teaching programs and programs for cancer patients have also provided opportunities for nursing role development and contributions of this kind.

However, case management that views hospital discharge as the goal is criticized by many health care consumers and policymakers as being too limited. Although it is important to minimize fragmentation and inefficiency within a particular acute care episode or hospital admission, a more important, and often more challenging, goal is to manage and coordinate the encounters of a client or family with various health care providers and agencies over a period of time. Such horizontal models of case management can be found in some community mental health programs (Pyke, Clark, and Walters, 1991) and palliative care programs, in programs for end-stage renal disease and certain other chronic illnesses, and in models such as single point of entry to long-term care. Nurses have much to offer in the development, implementation, and improvement of case management systems, and, within the acute care setting, case management roles offer nurses the support of the organizational structure for the exercise of expert professional knowledge and skill. The Toronto Hospital is believed to be the first institution in Canada to fully implement case management ("Hospital Develops . . . ," 1990).

Rationing and Reallocation

For the last two decades, the federal government stressed the importance of primary and preventive health. However, with the exception of a few federally controlled programs, implementation of health services is a provincial responsibility in Canada. Acute care hospitals, the most visible and familiar component of the Canadian health care system, still account for the highest proportion of all health care expenditures and employ the majority of health care workers.

Escalating hospital expenditures have resulted in the imposition of cost-containment initiatives by funding agencies and numerous strategies within individual hospitals, which sometimes include formal service reductions in the form of bed closures, "capping" of programs, and redefinition of waiting lists. Often the rationing of acute care services is left to nurses and other health care professionals involved in direct care. They must make decisions regarding how to manage the clinical care of persons whose conditions are more critical and whose treatment is more complex than was the case a few years ago when resources were more plentiful. In the absence of a policy framework that identifies goals and priorities for care in the health care system (in particular, in hospitals) and in individual nursing units, the need to give more care with constant or decreasing resources will remain a source of stress and burnout. This concern is reflected in the demands for "professional responsibility" clauses and committees in nurses' collective bargaining.

Public skepticism about the benefits of "high tech" medicine and concern about its cost in relation to the achievement of health outcomes has been gaining momentum. In the last several years, a majority of Canadian provinces appointed high profile commissions to inquire into the health care system. A common theme emerging from these inquiries is the need to refocus the health care system toward people and the empowerment of individual health care recipients. Another is the need to reallocate resources from traditional, medically driven acute care services to other domains of health care that may be more effective in achieving desired health outcomes and usually are less costly.

Organizational Instability

Acute care hospitals are multimillion-dollar, public service organizations that incorporate complexities not present in most other large bureaucracies. As public expectations continue to increase, the resource base for acute care hospitals becomes unpredictable. This is caused, in part, by the cycles and policies of funding agencies, but it is also a result of stakeholder pressure to reallocate resources from the acute care sector to other care modalities and settings.

The economic incentives imbedded in physicians' fee schedules have a profound effect on the use and application of acute care resources (Evans, 1984; Rachlis and Kushner, 1989). As independent professionals and as a professional lobby group, physicians enjoy unparalleled autonomy. Their social status also affords a high degree of access to political decision makers, both in government and at the level of hospital boards. Unlike all other hospital employees, including the chief executive officer, the medical staff function "in" the organization, but they are not "of" it. Although medical practice patterns are the major driving force in increasing the costs of acute care hospitals, administrative authorities have seldom dealt directly with this problem. At the level of government, acute care is rationed by means of price-based reimbursement systems or by recognizing only a percentage of actual salary or inflationary increases. At the level of individual hospitals, the shrinking value of the dollar is usually dealt with by seeking to achieve greater efficiencies in operating departments such as nursing, dietary, housekeeping, and maintenance.

The past two decades have been characterized by unparalleled, and largely unevaluated, experimentation in hospital administration. The tenure of chief executive officers is now often 5 years or less, in contrast to a previous era when corporate values and a personal commitment to a particular institution might be embodied in the same organization leader over a period of 15 or 20 years (Noble, 1990). In their search for internal, organization-based solutions to financial challenges, boards and chief executive officers eagerly embrace a "business" approach to hospital management. Organizational charts are drawn and redrawn; long-standing committees are abolished; new task forces are created; and new departments, administrative arrangements, and terminology appear as the organization is "flattened," "downsized," "decentralized," or "restructured." When organization redesign results in dismissal of a familiar and respected supervisor or clinical resource person or when it results in layoffs among colleagues, there is an obvious effect on direct caregivers. It is reasonable to assume that organizational instability is a major source of stress in acute care hospitals, and that this type of stress will continue to increase in the foreseeable future.

Little is known about the process by which administrative changes actually diffuse through a large organization, or how long it takes for such changes to be internalized and consolidated by workers. The effect of any single change on the overall organization and its performance is rarely assessed; the effect of organizational changes on caregivers and patients or the inefficiency and waste that may be among the by-products of organizational change are not known. Structural changes at the level of the health care system are needed before the current unprecedented level of instability can be reduced within acute care hospitals.

STAKEHOLDERS IN ACUTE CARE NURSING

Acute care hospitals are complex and diverse organizations in which various individuals and groups have an interest. Three stakeholder groups concerned about nursing in acute care settings are the community, members of other health professions, and, of course, nurses. Becoming aware of the perspectives and concerns of their own and other stakeholder groups can enable nurses to understand the acute care environment and to have an influence within it.

Community Stakeholders

Patients and their families are the most important stakeholders in acute care services. At times, their individual needs require that hospitals and caregivers develop new and creative responses. A blind patient expects to have his seeing eye dog remain at the bedside during his hospital stay in a coronary care unit. A native family requests permission to remain in the hospital room with the body of their deceased family member for several hours after death to observe their traditional religious practices. The parents of a juvenile diabetic ask that the meal and snack times convenient to their lives be maintained while their daughter is in hospital. The wife of a patient writes a letter to the health minister complaining about a lack of privacy and consideration during her husband's hospital stay. Despite the diverse and sometimes contradictory expectations that patients and families may have of nurses, fulfillment of the professional mandate of nursing requires responsiveness to the needs and concerns that are important to patients' dignity, identity, and potential for future wellness.

In the broader community, consumer groups and elected or appointed community and government representatives on boards of trustees are responsible for funding, policy setting, and governing of health agencies. Understanding and responding to the priorities and expectations of these groups, which form the political context for health service delivery, is a necessity and affects the availability of resources and support for nursing in acute care hospitals.

Nurses must respond effectively as individuals and as members of a professional group as they care for patients with AIDS, with women seeking abortion, and with victims of violence and sexual abuse. Acute care nurses may find themselves in clinical and ethical dilemmas in which human rights concerns and the demands for fiscal responsibility are powerful and sometimes contradictory expectations. The ethnic, political, religious, and educational diversity within the community is reflected in the many, and sometimes conflicting, demands that consumer groups, governing boards, and legislators make on acute care hospitals.

Stakeholders from Other Health Disciplines

Other health care professionals have a vested interest in the outcomes of acute care nursing. The interdependency of nurses and physicians is a historical and current reality. Effective nursing practice can enhance the effectiveness of medical care, and incompetence can undermine it. Personnel shortages in nursing have an adverse effect on physicians' ability to admit and treat patients in hospitals. Adversarial relationships, poor judgment, or questionable competence by either partner in the vital relationship between nurse and physician can jeopardize patient well-being and create conditions of professional liability (Prescott and Bowen, 1985).

Health care administrators, including senior nursing leaders, are concerned with the overall effectiveness of health care organizations. Since nursing personnel costs constitute a large proportion of hospital expenditures, administrators, governing bodies, and the public expect increasing accountability from nursing professionals. Efficiency and effectiveness are usually considered to constitute productivity, and since measures of nursing effectiveness are still in a developmental stage, concern with efficiency tends to predominate. Nursing activities are sometimes scrutinized through workload measurement studies and other types of operations research in which indicators of the quality of care are seldom considered. Such studies usually focus on efficiency in the implementation of nursing care, disregarding the intellectual activities of assessment, goal setting, and evaluation that are also part of the nursing process. Achieving complete documentation and enhanced visibility of these intellectual activities is of critical importance to nursing in the retention and acquisition of resources for patient care, and in communicating with other professionals and the public about the scope and responsibilities of clinical nursing practice.

The availability of consistent nursing service of predictable quality is important to medical researchers and others who conduct studies within nursing units. The maintenance of protocols and records, the delivery of medications or treatments, the collection of specimens, or observation of patients are among the types of support that nurses provide to researchers. When these services are additional to those normally provided to patients in a particular nursing unit, incremental nursing costs may result. To ensure the necessary amount and quality of care for all patients on the nursing unit, researchers must be encouraged to assess the need for nursing services in their project and to include incremental nursing labor costs in their research budgets.

Nurses in acute care hospitals provide various educational services to other professional groups. Most of this education occurs informally, and the extent of it is, at present, undocumented. Medical residents, medical students, nursing students, and students in other health disciplines learn many of their clinical skills from nurses in the hospital. At present, costs of these educational services are absorbed by nursing service (i.e., patient care) budgets. Health sciences faculties, patients, and nurses would benefit from a more formalized approach to payment for provision of the clinical education that nurses provide to physicians and other health workers.

Members of other health professions have concerns about the outcomes of acute care nursing services because of their varying degrees of interdependence with nurses. The quality of interprofessional communication is an important factor in patient well-being and in the efficient use of health care resources by the interdisciplinary health care team. Nurses can facilitate or impede the work of colleagues in allied health professions in their role as coordinators of patient care.

Nursing Stakeholders

Although nursing was originally the predominant service provided in hospitals, physicians have acquired and monopolized the admitting function. However, patients are increasingly hospitalized because they need 24-hour nursing care; otherwise their care would be provided on an outpatient basis. As previously noted, a majority of nurses continue to be employed in acute care settings. Nursing salaries constitute the largest single expenditure in most hospitals. Therefore nurses themselves are significant stakeholders in the acute care milieu.

Like the larger community, however, nursing contains varied and sometimes contradictory elements. The goals of unionized nurses sometimes appear to be at odds with those of the leaders of professional nursing associations, nursing education programs, or hospital nursing departments. Nurse educators and representatives of professional associations are sometimes critical of nursing service administrators for what is perceived to be a lack of decisive professional leadership or for appearing to let administrative goals predominate over professional concerns. On the other hand, nursing service administrators express concern that educational programs do not address the current realities in clinical nursing, and that educators do not appreciate the complexities of hospital organizations. New clinicians often feel unprepared for their responsibilities as graduates. Senior nurses may feel that the sense of responsibility and attention to detail they learned as students is no longer valued. Nursing researchers in clinical environments are few and may experience a sense of professional isolation, even in nursing organizations in which there is strong administrative support for their role. Hospital nursing service administrators attempt to represent all nursing stakeholders to the corporate level and to the community but may be prevented from achieving optimum impact if collegial consensus and support are lacking or ineffectual.

The legitimate interest of nurses in the management of acute care hospitals was recently recognized by the governments of Alberta and Ontario. These governments directed hospital boards to appoint nurses as voting members to the hospital board and to major committees. This governmental direction was energetically opposed by organizations of administrators and board members, but the catastrophic results predicted by these groups have not materialized.

An appreciation of the philosophy and mandate of their hospital and an awareness of how their aims and aspirations and those of their colleagues will affect it are helpful to those who practice in the acute care environment.

ETHICAL ISSUES AND PROFESSIONAL ACCOUNTABILITY

Patients in acute care hospitals are often confused about who is "in charge" of their care. The many health team participants ranging from subspecialists to students and the sometimes contradictory demands of clinical, educational, and research programs may seem to make the fragmentation of care inevitable. Although the doctor-patient relationship is considered sacrosanct, problems of communication about, and accountability for, the medical care of patients are now recognized as a significant problem, particularly within teaching hospitals. As mentioned earlier, one reason for the emergence of case management systems is to prevent costly inefficiencies, mistakes, and public relations problems arising from fragmentation of the care process.

Nurses take pride and derive identity from their continuous contact with, and responsibility for, patients. However, continuous nursing responsibility can no longer be taken for granted in most hospitals. Twelve-hour shifts, functional and team nursing assignment systems, "treatment oriented" systems of assessment and documentation, and shortcomings in nurse-to-nurse referral between units of the same hospital or from one health facility to another are threats to accountability in the nurse-patient relationship. A positive example of nursing accountability in the acute care environment is presented below.

Marion Snowdon, a part-time registered nurse, was working the 3-11 shift. Among the patients in her care was a woman dying of the final complications of systemic lupus erythematosus. The patient's attending physician visited and said, "I've arranged to send her to the ICU." Knowing the wishes of the patient and her family, and knowing that death was inevitable and probably imminent, Marion said quietly, "Why don't you let me keep her. She'll be fine here with me." At that moment, the ICU resident arrived and said, "We've got a bed for her in ICU." The attending physician looked at his patient and at her nurse and said, "We won't need the bed. Mrs. Snowdon will be looking after her here."

In this situation, it was clear to the patient and physician that the nurse recognized and understood the patient's needs and wishes and had assumed personal responsibility for her care.

When patients ask, "Who is looking after me?" they should be able to feel confident that at any time of the day or night an individual nurse has responsibility for their care and will help to solve any problems that may arise. Educational preparation, job design, and systems of nurse-to-patient assignment should enhance the potential for individual accountability by nurses. Finding ways to preserve, enhance, and reward the acceptance of accountability in the nurse-patient relationship is the single most important ethical and professional challenge facing clinical and administrative nurses in acute care hospitals today. The extensive literature that suggests nurses have a unique role in patient advocacy will become meaningless unless the obstacles to fully accountable nurse-patient relationships are removed.

CONCLUSION

Nursing in acute care hospitals is sometimes assumed to be more important or more intellectually demanding than in other settings. Although this is not necessarily the case, it is true that unique stresses arise from the complexities and uncertainties of the acute care setting (Gilmore and Peter, 1987; Leatt and Schneck, 1980, 1982a, 1982b, 1984). If nursing as a profession is to have a significant role in the development and implementation of health care policy, all stakeholders in acute care nursing services, particularly patients and others in the community, must see evidence of true accountability by nurses. The challenge of preserving patients' safety, dignity, identity, and autonomy faces all health professionals and is a particular challenge as acute care hospitals experience unprecedented operational instability. Nurses in the acute care environment have the opportunity to provide insights and leadership that will help achieve this goal.

REFERENCES

Alberta Hospital Association. (1989, March). *Post-basic specialty education for Alberta nurses.* Edmonton: Author.

Alberta Social Services and Community Health. (1985). *Provincial senior citizens' advisory council annual report.* Edmonton: Government of Alberta.

Anderson, P. (1979). *Nurse.* New York: Berkley Publishing.

Bentley, D. W. (1990). Tuberculosis in long term care facilities. *Infection Control Hospital Epidemiology, 11*(1), 42.

Callahan, D. (1987). *Setting limits: Medical goals in an aging society.* Toronto: Simon & Schuster.

Canadian Lung Association. (1988). *Canadian tuberculosis standards* (3rd ed.). Toronto: University of Toronto Press.

Chaska, N.L. (Ed.). (1983). *The nursing profession: A time to speak.* Toronto: McGraw-Hill.

Chaska, N.L. (Ed.). (1990). *The nursing profession: Turning points.* St. Louis: C.V. Mosby.

deCrosta, T. (1987). Portrait of a nurse. *Nursing Life, 7*(1), 18-25.

Dracup, K., & Marsden, C. (1990). Critical care nursing: Perspectives and challenges. In N. Chaska (Ed.), *The nursing profession: Turning points* (pp. 304-312). St. Louis: C.V. Mosby.

Evans, R. G. (1984). *Strained mercy: The economics of Canadian health care.* Toronto: Butterworths'.

Feeny, D., Guyatt, G., & Tugwell, P. (Eds.). (1986). *Health care technology: Effectiveness, efficiency, and public policy.* Montreal: The Institute for Research on Public Policy.

Fryer, M. T. (1990). *Hospital resource need measures: A comparison of diagnostic related groups and nursing resource need.* Unpublished, master's thesis, Department of Health Services Administration and Community Medicine, University of Alberta, Edmonton.

Fuszard, B., et al. (1988). *Case management: A challenge for nurses.* Kansas City, MO: American Nurses Association.

Gilmore, T. N., & Peter, M. (1987). Managing complexity in health care settings. *Journal of Nursing Administration, 17*(1), 11-18.

Gino, C. (1982). *The nurse's story.* Toronto: Bantam Books.

Giovannetti, P., & Thiessen, M. (1983). *Patient classification for nurse staffing: Criteria for selection and implementation.* Edmonton: Alberta Association of Registered Nurses.

Government of Canada. (1988). *Canadian seniors: A dynamic force* (Catalogue No. H88-311-1988). Ottawa: Minister of Supply and Services.

Growe, S. J. (1991). *Who cares? The crisis in Canadian nursing.* Toronto: McClelland & Stewart.

Hartigan, E.G. (1990). Discharge planning and continuity of care. In N. Chaska (Ed.), *The nursing profession: Turning points* (pp. 387-393). St. Louis: C.V. Mosby.

Hartshorn, J. (1988). President's message: It's up to you. *Focus on Critical Care, 15*, 67-69.

Health and Welfare Canada. (1990). *Geriatric services in acute care hospitals: A: Geriatric assessment and treatment units, B: Geriatric day hospitals.* Report of the Subcommittee on Institutional Program Guidelines, Health and Welfare Canada. Ottawa: Author.

Hospital develops case management. (1990, August). *The Dispatch: A Canadian Health Care Management Supplement*, No. 56.

Kramer, M., & Schmalenberg, C. (1977). *Path to biculturalism.* Wakefield, MA: Contemporary Publishing.

Leatt, P., & Schneck, R. (1980). Differences in stress perceived by head nurses across nursing specialties in hospitals. *Journal of Advanced Nursing, 5*, 31-46.

Leatt, P., & Schneck, R. (1982a). Work environments of different types of nursing subunits. *Journal of Advanced Nursing, 7*, 581-594.

Leatt, P., & Schneck, R. (1982b). Technology, size, environment, and structure in nursing subunits. *Organization Studies, 3*(3) 221-242.

Leatt, P., & Schneck, R. (1984). Criteria for grouping nursing subunits in hospitals. *Academy of Management Journal, 27*(1), 150-165.

McConnell, E.A. (1982). *Burnout in the nursing profession.* Toronto: C.V. Mosby.

McCormick, K. A. (1986). Preparing nurses for the technologic future. In E. C. Hein & M. J. Nicholson (Eds.), *Contemporary leadership behavior: Selected readings* (2nd ed.) (pp. 393-398). Boston: Little, Brown.

Malloch, K. M., Milton, D. A., & Jobes, M. O. (1990). A model for differentiated nursing practice. *Journal of Nursing Administration, 20*(2), 20-26.

Mayer, G. G., Madden, M. J., & Lawrenz, E. (1990). *Patient care delivery models.* Rockville, MD: Aspen.

Myers, L.P., Schroeder, S.A., Chapman, S.A., & Leong, J. (1984). What's so special about special care? *Inquiry, 21,* 113-127.

Noble, R. (1990). Executive performance: Demands of the 1990's. *Health Care Management Forum, 3*(4), 16-20.

Noseworthy, J., & Jacobs, P. (1990). Economic and ethical considerations in the intensive care unit. *Health Care Management Forum, 3*(2), 4-9.

O'Malley, M. (1986). *Life and death in a major medical centre.* Toronto: Macmillan of Canada.

Prescott, P.A., & Bowen, S.A. (1985). Physician-nurse relationships. *Annals of Internal Medicine, 103,* 127-133.

Pyke, J., Clark, S., & Walters, J. (1991). Case management. *Canadian Nurse, 87*(1), 22-25.

Rachlis, M., & Kushner, C. (1989). *Second opinion.* Toronto: McClelland & Stewart.

Richardson, S. (1986). Articulation and baccalaureate entry to practice: The Canadian context. *Nursing Papers, 18*(3), 47-58.

Sanford, N. D. (1986). Nursing opportunity in the world of 21st century technology. In E.C. Hein & M.J. Nicholson (Eds.), *Contemporary leadership behavior: Selected readings* (2nd ed.) (pp. 383-391). Boston: Little, Brown.

Schumacher, M. (1977). Technical and professional - What's in a name? In B. LaSor & M. Elliot (Eds.), *Issues in Canadian Nursing* (pp. 73-82). Scarborough, ON: Prentice-Hall.

Skene, M.P. (1990, October). *Canadian hospital unit design.* Paper presented at the Second International Meeting - Safety in the Hospital and in Medical Establishments, Centro Nazionale per l'Edilizia e la Tecnica Ospedaliera Roma, Milan, Italy.

Smith, D. L. (1983). Implementing clinical career development programs in Canadian nursing service settings: A strategy for achieving baccalaureate entry to practice (pp. 51-62). In Canadian Association of University Schools of Nursing, *Baccalaureate nursing education for the 80's—Proceedings of the 1983 Western Region Canadian Association of University Schools of Nursing.* Ottawa: Author.

Smith, D.L., & Olinyk, G. (1986). *Matching complexity of patient care requirements with nursing education needs and nursing service resources: A model for improving patient assignments.* A paper presented to the Second National Joint Conference for Nurses in Administration, Education, and Continuing Education, Canadian Nurses Association, Ottawa.

Thorpe, K.E. (1987). The distributional implications of using relative prices in the DRG payment system. *Inquiry, 24,* 85-95.

Wright, S. L. (1990). *A study of the relationship between nursing resource consumption and resource intensity weighted case-mix groupings (CMGs).* Unpublished master's thesis, Faculty of Nursing, University of Alberta, Edmonton.

Zander, K. (1990). Managed care and nursing case management. In G. Mayer, M. Madden, & E. Lawrenz, (Eds.), *Patient care delivery models* (pp. 37-60). Rockville, MD: Aspen.

One of the fastest-growing employment areas for nurses in the 1990s will be in care of the elderly. A primary goal for nurses will be to create environments that facilitate healthy living. Photograph taken in the Hoyles/Escasoni Complex, St. John's, Newfoundland. (Photograph courtesy Prime Communications Consultants, St. John's, Lane Photographics Ltd., St. John's, and the Association of Registered Nurses of Newfoundland. Used with permission.)

CHAPTER SEVEN

Nursing Practice in Long-term Care Agencies

JESSIE MANTLE, RN, MSN

Jessie Mantle, RN, BN (McGill), MSN (California, San Francisco), holds a joint appointment as Professor, School of Nursing, University of Victoria, and Clinical Nurse Specialist (Gerontology), Juan de Fuca Hospitals, Victoria, B.C. Professor Mantle teaches Nursing Process and Geronotological Nursing, both on campus and through distance education, and practices in a long-term care facility. She has served as consultant on major task forces looking into care of the aged, including the Institute for Health Care Facilities for the Future, and on the federal government's working group on Services to Elderly Residents with Mental Health Problems in Long Term Care Facilities.

R ecent trends in Canada, and indeed around the world, reveal that the numbers of citizens who require ongoing care constitute a rapidly growing group. If nurses are to respond to health care needs of Canadian people, then the nursing perspective must include institutional long-term care as an area of valid, respected clinical practice. To help demonstrate that perspective, this chapter will focus on factors causing growth in this area, give a broad, general description of long-term care, describe institutional long-term care, and discuss critical issues in this area of nursing.

Because the majority of residents in long-term care agencies are elderly, the commentary in this chapter will deal primarily with institutions for care of older people. It is important, however, to recognize that facilities for ongoing care of such groups as the mentally disabled, the mentally ill, and the physically disabled of all ages are classified as long-term care facilities. Many of the comments made in this section apply equally well to these agencies, and it must be acknowledged that innovations in these care facilities have often led the way in humanizing long-term care for the elderly.

THE GROWING NEED FOR LONG-TERM CARE

Long-term care services and programs are required by those persons who have some degree of functional impairment because of physical and/or mental frailty or disability. A number of forces, such as increased longevity, reduction in mortality from acute illnesses, and improved care for victims of serious trauma and neonatal and childhood abnormalities, have increased demands for long-term care.

The first such force is the aging of the Canadian population. Changing demographics, caused by lower fertility rates and increased longevity, have led to "greying" of the population in many countries. Canada's population is young compared with some developed Western countries, such as the Scandinavian countries, France, West Germany, and even the United States. Sweden, for example, had a population pyramid in 1985 that is similar to that predicted for Canada in 2031 (see Figure 7-1) (Health and Welfare Canada, 1989). However, the so-called "baby boom" of the late 1930s through the early 1950s means that a wave of seniors will occur, peaking in the early years of the next century, which is less than a decade away. In recent years, there has been a marked increase in Canada of numbers of those age 85+, a group commonly called the very old or the old-old, and this trend will continue. All these changes have implications for today's health care planners—and for those who plan for nursing care.

Although estimates of future growth must be done with caution, population projections suggest that by the year 2000 the 65+ age group will constitute somewhere between 13.6% and 16.1% of the Canadian population; by the year 2031, these figures will increase to between 18.9% and 26.6%—or about one quarter of the population (McDaniel, 1986). These percentages will translate into large numbers needing health care.

Provincial and city variations will be evident. The 1981 census revealed that the Capital Regional District surrounding Victoria, British Columbia, had become the geriatric capital of Canada. The 65+ population was 17%—the highest proportion of seniors in the country; this compared to 11% in the province of British Columbia as a whole and 10% in Canada (Gallagher, 1985). In Alberta, the 65+ population is projected to rise from 8% in 1986 to 14% in 2016; this percentage shift will represent more than a doubling of the older population from 201,000 to 464,000 in just 3 decades (Premier's Commission on Future Health . . . , 1989, p. 12).

Although a large percentage of the aged are able to live independently and care for themselves, many persons of extreme age have a decrease in the physical stamina necessary to maintain a fully independent life-style. Old age is also a time of life when there is potential for multiple major stressors, such as losses of spouse, friends, standard of living, home, independence, freedom, choices, and mobility. Such losses affect the psychological outlook of both older people and their support networks;

Changes in the Age Structure

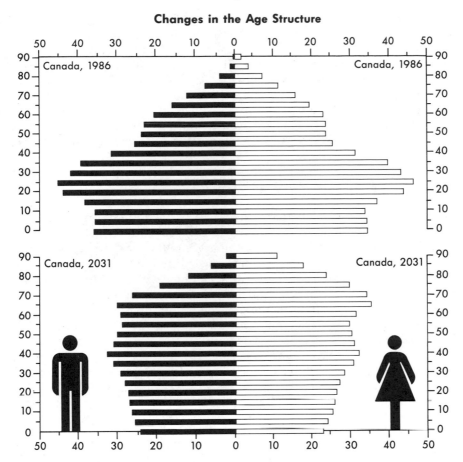

FIGURE 7-1 Canadian age structures (male and female) for 1986 and projected for 2031. (From Health and Welfare Canada, 1989. *Charting Canada's future: A report of the demographic review*. Ottawa: Author, p. 18. © Health and Welfare Canada. Used with permission.)

this, in turn, has a profound effect on the health status of the elderly.

A second factor related to the increased need for long-term care services is the shift in morbidity patterns away from a predominance of infectious diseases toward one of chronic illnesses, such as cancer, arthritis, cardiovascular disease, and Alzheimer-type dementias. Because many of these illnesses cannot yet be cured, affected individuals manifest varying degrees of disability as the disease progresses. Those suffering from mental illnesses also may need ongoing monitoring, periodic reassessment, management of acute episodes, and support in daily living activities. The rising age of the population also contributes to the increase in incidence of chronic illnesses because the elderly are particularly vulnerable to this type of disease.

Finally, growing numbers of individuals of all ages are needing long-term care because of permanent disabilities as a result of injuries or physiological damage. The growth in numbers reflects, in part, an improved ability to manage situations such as serious traumas, acute illness episodes, and childhood abnormalities that, in the past, have resulted in death. The needs of these affected individuals cannot be met by the acute care model, which was designed for episodic illnesses, crisis management, and curative treatment. The failure of the acute care model has been noted particularly in geriatrics and psychiatry (Heiskanen, 1988). Instead, the health care system needs a model suited to individuals attempting to maintain some normalcy in their lives while they experience ongoing functional deficits. Such a model comes under the rubric of long-term care.

THE CONCEPT OF LONG-TERM CARE

In contemporary terms, long-term care refers to provision of programs and services to functionally impaired individuals of all ages on an ongoing basis over a prolonged period of time. The length of contact with the long-term care sector may vary. Some clients may terminate contact because there is a significant improvement in their functional status. The majority of clients, however, will need to continue to receive some form of service for months or years, or until they die. The term *continuing care* has been used in many areas of the country to capture this notion.

The particular care package required differs for each individual but usually will include a mix of health care, personal care (e.g., assistance with meals or housekeeping), and social services (Kane and Kane, 1986). Rapelje, a Canadian leader in designing long-term care services for the elderly, describes this package as:

> a range of programs and services planned, organized, financed and co-ordinated that includes: preventive health, life enrichment, health promotion and "wellness" programs that promote overall well-being and independence as long as possible; community support programs and living options that enhance the quality of life and support the independence and needs of the community-based elderly and the family care giver; and a range of institutional settings [that] recognizes the varying degrees of physical and mental frailty and provides needed care and services for individuals who are severely disabled, limited in functional capacity or chronically impaired [so that these individuals may be maintained] at the highest possible level of health and well-being. (Rapelje, 1986, p. LT 1:1)

Within this context, the institution is but one option in a comprehensive system.

THE INSTITUTIONAL COMPONENT OF LONG-TERM CARE

Within the long-term care sector, institutions meet the needs of individuals for residential living arrangements in combination with 24-hour assistance in personal care, medical and nursing supervision, provision for addressing psychosocial needs, and, in some situations, a range of additional therapeutic services (Health and Welfare Canada, 1984; Forbes, Jackson, and Kraus, 1987). The types of care offered and the names used to describe the care differ from province to province, making comparisons difficult. Repeated attempts to find a universal nomenclature have failed. Figure 7-2 shows one attempt to portray a national profile of the types of care by province as they existed in 1986.

Types of Care

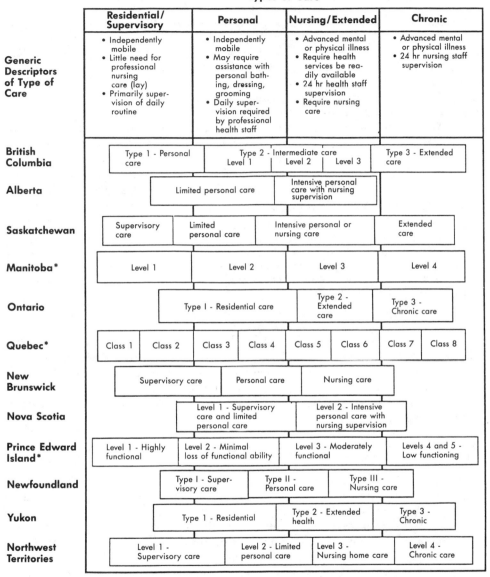

	Residential/Supervisory	Personal	Nursing/Extended	Chronic
Generic Descriptors of Type of Care	• Independently mobile • Little need for professional nursing care (lay) • Primarily supervision of daily routine	• Independently mobile • May require assistance with personal bathing, dressing, grooming • Daily supervision required by professional health staff	• Advanced mental or physical illness • Require health services be readily available • 24 hr health staff supervision • Require nursing care	• Advanced mental or physical illness • 24 hr nursing staff supervision

British Columbia	Type 1 - Personal care	Type 2 - Intermediate care — Level 1	Level 2	Level 3	Type 3 - Extended care			
Alberta	Limited personal care		Intensive personal care with nursing supervision					
Saskatchewan	Supervisory care	Limited personal care	Intensive personal or nursing care		Extended care			
Manitoba*	Level 1	Level 2	Level 3		Level 4			
Ontario	Type I - Residential care		Type 2 - Extended care	Type 3 - Chronic care				
Quebec*	Class 1	Class 2	Class 3	Class 4	Class 5	Class 6	Class 7	Class 8
New Brunswick	Supervisory care	Personal care	Nursing care					
Nova Scotia	Level 1 - Supervisory care and limited personal care		Level 2 - Intensive personal care with nursing supervision					
Prince Edward Island*	Level 1 - Highly functional	Level 2 - Minimal loss of functional ability	Level 3 - Moderately functional	Levels 4 and 5 - Low functioning				
Newfoundland	Type I - Supervisory care	Type II - Personal care	Type III - Nursing care					
Yukon	Type 1 - Residential	Type 2 - Extended health	Type 3 - Chronic					
Northwest Territories	Level 1 - Supervisory care	Level 2 - Limited personal care	Level 3 - Nursing home care	Level 4 - Chronic care				

*These provinces define Types of Care in a slightly different manner.

FIGURE 7-2 Types of Care by province and territory, 1986. Note the varying definitions of care and levels of care offered. (From Department of Energy, Mines and Resources (1986). *Energy survey of long term care health facilities: Phase 1—population profile.* Ottawa: Department of Supply and Services. © Energy, Mines and Resources Canada. Used with permission.)

Regardless of the name used, until the late 1980s, particular facilities generally have specialized in one level of care. More recently, multi-level care facilities have come into being, where several types of care have been combined (e.g., day care, intermediate care, and extended care). This may occur either in the same facility or in adjoining properties on the same grounds and under the same management. Such arrangements can reduce stress caused by relocation, help maintain personal relationships (such as when spouses need different levels of care), allow better responses to temporary variations in a resident's health state, and offer organizational advantages (such as allowing staff to have variety in kinds of care and allowing economies of scale) (Health and Welfare Canada, 1984).

The place of institutions within the broad spectrum of long-term care is controversial. The vast majority of persons express the wish to maintain themselves within the community setting. However, Kane and Kane (1986) suggest that, under the right conditions, living within an institutional setting can offer a life of greater freedom and more meaning than remaining in the community. In reviewing care of older people, Murakami (1983) states:

> Institutions [for long-term care] should be viewed not as the last resort after family care-givers and/or community health workers have made an heroic attempt to keep older adults in the community, but as a place where selected older adults go to receive the care they require from gerontological nurses, nurses who have special knowledge and expert skills, just as patients are admitted to intensive care units to receive the specialized nursing care they require. (p. 11-12)

Long-term care facilities are developing services that reach out to the elderly living in the community (Forbes, Jackson, and Kraus, 1987). Such institutions may offer respite or vacation relief to families, day care, foot care, bathing opportunities, meal services, health monitoring clinics, caregivers' support groups, or telephone monitoring systems that enable those who live at home to summon help from the institution should trouble arise. These programs will help make the long-term care facility a more familiar and less feared place for older citizens who ultimately may need to reside there.

THE RESIDENT POPULATION

As Rapelje (1986) noted, long-term care institutions serve the severely disabled, those limited in functional capacity, and the chronically impaired. It is difficult to obtain accurate statistical information about numbers of people who dwell in long-term care facilities because of the varied reporting systems and the differing provincial classification methods. Furthermore, these systems have changed markedly during the last 2 decades, making comparisons over time periods difficult. Using Statistics Canada data, Forbes, Jackson, and Kraus (1987) estimated that 240,000 individuals resided in long-term care institutions in 1981; almost three quarters (74%) were over age 65 and of this 65+ population, about 39% were 85+.

Development of community support services for the elderly and the physically disabled in the 1980s and the trend to deinstitutionalize the mentally disabled have resulted in more people remaining within the community for longer periods of time.

This has led to a change in the profile of long-term care residents in institutions in terms of age, acuity of illness, and complexity of needs.

Stone and Frenken (1988) compared the numbers of seniors living in Canadian institutions in the years 1976, 1981, and 1986. They found that there has been a decline in seniors below age 85 living in institutions, but that seniors over age 85 have increased steadily. These changes in age groups lend validity to the observation that institutionalized elders are older and frailer than in the past.

As well as being much older, elderly residents in long-term care facilities exhibit greater degrees of physical and mental frailty. Many enter in the final stages of dementia when home support systems collapse (Mental Health Division, 1988). In some instances, the resident group includes younger adults who need care because of chronic illnesses (e.g., multiple sclerosis, deficits resulting from accidents). In some settings it is common to have dying persons of various ages who require hospice care. A new group now coming on the scene is composed of young adults who have spent all or most of their early years in pediatric institutions. Such a mixture is a challenging one in which to provide quality care.

Because nurses are the daily interface between the institutionalized resident and the community, they must also decide whether they should extend the notion of "client" to include the families and significant others of the residents. Feelings of guilt often arise in family members who have admitted a relative to an institution and visiting cognitively and physically impaired family can cause extreme stress and anxiety (Rutenberg, 1988). Such intense emotions may affect the health of the family members and the resident. Recognition of this reality has led some organizations to develop guidelines for programs to prepare families for this stressful event (Council on Aging of Ottawa-Carleton, 1985).

NURSING PRACTICE IN LONG-TERM CARE

Just as it is difficult to obtain data about the kinds of facilities available for long-term care, it is equally difficult to find trends about staffing patterns of these institutions. Identifying the numbers of nurses working in long-term care facilities is complicated by the fact that the methods used to report nursing manpower statistics vary across the country. Information is supplied to Statistics Canada as a part of the registration process in the provinces and territories but the categories for data differentiate only between "hospitals" and "nursing homes/homes for the aged." This hides data about the number of nurses who work in extended care hospitals or in long-term care units in acute care hospitals, in psychiatric hospitals, or in other special hospitals caring for long-term stay patients.

The numbers of professional nursing staff in nursing homes and homes for the aged have remained relatively stable despite the increasingly complex medical and functional needs of the residents. The percentage of registered nurses in the work force in these agencies grew from 6.5% in 1984 to only 6.9% in 1987 (Statistics Canada and Canadian Nurses Association, 1986; Statistics Canada, 1989). Moreover, nearly 50% of these nurses are in managerial positions (head nurse, supervisor, director), although they report they are predominately diploma prepared and have neither post-basic preparation in management nor geriatrics (Statistics Canada and Canadian Nurses Association, 1986; Statistics Canada, 1989). In these facilities, the nursing aide, with limited short-term training, provides much of the front-line nursing care. This leads to the reality that registered nurses are supervising large groups of non-professional staff and may indicate that these agencies are understaffed with the kind of professional care needed. Much more data need to be collected and more research done to determine exactly what staffing ratios are needed to provide quality care in long-term care facilities.

Nursing practice in long-term care agencies has a different flavor than nursing in other clinical practice areas. Long-term care agencies differ from hospitals in that they are congregate living facilities that take the place of independent dwellings for those who are the recipients of care. In other words, the facility becomes the "home" of a "resident." A primary goal of caregivers, therefore, is to create environments that facilitate healthy living and dying even though the residents are experiencing varying degrees of illness. Health care needs represent only one facet, albeit an important one, in a person's daily life, and nurses must coordinate their activities and share their time with many groups. For this reason, the nurses' perspective on their work must include an emphasis on the psychosocial components of living in addition to biomedical understandings.

These ideas are well understood by Vera McIvor, a Canadian nurse who has received international acclaim for development of a model of care that has come to be known as the "Priory Method." It was her intent to liberate the older people in her institution from a life in which there had been exclusive emphasis on custodial, physical care (McIvor, 1978). The use of the term *resident* rather than the term *patient* was but one of the many ways in which McIvor helped others to recognize that long-term care institutions (an extended care agency in her case) were not hospitals, and people who lived there were not sick in the usual sense of that word. A recognition of the value of the residents' life experiences and of their needs for continuing self-development led to a clarification of the nursing role as one in which psychosocial concerns were as relevant as physical problems. She proposed various ways of making institutions more "normal": management of relocation trauma for residents who must be moved, training in group activity work for staff, imaginative planning of the environment to foster rehabilitation, using research data from studies on aging to plan care, abandoning uniforms, and involving family and friends in care (McIvor, 1978).

THE SCOPE OF NURSING

McIvor's ideas form a philosophical backdrop for contemporary nursing practice in long-term care agencies. The role is complex, and nurses who choose to practice in this area face many challenges. Three of these challenges are of particular interest:

1. The care of illnesses that affect individuals in long-term facilities
2. The critical role of *basic* care
3. The nature of the resident-nurse relationship

Nursing care needs for the diverse populations of long-term care settings are multiple and varied, but it is possible for nurses to achieve a full range of nursing goals, from health promotion to care of the dying. In many instances and over long periods of time, the overall health status of these individuals can be maintained with adequate monitoring and health education. Disability may be prevented, or at least compensated for, when nurses use team and community resources to activate a broad range of health and social services to strengthen the coping ability of the resident. Many residents require the assistance of nurses to help them manage treatment regimens, which may range from simple control of constipation to use of elaborate equipment such as respirators. A classification of interventions that addresses these broad goals has been developed (Mantle, 1978).

Because quality of life is an issue for residents, nursing care requirements go beyond needs for physical care to include programs that address the concerns of the whole person within the context of that person's developmental stage. Partnership models of care are being designed to enhance quality of life (Wells, Singer, and Polgar, 1986). When death is inevitable, the experiences of dying can be given meaning, and dignity and physical suffering can be alleviated as nurses make manifest the philosophy of hospice care.

Given the complexity of these situations, no one discipline has all the skills needed for management; this has led to an increasing emphasis on use of a multidisciplinary team. However, because of their continual presence on site, nurses are ideally suited to coordinate the plans and practices of the professional health care team, as well as the work of nonprofessional staff and volunteers.

Role in Illness Care

Opportunities for nurses to take an expanded role in illness care arise because physicians usually visit infrequently in these environments. Nurses therefore assume increased responsibility for monitoring and managing illness states. They will be consulted about minor events of everyday life, such as colds and upset stomachs. These must be discriminated from the more major acute illness episodes, which in the elderly may present in atypical fashion and must be detected rapidly if successful treatment is to be undertaken.

Chronic illnesses, however, predominate, and it is not unusual to find several illnesses present in one resident, which complicates selection of treatment and ongoing assessment. Rather than aggressive medical intervention and high technology, the chronically ill have a need for symptom management, rehabilitation, and health maintenance (Canadian Nurses Association, 1987).

Nurses in long-term care facilities must be knowledgeable about physical illness and also must be skilled in the management of mental health problems as manifested in older people. The term *mental health problem* has been used "to emphasize that what is at issue is not only individual pathology but a disruption in the interaction of the individual with his/her environment, necessitating attention to psychosocial and organizational factors as well as biological and intrapsychic factors" (Health and Welfare Canada, 1990, p. 1). Specific problems may include depression, loneliness, grief, dementia, fear, anxiety, adjustment disorders, psychoses, substance abuse, suicide, delirium, and other less common but disabling psychiatric symptoms (McEwan, Donnelly, Robertson, and Hertzman, 1991; National Advisory Council on Aging, 1989). While residents of institutions may experience any of these problems, depression and dementia are particularly common among the institutionalized elderly.

Much of this nursing activity comes under the heading of primary health care—and the Canadian Nurses Association (1987) has taken the position that, in nursing homes and long-term care facilities, these needs could be met by clinical nurse specialists.

Basic Care—A Critical Role

Any perspective on long-term care nursing must address the place of nursing activities designed to help people with acts of daily living, such as bathing, dressing, toileting, eating, and mobilizing. In long-term care facilities, these are complex acts of critical importance to a resident population either at risk of or already manifesting permanent functional loss. Professional nursing assessment and monitoring, as well as professionally delivered intervention at critical points, is required. Complexity in the assessment and management of these activities arises from three sources:

1. The manner in which physiological losses occur
2. The fact that accomplishment of these tasks is intimately bound up with a person's self-view
3. The availability of appropriate interventions

Loss of ability may occur over time—both in the course of a day, as when fatigue sets in, and over a long period, as when a disease progresses. Sometimes the shift is marked, but more often it is subtle, necessitating knowledge and skilled observation to detect alterations and make changes in routines so that an individual can optimize functional competence.

The behavior of nursing caregivers as they perform intimate tasks of daily living can leave a resident feeling either empowered or incompetent. When nursing staff have values and work opportunities that allow each resident to make choices and to take the time needed to function as independently as possible, then the resident continues to feel worthy as an adult. When an uneducated "do for" approach is taken and residents are not encouraged to use their skills (e.g., walking, eating, dressing), they quickly show losses in these abilities. As Rosendahl and Ross (1982) have shown, such an approach leads to increased dependence and loss of self-esteem. Thus staff who provide basic care must be skilled in human communication, especially nonverbal communication. In short, they should be nurses.

In striving to help residents with activities, nurses may need to adapt usual strategies or design new strategies to deal with the exact nature of a particular individual's loss. There is a dearth of knowledge about many of the common phenomena, such as incontinence or behavioral problems, experienced by residents. Not only is more clinical research needed, but long-term care facilities also need nursing practitioners who refuse to accept the status quo and who will problem-solve and find innovative ways to approach everyday situations.

Unfortunately, such activities of daily living have been stereotyped as *basic* nursing care in which the term *basic* is understood to mean care that requires little knowledge to perform other than minimal training in the mechanics of the performance. This inaccurate assumption has had serious consequences for staffing arrangements in long-term care settings and even for the ways in which nursing students are initiated into these settings.

Because basic activities are perceived to require little knowledge, they are delegated to nonprofessionals, and a staffing pattern has developed in which there is a low ratio of professional to nonprofessional personnel. The "doers" of these activities have been given low status, and this leads to difficulty in recruiting new staff because individuals develop self-concepts reflecting the value placed on their work. This can influence morale and also affect the way staff perform activities. Educators follow this pattern when they send a student to long-term care areas as a first experience because they believe, incorrectly, that these are simple situations. The experience is likely to set the tone for the student's perspective on nursing practice in long-term care facilities, thus perpetuating the myth. The residents are the real losers in that they are at risk of receiving basic care from ill-informed caregivers.

Resident–Nurse Relationships

In long-term care settings, the nurse usually will know the resident as a client for the rest of the client's life. Although this will give the nurse time to form a more meaningful relationship (time is a luxury most acute care nurses do not have), it also places heavy demands on the practitioner.

The long-term care nurse has to struggle, often many times a day, with questions of boundaries between nursing rights and obligations and the responsibilities and rights of the resident. Does a cognitively intact resident have a right to refuse treatment? Does a resident who often falls have the right to be mobile? Do families have the right to request that restraints not be used for their confused relatives? Issues surrounding death and dying are particularly difficult, especially such issues as living wills and do-not-resuscitate orders. Some provinces and some agencies have developed guidelines (e.g., British Columbia Ministry of Health, 1989).

Because a resident is captive, so to speak, his or her rights are at greater risk of violation. When this struggle is viewed against a backdrop of dependency and queries about mental competence, the resident is in a vulnerable position, needful of an advocate who has a clear personal set of values.

In long-term care, a great part of a nurse's day is spent in communication with the many residents who have difficulty with their human relationships because of cognitive impairment, agressive responses to stress, aphasia, or depression. To be truly available to these individuals, the nurse must give of self and be able to see through the outwardly disturbing behavior to the person within. This requires a high degree of communication competence and a philosophical stance that respects the personhood of every individual.

In long-term care settings, ways have to be found to support nurses through these intense and often draining encounters. Not only do these nurses require support, they also need communication strategies that can help staff reach these persons.

CRITICAL ISSUES IN LONG-TERM CARE

As long-term care assumes increasing importance in health care, nursing must pause and examine realities. A number of issues must be resolved if nurses are to use their skills to improve the quality of life of residents within the facilities. Discussions of these critical points have been grouped under educational issues, research issues, and workplace issues.

Educational Issues

Provision of quality service in any setting is based on the premise that caregivers have the requisite knowledge, skills, and attitudes to meet the client's needs. However, at the beginning of the 1990s, health care students are not receiving adequate training in geriatrics and gerontology in their basic programs. Attitude surveys conducted in the 1980s show that nurses do not find these fields attractive (Mantle, 1981; Podnieks, Laforet-Fliesser, and Brunton, 1988). To a large degree, this reflects a lack of understanding on the part of nurse educators about the complexity of nursing care required by long-term care populations, as well as an inability of service personnel to organize and change the perception.

In 1981, the National Advisory Council on Aging adopted the position that educational deficits about caring for the elderly could not continue (McDonald, 1981). In 1988, five national organizations (Canadian Hospital Association, Canadian Long Term Care Association, Canadian Medical Association, Canadian Nurses Association, and Canadian Public Health Association) reflected this position in a joint statement supporting undergraduate education in geriatrics and geronotology for health and social service professionals.

Earthy's (1991) survey of 20 Canadian generic baccalaureate programs suggests that there has been only minimal response to this position. In her survey, only 7.4% of the students' clinical experiences had a gerontological focus, and when a fourth-year practicum was offered it was chosen by only 2% of the students. The absence of adequate numbers of faculty role models is reflected in her finding that only 4.9% of the 550 faculty at the surveyed schools held a graduate degree with a gerontological focus.

Three issues must be addressed before this deficiency can be rectified. The first concerns the leveling of content between that required by generalists regardless of where they practice and that required by those wanting to specialize in long-term care. The emphasis in most nursing education programs on education only for acute care in hospitals is inappropriate. It would seem fruitful to expose all nurses to the long-term model of care so they might have greater sensitivity to the needs of this growing segment of the population. Such exposure would help all nurses provide better care when these individuals are in acute care facilities and serve as a base for successful career mobility into the long-term care sector.

Increasingly there are job opportunities for first-level positions in long-term care agencies. However, the complex nature of the health situations experienced by the residents means that even first-level clinical decision makers need a broad understanding of the multiple factors that affect health in the aged and in the chronically ill or disabled. Such first-level nurses must undertake the monitoring of health states on a day-to-day basis and often work alone on evening and night shifts without access to other team members. Basic educational programs do not purport to prepare specialists, but it would appear that some degree of concentration at the undergraduate level is essential for students interested in this field if nursing is to meet manpower demands in this growing health care sector.

Another educational issue concerns preparation of specialists for this field of practice. Long-term care, per se, is not a nursing specialty. With the growing heterogeneity of the resident populations, nursing specialists in various areas, such as rehabilitation, mental health, gerontology, and medical nursing, will be needed. More importantly, nursing education programs must address the special nature of long-term care so that differences in this field can be identified.

Controversy reigns over effective ways to help students gain knowledge in long-term care. For example, are there sensitizing experiences that will help learners overcome their own fears of aging and disability so that they are able to feel comfortable in these settings? How should learning experiences be sequenced? Because the educational experience will have a profound effect on a learner's attitude toward this (and other) fields of practice, educational research is needed to find answers that will enhance a student's views of long-term care.

Finally, how can one help nurses already employed in long-term care facilities? Many of these nurses lack not only formal knowledge but also contemporary nursing knowledge (e.g., knowledge about the nursing process). Until recently, long-term care nurses have been isolated and now need assistance in joining the mainstream of nursing.

Research Issues

Skilled practice and quality education depend on the availability of a relevant knowledge base. However, much knowledge about common long-term care clinical situations has not been tested, and researchers seem reluctant to become involved in this field. In many instances, the problems requiring study by nurses (e.g., wandering, constipation, incontinence, aggressive behavior) are defined as simple, uninteresting, or not worthy of the investment of time required to do rigorous investigations. This view reflects the social image about aging and disability.

Designing relevant research projects is difficult in this rapidly expanding and developing field. Much of the research has been done with the young-old or middle-old populations, and the approaches suggested are often inappropriate to the needs of the increasing numbers of old-old (age 85 +). The complexity of clinical situations for the old-old requires a multidisciplinary team for management, but research usually is undertaken by a single discipline, which leaves many parameters unexplored.

Communicating the findings of research and of clinical practice experiences has become a high priority for Canadian nurses working in long-term care. The biennial scientific and educational meetings of the Canadian Gereontological Nursing Association, formed in June 1985, serve as forums for presentation of knowledge about every aspect of gerontological nursing practice. The journal of the Ontario Gerontological Nursing Association, *Perspectives*, provides accounts about the practice of gerontological nursing in Canada, including that which occurs in long-term care settings.

Workplace Issues

Requirements essential for quality nursing care in long-term care institutions are often poorly understood by many architects, planners, facility designers, funding agencies, unions, and managers—yet these persons control the resources that set limits on how nursing will be practiced. Nurse managers must try to fulfill a complex mandate with an inadequate nursing service department profile.

Staffing issues center on quality and quantity of staff available. Nursing is the predominant group in long-term care facilities. Although this provides opportunities for independence not normally present in other health care sectors (Stryker-Gordon, 1982), inadequate staffing profoundly affects the residents and the goals that can be achieved. There are markedly fewer professional nurses and more nonprofessional staff and volunteers in long-term care institutions than in acute care hospitals. Most direct nursing care is undertaken by staff who have minimal education and who therefore lack the expertise necessary to manage the complex situations presented by the mentally frail and the extremely disabled. Rather than providing the broad range of care of which they are capable, nurses spend time supervising these workers and coordinating activities. Often a nurse must make complex, long-ranging decisions in isolation because he or she is the only professional in the facility.

Making current, useable, up-to-date information available to nursing practitioners is a critical ingredient for the delivery of quality care. In Alberta, the isolation of long-term care facilities from the mainstream of health education and service has been ameliorated by development of several Long Term Care Inservice Resource Centres. These centers distribute a wide variety of multimedia educational resources and educational opportunities to caregivers throughout the province (Church, 1991).

If residents in long-term care facilities are to receive the same high-quality care as users in other areas of the health care system, then reorganization of nursing work to facilitate the delivery of expert nursing care must be a priority.

NEW DEVELOPMENTS

Two developments that may address some of the problems and lead to resolution in exciting new ways are now evident: (1) use of the clinical nurse specialist and (2) introduction of the long-term care teaching unit. Use of a clincal nurse specialist provides a role model for excellence. During the late 1980s, this position became an established service position in several long-term care settings in Canada. Use of the long-term care teaching unit helps integrate practice, research, and education. A position paper describing teaching units was given at the Canadian Association on Gerontology in 1984 (Mohide, French, Caulfield, Chambers, and Bayne, 1984), and several such units now are available in Canada.

The Clinical Nurse Specialist

The opportunity to pursue a career in clinical nursing came into being in the late 1960s and early 1970s with development of the clinical nurse specialist role. The position was developed initially in acute care sectors in the United States to improve the direct care of clients by bringing the most advanced clinical nursing knowledge to bear directly on client situations through employment of an expert practitioner. Two functions are central to the role: (1) providing direct nursing care when specialized expertise is required and (2) influencing others to improve nursing care by acting as a consultant to other nurses (Canadian Nurses Association, 1986).

In long-term care, clinical nurse specialists undertake a number of activities in addition to acting as role model and giving direct care to residents and their families. A clinical nurse specialist may be involved in designing nursing strategies for improving care in particular situations (e.g., management of wandering patients). He or she may consult with staff nurses about specific difficulties (e.g., guidance on how to manage a depressed resident or on how to deal with physically aggressive individuals). The clinical nurse specialist may participate in clinical research projects, such as on use of restraints (Mitchell-Pedersen, Edmund, Fingerote, and Powell, 1986).

Gerontological clinical nurse specialists can do much to enhance the image of this specialty; they are leaders who have opportunities to publicize the complexity of the nursing contribution in long-term care (Mantle, 1986). Because they are prepared for their roles in a manner comparable to other health care professionals (i.e., through specialization at the graduate level of a university), they are more likely to achieve equality on the health care team and can argue for the nursing viewpoint when decisions on resident care or organizational methods are being made.

A number of long-term care agencies have expressed interest in having a clinical nurse specialist, but there is a shortage of appropriately prepared nurses. Until recently, nursing held a leadership role in long-term care, primarily because other disciplines were not interested. Now that emphasis is being placed on services for an aging population, this leadership role will be challenged. Unless the supply of clinical nurse specialists for long-term care can meet the demand, nursing may lose a critical avenue to demonstrate its contributions to health care.

The Long-term Care Teaching Unit

Another way to address problems in nursing practice, education, and research is by development of teaching units in long-term care. Clinical teaching units in acute care have been specially funded to serve as models in undergraduate and graduate medical education in Canada and have been used to enhance student learning, increase standards of care, facilitate research efforts, and act as development models in nonteaching facilities (Mohide et al., 1983). In the United States, where teaching projects in nursing homes have been tried for some years, progress has been made in developing learning opportunities and in increasing understanding about long-term care (Schneider, 1985; Mezey, Lynaugh, and Cartier, 1989). The first Canadian teaching nursing home was established in the Hamilton area and is affiliated with McMaster University ("First teaching nursing home . . . ," 1989).

Although teaching units are not proposed as substitutes for major centers for research and education, they have the potential to enhance the image of long-term care and to give meaning to the work and the nurses who do the work. Their development may be a critical step in improving quality of life for residents in long-term care settings.

CONCLUSION

Long-term care should perhaps be considered the most significant area for growth in health care for the next generation of nurses. Despite the stereotypes that such care is dull, simple, and uninteresting, nurses who work in long-term care have begun to demonstrate and articulate that such nursing practice is complex and challenging and that it offers unique personal satisfactions that compare to those found in other health care fields. The issues in this area are challenging, but their resolution will be significant and rewarding.

REFERENCES

British Columbia Ministry of Health. Continuing Care Division. (1989). *Death and dying in long term care facilities: Operational guidelines.* Victoria: Author.

Canadian Nurses Association. (1986). *Statement on the clinical nurse specialist.* Ottawa: Author.

Canadian Nurses Association. (1987). *The nursing contribution in health care for older adults.* Ottawa: Author.

Church, J. (1991). Long term care resource centres. *Alberta Association of Registered Nurses Newsletter, 47*(11), 10-11.

Council on Aging of Ottawa-Carleton. (1985). *Involving families: A guide for an educational programme for families of the institutionalized elderly.* Ottawa: Author.

Department of Energy, Mines and Resources. (1986) *Energy survey of long term care health facilities: Phase 1—population profile.* Ottawa: Department of Supply and Services.

Earthy, A.E. (1991). *Survey of gerontological curricula in Canadian generic baccalaureate nursing programs.* Unpublished master's thesis, University of British Columbia, Vancouver.

First teaching nursing home, Hamilton, Ont. (1989). *Dimensions, 66*(7), 10.

Forbes, W.F., Jackson, J.A., & Kraus, A.S. (1987). *Institutionalization of the elderly in Canada.* Toronto: Butterworths.

Gallagher, E.M. (1985). *A statistical profile of elderly people in the Capital Regional District.* Victoria: Greater Victoria Capital Regional District.

Health and Welfare Canada. (1984). *Adult long term institutional care.* Ottawa: Author.

Health and Welfare Canada. (1989). *Charting Canada's future: A report of the demographic review.* Ottawa: Author.

Health and Welfare Canada. (1990). *Guidelines for establishing standards for services to elderly residents with mental health problems in long-term care facilities.* Ottawa: Author.

Heiskanen, T.A. (1988). Nursing staff's perceptions of work in acute and long term care hospitals. *Journal of Advanced Nursing, 13,* 716-725.

Kane, R.A., & Kane, R.L. (1986). Health care for the elderly in the year 2000: A profile of service needs in the year 2000. Paper presented at the symposium *Health Care for the Elderly in the Year 2000,* November 16-18, 1986, Victoria, B.C.

Mantle, J. (1978). Nursing's contribution to the quality of care. *Journal of Gerontological Nursing, 4,* 34-37.

Mantle, J. (1981). Nursing's care of the aged in Canada. *Journal of Gerontological Nursing, 7,* 671-676.

Mantle, J. (1986). Role of the clinical nurse specialist in gerontology. In Canadian Hospital Association, *Papers from the third national conference on long-term care* (pp. 14-18). Ottawa: Author.

McDaniel, S.A. (1986). *Canada's aging population.* Toronto: Butterworths.

McDonald, S. (Ed.). (1981) *Report of the National Advisory Council on Aging: Priorities for action.* Ottawa: Health and Welfare Canada.

McEwan, K.L., Donnelly, M., Robertson, D., & Hertzman, C. (1991). *Mental health problems among Canada's seniors: Demographic and epidemiological considerations.* Ottawa: Mental Health Division, Health Services and Promotion Branch, Department of National Health and Welfare.

McIvor, V. (1978). Freedom to be: A new approach to quality care for the aged. *The Canadian Nurse, 74*(3), 19-26.

Mental Health Division. Department of National Health and Welfare. (1988). *Guidelines to comprehensive services to elderly persons with psychiatric disorders.* Ottawa: Minister of Supply and Services Canada.

Mezey, M., Lynaugh, J., & Cartier, M. (Eds.). (1989). *Nursing homes and nursing care: Lessons from the Teaching Nursing Homes.* New York: Springer.

Mitchell-Pedersen, L., Edmund, L., Fingerote, E., & Powell, C. (1986, February). Reducing reliance on physical restraints. *Today's Nursing Home, 40,* 42-46.

Mohide, E., French, S., Caulfield, P., Chambers, L., & Bayne, J. (1983, November). Needed: Teaching units in long-term care. *Dimensions,* pp. 18-21.

Mohide, E., French, S., Caulfield, P., Chambers, L., & Bayne, J. (1984). *Development of the long term care teaching unit model in Canada.* Position paper submitted to Canadian Association on Gerontology, Vancouver, B.C.

Murakami, R. (1983). Institutional care for older adults: Commitment to quality care. In E. Gallagher, M. Jackson, & G. Zilm (Eds.), *Proceedings of the First National Conference on Gerontological Nursing,* Vol. 1 (pp. 11-13). Victoria: University of Victoria School of Nursing.

National Advisory Council on Aging. (1989). *1989 and beyond: Challenges of an aging Canadian society.* Ottawa: Author.

Podnieks, E., Laforet-Fliesser, Y., & Brunton, B. (1988). Gerontological education: Meeting the challenge in nursing practice. *Perspectives, 12*(4), 6-10.

Premier's Commission on Future Health Care for Albertans. (1989). *The rainbow report: Our vision for health,* Vol 2. Edmonton: Author.

Rapelje, D.H. (1986, June). Long-term care: An overview. *Canadian Health Care Management,* LT 1:1- 1-6.

Rosendahl, P., & Ross, V. (1982). Does your behavior affect your patient's response? *Journal of Gerontological Nursing, 8*(10), 572-575.

Rutenberg, S. (1988). Reconnecting with the family. *Perspectives, 12*(4), 11-15.

Schneider, E. (Ed.). (1985). *The teaching nursing home: The Beverly Foundation.* New York: Raven Press.

Statistics Canada. (1982). *1981 census of Canada, Vol. 1, national series, populations: Age, sex and marital status.* Ottawa: Ministry of Supply and Services Canada, Catalogue No. 92-901.

Statistics Canada. (1989). *Nursing in Canada: 1987.* Ottawa: Ministry of Supply and Services.

Statistics Canada & Canadian Nurses Association. (1986, January). *Nursing in Canada, 1984.* Ottawa: Canadian Nurses Association.

Stone, L., & Frenken, H. (1988). *Canada's seniors: 1986 census of Canada.* Ottawa: Supply and Services Canada.

Stryker-Gordon, R. (1982). Leadership in care of the elderly: Assessing needs and challenges. *The Journal of Nursing Administration, 12,* 41-44.

Wells, L., Singer, C., & Polgar, A. (1986). *To enhance quality of life in institutions, an empowerment model in long-term care: A partnership of residents, staff and families.* Toronto: Governing Council, University of Toronto.

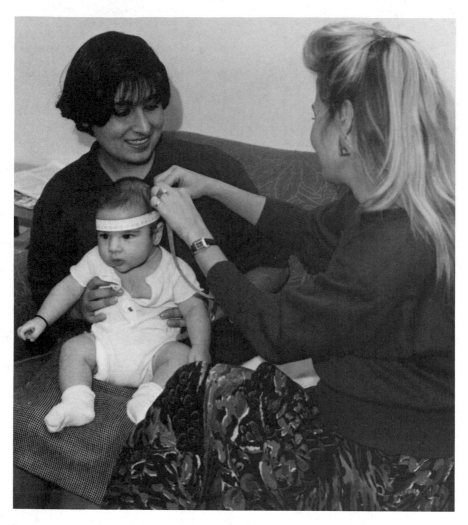

Kathy Knudsen (right), public health nurse for the City of Winnipeg Health Department, measures the head of 3-month-old Tyler during a home visit with new mother Anita Moore. (Photograph by Bob Talbot of the University of Manitoba Communication Services.)

CHAPTER EIGHT

Community Health Nursing Practice

KAREN I. CHALMERS, RN, PhD
LINDA J. KRISTJANSON, RN, PhD

Karen I. Chalmers, RN, BScN (McMaster), MSc(A) (McGill), PhD (Manchester), is Assistant Professor at the School of Nursing, University of Manitoba, where she teaches courses in family and community health. She has worked as a community health nurse in Canada, as well as trained primary health care workers in Nigeria through the Canadian University Services Overseas (CUSO). Her areas of research include community health nurse–client interactions, evaluation of community health nursing interventions, and abilities of clients to cope with long-term illness.

Linda J. Kristjanson, RN, BN (Manitoba), MN (Manitoba), PhD (Arizona), is Assistant Professor, School of Nursing, University of Manitoba. She conducts research, publishes, and has taught in the area of community health and family nursing. She has also maintained an independent practice in the community, helping families coping with terminal illness.

C ommunity health nurses in Canada are concerned with prevention of illness, promotion of health, and provision of home nursing care to clients of all ages living in the community. The work of the community health nurse includes early detection of disease and dysfunction, restorative and rehabilitative measures, and maintenance and promotion of a high standard of health. The range of health problems, of age groups, and of settings has implications for how community health nursing is conceptualized, structured within health care delivery systems, and carried out at the practice level.

This chapter explores issues central to the practice and development of community health nursing in Canada. Historical, societal, and health care factors that have shaped community health nursing practice are highlighted and issues that influence present and future practice are identified. It is our premise that community health nurses play a central role in promoting and maintaining the health of the Canadian population. However, for this practice to develop and flourish, community health nurses must develop their practice roles, re-examine current education for community nursing, and articulate more clearly the place of community health nursing within the discipline.

Although the term *community health nurse* is commonly used to refer to all nurses who practice in the community, some of these nurses are also referred to as public health nurses, community home care nurses, Victorian Order nurses, occupational health nurses, primary health care nurses, and health promotion nurses. In this chapter, the term *community health nurse* will encompass all of these categories.

HISTORICAL FORCES SHAPING COMMUNITY HEALTH NURSING

Several forces shaped the development of community health nursing. These include religious and informal service beginnings of community health nursing in Canada, development of public health practice, legislation that affects health care, and development of professional nursing.

Religious and Informal Service Beginnings

The earliest community health nurses in Canada were women in religious orders who settled in New France. In 1639, three Augustinian sisters arrived in Quebec City to not only provide care to the sick but also to provide necessities of shelter, food, and survival information to settlers and seamen (Allemang, 1985; Gibbon and Mathewson, 1947). In the Hôtel Dieu hospitals and through the sisters' visiting orders, health care was part of the provision of services for the community's survival.

In the century that followed the fall of New France in 1760, the population in Canada grew through immigration, primarily from Great Britain and the British colonies. Community health nursing services continued to be provided by religious orders such as the Grey Nuns (Allemang, 1985), as well as through informal caring networks of women in pioneer communities. This early work contributed to a philosophy of community health nursing concerned with not only the well-being of individuals, but also the health of the community as a whole.

This legacy also fostered a service-oriented approach and a volunteer philosophy that may have limited the recognition of the educational base required to provide nursing care. Consequently, community nursing, and, indeed, nursing as a whole, is still viewed by some today as an occupation of women requiring little formal education or remuneration. Limited resources and funding for community health nursing reflect, in part, this early history.

Public Health Practice

In the 1800s, public health efforts in Canada centered on protection of the new colonies from infectious diseases with quarantine legislation, public ordinances controlling the sale of meat from diseased animals, and organization of sanitary inspections of homes (see Chapter 2). The onslaught of typhoid, cholera, and smallpox epidemics, and the poor nutritional status of the settlers, inadequate housing, and poor water and sewage facilities in the colonies rendered these rudimentary public health measures relatively ineffective.

Although the early public health efforts were appropriate attempts to prevent and control the spread of communicable disease, they were not within an overall policy for community health, but were short-term crisis responses to health problems. The Public Health Act of Upper Canada (now Ontario) in 1833, for example, authorized the formation of a health board, but its power was limited to controlling infectious diseases only when, and if, outbreaks occurred (Rachlis and Kushner, 1989, p. 264). When the crisis was over, the local boards generally became inactive until the next crisis. Major improvements in public health in Canada did not occur until the late 1800s (see Chapter 2) with the development of knowledge about public health sciences.

The basic tenets of public health are illustrated in the classic definition by Winslow (1920) written in the early part of the twentieth century. Public health was defined as:

> the science and art of preventing disease, prolonging life, and promoting health and efficiency through organized community effort for 1) the sanitation of the environment, 2) the control of communicable infections, 3) education of the individual in personal hygiene, 4) the organization of medical and nursing services for the early diagnosis and preventive treatment of disease, and 5) the development of the social machinery to insure everyone a standard of living adequate for the maintenance of health. (Hanlon, 1950, p. 20)

This definition reflects what today is called the public health model. This model describes the relationship among host, agent, and environment as critical to the development and prevention of disease. The extent of exposure of the host (person) to the causative agent (e.g., bacteria), the host's level of susceptibility, and factors within the environment determine whether or not a disease outcome results. This relationship is often referred to as the *host-agent-environment* triangle (Freeman and Heinrich, 1981).

Public health departments were developed by municipalities and provinces early in the 1900s to control the spread of communicable diseases and to promote health. Nurses became the primary workers in bringing public health to families and communities (Emory, 1953). Within this model, the focus for the nurse was on screening programs to detect diseases early or to determine individuals at high risk. Measures then were taken to limit the spread of disease and thereby protect the health of the entire community. For example, case finding for tuberculosis centered in schools and mobile x-ray units; when tuberculosis was detected, contact tracing through follow-up home visiting was done to identify and treat the original source of infection.

With the passage of time, and as many communicable diseases were brought under control, the emphasis of public health nursing changed, and nurses addressed different health problems. Today, these health problems include: chronic illnesses, concerns of an aging population, complexities of high technology care now provided in the home, and health problems of families experiencing developmental changes and social stresses such as poverty. To a large extent, however, the predominant nursing interventions of nurses functioning within the traditional public health model remain active case finding through assessment and screening procedures, and ongoing surveillance and monitoring. Implications of this approach for current practice will be discussed later.

Legislation

Several legislative acts influenced the structure and delivery of community health nursing services. In 1867, the British North America Act allocated the federal government jurisdiction over quarantine practices and the establishment and maintenance of marine hospitals; the provinces assumed responsibility for the maintenance and management of hospitals, asylums, and welfare services. This historical event resulted in a provincially dominated yet federally influenced health care system that focused on immediate illness needs.

While the federal government assumed jurisdiction over quarantine practices at points of entry to Canada, protection of the local community's health was legislated through a series of provincial public health ordinances and acts. The development of public health sciences and legislation in Great Britain, however, led to recognition of the need for more permanent measures to protect the community's health. The British Public Health Act of 1875 became the model for similar acts in the Canadian provinces (Sutherland and Fulton, 1988). These acts provided for establishment of permanent boards of health to safeguard the community's health. Today the provinces have health acts that specify regulations regarding control of communicable diseases and sanitation. Nurses working in public health agencies have the authority, through these acts, to use measures to limit the spread of diseases. For example, a public health nurse in Manitoba may suspend from school a child who is infected with chickenpox.

A series of more recent acts also influenced the structure and delivery of community health nursing services. The implementation of the Hospital Insurance and Diagnostic Services Act of 1957 and the Medical Care Act of 1966 ensured Canadians access to medical and hospital care without concerns of direct payment (Iglehart, 1986). These acts also contributed to a trend toward illness-oriented, hospital and medically dominated health care services, an outcome that today has implications for public health services.

The Federal-Provincial Fiscal Arrangements and Established Programmes Financing Act of 1977 changed the financial payment system from 50-50 cost sharing between the federal government and the provinces to block funding linked to the growth of the gross national product (GNP). In addition, this act provided a per capita grant (indexed to the GNP) to assist provinces in providing less expensive support services. These support services include nursing home care, adult home care services, and ambulatory care services as alternatives to hospital care. Many provinces used these monies to develop more adequate long-term care facilities (Iglehart, 1986), and the primary outcome was a strengthening of services based in institutions and not in the community.

In 1984, the Canada Health Act replaced the Medical Care and Hospital Insurance and Diagnostic Services Acts in an attempt to protect the principles of the medical health insurance acts: universality, portability among provinces, comprehensiveness, and public administration and accountability (see Chapter 2). Although this is a laudable national achievement, the emphasis on funding for hospital and medical care in the provinces continues to overshadow preventive and community health services.

Professional Nursing

The development of professional nursing also influenced the structure and delivery of community health nursing in Canada. Florence Nightingale, although most widely known for the development of modern nursing, had a major impact on community health. As a sanitary and social reformer, she successfully campaigned for improved environmental health and workhouse reforms in Great Britain in the 1860s and 1870s (Monteiro, 1986). Florence Nightingale also influenced the development of what in Great Britain is called *district nursing,* a service initially for the poor. She emphasized the need for "health nursing" in addition to "sickness nursing."

Influenced by the success of district nurses in providing home nursing and sanitary education, the Victorian Order of Nurses (VON) was established in 1897 in Canada (see Chapter 30). VON nurses received additional preparation in midwifery and district nursing. Their practice involved not only care for the sick and dying and for women in childbirth, but also teaching about health and provision of practical services such as cleaning and preparing food. Despite the additional training of these early nurses and their recognized caring expertise, they responded to the needs in a particular situation, regardless of whether these were strictly nursing care needs. Because of this traditional concern for the overall needs of the client and the fact that other resources may simply be unavailable, nurses today still struggle to define appropriate nursing functions.

This history of responding to the needs of individuals, families, and communities characterized community health nursing during the twentieth century. Canadian community health nursing practice did not clearly distinguish between preventive community health nursing and direct home nursing, as for example occurred in Great Britain. Community health nursing in the twentieth century focused on both the provision of nursing care and the protection of the whole community's health. In addition to providing direct home nursing services, for example, the VON participated actively in public health efforts. One objective of the VON in 1929 related to assisting in training nurses in public health nursing (Emory, 1953). Funding difficulties in many small municipalities, particularly in the western and northern regions of Canada, prevented local governments from hiring public health nurses. Victorian Order nurses in many communities provided preventive community health functions, as well as home nursing, into the 1940s and early 1950s (see Chapter 30).

In some provinces, such as New Brunswick, VON continues to fulfill these dual roles.

Community health nursing's dual focus on (a) direct care of clients in the community and (b) promotion of the health of the entire community continued to characterize community health nursing in the 1960s and 1970s. This focus on multiple roles in the community, preventive and direct care to many different groups, and measures directed to communities, individuals, and families is reflected formally in a national definition of community health nursing. This national perspective is described in the booklet *The nurse and community health: functions and qualifications for practice* (Canadian Public Health Association, 1977; 1984). A review of this booklet was begun in 1989 by a task force coordinated by the Canadian Public Health Association with financial support from Health and Welfare Canada. In the 1984 document, community health nursing is defined as:

> professional nursing that focuses its attention on the health needs of people throughout their life span on a health-illness continuum. In collaboration with the client and other health workers, the nurse combines a knowledge of community health problems, practices, and resources, and the nursing process. She [sic] thus assists the individual, family, and/or community to assume responsibility for sound health practices and to achieve an optimum state of health and self reliance. (p. 3)

In this conceptualization, community health nursing encompasses both illness and health care to individuals, families, groups, and communities. Community health nursing is seen not simply as nursing "in" the community, but also as practice undertaken to improve the health of the entire community. It is this focus on breadth of roles, functions, and levels of community health nursing practice that is both an advantage to the community health care system and a source of some confusion regarding the role of community health nurses. The general role preparation of community health nurses allowed the VON, for example, to adapt to political and health care changes that influenced their practice. This resulted in innovative and progressive practice options such as adult day care programs in British Columbia and occupational health programs in Alberta. However, a more amorphous community health nursing identity can also contribute to a lack of control over practice and a less visible place in the health care system. The implications of this generalist role will be discussed in terms of present day and future practice.

COMMUNITY HEALTH NURSING TODAY

Community health nurses make up approximately 10% of all registered nurses in Canada (Table 8-1) and function in a variety of practices. These practices include: public health nursing, home care nursing, occupational health nursing, nursing in community health centers, and various health promotion roles.

Public health nurses are community health nurses who work in provincial, regional, or municipal public health departments. These departments receive funding from provincial, municipal, or combined sources. Public health nurses carry out many programs to prevent illness and promote the health of people, including prenatal classes, well baby clinics, immunization clinics, services to school age chil-

TABLE 8-1 **Nurses Employed in Community Health by Province, 1988**

Province	Total nurses	Number employed in community health	Percentage employed in community health (%)
Canada	210,506	20,890	10
Newfoundland	4304	300	7
Prince Edward Island	1064	73	7
Nova Scotia	8366	396	5
New Brunswick	6398	381	6
Quebec	53,832	5482	10
Ontario	75,116	8820	12
Manitoba	8996	653	7
Saskatchewan	8231	645	8
Alberta	20,171	2001	10
British Columbia	23,728	2096	9
Territories*	300	43	14

Compiled from Registered Nurses Management Data 1988, Health Manpower Statistics Section, Health Division, Statistics Canada, 613-951-1758.
*Because of the method of reporting, statistics from the Yukon and Northwest Territories are grouped together.

dren such as health teaching and screening for vision and hearing problems, foot clinics for the elderly, home visiting of new mothers and babies, and work with high risk or vulnerable groups. In some provinces (e.g., Manitoba and Saskatchewan), public health nurses also provide nursing services for postnatal mothers discharged from hospital within 48 hours and home-based nursing care for women with pregnancy-induced hypertension. A small but important part of public health nurses' day-to-day work is control of communicable diseases. This work is mandated through health acts in each province, such as the Health Protection and Promotion Act of 1983 of Ontario.

Other community health nurses provide home nursing services through government-run home care programs or nongovernmental health organizations such as the VON and the St. Elizabeth Visiting Nurses in Ontario. These services entail direct nursing care in the community and supervision and coordination of other workers who provide home-based services. One goal of these services is to maintain people in the community, delaying or eliminating the need for institutional care. These services are directed at different target populations in the community such as the mentally incompetent (e.g., Alzheimer's patients and their families) or those with terminal illness requiring palliative care.

Community health nurses may also provide services to children with disabilities who are integrated into regular community schools. This work involves interventions such as educating teachers about specific health needs of these children, training health aides to perform such procedures as catheterizations, collaborating with parents about care needs, and giving direct care.

Home care services are organized in different ways from province to province. Some are delivered as separate provincial programs (e.g., Manitoba), as part of regional public health services, (e.g., British Columbia and Ontario), through community ambulatory care centers (e.g., Quebec), or out of hospitals (e.g., some areas of Ontario) (Sutherland and Fulton, 1988).

Home care services may be organized into short- and long-term programs. Some agencies provide both types of programs (e.g., New Brunswick VON), and others provide only one type. For instance, in Winnipeg, short-term home care is provided by VON, and the long-term care needs are provided by a provincial home care program. As well, comparisons of services from province to province are difficult because definitions of what constitutes short-term and long-term care programs vary.

Occupational health nurses are community health nurses employed by industries and companies to provide health care and preventive services to workers. These services include education of workers about the use of protective equipment and procedures to protect health on the job, inspection of work sites for health hazards, screening for early detection of disease, health assessments, and general health education and counselling. Occupational health nurses may work with interdisciplinary teams of occupational physicians, industrial hygienists, and safety engineers, or function as the sole occupational health practitioner. Some companies that cannot afford to hire a nurse may purchase community health nursing services from nursing organizations such as the VON. At present, most occupational health nurses have additional training beyond diploma or degree preparation, but this is not mandatory or universal. Occupational health nurses have formed a national association, the National Association of Occupational Health Nurses. Through a related organization, the Canadian Council of Occupational Health Nurses, they are working toward certification. As with many groups in nursing, occupational health nurses are attempting to identify the unique body of knowledge needed for practice in occupational health settings and to provide a means of certifying nurses who meet the knowledge requirements. In 1984, occupational health nurses numbered approximately 4000 (Canadian Occupational Health and Safety News, 1984), approximately 2% of all registered nurses. Considering the opportunities for health promotion and illness prevention efforts within occupational settings, the small number of occupational health nurses limits the effect that this important community health nursing group could have on the health status of Canadians.

Community health nurses also work in community health centers, providing health assessments and nursing care, health education, and health counselling. In the 1970s, community health centers were introduced as a way to provide high-quality primary health care at reasonable costs. Through the use of multidisciplinary teams of physicians, nurses, social workers, and other health workers, a range of health, social, and health educational services are provided to meet local community needs. The Intercommunity Health Center in London, Ontario, for example, is located downtown in an underserviced area of the city. The health center attempts to reach out to "street people" and new immigrants and provide relevant health and social services.

Although many community health centers were developed in the provinces over the years, Quebec was the province that most ambitiously developed these centers. In Quebec today more than 160 Centres locaux de services communitaires, or CLSCs, provide community health and social services (Rachlis and Kushner, 1989). It is through CLSCs that nurses provide home care services, as well as other primary health care and health education services.

Community health nurses also provide primary health care services in remote areas of provinces and territories. As the entry point to the health care system, these community health nurses provide health promotion and support services, rehabilitation care, acute care, emergency treatment, and referral services. According to a 1990 survey (Recruitment and Retention Study, Northwest Territories, 1990), approximately 50% of nurses in the Northwest Territories are working in community health and public health centers, and the remainder are employed in hospitals of less than 100 beds. (This statistic is different from the figures shown in Table 8-1; the latter indicates that only 14% of nurses in the Northwest Territories are employed in community health. This discrepancy may be because a broader definition of community health nursing and/or more precise data collection methods were used in the Northwest Territories survey. This difference emphasizes the need for more consistent reporting methods across the country.)

Beyond the question of numbers is the importance of understanding the unique role of community health nurses in the North. In the absence of physicians and other secondary health services, the nurse in an isolated community performs an expanded role in primary health care and may perform procedures and treatments such as prescribing medication, providing x-ray interpretation, obtaining blood samples, and suturing (see Chapter 9). Through regional health boards and community health committees, a mechanism for participation of the public in the planning, administration, and evaluation of health care is ensured. The community health nurse has a key role as an advisor to these community health committees.

In more urban settings, health centers emerged that focus more specifically on health promotion services to individuals and groups. Although nurses in all community health nursing settings provide health promotion services, nurses working in these newer settings have a more focused role in health promotion through education and community development initiatives. The York Centre for Health, for example, is a health promotion center sponsored by the City of York Board of Health and Council and the Ministry of Health for Ontario. Community health nurses in this center work collaboratively with individuals and groups to help them identify their health needs and develop approaches to meet their health goals. The center also employs the services of a health promotion coordinator (a public health nurse with master's level preparation in health promotion) who provides community wide health promotive services.

Community health nurses also work in other roles and settings. For example, on Vancouver Island, community health nurses work for the Nuu-chah-nulth Tribal Council, providing health promotion and prevention services to aboriginal peoples on 14 reserves. These nurses are responsible to the health board of the Tribal Council. They work with residents to plan and implement health care programs that are congruent with cultural and social values and health beliefs.

TABLE 8-2 Frequency and Percent Distributions of Community Health Nurses in Each Province by Highest Level of Education in Nursing, 1988

Level of education	New-found-land		Prince Edward Island		Nova Scotia		New Brunswick		Quebec		Ontario	
	N	(%)	N	(%)	N	(%)	N	(%)	N	(%)	N	(%)
Registered nurse diploma	65	22	30	41	131	33	174	46	2581	47	4767	54
Post-basic diploma certificate	147	49	20	27	150	38	58	15	1881	34	1265	14
Baccalaureate	85	28	22	30	112	28	144	38	933	17	2698	31
Masters/higher	3	1	1	1	3	1	5	1	87	2	90	1
TOTAL	300	100	73	99†	396	100	381	99†	5482	100	8820	100

Compiled from Registered Nurses Management Data 1988, Health Manpower Statistics Section, Health Division, Statistics Canada, 613-951-1758.
*Due to reporting procedures, Yukon statistics are included with those of the Northwest Territories.
†Greater/less than 100% due to rounding.
N, Number of nurses.

The positions that nurses assume in the community health care system also vary. Data from Statistics Canada (1988) indicate that approximately 19% (3000) of community health nurses in Canada are in administrative roles. The majority, 61% (12,704), function at the field level of practice. Only 1% of those employed in community health nursing classify themselves as clinical specialists. These data indicate that 18% classify their positions as "other." When this figure is combined with "missing data" (3%), there is unspecified and incomplete information for 21% of the Canadian community health nursing work force.

Educational preparation for nurses working in community health positions varies from province to province. National work force figures for 1988 show that the highest educational level for 46% is the registered nurse diploma, whereas 24% have a post-basic certificate, 30% have baccalaureate preparation, and 1% have master's degrees or higher (see Table 8-2). Information showing a breakdown of education and practice area is not available, but information from provincial department sources indicates that nurses prepared at the diploma level generally provide home care and baccalaureate prepared nurses fill public health roles.

Unfortunately, information presented in Table 8-2 may be misleading because of

Manitoba		Saskatchewan		Alberta		British Columbia		Territories*		Canada	
N	(%)	N	(%)	N	(%)	N	(%)	N	(%)	N	(%)
240	37	307	48	705	35	541	26	9	21	9550	46
120	18	108	17	475	24	689	33	18	42	4931	24
293	45	230	36	804	40	816	39	16	37	6153	30
—	—	—	—	17	1	50	2	—	—	256	1
653	100	645	101†	2001	100	2096	100	43	100	20,890	101†

the data collection methods used, differing definitions of community health nursing, and individual and regional differences in coding. For example, data in Table 8-2 indicate that only 28% of community health nurses in Nova Scotia are prepared at the baccalaureate level. However, according to Janet Braunstein of the Nova Scotia Department of Health and Fitness, 47% of nurses employed by the department, which is the major employer of community health nurses, have baccalaureate preparation. This significant discrepancy suggests that broad conclusions should be avoided.

Despite the limitations of the data, it is still evident that the diversity of educational preparation of community health nurses contributes to a lack of solidarity within the discipline. As well, the lack of nurses prepared at the master's level results in a shortage of health care planners and community health nursing leaders. Therefore the blend of educational preparation among community health nurses is a factor that influences how roles and practice are defined.

The role of the community health nurse is partly determined, as well, by geography (e.g., rural versus urban), by the needs of a particular community (e.g., palliative care), and by the policy directions for community health care in the area.

CONCEPTUAL FRAMEWORK OF COMMUNITY HEALTH NURSING

After discussion with representatives of community health nursing from each of the provinces, we concluded that, despite regional variations in practice, a common conceptual framework for Canadian community health nursing practice today could be identified, and issues of mutual concern pinpointed.

Community health nursing has been influenced by structural factors such as setting, policy decisions, funding sources, and administrative frameworks for practice. The emphasis has been on multiple roles directed at various target groups across the age span and at different points along the health-illness continuum. Also, community health nurses practice at different levels of the system, from the individual to the large community aggregate. A representation of the framework of community health nursing practice today is presented in Figure 8-1.

Structural Factors

The structure within which practice occurs provides the boundaries and constraints for nursing roles and priorities. Structure is likely the key determinant of community health nursing practice. Nursing has had to struggle in the past and present to influence and direct decisions at the structural level of community health practice.

One aspect of structure is the funding base for community nursing services. Traditionally, there have been two ways of funding: per client contact or block. Funding influences the nature of the interaction between clients and nurses by shaping the purpose of the interaction, the available time, and the priority for service.

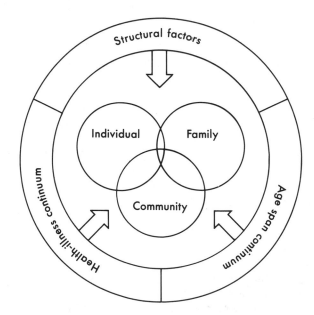

FIGURE 8-1 Conceptual framework for community health nursing practice in the 1990s.

For example, a nurse working within a home-visiting service funded on a per visit basis in response to a specific health concern, such as a dressing change, may not be able to allocate the time to address health issues of other family members. However, individual nurses who feel responsibility for these other needs may provide unfunded, but needed, services. This results in unfunded and unrecognized nursing practice—a kind of invisible nursing care. In contrast, a public health department funded by block funds may allow the nurse more scope to explore other health issues. Nurses in this system, however, may still be restricted by focused program objectives determined by funding priorities.

Ideally, the funding structure should permit the nurse and the nursing service to respond flexibly and to anticipate health issues. This structure could allow a greater proportion of resources to be directed toward primary health care efforts to address health concerns early before health problems become more entrenched.

The stability of the funding base is critical to effective community health nursing practice and planning. In the 1950s and 1960s government health care funds were more plentiful, and fund-raising efforts by agencies such as the VON declined. Recently, government funds have become more scarce and the VON is identifying the need to resume fund-raising efforts to supplement operating budgets. In some provinces (e.g., British Columbia), the government has taken over home care service delivery, believing that centralized control might be more cost effective than contracting with a number of different agencies for services. In fact, this has not happened. The VON has adapted by identifying gaps in health care service delivery and targeting programs in these areas. Provision of community health nursing care in this type of unstable financial arrangement does not permit long-term planning and evaluation of services. Coordination of services is often a problem when a number of governmental departments share the responsibility for community health care delivery (e.g., home care). A home health aide from the VON, for example, may report to both a supervising nurse in the VON and a provincial home care nurse who coordinates a specific case. Duplication and fragmentation of health care services in this approach to service delivery cannot be cost effective.

The administrative structure of community health delivery systems also affects practice. Practice may be organized around a discipline-specific model or a multidisciplinary program delivery model. For example, public health nurses may work in a system that is organized with a nursing supervisor as the first-line manager and a director of public health nursing as the senior administrator. When the client's needs are beyond the scope of public health nursing services, consultation with other professionals in other agencies is sought.

Other public health nurses may work as part of a multidisciplinary team of social workers, home care nurses, home economists, and other professionals who provide services to designated target groups in the community. Multidisciplinary program delivery may result in less duplication of services at the field level and a system more responsive to the multiple needs of clients (although this assumption has yet to be empirically evaluated). However, program-focused delivery creates difficulty in identifying accountability and in isolating and evaluating the nursing component of care. As a result, effective nursing input may not be specifically identifiable. Also, the manager of the team may be any one of the previously mentioned professionals. Consequently, community health nurses working within this structure may be accountable to a non-nurse manager who does not share the same knowledge base and professional concerns. Therefore this organizational structure may perpetuate the absence of community health nursing representation at administrative and decision-making levels of the system.

An additional problem facing current community health nurses is the lack of control over practice that derives from multiple administrative structures. For example, in Saskatchewan, regional boards administer community health services for a particular geographic community. Funding for these services comes from the provincial government. These regional boards are composed primarily of lay representatives and local politicians. The boards may or may not have formal input from a community health nurse yet wield considerable power in terms of funding and resource allocation. Consequently, community health nursing goals, control of educational requirements for community health nurses, and standards for practice are determined to a large extent by these external forces.

In Nova Scotia, a comprehensive home care program was recently developed. This program is administered by five government departments. This may create problems in terms of practice control, achieving consensus on budgetary allocations, and program accountability. However, Nova Scotia recently instituted an interim computerized central data base system that will provide information about community health nursing, homemaker, volunteer, and housing services, and program outcomes. This is a laudable achievement and is one needed in all provinces.

The conservative versus progressive orientation of the community health structure further determines the roles and functions of community health nursing at the discipline level and at the individual practitioner level. For instance, those in community health nursing leadership roles may take a progressive, pro-active stance by initiating health care delivery changes. This requires leaders with political prowess and a goal-oriented approach who will question and use the system to improve health and health care delivery. A good example of this type of pro-active effort occurred in Alberta recently when the government assumed home care services previously provided by VON. The VON responded by identifying gaps in health care delivery and developed a "People in Crisis" program to meet the needs of battered women and their children and homeless teenagers. This program is now administered in seven shelters by nurses and social workers. Nurses conduct health assessments and provide health education and counselling. In contrast to a progressive orientation, nursing leaders may take a more conservative, "status quo" stance that results in maintenance of the present structure. Although there may be promotion of some changes within the system, overall a tolerance or an acceptance of current conditions prevails.

The point of this dichotomy is that leadership in community health nursing is critical to the direction of community health policy and warrants progressive, politically astute leaders. Community health nursing in recent years has lacked a cadre of highly visible and influential leaders. A notable exception is Dr. Helen Glass, past president of the Canadian Nurses Association and former first vice president of the International Council of Nurses. At provincial, national, and international levels, she has been a central force in the primary health care movement (WHO, 1978). Furthermore, she has advocated strongly that nursing has a key role in delivering primary health care services, and that nurses can be used as the "point of first contact" for people into the health care system (Glass, 1984). Her philosophy of community-based health care is well respected and known throughout international health care organizations. It is this type of leadership that is needed. Without such direction, community health nursing will not have an active role in strengthening and developing community health programs and may also run the risk of losing current program resources.

Age Span Continuum

A second influence within the conceptual framework of community health nursing practice is the fact that community health nurses provide services to clients across the age span from birth to death and in the bereavement period that follows. The fact that community health nurses provide care to this range of clients is one of the primary reasons for the traditional generalist role. To provide this breadth of care, community health nurses must have a sound understanding of normal growth and development and the impact of illness and situational crises at each stage of the life span. Focusing on this broad client age range further requires specific knowledge of health concerns and problems unique to different life stages (e.g., baby bottle caries, pregnancy, Type II diabetes, osteoporosis).

Considering the increasing volume of science related to health issues in different age groups (e.g., gerontology, neonatology) and changes in health care needs, the expectation that all community health nurses continue to be knowledgeable about all health concerns for all target groups warrants re-examination for future practice. For instance, approximately 80% to 85% of community home care services are provided to the elderly. In the future it may become more feasible for community health nurses to concentrate their education and practice on a particular age group (e.g., elderly) or client focus (e.g., chronically ill).

Health–Illness Continuum

Community health nurses also provide services to clients experiencing a range of health concerns. For example, public health nurses offer preventive health teaching and care to new mothers, well babies, and children. The same nurses provide care to elderly individuals experiencing limitations from chronic illness and social isolation. These nurses may also address the needs of a low income family dealing with problems of poverty, inadequate housing, and lack of social support. Interventions directed during this encounter might include an advocacy role and teaching and counselling functions. Today's public health nurses may also be dealing with communicable diseases, drug related problems in the adolescent school population, and educational needs of expectant parents and special needs groups. The cross cultural dimension of the role only adds to the complexity and demands on this health professional.

A similar practice situation may exist for nurses involved in the delivery of home nursing services. For example, a home visiting nurse is expected to be knowledgeable about psychosocial and physiological health problems across the age span. The nurse is also required to have specific content knowledge related to disease specific conditions such as symptom management of cancer, medications and treatments, and specific technical skills (e.g., oxygen therapy). Patients are now being discharged home with specialized nursing care needs; a few years ago these same patients were nursed in the acute care hospital in which the nurse had ready access to nursing and medical consultation. For example, in Ontario a number of early discharge programs resulted in more high technology care being given at home (e.g., home dialysis). Therefore, today's community health nurse is assuming greater responsibility for a higher risk, more acutely ill population without on-site health team back-up resources. The implications of this change for education and service structure are considerable.

Levels of Practice

Figure 8-1 also illustrates the levels of practice that community health nursing addresses. These levels are the individual, the family, and the community. Attention to the health needs of each of these levels requires different skills and reflects different priorities.

Depending on the structure within which practice is defined, the level of service may vary. For example, the community health nurse may focus on individuals and the family level of care as directed by community health policy and program delivery decisions (e.g., well baby clinics, home visits). The agency may also direct services at the community level through immunization efforts and public education programs about target health problems (e.g., risks associated with alcohol use during pregnancy).

A good example of an agency's ability to provide service at the aggregate level comes from the work of the VON. In one Newfoundland community, the VON provides a "health club" service to individuals needing exercise and weight control assistance. This is a particular problem in certain areas of Newfoundland where the diet is rich in high-salt fish and obesity is a health risk. Such a program is effective in addressing a concern common to residents in a community and makes more effective use of nursing time than individual health teaching or counselling sessions.

Although today's community health nurses demonstrate considerable flexibility and range in terms of the levels of service they provide, there is an emerging sentiment that the generalist approach across practice levels is more difficult to maintain given the increasing complexity of communities and the community health care system. Therefore the knowledge and skills required to function at the various levels must be acknowledged in view of this increasing complexity. This range and complexity of practice necessitates a critical re-examination of future nursing education and practice.

ISSUES

Various issues arise from this brief examination of community health nursing practice. Some issues involve the broader discipline level of community health nursing. Others are classified as practice level issues related to the day-to-day concerns of the front-line community health nurse.

Issues of the Community Health Nursing Profession

The three major issues facing community health nurses at the broader professional level are:

1. The theoretical basis of community health nursing
2. Educational preparation
3. Sociopolitical factors

The first issue concerns the theoretical basis for community health practice. Community health nursing developed in response to needs of individuals and communities. Many community health nursing practices were based on common sense, intuition, ritual, and tradition, as well as medical and public health science (Hamilton and Bush, 1988). Until recently there has been little empirical research and theory development in community health nursing. Many theories and models that are used to conceptualize and direct practice, such as systems theory and community change theory, are largely borrowed from other disciplines without a careful examination of their applicability with the assumptions underlying practice. This is not surprising given nursing's state of theory development (see Chapters 16 and 22). In addition, much of the theory applied in community nursing practice is based on the individual as the recipient of care rather than on the community as a whole or aggregates such as the family. Community health nursing also lacks diagnostic categories related to the community as the focus of care. As Higgs and Gustafson (1987) state, most of the nursing diagnoses used by the profession are based on care for the ill, hospitalized individual.

Existing models used to direct practice may no longer provide an adequate conceptualization for today's practice. The traditional public health model, for example, which was developed during the period of devastating epidemics, places emphasis on the public health professional as the definer of the health problem. When applied to nursing, the nurse detects the problem, seeks out the client, and attempts to intervene. The client may or may not be aware of, or interested in, the health concern as the nurse defines it and may not be wanting service. The preventive perspective and concern for the health of the total population that this history emphasizes are aspects of the model that should be retained and fostered. However, specific efforts to establish collaborative relationships with clients to secure mutual goals for health are more appropriate to today's practice environment and health problems. For example, the McGill Model of Nursing emphasizes collaborative work between the nurse and client (Gotlieb and Rowat, 1989). A nurse working within this model uses the client's definition of the health situation as a starting point for a working relationship. A client concerned about a sleeping problem, for example, might be encouraged to monitor, observe, and record circumstances related to the problem. In doing so, the client actively participates in clarifying the health concern, invests energy in seeking a solution, and helps to identify workable interventions. This more collaborative approach to working with people is currently being used to some extent and is recommended in the more recent public health literature (Baum, 1988; Kickbush, 1987; Labonte, 1989; Martin and McQueen, 1989).

In addition to the lack of community health nursing theories and models, there is also a paucity of empirical research on practice, particularly community level of practice (Highriter, 1984; Sills and Goeppinger, 1985). This lack of research results in practice that is not grounded in well-tested and evaluated interventions. With little research, "good" community health nursing practice remains largely invisible. For community nursing care to be identifiable and therefore open to evaluation, attention to defining community nursing interventions, articulating the community nurse-client relationship process, isolating outcome criteria, and developing reliable and valid measurement tools must be the focus of ongoing research.

The second major issue facing community health nurses is the educational preparation needed for practice today. In 1982 the Canadian Nurses Association adopted the position statement that by the year 2000 baccalaureate nursing education will be the entry level for nursing practice (Canadian Nurses Association, 1982; see Chapter 21). The nature of this education and the implications of this recommendation for community health nursing are significant. Community health nursing has a tradition of recognizing baccalaureate preparation as the desirable level of entry into practice (Spelman, 1981). However, questions related to the characteristics, goals, and functions of baccalaureate nursing education have concerned nursing educators, administrators, and practitioners in recent years. Traditionally, baccalaureate nursing education prepares nurses for a generalist role. Can nursing continue to do this given the increasing complexity and diversity of roles within which nurses are expected to function? Furthermore, is it reasonable to continue to prepare all baccalaureate nursing students for a generalist community role? Is community health nursing a specialty requiring further preparation? And if so, what should this specialty entail? Should it be a focused area of community health practice or further preparation as an advanced generalist? The issue of specialization within nursing is currently under discussion by many provincial and national nursing organizations (see Chapter 17).

The community health nurse has been described as a teacher, coordinator, planner, counsellor, facilitator, evaluator, caregiver, and consumer advocate (Searl, Stewart, and Kociol, 1985; Spelman, 1981; Stanhope and Lancaster, 1988; Stewart, 1985). Spelman (1981) further argues that university based education that includes knowledge of social, biological, organizational, behavioral, and educational sciences is necessary to produce competent community nurses. We concur and state further that the position of "advanced generalist" in the Canadian community health care system is imperative. Such an individual provides a holistic and systemic perspective that is lacking in the current highly specialized and fragmented health services.

Unfortunately, conflict still arises among community health nurses who cannot agree on educational requirements for practice and who see themselves in a more competitive rather than collaborative role. This internal divisiveness thwarts the profession's advancement and must be halted if community health nursing in the health care system is to flourish.

A third group of issues affecting community health nurses as a professional group is based on sociopolitical factors. For instance, community health nurses are informally organized nationally and voluntarily under the Canadian Public Health Association and the Community Health Nurses Association of Canada. These groups provide a mechanism for communicating public health concerns, taking leadership in community health problems, and stimulating continuing education for community health professionals. Many community health nurses have provided constructive leadership and direction within the Canadian Public Health Association. The Community Health Nurses Association of Canada was founded in 1987 (Community Health Nurses Association of Canada, 1990). This group has a membership of more than 2000 nurses representing approximately 10.5% of community health nurses in Canada. This organization is making efforts to increase its membership, to lobby decision-making bodies at the national level, and to develop position statements related to community health issues.

A particular obstacle to the development of a national voice, however, has been that power and control of community health nursing practice are more difficult to amass when nurses are divided into small groups with community nursing practice delivered under different municipal, regional, provincial, and voluntary structures. Although the preservation of local autonomy and provision of services that are responsive to particular regional needs is a positive feature, this regionalization creates disparity in Canada in terms of availability, type, and quality of community health nursing services. For example, Centretown Community Health Centre in Ottawa provides provincially funded health promotion programs to adults, the elderly, and low-income women (Healthstyles: A Report of a Community Health Promotion Demonstration Project, 1986; Healthstyles '87 (1989); Keep Well, 1988; Turning Point, 1987). In other jurisdictions, such as Manitoba, home care services consume a greater proportion of the community health care dollar. Although development of regional programs in response to local needs is valuable, there may still be gaps in services (e.g., home care). Regional efforts to address these service gaps are more effective when a large national organization can provide assistance such as background position papers, statistical data, and planning and implementation advice.

As well, Canada's enormous size and the relative isolation of some regions make easy collaboration and frequency of dialogue regarding community health issues another barrier to national solidarity. Still, if community health nurses want to have an effect on policies and legislation related to the delivery of community health nursing and community health care, strengthening this national organization is imperative. Community health nurses must lobby for provincial and regional health goals, a secure funding base for their services, and representation of community health nursing at all decision-making levels of community health care delivery.

A related issue involves the fact that a number of social policies and legal mandates emanating from different political sources affect community health care. For example, child abuse reporting and prevention legislation, organization of delivery of services to AIDS victims, environmental hazards legislation, public health smoking ordinances, legislation related to health care insurance, and changes in mental health care policy are just some of the directives that influence community health nursing practice. For community health nurses to have a voice at regional and federal levels of policy decisions and legislation, knowledge related to these issues and forces is required.

As well, community health nurses must recognize and respect philosophies and priorities unique to different regions of Canada, while maintaining open dialogue with each other. This can occur, for example, through the auspices of the provincial and national community health nursing associations. Nurses can work collaboratively and collectively to develop position statements and briefs on issues that have national or provincial importance for the health of Canadians. The protection of the environment and child abuse prevention policies are examples of issues that transcend regional concerns.

There is also a need for leaders in community health nursing who are prepared with the requisite sociopolitical skills to function at the regional, municipal, and federal levels of the system. This is a particular concern in a female dominated profession in which the majority of professionals may lack experience, educational preparation, or confidence to function at the sociopolitical level. Cohesion through formal and informal networks, commitment to long-term goals, and development of community health nursing leaders is essential. For example, in Saskatchewan the Community Health Nurses Interest Group is developing a position statement on the role of community health nurses in health promotion and illness prevention to present to the provincial government. This action is in response to a growing concern that community health nursing and its role in health promotion is being eroded. Representatives from that province believe that the reason for the erosion is partly a lack of understanding by governments about what community health nurses actually do. The public may equate community health nurses with only looking after babies and may not recognize the broader role of community health nursing with different age groups, target groups, and levels of practice. This may also be influenced by stereotypical views about nurses in general and historical undervaluing of "women's work." Therefore formal action to correct these misconceptions is critical.

Cohesion among community health nurses, along with sociopolitical competence, is imperative if the range of community health nursing services is to be maintained and strengthened. Community health services today receive a small proportion of provincial health care budgets. Although the precise amount is difficult to determine because of differing methods of reporting, estimates range from 5% to 10% of the provincial health budget (Canadian Nurses Association, 1988; Health and Welfare Canada, 1987). Restricted community health budgets influence the kinds and scope of community health nursing programs.

The current practice in some jurisdictions of early discharge of hospitalized patients is another threat to the preventive and health promotion component of community health nursing. Early discharge programs transfer patients to public health nursing care without an adequate transfer of funds to the community health nursing program. This is occurring at the same time that more health promotion and prevention is being advocated (Epp, 1986; Podborski et al., 1987) and new roles such as community development are being encouraged for community health nursing (Doucette, 1989; Flynn, Ray, and Selmanoff, 1987).

Limited budgets have contributed to a community nursing delivery system aimed primarily at "hands on" home care services (e.g., vitamin B_{12} injections), preventive and health promotion programs limited to specific population groups (e.g., pregnant adolescents), and an emphasis on high-risk groups (e.g., isolated elderly). For example, in some regions of Saskatchewan, community health nurses are expected to assume two public health districts instead of one, and nurses report feeling over-loaded. With additional funding, more primary health care and health care services could be implemented for a wider range of clients and more nursing action directed at the community level.

With the need for adequate funding is a growing demand for accountable services. In Saskatchewan, for example, the provincial government is requiring greater ac-countability from regional boards related to funding and services provided. This pressure will contribute to the belief among community health nurses that a data base that captures services and health outcomes and isolates more clearly the role of a community health nurse in the system will result in better planning and service delivery.

Practice Level Issues

There are two major practice issues affecting the day-to-day work of community health nurses: educational needs specific to the role and legal and ethical issues.

First, many of the skills used in community health nursing practice are similar to those needed by nurses in other areas and might be argued to be basic and common to general nursing. However, closer examination of community health nursing prac-tice reveals that certain skills require attention and training. For example, recent research (Kristjanson and Chalmers, 1987; 1990) to examine the nurse-client rela-tionship in public health nursing practice revealed that nurses' abilities to "pace" the interactions, or to vary the speed with which they conducted interviews to match the client's conversational and nonverbal tempos, was central to the success of the interaction. Another important interactional skill involves a nurse's ability to use an "engaging style" of interaction. This refers to the nurse's ability to enlist the client's interest in working on a potential or actual health problem, a skill critical to a suc-cessful working relationship because most often the nurse is a guest in the client's home and the rules of nurse-client interaction and the reason for contact are not always clear to clients.

In many ways the community health nurse "sells health door-to-door." Although the core skills necessary for this practice are learned through interpersonal nursing skills courses, the refinement and development of the process abilities are best gained through supervised clinical training in the field. Such training may be expensive and time-consuming; however, given that the primary mode of health care intervention in public health nursing is the interpersonal relationship, this effort is warranted.

A second set of issues relates to legal and ethical concerns that are revealed in day-to-day practice. The nature of community health nursing makes the nurse ac-countable to the community as a whole, as well as to the individual or family being nursed (CPHA, 1977; 1984). These multiple responsibilities may be in conflict if the nurse is torn between implementing the standards of practice mandated by the community health agency (e.g., required home visits to all new infants) and the professional code of ethics by which he or she practices. For instance, the Canadian Nurses Association code of ethics for nursing emphasizes the obligation of all nurses to respect clients' individual needs and values and their rights to control their own care (Canadian Nurses Association, 1989, pp. 13-14). The conflict is most intensely felt by the individual nurse who struggles to provide accountable care and deals with resistant or uncooperative clients who use whatever veto power is at their disposal to limit interventions that they consider intrusive. This dilemma is relatively unreported in the community health literature and is seldom discussed in practice situations.

Part of the problem may arise because of the influence of the historical stereotype of a public health nurse held by some clients who see the nurse as someone coming to "check" on them and report them to some unknown authority. Further, some nurses may see themselves as authority figures who can define the family's problem and give advice and teaching. This may be perceived by clients as unhelpful and may not be aimed at concerns that clients may be experiencing.

As well, problems may occur because clients do not understand the reasons for referral to the community health nurse. Many clients today expect to have a collaborative role in health care encounters and would benefit from more precise information regarding the reasons for referral, standard practices, and intended goals of service as seen by the community health nurse and health care system. We further argue that the decision to receive services is primarily the client's, except for the few health problems that legally require the nurse to contact the client (e.g., tuberculosis, sexually transmitted diseases).

FUTURE TRENDS IN COMMUNITY HEALTH NURSING

A future issue facing community health nursing involves the question about preserving the generalist role or further developing specialist areas within community health. This issue will, no doubt, be influenced by broader forces within the health care system. Pressure on provincial governments to decrease health care costs will likely increase the trend toward earlier discharge of hospitalized patients into the community. Community health nurses will be expected to provide nursing services in the home to patients of higher acuity levels. At the same time, national and provincial policy directives are stressing the importance of health promotion efforts (Epp, 1986; Epp, 1988; Manitoba Health, 1989; Podborski et al., 1987) with the intent of improving the health of the population and decreasing health care costs. The implications of these trends are that different community health nurses will be needed to address these varied and, in some instances, increasingly specialized health concerns.

Political action, community development, and collaborative work with groups are intervention skills that community health nurses will increasingly require if they are to make health care changes and decisions at the community level. Furthermore, community health nurses need to continue to ensure that the preventive and health promotive focus at the individual and family level is maintained and strengthened.

Additional health care trends and forces will also affect the shape of community health nursing in the future. The demographic trend of decreasing birth rates and increasing numbers of elderly Canadians will continue. With the increasing elderly population, the dominant client group of the future will no longer be the young family but the sick and well elderly and their families in the community. Another trend that may be expected to continue is that more women will enter the work force, combining family role responsibilities with career expectations. Community health nurses will likely need to develop creative ways of providing preventive and promotive health care to these families. Routine postnatal visits to new mothers and babies may become a less useful way of accessing the beginning families. Community health nurses may develop new roles for themselves in day care facilities or in occupational health settings that employ large numbers of women of child-bearing age. The use of computers to access community health information may become a convenient and efficient method of information exchange between community health nurses and clients. Although health promotion strategies must continue for the benefit of the health of the population as a whole, we envision increasing emphasis on high risk groups with a particular need to take "positive discrimination" health and social actions to address the underserved communities of the North and needs of the aboriginal peoples. Lifestyle interventions such as nutrition counselling or stress reduction groups are effective but tend to benefit the already privileged class. Community health nurses must continue to act as advocates of those most in need of basic health care services.

To prepare community health nurses for future roles, nursing education programs must offer learning opportunities that build on past learning and that introduce new concepts and practice experience. In the future, a mixture of community health nurses with knowledge and practice skills will be required. A proposed educational framework for future community health nurses is shown in Figure 8-2.

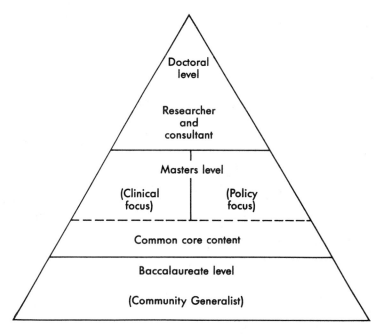

FIGURE 8-2 Proposed educational framework for community health nursing.

We envision two practice levels for community health nursing practice. One level is a "community generalist" role with preparation in individual and family assessment and interventions, communication skills, health promotion, and primary health care concepts. In addition, baccaleaurate prepared nurses must increase their skills and comfort in working with groups. The generalist focus of undergraduate baccalaureate programs must continue. Concepts related to promoting health at the individual, family, and community levels are important and need to be introduced to all professional nurses. The baccalaureate community health nurse prepared as a generalist can provide flexibility in the health care system to meet new health problems, such as the AIDS epidemic, the special health needs of new Canadians, and the health concerns of the homeless.

A second level of practice is envisioned for the graduate at the master's level. This individual is viewed as an advanced community practitioner with a focus on one of two pathways: (1) client-focused practice for specific client groups defined by parameters such as age category or illness, or (2) community-focused practice. At the master's level, students need various routes to follow to build on past work experiences and particular talents. A client-focused clinical pathway might be maternal and infant community care, community nursing of the elderly, or community nursing of the terminally and chronically ill. An alternate path would provide additional preparation for nurses to work at the community level by providing advanced learning experiences in community development, community health planning, and community system change strategies.

The doctoral level of educational preparation is considered the avenue for development of research abilities and theory. These individuals would offer leadership and consultation to community health planners and decision-making bodies. This group would also be important as a source of knowledge development for community nursing practice. For community health nurses to articulate their contribution to health care, evaluate interventions, and make policy decisions about directions for health care, a systematic empirically grounded knowledge base is imperative.

CONCLUSION

Community health nurses in Canada in the past and at present have maintained a strong focus on preventive and nursing care services to the individual and family and, at the same time, have attempted to address the overall health needs of the community. Community health nurses in the future must continue to work with individuals, families, and community groups to influence health. The knowledge base and skills needed for varying levels of practice will become more specialized, practice roles will be redefined, and the position of community health nursing within the discipline and as a force within the Canadian health care system will be stronger.

Community health nurses need to document their services through a systematic data base that makes their work more visible and allows evaluation of services. This information is critical if community health nursing is to obtain a predictable and solid funding base, participate in health care policy decisions, and significantly affect the health care of Canadians.

ACKNOWLEDGEMENT

The authors gratefully acknowledge the generous assistance of the following nursing leaders who helped by discussing key issues in community health, informing us of provincial and territorial community health concerns, providing expert critique of our work, and sharing useful local resources:

Elizabeth Adey, Executive Director, Newfoundland Association of Registered Nurses; Janet Braunstein, Director of Nursing, Community Health Services, Nova Scotia Department of Health; Beverley Cann, Occupational Health Nurse, Manitoba Federation of Labour Occupational Health Centre; Geraldine Cradduck, President, Community Health Nurses Association of Canada, and Director, Public Health Nursing, Elgin-St. Thomas Health Unit, Ontario; Helen Glass, Professor Emerita, School of Nursing, University of Manitoba; Marjorie Hayes, Director of Nursing Services, Community Health Facilities, Northwest Territories Health, Yellowknife; Mary Heatherington, Nursing Supervisor, and Simon Read, Manager, Nuu-chah-nulth Health Board, Port Alberni, British Columbia; Sue Hicks, Consultant, Maternal and Child Health Directorate, Manitoba Health; Cheryl Jackson, Lecturer, McGill University School of Nursing; Joan Jasinski, Assistant Professor, Faculty of Nursing, University of Western Ontario; Lynda Kushnir-Pekrul, Acting Executive Director, Saskatchewan Association of Registered Nurses; Margaret Mackling, Past Executive Director, Victoria Order of Nurses, Winnipeg Branch; Ruth Mellor, Director of Communication, Victorian Order of Nurses of Canada, Ottawa; Joan Mills, Executive Director, Registered Nurses Association of Nova Scotia; Elaine Pollett, Director of Health Education and Promotion, City of York Health Unit, Ontario; and Dale Walker, Executive Officer—Nursing, Vancouver Health Department.

REFERENCES

Allemang, M. (1985). Development of community health nursing in Canada. In M. Stewart, J. Innes, S. Searl, & C. Smillie (Eds.). *Community health nursing in Canada* (pp. 1-29). Toronto: Gage.

Baum, F. (1988). Community-based research for promoting the new public health. *Health Promotion, 3*(3), 259-268.

Calkin, J., Fitch, M., & Larsen, J. (1989). *Discussion paper: Specialization in nursing and nursing education*. Ottawa: Canadian Association of University Schools of Nursing.

Canadian Nurses Association. (1982). *Entry to practice: A background paper*. Ottawa: Author.

Canadian Nurses Association. (1988). *Health for all Canadians: A call for reform*. Ottawa: Author.

Canadian Nurses Association. (1990). *Code of ethics for nursing*. Ottawa: Author.

CNA connection. (1990). *The Canadian Nurse, 86*(1), 12-16.

Canadian Occupational Health and Safety News. (1984), *7*(4), 1.

Canadian Public Health Association (1977; 1984). *The nurse and community health: Functions and qualifications for practice in Canada*. Ottawa: Author.

Community Health Nurses Association of Canada. (Winter, 1990). Greetings from the president. *Newsleaf, 1*(2).

Doucette, S. (1989). The changing role of nurses: The perspective of medical services branch. *Canadian Journal of Public Health, 80*(2), 92-94.

Emory, F. (1953). *Public health nursing in Canada: Principles and practice*. Toronto: Macmillan of Canada.

Epp, J. (1986). *Achieving health for all: A framework for health promotion*. Ottawa: Health and Welfare Canada.

Epp, J. (1988). *Mental health for Canadians: Striking the balance*. Ottawa: Health and Welfare Canada.

Flynn, B.C., Ray, C.W., & Selmanoff, E. (1987). Preparation of community health nursing leaders for social action. *International Journal of Nursing Studies, 24*, 3, 239-248.

Freeman, R., & Heinrich, J. (1981). *Community health nursing practice*. Toronto: W. B. Saunders.

Gibbon, J. M., & Mathewson, M. S. (1947). *Three centuries of Canadian nursing*. Toronto: Macmillan.

Glass, H. (1984). *Primary health care: Nursing developments and responsibilities*. Address to the 12th Annual Federal/Provincial Nursing Consultants Meeting, Winnipeg, Manitoba, May 28-30.

Gottlieb, L., & Rowat, K. (1987). The McGill model of nursing: A practice-derived model. *Advances in Nursing Science, 9*(4), 51-61.

Hamilton, P., & Bush, H. (1988). Theory development in community health nursing: Issues and recommendations. *Scholarly Inquiry for Nursing Practice: An International Journal, 2*(2), 145-160.

Hanlon, J. (1950). *Principles of public health administration*. St. Louis: Mosby.

Health and Welfare Canada. (1987). *National health expenditures in Canada 1975-1985* (Cat. No. h21-99/1985 E.). Ottawa: Minister of Supply and Services Canada.

Healthstyles: A report of a community health promotion demonstration project. (1986). Ottawa: Centretown Community Health Centre.

Healthstyles '87. (1989). Ottawa: Centretown Community Health Centre.

Higgs, Z.R., & Gustafson, D.D. (1985). *Community as client: Assessment and diagnosis*. Philadelphia: F. A. Davis.

Highriter, M. (1984). Public health nursing evaluation, education, and professional issues: 1977 to 1981. *Annual Review of Nursing Research, 2*, 165-189.

Iglehart, J. (1986). Health policy report: Canada's health care system. Part I. *New England Journal of Medicine, 315*(3), 202-208.

"Keep Well." (1988). Ottawa: Centretown Community Health Centre.

Kickbusch, I. (1987). Issues in health promotion. *Health Promotion, 1*(4), 437-442.

Kristjanson, L., & Chalmers, K. (1987). *Nurse-client interactions in community based practice: A pilot study.* Research Report, University of Manitoba, Winnipeg.

Kristjanson, L., & Chalmers, K. (1990). Nurse-client interactions in community based practice: Creating common meaning. *Public Health Nursing, 7*(4), 215-223.

Labonte, R. (1989). Community health promotion strategies. In C. Martin & D. McQueen (Eds.). *Readings for a new public health* (pp. 235-249). Edinburgh: Edinburgh University Press.

Manitoba Health. (1989). *Partners for health: A new direction for the promotion of health in Manitoba.* Winnipeg: Author.

Martin, C., & McQueen, D. (1989). Framework for a new public health. In C. Martin & D. McQueen (Eds.), *Readings for a new public health* (pp. 1-10). Edinburgh: Edinburgh University Press.

Monteiro, L. (1986). Florence Nightengale on public health nursing. In B. Spradley (Ed.), *Readings in community health nursing* (pp. 74-82). Toronto: Little, Brown & Co.

Pender, N. (1987). *Health promotion in nursing practice* (2nd ed.). Norwalk, CT: Appleton & Lange.

Podborski, S., Pipe, A., Jette, M., Knox, M., Panzica, N., Robbins, S., & Shosenberg, N. (1987). *Health promotion matters in Ontario: A report of the minister's advisory group on health promotion.* Toronto: Ontario Ministry of Health.

Rachlis, M., & Kushner, C. (1989). *Second opinion: What's wrong with Canada's health care system and how to fix it.* Toronto: Collins.

Recruitment and Retention Study, N.W.T. (1990). Internal document provided by Nursing Services Division, Department of Health, N.W.T.

Searl, S., Stewart, M., & Kociol, L. (1985). Advocate for consumer participation. In M. Stewart, J. Innes, S. Searl, & C. Smillie (Eds.), *Community health nursing in Canada* (pp. 194-202). Toronto: Gage.

Sills, G., & Goeppinger, J. (1985). The community as a field of enquiry in nursing. *Annual Review of Nursing Research, 3,* 1-57.

Spelman, S. (1981). Strengthening and extending community-health nursing services. In C.O. Helvie (Ed.), *Community health nursing: Theory and process.* New York: Harper and Row.

Stanhope, M., & Lancaster, J. (1988). *Community health nursing: Process and practice for promoting health.* Toronto: Mosby.

Stewart, M. (1985). A comparison of community health content in curricula of Canadian university schools of nursing. In M. Stewart, J. Innes, S. Searl, & C. Smillie (Eds.), *Community health nursing in Canada* (pp. 579-590). Toronto: Gage.

Sutherland, R., & Fulton, M.J. (1988). *Health care in Canada: A description and analysis of Canadian health services.* Ottawa: The Ottawa Health Group.

Turning point: A health promotion demonstration project with women on social assistance. (1988). Ottawa: Centretown Community Health Centre and South East Ottawa Community Resource Centre.

Winslow, C.E.A. (1920). The untilled field of public health. *Modern Medicine,* March 20.

World Health Organization. (1978). *Primary health care: Report of the international conference on primary health care, Alma-Ata, USSR, September, 1978.* Geneva: World Health Organization.

Provision of primary nursing care to Indian, Inuit, and Metis people in rural and northern areas of Canada can be a most rewarding nursing experience. This photograph shows a native nurse conducting a home visit. (Photograph courtesy of the Communications Branch, Health and Welfare Canada. Used with permission.)

CHAPTER NINE

Nursing Practice in Native Communities

DAVID M. GREGORY, RN, Ph(C)

David M. Gregory, RN, BScN (Ottawa), MN (Manitoba), Ph(C), is Assistant Professor at the School of Nursing, University of Manitoba, and a doctoral candidate at the College of Nursing, University of Arizona, Tucson. Before joining the faculty at the University of Manitoba, he worked as a community health nurse with Medical Services Branch, Health and Welfare Canada. His areas of recent research include native health concerns, suffering, and men's health.

Provision of health care in isolated and semi-isolated communities throughout Canada relies heavily on the services of registered nurses. Nurses are often the sole health care workers in these areas and must function as primary health care providers, a concept that raises many important issues for nurses and nursing.

This chapter focuses mainly on nursing practice issues in isolated Indian and Inuit communities, an area of serious concern for nursing in the 1990s. Health care for Canada's native peoples has been a problematic area for several decades, and the organization of health care by federal, provincial, and territorial governments is briefly described and discussed. Specific practice-related issues in the field such as isolation, high turnover rates of nursing personnel, and discussion of cross cultural nursing are presented. Finally, some directions for future practice are suggested.

When appropriate, issues relative to nursing practice in rural communities generally are also discussed. Chapter 5, which introduces this nursing practice section, and chapters 4 and 30 also contain discussion of pertinent trends and issues related to these topics.

CONTEXT OF PRACTICE: NATIVE HEALTH STATUS

Numerous governmental inquiries, reports, and commissions identify and confirm the great inequality between the health status of native Canadians and the remainder of the population (Berger, 1980; Health and Welfare Canada, 1983; Indian Affairs and Northern Development, 1980; Manitoba Department of Health, 1981). These reports are reconfirmed by more recent studies, which emphasize the presence of a poor state of health for Indian and Inuit people. Although the health status of native Canadians in urban settings is similar to that of rural and northern communities, there are distinct differences associated with the delivery of health care to urban natives. Discussion of native health in this chapter is limited to delivery on reservations and in northern and rural locations.

Tremendous gains have been made in improving the health status of native people. They continue, however, to suffer disproportionately poor health compared to other Canadians (see box). There is a marked decline in deaths from infectious diseases, but a rapid increase in deaths due to accidents, poisoning, violence, and suicide (Bobet, 1989; Weller, 1981; Weller and Manga, 1985; Young, 1988). Reasons for the disparities go beyond the disease process and the health care system (Mar-

Reasons for Concern about Native Health Care in Canada

- The loss of whole generations, the enfeeblement of those who remained, the fear of demographic destruction, the loss of faith in their own institutions and values has resulted in a demoralization and sense of powerlessness in Indian communities throughout this country (Berger, 1980, pp. 2-3)
- Neonatal mortality on Indian reserves is one third higher than that experienced by a comparable non-reserve population; postneonatal mortality is almost four times higher with the causes attributed to infective and parasitic diseases, pneumonia, Sudden Infant Death Syndrome, and fires (Morrison et al., 1986, p. 269)
- Mortality rates on Indian reserves for violent deaths are three to four times higher than Canadian rates in general. Violent deaths account for half of all deaths to residents of Indian reserves (Mao et al., 1986, p. 267)
- Native Indians and Inuit, particularly those residing in northern communities, have substantially worse reproductive health than the national population (Young, Horvath, and Moffatt, 1989, p. 277)
- Native people between age 15 and 24 are five to six times more likely to commit suicide than non-natives of those age groups ("Social studies . . .," 1990)
- Indian children and even adults, like their Third World counterparts, excessively suffer the effects of infective and parasitic disease, such as meningitis, otitis media, and tuberculosis (Postl, 1986, p. 253)

diros, 1987; Young, 1983), and it is suggested that the health care system is simply treating the symptoms of much deeper problems (Weller and Manga, 1985). T. R. Berger notes in the classic Royal Commission Report on the North: "the problems of Indian health are the outcome of centuries of oppression, of the domination of one society by another" (1980, p. 4). Historically, native people have been subjected to intense cultural, social, economic, and political stressors. These forces continue to have a negative effect on their health.

At the level of the family or individual, substandard housing with an absence of central heating, the lack of indoor plumbing and consistently safe drinking water, and inappropriate waste and sewage disposal contribute to the distressing level of native health (Bobet, 1989; Maslove and Hawkes, 1989; Spreitzer, 1991). Community unemployment rates reach 90% with concomitant welfare dependency (Stewart, 1986, p. 51). A loss of self-esteem, depression, family and social breakdown, and violence is frequently associated with this situation. Alcohol and drug abuse also affect the health of many native people. Alcohol and drug consumption serve to dull the harsh realities in communities in which life is often bleak and the standard of living well below the national average. This drug abuse must be recognized as a symptom of complex socioeconomic, political, and cultural problems.

The distressing health status of Indian and Inuit Canadians remains a paradox in a country that is considered a leading industrial nation and that contributes millions of dollars to Third World countries for health improvement purposes. The physical and mental health of native Canadians is referred to as "a nation's disgrace" (Grescoe, 1987, p. 127).

ORGANIZATION OF HEALTH CARE

The federal government of Canada assumes responsibility for providing health care to native people, even though constitutionally, and under the terms of the treaties, it may not legally be bound to do so (see also Chapter 30). Native political groups such as the Assembly of First Nations hold the federal government legally responsible for the provision of health care based on treaties signed by their forefathers. The provision of health services to Indians has been a matter of policy for the federal government since 1945. In addition, the provincial and territorial governments and various religious and voluntary organizations provide native health services. The federal government transferred responsibility for native health services to the territorial governments in April 1988.

The Department of National Health and Welfare, through the Medical Services Branch, possesses a comprehensive organizational structure with a central headquarters in Ottawa to deliver health care to native Canadians. For the purposes of administration, Canada is divided into regions, and each region is subdivided into zones. Health services for the Indian and Inuit people are provided through a network of more than 450 health care facilities in native communities throughout Canada. These range from hospitals and nursing stations to health centers. Nurses and community health representatives (CHRs) form the backbone of this health care delivery system. Nursing staff account for more than one quarter of the Medical

Services Branch's work force, and nurses have a vital role in the delivery of health care. Scheduled visits by general practitioners, specialists, and dentists support nurses as they function in a primary health care practitioner role.

The community health representative (CHR) program involves local native individuals in the delivery of care. The federal government initiated this program in 1961 to provide basic education in health related programs and health promotion techniques to members of native communities. These men and women are recruited from their home communities and, in theory, they work under the guidance of the nurses to provide a liaison between the native community and the health system.

Nurses new to Indian and Inuit communities may have a limited understanding of the CHR's role and perceive these workers simply as translators, or as chauffeurs for patients. This perspective undermines the effectiveness of CHRs. Most CHRs are currently employed by the Indian bands or northern communities. Working with Medical Services Branch staff while salaried by the band places many CHRs in a double bind when the expectations and demands of these groups are in conflict. Whether these individuals are sufficient in number is also an issue. The number of CHRs relative to reservations and native communities in Canada is small.

Over the years, a significant improvement in the quality, continuity, and availability of acute care has been achieved by Medical Services Branch. Health services characterized by dedication, competence, and a generous budget are not enough. Long-term improvement in the health status of native communities is seriously restricted considering the limited opportunities for social and economic development and the cultural displacement endured by native people. As well, involvement of outside agencies in community health services delivery contributes to a perception of paternalism by Indian and Inuit people. One consequence of a paternalistic approach to health care delivery is the promotion of passivity. Native people are conditioned to assume a dependent role in their health care.

As Jull (1987) notes, native people must shape their culture themselves; this is the only way they can secure their future. In terms of health care, native people must be involved in the planning, operation, and delivery of their health programs. Health Committees composed of local residents and nursing staff have assumed aspects of this task in many native communities, with varying degrees of success. Although the merits of such committees are acknowledged, they usually function as marginal entities in guiding health care delivery.

The Indian Health Transfer Policy developed by Health and Welfare Canada in 1986 serves as the formal blueprint for the involvement of native people in the planning and delivery of health care programming. This transfer policy is described by the federal government as a means to achieve self-determination in health by the First Nations people. Whereas the policy is viewed by the federal government as meeting the demands for autonomy and band-level control of health care services, it has been criticized and generates considerable controversy (Speck, 1989). Some of the major points of contention include noninsured health benefits, transfer of existing resources, and inadequate levels of funding. Noninsured health benefits such as medical transportation, eye glasses, prescription drugs, and dental services are not open to negotiation in the transfer process. These benefits, which are currently uncapped, have a great potential for creativity in terms of health care delivery and the redirecting of funds into preventive programming, yet they are not on the negotiating table.

The policy also identifies that only existing resources are available for transfer. Native people argue that available health services are below national standards and health transfer would entrench these current shortcomings. For example, home care services are not available on many reservations, and community mental health services are also severely lacking. The Assembly of First Nations submits that present levels of health care funding are inadequate. Furthermore, the Assembly cautions that the health transfer policy reflects assimilationist ideology (Assembly of First Nations, 1988).

Speck (1989) observes that, in reality, the policy provides bands with a restricted role in the lowest echelons of local health administration. Local administrative health control does little to alter the health of the community, particularly when this control pertains to inadequate existing health services. Gregory, Russell, Hurd, Tyance, and Sloan (in press) note that in terms of achieving self-determination in health, the policy is constrained, since the major causes of poor health among native people are beyond its mandate. Implementation of innovative and locally based programs is curtailed as a result of the economic and developmental restrictions inherent in the transfer policy. Community expectations regarding changes in the health care infrastructure may not be met under the current policy guidelines. Moreover, the health care delivery system historically and currently employed by Medical Services Branch consistently demonstrates its tenacity for keeping native people powerless. It is this model that is essentially preserved by the policy. Thus the policy, while seductive in its promises for self-determination in health care, is impotent in its abilities to effect actual change in health status at the community level. Evaluation research demonstrating the effects of transfer on the health of native communities is urgently required.

Nationally, only a few native communities have completed transfer of health control. In the Manitoba Region, Pukatawagon successfully negotiated transfer, and the band is currently hiring nurses to staff its nursing station. Some tribal councils (e.g., Swampy Cree Tribal Council in Manitoba) note that the funding for preparation of transfer (pretransfer phase) is inadequate considering the tremendous growth required by the band to administer and manage such an undertaking.

NURSES AS HEALTH CARE PROVIDERS

Nurses who work in northern or in rural or remote areas must function as generalists and as specialists; a broad knowledge base is required to care for a variety of patients who present with specific health care problems. Nurses also exercise a great degree of autonomy as primary care practitioners. Health care delivery in native and rural communities involves independent and interdependent roles with physicians and other health care professionals. Few technological resources are available, and the presence of other health care professionals and support staff is limited. Role diffusion usually occurs among these nurses. Rural and northern nurses often assume various nursing and non-nursing functions (Canitz, 1989; Moreno, 1987). For example, it is not uncommon for northern and rural nurses to assume the roles of pharmacist, environmental health officer, and clerk while providing health care to patients.

In isolated and semi-isolated communities, nurses are responsible for the development and maintenance of community health programs, which may include maternal-child health, school health, environmental health, communicable disease control, accident prevention programs, and nutrition counseling. Special clinics (e.g., pre- and postnatal, well baby, immunization, and chronic disease) are held. Home visit programs are undertaken. Nurses also perform procedures historically considered to be the prerogative of physicians. These procedures include suturing, application of temporary casts, venous cutdowns, x-ray examinations, prescribing medication, and emergency care (Christensen, 1987).

Nursing stations have been established in isolated native communities. Frequently they are accessible only by air or have limited road access. Nursing stations are self-contained units composed of clinic facilities and living quarters for nurses and other health care professionals. A limited number of beds (from 2 to 12) for in-patient treatment or temporary admissions are available in the stations.

Nurses may also be responsible for one or more satellite health stations in addition to the nursing station. Health stations are located in more remote villages where a limited population base precludes the presence of a nursing station. Health stations, which are usually in the charge of a CHR, accommodate emergency cases and provide a base of operations for the nurses, visiting doctors, and other health care providers. Nurses regularly conduct clinics at the health stations and orchestrate community health programs in these villages.

PRACTICE RELATED ISSUES

Nurses function as primary health care practitioners within a milieu of poor client health. Although the quality of nursing care is praised and documented as effective (Arnoti, 1984), there are issues inherent in this practice model. These include the legal status of nurses, limited preventive programming, heavy workloads, and the changing epidemiological profiles of native communities. Frequently the legal status of nurses in the north and in rural communities is ambiguous. Nurses routinely perform interventions that are within the realm of medicine and, although physician approval is necessary, it cannot always be obtained for various reasons (e.g., emergency situation, poor communications). Where this leaves nurses, in a legal sense, is uncertain.

Medical Services Branch encourages preventive health programming, but the health system still remains curative or treatment oriented. A considerable amount of time is spent on treatment services. For example, Medical Services Branch statistics indicate that nurses spend 41% of their time on treatment activities and 33% of their time on indirect services such as office management, travel, and maintenance; preventive activities accounted for only about 20% of the nurses' total interventions (Stewart, 1986, p. 59).

Nurses are frequently hindered from engaging in well orchestrated preventive programs because of demanding workloads involving patients who present for acute treatment. Greater investment in broad preventive programs would probably yield an improved population health status, but there is frequently neither the time nor personnel to initiate or maintain these preventive activities on a large scale. As previously mentioned, native people are conditioned to expect a curative health system. Furthermore, socioeconomic conditions greatly contribute to the poor health status of the majority of Indian and Inuit communities. These abject conditions also impede the engagement and effectiveness of preventive health programming. Nurses are greatly challenged in their efforts given these constraints.

Nurses in rural and northern communities must possess a range of expertise. There may be considerable passage of time between uses of specific clinical skills, such as establishing an IV in the scalp vein of an infant, but when the need arises, the nurse is expected to perform as if the event were a regular occurrence (Fort, 1986). Maintaining clinical competence within the sporadic demand for a broad array of nursing skills is a challenge for northern and rural nurses. Limited opportunities for continuing education exist (Hanson and Hilde, 1988; Jezierski, 1989), although attempts are being made to remedy this situation.

Medical Services Branch does provide opportunities for nurses to attend clinical workshops. The frequency with which these occur, however, is limited. Procedure manuals developed by Medical Services Branch are of assistance to nursing staff. Videotapes focusing on topics such as laboratory procedures are also available to nurses, but the range of topics is somewhat restricted. However, workshops conducted in tertiary care health care facilities would expose nurses to a broad array of clinical skills and afford them the opportunities for advanced clinical practice. Alternatively, visiting clinical nurse specialists could provide regular on-site inservice for nursing staff. From a more economical perspective, context-appropriate videotaped lectures on acute primary care interventions, community health nursing, and pharmacology, for example, would be of great value to nurses working in isolated communities. Although advanced technology permitting remote communities to connect with tertiary health care centers currently exists (e.g., ECG transmission via telephone line), the wide scale application of this technology remains underdeveloped.

The epidemiologic and demographic characteristics of native communities are changing. There are many emerging practice issues related to these changes in morbidity and population profiles. An expanding elderly population and the absence of long-term care facilities, for example, present native communities and nurses with a host of issues. Increasing levels of chronic disorders in native communities and the special health care needs of this group are other main issues. Spreitzer (1991) discusses pain control in a patient with adenocarcinoma of the cervix (stage IV) in a northern isolated community. The nurses, working in collaboration with native families, provided the necessary leadership and nursing practice solutions to this patient's experience with cancer and ultimately her death. There is a dearth of knowledge regarding the presence of chronic diseases in native communities and how nurses are attending to these states with limited technological support.

Patients requiring emergency care beyond the expertise of the nurse are transferred as medical evacuations to larger treatment facilities. The method of evacuation varies, with fixed-wing aircraft (single- or twin-engine) the most common mode. Nurses usually escort their patients and provide care until transfer is completed, and this can vary from minutes to hours. Climatic conditions sometimes delay evacuation, in which case the nursing staff must administer care for the patient until the weather permits transfer. Transfer of patients by air is, in itself, a specialized field of nursing practice. The formal preparation of most Medical Services Branch nurses in this area is minimal. Recognizing the need to adequately prepare health care personnel in medevac procedures, Alaska initiated a statewide medevac escort training program (Bernard and Williams, 1988). This development warrants serious consideration by Medical Services Branch.

NURSES IN ISOLATION

Personal and professional isolation is a reality in rural and northern communities. Culture shock, environmental differences in climate and terrain, unfamiliar modes of transportation, and a geographical and psychological sense of distance from significant others contribute to a nurse's feeling of personal isolation. Professional isolation occurs as a result of limited contact with other health care practitioners and colleagues, reduction in health care resources available, and breakdown in communication links with support systems. Personal and professional isolation may produce considerable anxiety and strain. These are powerful forces affecting a nurse's ability to function in rural and northern communities. Canitz (1989) cogently notes that most nurses in the north are single women who are alone, "with little social support and with little opportunity to separate themselves from the government's health care apparatus and their professional posts" (p. 8).

Nursing stations also isolate nurses from their communities. All amenities of modern living, such as plumbing, central heating, and electrical appliances, are found in the stations, in stark contrast to the majority of buildings and homes in the native community. Nursing stations need to be comfortable and provide nurses with the living standards they have come to expect. However, differences in the standards of living isolate and distance nurses from the local native population. Because nurses work, sleep, and spend their leisure time in the nursing station, this further enforces social isolation (Hodgson, 1982). Nonparticipation in local activities can also contribute to alienation from the community. Social relationships often tend to be with the non-native population such as the Royal Canadian Mounted Police staff, Hudson's Bay Company workers, and teachers, and this also distances nurses from the native community.

On the other hand, nurses in a small community get to know their patients extremely well. This may be viewed positively in that nurses can provide tailored care. Conversely, providing care for family and friends can be frightening (Scharff, 1987, cited in Long and Weinert, 1989). For some nurses, socializing with patients and potential patients is distressing. Role ambiguity develops, with the nurse caught between being a professional health care provider and a friend, neighbor, and community member. A lack of anonymity for rural and northern nurses limits their abilities to have private areas of their lives (Long and Weinert, 1989).

NURSE TURNOVER RATE

A consistently high turnover rate of nursing personnel in northern and rural communities is a serious and constant problem (Ross, 1989). In 1988-1989, a 50% turnover of nursing station staff occurred in the Medical Services Branch, Manitoba Region (personal communication with Bill Rutherford, Manitoba Regional Nursing Officer, June 1990). Because of the rapid turnover, continuity of care is compromised and community health programs are often disrupted. New nursing personnel need time to orient to a community and to assess its strengths and weaknesses. Trust is a crucial element in the nurse-patient, nurse-community relationship, and time is required to develop this trust. Establishing relationships is difficult when nurses remain in a community for relatively short periods of time. Native people have learned to expect that health care personnel will remain only briefly in their communities. One of the first questions posed to a new nurse by community members is, "How long are you staying?"

Reasons for a high nurse turnover rate include the following:
- Transfers to another Branch region or to another facility within the same region
- Burnout
- Family situations
- Educational upgrading
- Environmental differences
- Culture shock
- Satiation with the northern or rural experience

Attracting and maintaining adequate nursing staff is a major concern in northern and rural communities. Furthermore, staffing problems are created when nurses require sick leave or vacation time. Although Medical Services Branch attempts to provide relief staff, a station will often operate with reduced nursing staff. In nursing stations, even a temporary loss of a nurse can constitute a significant staffing crisis. Fatigue among nurses in the north is a major problem. This situation is equally true in rural hospitals, where it is not always possible to find replacements for ill or vacationing staff (Fort, 1986; Henry and Moody, 1986).

Strategies that address relief staffing vary from region to region. For example, in Manitoba Region, Medical Services Branch has a relief pool of nurses that is managed at the zone and nursing station level. The zone nursing officer and the nurse-in-charge assume the responsibility for planning the staffing of nursing stations. From a financial perspective, Manitoba Region prefers to hire pool nurses for a minimum of three weeks. Also, nurses are matched to communities; that is, nurses are consistently assigned to particular native communities. Additionally, contingency plans list the prioritization of community programs in the event a reduction of nursing staff occurs. These plans are approved by the nurse-in-charge and the community.

Alberta manages its relief pool at the regional level. In Saskatchewan, relief nurses are hired on a contractual basis (personal communication with Bill Rutherford, Manitoba Regional Nursing Officer, June 1990). Although attempts are made to address this staffing problem, there remains an urgent need to replace nurses on a short-term basis. The effect of understaffing on the morale of nurses and the turnover rate should not be underestimated by Medical Services Branch. Providing a full complement of nursing staff is an expensive enterprise; however, benefits may outweigh costs in terms of the nurse turnover rate.

POLITICS OF NURSING IN NATIVE COMMUNITIES

Health care is a paramount political issue for native people. Nurses who practice in native communities will, of necessity, have to become involved in an increasingly militant political arena. This results in other nursing issues. For example, the nurse-in-charge is the administrative head of the health care facility and is responsible for the functioning of the nursing station. He or she is also responsible for health programming in the community. Consequently, these nurses often must engage in political sparring with official community representatives, which may include the chief and council or mayor and council. Innocent and relatively minor misunderstandings concerning health care can escalate into major political events. Nurses require cultural sensitivity, political tact and diplomacy, and a clear sense of purpose when dealing with these situations.

Many native community leaders have a wealth of experience with local power and politics and possess a fine sense of political savvy. They want to actualize the best interests of their people and will challenge the nurse-in-charge to meet these desired outcomes. Nurses unaware of political realities may face a significant power struggle in their interactions with community leaders.

What many inexperienced nurses in native communities do not realize is that the federal health care bureaucracy is quite sensitive to the demands of the chief or mayor. For example, chiefs and mayors have direct access to powerful individuals in the departments of Indian Affairs and Health and Welfare. If a nurse-in-charge is perceived as unreasonable regarding a health matter, a chief can initiate a flurry of activity by contacting senior management in Medical Services Branch. Considerable pressure may then be exerted on the nurse by the senior managers. Nurses, however, are subject to the established lines of communication; their concerns must rise from the individual nurse upward through all levels in the organization to the major decision makers. To compensate for this imbalance of power at the local level, the wise nurse-in-charge develops and maintains a positive relationship with community leaders. Meeting with the chief or mayor on a regular basis is a good strategy for nurses to employ. An informed zone nursing officer is fundamental to supporting nurses in the field. Nurses must keep their zone nursing officers apprised of health care matters in their communities. Responsible zone nursing officers should encourage regular communication with nurses in the field.

Councils have the power to pass a band council resolution, which can effectively remove a health care professional from the community. Although the legal status of this action is uncertain, Medical Services Branch will usually remove the personnel in question. A band council resolution requesting expulsion of nursing or medical staff is the ultimate step a community can initiate to solve their problems associated with health care professionals.

PREPARATION OF PRIMARY HEALTH CARE NURSES

Nurses in northern and rural settings come from various educational backgrounds, including diploma, baccalaureate, master's, and doctoral programs. However, many of these nurses have not received appropriate education considering the kinds of care they must deliver. Consequently, nurses may be placed in positions in which they are required to provide interventions they have not been educated to perform. The ethical and legal implications associated with this situation are profound for both the nurses and the communities receiving this care. Patients are placed in jeopardy when they do not obtain the care they require. Anxiety levels for nurses and community members can be tremendous when these deficiencies exist.

Meeting the market needs of society as a whole is a principle on which educational systems operate. The majority of nursing education programs in Canada are urban based and prepare practitioners to function in technologically advanced health care centers. Northern nursing programs are available, but most are currently at the diploma level and do not provide the theoretical base and clinical skills required for nursing practice in more isolated communities. Although these programs tailor their curriculum to reflect cultural sensitivity with northern populations, they lack the systematic development of nurse-practitioner skills. Addressing these issues is the responsibility of the nursing profession and Medical Services Branch. Standards of practice for nurses who function in an expanded role have not been clearly articulated by nursing associations in Canada. Whether nursing care in isolated communities should be considered a specialty practice is another issue that warrants attention.

Medical Services Branch conducts a national outpost nursing program for its employees on a three-year contract with various universities. Theoretical foundations and clinical skills necessary to practice nursing in northern and rural communities are provided. University degree credits are allocated for specific courses within the program. The number of graduates from this program, however, does not meet the demands of the Branch. Outside this Branch program, there is only one other outpost nursing program in Canada. Memorial University in Newfoundland offers degree credits to nurses who complete a program in community care, primary health care, or midwifery. Several regions within Medical Services Branch now operate "in-house" programs in which nursing staff learn clinical skills required to practice in isolated areas. No university degree credits are currently associated with these programs, a limiting factor for nurses who wish to pursue advance education.

If the nursing profession is seriously committed to nursing practice in isolated and rural communities in Canada, then increased opportunities for nursing education must be available. Clearly the existing structure is deficient in meeting the needs for nursing practice in these communities. Specialty education in primary health care is warranted throughout the country. Specifically, collaborative efforts between universities and each region within Medical Services Branch may be of benefit. University based courses offered to Branch and other nurses who are interested in nursing in remote areas is a possible strategy to remedy this situation.

CROSS CULTURAL NURSING: PREPARATION AND PRACTICE

Concepts and principles of cross cultural nursing have been lauded as essential to effective nursing practice for more than a generation. Nurses provide care to people and communities whose cultural beliefs and assumptions about health, illness, and healing may fundamentally differ from their own perspectives. Such is the situation with the majority of Canada's indigenous population.

It is postulated that nursing is increasingly encouraging holistic health care and is beginning to focus on cross cultural and holistic approaches to better client care (Mardiros, 1986). Hodgson (1980) found, however, that many nurses find it difficult to overcome the linguistic, cultural, and educational barriers between themselves and the majority of their native patients. Cross cultural nursing concepts are applied in the Canadian North primarily on individual initiative. Cultural sensitivity among nurses who provide care in native communities is inconsistent.

Cultural and linguistic differences between natives and non-natives can affect communication in many ways. For example, in the North there may be several different languages or dialects within a region. Most nurses do not speak even the main Indian or Inuit language of the region and native interpreters are needed. Furthermore, the use of translators in the provision of health care is a skill that must be learned by nurses who practice in native communities. O'Neil (1989) engages in a critical discussion of the historical and sociopolitical influences on communication in Inuit communities. According to O'Neil, the medical interpreter as patient advocate is essential to improving health care rendered by Medical Services Branch staff.

Scollon and Scollon (1981) explore discourse systems and note, for example, that problems may arise when two speakers have different approaches to the use of pauses in conversation. In general, Athabaskan and Algonkian (e.g., Cree) speakers allow slightly longer pauses between sentences than do English speakers. Although the difference may be no more than half a second, it can have important consequences. An Athabaskan patient may feel that the English-speaking nurse continually interrupts and will not wait for the entire story. The nurse may assess the native speaker as slow or reluctant to disclose a history.

This example is one of many aspects of interethnic communication that needs to be explored. Nursing education programs are, for the most part, remiss in providing a solid foundation in cross cultural nursing. In a country as culturally diverse as Canada, cross cultural nursing content must be acknowledged as essential in the preparation of nurses. As well, there is a need for nursing research into native Indian and Inuit cultures, including approaches to illness and health care.

The job orientation provided by Medical Services Branch does not adequately explain native culture to new nurses (Gregory, 1986; O'Neil, 1987). As Hodgson (1980) states, "nurses must pick up knowledge largely through trial and error, a slow and costly way of learning" (p. 11). A trial and error approach is neither sufficient nor appropriate in providing cross cultural health care to others. Despite the concerns, this approach continues to occur in the north (Canitz, 1989; Ross, 1989).

Additional substantive knowledge and understanding of traditional health care systems are also required if northern and rural nurses are to effectively carry out cross cultural health care services. Kennedy (1984) suggests the health demands of Canada's Indian population are not being met by Western medicine, and Indian people are augmenting the health services offered with resources available to them in the folk sector. Many Indian people use the Western health care system and their own traditional healing system: they engage in the services of healers in both systems (Gregory, 1988, 1989; Kennedy, 1984; O'Neil, 1986). Traditional native healers in urban and rural or northern settings are active in the provision of health care. The Medical Services Branch in Manitoba Region recognizes the legitimacy of some traditional health care practices. For example, transportation is provided for patients who wish to be attended by a traditional healer. Additionally, traditional healers are flown into native communities to provide care (Gregory, 1989). There is a need, however, for more efforts by the federal government and other health institutions to recognize the importance of this care to native peoples. Many native people diverge from the Western medical model and often hold quite different perspectives about health, illness, disease processes, and the role of the family and community in relation to the sick (O'Neil, 1986).

NATIVE NURSES AS PRIMARY HEALTH CARE PRACTITIONERS

In Regina in 1982, the World Assembly of First Nations contended that the insignificant number of natives in the health care professions is a contributing factor to the poor overall health status of native people (Saskatchewan Indian Federated College, 1985).

> It is recognized that perhaps the best people to provide health care to native people are fully qualified nurses who are part of that culture and likely to remain part of it. (Irvine, 1987, p. 16)

This viewpoint is reinforced provincially and nationally by the Indian and Inuit Nurses' Association, which presses for a greater involvement of native people in Canadian health care (see Chapter 30). Although native nurses are not a panacea for health problems experienced by native people, native nurses recruited from rural and northern communities may possess an intimate link with native culture, a command of the local language, an awareness of the socioeconomic realities of native communities, and familiarity with the harshness of the environment.

There are distinct issues encountered by native nurses who practice in native communities. Native nurses may be subject to different expectations by community members compared to non-native nurses. Community politics encountered by native nurses can be intensified, particularly when the community power broker is known to the native nurse, perhaps as a relative or friend. Many native nurses may be young and female, trying to assert their authority in a male-dominated culture.

REWARDS OF NURSING IN NATIVE COMMUNITIES

The provision of primary health care to Indian and Inuit people in rural and northern Canada can be a rewarding experience, from both a personal and professional perspective. Nurses in isolated and semi-isolated communities are challenged to the upper limits of their abilities. A great sense of satisfaction is often achieved with this type of nursing. Indeed, there are nurses who make caring for the First Nations people a career. Autonomy, creativity, and resourcefulness in practice are frequently cited as the main benefits of nursing with Medical Services Branch. Nurses displaying critical thinking skills, competence, and confidence are actively sought by the Branch.

Nurses who practice in native communities develop an impressive repertoire of clinical, administrative, and life-skills. Independence, self-reliance, and self-confidence are fostered in this practice setting. Physicians and other health professionals have considerable admiration for these nurses, and true collegial relationships are not uncommon. As well, nurses who work in native communities discover the warmth, beauty, and humor of the native people despite the health and social sequelae associated with unemployment and poverty. A unique cross cultural experience is offered to nurses who are receptive to native people. Many of these isolated and semi-isolated communities are also located in startlingly beautiful settings.

FUTURE DIRECTIONS

Understanding the realities of the context in which this type of nursing care is provided is essential if the difficulties nurses may experience in native communities are to be understood and anticipated. Too often a romantic vision of the north is held by southern, urban nurses who wish to engage in a journey to one of Canada's last frontiers. Nurses without an appropriate educational background and experience can become overwhelmed with the practice situation in which they find themselves. Descriptions of nursing experience in the north provide valuable information to prospective nurses (Spooner, 1989; "The last outpost . . . ," 1988). However, there is a need for thorough discussion of critical issues associated with this type of nursing practice.

Primary health care nurses, with reliable medical support, contribute to a decrease of acute illness and its complications among native people. The current poor health statistics do not directly reflect the quality of the health care system but mirror a situation of considerable economic and social deprivation. Nurses have the opportunity and the responsibility to be agents of change with energies directed toward improving the living conditions in native communities. Realistically, this is not a simple task, and it requires concerted political efforts by nurses and their associations in conjunction with native people.

To be effective, primary health care services must be tailored to the community's needs and resources (Brash and McClellan, 1989), and they must be developed collaboratively. Medical Services Branch, Manitoba Region, recently initiated "unit workplans" that establish a definite schedule of activities performed by the health care team. Community health needs are assessed, and realistically achievable methods and strategies to meet these needs, based on resources available in the community, are implemented. Representatives of the native community and members of the health care team are responsible for developing the unit workplans. Unit workplans reflect an attempt by Medical Services Branch to facilitate mutual goal setting and health programming between the community and the health care team (personal communication with Laurel Tornquist, Manitoba Assistant Regional Nursing Officer, January 1990).

One area requiring urgent development is nursing research that focuses on native health and on nursing practice in rural and northern settings. Only a few Canadian nurses are engaged in research in the area of native health (e.g., Anderson, 1988; Burke, Sayers, Baumgart, and Wray, 1985; Gregory et al., in press; Hagey, 1984, 1989; Neander and Morse, 1989; Young, Morse, Swartz, and Ingram, 1988). An interdisciplinary and collaborative approach is required, with nurses providing critical input into research projects. Considering the vital role nurses have in the delivery of health care to native people, it is incumbent on nurse researchers to mobilize their efforts in this area.

There is a strong demand for native nurses. Native people must have direct input into their health care programming, and native nurses could greatly facilitate this process. At present, the majority of native people are employed by Medical Services Branch in supportive roles within their communities (e.g., interpreters, custodians, housekeepers).

Several university and college programs are responding to the need for native health professionals as a result of funding from Health and Welfare Canada. The Saskatchewan Indian Federated College established a multidisciplinary Indian Health Career Program that is designed to prepare native people for entry into professional health and allied health programs. The University of Saskatchewan offers a nine-week summer preparatory program for native students who are considering nursing as a career. Graduates from this summer program are eligible to apply to 16 university nursing programs in Canada. These graduates are offered conditional acceptance by the universities based on the successful completion of the preparatory program. Lakehead University at Thunder Bay, Ontario, recently mounted a Native Nurses Entry Program. It is designed to facilitate the entry of native people into Lakehead University's nursing degree program. The University of Toronto also has a Native Health Career Access Program.

At the University of Manitoba, the School of Nursing has engaged in a collaborative educational project with the Swampy Cree Tribal Council to deliver a Northern Baccalaureate Nursing Program for Registered Nurses. The program admitted its first class in September 1990 at a location off the Winnipeg campus in The Pas, Manitoba. The program design features a remedial component, an advanced clinical knowledge base, and appropriate clinical skills to enable graduates to practice in isolated and semi-isolated communities. Funds for implementation have been approved by the federal government and the Province of Manitoba. The program is unique in North America.

Both native and non-native nursing students must be provided with an education appropriate to the roles they will perform. Obtaining an education suited for northern or remote area nursing is a difficult task for Canadians within the limited availability of existing programs. Health care preparatory programs for native people usually channel students into diploma and urban baccalaureate nursing programs, and this is a positive movement. Such graduates, however, do not exist with adequate preparation for nursing in northern or remote areas. This situation is serious, since there is a substantial need for nurses who possess nurse practitioner skills. If the principles of universal access to quality health care are to be upheld, the nursing profession must press for the establishment of appropriate primary health care programs.

Primary health care nurses in rural and northern communities have shown that nursing contributes positively to the health care system. Adequate preparation of these nurses should include the following:

1. An advanced knowledge base and clinical skills to competently practice primary health care nursing
2. Excellent physical assessment skills
3. A solid theoretical foundation in community health nursing
4. Principles and concepts of cross cultural nursing care
5. A sound orientation to Indian, Inuit, and Metis culture and communities

Primary health care offers great potential for the entire nursing profession. Nurses are capable of accepting greater responsibility and accountability in the health care delivery system for all areas of Canada. The Northwest Territories Registered Nurses Association strongly believes that this futurist role is already being achieved in the north. Nurses in the north have been providing primary health care for many years and the public accepts their extensive role. As well, the northern setting supports increased roles for nursing in the future (NWT RNA, 1985). Thus, nursing practice in northern and rural communities will continue to affect the future of the nursing profession in Canada.

ACKNOWLEDGEMENT

The author acknowledges the assistance of Cindy Russell, RN, MSN, for critical commentary in this chapter.

REFERENCES

Assembly of First Nations. (1988). *Special report: The national Indian health transfer conference.* Ottawa: Author.

Anderson, K. (1988). Health care needs of a Canadian native population. *Recent Advances in Nursing, 22,* 137-148.

Arnoti, B. (1984). Yukon medicine: The vital role of public health nurses. *Canadian Medical Association Journal, 130*(4), 492-496.

Berger, T.R. (1980). *Report of advisory commission on Indian and Inuit health consultation.* Ottawa: Department of National Health and Welfare.

Bernard, N., & Williams, C. (1988). An Alaskan medevac training program. *Journal of Emergency Nursing, 14*(5), 40A-43A.

Bobet, E. (1989). Indian mortality. *Canadian Social Trends, 15*(Winter), 11-14.

Brash, J., & McClellan, V. (1989, February). Eketahuna health centre: A recipe for success. *New Zealand Nursing Journal,* pp. 20-22.

Burke, S.O., Sayers, L.A., Baumgart, A.J., & Wray, J.G. (1985). Pitfalls in cross-cultural use of the DDST: Cree Indian children. *Canadian Journal of Public Health, 76*(5), 303-307.

Canitz, B. (1989). Nursing in the north. *Northern Perspectives, 17*(3), 8.

Christensen, B. (1987). On call. *RNABC News, 19*(5), 18-20.

Fort, J. (1986). Rural nursing. *RNABC News, 18*(4), 14-16.

Gregory, D. (1986). Nurses and Indian elders/traditional healers: An exploration of the contact between non-traditional and traditional health care providers in Manitoba. *Indian and Inuit Nurses of Canada Newsletter, 1*(5), 5-8.

Gregory, D. (1988). An exploration of the contact between nurses and Indian elders/traditional healers on Indian reserves and health centres in Manitoba. In David Young, (Ed.), *Health care issues in the Canadian north* (pp. 39-43). Edmonton: Boreal Institute for Northern Studies.

Gregory, D. (1989). Traditional Indian healers in northern Manitoba: An emerging relationship with the health care system. *Native Studies Review, 5*(1), 163-174.

Gregory, D., Russell, C., Hurd, J., Tyance, J., & Sloan, J. (In Press). Canada's Indian Health Transfer Policy: The Gull Bay Band Experience. *Human Organization.*

Grescoe, P. (1987). A nation's disgrace. In D. Coburn, C. D'Arcy, P. New, & G. Torrance (Eds.), *Health and Canadian society: Sociological perspectives* (pp. 127-140). Toronto: Fitzhenry & Whiteside.

Hagey, R. (1984). The phenomenon, the explanations and the responses: Metaphors surrounding diabetes in urban Canadian Indians. *Social Science and Medicine, 18*(3), 265-272.

Hagey, R. (1989). The native diabetes program: Rhetorical process and praxis. In J. Morse (Ed.), *Cross cultural nursing: Anthropological approaches to nursing research* (pp. 7-33). New York: Gordon and Breach Science Publishers.

Hanson, C., & Hilde, E. (1989). Faculty mentorship: Support for nurse practitioners, students and staff within the rural community health setting. *Journal of Community Health Nursing, 6*(2), 73-81.

Health and Welfare Canada (c 1983). *Medical services annual review 1982-1983.* Ottawa: National Health and Welfare.

Henry, B., & Moody, L. (1986). Nursing administration in small rural hospitals. *Journal of Nursing Administration, 16*(7,8), 37-44.

Hodgson, C. (1980). Transcultural nursing: The Canadian experience. *The Canadian Nurse, 76*(6), 23-25.

Hodgson, C. (1982). Ambiguity and paradox in outpost nursing. *International Nursing Review, 29*(4), 108-111, 117.

Indian Affairs and Northern Development. (1980). *Indian conditions: A survey.* Ottawa: Indian Affairs and Northern Development.

Irvine, R. (1987). Nursing education moves to the north. *The Canadian Nurse, 83*(2), 16-18.

Jezierski, M. (1988). Profiles: Rural nursing: The challenge. *Journal of Emergency Nursing, 14*(5), 326-328.

Jull, P. (1987). How self-government must come. *Policy Options, 8*(6), 10-13.

Kennedy, D. (1984). The quest for a cure: A case study in the use of health care alternatives. *Culture, 4*(2), 21-31.

Long, K., & Weinert, C. (1989). Rural nursing: Developing the theory base. *Scholarly Inquiry for Nursing Practice: An International Journal, 3*(2), 113-127.

Manitoba Department of Health. (1981). *The Manitoba native Indian mother and child: A discussion paper on a high risk population.* Winnipeg: Author.

Mao, Y., Morrison, H., Semenciw, R., & Wigle, D. (1986). Mortality on Canadian Indian reserves 1977-1982. *Canadian Journal of Public Health, 77*(4), 267.

Mardiros, M. (1986). Part I: Cultural relevance in nursing education - A native Indian model. *RNABC News, 18*(1), 13.

Mardiros, M. (1987). Primary health care and Canada's indigenous people. *The Canadian Nurse, 83*(8), 20-24.

Maslove, A., & Hawkes, D. (1989). The northern population. *Canadian Social Trends, 15*(Winter), 2-7.

Moreno, M. (1987). Rural nursing. *Arizona Nurse, 40*(4), 13.

Morrison, H., Semenciw, R., Mao, Y., & Wigle, D. (1986). Infant mortality on Canadian Indian reserves 1976-1983. *Canadian Journal of Public Health, 77*(4), 269.

Neander, W., & Morse, J. (1989). Tradition and change in the northern Alberta Woodlands Cree: Implications for infant feeding practices. *Canadian Journal of Public Health, 80*(3), 190-194.

Northwest Territories Registered Nurses Association. (1985). *The future role of nursing in the NWT*. Yellowknife: Author.

O'Neil, J. (1986). The politics of health in the fourth world: A northern Canadian example. *Human Organization Journal of the Society for Applied Anthropology, 45*(2), 119-128.

O'Neil, J. (1987). Health care in a central Canadian arctic community: Continuities and change. In D. Coburn, C. D'Arcy, P. New, & G. Torrance, (Eds), *Health and Canadian society: Sociological perspectives* (pp. 141-158). Toronto: Fitzhenry & Whiteside.

O'Neil, J. (1989). The cultural and political context of patient dissatisfaction in cross-cultural clinical encounters: A Canadian Inuit study. *Medical Anthropology Quarterly, 3*(4), 325-344.

Postl, B. (1986). Native health: A continuing concern (Editorial). *Canadian Journal of Public Health, 77*(4), 253.

Ross, D. (1989). Nursing up north. *The Canadian Nurse, 85*(1), 22-24.

Saskatchewan Indian Federated College. (1985). *Program description*. Regina: Author.

Scharff, J. (1987). *The nature and scope of rural nursing: Distinctive characteristics*. Unpublished master's thesis, Montana University, Bozeman, Montana.

Scollon, R., & Scollon, S. (1981). *Narrative, literacy and face in interethnic communication*. Norwood, NJ: Ablex Publishing.

"Social studies: Native poverty." (1990, September 23). *The Globe & Mail*, p. D3.

Speck, D. (1989). The Indian health transfer policy: A step in the right direction, or revenge of the hidden agenda? *Native Studies Review, 5*(1), 187-213.

Spooner, L. (1989, June). Nursing on Baffin Island, Part I (of two). *AARN*, pp. 11-13.

Spreitzer, E. (1991). Pain control in a patient with adenocarcinoma of the cervix stage IV in a northern isolated community. *Cancer Nursing, 14*(3), 155-158.

Stewart, P. (1986). *Bachelor of nursing feasibility study report*. The Pas, Manitoba: Swampy Cree Tribal Council.

The last outpost. (1988). *RNABC News, 20*(5), 10-14.

Weller, G. (1981). The delivery of health services in the Canadian north. *Journal of Canadian Studies, 16*(2), 69-79.

Weller, G., & Manga, P. (1985). *The politics of health in the circumpolar north*. Paper presented at the annual meeting of the Canadian Political Science Association, Montreal, June 2.

Young, D., Morse, J.M., Swartz, L., & Ingram, G. (1988). The psoriasis research project: An overview. In David Young (Ed.), *Health care issues in the Canadian north* (pp. 76-88). Edmonton: Boreal Institute For Northern Studies.

Young, T. (1983). The Canadian north and the third world: Is the analogy appropriate? *Canadian Journal of Public Health, 74*, 239-241.

Young, T. (1988). *Health care and cultural change: The Indian experience in the central subarctic*. Toronto: University of Toronto Press.

Young, T., Horvath, J., & Moffatt, M. (1989). Obstetrical ultrasound in remote communities: An approach to health program evaluation. *Canadian Journal of Public Health, 80*(4), 276-281.

Canadian nurses have a long history of work in international health. In this photo from January 1964, Miss T. Fortier, World Health Organization nurse from Canada, is shown giving advice on child care to mothers in Louis, near Libreville, Gabon. (Photograph courtesy United Nations. Used with permission.)

CHAPTER TEN

Nursing Practice in International Areas

KATHLEEN A. DIER, RN, MScN

Kathleen Dier, RN, BScN (Alberta), MSc(N) (McGill), is Professor Emeritus (Nursing), University of Alberta. She was formerly a Senior Nurse Educator with the World Health Organization in Iran, Ghana, Malawi, and Thailand, where her main function was integration of community health nursing and primary health care principles into nursing curricula. Since her return to Canada she has been involved in a number of short-term consultancies with the World Health Organization, the Canadian International Development Agency, the Canadian Nurses Association, the Aga Khan Foundation, and the Canadian Public Health Association in Thailand, India, Pakistan, Columbia, and Australia.

International nursing has been defined as "any nursing care activity carried out by a nurse from a donor country in a host nation" (Douglas and Meleis, 1985, p. 84), and it is usually understood that the services are requested by the host country for a contracted period. This chapter will focus on services provided by Canadian nurses who have lived and worked overseas. The discussion will center on international nursing in the context of Third World development, as this has been the major area of activity to the present time. It is not possible to mention the many outstanding international nurses by name, but some contributions will be shared to provide an insight into the Canadian experience.

HISTORICAL BACKGROUND

Canadian involvement in international nursing has a long history; records from the Presbyterian Mission Board of Canada indicate that nurses were sent to the field more than 100 years ago, mainly to Taiwan, China, and India. Nurses continued to serve abroad between the two World Wars. Jean Ewan, from Winnipeg, recounts that the scarcity of jobs during the depression influenced her to go to a Franciscan Mission in China in 1933. She came home to Canada after 4 years, then immediately returned to China with Dr. Norman Bethune, this time under the sponsorship of the Canadian Communist party. They were assigned to the army of Mao Tse-tung, but war conditions and a stormy working relationship with Bethune prompted Ewan to return to Canada in 1939, on the last boat to leave before the Japanese invasion of China (Ewan, 1981). Some nurses were not as fortunate. Ella Foerstel, an Alberta nurse serving with the Episcopal Church in the Philippines at the beginning of World War II, was interned in a Japanese prison camp for 4 years (Cashman, 1966).

The Red Cross Society, or Red Crescent as it is known in Muslim countries, responds to disasters worldwide, and nurses have been members of its relief teams for many years (de Grace, 1989). In 1946, Helen McArthur became director of nursing services of the Canadian Red Cross. She was previously a leader in public health and education in Alberta and president of the Canadian Nurses Association (CNA). McArthur was posted to Korea from June 1954 until December 1955 as associate coordinator of the League of Red Cross Societies. Her major concern was the care and placement of 100,000 war orphans, many suffering from tuberculosis. For her contributions to nursing she was awarded the Coronation Medal honoring Queen Elizabeth's coronation in 1953, the Florence Nightingale Medal from the International Red Cross in 1957, and an honorary Doctor of Laws from the University of Alberta in 1964. In 1971 she was also honored by CNA for her outstanding contributions to nursing.

The United Nations Relief and Rehabilitation Administration was established immediately after World War II to assist in repatriating the millions of displaced persons in Europe. By November, 1945, there were 211 nurses in the service, 16 of whom were Canadian (Creelman, 1947a). The Relief and Rehabilitation Administration closed its operations as the refugees returned home, and any remaining matters were assumed by the newly formed World Health Organization (WHO), which replaced the numerous international health groups that existed before the war. The WHO charter was signed on April 7, 1948; its role was to monitor health matters on a global scale (WHO, 1976).

In Canada, the Colombo Plan was initiated in 1950. It offered scholarships to foreign nurses studying at Canadian universities and sent Canadian nurses overseas. With the establishment of the Canadian International Development agency (CIDA) in 1968, more funds became available for development, which expanded the number of health related projects (Landry, 1988). Thus the demand for international nurses increased dramatically as agencies responded to urgent health needs around the world. To understand the nurses' role, it is necessary to briefly discuss the major international agencies and how their approach to development has evolved over the past 45 years.

AGENCIES INVOLVED IN INTERNATIONAL HEALTH

Religious organizations were the first to send nurses abroad. The goal of the original Christian missions was to spread the gospel. It soon became apparent that they could not serve the spiritual needs of the people without addressing the health and educational problems. Therefore the missions established schools and hospitals.

In the 1960s the World Council of Churches, which represents more than 300 Protestant and Orthodox denominations, conducted a study that found an overlap of health services and a focus on curative medicine that benefitted only 20% of the population. In 1968 the Christian Medical Council was formed to promote community health and to "search to understand health, healing and wholeness beyond the medical model" (Ray, 1989, p. 295). Various denominations now support WHO's concept of primary health care, which states that health care should be universally accessible, affordable, employ appropriate technology, and involve the community in the planning process (WHO, 1978). Mission boards now fund projects submitted by developing countries that have primary health care as a goal (Ray, 1989). The religious missions still have a significant impact on health worldwide. For example, in 1982 more than 15% of all hospital beds in India were in the 600 Christian hospitals (Missionfax, 1982).

A missionary nurse's assignments were usually long term and in one country; the nurse therefore became familiar with the language and culture of the people. For example, Sister Jeannine Gagnon, from Quebec, went to Haiti in 1956 with the Missionary Sisters of the Immaculate Conception. She has seen many changes over the years and applauds the present emphasis on primary health care and community development that helps people to gain control over their lives. Sister Jeannine stresses the "inextricable link between missionary work and commitment to social justice" (Degarie, 1988, p. 31).

The Aga Khan Foundation has been active in promoting the health of the Ismaili community of more than 2 million people in India, Pakistan, Kenya, Tanzania, and Bangladesh since the end of the nineteenth century (Aga Khan University Medical Centre, 1989). In 1979, Dorothy Kergin, then dean of McMaster School of Nursing, signed an agreement with Aga Khan University in Karachi to enable nurses from Pakistan to study at McMaster University. In turn, nursing faculty from McMaster assist in teaching and advisory duties for the Aga Khan Medical Services. The McMaster University School of Nursing continues to support the project, which is funded by CIDA. Winnifred Warkentin, a nurse from Manitoba with 16 years experience with CIDA and WHO, became the first director of the School of Nursing in Karachi in 1979, a position she held for 10 years. In September 1989, Aga Khan University began the first baccalaureate program in nursing in Pakistan.

The World Health Organization (WHO) is a United Nations (UN) agency. WHO has 166 member countries, and each has equal representation in the World Health Assembly, which meets annually in Geneva. The Assembly sets health goals and policies. WHO works directly with member governments and only responds to requests presented through official channels (WHO, 1976).

After World War II, many new countries came into existence as former colonies gained independence. These new countries inherited meager health services from the colonial powers, and therefore they requested assistance from WHO. Lyle Creelman, a Canadian who became WHO's Chief Nurse, reported that initially countries requested a "pair of hands" to do the work but soon were persuaded to plan for the future and began training their own people. Nurses from around the world testify that this policy has been highly successful ("WHO's contributions to . . . ," 1988). Eunice Muringo Kiereini, former chief nursing officer in Kenya and a president of the International Council of Nurses, credits WHO for aiding the progress of nursing in Africa. WHO was responsible for helping to upgrade the "varied and inconsistent" nursing education programs introduced during the colonial period before 1953 (Kiereini, 1988, p. 65).

WHO recruited many Canadian nurses because they were well prepared and politically acceptable. Creelman estimated that in number they were second only to the British. Unlike mission nurses, WHO staff were moved frequently as projects were completed or contracts expired. As international civil servants, they took an oath of office that required them to remain apolitical and loyal to the organization (United Nations, 1965). The need for discretion prohibited publication of articles or pictures and this is probably why so little has been written about the service. In 1986 there were 55 full time nurses working in WHO (Maglacas, 1986), but the current

Canadian Nurses Who Served in Senior Positions in WHO

WHO Headquarters, Geneva

Lyle Creelman, MCH Advisor   1954-1968
  Chief Nurse   1949-1954
Lily Turnbull, Chief Nurse   1968-1976

Regional Nursing Officers
AFRO-Regional Office for Africa
Brazzaville, Congo (44 countries)
Dorothy Potts: 1966-1973

EURO-Regional Office for Europe
Copenhagen, Denmark (34 countries)
Dorothy Hall: 1972-1981

AMRO-Regional Office for the Americas
Washington, DC (34 countries)
Margaret Cammaert: 1968-1975

SEARO-Regional Office for South-East
  Asia
New Delhi, India (11 countries)
Dorothy Hall: 1962-1972

EMRO-Regional Office for the Eastern
  Mediterranean
Alexandria, Egypt (23 countries)
Dorothy Potts: 1958-1966
Evelyn Matheson: 1965-1970

WPRO-Regional Office for the Western
  Pacific
Manila, Philippines (34 countries)
Lily Turnbull: 1957-1968

number of Canadian nurses has not yet been released. (Canadian nurses who held senior positions in WHO are listed in the box.)

The status of nursing in WHO has not been one of steady progress. The nursing unit was established in 1949 and had a high profile. Nurses provided input into all interdisciplinary projects at headquarters and in the six regions. Several "Expert Committee Reports on Nursing" were published, and Dr. Moyra Allen, of the School of Nursing at McGill University, produced the WHO document *Evaluation of Education Programmes in Nursing* in 1977.

In the mid-1970s, a reorganization at WHO head office eventually eliminated the position of Chief Nurse, and the two senior nurses were absorbed into other units and given the title of Nurse Scientists. The change was not welcomed by nurses in the field or by the International Council of Nurses (ICN). In writing about the move years later, Martha Quivey of Norway, a member of the ICN Board, viewed the dismantling of the nursing offices, which left only WHO Europe with a nursing section, as a "disheartening move" (Quivey, 1988, p. 67).

In 1978, shortly after this change, primary health care was officially accepted as a WHO strategy with "Health for All by the Year 2000" as the rallying cry (WHO, 1978). Unfortunately, the implementation plans completely ignored the contribution that nurses made to health care in the past and could make in the future. As a result nurses were pushed to the periphery and "to date . . . nursing's response to the health-for-all challenge has been fragmented, sporadic, unplanned, and uncoordinated, and has involved few, if any, other disciplines" (Maglacas, 1988, p. 67). In a public statement in 1985, Dr. Halfdan Mahler, director general of WHO, admitted that nurses had practically been eradicated from the organization, but that he now recognized nursing was much more ready for change than any other professional group, and that nurses were crucial to the success of the primary health care movement (Mussallem, 1985).

Throughout the years ICN has maintained close contact with WHO and has lobbied hard for such recognition. The Canadian Nurses Association (CNA) has been an active member of this international nursing body, and Alice Girard, former dean of the University of Montreal and past president of CNA, served as president of ICN from 1965 to 1969. In 1985, CNA submitted the resolution to the ICN Board that initiated the formal definition of the role of the nurse in primary health care ("WHO promises nursing changes," 1985).

Several Canadian agencies are involved in international health. Canadian University Service Overseas (CUSO) and its francophone equivalent Service universitaire canadien outre-mer (SUCO) were established in 1961, originally to recruit university students to serve overseas. In 1967, near the peak of volunteer activities, more than 60 nurses served with CUSO. Today there are only about 40 health personnel and they are older (average age 37). This is in keeping with CUSO's new policy of funding larger projects that require fewer but more specialized placements and more emphasis on community development projects. CUSO does not discourage its workers from being politically active if their work warrants it. Over the years CUSO provided excellent experience for nurses, many of whom are now leaders in international health.

The Canadian International Development Agency (CIDA), a federal agency, was established in 1968 and since its inception has used nurses in its health related projects. Connie Swinton, a graduate of the Royal Alexandra Hospital in Edmonton, served with this organization for many years and in 1987 was awarded the Order of Canada for her "remarkable contribution to improvement of health services in Nepal" ("Unsung heroes," 1988, p. 2). It was announced in 1988 that half of CIDA's funding would be allotted to Partnership Programs, which are usually initiated by voluntary organizations (Landry, 1988). The International Development Research Centre (IDRC) complements the work of CIDA by supporting research endeavors that benefit developing countries ("Overview of IDRC . . . ," 1988). However, in the 1989 federal budget there was a 12% reduction in international aid, which resulted in a drastic cutback in projects and raises the question of the government's commitment to global health and development (Best, 1989). A further concern is the recent change in overseas development policy, based on the World Bank model, that downplays humanitarian considerations in favor of economic gains. This approach inevitably leads to cuts in health and education, and "the social disruption such efforts cause is often catastrophic for the poor" (Todd, 1991, p. 83).

In the late 1960s, the Canadian Nurses Association began small technical assistance programs in the Caribbean and Africa with aid from CIDA. In 1980, CNA took advantage of a new CIDA program that encouraged joint projects with national nursing associations in developing countries. In 1984, CNA established an International Division with Joan McNeil, a graduate from the Faculty of Nursing, University of Alberta, a nurse with extensive experience in francophone Africa, as the first Director (Dier, 1987). In 1988, McNeil was replaced by Lorraine Tinivez, originally from Saskatchewan, who had 15 years experience working in South America. In September 1990, Debbie Grisdale, from Ontario, assumed the director position, having previously been a CUSO volunteer in Colombia and Nicaragua. CNA's International Division assisted nursing associations in Africa, South America, Mexico, the Caribbean, Thailand, Nepal, and China, and several new projects are being investigated. Canadian nurses usually participate in the feasibility and evaluation studies, whereas nurses in the host country implement the projects.

The Canadian Public Health Association (CPHA) is also involved in strengthening public health associations in various countries, and Canadian nurses have been involved in these projects. Margaret Hilson, from Ottawa, is the assistant executive director of the CPHA International Program. She is a nurse who formerly worked for CUSO and WHO in India. CPHA has also received funding to participate in the International Immunization Program, and CNA and CUSO have cooperated with this endeavor in several countries ("CPHA/NGO partners . . . ," 1989; Dafoe, 1989).

Other nongovernmental organizations (NGOs) such as World University Services and the Oxford Committee for Famine Relief (OXFAM) raise money privately and also apply to CIDA and provincial governments for grants. Nursing involvement depends on the health focus of the various projects.

Universities, colleges, and health agencies also are becoming involved in international "linking arrangements" with other countries. For example, the University of Ottawa's School of Nursing is collaborating with Tianjin Medical College School of Nursing in China, Newfoundland's Memorial University School of Nursing runs a project with a School of Nursing in Belize, and the University of Manitoba School of Nursing has a program in conjunction with the Department of Nursing, West China University of Medical Sciences. Dalhousie's School of Nursing has also initiated a project with the nursing program at the University of Dar-es-Salaam in Tanzania (Nova Scotia, 1989), and a rehabilitation project has begun between Ottawa Civic Hospital and a hospital in Beijing, China (Shay, 1988). International offices at various Canadian colleges and universities are being established to coordinate activities. CIDA is now funding an International Office at the University of Calgary, which is designated as a Centre of Excellence in International Development. The Canadian University Consortium for Health In Development (CUCHID) was organized in 1989 with the help of the International Development Research Centre. It represents a collaborative effort by many Canadian universities to pool their resources and strengthen international health programs. CUCHID's secretariat is located in the offices of the Canadian Public Health Association in Ottawa ("International health community . . . ," 1991).

NURSING PRACTICE

The nurse's role in international health has evolved over the years and still varies a great deal, depending on the stage of development of nursing in the country (Dier, 1988). (See box on p. 208 for a description of various phases.) In the past, nurses reported assuming a range of duties that included administering hospitals, performing laboratory tests, making medications such as cough syrups and ointments, setting up emergency rooms, discovering how to sterilize equipment in innovative ways (such as in a pressure cooker), giving anesthetics, diagnosing and treating patients, and practicing midwifery in hospital and in home. Outreach clinics were also established; one interesting innovation was a floating clinic operated on several rivers in Bolivia by Catherine McGorman, a Baptist missionary nurse from New Brunswick.

Education of local nurses and auxiliary level workers is invariably an integral part of international nursing practice, requiring preparation of curricula, course materials, and manuals, often in the local language. In some countries, nursing was considered to be "servant's work," or not an activity appropriate for a young woman. Consequently the expatriate nurses had to roll up their sleeves and demonstrate good nursing care so the profession would be accepted by students and others. Teaching was often complicated by a lack of supplies, such as bed linen and syringes. Even when supplies were available, they could be locked up by the nurse in charge. This action was understandable, since the charge nurse on each ward was responsible for equipment, and if any item disappeared the cost was deducted from her government salary. This strategy kept the inventory balanced but created many a crisis in patient care.

Field work was often challenging. Sarah Ste. Marie, from Longueil, Quebec, who worked for many years in the francophone countries of Burkina Faso, Zaire, Benin, and the Congo, as well as in Vietnam, recounts with pride the 3-month block of community health experience that she arranged for students in Burkina Faso in West Africa. And Madeleine Bissonnet, from St. Hyacinthe, Quebec, who had experience in Cambodia, Laos, Papua New Guinea, and the Philippines, describes the problems

Phases of International Nursing Practice

Doing Phase

The "doing" phase involves the actual rendering of services. This was the role of pioneer nurses who were faced with a complete lack of facilities or trained personnel. Today it is not a recommended role, except perhaps for a short period in the case of disasters when people are unable to act for themselves.

Training Phase

The "training" phase denotes the establishment of education programs for all levels of nursing personnel. It has two components: (1) selection of the best candidates available to send away for training and (2) institution of local training programs that are appropriate for the level of education of the students available and that address the health needs of the country.

Supporting Phase

The "supporting" phase provides assistance and guidance to national nurses until they are capable and confident enough to take over responsible posts. International nurses are named as "counterparts" to provide support and advice as needed and gradually phase out as the national nurse takes over. As more experienced nurses are available this role is disappearing.

Consulting Phase

In the "consulting" phase, nurses with specific expertise may be required for limited periods of time. Requests are usually to give workshops on new developments, to establish a project or program, or to conduct feasibility or evaluation studies.

Collaborating Phase

The "collaborating" phase means a two-way support and exchange of information. This is the model for the future. It means nurses from other countries are considered as partners in an undertaking, and there are mutual benefits and obligations involved.

of trying to place 800 students in Singapore hospitals. In some cases it was impossible for nurses to arrange experience in the community because of a sensitive political situation or restrictions against women appearing in public.

Nearly all international nurses state that the opportunity to work and make friends with people from other countries is a positive experience, in fact a privilege. For those who spent many years abroad the final return to Canada was a shock. As one nurse explained, "it was difficult fitting the changed 'me' into the Canadian scene." Re-entry affects all nurses to some extent. Common initial reactions relate to Canada's affluence. Professionally, there seems to be a lack of interest in international health, and repatriated nurses report they are seldom asked to share their cross-cultural experiences or their knowledge about primary health care.

Anne Dyck, from Saskatchewan, was in Indonesia for 18 years with the Mennonite Mission, returning to Canada in 1973. She was awarded the Queen's Medal for distinguished service in 1977. She captured the evolution of the international nurses' role when she said that her greatest satisfaction was:

> . . . working myself out of a job (OR was the most painful one to step back from), and being instrumental in installing independent department heads in every department . . . then being able to stay around long enough to help make it workable and experience how responsibly they carried out their tasks. (Dyck, personal communication, Nov. 22, 1989)

LEADERS IN INTERNATIONAL NURSING

Although it is impossible to list the contributions of all Canadian nurses, four in particular stand out. Their names should be known by their nursing colleagues.

Anne Munro was born in 1899 in Oxford County, Ontario, received her nursing diploma in Winnipeg, and took postgraduate studies in pediatrics in New York. In 1920 she went to India with the Canadian Baptist Mission Board. Her main work was with the Soras, an oppressed people living in the hills of Orissa state. Munro visited the homes and learned about local customs. She learned to understand the reason that the Soras abandoned babies: if the mother died they feared her spirit would come back to haunt the foster parent. Munro reacted to this by adopting an abandoned baby. When no harm came to her she was gradually able to establish a project to save other infants. She also understood the importance of making allies of powerful people who could support her work. The respect she engendered is illustrated in the incident when the Maharajah of Parlakamundi "sent her half-way across India in his private rail coach, bearing a gift of jewels to a woman being considered as a son's bride" ("The enterprisers," 1987/88, p. 23). So great was the trust of the people that in 1946 Munro was appointed as a representative of the Soras to the first legislative assembly of Orissa state. In the same year she was recognized by the British government with the highest award the King could give for service in India, the Kaiser-i-Hind Gold Medal for humanitarian service. Her story illustrates that Anne Munro understood the importance of power and practiced transcultural nursing long before these concepts became part of the nursing lexicon.

Lyle Creelman was born in Nova Scotia in 1908 and moved to Richmond, British Columbia, where she attended high school and Normal School. She went to the University of British Columbia for her bachelor's degree in nursing in 1936, followed by a master's degree in public health in 1939 from Teacher's College, Columbia University, New York. Creelman worked in public health and soon advanced to the position of director of nursing of the Metropolitan Health Unit in Vancouver. Her international career began in 1944 when she joined the United Nations Relief and Rehabilitation Administration. On June 11, 1945, 1 month after the victory in Europe, Creelman followed the army into war-ravaged Europe as UNRRA's Chief Nurse in the British Occupation Zone. Her task was to organize the health services for the refugees (Creelman, 1947b). She began training programs for the women in the camps to help them improve their status and to enable them to care for their own people (Creelman, 1947a). The United Nations project was phased out, and Creelman returned home in 1947.

In 1948 she collaborated with Dr. J.H. Baillie of the Canadian Public Health Association in an intensive study of public health practices in Canada (Nursing profiles, 1954, p. 484). The stay at home was short. Creelman arrived in Geneva on July 31, 1949, as the Maternal-Child Health Nursing Advisor in the newly formed Nursing Unit of WHO. The first task was to recruit nurses to fill all the positions requested. Creelman succeeded Olive Baggallay, a British colleague, as Chief Nurse in 1954, a post she held until her retirement in 1968. Creelman's clear judgment and exceptional administrative ability won her respect from other colleagues both within and outside WHO. Her contributions did not go unnoticed and she received an honorary doctorate from the University of New Brunswick (1963), the Canadian Centennial Medal (1967), and the Order of Canada (1971), and she was honored by CNA in 1974.

Lily Turnbull was born in Saskatchewan in 1915. She graduated from Regina General Hospital in 1941 and joined the Canadian Army Medical Corps, serving overseas until 1946. On her way home she stopped in Montreal and decided to enroll at McGill University. She obtained her bachelor's degree in 1947 and a masters in public health from Johns Hopkins in Baltimore in 1968. In 1952 Turnbull went to Malaysia as a WHO Nurse Educator. The British were evacuating and the country was still in the midst of internal struggles, which made the organization of health services difficult. Turnbull remained for 5 years and saw great progress as young men and women struggled to put their lives together and obtain training. In 1957 she became Regional Nursing Officer of the Western Pacific Region in Manila. She made frequent visits to nurses in the field, where conditions were difficult since many countries were still at war. She recalls sadly how many bright Cambodian and Vietnamese nurses did not survive these conflicts. In 1968 Turnbull was promoted to the post of Chief Nurse in Geneva, where she remained until her retirement in 1976. While in that position she organized several important WHO Nursing Expert Committees dealing with nursing education, maternal and child health, and working conditions of nurses. Turnbull retired in Saskatoon where she continued to be active in community activities until her death in November 1991. The University of Saskatchewan awarded her an honorary doctorate in 1988.

Rae Chittick was born in Ontario and educated in Calgary. She obtained her nursing diploma from Johns Hopkins in 1922 and a baccalaureate in science from Teacher's College in 1931. She held two master's degrees, one in education from Stanford and a master's in public health (cum laude) from Harvard. Chittick worked in public health and as a faculty member and director of the School of Nursing at the University of Alberta before becoming director of the School of Nursing at McGill University from 1953-1963.

Although Dr. Chittick's international nursing career did not commence until after her retirement, her global vision was evident in the innovative program that she initiated at McGill, which enabled foreign students to qualify for a baccalaureate in nursing. She and her staff were sensitive to the needs of nurses from other countries and this consideration and concern resulted in the goodwill directed toward McGill and Canada from nurses around the world. In 1962 Dr. Chittick did a study of nursing needs in Ghana. A linkage was established to provide scholarships for Ghanian nurses at McGill while Dr. Chittick became the first director of the post-RN program at the University of Ghana from 1963-1965. Her retirement was again interrupted when she accepted a contract to become advisor to the government of Jamaica and visiting professor to the University of the West Indies for 2 years (1965 and 1966). She concluded her career by conducting a study of nursing in Australia for WHO.

Dr. Chittick brought a wealth of wisdom from her previous nursing experiences and was able to share these with other nurses throughout the world. Her remarkable accomplishments on behalf of nursing were recognized by an honorary Doctor of Laws from the University of Alberta in 1954, followed by the Order of Canada in 1975, an honorary Doctor of Science from McGill in 1976, and the CNA Award of Merit in 1977.

FUTURE TRENDS

In this rapidly changing world it is difficult to predict the future. However, it is fairly certain that technology will continue to proliferate in biotechnology and communications. Biotechnology will increase the demand for surgical procedures, which will exert pressure on Third World countries to equip hospitals at the expense of community-based primary health care. Improved communication systems such as hand-held computers are being investigated to improve data collection ("Infomatics and health," 1989). Rapid communications such as fax can facilitate international nursing collaboration in publishing and research. If computers achieve translation capability, nursing studies published in other languages will become available. Translation of textbooks and journals into local languages would also be possible. The impact would be revolutionary, giving equal access to nursing knowledge worldwide.

Socioeconomic trends that have particular relevance to health care include an aging population, changing patterns of disease, environmental issues, the status of women, and the holistic health movement. The demand will be for more chronic health care and rehabilitation services, not only for the elderly but also for those who are disabled. Traditional medicine and holistic health practices will become accepted as appropriate options, particularly for nonacute conditions (Bannerman, Burton, and Wen-Chieh, 1983). Industrialization adds problems such as accidents, heart disease, mental illness, and social pathology as manifested by substance abuse, torture, and violence. The AIDS epidemic has ominous economic and social ramifications. It is hoped that the environmental concerns of the West will lead to more ethical development policies that, while still promoting growth in the Third World, will not destroy the health and well-being of individuals and their society.

Women's health must be a priority in the future. In Africa there are almost 700 maternal deaths for every 100,000 live births; in South Asia the rate is 500 per 100,000 live births. In the industrialized world, the rate is less than 10 ("Maternal deaths . . . ," 1989, p. 120). Urgent issues related to this problem are literacy, access to family planning, and the training of midwives. There have been some positive policy initiatives. A 1988 WHO report stresses the importance of nurse midwives in primary health care and the necessity of raising their status and involvement in health decision making. The report, however, adds that to date this approach has received little support from member states (WHO, 1988). On a positive note, a 1990 WHO publication stresses that nurses and midwives in developing countries must become involved in research if improvements are to be made in maternal and child health (Okafor, 1990). CIDA has a "Gender in Development" policy, which states that all projects must clearly identify how the projected outcomes will benefit women. A troubling trend, at a time when nurse power is urgently needed, is the shortage of nurses in most countries. WHO and ICN warn that positive steps must be taken to recruit and retain nurses or the situation will become more acute (WHO, 1989; "International team . . . ," 1990).

Politically, developing countries have accepted the principles of primary health care and most draw up health plans every 5 years to outline health priorities and goals. The commitment to equity, inherent in the primary health care concept, is a difficult one for politicians. It means that scarce resources should be shared with the relatively powerless, such as the rural poor, although powerful well-to-do citizens and physicians pressure for the funds to be spent on modern urban hospitals. In a courageous step the European community has endorsed primary health care and its goals for the year 2000. Its definition of health is broad, encompassing housing, employment, and lifestyle issues (Bryant, 1988). The United States is ignoring primary health care, and the American approach has resulted in a two-tiered health care system, one for the rich and one for the poor (Blum, 1985).

Although Canada has always promoted equity in health care, two federal government initiatives place this principle in jeopardy. The 1989 budget introduced a tax recovery on old-age pensions and family allowance, which undermines the principle of universality of social programs (National Council of Welfare, 1989). In February 1991, the Government Expenditures Restraint Act cuts back, and will eventually eliminate, all payments to the provinces for health and secondary education. This, in effect, means that "the Canada Health Act will be toothless . . . [and] equity and fairness, the underlying principles of our health care system are likely to disappear" (Bryce, 1991, p. 75). This is unfortunate because the Epp framework, presented in 1987, provided a vision for the future that emphasized many of the aspects of the primary health care philosophy.

WHO proposes that primary health care can be strengthened by improved health planning, integrating hospitals more fully into the system, and training leaders. Smith (1987) regards the need for leadership as an opportunity for nurses to shape their own destiny. Bryant (1988) supports this view; he believes nurses could be the potential moving force in primary health care, because doctors often obstruct teamwork.

Research is a priority for the future. WHO delineates the need to study the health care delivery system and the various parameters of health. The European Region followed up on this theme and prepared an excellent document outlining research priorities and target dates ("Priority research . . . ," 1989). The growing interest in "participatory research," which aims to share knowledge democratically and promote community development, should also contribute to the impetus of research in primary health care (Pyrch, 1988).

FUTURE ROLE OF THE INTERNATIONAL NURSE

The structure of international nursing will be different in the future. Long-term appointments will be replaced with frequent, short-term assignments. The use of independent international consultants is also a possibility. Dr. Yolanda Mousseau-Gersham, a Canadian who received her nursing degree from the University of Montreal and a doctorate in education from the University of Ottawa in 1965, has an extensive background with WHO and the International Development Research Centre. She is a role model in this regard. Working independently, she has accepted contracts in all parts of the world, as well as visiting professorships in international health at three American universities. She is currently a consultant to the Aga Khan Foundation and is residing in Egypt. (The boxed information (see pp. 214 and 215), although not comprehensive, is designed to give interested nurses some idea of the preparation required for international work and agencies to contact for information about positions in the field.)

The role of the international nurse will increasingly become a collaborative relationship encompassing all countries, not just the Third World. It is imperative that we move quickly to a partnership and dispel the growing resentment toward the "imperialism" some Canadian and American nurses display toward international colleagues (Holleran, 1988). Other countries are preparing world leaders as well, and there are doctoral programs in Britain, Egypt, Korea, and Japan, to name just a few.

New orientations to nursing care are needed. Kiereini (1985) identifies one of the main barriers to the implementation of primary health care as the inability to delegate duties to nonprofessionals. This problem of "sharing power" is addressed in Stewart's (1990) conceptual framework, which is based on a primary health care model that emphasizes social support, consumer collaboration, and the patient as "partner." Another dilemma international nurses face is the emphasis on the nurse-client relationship, which is impossible to maintain when there are so many in need of help. Butterfield (1990) proposes that this one-to-one focus in nursing limits vision. She advocates a population-centered practice that seeks collective solutions to health problems and provides a "conceptual foundation to enable its practitioners to understand health problems manifested at community, national, and international levels, as well as the individual and family levels" (p. 7). She adds that the societal perspective is necessary to promote change. The focus on primary health care and the growing importance of midwifery has implications for nursing education programs. If nurses are to become leaders in the primary health care movement, outdated modes of practice must be eliminated and curricular changes introduced to expand the nursing role and to include skills in community assessment and manpower development (WHO, 1989). That nurses are accepting the challenge is evidenced by the recognition they have received for their contributions to primary health care in Botswana and Finland (Rojas, Stark, and Tembo, 1990; Siivola and Martikainen, 1990).

International nursing research in the future should be collaborative because scattered individual projects will have little effect (Meleis, 1989). European nurses are using the WHO framework to develop research guidelines ("Priority research . . . ," 1989). To ensure that international nursing research is collaborative it should be

Information for Nurses Interested in International Health

Strategies to gain background knowledge and experience

Travel abroad

Study tours

Student exchange programs (See below)

Join an international organization (e.g., UN Assoc)

Join an NGO involved in development (e.g., church or community affiliated group)

Become a member of the CCMH*

Become fluent in more than one language

Participate in foreign student activities

Attend workshops on cross-cultural nursing, international health, or tropical diseases

Practicum or experience in a nursing station, health centre, or community health

Volunteer or take a position with refugee or immigrant services

Employment with Native Health Services

*CCMH (Canadian Coalition on Multicultural Health, Suite 406, 1017 Wilson Ave., Downsview, Ontario M3K 1Z1. There are branch organizations in each province.

Examples of useful courses for international nursing

Cross-cultural nursing

Anthropology with emphasis on religion and family structures

Tropical diseases

Program planning and evaluation

Health promotion

Midwifery

Nursing education

Community development

International health

Primary health care skills (assessment, community health)

Epidemiology

Health administration

Research

Economics

Political science

Sources of information regarding positions in international health

Apply to have your name placed on the Resource Registries of CIDA, CNA, and CPHA

Request CIDA brochure *Signposts: Looking for work in international development*

Obtain a copy of "Opportunities Abroad for Canadian Health Personnel" from the International Division, Canadian Public Health Association. The list gives an address and a brief description of organizations involved in development and the type of health professionals required

Read Cumyn A (1988). *What in the world is going on: a guide for Canadians wishing to work, volunteer or study in other countries*, Ottawa: Canadian Bureau for International Education. [85 Albert St., Suite 400, Ottawa, Canada K1P 6A4]

Write to CUSO (Regional or Ottawa office) for current positions being advertised

Write Overseas Development Associate Program, Institute for Development and Co-operation, University of Ottawa, Canada 25 University St. Ottawa, Canada K1N 6N5 (Recent university graduates only)

Abe,

Thanks for the 10 but
if you find a stray $50
around the house, kindly
give it to me.

:)

Mutt

Information for Nurses Interested in International Health—cont'd

Students: Graduate Fellowships available for student research in international health. International Development Research Centre (IDRC), P.O. Box 8500, Ottawa, Canada K1G 3H9

Undergraduate students: Elective in a developing country. International Health Exchange Program, 1565 Carling Avenue, Suite 400, Ottawa, Canada K1Z 8R1

Other opportunities advertised in: *The Canadian Nurse*, Newspapers, Church Bulletins, NGO newsletters, *Synergy*, Canadian Initiatives for International Health, c/o AUCC, 151 Slater Street, Ottawa, Canada K1P 5N1. Increasingly there will also be opportunities to become involved in projects sponsored by universities, colleges, and health agencies

National Council for International Health, 1101 Connecticut Ave. NW, Suite 605, Washington, DC 20036-4390 (Vacancies in health and development. Fee for the job list)

carried out jointly with nurses from another country, address a priority topic identified for research on primary health care, and indicate clearly how the findings will contribute to the goals stipulated in the host country's national health plan. It is exciting that support will be available through the global network of WHO Collaborating Centres for Nursing Development, which was inaugurated in 1987 and is being established around the world to promote research on primary health care. The College of Nursing, University of Illinois, was named the first center in North America, and work is underway to establish one in Canada in the near future.

The future of international nursing depends on the strength of the national nursing associations in each country. In Canada, two successful workshops were led by Dorothy Hall, from London, Ontario, who is a former WHO Regional Nursing Advisor, to educate Canadian nurses about primary health care. Hall is presently coordinator of a joint pilot project between the Danish Nurses Organization and the Association of Registered Nurses of Newfoundland, the purpose of which is to monitor the effectiveness of nurse-managed primary health services in selected communities ("Denmark/Canada: a nursing . . . ," 1991).

The next challenge for Canadian nurses will be to convince the government to endorse primary health care, because to be truly effective it must be a rationally planned national policy. At the same time support must continue for nursing colleagues in other countries, many of whom struggle against overwhelming odds.

Since the Gulf War, there has been growing dissatisfaction about the proliferation and use of military armament, which threatens the health and in many instances the lives of people, to say nothing of the well-being of the planet that we share. UNICEF and other agencies are now making public statistics that dramatically illustrate the negative relationships between military spending and poverty, suffering, and poor health. ICN exhorts its members to become informed and to pressure governments to invest in health and social programs rather than in instruments of destruction ("Health needs, budget cuts . . . ," 1991).

Recent world events dramatically illustrate that "people power" can move governments. With will and determination it is possible to mobilize "international nurse power" and transform "Health for All" from a slogan into a reality.

ACKNOWLEDGEMENT

Professor Dier wishes to acknowledge the input from numerous nursing colleagues in the international field and in particular the support received from Ginette Rodger, former CNA Executive Director, and Hazel Wilson, retired World Health Organization Nursing Consultant.

REFERENCES

Aga Khan University Medical Centre. (1989). *Report*. Karachi: Islamic Publications, Inc.

Allen, M. (1977). *Evaluation of education programs in nursing*. Geneva: World Health Organization.

Bannerman, R.H., Burton, J., & Wen-Chieh, C. (1983). *Traditional medicine and health care coverage*. Geneva: World Health Organization.

Best, J. (1989, November 24). Federal budget cuts hurt poor, diseased in the Third World. *Winnipeg Free Press*, p. 7.

Blum, H.L. (1985). Health trends around the world. *Mobius, 5*(3), 51-83.

Bryce, G.K. (1991). Medicare on the ropes. *Canadian Journal of Public Health, 82*(2), 75-76.

Bryant, J.H. (1988). Health for all: The dream and the reality. *World Health Forum, 9*(3), 291-302.

Butterfield, P.G. (1990). Thinking upstream: Nurturing a conceptual understanding of the social context of health behavior. *Advances in Nursing Science, 12*(2), 1-8.

Cashman, T. (1966). *Heritage of service: The history of nursing in Alberta*. Edmonton: Alberta Association of Registered Nurses.

CPHA/NGO partners workshop. (1989). *CPHA Health Digest, 13*(2), 7.

Creelman, L. (1947a). With UNRRA in Germany. *The Canadian Nurse, 43*(8), 605-610.

Creelman, L. (1947b). With UNRRA in Germany. *The Canadian Nurse, 43*(7), 532-556.

Dafoe, G. (1989). Executive director's report. *CPHA Health Digest, 13*(2), 2.

Degarie, R. (1988, Summer-Autumn). Canadians in the Third World. *Development*, pp. 30-34.

de Grace, R. (1989). Canadian Red Cross. In R. Masi (Ed.), *Multiculturalism and health care: Proceedings of the Canadian Council on Multicultural Health First National Conference* (pp. 288-290). Downsview, ON: Canadian Council on Multicultural Health.

Denmark/Canada—A nursing model in primary health care. (1991). *International Nursing Review, 38*(1), 4.

Dier, K.A. (1987). *Evaluation of the Canadian Nurses Association international projects funded by the Canadian International Development Agency*. Unpublished manuscript. Available from CNA Library, Ottawa.

Dier, K.A. (1988). International nursing: The global approach. *Recent Advances in Nursing, 20*, 39-60.

Douglas, M.K., & Meleis, A.I. (1985). International nursing challenges and consequences. *Mobius, 5*(3), 84-92.

Epp, J. (1987). *Achieving health for all: A framework for health promotion*. Ottawa: Health and Welfare Canada.

Ewan, J. (1981). *Canadian nurse in China*. Toronto: McClelland and Stewart.

Health needs, budget cuts & military spending. (1991). *International Nursing Review, 38*(2), 41-44.

Holleran, C. (1988). Nursing beyond national boundaries: The 21st century. *International Nursing Review, 36*(2), 72-75.

Infomatics and health. (1989, August/September). *World Health*, pp.1-29.

International health community in Canada. (1991). *Synergy, 3*(4), 6.

International team addresses nursing shortages. (1990). *International Nursing Review*, 37(4), 293-294.

Kiereini, E.M. (1988). WHO's role in the development of nursing in the African region. *International Nursing Review*, 35(3), 65-66, 68.

Kiereini, E.M. (1985). What's happened since Alma Ata? *International Nursing Review*, 32(1), 17-19.

Landry, M. (1988, Summer/Autumn). Minister's message. *Development*, pp. 1-2.

Maglacas, A.M. (1986). Nurses must look towards the future. *International Nursing Review*, 33(6), 178-179.

Maglacas, A.M. (1988). Health for all: Nursing's role. *Nursing's Outlook*, 36(2), 66-71.

Maternal deaths: Statistics of shame. (1989). *International Nursing Review*, 36(4), 120.

Meleis, A.I. (1989). International research: A need or a luxury? *Nursing Outlook*, 37(3), 138-142.

Missionfax - India. (1982). *The Enterprise*, 29(5), 13-16.

Mussallem, H.K. (1985). Thank you, Dr. Mahler. *The Canadian Nurse*, 81(4), 5.

National Council of Welfare. (1989, September). *The 1989 budget and social policy*. Ottawa: Minister of Supply and Services Canada.

Nova Scotia. (1989). *Synergy*, 1(4), 6.

Nursing profiles. (1954). *The Canadian Nurse*, 50(6), 484.

Okafor, C. (1990). Nurses, midwives and health research. *World Health Forum*, 11(1), 98-101.

Overview of IDRC international health priorities. (1988). *Synergy*, 1(1), 5.

Priority research for health for all. (1989) *International Health Review*, 36(1), 30-31, 24.

Pyrch, T. (1988). International Centre, University of Calgary. *Update*, 1(1), 1-2.

Quivey, M. (1988). ICN's relationship with WHO: A view from Europe. *International Nursing Review*, 35(3), 67-68.

Ray, J. (1989). Canadian participation and collaboration abroad: Christian Medical Commission of the World Council of Churches. In R. Masi (Ed.), *Multiculturalism and health care: Proceedings of the Canadian Council on Multi-cultural Health First National Conference* (pp. 294-299). Downsview, ON: Canadian Council on Multicultural Health.

Rojas, P., Stark, R., & Tembo, P. (1990). Nurses bring primary health care to industrial workers. *World Health Forum*, 11(1), 108-113.

Shay, C. (1988). Rehabilitation in China inspired by Ottawa hospital. *Synergy*, 1(3), 5.

Siivola, U., & Martikainen, T. (1990). The public health nurse—the linchpin of primary health care. *World Health Forum*, 11(1), 102-107.

Smith, J.P. (1987). Targets for health for all: Implications for nurses, midwives and health visitors. *Journal of Advanced Nursing*, 12(1), 1-2.

Stewart, M.J. (1990). From provider to partner: A conceptual framework for nursing education based on primary health care premises. *Advances in Nursing Science*, 12(2), 9-27.

The enterprisers. (1987/88). *The Enterprise*, p. 23.

Todd, D. (1991, May 22). Ottawa to shift foreign aid focus. *Edmonton Journal*, p. A3.

United Nations. (1965). *Report on standards of conduct in the international civil service 1954* (Rev.). New York: Author.

Unsung heroes. (1988). *Synergy*, 1(1), 2.

WHO promises nursing changes. (1985). *The Canadian Nurse*, 81(3), 9.

WHO's contributions to nursing—reflections from the field. (1988). *International Nursing Review*, 35(3), 69-72.

World Health Organization. (1976). *Introducing WHO*. Geneva: Author.

World Health Organization. (1978). *Alma-Ata 1978 Primary Health Care*. Report of the International Conference on Primary Health Care, Alma-Ata, USSR, September 1-12, 1978. Geneva: Author.

World Health Organization. (1988). *The work of WHO: Biennial report of the director general*. Geneva: Author.

World Health Organization. (1989). *Nursing in primary health care: Ten years after Alma Ata and perspectives for the future*. Report on the joint WHO/ICN consultation August 1-3, 1988. Geneva: Author.

NURSING WORKPLACES

Nursing has long been a female-dominated profession, but male nurses, such as Kevin Bigham, director of patient services at Prince Rupert (British Columbia) General Hospital, account for slightly less than 3% of registered nurses in Canada. The photograph, with Cathy Maestrello *(left)* and Hardev Toor *(right)*, was taken in a nursing station at the hospital. (The photographer was Gerry Deiter for *Nursing BC*, the journal of the Registered Nurses Association of British Columbia. Used with permission.)

CHAPTER ELEVEN

Overview: Inside Nursing Workplaces

JENNIECE LARSEN, RN, PhD
ALICE J. BAUMGART, RN, PhD

Nursing is the most important element of modern health care facilities. This importance is derived from a central role in providing patient care and in coordinating essential organization activities and from the political, technical, and cultural complexities of the health care environment. As Meilicke (1991) observes, these factors put nursing at the leading edge of issues facing all sectors of health care in recent years. As a result, work experiences of nurses are shaped by complexities and uncertainties that are usually not recognized by administrators, colleagues, and nurses themselves. As well, the position of nurses in the organizational hierarchy often adversely affects nursing practice. In recent years, these factors have been intensified by a heightened sense of entitlement to meaningful work, to career advancement, to a voice in decisions, and to workplaces that reflect the nursing concerns of health and safety. In spite of many problems, nurses want to invest in their work; they find patient care rewarding, and they want to give high quality nursing care.

This section of the book analyzes recurrent issues and emerging trends that arise from the turbulent environments in nursing workplaces. In large measure these trends and issues are a function of tensions generated by nurses' unique relationships with patients, physicians, and the health care organization. A brief discussion of these unique features is the first purpose of this overview chapter. A second purpose is to introduce the chapters that follow in this section, all of which examine prominent features of nursing workplaces. Issues of power and issues of relationships are critical themes. The issues surrounding these two themes are, in many ways, shared by other professionals who work in large, complex organizations.

Much literature exists describing the uneasy nature of the relationships professionals often experience in organizations. As early as 1965, Kornhauser captured the essence of this literature in his description of four major sources of conflict that professionals encounter as organizational employees. The first source of conflict concerns the nature of goals. Professionals are concerned with providing service to clients in accordance with professional standards. In organizations, the pursuit of professional excellence usually must be tempered by other considerations such as cost. A frequent concern expressed by nurses is that there often are inadequate numbers of nursing staff to provide a level of patient care to meet professional nursing standards. This situation is aggravated by staff reductions in departments that support the nursing unit, a situation that, in effect, increases the work of the nurse. Reduction of human and other resources for patient care has a direct effect on nurses, who seem to have few means to rectify the situation.

The second source of conflict involves control of professional work. Organizations rely on hierarchical control, and this may be at variance with professional control, which emphasizes experience and expertise. Braverman (1974) argues that a bureaucratic system of control separates conceptualization of work from implementation of work and, when work processes are standardized, contributes to deskilling of workers. Professionals usually struggle to avoid highly standardized work processes. In nursing workplaces, however, heavy reliance is placed on hierarchical structures to control professional nursing practice and considerable authority is invested in nursing administration. To cope with the need to eliminate or reduce potential errors by caregivers, nursing administrators establish highly bureaucratic structures and processes. As a result, nursing administrators often make decisions that in other disciplines in the same organization would be made by the individual caregiver. This situation is further complicated by the fact that much good nursing practice has an intangible quality not amenable to rigid decision-making strategies. This conflict between control by professional expertise and control by hierarchy is evident in a stark fashion when cuts to operating budgets occur while quality patient care and staff morale must be maintained.

A third source of conflict concerns reward systems. Organizational reward systems are usually related to movement up the hierarchy and away from direct service to clients, whereas professionals often rely on rewards derived from patient care expertise and peer recognition. Progression up the hierarchy on administrative or educational career ladders is well established in nursing workplaces. Similar career opportunities in clinical nursing practice remain underdeveloped, with even less attention directed to creation of peer rewards such as opportunities for in-depth study with recognized nursing clinical experts or nurse-to-nurse consultation practices. Moreover, financial rewards for staff nurses are constrained by compressed salary scales and lack of salary differentials to reward individual expertise. As Kanter (1989) illustrates, the consequences of blocked opportunity structures are that people limit their aspirations, stop future planning, lower their work commitment, and feel demoralized.

The fourth source of conflict involves ability to influence decision making concerning organizational and professional issues. Nurses are the largest professional group in any health care facility, but most nurses believe they have few formal and informal opportunities to influence decisions that affect their practice. This perceived lack of opportunity to influence begins at the nursing unit level and progresses to include policy-making committees and boards within the facilities. Staff nurses seem to believe that nursing administration does not represent their interest, and they are now demanding an independent voice in decision making.

Beyond the traditional sources of conflict just noted, nursing work is also shaped by several unique factors. Some of the most important follow:
1. The dual roles of the nurse as caregiver and coordinator
2. The knowledge base of the nurse compared to that of other health occupations
3. The relationship between nurse, physician, and patient
It is important to remember that being a "woman's profession" and doing "traditional women's work" also is an implicit theme in the following discussion of the other three factors.

CAREGIVER ROLE

In most organizations in which nurses work, they have two major roles. One is the patient caregiver role, which involves nursing assessment and care for an individual patient or a group of patients. Although this caregiver role is the most visible aspect of nursing practice, its importance is often underestimated and misunderstood. The nurse's role in patient care is often viewed by the public, other professionals, and patients as being implemented under the close supervision of a physician. Although some aspects of the nurse's role derive from the medical plan of care, other aspects (e.g., educating patients about their illness or providing skin care for an immobilized patient) derive from nursing expertise. Flood and Diers (1988) assert that the main reason most patients are admitted to hospital is to receive skilled nursing care. For example, patients are admitted to hospitals before surgery because of their perioperative nursing care needs, and they are discharged when they no longer need nursing care (McClure and Nelson, 1982).

The importance of the caregiver role is confirmed in various research studies. For example, studies of differential mortality rates for critically ill patients in various hospitals indicate that education and experience of nursing staff is a major variable in determining patient outcomes (Knaus, Draper, Wagner, and Zimmerman, 1986; Scott, Forrest, and Brown, 1976). The complexity of the caregiver role is reflected in significant differences that exist in nursing work throughout nursing units in a single agency and between agencies. Nursing units in contemporary hospitals have different levels of complexity in patient care, face major variations in turnover rates, and require use of specialized equipment and procedures (Medcof and Wall, 1990). Grouping nurses as if they all did exactly the same kind of work is an outdated notion.

Furthermore, steady advances in biomedical knowledge and accelerating technological change have resulted in highly specialized medical practice and an increasingly specialized clinical nursing practice. Specialization of nursing practice is now common in large health science centers and is increasing in public health units. With time, diffusion of knowledge and technology to small centers, with accompanying specialized practice, is inevitable; specialized clinical approaches of today become standard practices of tomorrow.

The effect of specialization on the caregiver role of nurses has been and will continue to be profound. In Chapter 17, Calkin outlines the challenges of Canadian nursing when confronted with specialization in nursing practice. These challenges concern the position of nursing specialty roles within the health care organization, the effect of specialization on job satisfaction of nurses, and the changes in design of basic and advanced education that might be required.

Similarly, work of nurses in nursing workplaces is being transformed by advances in technology. Campbell (1988) argues that use of management information systems is an attempt to increase nurses' productivity, with the consequence that time available to give nursing care to individual patients is reduced. The quest for objectivity, efficiency, and cost-cutting has caused a "speed-up" in nurses' work and increased nurses' militancy about work load issues (Thompson, 1991).

For more than a decade, computer programs performed such functions as taking complete health histories, maintaining patient records, and accessing up-to-date clinical electronic data bases. Information technology can give to all who have training to operate the equipment, including patients, the possibility of having access to knowledge previously known only by practitioners. Computers that use artificial intelligence to derive nursing diagnoses may be possible in the near future. There will be a tremendous increase in the diffusion of these technologies to all parts of the health care system in the next decade. Such technologies will enhance organizational supports to nurses and other caregivers by transforming manual systems of patient care documentation, methods of work load measurements, and interdepartmental communication, and by automating medical records (Sinclair, 1991). Concurrently, information technologies in health care institutions may reduce the need for all types of workers. The use of an electronic patient information chart (EPIC) may reduce the time nurses spend on paperwork by 25% to 40% (Dowling-Smout, 1991). However, these savings in time only occur after a long period of inservice training and learning. Furthermore, resources are required to customize an electronic system to the main information system already installed in the agency.

In Chapter 15, Maloney discusses the need for assessment of technologies used in health care organizations for their effect on patient care and on health human resources (including nurses). Unlike most information technologies, most biomedical technologies increase rather than decrease the need for nursing care. As well, part of the assessment of new technology must include finding a balance between social concerns such as the human/machine interaction and the economic effect of technology on nursing practice. Maloney presents a concise summary of the current issues confronting nursing in highly technological environments. The most significant issues are the perceived scarcity of programs of continuing education to keep nurses current with the changing patient care and safety requirements when new technologies are introduced into the setting. An equally difficult problem is how to keep basic educational curriculum current in a situation of rapid change. There is a critical need for nurses to participate on committees that assess new technologies. For example, nurses need to be involved in agency committees that consider the effect of any new technology on the need for nursing resources, on nurses' education, and on the nature and location of nursing work.

The increasing specialization of medical practice results in fragmentation of patient care and higher levels of acuity in hospitalized patients. Physicians are absent from most clinical units for extended periods during the day, and nurses must synthesize the treatment plans of several specialists and participate in new levels of clinical decision making. The reality of the work situation casts nurses in new caregiving roles, but continues to acknowledge only the physician as an independent clinical decision maker. As nurses are the only constant source of continuing professional surveillance in health care institutions, their knowledge base and skill base required to assess patient status, detect problems, and prevent crises must constantly become more sophisticated.

In the 1980s, a major change occurred in the composition of workers on nursing units, commonly referred to as a change in the skill mix. Although the number of nurses per patient increased as a function of greater patient acuity, corresponding increases did not occur in other categories of hospital personnel, particularly those who directly support or assist nurses. In fact, hospitals reduced the total number of licensed practical nurses and registered nursing assistants employed, particularly in acute care workplaces. These workers, in effect, were replaced by nurses. Further, in many hospitals, the use of nursing aides, orderlies, and attendants also was reduced and, at the same time, many support departments had personnel reduced, resulting in fewer workers available or available for fewer hours in areas such as patient transport, housekeeping, admissions, clerical, central supplies, and pharmacy. As a result, additional responsibilities, often of a non-nursing nature, have by default fallen to nurses. This change in the skill mix and in support personnel means nurses perform many support and clerical tasks not requiring their professional expertise. A careful examination of the adequacy of support and auxiliary services for nursing units 24 hours a day and on weekends is needed so that nurses will not be expected to perform tasks that should be the responsibility of other workers (McKibbin, 1990). During the 1991 nursing strike in Manitoba, the amount and nature of non-nursing tasks performed by nurses became visible to nursing, as well as to non-nursing management personnel and to board members because many of them were required to work on nursing units. The reintroduction of support workers is now under discussion in Manitoba—but may be obtained only with an overall reduction in the numbers of nurses on nursing units, resulting in a Catch-22 situation.

In the past few years, Canadian nurses have become increasingly concerned about the legal consequences of nursing practice, especially because practice is constantly changing. The visibility of nursing practice legislation and the requirement for nurses to be held accountable for their practice trigger much interest in legal matters. In Chapter 14, Wiebe provides examples from recent legal cases that reflect trends in nursing law and identify legal issues. These issues deal with matters arising from criminal law, which are relatively rare, and with matters arising from the private law, such as liability, which are becoming much more prominent. Wiebe identifies negligence as an important issue because unintentional acts may lead to legal consequences for nurses. Wiebe's comprehensive work on legal issues emphasizes the importance of nurses being able to understand patients' rights and nurses' rights, and on nurses' obligations for patient care.

The requirement for professions to be accountable to the public for their actions to protect the public interest has also thrust increasing attention toward issues surrounding regulation of nursing practice. As Risk discusses in Chapter 19, several issues in professional regulation are undergoing intensive debate as governments scrutinize professional legislation. The outcome may have significant impact on nursing workplaces. Risk examines prominent issues such as scope of practice, regulation of auxiliary personnel, demands for outcome standards for quality assurance, professional discipline, and interrelationships with occupational health and safety legislation, as well as labor and human rights legislation.

COORDINATOR ROLE

The second major role of the nurse in nursing workplaces is that of coordinator. How coordination of the various tasks occurs is a fundamental issue for the structure of health care organizations. Health care organizations such as hospitals or public health agencies are structured into highly specialized departments (e.g., nursing, medicine, dietary, social services, environmental safety, among others). These departments perform different aspects of the work of the organization. To ensure effective patient care, the work of various professionals from these highly specialized departments must be coordinated. Coordination consists of facilitating the flow of relevant patient data and managing the conflicts that are often inherent in activities that involve numerous participants (Charns and Schaefer, 1983). At the patient care level in most health care organizations, the person who undertakes much of this coordination role is the nurse assigned to the patient, supported by the head nurse of the nursing unit. A recent study by Raber (1988) illustrates the heavy demands placed on head nurses for exchange of information about patients as the nurse functions in this coordinator role. She found that head nurses had three times as many daily encounters with their professional colleagues than the senior corporate managers studied by Mintzberg (1973) had with their business associates.

Coordination is complex work and has not received much attention from organizational theorists. Stelling's (1987) observations of nurses in a Montreal hospital show that a significant portion of nurses' time is devoted to coordination, but this work is invisible work. She observes, "Nobody sees it, unless it's not well done; then it becomes visible" (p. 90). Being invisible is important for patient care and the smooth operation of the organization, but the work goes unrecognized by most people outside of the nursing profession. Moreover, its value is unacknowledged.

Coordination of patient care is particularly difficult when the work to be coordinated originates with professionals in different departments of the health organization. The differences in objectives, values, and treatment orientation of these specialized groups increase the difficulty in achieving coordination and may result in interprofessional conflict. Furthermore, coordination is hampered by formal organizational structures and highly bureaucratic decision-making methods. The work of nurses in these multidisciplinary groups is handicapped by the expectation for subordinate behavior. The use of mechanisms such as joint task forces, interlocking committees, and dual authority for budgets would provide more adequate coordination (Meilicke, 1990). As well, the fostering of an organizational culture that values and rewards teamwork could provide more recognition of nursing's central role in the process.

Effective functioning in the coordination role requires highly developed skills to extract information from conversations and observations, the ability to talk easily with other professionals, and skills in negotiation and conflict management, as well as a thorough grounding in operations of a complex professional bureaucracy. Education for this difficult but important role is usually not an explicit part of professional nursing education.

KNOWLEDGE BASE OF NURSING

Although nursing roles in health care organizations have become more demanding, the educational and research bases for nursing practice have experienced much slower development. Physicians respond to technology and advanced biomedical knowledge by developing an elaborate system of subspecialties and related training programs. Most nursing education opportunities are confined to initial preparation for generalist practice and ad hoc and unsystematized training programs for specialty work. In today's workplaces, nurses experience difficulties in remaining generalists and yet obtaining sufficient expertise to practice nursing competently. A second and related problem concerns the implicit belief by employers that nurses are interchangeable and can be sent anywhere to any part of the hospital at any time of the day or night. Further, the effect of constant changes in medical practice imposes new knowledge and skill requirements on staff nurses, and these have been virtually ignored by health care organizations and government funders.

The gap in training at basic and specialty levels between nurses and most other health care professionals is already wide and is increasing. The lack of opportunities for specialized training has serious consequences for development of a research-based nursing practice. Advanced training in research is essential to unlock the knowledge embedded in the everyday work of expert nursing practitioners. Without systematic study, nursing knowledge will remain underdeveloped and unrecognized. Currently, only a few Canadian nurses have the research training, experience, and academic qualifications to be competitive for national research awards. After several years of lobbying, the National Health Research Development Program and the Medical Research Council of Canada belatedly recognized the need to fund the development of nursing research systematically and in late 1987 announced a jointly funded program. Unfortunately, the program was suspended in 1991 for evaluation to determine the effectiveness and suitability of the program for nursing's circumstances.

In Chapter 16, Ritchie chronicles the development of nursing research in Canada.

She devotes considerable attention to the problems and challenges faced by Canadian nurses in the struggle to establish a research base for nursing practice. Not only does research-based practice require a mass of highly trained nurse researchers and clinical nurse specialists, resources such as money, space, and time are also essential.

Progress in science usually occurs as a result of collaborative endeavors that build on past achievements of others. Such endeavors in nursing research may involve clinical nurse specialists and nurse researchers who draw on the expertise of basic scientists, physicians, and social scientists and who provide training for graduate students. The cancer nursing research team, headed by Dr. Lesley Degner at the University of Manitoba, is an example of a collaborative effort to improve the quality of nursing care for cancer patients; the team involves nurse scientists, clinical nurse specialists, physicians, and other scientists and caregivers. The outcome of such collaborative research efforts could be findings that, if applied, could revolutionize nursing practice. As long-time American nursing leader Virginia Henderson recommends, in pursuit of scientific excellence nursing must "cherish the 'poets' among us—the visionaries," whose courage and determination will contribute to "the betterment of the lot of mankind" (1977, p. 164).

NURSE–PHYSICIAN–PATIENT RELATIONSHIP

Another unique and often problematic feature of nursing workplaces is the interdependent relationships between nurses, patients, and physicians. The common goal of patient care necessitates effective and close collaboration. Yet the long-standing problems of status, authority, and gender so much a part of these relationships remain neglected issues inside nursing workplaces. The disparities within the relationship are widely discussed in the literature using the family metaphor of physician–fathers and nurse–mothers, with patients assuming the role of children (Ashley, 1976; Leeson and Gray, 1978).

Physicians' contacts with patients are usually brief and highly structured, with many ceremonial qualities. Nurses' contacts with patients, on the other hand, span 8 to 12 hours a day and are more loosely structured, ranging from casual conversation to assisting with intimate body functions. As Campbell-Heider and Pollock (1987) note, "the nurse's closeness to the patient and the physician's remoteness are pervasive features of the ideology of social relations within hospitals, in which status is proportional to separation from patient" (p. 422).

The pattern of communication that has evolved between nurses and physicians about patients is highly ritualized, embracing "a host of status symbols and a differential use of time, space and numerous nonverbal clues" (Tellis-Nayak and Tellis-Nayak, 1984, p. 1065). Nonverbal clues, which include facial expressions, use of touch, interrupting in conversation, self-disclosure, and staring, are as integral to the communication process as are spoken and written words. Aspects of this process are now being documented (Keddy, Gillis Jones, Jacobs, Burton, and Rogers, 1986). These ritualistic patterns of communication reflect the status differences between physicians and nurses and actually support and fortify the disparities in the relationship (Tellis-Nayak and Tellis-Nayak, 1984).

Closely linked to this ritualistic pattern of communication is the issue of authority for patient care. Historically, nurses gained much of their professional status and legitimacy from performing functions delegated by physicians, but nurses' dependence on physicians hinders the quest for greater independence. In spite of the fact that physicians typically spend little time with patients, nurses who are with patients constantly must ask permission to institute simple measures necessary for the safety and comfort of patients (e.g., giving an aspirin to a patient with a headache). A change in this traditional relationship is being introduced in Britain. The National Health Service recently accepted in principle that the practice of some nurses (community psychiatric nurses, specialist nurses working with the terminally ill) should be expanded to encompass adjusting dosages and timing of medications for specific types of patients, prescribing from a set list of drugs and products such as laxatives, mouthwashes, and gargles, and removing ear wax ("U.K. nurses to get . . .," 1990). New legislation is required to implement this policy.

Nurses are generally expected to defer to medical authority even in situations in which a physician is clearly less knowledgeable and less experienced. When physicians and other professionals are not available to provide patient services, nurses substitute (e.g., deliver babies or prescribe a required medication). Often, nurses must exercise authority beyond that allocated in the formal structure just to do their jobs. As Hughes, Hughes, and Deutscher (1958) observe, "The person at the top of the hierarchy of authority is invested with more power than he [sic] can ordinarily use, while the second in command must often exercise more than she [sic] is formally allowed" (p. 6). In these situations, nursing knowledge is simultaneously undervalued and taken for granted, causing considerable frustration and discontent among nursing staff.

However, in a recent article, Stein, Watts, and Howell (1990) note major changes in the doctor–nurse relationship in the past 20 years. Physician authority is threatened by several factors, including:

- Deterioration of public esteem for physicians
- Nursing shortages that focus more attention on the value of nursing in health care
- Strong nursing roles in the media
- New roles for nurses in utilization review committees and quality assurance
- More female physicians

Combined, these factors could foster more interdependence between physicians and nurses. Stein and his colleagues observe that subservience and dominance are psychologically and professionally restricting for both doctors and nurses.

Ethical concerns of the nurse are another set of largely ignored issues germane to the nurse–physician–patient interactions. Freedman (1981) states that discussions of medical ethics tend to concentrate on physician–patient interaction "to the relative exclusion of patient–nurse or nurse–physician relationships" (p. 175). He continues, that the ethical issues in nursing practice are complicated by nurses' place in the hierarchical structure of health care organizations. For decision making that is informed and shared with patients, better ethical relationships between nurses and physicians and between nurses and nursing administration must be fostered (Rodney, 1989). These relationships result from mutual respect and acknowledgement of the unique and valuable contributions to patient care that each professional has to offer.

Although there is a growing body of literature about ethical issues in nursing practice, limited discussion of the ethical problems for the nurse, which arise from the nurse's responsibility to the patient, to the physician, and to the organization, has occurred. As Storch observes in Chapter 13, the complexity and uniqueness of nursing ethics is a function of always being there, of having multiple obligations, of having a subordinate position in a hierarchy, and of experiencing the daily dilemmas of patient care. Numerous mechanisms to enhance ethical decision making have been tried, including ethical rounds, institutional ethics committees, and nursing ethics councils.

Genuine collaboration and recognition of the complementary roles between nurses and physicians are crucial for quality patient care and for job satisfaction of nurses and physicians. Examples of mechanisms could include joint practice committees, joint patient care planning teams, and integrated patient records. Strategies to improve working relationships between nurses and other members of the health team, including physicians and hospital administrators, are essential. Without these strategies, the phenomenon of "problem-shifting" may occur (i.e., the professional may transfer these difficulties into relationships with their patients) (Nievaard, 1987).

QUALITY OF WORK EXPERIENCE

Quality of nurses' work experience is a long-standing, unresolved problem in nursing workplaces and has direct impact on productivity of nurses and on quality of patient care. This issue more than any other is the reason for continued unrest in nursing workplaces. Kopinak (1990) describes the situation as a revolt by nurses against unacceptable conditions, noting that "nurses all over the country are mad" (p. 314). The quality of nurses' work experience has been repeatedly studied in Canada and in other Western countries such as the United States and Britain with similar results and recommendations, yet little has changed. What is now different is that nurses themselves are beginning to organize inside nursing workplaces to ensure that their concerns are heard and that changes occur.

A recent report concerning nurse retention and quality of work life, jointly undertaken by the Canadian Nurses Association and Canadian Hospital Association (1990) analyzed 23 Canadian nursing work force studies from the 1980s. The analysis showed that factors leading to dissatisfaction involved lack of educational opportunities, inflexible schedules, lack of involvement in organizational decisions, inadequate staffing, and too many non-nursing tasks. Other issues involved limited professional autonomy, lack of respect from other health care team members for nursing's contribution to patient care, and inadequate salary and benefits. The board of directors of the Canadian Nurses Association recently approved position statements on the quality of worklife and safe workplace environments, and these statements call for major reform in nursing workplaces. Creating "nurse friendly" work environments requires intensive and urgent attention.

The importance of finding solutions to these concerns was recognized with the establishment of the Quality of Nursing Worklife Research Unit at two sites—

McMaster University's Faculty of Health Sciences and the University of Toronto's Faculty of Nursing. Funding for this five-year initiative was provided by the Ontario Ministry of Health. The unit's purpose is "to promote, coordinate and conduct research in the quality of nursing worklife" (O'Brien-Pallas and Baumann, 1991). The current activities of the unit include sponsoring a quarterly newsletter (*The Review*), offering seminars for nurses and researchers to exchange ideas about nursing worklife, and generating research initiatives such as development of instruments to measure recruitment and retention in nursing. Funding for this project is part of a $15.5 million, 5-year envelope allocated by the Ontario government for improving nurses' quality of working life. Similar funding has been provided by the governments of Alberta and British Columbia.

Quality of worklife encompasses environmental concerns such as lighting, acoustics, temperature, humidity, and air quality in the workplaces, as well as ergonomic and worker safety issues. These concerns reflect the expectations of an educated, skilled, and informed work force. Workers increasingly stress workplace factors as reasons for accepting employment in specific places (Curry, 1991). In nursing workplaces, attention to ergonomic issues by redesigning patient care areas to reflect physical and psychological demands of delivering nursing care is essential. Nursing workplaces need to be modified to suit nurses instead of nurses having to adapt to the workplace.

Recent studies on the effect of new technologies promote the application of ergonomics as an integral part of health facilities design (CHA, 1990). Moreover, Messing (1990) notes that research is needed to examine women's occupational health. Areas for study include effects of involuntary employment (part-time, short-term work) on mental and physical health, development of more sensitive methods for study of exposure levels to chemicals on pregnant women, global physiological effects of stressful workplaces, and research to support standards that truly reflect the extent of physical exertion in a particular job. Currently, work that is considered light may in fact require considerable physical exertion—yet this is not reflected in usual workplace standards. Limited research and small attention to these issues occurs in most nursing workplaces.

The available research about nursing work is primarily on factors such as job dissatisfaction, turnover, stress, and burnout while essentially neglecting environmental and ergonomic concerns. For example, Parasuraman and Hansen (1987) found that work overload, assignment changes, and resource inadequacy contribute to stress and negatively affect job satisfaction and organizational commitment. However, as Hinshaw and Atwood (1984) state, many of these studies do not include a multifactorial perspective and often lack adequate theoretical grounding. A recurrent theme in much of this research suggests that nurses respond to their work experience in ways characteristic of other groups with limited organizational power and blocked opportunities for career growth. In these circumstances, workers tend to lower their aspirations, appear to be less motivated to achieve, are less likely to make their skills and abilities known to supervisors, tend to seek psychosocial rewards from peers and not from their work, and frequently develop hostility to people outside of the work group and to administrative personnel (Kanter and Stein, 1979).

Strategies for improving the quality of work experiences of workers, including nurses in low-power and low-opportunity positions, need to focus on job restructuring and putting more control in the hands of individuals and groups who actually perform tasks. Research comparing nurses with accountants and teachers shows that nurses had significantly lower levels of job satisfaction with respect to salary, participation in decisions, and job security (Wright, McGill, and Collins, 1990). This and similar studies focus attention on the most critical question to be addressed about nursing workplaces: to what extent is it possible to modify the structure of health care organizations to ensure more autonomy, more recognition for clinical expertise, and more access to opportunities for growth and change in the design of nursing work?

Cohen (1976) observes that most organizations do not have a way to implement the intelligence and capabilities of most workers to generate innovative solutions for organizational problems. The human and financial cost to health care organizations because of the lack of this adaptive capacity is tremendous. Kanter and Stein (1979) argue that "people would rather vest themselves in work than not and will find ways to do so even if their own organization does not provide the tools for doing it" (p. 189).

One big issue facing health care organizations in the next decade will be competition for highly educated and highly talented nurses for a broad spectrum of positions. More attention to what attracts, motivates, and retains nurses will be essential. Nursing "talent" will be health care's newest form of "capital" in the future. Treating nursing talent as capital necessitates considerable reorientation of managerial thinking and practice (Light, 1990). Nursing staffs need opportunities to learn as patient care requirements change, the authority to get the job done, opportunities for individual initiative and creativity, and support in ways that enable them to do their very best. Initiatives such as job redesign by the employee (Perlman, 1990) and lateral movement and career planning for expert practitioners who may not want to move to management or education (Winstead-Fry, 1990, p. v) are some strategies that can be used to show value for "bedside nurses."

Nursing divisions of most health care organizations have few resources to support innovation and change. Yet the need for innovation is acute. Strategies to foster critical questioning of established practices and to support nurses to take risks are the foundation of innovation. Linkages to external agencies such as universities and consumer groups have potential to bring new ideas into the organization, another essential element of innovation. Securing new resources, often from special project funds of governments or private foundations, to test a nursing intervention or to implement a workplace strategy offers opportunities to try out new ideas and, if successful, aids in securing permanent funding at a later stage.

How nurses establish their careers and what factors within the work and educational environment contribute to career development are continuing issues in nursing. Career development has two dimensions: vertical progress along a career ladder and horizontal progress to develop personal and professional expertise. In nursing, this complementary relationship is largely absent. A major concern of nurses is the absence of opportunity for career development in clinical practice. Yet clinical practice is where nurses develop their educational, technical, professional, and personal expertise. Career advancement and recognition occur most frequently when nurses leave clinical settings and accept administrative or educational appointments. In Chapter 18, Donner discusses professional socialization, career development, and mobility in nursing workplaces. She identifies changing expectations of nurses, need for social support, and structural barriers inside nursing workplaces as key variables that require attention by individual nurses and by their employers to ensure increased career opportunities, particularly in clinical nursing practice.

Studies concerning nurses' perspectives of the quality of their work environments echo recurring themes of the importance of having supportive colleagues, autonomy, control over work activities, and adequate human and other types of resources with which to provide patient care (Attridge and Callahan, 1990; Lindsey and Attridge, 1989; McCloskey, 1990). Having supportive colleagues and adequate resources is particularly significant considering recent budget reductions within the health care sector. The consequences of budget reduction on nursing work seem to be forgotten in the ongoing debates about costs of health care services. Attridge and Callaghan (1987) observe that individual nurses "lacking the power and strategies to manage what is in effect a system problem, not of their making, experience dissatisfaction, disillusionment with work and . . . experience [a sense of] failure whose impact on self-worth is less than positive" (p. 34).

Nursing workplaces also suffer from a lack of support systems (services) such as secretaries, porters, dietary aides, and housekeepers, particularly after normal working hours and on weekends. Consequences of staff reductions in other departments (e.g., housekeeping and dietary) often mean an increased nursing workload because these services still must be maintained. Nurses forced to decide whether or not to provide the service may face increased stress levels (Meilicke, 1991). Nurses have traditionally filled these non-nursing roles to ensure adequate care to patients but in doing so have masked the inadequacy of the system. Devereux (1981) observes: "Despite inadequate delivery systems, nurses will always manage to get what they need. They hoard supplies, borrow from each other, take more than they need and hide the extras, and keep emergency stashes in unlikely places" (p. 20). However, such tactics do not force system-wide change. Sabo's (1990) recent studies reinforce the need for unit aides to provide general maintenance of the nursing unit by cleaning equipment and stocking cupboards, for expanding the role of the unit clerk to include more secretarial and related documentation activities, for reviewing and enhancing the role of volunteers on nursing units, and for other disciplines (physiotherapy, pharmacy, respiratory therapy) to provide expanded coverage to better meet patient and nursing unit needs. These measures will reduce the amount of time nurses spend performing "non-nursing" tasks. However, unless new financial resources are obtained, converting nursing positions to support staff positions or transferring money from the nursing budget to other departments so they can provide expanded service to the nursing unit will result in a loss of nursing jobs.

Nurses who occupy middle management positions are often laden with budgeting, staffing, and related functions as a consequence of decentralization and frequently have little time to provide necessary "support work" to ensure that nurses will feel valued and will take risks to find creative solutions to workplace problems

(Owens and Glennerster, 1990, p. 156). This support work entails being there to provide timely feedback and encouragement, identifying approaches for the handling of difficult situations, or finding extra staff in emergencies. Thus there is a concomitant need to enhance staff support resources to nursing managers at all levels (Meilicke, 1990). Enhanced staff support includes more clinical experts to work with nursing staff; more administrative assistants to handle the myriad of paperwork tasks; and more experts to develop budgets, supervise computerization, and organize related planning activities.

Meilicke (1991) notes that the shifts to ambulatory care and reduced length of stay, with no or limited reductions in rates of admission, also contribute to increased nursing workload and stress; the stress related to increased workload often exceeds even that generated by budget reductions within the nursing division. Effective management in these circumstances requires development of strategies to better use nursing resources. These are strategies that have been labeled work force extenders and include the following (Kramer, 1990):

- Using case managers
- Assigning nursing aides to nurses and not to patients
- Limiting the practice of floating nurses to other units in hospitals
- Reducing the use of contract agency nurses and employing more permanent nurses
- Hiring educated, experienced nurses and limiting the hiring of new graduates
- Creating self-managed work groups at the nursing unit level

Lack of involvement in organizational decision making has also been acknowledged as a source of dissatisfaction for nurses. For involvement to be meaningful, the purposes and level of participation expected from the nurse must be delineated so that congruence between the nursing administrator's expectations and expectations of the staff nurses is maintained (Fried, 1991). Recently, legislative initiatives in Ontario mandated staff nurse representation on various hospital committees, including the fiscal advisory committee, which reports to the hospital's board. This represents an attempt to provide meaningful involvement in decisions that affect nursing practice and quality of work life (Dowling-Smout, 1990). Nurses who sit on these committees will need adequate training and orientation to aid effective participation. These strategies represent an attempt to empower staff nurses by extending their control over their work environment.

Donovan (1990) outlines other measures for empowerment, some of which include improving nurse retention by rewarding seniority, by legitimizing the role of the charge nurse, by having reporting relationships reflect authority for the unit-based activities of housekeeping and dietary staff, by developing active long-range recruiting plans, and by negotiating with medicine and administration with respect to appropriate patient census and staffing for the size of nursing unit. Other initiatives include having meaningful involvement in the formulations of mission statements, objectives, and priorities of the organization and having control of nursing staff travel and training budget by a staff nurse committee (Thomas, 1990). Staff nurses can learn politically astute strategies for change in the workplace. Mason, Costello-Nickitas, Scanlan, and Magnuson (1990) note that 88% of participants involved in a continuing education program aimed at developing these strategies increased their professional connections or networks. Most also had accomplished small changes in their workplaces, such as reducing non-nursing duties assigned to nursing staff.

Highly competent nurse administrators are central to the creation of change in nursing organizations. Such nurse administrators must be "capable of specifying multiple goals, weighing them, interrelating them, and finding synergetic policies that will accomplish more than a single goal at a time" (Gardner, 1965, p. 66). These administrators can build learning organizations—organizations in which "people are continually expanding their capabilities to shape their future" (Senge, 1990, p. 9). Nurse administrators must work with "multiple bottom lines—social, environmental, political and ethical—and ensure that all of them are interconnected" (Poulin, 1984, p. 38)

In Chapter 12, Lemieux-Charles and Wylie examine the roles and functions of nurse administrators in relation to emerging trends in nursing, in management, and in the delivery of health care services. These trends include megastructures, participative management, outcome-oriented nursing research, quality assurance, nurse-managed care, and case management. These authors stress the importance of appropriate educational preparation for nursing administrators so they may fulfill the corporate and professional dimensions of the job.

Effectiveness in nursing administration is central to quality nursing care and to quality work experience of the nurse. Good administrators develop a complex range of leadership, managerial, and cognitive skills for the successful orchestration of the various components of the nursing division. Effective nursing administrators must be able to act flexibly, to accomplish goals, and to gain cooperation from various people in the organization. The management of knowledgeable workers requires radical rethinking of an organization's values and ways of approaching problems. This can be accomplished by lessening the distinction between administrators and staff nurses in terms of access to organizational information, control over work assignments, and visibility outside of nursing units within the organization and external to the health care setting. This also entails being consistent and providing challenging projects, rewards, and innovation (Gellman, 1990). The effective nurse administrator demonstrates consistency in what is said and done, and rewards and encourages innovation. Sadly, innovation in nursing practice is an unusual rather than expected event. Most health care organizations do not reward or encourage innovation at the grass roots level. Innovation advances nursing practice by highlighting and testing new and possibly better ways to deliver and/or organize patient care. By valuing innovation, the nursing administrator verifies that the staff nurses' ideas are important and meaningful. Thus a sense of heightened commitment to the organization may be engendered in staff. Most importantly, however, the effective nursing administrator must be able to obtain the resources required for staff nurses to provide quality patient care.

Meilicke (1990) believes that the nursing division can be strengthened if board members and non-nursing managers know and understand nursing's contributions within the organization; thus a broader perspective concerning patient care may be achieved and the profile of the nursing profession may be enhanced, paving the way for heightened interdisciplinary cooperation. DeBack (1991, p. 127) emphasizes the need for recognizing and working with "organized, funded interdisciplinary coalitions with focused plans and objectives," rather than depending on nursing resources alone. The approach reflects the trend toward integration of health care and the globalization of activities through interdisciplinary networks. To effect workplace change, nurses must strengthen their unity of purpose and become empowered through and with the support of others in the health care enterprise.

CONCLUSION

Many of the issues discussed in this overview and in the chapters that follow are derived from the structure of nursing workplaces. Recognition of the fact that nurses will continue to practice within these turbulent environments is a first step to development of individual and collective strategies to survive in and cope with the present situation and to shape future workplaces. For these reasons and others such as lack of financial resources, shortage of specialized staff, and more demands on nursing time, leadership of the nursing division will be more difficult and more challenging than ever before—but for those able to meet this challenge, perhaps ultimately more satisfying than ever before.

REFERENCES

Ashley, J.H. (1976). *Hospitals, paternalism and the role of the nurse*. New York: Teacher's College Press.

Attridge, C., & Callahan, M. (1987). *Women in women's work: Nurses' perspective of quality work environments* (Research Report #1). Victoria: University of Victoria, Faculty of Human and Social Development.

Attridge, C., & Callahan, M. (1990). Nurses' perspectives of quality work environments. *Canadian Journal of Nursing Administration, 3*(3), 18-24.

Braverman, H. (1974). *Labor and monopoly capital*. New York: Monthly Review Press.

Campbell-Heider, N., & Pollock, D. (1987). Barriers to physician-nurse collegiality: An anthropological perspective. *Social Science Medicine, 25*(5), 421-425.

Campbell, M. (1988). The structure of stress in nurses' work. In B.S. Bolaria & H.D. Dickinson (Eds.), *Sociology of health care in Canada* (pp. 393-405). Toronto: Harcourt Brace Jovanovich.

Canadian Hospital Association. (1990). *The impact of technological change on human resources in health care*. Ottawa: Employment and Immigration Canada.

Canadian Nurses' Association & Canadian Hospital Association. (1990, November). *Nurse retention and quality of work life: A national perspective*. Ottawa: Canadian Nurses Association.

Charns, M.P., & Schaefer, M.J. (1983). *Health care organizations: A model for management*. Englewood Cliffs, NJ: Prentice-Hall.

Cohen, L.B. (1976). The structure of workers' decisions. *Journal of Economic Issues, 10*, 524-537.

Curry, B. (1991). Your office can be harmful to your health. *Policy Options, 12*(2), 11-12.

DeBack, V. (1991). The National Commission on Nursing Implementation project. *Nursing Outlook, 39*(3), 124-131.

Devereux, P.M. (1981). Essential elements of nurse-physician collaboration. *Journal of Nursing Administration, 11*(5), 19-23.

Donovan, M. (1990). What we need to change about nursing: Staff nurses share their ideas. *Journal of Nursing Administration, 20*(12), 38-42.

Dowling-Smout, C. (1991, July). Computerized patient care systems: Potential problems and how to reduce them. *Canadian Health Care Management* (*Dispatch* Supplement No. DP 67:30-35). Toronto: Methuen.

Dowling-Smout, C. (1990, April). Beneficial or bureaucratic? Giving nurses a voice on hospital committees. *Canadian Nursing Management (Special Reports* Supplement No. SR 7:1-7:7). Toronto: MPL Communications Inc.

Flood, S., & Diers, D. (1988). Nurse staffing, patient outcome and cost. *Nursing Management, 19*(5), 34-43.

Freedman, B. (1981). A prolegomenon to the allocation of responsibility in hierarchical organizations: Nurses and physicians. In M.S. Staum & D.E. Larsen (Eds.), *Doctors, patients and society* (pp. 175-192). Waterloo, ON: Wilfred Laurier University Press.

Fried, B. (1991, January). Employee participation in decision making. *Canadian Health Care Management (Organizational Behaviour* Supplement No. OB 13:1-13:7). Toronto: Carswell.

Gardner, G. (1965, October). How to prevent organizational dry rot. *Harper's Magazine*, pp. 66-81.

Gellman, H. (1990, Spring). Knowledge workers require special touch. *Inside Guide, 4*(1), 22, 24, 29.

Henderson, V. (1977). Guest editorial. *Nursing Research, 26*(3), 163-164.

Hinshaw, A.S., & Atwood, J.R. (1984). Nursing staff turnover, stress and satisfaction: Models, measures and management. In H.H. Werley & J.J. Fitzpatrick (Eds.), *Annual Review of Nursing Research* (pp. 133-153). New York: Springer.

Hughes, E., Hughes, H., & Deutscher, I. (1958). *Twenty thousand nurses tell their story.* Philadelphia: Lippincott.

Kanter, R. M. (1989). *When giants learn to dance: Mastering the challenges of strategy, management and careers in the 1990s.* New York: Simon & Schuster.

Kanter, R.M., & Stein, B.A. (Eds.). (1979). *Life in organizations: Workplaces as people experience them.* New York: Basic Books.

Keddy, B., Gillis Jones, M., Jacobs, P., Burton, H., & Rogers, M. (1986). The doctor-nurse relationship: An historical perspective. *Journal of Advanced Nursing, 11*, 745-753.

Knaus, W., Draper, E., Wagner, D., & Zimmerman, J. (1986). An evaluation of outcome from intensive care in major medical centers. *Annals of Internal Medicine, 104*, 410-418.

Kopinak, J. (1990). Nursing in Canada: A profession in revolt. *International Nursing Review, 37*(4), 312-314.

Kornhauser, W. (1965). *Scientists in industry.* Berkeley: University of California Press.

Kramer, M. (1990). Magnet hospitals: Excellence revisited. *Journal of Nursing Administration, 20*(9), 35-44.

Leeson, J., & Gray, J. (1978). *Women and medicine.* London: Tavistock.

Light, W. (1990, November/December). Walter's megatrends for the 1990s. *The Equal Times,* pp. 72-74.

Lindsey, E., & Attridge, C. (1989). Staff nurses' perceptions of support in an acute care workplace. *Canadian Journal of Nursing Research, 21*(2), 15-25.

Mason, D.J., Costello-Nickitas, D.M., Scanlan, J.M., & Magnuson, B.A. (1991). Empowering nurses for politically astute change in the workplace. *Journal of Continuing Education in Nursing, 22*(1), 5-10.

McCloskey, J.C. (1990). Two requirements for job contentment: Autonomy and social integration. *Image: Journal of Nursing Scholarship, 22*(3), 140-143.

McClure, M.L., & Nelson, M.J. (1982). Trends in hospital nursing. In L.H. Aiken (Ed.), *Nursing in the 1980s: Crises, opportunities, challenges* (pp. 59-73). Philadelphia: Lippincott.

McKibbin, R.C. (1990). *The nursing shortage and the 1990s: Realities and remedies.* Kansas City, MO: American Nurses Association.

Medcof, J.W., & Wall, R.W. (1990). Work technology and the motive profiles of nurses. *Canadian Journal of Nursing Research, 22*(3), 51-65.

Meilicke, C. (1990, April). Nurses and physicians in the modern hospital: Watering the garden. *Canadian Health Care Management (Organizational Design* Supplement No. OD 11:1-11:6). Toronto: Methuen.

Meilicke, C. (1991, July/August). The nursing division: Environment and strategy. Part 1: Management problems. *Canadian Health Care Management (Organizational Design* Supplement No. OD 12:1-12:6). Toronto: Carswell.

Messing, K. (1990). Are women "the weaker sex" or do they just have hard jobs? The need for research on women's occupational health. *Chronic Diseases in Canada, 11*(2), 25-27.

Mintzberg, H. (1973). *The nature of managerial work*. New York: Harper & Row.

Nievaard, A.C. (1987). Communication climate and patient care: Causes and effects of nurses' attitudes to patients. *Social Science Medicine, 24*(9), 777-784.

O'Brien-Pallas, L., & Baumann, A. (1991). Welcome to the unit. *The Review, Quarterly Newsletter of the Quality of Nursing Worklife Research Unit, 1*(1), 1.

Owens, P., & Glennerster, H. (1990). *Nursing in Conflict*. London: Macmillan Education.

Parasuraman, S., & Hansen, D. (1987). Coping with work stressors in nursing: Effects of adaptive versus maladaptive strategies. *Work and Occupations, 14*(1), 88-105.

Perlman, S.L. (1990). Employees redesign their jobs. *Personnel Journal, 69*(11), 37-40.

Poulin, M.A. (1984). Future directions for nursing administration. *Journal of Nursing Administration, 14*(3), 37-41.

Raber, W.J. (1988). *The work activities and behavior of first-line nursing managers*. Unpublished thesis, School of Nursing, Faculty of Graduate Studies, University of Manitoba, Winnipeg.

Rodney, P. (1989). Towards ethical decision-making in nursing practice. *Canadian Journal of Nursing Administration, 2*(2), 11-14.

Sabo, K. (1990). Protecting the professional role: A study to review non-nursing activities and recommendations for change. *Canadian Journal of Nursing Administration, 3*(4), 15-18.

Scott, W.R., Forrest, W.H., & Brown, B.W. (1976). Hospital structure and postoperative mortality and morbidity. In S.M. Shortell & M. Brown (Eds.), *Organizational Research in hospitals* (pp. 72-89). Chicago: Blue Cross Association.

Senge, P. M. (1990, Fall). The leader's new work: Building learning organizations. *Sloan Management Review, 31*(3), 7-23.

Sinclair, V. (1991). The impact of information systems on nursing performance and productivity. *Journal of Nursing Administration, 21*(2), 46-50.

Stein, L., Watts, D.T., & Howell, T. (1990). The doctor-nurse game revisited. *New England Journal of Medicine, 322*(8), 546-549.

Stelling, J. (1987). Summary remarks. In C. Attridge & M. Callahan, *Women in women's work: Nurses' perspective of quality work environments* (Research Report #1) (pp. 90-92). Victoria: University of Victoria, Faculty of Human and Social Development.

Tellis-Nayak, M., & Tellis-Nayak, V. (1984). Games that professionals play: The social psychology of physician nurse interaction. *Social Science Medicine, 12*(18), 1063-1069.

Thomas, C. (1990). Power struggles ... hospital decentralization. *The Registered Nurse, 2*(3), 9, 11, 12, 14.

Thompson, L.G. (1991, June). The transformation of the nursing work process: "The separation of hand and brain." Paper presented at the meeting of the Canadian Sociology and Anthropology Association, Kingston, ON.

U.K. nurses to get drug prescribing privileges. (1990, May 29). *The Medical Post, 26*(21), 4.

Winstead-Fry, P. (1990). *Career planning: A nurse's guide to career advancement*. New York: National League for Nursing.

Wright, V.B., McGill, J., & Collins, J. (1990). Are nurses less satisfied than other workers? *Nursing Economics, 8*(5), 308-313.

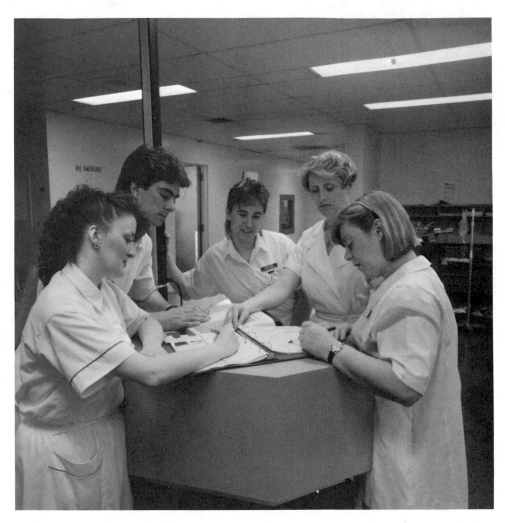

Communication and team work are important aspects of nursing practice. This photograph, taken for a poster by the Association of Registered Nurses of Newfoundland, shows a team of health care workers at a nursing station at St. Clare's Mercy Hospital, in St. John's, Newfoundland. (Photograph courtesy Prime Communications Consultants, St. John's, Lane Photographics Ltd., St. John's, and the Association of Registered Nurses of Newfoundland. Used with permission.)

CHAPTER TWELVE

Administrative Issues

LOUISE LEMIEUX-CHARLES, RN, PhD
DOROTHY WYLIE, RN, MSc(HRD)

Louise Lemieux-Charles, RN, BScN (Ottawa), MScN, PhD (Toronto), is an Assistant Professor in the Department of Health Administration, University of Toronto, where she is also Program Director of the Hospital Management Research Unit. Her main research areas include ethical issues arising for clinicians and managers in resource allocation and utilization decisions, processes of team functioning in quality improvement, and impact of job design on nurse staff satisfaction and perceived effectiveness. At the time this chapter was conceived, she was Member-At-Large Nursing Administration for the Canadian Nurses Association, where she was also a member of the Board of Directors (1984 to 1988) and chaired the committee that revised the standards for nursing administration. Her interests in organization design and its impact on staff date back to studies she conducted in the early 1980s on nurse satisfaction, turnover, and retention.

Dorothy M. Wylie, RN, BScN (New York), MA (Nsg Admin) (Columbia), MSc(HRD) (American University), is Principal of the consulting firm of Dorothy M. Wylie and Associates and has been consulting in health care for several years. She has held positions in nursing administration in the United States and Canada and was Vice President, Nursing at the Toronto General Hospital for 9 years. She currently teaches nursing administration in the graduate program of the Faculty of Nursing, University of Toronto, and holds the rank of Associate Professor. She is Associate Editor of the Canadian Journal of Nursing Administration *and a Surveyor with the Canadian Council for Health Care Facilities Accreditation.*

N urse administrators in the 1990s know that they are in key positions to ensure that nursing staff are providing quality care in acceptable working environments and to influence organizational policies related to overall delivery of health care. This chapter describes the challenges that nursing administration may confront in the future, given past and present trends.

These challenges must be defined in the context of the environment in which health care is delivered. Because nurse administrators occupy different positions depending on the agency and its size, differences in roles and functions will be described. Nursing administration is well positioned to influence the organizational environment and, consequently, to manage future challenges and ensure that nursing services are delivered in an effective and efficient manner.

NURSE ADMINISTRATOR

Size and complexity of the health organization will dictate the number of levels of nursing administration. The degree to which an organization is complex depends on the number of its divisions and departments, the number of specialties within divisions, and the number of supervisory levels in the organization as a whole. Figure 12-1 illustrates three common nursing administration levels and gives the general titles most often used.

Because health organizations are reviewing the ways in which they are organized,

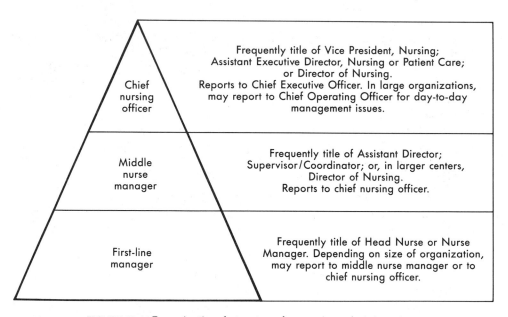

FIGURE 12-1 Organizational structure for nursing administration.

many nursing titles and, in some cases, functions are changing. Figure 12-2 illustrates the most common type of organizational structure in hospitals. However, divisions such as information systems, public relations, or planning may not be in smaller hospitals, or some positions may be combined.

The differences in titles and functions are often confusing to staff nurses, who are mainly concerned with patient care issues and who often wonder what nurse administrators or nurse managers do. As noted in Figures 12-1 and 12-2, there is little consistency among organizations in use of titles. For this reason, the terms *first line manager, middle manager,* and *chief nursing officer* will be used in this chapter to describe levels of nursing administration.

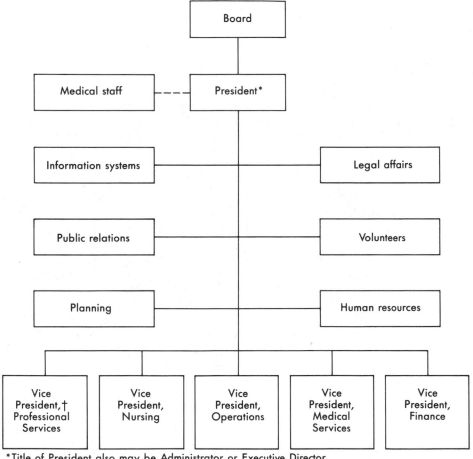

*Title of President also may be Administrator or Executive Director
†Title of Vice President also may be Director or Assistant Executive Director

FIGURE 12-2 Typical organizational structure for hospitals.

Nurse managers perform functions similar to other non-nurse managers. These functions include:
- Setting objectives, planning, and organizing
- Communicating, motivating, and leading
- Measuring and evaluating to ensure plan implementation
- Instituting quality assurance mechanisms

However, they also have a responsibility to advance professional knowledge and ensure integration of that knowledge into practice (Canadian Nurses Association, 1988). This latter responsibility requires that those in nursing management positions be nurses and that they understand the nature of nursing.

Mintzberg (1975) notes that the aforementioned functions do not fully address the difficulties and complexities of a manager's role. In reference to first-line managers, Simpson (1988) notes that they "work at an unrelenting pace . . . yet are required to be strongly oriented to both action and people in order to succeed in keeping their units viable, competitive and in step with organizational goals and objectives" (p. 18). To assist nurse administrators in defining their roles and evaluating their effectiveness, the Canadian Nurses Association (CNA) has developed standards for nursing administration (see box).

CNA supports Leatt's statement (1982) that nursing administration contains a professional component and a corporate component. The professional component refers to the nurse administrator's knowledge and expertise with respect to professional nursing, to the ability to exert nursing leadership, and to the ability to act as advisor on nursing matters to the executive team of the organization (e.g., to the executive director, president, or administrator; the chief medical representative; and other chief administrative officers such as directors of finance, human resources, hospital services). The corporate dimension refers to the nurse administrator's involvement in organization-wide policies and participation in the organization's executive team to determine policies, priorities, allocation of resources, and other general management issues (CNA, 1988).

The proportions of these two dimensions—corporate and professional—as performed by nurse administrators vary according to the level in the management hierarchy. For example, in relation to CNA's standard for setting and implementing organizational goals, priorities, and strategies (Standard II in the box), the first-line manager is concerned with the professional component when he or she translates the organization's patient-related goals into nursing actions. Such translation requires clinical expertise and an understanding of nursing's unique contribution to patient care. The corporation component is reflected in such activities as the development of programs that are part of the organization's overall plan.

On the other hand, the chief nursing officer is involved to a greater degree in working with other senior non-nurse directors and with board members to determine the goals and objectives for the organization and the allocation of resources, keeping in mind how nursing contributes to the goals. The chief nursing officer is responsible "to improve the knowledge and understanding of non-nurse managers and board members regarding the nursing enterprise" (Meilicke, 1990, p. 31).

**Standards for Nursing Administration
Canadian Nurses Association 1988**

Standard I

Nursing administration plans for and implements effective and efficient delivery of nursing services.

Standard II

Nursing administration participates in the setting and carrying out of organizational goals, priorities, and strategies.

Standard III

Nursing administration provides for allocation, optimum use of, and evaluation of resources such that the standards of nursing practice can be met.

Standard IV

Nursing administration maintains information systems appropriate for planning, budgeting, implementing, and monitoring the quality of nursing services.

Standard V

Nursing administration promotes the advancement of nursing knowledge and promotes the utilization of research findings.

Standard VI

Nursing administration provides leadership that is visible and proactive.

Standard VII

Nursing administration evaluates the effectiveness and efficiency of nursing services.

From the Canadian Nurses Association (1988): *The role of the nurse administrator and standards for nursing administration,* Ottawa: Author, p. 10. © Canadian Nurses Association. Used with permission.

CONTEXT OF NURSING ADMINISTRATION

The CNA (1988) states that nursing administration "is concerned with knowledge of systems, organizations and groups within the context of the environment, health and nursing" (p. 3). Nursing administration is practiced in a climate of rapid change and in organizations that are experiencing increased pressures to re-examine delivery of care so that resources are used efficiently and effectively. These pressures are primarily the result of such external factors as increased regulation by governments, increased attention to cost containment measures, better informed consumers, and continued technological development. Many task forces (e.g., British Columbia Royal Commission, 1991; Evans, 1987; Gallant, 1989; Hyndman, 1989; Spasoff, 1987) conclude that there is sufficient money. However, a major policy question involves appropriate allocation of the monies to various health care programs. For example, should additional monies be allocated to neonatal intensive care or given to health promotion programs for disadvantaged children? The organization's internal environment—which includes its mission, goals, and its various disciplines, technology, managers, staff, and clients—must consider the external environment when it is defining its role.

PERSPECTIVES ON NURSING ADMINISTRATION

Roles and functions of nurse administrators are being redefined in the context of emerging trends in nursing, management, and delivery of health care services. Table 12-1 compares past, present, and emerging trends. Each trend is discussed in more detail and the implications for nurse administrators are elaborated in the following section.

Setting for Delivery of Care

In the 1940s, nursing services were delivered in hospitals and in homes. The latter required services of visiting nurses and community health agencies. With the federal government's Hospital Incentive Grants in the late 1940s, more than 46,000 new hospital beds opened between 1948 and 1953 (Taylor, 1987). This addition increased the need for nurses to staff growing hospitals and changed the pattern of nursing practice. Whereas in 1930, 60% of nurses worked as private duty nurses, this number decreased to 9% in 1960. In contrast, nurses working in hospitals increased from 25% in 1930 to 59% in 1960 (Hall, 1964).

Hospital growth and expansion continued into the 1970s—until governments questioned the costs incurred by such expensive services. Governments became aware that hospitalization was not necessarily the best alternative to treatment and encouraged hospitals to shift to ambulatory care services. The move to examine alternatives to hospitalization was supported by various task forces and royal commissions, described previously in the chapter. These reports recommend that further improvements in the cost-effectiveness of health services can be achieved, particularly by more appropriate use of services, including a shift in emphasis from institutional to community-based services and better integration and coordination of care. The basis is that a significant portion of hospital admissions could be avoided and length of stay reduced; that a number of patients in institutions could be cared for in their homes. The so-called "hospital-in-the-home" and "hospital without walls" approaches illustrate these trends. However, what is occurring in clients' homes today is very different than what occurred 40 years ago. As governments examine community alternatives and seek to harmonize health and social service delivery systems, they must think more fundamentally about the meaning of community health in relation to caring for individuals in the community.

TABLE 12-1 **Summary of Past, Present, and Emerging Trends in Health Care and Nursing**

	Past (1940s to 1960s)	Present (1970s to 1980s)	Emerging (1990s and beyond)
Setting for care delivery	Client's home Hospital	Hospital Community Ambulatory	Hospital Ambulatory Client's home
Organizational structure	Functional	Shared services	Programmatic Mega structures Alternative systems (CHOs, OSISs, HSOs)*
Management approach	From top down	Participatory	Democratic
Focus of quality assurance	Standard development structures	Assessment control processes Blame	Outcomes of care Total quality management Continuous improvement
Nursing care delivery system	Team	Total patient care Primary nursing	Nurse-managed care Case management
Nursing research	Negligible	Process oriented	Outcome oriented

Compiled by the Authors. ©1991 Louise Lemieux-Charles. Used with permission.
*CHO, Comprehensive Health Organization; OSIS, Organizations de soins intègres de santé (Quebec); HSO, Health Service Organizations.

Organizational Structure

The move to coordinate and integrate patient care requires different organizational structures than existed previously. The traditional hospital structure was a functional one that emphasized services provided by individual departments such as nursing, nutrition, and pharmacy. Because governments are increasingly interested in costs associated with specific patient groups, the concept of programs emerged. In addition, because physicians "drive" approximately 70% of all costs generated in a hospital, there are attempts to involve them more closely in management of critical resources (e.g., budget and staff allocations), and they emerge as new factors in the management structure. The definition of programs facilitates the identification of costs associated with caring for one particular group of patients. For example, programs such as oncology, transplantation, neurosciences, or geriatrics are defined and may be managed by a physician manager or by a team that consists of a physician, nurse, and administrator. Nurse managers experience this change with uncertainty because they perceive erosion of their responsibility for managing a nursing unit.

Also, it is often unclear to whom nurse managers should report (i.e., through nursing to the chief nursing officer, or to the physician manager, or to both).

This program approach is popular in public health because governments identify certain core programs (e.g., AIDS programs or introduction of care for neonatal alcohol syndrome) to be made available to the public. Some major teaching hospitals in Canada (e.g., Sunnybrook Medical Health Centre) are exploring or implementing such an approach or have developed what Stuart and Sherrard (1987) describe as a programmatic approach to decision making. In all cases, nursing administration remains responsible for the development and monitoring of nursing standards within the organization.

Such approaches have implications for the chief nursing officer role: if the programmatic structure is adopted, the role may become totally policy oriented. If this happens, the chief nursing officer may be displaced from the traditional position of line authority (whereby nursing staff report to him or her). This would result in a loss of a position of power in a formal organization.

Kanter (1979) maintains that power derives from two kinds of capacities: "access to resources, information and support necessary to carry out the task; and . . . ability to get cooperation in doing what is necessary" (p. 66). In program management, the chief nursing officer may lose access to resources, which would necessitate development of other means of power and influence. Personal power then assumes new significance. It is essential that nursing retain its strong influences over standards of nursing practice and quality of care. Meilicke (1990) suggests that restructuring may be unnecessary because the basic problem in hospitals is inadequate management of medical decision making. The debate is likely to continue through the 1990s because organizations continue to seek better ways to deliver care within specified resources. However, nurse managers must be sensitive to changes in management structure to ensure that they are not excluded from involvement in decisions that affect the way patient care is delivered.

As management structures within hospitals have begun to change, there have been changes in organizational structure that have affected hospitals on a broader scale. The move to share services (e.g., laundry services, nutritional services) and the development of formal and informal linkages (e.g., diabetic services, pharmacy) with other hospitals are the first signals of pressures for rationalization and containment of costs. An obvious way to rationalize services and use resources effectively is to amalgamate, into one hospital, services that previously existed in several hospitals (e.g., obstetrical or pediatric). This type of consolidation first occurred in small, two-hospital communities, but now has spread to larger urban centers.

In the 1980s, better coordinated and more integrated services continued with amalgamation of hospitals. In the 1990s, hospital megastructures, combining two or more hospitals and agencies under one administration, are common. Examples include University Hospital in Vancouver, Victoria (British Columbia) Hospital Corporation, The Toronto Hospital, and the Camp Hill Medical Centre in Halifax. Breaking hospital traditions has significant ramifications for nursing, especially when many nursing leaders are concerned that quality of care is overlooked in the effort to contain costs (Kooi, White, and Smith, 1988; Kaluzny and Shortell, 1988).

When linkages occur, nurses must communicate more effectively with outside organizations to ensure continuity of care for patients and clients. When hospitals or agencies merge, nurses may experience a loss of identity with programs to which they were loyal. Such restructuring requires nurse managers who can translate the goals of the new structure to staff nurses while also communicating the impact of the changes on nursing practice to non-nurse managers (Kooi, White, and Smith, 1988).

During the 1990s, the trend to coordination and integration of services within regions likely will continue. The 1990s will see development of alternative systems of care delivery such as early discharge and home care programs linked with hospitals. In large health care regions, which are likely to include linkages with community services, nurse managers at all levels will interact with a greater number of professionals within and outside the organization. Such interactions will further increase the complexity of their work. To be effective they will require additional support staff (e.g., clerical) and information systems to assist them in balancing their clinical and administrative responsibilities.

Management Approach

Florence Nightingale, in her role as superintendent of a field hospital in Scutari in 1857, is often portrayed as the first great nursing administrator. The influence of the military, as well as that of the religious orders, was still evident in nursing departments in the 1950s. Multiple layers of administration created communication and decision-making systems that often were slow to respond to staff and patient needs.

In the 1960s, Douglas McGregor pioneered development of Theory X and Theory Y assumptions about man that led to new managerial styles. McGregor (1960) viewed the individual as being responsible, wanting to do a good job, and having a need for growth and achievement (the Theory Y assumption). His contention was that managers often made incorrect assumptions about those who worked for them; they assumed that the individual was lazy and that personal goals ran counter to organizational goals (the Theory X assumption). About this same time, the works of Abraham Maslow (described in Goble, 1970) and Kurt Lewin (described by Weisbord, 1987) were developing along similar lines, fostered by the movement toward humanistic psychology. The result was a new organizational approach called participative management.

In the late 1970s, senior nurse administrators became aware that first-line managers were in the best position to make decisions about their specific units and therefore required the authority to perform their responsibilities. Many layers of assistant directors and supervisors were removed and communication lines were shortened. The scope of the first-line manager (formerly known as the head nurse) expanded as decision making extended farther down into the organization. Consequently, nurse managers at all levels needed additional managerial preparation for their roles so that they could accomplish leadership and management functions. In addition, first-line managers' input was sought in the formulation of hospital policies.

As hospitals have grown in size and complexity, the role of the chief nursing officers also enlarged; some control budgets in the tens of millions of dollars. As Huckaby (1989) notes, in addition to a sound knowledge of nursing, the chief nursing officer is also required to understand and possess skills in "management science; marketing; finance; policy-making; labor relations and negotiations; ethical-moral issues; politics of health care and health policy formation; research methodology; human relations; personnel psychology; and current trends in health care including their impact on nursing" (p. 534).

The 1990s will be an era when individual and collective rights gain prominence. Democratization of decision making in the workplace is being legislated or is resulting from new approaches to work. These changes will require meaningful worker involvement in determining effective work processes. For example, under new regulations in the Public Hospitals Act in Ontario, staff nurses are included on hospital committees that make administrative, financial, planning, and operational decisions. In Alberta, the Health Minister has requested that nurses be appointed not just to hospital committees but to hospital boards.

For some nurse managers, participation of staff nurses on committees that, in the past, have been restricted to management levels may be threatening. This is especially so if membership on these committees previously was closed to nurse managers. The challenge will be to develop a management style congruent with a high involvement approach and to acknowledge that staff nurse input on these committees probably will lead to formulation of policies that are more easily implemented. New management skills that will be required include negotiation, collaboration, and group process skills, as well as highly developed communication abilities.

Focus of Quality Assurance

Arnold Relman, editor of the *New England Journal of Medicine,* argues that health care is on the threshold of a "third revolution" (Relman, 1988). The first revolution was a revolution of expansion, in which concern for quality related primarily to soundness of building structures and organizational structures (e.g., qualifications of staff, appropriate committees). All this growth forced a second revolution, one of cost containment. However, cost-cutting measures are insensitive to needs of consumers and providers. The emphasis of quality assurance was on measurement and, sometimes, on comparison with a standard, but the critical element of improved performance was not key. For example, there generally was more concern with finding "bad apples" and blaming them for the problem. In the 1990s, the spotlight is shifting from costs to quality, from worrying about how much health care is costing to the fundamental question: "Is it doing any good?" Hence the focus is on outcomes. Two areas have had particular impact: the study of "small area variation," in which comparisons of communities with vastly differing rates for certain procedures (e.g., cholecystectomies) lead to no difference in overall health status: and appropriateness of care, in which those who may benefit from an intervention should receive it and those who would not benefit would not receive it.

Quality assurance in the 1990s will emphasize outcomes management and continuous improvement. Outcomes management is generally characterized by a reliance on standards and guidelines, measurement of functioning and well-being of patients, pooling of clinical and outcome data on a massive scale, and analysis and dissemination of results. Continuous improvement stresses improvement of work processes and systems of service delivery. The belief is that quality problems generally result from inadequacies of the system and work processes rather than from specific individuals. Teams of workers generally participate in the process.

Because this approach also emphasizes the importance of quality assurance as an integrated activity, the standards must reflect the input of the various professional groups about the outcomes of care. Nursing is responding to these challenges by re-examining its methods of nursing care delivery. The difficulties inherent in interdisciplinary teamwork must be addressed, however, and there must be opportunities for resolution of conflicts.

A major challenge for nurse managers is their ability and commitment to institute corrective action when nursing practice does not meet acceptable standards. First-line managers must be supported by chief nursing officers when organizational constraints affect staff nurses' abilities to deliver effective care. In such cases, the organization must reassert its commitment to continuous improvement (Wylie, 1991).

Nursing Care Delivery Systems

Systems used for delivery of care have changed significantly over the last 50 years. New directions in quality assurance mean that nursing must examine whether present models of care are compatible with the new emphases.

After World War II, a shortage of registered nurses resulted in the introduction of team nursing. In team nursing, a registered nurse heads a team of nursing students and auxiliary personnel and supervises them in supplying care to a group of patients. When the supply of nurses increased in the 1960s and 1970s, emphasis was placed on the professional practice of nursing, including all-RN staffing. "Total patient care" and "primary nursing," whereby one nurse was responsible for every facet of care for the assigned patients, were the delivery systems of choice. These delivery systems emphasize the five A's (accountability, advocacy, assertiveness, authority, and autonomy) and the five C's (collaboration, continuity, communication, commitment, coordination) (Kerouac, Duquette, and Sandhu, 1990). However, Loveridge, Cummings, and O'Malley (1988) note that primary nursing does not satisfactorily bridge the financial and quality of care issues that arise in an era of cost containment. Therefore the early years of the 1990s introduce "nurse-managed care" and "case management" as delivery systems that may be more suited to modern health care. Nursing case management is described as one delivery system that is compatible with the new directions in organizations (Loveridge, Cummings, and O'Malley, 1988; Olivas, Togno-Armanasco, Erickson, and Harter, 1989a, 1989b; Zander, 1988a). The nurse case manager is responsible for managing a group of patients (in contrast to the nurse manager who manages a group of nurses) in collaboration with a physician case manager; their authority extends throughout all units. This approach requires that all members of the health care team work collaboratively to achieve expected patient results, which have been developed by the team and are detailed in a case management plan.

Another new model for delivering nursing care is that of nurse managed care (del

Bueno and Leblanc, 1989). Nurse managed care builds on primary nursing but frees the nurse from institutional constraints such as working specific hours. This system addresses the issues of appropriate nurse use and nurse satisfaction. The registered nurse delegates tasks to support staff so that the professional role is emphasized. In this approach, nurses define the care required by a group of patients and determine how best that care can be delivered.

Both methods of care delivery require a management approach in which staff nurses have the freedom to determine what is best for the patient and family. These approaches increase staff nurses' authority and accountability for clinical and case cost activities (Zander, 1988b). These changes will require a redefinition of first-line nurse managers' roles and their relationship to case managers. Nurse managers must have a high degree of trust in staff nurses as professionals and a commitment to a delivery system that nursing administration does not fully control. The Toronto Hospital was the first hospital in Canada to implement nursing case management, but interest was high among some 300 nurse administrators who attended an international conference held in Toronto in Spring of 1990.

Nursing Research

Graduate programs in nursing hastened the thrust toward scholarship and research. The establishment of the *Canadian Journal of Nursing Administration* in the Spring of 1988 and the continued development of the *Canadian Journal of Nursing Research* (formerly *Nursing Papers*) confirm this direction. Most major teaching hospitals have a department of nursing research within the nursing portfolio. These departments are beginning to generate research on nursing practice issues and patient outcomes, which will strengthen nursing's role (Thurston, Tenove, and Church et al., 1989). Also, nursing practice research will give nurse managers information they need to support required changes to patient care delivery.

Nursing research is an area in which first-line managers are not always comfortable, because they have not seen the applicability of findings for their units. However, they now have opportunities, through quality assurance programs, to collaborate with nurse researchers in examining the effectiveness of corrective actions that ensure ongoing improvement in nursing care.

ADMINISTRATIVE ISSUES

The overall challenge facing nurse managers, given these present and future trends, will be to make the work setting a place in which nurses want to work while at the same time ensuring that nursing care is delivered in an effective, efficient manner. The common future thread is accountability for use of resources, especially because resources affect outcomes of care. Ensuring efficiency and effectiveness is a balancing act that may prove difficult for some nurse managers. A study of the ethical dilemmas faced by nurse managers (Youell, 1986) shows that many nurse managers experienced problems with resource allocation, technology, conflicting loyalties and values, staff relationships, conflict between nursing staff and physicians, and promotion of quality of care.

The *critical issue* for nursing administration in the future concerns human resources planning. The nursing shortage led health care organizations to examine on one hand the type of nursing personnel required to deliver nursing care and on the other hand the recruitment and retention strategies needed to ensure a satisfied and competent work force.

Concerns over costs and shortages caused governments to take an interest in human resources planning as well. Governments evaluate whether professionals (physicians, nurses, and others) are providing the services for which they are trained and leaving the performance of simpler tasks to others. Although nursing has a history of working with auxiliary personnel, nurses have not always been successful in using them appropriately (Manthey, 1989). Nor, in recent years, has nursing education prepared nurses to work in team settings and to allocate some tasks while successfully keeping the concept of total care for patient and family. Nursing managers, believing wholeheartedly in giving "the best possible care," are learning that this may need to be amended to "the best possible care that society can afford." Such a stance may not mean that nursing must be the only group of health care workers in an organization to face changes—but nursing must be prepared to help nursing managers evaluate what is best and how to achieve it. The challenge will be to skillfully blend many different levels of practitioners into a cohesive and unified group.

If they are to deliver quality care, health care institutions must have the staff to perform the activities. Nurses have not been satisfied with what they perceive to be a lack of control over their working environments and a lack of respect for their knowledge and skills. Allen, Calkin, and Peterson (1988) warn that involving staff nurses in decision making does not necessarily guarantee satisfaction. These authors stress that, above all, "nurses must be involved in decisions that they *perceive* as being most important to them" (p. 41). One challenge, then, for nurse managers at all levels is to create channels of communication that will allow them to detect what is important to staff nurses and to respond appropriately.

ORGANIZED NURSING'S RESPONSE TO ADMINISTRATIVE ISSUES

In Canada, there are few educational programs that prepare nurse administrators for their role. The literature (e.g., Leatt, 1982) debates whether preparation for nursing administration should be clinical or administrative in nature—that is, should a nurse manager hold a master's degree in nursing or a master's degree in business administration? Recently, because interdependence in the health care system is increasing, the view is that nurses should interact with other fields or disciplines, and this should occur during the educational process through faculty cross appointments and integrated programs. The future will require nurse managers who understand the "business" of nursing, including new developments in the field, as well as the "business" of health service delivery.

Recognition of the need for education for nursing administration by the CNA in 1981 resulted in development of a discussion paper on education for nursing administration in Canada (Leatt, 1981). A *Position Paper on the Role of the Nurse Admin-*

istrator and Standards for Nursing Administration was subsequently developed and was revised in 1988 as a result of feedback from nurse administrators throughout Canada and from national health organizations. Because CNA believes that nursing administration can be strengthened through improved educational preparation, CNA researchers analyzed data on the educational preparation of nurse administrators to identify specific educational needs. Table 12-2 compares levels of educational preparation of nurse administrators in 1980 and 1988.

Table 12-2 also illustrates that a large percentage of nurse administrators have no additional academic preparation beyond a basic nursing education. This situation existed in 1986 when CNA requested support from the Canadian Association of University Schools of Nursing, the Canadian College of Health Service Executives, the Canadian Hospital Association, and the Canadian Public Health Association in creating opportunities for nurse administrators to obtain advanced education and in improving opportunities for continuing education. These groups recognize that not all nurse managers—especially first-line managers—can pursue a baccalaureate ed-

TABLE 12-2 Registered Nurses by Type of Nursing Administrative Position Held, Highest Level of Education Canada, 1980 and 1988

Position	RNs	1980 Work force (%)	Diploma (%)	Baccalaureate (%)	Masters (%)
Director/Assistant	3792	2.4	76.1	19.6	4.3
Supervisor/Coordinator/Assistant	7672	4.9	83.5	15.5	1.0
Head Nurse	16,263	10.5	92.9	6.8	0.3
TOTAL RNS EMPLOYED	155,178	100.00	89.7	9.6	0.7

	RNs	1988 Work force (%)	Diploma (%)	Baccalaureate (%)	Masters (%)
Director/Assistant	5160	2.5	67.8	25.8	6.4
Supervisor/Coordinator/Assistant	10,834	5.1	77.7	20.6	1.7
Head Nurse	15,872	7.5	87.1	12.0	0.9
TOTAL RNS EMPLOYED	210,506	100.00	86.0	13.0	1.0

Prepared by Research Department, Canadian Nurses Association, January 1990, for the authors of this chapter. Used with permission.

ucation, yet they need to acquire additional management skills. These groups meet annually to plan for and monitor progress in development of management programs and graduate education programs.

CONCLUSION

This chapter discusses the evolution of nursing administration in the context of a changing health care environment. Explored areas include the changing setting for care delivery, management approaches, organizational structures, focus of quality assurance, nursing care delivery systems, and nursing research. Because health care organizations throughout Canada are at different stages of development, Canadian nurses will practice in health care workplaces characterized by many of the past, present, and future trends summarized in Table 12-1.

The challenges faced by nurse managers as a result of changes in these areas are described. Human resource planning is emphasized as a major administrative issue that must be addressed and resolved in the immediate future.

The future will require that nurse managers at all levels be highly adaptable, creative, and responsive to the needs of client groups and nursing staff, as well as to the corporate needs of the organization. Dealing with these different perspectives, at times, creates conflict for nurse managers, especially when cost containment efforts are perceived as threatening the quality of patient care. In such instances, the chief nursing officers must translate these concerns to the executive team in an attempt to span the corporate and professional dimensions of the role. Influencing future directions in administrative issues will depend on what Kaluzny and Shortell (1988) call "a critical mix of abilities, insight and courage" (p. 504). Organizational theorists predict that nurses will be an important coalition in influencing the future direction of the health care system. Nurses must discover ways to address that challenge through their professional expertise and their management approaches.

REFERENCES

Allen, A., Calkin, J., & Peterson, M. (1988). Making shared governance work: A conceptual model. *Journal of Nursing Administration, 18*(1), 37-43.

British Columbia Royal Commission on Health Care and Costs. (1991). *Closer to Home: Volume 1 — Summary of the Report.* Victoria: Author.

Canadian Nurses Association. (1988). *Position paper on the role of the nurse administrator and standards for nursing administration.* Ottawa: Author.

del Bueno, D.J., & Leblanc, D. (1989). Nurse managed care: One approach. *Journal of Nursing Administration, 19*(11), 24-25.

Evans, J. (1987). *Toward a shared direction for health in Ontario: Report of the Ontario Health Review Panel.* Toronto: Queen's Printer.

Gallant, C. (1989). *The report of the Nova Scotia Royal Commission on Health Care: Toward a new strategy.* Halifax: Nova Scotia Government Bookstore.

Gillies, D.A. (1989). *Nursing management: A systems approach* (2nd ed). Toronto: Saunders.

Goble, F. (1970). *The third force: The psychology of Abraham Maslow.* New York: Washington Square Press.

Hall, E. (1964). *Royal Commission on Health Services: Report* (Vol. 1). Ottawa: Queen's Printer.

Huckaby, L. (1989). Professional issues facing the field of nursing administration. In B. Henry, C. Arndt, M. Di Vincenti, & A. Marriner-Tomey (Eds.), *Dimensions in nursing administration: Theory, research, education, practice* (pp. 515-535). Boston: Blackwell.

Hyndman, L. (1989). *The rainbow report: Our vision for health: Premier's Commission of Future Health Care for Albertans*. Edmonton: Queen's Printer Bookstore.

Johnson, J., & Bergmann, C. (1988). Nurse managers at the broker's table: The nurse executive's role. *Journal of Nursing Administration, 18*(6), 118-21.

Kaluzny, A.D., & Shortell, S.M. (1988). Creating and managing the future. In S.M. Shortell & A.D. Kaluzny (Eds.), *Health care management* (2nd ed.) (pp. 492-522). Toronto: John Wiley & Sons.

Kanter, R.M. (1979). Power failure in management circuits. *Harvard Business Review, 57*(4), 65-75.

Kerouac, S., Duquette, A., & Sandhu, B.K. (1990). Les systèmes de prestation des soins. *The Canadian Nurse/L'infirmière canadienne, 86*(6), 39-42.

Kooii, D., White, R., & Smith, H.L. (1988). Managing organizational mergers. *Journal of Nursing Administration, 18*(3), 10-16.

Langill, G. (1989, Winter). Who's managing the care givers—A nursing dilemma. *Health Management Forum*, pp. 6-11.

Leatt, P. (1981). *Education for nursing administration in Canada: A discussion paper*. Ottawa: Canadian Nurses Association.

Leatt, P. (1982). Educational preparation for nursing administration in Canada. *Health Management Forum, 3*(1), 56-65.

Loveridge, C.E., Cummings, S.H., & O'Malley, J. (1988). Developing case management in a primary nursing system. *Journal of Nursing Administration, 18*(10), 36-39.

Manthey, M. (1989). The role of the LPN or the problem of two levels. *Nursing Management, 20*(2), 27-28.

McGregor, D. (1960). *The human side of enterprise*. New York: McGraw Hill.

Meilicke, C. (1990, June). Nurses and physicians in the modern hospital: Watering the garden. *Canadian Nursing Management, 29*, 27-32.

Mintzberg, H. (1975, July-August). The manager's job: Folklore and fact. *Harvard Business Review*, pp. 49-61.

Olivas, G.S., Togno-Armanasco, V.D., Erickson, J.R., & Harter, S. (1989a). Case management—a bottom-line care delivery model: Part 1—the concept. *Journal of Nursing Administration, 19*(11), 16-20.

Olivas, G.S., Togno-Armanasco, V.D., Erickson, J.R., & Harter, S. (1989b). Case management—a bottom-line care delivery model: Part 2—adaptation of the model. *Journal of Nursing Administration, 19*(12), 12-17.

Relman, A.S. (1988). Assessment and accountability—the third revolution in medical care. *New England Journal of Medicine, 319,* 1220-1222.

Simpson, P. (1988). Motivational theories: Reflection on their application by nurse managers. *Canadian Journal of Nursing Administration, 1*(1), 16-19.

Spasoff, R. (1987). *Health for all Ontario: Report of the Panel for Health Goals for Ontario.* Toronto: Queen's Printer.

Stevens, B. (1980). *The nurse as executive* (2nd ed.). Wakefield, MA: Nursing Resources.

Stuart, N., & Sherrard, H. (1987, Spring). Managing hospitals from a program perspective. *Health Management Forum,* pp. 53-63.

Taylor, M.G. (1987). The Canadian health care system: After Medicare. In D. Coburn, C. D'Arcy, G. Torrance, & P. New (Eds.), *Health and Canadian society* (2nd ed.) (pp. 73-101). Markham, ON: Fitzhenry & Whiteside.

Thurston, N., Tenove, S., Church, J., et al. (1989). Nursing research in Canadian hospitals. *Canadian Journal of Nursing Administration, 2*(1), 8-10.

Trist, E. (1981). *The evolution of socio-technical systems: A conceptual framework and an action research program* (Occasional Paper No. 2). Toronto: Quality of Working Life Centre.

Weisbord, M. (1987). *Productive workplaces: Organizing and managing for dignity, meaning and community.* San Francisco: Jossey-Bass.

Wylie, D.M. (1991). Continuous quality improvement. *Canadian Journal of Nursing Administration, 4*(2), 5.

Youell, L. (1986). A question of balance. *The Canadian Nurse, 82*(3), 26-33.

Zander, K. (1988a). Nursing case management: Resolving the DRG paradox. *Nursing Clinics of North America, 23*(3), 503-520.

Zander, K. (1988b). Nursing case management: Strategic management of cost and quality outcomes. *Journal of Nursing Administration, 18*(5), 23-31.

Nurses frequently must make ethical judgments and live with the consequences. Knowledge of ethical principles and models that assist in decisions can assist nurses. Janet Storch, professor and dean, Faculty of Nursing, University of Calgary, *(right)* discusses ethics codes and models with graduate students Brenda Conrad *(left)* and Barbara Boyer *(center)* in a class in January 1992. (Photograph courtesy Campus Photography University of Calgary.)

CHAPTER THIRTEEN

Ethical Issues

JANET L. STORCH, RN, PhD

Janet L. Storch, RN, MHSA, PhD (Alberta), is Dean, Faculty of Nursing, University of Calgary. She is author of a benchmark textbook, Patients' Rights: Ethical Issues in Health Care and Nursing *(1982), and more recently two articles, "Caring for the Caregiver" (1990) and "Ethics Committees in Canadian Hospitals" (1990), which also deal with ethical issues. She has published numerous articles and made many presentations on patients' rights, ethics, and ethical-legal issues.*

E very working day, nurses must make continuous choices—and many of these involve distinction between a greater and a lesser good for the patient (Lanara, 1981). One of the most critical areas in which nurses face choices involves questions of ethical judgment.

What does it mean to be an ethical practitioner in health care today? And how do nurses fulfill that mandate?

This chapter will attempt to respond to these questions by focusing on the unique aspects of nursing ethics and by identifying several central ethical issues confronting nurses. Some of the measures that will assist nurses toward ethical practice will then be explored, and some of the challenges that face nurses who would be ethical in their practice will be described.

UNIQUENESS OF NURSING ETHICS

With changing technologies, increasing specialization, and burgeoning bureaucracies, ethics in patient care has involved re-examination of the basic values and belief systems that govern society and the health care system that is part of that society. In part, this renewed attention arises with the realization that technology cannot solve society's problems. Instead technology itself has become a source of problems, often highly detrimental to the quality of human life. In fact, technological advances and fragmentation of care may only emphasize the "looseness and cloudiness" of present beliefs and values (Lanara, 1981, p. 45).

Clearly, the basic problems, such as prolonging treatment or ensuring patient autonomy, are shared with other health care providers. What is unique to nursing, however, is the type of relationship the nurse has with the patient, and the different role relationships the nurse has with other health professionals and the employing organization. In respect to the latter, the way in which nurses are involved in, or participate in, the situations giving rise to ethical conflict is frequently a function of institutional policy and of the place of the nurse in the organizational hierarchy and the professional division of labor. These realities often create additional dilemmas for nurses, particularly when their legitimate authority is usurped.

> When a nurse faces an ethical dilemma it is typically far more complex than a dilemma faced by a physician. Among the complicating factors are the facts that the nurse has multiple obligations derived in part from having a subordinate position in a hierarchy, little professional autonomy, an often ambiguous definition of role, and the historical and social onus of being a member of a woman's profession. When these factors are taken into consideration, it is easy to argue that physician ethics is a rather simpler case than nursing ethics. (Pence, 1983, p. iii)

Essentially, the uniqueness of nursing's ethical dilemmas can be summed up as a function of the nurse-patient relationship, the presence of the nurse with the client or patient during a health or an illness episode on a more constant basis than other health professionals, and the need to respond to multiple obligations.

Nurse-patient Relationship

To be a patient or client in today's health care system involves certain realities. If one is diseased or disabled there may be loss of independence, loss of freedom of action, interference with one's ability to make choices, and subjugation to the power of health care professionals and institutions (Curtin, 1979). To be a professional, on the other hand, is to profess to "know better than others the nature of certain matters" (Hughes, 1963, p. 656). Being a professional obligates one to use one's special skills for the benefit of others (Goode, 1969). There are many health professionals involved in patient care, with each type of professional involved in a specific set of relationships with the patient based on that professional's unique philosophy, knowledge, and skill. Nursing's philosophical base is advocacy and caring; nursing's theory has as its core of distinctiveness the process of maintaining health. Thus the nurse's unique role with the patient is based on a commitment to holistic care and healing, which rejects paternalistic actions and engages in patient-centered goals. The relationship is one of "presence" and "reciprocal nuturance" (Twomey, 1989; Yeo, 1989). Nurses are being called to use their knowledge and skills in the kind of care that desires the welfare of another, not because it is a duty but because of a connection to the humanness of that person (Benner and Wrubel, 1989).

Being Present

Because providing nursing care often involves 24-hour coverage, the nurse work-ing in an institutional setting or providing care in the home or community is generally the health professional who is with the patient on a more constant basis than other health care providers. Thus the nurse is "there" to witness instances of the patient's loss of autonomy and submission to the health care ministrations. When these ministrations are contrary to the patient interests or in violation of the patient's wishes, the nurse is present and has to make a choice to act or remain a silent observer of a wrong. Because obedience and absolute silence, once demanded of a nurse who would be a good and faithful practitioner (Coburn, 1981, p. 199), are no longer considered appropriate behaviors for the nurse who would be an ethical practitioner, many nurses experience conflict and a substantial degree of stress in fulfilling their ethical obligations. And because the nurse is present, the ethical and moral dilemmas of practice become even more acute when there is a lack of oppor-tunity for the nurse to participate in the process of decision making on matters of treatment. This exclusion places nurses in a most difficult position, particularly when those same nurses must implement decisions with which they disagree. Moral dis-tress is a product of these types of situations (Fenton, 1988).

Having Multiple Obligations

A third reality of nursing practice pertinent to nursing ethics is that nurses must assume different roles and take on responsibilities that demand different allegiances (Huckabay, 1986). Nurses have professional obligations to patients, to families, to physicians, to colleagues, and to employing institutions. The problem of ordering these multiple obligations is at the root of many ethical dilemmas for nurses in health care. Codes of nursing ethics, nursing textbooks, and other guidelines long main-tained that a nurse's primary loyalty was to the physician. The Florence Nightingale Pledge emphasizes this value, and early nursing textbooks warn against questioning or openly criticizing the physician's decisions, treatment plans, or techniques. How-ever, since the 1970s the priority of the nurse's obligation to the patient has been affirmed in codes of ethics, bills of patients' rights, standards for nursing care, and nursing textbooks (Woodruff, 1985). The International Council of Nursing Code of Ethics for Nurses (as revised in 1973) contains the clear statement of the priority of the patient: "The nurse's primary responsibility is to those people who require nurs-ing care" (cited in Storch, 1982, p. 201).

Yet the problem of multiple obligations, particularly for nurses who work in institutional settings such as hospitals and nursing homes, continues to be a source of role conflict for nurses. In many cases, including those that involve ethical decision making, it appears that nurses often make decisions in keeping with the bureaucratic authority of the institution. A study of senior nursing students found that students adopted a bureaucratic-centered approach to their ethical dilemmas rather than a patient-centered approach (Swider, McElmurry, and Yarling, 1985). Other studies suggest that the workplace can strongly influence the moral judgment of profes-sionals (Mayberry, 1986). Some even conclude that nurses are not always free to be moral (Yarling and McElmurry, 1986), particularly when loyalty to the organization, physician, and colleagues competes with that of loyalty to patient and family.

For all nurses, but particularly those in community health nursing, conflicting obligations of individual ethic versus aggregate ethic is also a present reality. Nursing codes of ethics reflect this need to consider the individual while also promoting the good of society (Fry, 1985, p. 305). The tension of balancing these two ethics is likely to increase for all nurses as pressures for cost containment increase and as nurses try to balance ethics and economics of care. Fry (1988) contends that nursing shortages resulting in unsafe staffing patterns undercut the opportunity for nurses to realize an ethic of care in nursing care. In contrast, Bishop and Scudder (1987) argue that a prime "moral obligation of a nurse is to sustain excellent practice in the face of unreasonable demands and lack of appreciation on the part of patients" (p. 37). The impact of scarce resources will likely be felt most acutely by nursing administrators as they strive to meet individual needs of patients while attempting to uphold the utilitarian goals of the hospital or other agency. This impels nurse managers to monitor and manage nursing manpower to ensure nursing care is decided by professional nurses and not solely by management engineers (O'Leary, 1984).

CENTRAL ETHICAL ISSUES FOR NURSES

Being more constantly present with the patient and having multiple obligations means that maintaining the patient's or client's interest as top priority is made more difficult. These realities require that nurses recognize and manage several important tasks: being a patient's advocate; dealing with clinical disagreement, incompetence, or unprofessional practice; and being a competent practitioner.

Patient's Advocate

Although the nurse has always functioned as the patient's advocate to some extent, the priority of patient advocacy has sometimes been in conflict with advocacy for the physician or the institution.

Winslow (1984) describes the changing role of the nurse in patient advocacy by noting the military influence on nursing, characterized by training and discipline, uniforms, ranks and stripes, and barriers across ranks. In this context, loyalty was a key value, and loyalty to physician and patient were seen as one. Thus nurses functioned as physicians' advocates or hospital advocates. As nurses began to realize that they were accountable for their own actions and became increasingly sensitized to patients' rights, they became influenced by a model in which advocacy is seen as an appropriate basis for nursing practice (Winslow, 1984).

Curtin (1979) describes advocacy as the philosophical foundation of the nurse-patient relationship; an advocacy based on common needs, common human rights, and common humanity:

> Explanations and working together with patients are not extras that nurses may choose to do; they are the essence of nursing, the essence of nurse-patient relationships, the profession. (p. 8)

The ethics of patient advocacy is based on ethical principles of autonomy, veracity or truth telling, and justice. Because illness may interfere with a person's ability to make decisions, the nurse as advocate can play a vital role in guarding the right to choice and decision (Leddy and Pepper, 1985). Respect for patient autonomy essentially means that patients be kept as much in command of themselves, their symptoms, and their situation as possible.

Ensuring that patients receive the information necessary to make sound decisions (i.e., adherence to the principle of autonomy) requires nurses to play a role in obtaining consent to treatments, in interpreting and reinforcing information given, in encouraging the patient to voice questions and concerns, and in supporting the patient in decisions (Kohnke, 1982). This is a difficult role for a nurse, considering that legal statutes generally specify that the physician is responsible for matters of diagnosis, treatment, and prognosis, which would seem to include the right to determine the amount of information the patient might receive and the timing of its release (Yeo, 1991). Until such professional legislation is modified to reflect the modern realities of a health care team, nurses must often tread the difficult line of gaining permission from physicians to teach and to disclose information to patients. Unfortunately, when the withholding of information involves a terminally ill patient, the claim that this is a medical decision is often erroneously confused with what, in fact, is an ethical decision (Huckabay, 1986).

To ensure that patients have needed information, nurses must seek to know each individual patient and determine what he or she wants to know. The College of Nurses of Ontario (1988) suggests that nurses should distinguish among three areas of information: that which the patient requests and wants to know; that which the client neither requests nor wants to know; and that which is not requested because the client does not know it exists. The first type of information requires a direct, honest response from the nurse, the second a respect for the client's wishes, and the third, a judgment regarding an appropriate time and place to share sometimes unwelcome news. Gadow (1985) reminds us that if patients are "treated" with information without regard to their wishes, we are relating to them as objects as clearly as we would if we administered treatment without their consent.

The principle of veracity or truthfulness applied to nursing practice necessitates a respect for a patient's right to know in order to make wise choices. It means, for example, that patients will be told they are dying when they want to know, and that other difficult diagnoses will not be withheld from patients. Yeo (1991) argues that, although there may be occasional exceptions to this principle, the presumption in favor of "openness and disclosure" means that any exceptions must be justified (p. 93). It also means that errors in care will be discussed frankly and openly with the patients involved.

The principle of justice means that patients will be treated fairly in their access to treatment and assured of quality of care. A caring person is committed to an advocacy role, which seeks to conserve those social structures that function to treat others fairly but also seeks to change those that do not (Shogan, 1988).

Being a patient's advocate is a complex role for nurses, involving risk and challenge. It involves risk because the nurse often must choose to speak out, to break silence, at times when it is uncomfortable to do so. Advocacy poses a threat to the traditional nurse-physician relationship that has relied on unswerving loyalty and game playing to achieve patient-oriented goals. The challenge in the advocacy role is that it can lead to better, healthier relationships among physicians, patients, and nurses, as each patient's goals, values, and well-being become the central focus for all team members (Aroskar, 1985).

Clinical Conflict and Incompetence

Within any work group, some degree of conflict is inevitable. When that work group is dealing with matters of patient care, which may involve life and death issues, the conflicting points of view may be particularly acute, especially when other professionals believe their clinical judgment is being questioned. In keeping with an ethical obligation to the patient, which involves a duty to benefit others and to do no harm, these disputes must be handled as quietly and as judiciously as possible. Nurses are accountable for the well-being of assigned patients, and they must take action when medical orders appear inappropriate. Generally, acknowledgement of such "disputes" is rare and guidance for the handling of such disputes even more rare. But evidence of some beginning awareness of the problem is reflected in the 1985 Ontario Hospital Association Board's guidelines for the handling of such disputes between nurses and physicians. Although these guidelines are limited to specific physician actions, such mechanisms should be available to help nurses handle conflicts with other professionals and between nurses.

Matters of clinical incompetence and professional misconduct are of a more serious nature. In these cases, being present as a nurse necessitates action, whether in regard to a nursing colleague, a physician, or any other health care professional. The 1991 Canadian Nurses' Association Code of Ethics provides some clear and compelling guidance for nurses in handling these difficult situations. The nurse must ascertain the facts of a situation that indicate incompetent or unethical conduct, then use institutional reporting channels whenever possible, and do so without undue disruption of the health care team. But most importantly, the CNA Code states that "it is unethical for a nurse to participate in efforts to deceive or mislead clients about the cause of alleged harm or injury resulting from ethical or incompetent conduct" (p. 16).

Being a Competent Practitioner

Although reporting incompetence in others becomes an ethical obligation of nursing practice, an obligation of equal importance is to maintain one's own competence as a practitioner and be ready to report one's own errors. "Since nursing practice aims at the well-being of the patient, the first moral responsibility of any nurse is excellent practice" (Bishop and Scudder, 1987, p. 36). This means that nurses take advantage of both formal and informal opportunities for continuing education; that they read and study professional journals; that they take responsibility for advising supervisors of limitations they might have; and that they work to ensure they are providing a high quality of patient care. In a sense, a nurse must show a dedication to being a master craftsman whose hallmark is "an inquiring mind and a commitment to continuous learning" (Flaherty, 1985, p. 101). In addition, such master craftsmanship involves a continued commitment to caring.

At least one study shows that nurses had different perceptions of what constituted good care than did their patients. The nurses valued comfort, care, and the development of a trusting relationship, whereas their patients placed greater value on technical skill, monitoring, and follow-through (Larson, 1987). This study underscores the point that a fundamental aspect of caring is clinical competence.

There may be times when the rights as a nurse are in conflict with the rights of the patient. Such instances can occur when, for example, the nurse's values conflict with those of the client. In such cases the competent practitioner must be able to respect the client's point of view and provide for necessary care by giving it or by arranging for someone else to care for the patient. This dilemma often arises in relation to nursing care of patients receiving abortion services. Nurses have an obligation to settle their conditions of employment in advance whenever possible to minimize jeopardy to patients (CNA, 1991).

MEANS TO ETHICAL NURSING PRACTICE

All too frequently nurses regard themselves as helpless victims of circumstances, even in matters involving ethical dilemmas. It is important to shake this belief and to recognize that nurses can change and influence forces both within and without nursing (Lanara, 1981). Nursing has a tremendous potential to make a difference in health care, to foster and enhance humanistic and ethical practice. Because nurses are caught between the rights of the patient, the authority of the physician, and the power of administrators, their contribution to moral decisions increases in significance by being "persons in between." As such, they can increase the consciousness of other team members regarding the need to focus on the patient's well-being and can encourage team members to ensure that different perspectives on a patient's care are heard and valued (Bishop and Scudder, 1987).

Various means are already available, and other means can become available to facilitate this end. These include codes of ethics; guidelines and policy papers of nursing associations; educational programs; and organizational supports such as strong and committed leaders in the nursing department, patient ombudsmen, and ethics consultation committees. Each of these means will be discussed briefly.

Codes of Ethics and Guidelines for Practice

Although it is clear that codes of ethics and guidelines cannot possibly address all ethical situations of nursing practice, recent revisions and modifications to such guidelines provide a much clearer direction to nurse practitioners, as well as a much clearer statement of nursing ethics to the public. Until the mid-1970s, codes of ethics for nursing practice provided only general guidelines, leaving much to the imaginative nurse to devise.

In the early 1970s, patients' bills of rights began to appear, making more explicit the rights of patients and the correlative duties of health care providers. In the United States, the American Hospital Association adopted a 12-point statement of patients' rights; in Canada, the Consumer's Association of Canada developed a four-point charter of consumer rights. These associations claimed that professional codes of ethics did not sufficiently address issues of patients' rights and that more guidance was required for patients and for health care providers (Storch, 1982). These were among the many factors that led to the reformulation of existing codes and the development of further guidelines by professional nursing associations. Such initiatives are evident throughout Canada and only a few examples are provided here.

The Registered Nurses Association of British Columbia has a *Position Statement* on informed consent (1989) outlining the responsibilities of the nurse in the consent process. In the Statement, the Association stresses that nurses who witness a signature for consent "are ethically obligated to assess the patients' understanding of the proposed treatment" and to apprise others (e.g., the physician) if the nurse believes the patient does not understand the treatment. The Saskatchewan Registered Nurses' Association's *Guidelines for Nursing Practice* includes a section on consent for treatment and/or surgery, which states that the nurse "may witness the client's signature on the consent form" if satisfied that the conditions of consent have been met (SRNA, 1988). The College of Nurses of Ontario also has *Guidelines for Ethical Behaviour in Nursing* as a preliminary statement of standards in developing and assessing the ethical component of professional nursing practice (1988). The Alberta Association of Registered Nurses developed a document entitled *Guidelines for Registered Nurses as Client Advocates* (1990) providing, in question and answer format, guidance for nurses in fulfilling their professional responsibilities relative to clients' rights and client advocacy.

The Canadian Nurses Association has an Ad Hoc Committee to review the CNA *Code of Ethics for Nursing* and to recommend changes as required. Minor modifications to the 1985 Code were approved by the CNA Board in 1991 with agreement for another review in 5 years (CNA, 1991).

Ethics Education

Codes and guidelines can be of considerable value in dealing with ethical dilemmas of patient care. However, these often cannot address the total range of issues and conflicting demands experienced by the average nurse. For this reason, ethics education is important in all formal and continuing nursing education programs. In these educational endeavors, nurses need to become sensitized to ethical issues and ethical principles to become skilled in applying the ethical principles to practice (Fromer, 1982). Ethics involves the study of rational ways for determining better courses of action when faced with conflicting choices (Gilbert, 1982), and principles serve to clarify the issues at stake. Case studies reflective of nursing dilemmas can provide a practical and relevant means for the study of ethics.

There are various models for ethical decision making. Figure 13-1 shows one such model. This three-step process stresses the importance of, first, determining the facts of the situation and identifying the dilemma. The problem, the people involved, and the ethical components should be identified and information collected. In the second step, seeking to clarify the dilemma, the Canadian Nurses Association *Code of Ethics for Nursing* (1985, 1991), provincial statements, and mission statements from the agency provide a basis for assessment. The four ethical principles (beneficence, nonmaleficence, autonomy, justice) serve to locate and clarify the fundamental nature

1. Information and • Problem
Identification • People
• Ethical components

2. Clarification and Evaluation

Ethical priniciples

• Beneficence
• Nonmaleficence
• Autonomy
One's values/beliefs • Justice

Social expectations

Values/beliefs of others

Legal reqirements

Value conflicts

Range of actions/ anticipated consequences

Professional Codes of Ethics

3. Action and Review

FIGURE 13-1 Model for ethical decision making.

of the dilemma. A major consideration involves identifying one's own values and beliefs, as well as the values and beliefs of all other stakeholders (i.e., the patients, foremost; the family; the physicians; other colleagues involved in care). Other important considerations include identifying social expectations and legal requirements to ensure that informed choices of action are proposed and taken. Third, as in any problem-solving model, action and review are critical elements of the process.

The review step has added significance in ethical decision making since few ethical problems can be anticipated or resolved in advance. However, nurses who devote time to consideration of past dilemmas, and who take time to ponder the resolution of hypothetical problems, can develop a clearer sense of personal values and priorities so that choices in ethical dilemmas can become more coherent and reasoned.

Organizational Supports for Ethical Practice

It is critical that the nurse knows what constitutes right conduct and knows how to determine an ethical course of action. It is also imperative that the nurse is given support in practicing ethical behavior. Such support must come from nursing colleagues, the nursing department, and the organization as a whole and may be provided in many forms.

The support of colleagues constitutes an informal structure in which support is provided in one's work-group and (formally and informally) in professional associations. Nurses have not been noted for unification in difficult situations, and it becomes increasingly important that nurses trust and rely on one another for help, teaching, and support (Flaherty, 1985). To be present and to speak out involves risk. Any nurse who risks needs the support and backing of colleagues.

In addition, the nurse needs the support of nursing department supervisors. This support is more likely to be forthcoming if a formal statement of such support is embodied in a philosophy and objectives statement of the nursing department. Nurses can work toward developing a departmental philosophy and objectives, as well as guidelines for ethical decision making. And nursing administrators need to place a high priority on establishing an environment in which "moral conflict can be addressed with tolerance, mutual respect, and commitment to the best interests of present and future patients" (McCullough, 1985, p. 74). Nursing administrators can be role models by maintaining a management style that is "caring and respectful of staff as individuals" (Fenton, 1988, p. 11) and in which ethical decision making is strengthened (Mayberry, 1986).

At an institutional level, support can be provided through philosophy and goals statements that direct attention to patients' rights and provide ombudsmen services and ethics consultation committees. A patient ombudsman, to whom patient advocacy problems can be directed when the nurse cannot resolve the situation, is a tangible means of support. Ethics consultation committees can also serve as support for nurses by providing opportunities for nurses to express their concerns and to be in consultation with other members of the health care team in addressing particular ethical problems. More importantly, ethics committees can adopt a proactive stance and develop institutional guidelines for difficult problems, such as orders not to resuscitate or matters of providing information to patients (Storch et al., 1990).

More fundamental support can be provided by ensuring that the safety and security needs of nurses are addressed through attention to practices that protect and support nurses as they work with potentially harmful substances, and as they care for those who suffer from AIDS (Storch, 1990).

CHALLENGES INVOLVED IN ETHICAL NURSING PRACTICE

Clearly, ethical dilemmas are a part of nursing practice because the nurse has a unique, more intensive, and constant relationship with the patient, and because the nurse faces demands of different allegiances. Nurses are therefore required to make ethical judgments and must live with the consequences of their actions. Although in many instances there are no "right" or "wrong" solutions to ethical dilemmas, there are better and worse ways of trying to deal with them (Callahan, 1980). Acknowledging one's professional and ethical responsibilities for patient advocacy, dealing with conflict, and maintaining competence can make significant differences in the lives of patients and nurses alike. To be an ethical nursing practitioner involves taking responsibility for moral choices and being equipped to make responsible choices through a serious deliberation of ethical issues. In this undertaking, the support of the employing organization can be a critical factor and must be a goal nursing strives to achieve.

For the present, the use of ethical principles and models for decision making seem to provide a preliminary understanding and a workable means to ethical decision making. The challenge for nursing ethics now and in the future is to incorporate the best of feminist ethics into nursing ethics and to integrate nursing theory and nursing ethics (Yeo, 1989).

REFERENCES

Alberta Association of Registered Nurses. (1990). *Guidelines for registered nurse as client advocate*. Edmonton: Author.

Aroskar, M.A. (1985). Ethical relationships between nurses and physicians: Goals and realities—a nursing perspective. In A.H. Bishop & J.R. Scudder, Jr. (Eds.), *Caring, curing, coping* (pp. 44-61). Mobile, AL: University of Alabama Press.

Benner, P., & Wrubel, J. (1989). *The primacy of caring*. Don Mills, ON: Addison Wesley.

Bishop, A.H., & Scudder Jr., J.R. (1987). Nursing ethics in an age of controversy. *Advances in Nursing Science, 9*(3), 34-43.

Callahan, D. (1980). Goals in the teaching of ethics. In D. Callahan & S. Bok (Eds.), *Ethics teaching in higher education* (pp. 61-80). New York: Plenum Press.

Canadian Nurses Association. (1985). *Code of ethics for nursing*. Ottawa: Author.

Canadian Nurses Association. (1991). *Code of ethics for nursing* (Rev.). Ottawa: Author.

Coburn, J. (1987). "I see and I am silent": A short history of nursing. In D. Coburn, C. D'Arcy, P. New, & G. Torrance (Eds.), *Health and Canadian society* (pp. 441-462), Toronto: Fitzhenry and Whiteside.

College of Nurses of Ontario. (1988). *Guidelines for ethical behaviour in nursing*. Toronto: College of Nurses of Ontario.

Curtin, L. (1979). The nurse as advocate: A philosophical foundation for nursing. *Advances in Nursing Science, 1*, 1-10.

Fenton, M. (1988). Moral distress in clinical practise: Implications for the nurse administrator. *Canadian Journal of Nursing Administration, 1*(3), 21-23.

Flaherty, M.J. (1985). Ethical issues. In J. Innes, S. Searl, & C. Smillie (Eds.), *Community health nursing in Canada* (pp. 97-113). Toronto: Gage.

Fromer, M.J. (1982). Solving ethical dilemmas in nursing practice. *Topics in Clinical Nursing, 4*, 15-21.

Fry, S.T. (1985). Individual vs. aggregate good: Ethical tension in nursing practice. *International Journal of Nursing Studies, 22*(4), 303-310.

Fry, S.T. (1988). The ethic of care: Can it survive in nursing? *Nursing Outlook, 36*(1), 48.

Gadow, S.A. (1985). Nurse and patient: The caring relationship. In A.H. Bishop & J. Scudder, Jr. (Eds.), *Caring, curing, coping* (pp.31-43). Mobile, AL: University of Alabama.

Gilbert, C. (1982). The what and how of ethics education in nursing. *Topics in Clinical Nursing, 4*, 49-56.

Goode, W.J. (1969). The theoretical limits of professionalization. In A. Etizoni (Ed.), *The semiprofessions and their organization* (pp. 166-313). New York: The Free Press.

Huckabay, L. (1986). Ethical-moral issues in nursing practice. *Nursing Administration Quarterly, 10*(3), 61-67.

Hughes, E.C. (1963). Professions. *Daedalus, 92*, 665-668.

International Council of Nurses. (1973). *Code of Ethics*. Geneva: Author.

Kohnke, M. (1982). *Advocacy: Risk and reality*, St. Louis: Mosby—Year Book, Inc.

Lanara, V.A. (1981). *Heroism as a nursing value: A philosophical perspective*. Athens, Greece: Sisterhood Evniki.

Larson, P.J. (1987). Comparison of cancer patients' and professional nurses' perceptions of important caring behaviors. *Heart and Lung, 16*(2), 187-193.

Leddy, S., & Pepper, J.M. (1985). *Conceptual bases of professional nursing*. New York: J.B. Lippincott.

Mayberry, M.A. (1986). Ethical decision-making: A response of hospital nurses. *Nursing Administration Quarterly, 10*(3), 75-81.

McCullough, L.B. (1985). Moral dilemmas and economic realities. *Hospital and Health Services Administration*, 30(5), 63-75.

O'Leary, J. (1984). Do nurse administrators' values conflict with the economic trend? *Nursing Administration Quarterly*, 8(4), 1-9.

Ontario Hospital Association. (1985). *Policy: nurse/physician disagreement*, Don Mills, ON: Author.

Pence, T. (1983). *Ethics in nursing practice: An annotated bibliography*. New York: National League for Nursing.

Registered Nurses Association of B.C. (1989). *Position statement: Informed consent*. RNABC News, 21(1), 27.

Saskatchewan Registered Nurses Association. (1988). *Guidelines for nursing practice*. Regina: Author.

Shogan, D. (1988). *Care and moral motivation*. Toronto: OISE Press.

Storch, J. (1982). *Patients' rights: Ethical and legal issues in health care and nursing*. Toronto: McGraw-Hill Ryerson.

Storch, J. (1990). Caring for the care-giver. *Hospital Trustee*, 14(3), 10-11.

Storch, J.L., Grienier, G.G., Marshall, D.A., & Olineck, B.A. (1990). Ethics committees in Canadian hospitals: Report of the survey. *Health Care Management Forum*, 3(4), 3-8.

Swider, S.M., McElmurry, B.J., & Yarling, R.R. (1985). Ethical decision-making in a bureaucratic context by senior nursing students. *Nursing Research*, 34, 108-112.

Twomey, J.G. (1989). Analysis of the claim to distinct nursing ethics: Normative and non-normative approaches. *Advances in Nursing Science*, 11(3), 25-32.

Winslow, G.R. (1984). From loyalty to advocacy: A new metaphor for nursing. *The Hastings Center Report*, 14, 32-40.

Woodruff, A.M. (1985). Becoming a nurse: The ethical perspective. *International Journal of Nursing Studies*, 22(4), 295-302.

Yarling, R.R., & McElmurry, B.J. (1986). The moral foundation of nursing. *Advances in Nursing Science*, 8(2), 63-73.

Yeo, M. (1989). Integration of nursing theory and nursing ethics. *Advances in Nursing Science*, 11(3), 33-42.

Yeo, M. (1991). *Concepts and cases in nursing ethics*. Peterborough, ON: Broadview Press.

In 1981-1982, Canadian nurses were awakened to the importance of legal issues through the charges brought against Susan Nelles, RN, in a widely publicized criminal trial. Charges against Nelles were—eventually—dismissed as unfounded, and she became a well-known speaker to nurses' groups throughout Canada on the need to understand legal implications of nursing practice. (News photograph supplied by Canapress Photo Service. Used with permission.)

CHAPTER FOURTEEN

Legal Issues

SHERRY WIEBE, BN, LLB

Sherry Wiebe, RN, BN, LLB (Manitoba), is a fully qualified nurse and lawyer with a consulting practice in health law. The clients in her law practice include nurses and other health care professionals. As a member of the Advisory Council to the Federal/Provincial/Territorial Review on Liability and Compensation Issues in Health Care, chaired by Robert Prichard, President, University of Toronto, and as Past Chair of the National Health Law Section of the Canadian Bar Association, Ms. Wiebe is involved in national health law and policy development and in teaching health care professionals about legal issues. She is the former Executive Director of a provincial professional nurses' association.

"I 'll sue!" Few words engender a stronger response in the hearts and minds of health care professionals. Increasingly doctors and nurses are involved in legal actions, which exact their cost financially and emotionally. Prichard (1990) reports that escalation of health care malpractice litigation in Canada over the last 15 years is similar to that experienced in the United States. The sixfold increase in the frequency of lawsuits in the health care field is much greater than the growth of legal actions against lawyers, engineers, and other professionals and therefore has generated concern and anxiety among health care professionals.

The legal accountability of nurses has been down-played through the years, in large part because of a commonly held belief that the physician is ultimately responsible for the entire course of treatment and care of the patient. In the past, nurses took comfort that legal liability stopped short of them. This misperception was laid to rest with the arrest of nurse Susan Nelles, RN, for the deaths of four babies in Toronto in 1981 (Grange, 1984, p. 194). Nelles was subsequently discharged on all four counts of murder (Grange, 1984, p. 207), and the Supreme Court of Canada in 1989 contended that Nelles could sue the Ontario Attorney General and

Crown prosecutors for malicious prosecution (*Nelles v. Ontario*, 1989). The impact of this case on every nurse in Canada—after some of the most sensational news coverage Canada has witnessed—was profound. Nurses began to demand education and advice on legal matters from their employers, educational institutions, and professional associations. No longer satisfactory were assurances that they were "covered." A heightened awareness of the potential for personal liability, as well as nurses' perceptions of lack of employer support and inevitable legal action, precipitated a dramatic change in nurses' perspectives of their own vulnerability.

Nurses as primary caregivers in the health care system are increasingly exposed to risk of legal liability, not only because of the increased tendency of health care consumers to resort to legal remedies but also because of pre-trial legal procedures. These render it advantageous to personally name nurses in legal actions (Prichard, 1990, Appendix A, p. 33). Other factors also contribute to the increased incidence of legal actions alleging nurses' negligence. Notably, the advances of medical science and technology with the continuing evolution of professional nursing practice have created a demand for high-risk and autonomous nursing interventions (Prichard, 1990, Appendix A, p. 19), which are fraught with the potential for harm.

Nurses today decry the lack of recognition of their professionalism and advanced knowledge and skills. Such recognition, however, is a double-edged sword with both benefits and burdens. For example, one case in which an experienced nurse in charge during the birth of a child delivered with birth injuries was absolved of liability might have had a different outcome if nursing's autonomous role had been recognized. The obstetrician was delayed and the nurse assumed control of all aspects of the birth until the doctor arrived, just as the baby was being born. Yet in discussions regarding apportionment of liability for the injuries, the lawyers concluded the nurse was not legally accountable because she had no responsibility for the delivery. Despite the fact that the nurse had a major part in the delivery, her role was summarily dismissed. No doubt, heightened recognition of a nurse's autonomous and professional role will render obsolete such offhand immunity. In the future, nurses must be prepared to accept the risk of legal action as an occupational hazard for which the most effective shield is the application of due skill and knowledge while delivering nursing care.

The purpose of this chapter is to explore current legal issues in nursing practice in the context of the Canadian legal system. Although comprehensive discussion of all the nurse's legal concerns is impossible, this chapter will provide an overview of the concepts of duty and liability, professional regulation and discipline, tort including negligence, and patients' rights. There will also be reference to legal issues arising from employment, risk management, and the continued evolution of medical technology. Consent and documentation are discussed in the context of minimizing risks of legal liability.

INTRODUCTION TO THE CANADIAN LEGAL SYSTEM

Law, states Gall (1990, p. 17), a noted author of legal texts, is elusive, and hence difficult to define. He regards the law as the core matter used by persons and institutions in any legal system to regulate the affairs and conduct of persons in society. The law encompasses a number of concepts that have been widely accepted as a means by which to analyze legal problems (Gall, 1990, p. 13). One of the most important concepts is the jural correlative, which entails the presence of corresponding characteristics in two persons (Gall, 1990, p. 15). For example, the presence of a right (e.g., a legally actionable claim) of one person to expect a medication to be administered properly corresponds with a duty or obligation of the nurse to perform accordingly. If the nurse who owes the duty fails to satisfy it, the party to whom the duty is owed, the patient, has the right to take legal action (Philpott, 1985, p. 26). Hence analysis of legal institutions includes the identification of one person's rights and another person's corresponding duties or obligations. Although there are many nuances in analyzing legal rights and duties, this analysis is an approach that may be used to clarify legalities in the nurse/patient relationship. Considering American estimates that one in ten negligently injured victims initiates legal action (Duff, 1987, pp. 18-19), it is apparent that legal analysis will be determinative of respective rights and obligations but will not be conclusive as to findings of liability, in that the latter requires initiation and completion of formal legal proceedings.

The Canadian legal system may be described variously. However, Gall divides it into two main divisions: Law involving the public and law involving disputes between private citizens (Gall, 1990, p. 24). Four areas of public law described by Gall include constitutional, administrative (including regulation of professionals), criminal, and taxation law. The private law encompasses private interests in the areas of contracts, torts, and property. Traditional subdivisions of private law also include wills and trusts, family law, real estate, trademarks and patents, sale of goods, and corporate law (Gall, 1990, p. 26).

PUBLIC LAW

The private law of Canadians is characterized as either a common law or a civil law system. The systems are distinguished principally by their differing legal processes. In the common law system, the courts extract principles of law from decisions of previous cases. Hence precedent is a hallmark of the common law system, which is the system in force in all provinces but Quebec. In Quebec, the civil law system prevails. It is a codification of laws, that is a conclusive statement of law, which is applied to the facts of each case. Precedent is not ascribed the importance in a civil system that it is in a common law jurisdiction (Gall, 1990, p. 173). Whereas Canada has both a common law and civil law system applicable to private law, one common approach is used throughout all of Canada with respect to public law. Thus criminal matters are handled similarly throughout Canada (Gall, 1990, p. 98). The Supreme Court of Canada, consisting of six judges from common law provinces and three judges from the civil law Quebec, constitutes the highest court for both systems of law (Gall, 1990, p. 150).

Gall describes the principal source of law as legislation, which, if relevant, is applied to a set of facts in priority to other sources of law. Another source of law, but secondary to legislation, is caselaw, or precedent. Custom is a third and inferior source of law, as are the subsidiary sources such as books of authority and Canon (religious) laws (Gall, 1990, p. 34).

Liability is a broad legal term that includes almost every kind of legal obligation, responsibility, or duty (Black, 1990, p. 914). Failure to satisfy a legal obligation of duty may give someone the right to enforce it. In legal proceedings, respective rights and duties are ascribed, and a judicial pronouncement of liability is made. The judgment describes who is responsible, for what they are responsible, and what the remedy will be.

Nurses, like other professionals, are exposed to liability in both public and private law divisions. Their exposure is not due solely to professional practice but is due as well to being a citizen subject to the laws of the land.

Criminal Matters

Liability in the public law arena includes accountability for criminal actions as outlined in The Criminal Code (1970). Susan Nelles, RN, was charged in the realm of the criminal law. Rarely are criminal charges brought against nurses in the course of their professional duties. Historically, nurses have been involved with the criminal law as witnesses. It is not uncommon for nurses in emergency departments or nursing stations to be called as witnesses to the injuries and behaviors of the victim or the accused in a criminal charge. The nurse's responsibilities as witness are to provide evidence or personal knowledge in response to questions asked by legal counsel to assist the court in the determination of the guilt or innocence of the accused.

This limited involvement has broadened since the early 1980s, when the profession began to change its attitude toward injuries suffered at the hands of patients, and nurses began to become involved in the criminal justice system as complainants. Nurses who are abused or assaulted may initiate a private lawsuit against the patient, but civil action is often seen as neither satisfactory nor viable by the nurse complainant, who chooses instead to seek more timely and affordable redress through the criminal courts. Kenn Cust was a nurse assaulted in a psychiatric assessment unit by a coherent patient swinging his encasted arm. Cust spent 4 months in physiotherapy and ultimately brought a criminal complaint against his patient, who was later found "not guilty." Cust (1986) suggests nurses have been reluctant to bring charges against their patients. He also alludes to the difficulty in obtaining information and support from hospital superiors and peers when laying such charges. Furthermore, the nurse has to challenge the commonly held view that nurses consent to assault by virtue of their choice of work settings (Cust, 1986). Current data regarding the ratio of nurse assaults to nurse-initiated legal action suggests that little has changed during the last decade. However, there is a growing awareness of the problem of nurse assault.

In 1986, the Manitoba Association of Registered Nurses, with the Registered Psychiatric Nurses Association of Manitoba and the Manitoba Association of Licensed Practical Nurses, began a review of physical, verbal, and sexual abuse suffered by nurses from their patients and also from their colleagues and employers (Manitoba Association of Registered Nurses, 1989). The report, based on the responses of half of Manitoba's 10,000 nurses, was released in 1989 and suggested that nurse abuse was a pervasive and complex problem. One recommendation contained within the report suggests that legislation relevant to nurse abuse be defined and clarified

(MARN, 1989). Physical assault, including sexual assault, is governed by federal legislation in The Criminal Code (1970), whereas sexual harassment and discriminatory actions are prohibited by human rights codes within both federal and provincial jurisdictions.

Administrative Law

A second subdivision of the public law in which a nurse is exposed to liability is administrative law. This includes statutes passed by provincial legislatures delegating powers of self-regulation to specified professional groups. These statutes are to act as legislative safeguards for the protection of the public from unsafe, incompetent, and unethical practices of individuals presenting themselves as members of a recognized profession (Philpott, 1985, p. 141). Self-regulatory legislation generally incorporates entry to practice and renewal prerequisites, definition of practice, standards of performance, disciplinary action, and ethical standards that the nurse member must fulfill. Failure entitles the professional association to take legal action specified in the statute, which includes suspension or revocation of license.

The acts governing nursing in each province provide for either mandatory or permissive registration with the professional nursing association. Mandatory regulation entails that individuals obtain a license to engage in a given profession without which practice is prohibited (Young, 1987, p. 5). This is true for the practice of medicine but not for the practice of nursing, which is generally protected as to name and to a lesser extent, practice. Most jurisdictions provide that no one except a nurse registered with a professional association may use the initials "RN." Practicing as a registered nurse or presenting oneself for employment as a registered nurse if not registered may constitute a breach of the provincial nurse practice act. Sanctions against nonmembers include fines.

Renewal of registration for practice is an obligation set by the professional practice acts, which also set criteria for initial registration. In 1987, provincial nursing association registrars agreed that a uniform standard of 1125 hours of nursing practice in 5 years be required by 1990 for renewal of registration in each province (Provincial/Territorial Registrars, 1987), an agreement that most jurisdictions have met. The purpose of this legislated requirement is satisfaction of the self-regulating association's mandate to protect the public from incompetent practitioners.

Another statutory provision affecting professional nursing practice is the definition of nursing, which outlines the scope of practice in which a registered nurse may engage. This definition is important in that it is frequently used by employers and insurers to describe the limits of employee duties and of insurance coverage. Practicing outside of the legal scope of nursing may entitle the employer to deny responsibility for the nurse, the insurer to deny coverage for the nurse, and the professional regulating association to take disciplinary action against the nurse. Venturing outside the scope of professional nursing practice (i.e., as occurs in the preparation and dispensing of medications) is fraught with risk of legal liability, particularly as this may involve nurses engaged in activities beyond their education and competence.

The legislated scope of practice also generates concerns regarding the legalities of nurses practicing in so-called "extended roles," including nurse midwives and nurse practitioners. Midwifery is a practice outside the legislated scope of ordinary nursing practice and has therefore been a prohibited area of practice for nurses in Canada. In recent years, however, public demand has arisen for legalization of midwifery as an alternative to traditional birthing practices in Canada. The controversy generated by this issue resulted in a plethora of studies and recommendations. One such report from the Ontario Task Force on Midwifery (1987) recommends the establishment of independent midwifery practices and services regulated by the Ministry of Health. The law to legalize midwifery independent of both nursing and medical practice arts was passed in Ontario in 1991.

There are other legal obligations pursuant to the disciplinary provisions of nurse practice acts. The disciplinary process commences in many jurisdictions by the filing of a complaint or report. In some provinces, the employer is required to notify the licensing body when a nurse employee is dismissed because of incompetence. These statutes may also impose a positive duty to maintain competence, as well as physical and mental ability to practice. The statutes also prohibit conduct unbecoming a professional. In that professional regulation is within provincial jurisdiction, each province imposes varying obligations in this regard. For example, in Manitoba a registered nurse is subject to disciplinary sanction when that nurse is found guilty of professional misconduct or conduct unbecoming a member (Registered Nurses' Act, 1980, s.26). In British Columbia, by contrast, discipline will be taken against a member guilty of incompetence, conduct contrary to ethical standards, or impaired ability to nurse (Nurses (Registered) Act, 1979). Similarly, the Ontario government delegated responsibility to the College of Nurses of Ontario to define professional misconduct subject to the approval of the Lieutenant Governor (Health Disciplines Act, 1980, s.73). Furthermore, the Discipline Committee of the College of Nurses, struck in accordance with the Health Disciplines Act (1980), is to determine allegations of professional misconduct or incompetence of members of the College of Nurses (Health Disciplines Act, 1980, s.83).

The behavior of nurses that may be disciplined is generally outlined in legislative terms sufficiently vague and broad enough to cover a range of actions. This however means that the legislated terms are subject to interpretation. Discipline committees and, if necessary, courts may be required to rule on whether complaints about nurses warrant discipline. These rulings and interpretations then become the precedents binding future decisions.

PRIVATE LAW

Nurses are exposed to liability in the division of law known as private law and are particularly subject to the laws of contract and tort. The greatest exposure is in tort, which governs civil wrongs occurring within the context of the nurse/patient relationship.

Contract

The courts deem that the law of contract as it relates to nurse/patient relationships has limited application and usefulness (Philpott, 1985) and is therefore not considered in this discussion of a nurse's contractual obligations. Nursing interventions involving "patient contracting" are nursing rather than legal instruments.

Nurses are usually employees and hence are subject to the laws and obligations that apply to employment or labor agreements. A contract is an agreement between two or more persons; it creates obligations and may be written or verbal. The parties to the contract (i.e., the employer and the nurse employee or the nurse's union) are obligated to fulfill the express terms of the contract. Failure enables the nonoffending party to enforce the terms of the contract in accordance with the remedies specified within it. For example, if an employer fails to provide the employee with the agreed vacation time, the union employee may enforce this term by filing a grievance under a union contract, or the non-union employee may make application to a statutory body with the appropriate jurisdiction. If the employment contract is non-union and perhaps unwritten, the express understandings between employer and employee, as well as the relevant provincial legislation, impose terms on the parties. Where a union contract exists, legislated labor codes and essential services agreements will impose additional rights and obligations.

Although comprehensive discussion of the legal issues of employment and labor is beyond the scope of this chapter, it is worthwhile to note that the burgeoning area of wrongful dismissal and the duty of fair representation owed by a union to its members raise important issues for consideration by practicing nurses.

Tort: Intentional Tort

The area with the most dramatic rise in legal action is tort law, a civil wrong or injury for which the court provides a remedy in the form of an action for damages (Black, 1990, p. 1489). There are two main categories of torts. Intentional torts are those in which a defendant intentionally causes injury to others, causing the law to be more heavily weighted in favor of the person harmed (Fleming, 1987, p. 93). The unintentional tort, in contrast, is more difficult to establish and may have been caused either negligently or without any fault at all (Fleming, 1987, p. 93).

Intentional torts include battery, assault, and false imprisonment. Battery is committed by intentionally harmful or offensive contact with another person (Fleming, 1987, p. 23), such as that which occurs when a mentally competent patient refuses an intramuscular injection that has been ordered to be given if needed and the nurse administers the injection against the patient's wishes. Injury is unnecessary. The Supreme Court of Canada ruled that a finding of battery is limited to those circumstances in which there is no consent at all, in which the treatment goes beyond consent, or in which the consent was obtained by fraud or misrepresentation (*Reibl v. Hughes*, 1980). Only infrequently is assault or false imprisonment the basis of an action against a nurse.

Tort: Unintentional Tort

Negligence is fertile ground for legal action against health professionals and/or hospitals (Picard, 1984, p. 28). Fleming (1987, p. 96) describes negligence as conduct that falls below the standard that is regarded as normal or desirable in a given community. This standard of performance is that of the "reasonable man," a measure intended to be somewhat objective.

Four elements of a cause of action must be present for a successful action in negligence:

1. A legally recognized duty of care to protect others against unreasonable risk (Fleming, 1987, p. 95)
2. Failure to perform according to a specified standard of conduct (which is a breach of duty or negligence)
3. There must be damage
4. There must be a connection between the defendant's conduct and the resulting injury (referred to as "remoteness of damage" or "proximate cause" (Fleming, 1987, p. 95)

If any one of these elements is absent, the negligence action cannot succeed (Fleming, 1987, p. 95).

Because negligence is such an important topic, one of the necessary elements— standard of care—will be discussed in more detail, and then examples of negligence that have resulted in suits will be examined.

Standard of care. The nurse is required to bring to the task of caring for a patient a reasonable degree of skill and knowledge, as well as to exercise a reasonable degree of care. This principle was applied to a nurse's action in *Dowey v. Rothwell and Associates* (1974). In this case, a young woman who was epileptic went into a doctor's office and requested assistance, saying she was about to have a seizure. The registered nurse placed the patient on an examination table and left the patient unattended. The patient had a seizure and suffered a severe comminuted fracture of her arm. The judge in rendering judgment stated that the standard to be expected of the nurse is that of the normal, prudent practitioner of the same experience and standing, which the nurse had failed to meet. The judge further stated that a person who possesses special skill and knowledge and is consulted by a patient because of this owes a duty to that patient to use due caution. In considering whether this was an error in judgment, as distinct from an act of carelessness or lack of skill (negligence), the judge outlined the three-point test provided by the Supreme Court of Canada:

1. The professional must have undertaken to possess the skill, knowledge, and judgment of the average professional of that group
2. The average standard of the professional group is defined
3. The decision must have resulted from an exercise of the average standard

If the facts reflect these three steps, then it was an error and there is no liability.

The caselaw substantiates that the expert or specialist is expected to exercise a higher degree of skill in his or her particular area of expertise than is the so-called general practitioner (Picard, 1984, p. 155). Further, the courts have held that the standard of care for novice practitioners is not lowered to accommodate their lack of experience. This precedent may be applied to nursing students and novice nurses. Picard outlines cases in which nonphysicians have undertaken responsibilities similar to that of a physician and have been held accountable for failing to perform in accordance with the higher standard of care of the general practitioner, irrespective of the lack of medical training (Picard, 1984, p. 161). These cases may be compared to circumstances in which a nurse acts as an expert and/or undertakes to perform certain medical functions that are commonly described as sanctioned medical acts or transferred functions. Although this standard has not been judicially considered, a court may require the higher standard of performance of any nurse undertaking transferred functions. Clearly, health professionals are expected to recognize their limitations (Linden, 1988, p. 145).

The standard of care expected is also affected by the degree of risk to which the patient is subject in the circumstances. For example, in a case in which a patient being recovered in the postanesthesia room following routine and uneventful surgery suffered respiratory arrest, the judge commented on the higher standard of care required in areas such as recovery rooms (*Krujelis v. Esdale*, 1972, p. 499). The extreme dependency of the patients on the care of the staff in a recovery area entails more attentive monitoring, a standard that the nurses in this case failed to meet.

Evidence pertaining to the standards of performance applicable in contested legal situations is introduced into court by expert witnesses. However, the court must often decide to accept the evidence of one or more experts, while disregarding others. In *Robertshaw Estate v. Grimshaw et al.* (1987), a nurse expert gave evidence of the standard of care to be met by nurses in an Emergency Department. The judge held these standards to be ideal and applicable to the future and chose instead to accept the evidence of another nurse expert that he judged to be less ideal and more in line with the approved practice at the time of the incident. It is incumbent on the nursing profession to identify common standards of practice and to distinguish the ideal standard from approved practice. Lack of certainty about the reasonable standard of performance may lead to confusion among nurses and adverse positions in the courtroom.

Instances of negligence. The standard of care provides the measure by which a nurse's care is judged. A wide range of nursing activities have been held up to accepted standards of performance. Klein (1986, p. 78) identified the areas of greatest risk for assessment of liability for negligence against nurses in the United States: foreign objects left in patients, burns, falls, failure to observe and take appropriate actions, medication errors, mistaken identity, failure to communicate, failure to exercise reasonable judgment, abandonment, and infections. The available statistics regarding nursing actions that resulted in judicial pronouncement of negligence in Canada are limited. However, a review of the Canadian caselaw shows nursing activities that have been the subject of litigation are similar to the American experience, including burns, medication errors, inadequate monitoring of patient status or whereabouts, failure to communicate, and errors in procedures (Prichard, 1990, Appendix B).

The observation, supervision, and monitoring of patients are nursing duties that have been brought to the attention of Canadian courts. In *Child v. Vancouver General Hospital et al.* (1970), a nurse was assigned to only one patient, who was intermittently restless and confused. The nurse went for coffee and approximately 15 minutes later the patient was found on a canopy below his open window. The Supreme Court of Canada found that the nurse was not negligent on the basis that it was reasonable to believe that the patient would remain quiet and therefore that the nurse could leave the room.

However, in other so-called "coffee break" cases, the court found nurses negligent in going on coffee break and failing to adequately monitor the patients being recovered in the postanesthesia area (*Laidlaw v. Lions Gate Hospital*, 1969; *Krujelis v. Esdale*, 1972). The head or charge nurses involved agreed to allow nursing staff to take their breaks. The nurses who stayed were unable to monitor all patients and, consequently, in each case, a patient suffered respiratory arrest with permanent damage. In *Meyer v. Gordon* (1981), a newborn suffered brain damage as a result of negligent nursing care; the three nurses available failed to take a history, monitor, and record the progress of an expectant mother. A nurse in *Joseph Brandt Memorial Hospital v. Koziol* (1977) was found to be negligent for allowing a patient on a Stryker frame, who required frequent turning, deep breathing and coughing, and close monitoring, to sleep through the night. The patient died from aspirating gastric fluid. It was held that the nurse should have roused the patient hourly for deep breathing and coughing.

Nurses' duties include effective management of crisis situations. In *Bergen v. Sturgeon General Hospital et al.* (1984), a woman was admitted to hospital with abdominal pains. She died several days later of appendicitis. In this case, the patient was misdiagnosed, went into crisis, and experienced an "abdominal snap," which was later identified as the acute onset of sepsis. The charge nurse, who was 25 feet away from the patient's room, was aware of the crisis but made no personal assessment of the situation. The nurse caring for the patient and the charge nurse were found negligent, the latter for her failure to more closely assess the situation and for failing to inform fully the oncoming charge nurse of the serious turn of events.

In a 1986 decision of the Ontario High Court of Justice (*Kahn v. Salama*, 1986), which was upheld by the Ontario Court of Appeal (1988), a nurse certified to administer "top-up" doses of epidural anesthetic, administered the same. She checked the patient's blood pressure, which registered 100/70 mm Hg and immediately palpated another reading of 50 mm Hg systolic. The nurse again used her stethoscope and obtained a reading of 50/20 mm Hg. This experienced obstetrical nurse turned the patient on her left side, applied an oxygen mask, turned off the pitocin drip, and checked the blood pressure again. At this moment, the patient stopped breathing. The nurse pulled the emergency bell and commenced cardiopulmonary resuscitation. It was alleged that the nurse was negligent in failing to pull the emergency bell earlier. An expert nurse witness gave evidence at the trial that the nurse's performance was substandard. However, the judge, relying on the experience of the nurse defendant, determined that the nurse made only an error in judgment and hence no liability was ascribed for not calling for help earlier. The judge relied on the fact that the nurse had considerable experience in resuscitating patients in similar circumstances.

The administration of medications has significant potential liability, as was found in *Fiege v. Cornwall General Hospital* (1980), in which the nurse improperly mapped an injection site for an intramuscular medication. However, the Supreme Court of Canada in 1974 reversed a lower court finding of negligence in which a nurse injected Bicillin into the circumflex artery causing gangrene of the fingers; the court stated that nurses cannot be guarantors that accidents will not occur (*Cavan v. Wilcox*, 1975). In another case, two nurses were judged negligent when one nurse asked another for Novocaine and was handed a container of adrenaline. The first nurse, without looking at the label, handed it to the physician who had requested Novocaine. The physician injected the medication without checking the label and caused the death of the patient. The judge held the physician was not negligent and was entitled to rely on the nurses (*Budgen v. Harbour View Hospital*, 1947; see also *Walker v. Sydney City Hospital*, 1983). In a 1983 decision (*Misericordia Hospital v. Bustillo*, 1983), it was held that the hospital pharmacy and a nurse had negligently delivered the wrong solution to an ophthalmologist during cataract surgery. The physician had requested to see the bottle but "by a very serious oversight" failed to notice that the bottle contained the wrong solution. The Alberta Court of Appeal varied the degree of liability of the pharmacy and nurse from 87.5% to 60% with 40% assessed against the doctor.

Another area that has been the subject of considerable judicial comment is the doctor/nurse interface. It is the duty of the nurse to advise a physician of changes in a patient's condition so that the physician may adapt the medical treatment as necessary. This obligation was discussed in *Bergen v. Sturgeon General Hospital et al.* (1984), in which a charge nurse was found negligent in failing to give a complete report on the condition of a patient to the oncoming charge nurse and in failing to call the physician regarding a critical downturn in the condition of his patient.

The balance between the nurse's duty to carry out a physician's order and the obligation to intervene on a physician's order can be precarious. In *Villeneuve v. Sisters of St. Joseph* (1975), a child received a Pentothal injection in the brachial artery, consequently necessitating amputation of the hand. Negligence was alleged against a doctor for the injection and against two nurses for failing to completely immobilize the child's arm. It was also alleged that the nurses should have intervened on behalf of the child. The judge ruled that the doctor should not have attempted the injection when he realized that three persons could not immobilize the patient. He continued to say that the child's movement was not evidence of the nurses' lack of care and that the responsibility for persisting with the injection lay solely with the physician. Furthermore the judge, in absolving the nurses of liability, pointed out that if they had been negligent it was expected the physician would have alleged so in his defense.

Negligence was alleged in *Serre v. de Tilly et al.* (1975) in which two nurses saw the same patient for the same complaint in different Emergency Departments. Physicians gave orders that required the patient be sent home, since her symptoms were thought to be related to "hysteria." One nurse delayed in implementing the physician's orders out of concern for the patient, but ultimately carried them out and sent her home. The patient died of a brain hemorrhage, which the judge accepted on the evidence as a very rare occurrence. The physicians were found to have met the standard of care. The judge commented as follows:

> I cannot accept the argument that if any of the nurses or the hospital servants disagreed with the findings or direction of the family doctor, that they should have acted independently or called in other medical advice. Diagnosis is surely not a function of the nurse; and unless there were clear and obvious evidences of neglect or incompetence on the part of the family doctor, it would be unthinkable that the hospital or its agents should interfere or depart from his instructions. (*Serre v. de Tilly et al*, 1975, 8 O.R. (2d) 490 at 495)

However, in *MacDonald v. York County Hospital et al.* (1976), the trial judge commented that the nurses were negligent in failing to monitor more frequently the condition of a patient with a leg cast when signs of circulatory impairment appeared. The nurses also failed to advise a doctor of the changes. A Supreme Court of Canada unanimous decision agreed with the Ontario Court of Appeal that the nurses who observed circulatory impairment in the patient with a leg cast and advised the doctor of their concerns once but took no further action for at least 18 hours were remiss and probably negligent. As the judge accepted that the doctor would have taken no action even if the nurses had called, the nurses were held not to have contributed to the patient's loss.

In a judgment following the inquiry into the death of a child in Nova Scotia (In Re *The Fatality Inquirers Act,* 1986), the judge referred to the Canadian Nurses Association (CNA) Code of Ethics in discussing the duties of the staff nurse and nurse supervisor to a child who was not awakening from anesthesia after a tonsillectomy. The night nurse supervisor failed to respond appropriately to the staff nurse's requests to check the child and call the physician. It was accepted in evidence that the hospital had a policy not to call a doctor during the night without approval of the supervisor. The judge held the supervisor to have compounded her negligence by breaching the CNA Code of Ethics obligation to take measures on behalf of the patient.

It is apparent from the foregoing discussion that the duties to the patient of the nurse and nurse manager are manifold. The caselaw demonstrates that patients are entitled to rely on nurses in numerous ways, and the failure for nurses to act in these ways is legally actionable. Obviously the duty to patients is paramount, particularly with respect to a nurse's personal concerns, and affects not only the nature, scope, and standard of care, but also the communication and interactions with others.

PATIENTS' RIGHTS

Sensitivity to patients' rights has been raised in relation to a society that has become more consumer oriented and values the observance of individual rights above group rights. The passage of human rights legislation and, in 1982, of the Canadian Charter of Rights and Freedoms hails a new era in individual rights. Concomitantly, the Supreme Court of Canada decided two landmark cases affirming the patients' right to self-determination and inviolability (*Hopp v. Lepp,* 1980; *Reibl v. Hughes,* 1980). In 1988, the Supreme Court of Canada handed down another decision regarding individual rights. It struck down the federal abortion law contained in the Criminal Code—it was held to infringe on the individual's right to "life, liberty and security of the person" guaranteed in the Charter of Rights and Freedoms ("Upsetting a law . . . ," 1988, p. A7). A bill to introduce a new provision regarding abortion into the Criminal Code was passed by the House of Congress but was defeated in the Senate in January 1991; thus the common law prevails in the absence of applicable legislation. The rights of any patient are ensconced in various statutes throughout the common law and are rights assigned to all persons. Although organizations such as the Law Reform Commission of Canada (1983) recommend that patients' rights be expressly recognized, provincial governments have not done so.

Despite the lack of one statute of consolidated rights, patients have numerous remedies available to them. For example, a complaint may be filed with the licensing body against a nurse. In addition, a patient may also initiate a private lawsuit against a hospital, nurse, or other health professional who has failed to fulfill all the duties or obligations that are owed to the patient. Furthermore if a patient were the victim of any criminal action within the health system, a complaint may be filed with the police. Ellis (1981) identifies a number of specific rights of patients, including the freedom to receive service in a hospital of their choice, the freedom to select a physician, and the right to confidentiality. However, it is also recognized that statutory restrictions may be imposed on these rights. Provincial public health statutes require reporting and mandatory treatment of sexually transmitted diseases. The nature and extent of the duty to warn unsuspecting partners of persons who are HIV seropositive remains controversial (Macmillan, 1988). Child protection legislation supersedes the common law duty of confidentiality by mandating the reporting of suspected child abuse. Patients or residents in some jurisdictions may be restrained when it is necessary to prevent injury (Public Health Act, R.S.M. 1987, cP210).

Other rights issues causing debate are the right of persons who are HIV seropositive to expensive and experimental drugs and treatments. The entitlement to donor organs, especially of elderly persons, has sparked controversy as it relates to age discrimination prohibited by human rights legislation and the limited resources of the health care system. Furthermore, the rapid advancement of reproductive technologies and public health demand for clarification of the issues has resulted in the establishment of a Royal Commission on Reproductive Technology, which will provide its report in 1992. Following a decade of growth of individual rights, the 1990s promise clarification of group and individual rights, as well as of issues heretofore unregulated. Decisions that are now being made on an ad hoc basis by health professionals will be facilitated by new laws and jurisprudence.

The right of refusal of treatment comes directly from the basic rights of self-determination and inviolability; although it is widely accepted and has been articulated by the Supreme Court of Canada (*Hopp v. Lepp*, 1980) that treatment should not be imposed against a patient's will, such a decision evokes great anxiety regarding legalities among health professionals. There are no known cases in which a health professional has been successfully prosecuted for observing a competent patient's desire to have treatment terminated, but federal criminal legislation permitting prosecution when life has not been preserved has not yet been repealed or made inapplicable to health professionals. The courts recognize the right of the patient or parent to make a choice, even when that choice may result in death. A well-publicized case in January 1992 involved "Nancy B," a 25-year-old quadraplegic who required mechanical ventilation to survive. The Quebec Superior Court ruled that "Nancy B," had the right to tell doctors to disconnect her respirator, and acknowledged her right to die. In a 1986 decision of the Quebec Court of Appeal (*Montreal Children's Hospital v. J.*, 1986) a mother refused to authorize a hospital to administer chemotherapy to her infant daughter who was suffering from cancer. Under Quebec public health legislation, the hospital required parental consent, but if the parent refused, the hospital could petition the court showing the refusal was not in the child's best interest. The court held against the hospital, saying that a 10% to 20% chance of

cure with chemotherapy was not comparable to the serious and permanently inca-
pacitating side effects suffered by the child.

The Ontario Court of Appeal in 1990 unanimously ruled that a person has the
right to reject lifesaving treatment, in this case a blood transfusion, even if it results
in death (*Mallette v. Shulman*, 1990). It was held that a card rejecting blood transfusions, which was found on an unconscious and seriously injured woman, was
sufficient to deny treatment.

It is important to note that a patient's rights generally correspond with the imposition of duties or obligations on others, such as the hospital and health professionals caring for the patient. It is equally important to note that, while the rights
exist, the decision to exercise these rights rests with the patient.

RISK MINIMIZATION

Steps that may be taken by each nurse to minimize the risk of liability should not
be confused with the risk management programs being established or already implemented in health care facilities. Although the purpose and principles may be
similar, the approaches taken by the individual and the institution will differ. The
risk of legal liability in contemporary nursing practice is as much a characteristic of
that practice as is change. The nature of risk experienced by the nurse varies in
relation to whether the nurse is employer, employee, or self-employed.

A health-care-provider/employer has both direct and indirect obligations to patients or clients (Kolber, 1984a, p. 72). Direct duties are legally actionable obligations
imposed on the provider/employer by virtue of the nature of service it purports to
provide. For example, nurses employed in a health care institution are represented
to be duly qualified, and a patient entering this setting is entitled to expect hiring
practices to ensure this (Kolber, 1984b, p. 47). Similarly the institution is obligated
to provide a safe system of care, including safe levels of staffing. A patient who is
harmed directly as a result of an employee who is not qualified or as a result of
inadequate staffing may have the basis for a direct civil action against the provider/
employer.

Corporate liability is the imposition of a direct nondelegable duty of care to provide
all patients with a reasonable standard of care (Duff, 1987). This duty was first
recognized by the American courts in 1965 in *Darling v. Charleston Community Memorial Hospital* (1965). Support for this position was strongly endorsed in the dis-
senting judgments of the Ontario Court of Appeal in *Yepremian v. Scarborough General
Hospital* (1980). Although direct corporate liability is not yet law in Canada, there is
strong support favoring it.

The provider/employer is exposed to risk in a second manner, that is, vicariously
or indirectly. An employer is responsible for the acts of its employees performed
within the scope of their employment (Sneiderman, 1989, p. 110). The Supreme
Court of Canada has held hospital employers vicariously liable for the negligence
of their employees (Prichard, 1990, Appendix B, Vol. 1). A finding of vicarious liability
is a two-step process: first, the acts of the employees must be held negligent; second,
the acts must have been performed within the scope of the negligent person's employment. Negligence actions involving nurses as employees always name the hos-

pital employer as a defendant in the action and, increasingly, also name the individual nurse. There are no reported cases in which a Canadian hospital avoided liability by disavowing responsibility for the negligent actions of a staff nurse. This is important to note in that many nurses have voiced concern over the potential conflict of interest between the hospital and its insurers who wish to avoid liability and the nurse who is the perpetrator of the alleged negligent acts. Unfortunately, tensions between management and staff may exacerbate perceptions of conflict. Institutional employers will have liability insurance as a result of exposure to vicarious liability for the actions of their employees. Also, if the facility has been named as defendant in a legal suit, the institutional employer will retain legal counsel to defend the action. Often the individual staff nurse alleged negligent is not notified of the measures taken by the institution to defend these actions, thereby isolating the nurse, who may consequently feel suspicious that there is no defense. The nurse should inquire of administration what steps have been taken and whether the institution's insurance policy adequately provides for the claim. Nurses may also wish to consult independent legal counsel to ensure that their best interests are represented. National liability coverage was made available to members of the CNA through the Canadian Nurses Protective Society (CNPS), which came into being in 1988. The protection will generally be secondary to the primary insurance of a nurse's employer. However, the nurse is nonetheless required to notify the CNPS of any potential claims as a condition of coverage (McLean, 1989).

Self-employed nurses have direct legal liability. Their risk minimization strategies should include obtaining adequate primary insurance coverage with regard to the risk inherent in their practices.

Nurses, whether employees or not, are personally accountable for their actions. Although the employer's insurer may be required to pay the damages awarded due to negligent actions of its nurse-employee, the nurse will nonetheless be central to the legal action. Furthermore, the employer may seek to indemnify itself from the nurse, (Sneiderman, 1984, p. 112), although this rarely, if ever, has been exercised by a Canadian hospital. A nurse involved in a lawsuit may also be reported to the licensing body for discipline. A finding of negligence does not automatically justify disciplinary action, but the negligent actions may nonetheless be the source of a complaint.

Minimizing risk entails recognition of the nature of the risk, as well as ensuring adequate insurance coverage. Many Canadian hospitals are currently implementing risk management programs, including risk identification and evaluation, policy development, education, claims management, and annual review (McKerrow, 1987, p. 69). Prichard (1990, Appendix A, p. 219) recommends increasing the legal responsibility of health care institutions for care provided within them, thus supporting the concept of team-delivered care. He also suggests that quality assurance, risk management, and peer review programs be made mandatory by statute. Further, the report recommends that all health care professionals, including physicians, be required to participate in these programs, with severe penalties assessed against those failing to fullfill their responsibilities.

Individual nurses would do well to analyze their practices with regard to the nature of the practice, inherent risks, skill/knowledge levels and limits of competence, currency of practice, and communication skills. Awareness of the risk will enable nurses to incorporate risk minimizing activities into practice.

The first of such activities is the need to keep knowledge current. Several judgments have specifically stated the need for nurses to maintain their knowledge and skill levels in relation to approved practice of the time (*Murphy v. St. Catharine's General Hospital*, 1964; *Bernier v. Sisters of Service et al.*, 1948; *Dowey v. Rothwell and Associates*, 1974).

The right of the patient to self-determination, hence consent to treatment, is critical in reducing exposure to risk. Consent is required generally with respect to admission to a health care facility and specifically with regard to particular treatments, usually medical procedures that are associated with risk of adverse effects. Consent must be valid and must not have been revoked or withdrawn. The mere signing of a consent form does not guarantee validity of consent. A valid consent is one provided by a mentally competent person and obtained without coercion, influence of drugs, deceit, or fraud (Fleming, 1987, p. 73). The consent must also be specific to the treatment and the caregiver. Moreover, the patient must be informed if the consent is to be valid (Sneiderman, 1989, p. 52).

The contemporary concept of "informed consent" was introduced in two 1980 Supreme Court of Canada decisions (*Hopp v. Lepp*, 1980; *Reibl v. Hughes*, 1980). Informed consent reflects that a surgeon (or other health professional) is not immune from negligence or battery if there has been a failure to disclose the required information, most notably risks. Entwined in the issue of informed consent is the existence of a duty of disclosure (Sneiderman, 1989, p. 53). The performer of the treatment or procedure (e.g., surgery) is required to answer any specific questions posed by the patient; to disclose the nature of the proposed operation and its gravity; and to disclose any material risks, probable risks, and any unusual or special risks (*Hopp v. Lepp*, 1980). In addition, reasonable alternatives must be disclosed. The scope of disclosure must be decided in relation to the facts in each set of circumstances. To find liability it is necessary to conclude that the patient would not have undergone the treatment and would not have suffered the harm if the risks had been outlined. This is an objective test (Sneiderman, 1989, p. 55). Therefore if the patient would have undergone the procedure even knowing the risks, no liability will be assessed. Clearly this is an important area of law for health professionals.

When nurses conduct procedures for which informed consent must be obtained, and these are generally elective procedures that create a risk to the future well-being of the patient, then nurses could be expected to meet the aforementioned standard. However, nurses may become involved in informed consent by default; that is, the nurse may discover just before a procedure that informed consent has not been obtained. A number of cases suggest that a doctor can delegate the duty to inform, but this delegation must be to someone who has sufficient knowledge to inform the patient (Rozovsky and Rozovsky, 1987, p. 8). It has also been decided that one doctor does not have a duty to warn a patient of a procedure to be carried out by another doctor (*McLean v. Weir*, 1980). It is open for a court to apply this principle to a situation involving a nurse. However, this raises the issue of whether the CNA Code of Ethics imports the duty to answer questions and advocate for the patient into the realm of a nurse's legal duties (Canadian Nurses Association, 1991, p. 21). This question has not been specifically contemplated by the courts. Undoubtedly, nurses are exposing themselves and their employers to risk by undertaking the responsibility to inform patients about medical procedures. Rozovsky and Rozovsky (1987, p. 60) suggest nurses refrain from becoming involved in obtaining informed consent. Whereas the duty is that of the performer, hence usually the physician, any nurse undertaking such responsibility should be thoroughly aware of hospital policy on this issue and make every effort to ensure communication of all the requisite information, thereby limiting the risk.

In the context of legal risk minimization, the purpose of the chart is to serve as a record of all care provided to the patient. The common law, since *Ares v. Venner* in 1970, has rendered hospital records admissible in court. Some jurisdictions have legislation that authorizes the admissibility of these records into court. The court in *Ares v. Venner* addressed the issue of the trustworthiness of the record, which is an essential element of its worth to the court. Trustworthiness is enhanced by the duty to record, in one's own handwriting, at the time events occur. Furthermore, the record is to be made by a person with first-hand knowledge.

There are no immutable rules for documentation, but there are several significant principles and guidelines. The chart must meet statutory requirements. Also it must reflect the status of the patient, the care provided, and the response to care. Since litigation often occurs years after an incident, the record may constitute a nurse's only "memory" of the event. It is therefore critical that the language of the record be clear, precise, and objective. An issue frequently arises regarding the degree to which conditions, actions, and events must be recorded. The approaches range from recording only in a detailed, narrative format to documentation-by-exception, as in recording only "significant changes."

In this regard, judges in numerous cases have commented on the "custom" of recording all activities, events, and conditions. This traditional practice, as well as accreditation requirements, led the judge in *Kolesar v. Jeffries et al.* (1978) to infer that if it was not written it was not done. Furthermore, the absence of documentation at a critical time in the patient's course of illness has led to an inference that there was no great concern for the patient during that time (*Holmes v. Board of Hospitals Trustees of London*, 1977). Nonetheless, the court in *Hajgato v. London Hospital Association* (1982) found no negligence when the nurses were alleged to have failed to diagnose infection in a surgical incision and were also alleged to have inadequately recorded the clinical indicators of infection. The hospital policy of charting only significant changes in the patient was followed and was accepted by the court. In *Ferguson v. Hamilton Civic Hospital et al.* (1983), the judge stated that the lack of recording normal results by nurses engaged in "routine patient monitoring" would not lead to the automatic conclusion that no monitoring took place.

The quality of the record is important and will create an impression of the quality of care (Picard, 1984, p. 332). Alterations and late entries, as well as inconsistencies, undermine the reliability of the records. Lack of chronological recording may also call the timing of events into question. The hallmarks of trustworthiness include objective, complete, accurate, clear, and contemporaneous recording.

CONCLUSION

This chapter discusses the broad scope of legal issues and concerns affecting a nurse's professional practice. Many of the legal aspects are not new concepts or trends but are an overview of the liability of the nurse within contemporary Canadian society. The obligations of the nurse may be associated with corresponding rights in employers, patients, and professional associations. The duties of the nurse must be discharged with due caution. Whether a nurse is held accountable personally or a nurse's employer is held responsible for vicarious liability, the ramifications for the nurse are no less significant. The successful practice of nursing entails the implementation of measures to minimize exposure to liability. Defensive professional practice is not the answer. Instead, nurses are encouraged to seek out sources of information and education to keep abreast of the law—that vague and dynamic order that is omnipresent in the professional practice of the nurse.

REFERENCES

Ares v. Venner, [1970] S.C.R. 608, 73 W.W.R. 347, 12 C.R.N.S. 349, 14 D.L.R. (3d) 4, rvsg 70 W.W.R. 96.

Bergen v. Sturgeon General Hospital et al, (1984) 28 C.C.L.T. 155 (Alta. Q.B.), 52 A.R. 161 (Q.B.).

Bernier v. Sisters of Service et al, [1948] 1 W.W.R. 113 [1948], 2 D.L.R. 468 (Alta. S.C.).

Black, H.C. (1990). *Black's law dictionary* (6th ed.). St. Paul, MN: West Publishing.

Bugden v. Harbour View Hospital, [1947] 2 D.L.R. 338 (N.S.S.C.).

Canadian Nurses Association. (1985). *Code of ethics for nursing.* Ottawa: Author.

Cavan v. Wilcox, [1975] 2 S.C.R. 663, 50 D.L.R. (3d) 687, 9 N.B.R. (2d) 140, 2 N.R. 618 rvsg 44 D.L.R. (3d) 42, 7 N.B.R. (2d) 192.

Child v. Vancouver General Hospital [1970], S.C.R. 477, 71 W.W.R. 656, 10 D.L.R. (3d) 539.

Criminal Code, R.S.C. 1970, c. C-34.

Cust, K. (1986). Nurse don't consent to assaults from patients. *The Lawyers Weekly,* 6(32),4.

Darling v. Charleston Community Memorial Hospital (1965), 211 N.E. (2d) 253 (Ill. C.A.).

Dowey v. Rothwell & Associates, [1974] 5 W.W.R. 311 (Alta. S.C.).

Duff, D.G. (1987). *Medical malpractice: Relevant data for an investigation as to the impact of civil liability on professional behaviour.* Unpublished manuscript.

Ellis, R.G. (1981). *Patients' rights.* Saskatoon: Public Legal Association of Saskatchewan.

Ferguson v. Hamilton Civic Hospital et al, (1983), 40 O.R. (2d) 557, 23 C.C.L.T. 254, 144 D.L.R. (3d) 214 (H.C.).

Fiege v. Cornwall General Hospital (1980), 30 O.R. (2d) 691, 117 D.L.R. (3d) 152 (H.C.).

Fleming, J.G. (1987). *The law of torts* (7th ed.). Sydney, Australia: Law Book.

Gall, G.L. (1990). *The Canadian legal system* (3rd ed.). Toronto: Carswell Legal Publications.

Grange, S.G.M. (1984). *Report of the Royal Commission of Inquiry to Certain Deaths at the Hospital for Sick Children and related matters.* Toronto: Ontario Ministry of the Attorney General.

Hajgato v. London Hospital Association, (1982), 36 O.R. (2d) 669, affd 40 O.R. (2D) 264 (C.A.).

Health Disciplines Act, R.S.O. 1980, c. 196, as am S.O. 1983, c. 59; am 1986, c. 34; am 1989, c. 72, s. 4.

Holmes v. Board of Hospital Trustees of London, (1977), 17 O.R. (2d) 626, 5 C.C.L.T. 1, 81 D.L.R. (3d) 67 (H.C.).

Hopp v. Lepp, [1980] 2 S.C.R. 192, 13 C.C.L.T. 66, [1980] 4 W.W.R. 645, 112 D.L.R. (3d) 67, 4 L. Med. Q. 202, 22 A.R. 361, 32 N.R. 145, reversing 8 C.C.L.T. 260, [1979] 3 W.W.R. 409, 98 D.L.R. (3d) 464 4 L. Med. Q. 191, 15 A.R. 472, which reversed 2 C.C.L.T. 183, 77 D.L.R. (3d) 321, 4 L. Med. Q. 187, 5 A.R. 267.

In Re *The Fatality Inquiries Act,* R.S.M.S., 1963 c. 101 (as am) and the Death of Diana Michelle Strickland, North Sydney, Nova Scotia, 1986.

Joseph Brandt Memorial Hospital v. Koziol (1977), 2 C.C. L. T. 170 (S.C.C.).

Kahn v. Salama [1986] 12 A.C.W.S. (3d) 231 (Ont. C.A.) aff'g. [1986] O.J. No. 619 (unreported) (S.C.).

Klein, C.A. (1986). Preventing malpractice suits. *The Nurse Practitioner: American Journal of Primary Health Care,* 11(3), 78.

Kolber, S.M. [1984a]. Toward the finding of greater hospital liability (Part 1). *Health Law in Canada,* 4(3), 72.

Kolber, S.M. (1984b). Toward the finding of greater hospital liability (Part 2). *Health Law in Canada,* 5(2), 47.

Kolber, S.M. (1985). Toward the finding of greater hospital liability (Part 3). *Health Law in Canada*, 5(3), 72.

Krujelis v. Esdale, [1972] 2 W.W.R. 495, 25 D.L.R. (3d) 557 (B.C.S.C.).

Laidlaw v. Lions Gate Hospital, (1969), 70 W.W.R. 727, 8 D.L.R. (3d) 730 (B.C.S.C.).

Law Reform Commission of Canada. (1983). *Report on Euthanasia, Aiding Suicide and Cessation of Treatment.* Ottawa: Law Reform Commission of Canada.

Linden, A.M. (1988). *Canadian tort law* (4th ed.). Toronto: Butterworths.

MacDonald v. York County Hospital et al, 1 O.R. (2d) 653, 41 D.L.R. (3d) 321 affd (sub nom *Vail v. MacDonald*) [1976] 2 S.C.R. 825, 66 D.L.R. (3d) 530, 8 N.R. 155.

Macmillan, R.M. (1988). *Report of the Federal/Provincial/Territorial Working Group on Confidentiality in Relation to HIV Seropositivity.* Ottawa: Health and Welfare Canada.

Malette v. Shulman, [1990] 72 O.R. (2d) 417 (Ont. C.A.).

Manitoba Association of Registered Nurses: (1989). *Nurse abuse report.* Winnipeg: Author.

McKerrow, L.W. (1984). Litigation and the health care professional—defensive practice is not the answer. *Health Law in Canada,* 5(2), 35-38.

McKerrow, L.W. (1987). The whys and hows of hospital risk management programs. *Health Law in Canada,* 7(3), 67-69.

McLean v. Weir, [1980] 4 W.W.R. 330, 18 B.C.L.R. 325 (C.A.).

McLean, P. (1989). Professional liability: A successful year of self-protection for Canadian nurses. *The Canadian Nurse,* 85(5), 26.

Meyer v. Gordon (1981), 17 C.C.L.T. 1 (B.C.S.C.).

Misericordia Hospital v. Bustillo, [1983] Alta.D. 2632-01 (unreported) (C.A.).

Montreal Children's Hospital v. J. No. 500-09-000105-866, 500-05-009297-845, (unreported) Feb. 4, 1986 (Que. C.A.).

Murphy v. St. Catherines General Hospital, [1964] 1 O.R. 239, 41 D.L.R. (2d) 697 (H.C.)

Nurses (Registered) Act, R.S.B.C. 1979, c. 392, as am 1980, c. 10, s. 118; am 1983, c. 10 Sch. 2; am 1988, c. 51, ss. 4-38.

Nelles v. Ontario, (1989), 49 C.C.L.T. 217 (S.C.C.); [1989] 2 S.C.R. 170.

Philpott, M. (1985). *Legal liability and the nursing process.* Toronto: W.B. Saunders.

Picard, E.I. (1984). *Legal liability of doctors and hospitals in Canada* (2nd ed.). Toronto: Carswell Legal Publications.

Prichard, J.R.S. (1990). *Liability and compensation in health care.* Toronto: University of Toronto Press.

Provincial/Territorial Registrars. (1987). *Minutes.* Unpublished document available Alberta Association of Registered Nurses, Edmonton, July 24.

Public Health Act, R.S.M. 1987, c. P210, Regulation 337/88R.

Registered Nurses' Act, S.M. 1980, c. 45.

Reibl v. Hughes, 16 O.R. (2d) 306, 78 D.L.R. (3d) 35, 1.L. Med. Q. 50, reversed 21 O.R. (2d) 14, 6 C.C.L.T. 227, 89 D.L.R. (3d) 112, 2 L. Med. Q. 153, which was reversed [1980] 2 S.C.R. 880, 14 C.C.L.T. 1, 114 D.L.R. (3d) 1.33 N.R. 361.

Richards, E.P., II. (1983). Patients' rights issues in health care administration. *The Health Lawyer,* 1(3), 13.

Robertson Estate v. Grimshaw et al, (1988), 49 Man.R. (2d) 20 (Q.B.); (1989) 57 Man. (2d) 140 C.A. affg.

Rozovsky, F.A. (1984). *Consent to treatment: A practical guide.* Toronto: Little Brown and Company.

Rozovsky, L.E., & Rozovsky, F.A. (1986). Why some patients do not sue. *Canadian Critical Care Nursing Journal,* July/August, p. 20.

Rozovsky, L.E., & Rozovsky, F.A. (1987). Should nurses be involved in consent? *Critical Care Nursing Journal.* March/April, p. 8.

Serre v. de Tilly et al (1975), 8 O.R. (2d) 490, 58 D.L.R. (3d) 362 (H.C.).

Sharpe, G. (1987). *The law and medicine in Canada* (2nd ed.). Toronto: Butterworths.

Sneiderman, B., Irvine, J.C., & Osborne, P.H. (1989). *Canadian medical law.* Toronto: Carswell.

Steed, J. (1987). Where has all the money gone? *The Globe and Mail,* July 4, p.D5.

Task Force on Midwifery, (1987). *Report of the Task Force on the Implementation of Midwifery in Ontario.* Toronto: Author.

"Upsetting a law of the land." (1988). *The Globe and Mail,* Jan. 29, p.A7.

Villeneuve v. Sisters of St. Joseph, [1971] 2 O.R. 593, 18 D.L.R. (3d) 537, rvsd in part [1972] 2 O.R. 119, 25 D.L.R. (3d) 35, rvsd [1975] S.C.R. 285, 47 D.L.R. (3d) 391.

Walker v. Sydney City Hospital (1983), 19 A.C.W.S. (2d) 57 (N.S.S.C.).

Yepremian v. Scarborough General Hospital [1980], 28 O.R. (2d) 494, 13 C.C.L.T. 105, 110 D.L.R. (3d) 513 (C.A.).

York, G. (1986). Suits against MDs rise 33%. *The Globe and Mail,* July 8, p.A3.

Young, S.D. (1987). *The rule of experts: Occupational licensing in America.* Washington, DC: Cato Institute.

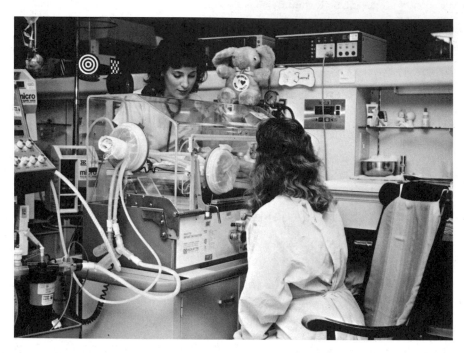

Nurses need an acute awareness of technology's impact on care. This photograph shows a mother being encouraged about the care of her premature infant by Jean Cress, RN *(behind isolette)*. (The photograph was taken in 1987 in the Neonatal Intensive Care Unit, University of Alberta Hospitals, Edmonton, by Pat Marston, and was supplied courtesy of University of Alberta Hospitals. Used with permission.)

CHAPTER FIFTEEN

Technological Issues

RITA MALONEY, RN, MEd

Rita Maloney, RN, BNSc, MEd (Queen's), is Associate Professor and Dean, School of Nursing, Queen's University. Her teaching and scholarship are in the areas of maternal-child nursing, new reproductive technologies, and women's health issues.

Technology has been hailed as progress—and denounced as counterproductive to a holistic view of health. Certainly, however, its advance is changing the nature of nursing practice and will continue to change it for years to come. Why, and in what ways, is technology causing change? How can nurses ensure that the change is beneficial for them and for their patients? What key issues attend the use of health care technologies? Finally, what lies ahead? This chapter attempts to answer these questions, but first examines another: What is technology?

TOWARD A DEFINITION

Capturing the essence of technology is a difficult task. As Franklin (1990) asks: "How does one speak about something that is both fish and water, means as well as end?" (p. 15). One approach, and that used here, is to apply what Franklin calls context-specific rather than global definitions. As the words suggest, such definitions provide a frame of reference for discussing technology within a specific context—in this case, nursing. Two definitions shape the view that guides this discussion.

Pillar, Jacox, and Redman (1990) regard technology as the practical application of science, citing as its two components physical artifacts, or "hardware," and social instruments, or "software." Software includes laws, information systems, and work patterns; hardware focuses on machinery, equipment, and pharmaceuticals. Although Campbell (1990) uses this definition in *Technology and Nursing,* a literature review commissioned by the Canadian Nurses Association, she also finds it lacking. Technology, she says, is more than devices, products, things, procedures, and techniques; it is, as Noble (1977) has shown, also a social phenomenon, growing out of real-world conditions and shaping human responses. As such, an examination of technology's effect on what Campbell calls the "very human enterprise" of nursing must consider the interplay of all actors in the health care system.

In adopting these definitions of technology for the purposes of discussion, it is important to remember that definitions are of themselves limiting. Above all, then, technology should be thought of as a fluid and multifaceted entity (Franklin, 1990, p. 14) and a subject to be approached with an open and flexible, if questioning, mind.

TECHNOLOGY'S EFFECT ON SOCIETY

According to Campbell (1990, p. i), technology continually transforms the contexts and ideas people use to think about it, making it difficult for nurses or anyone else to stand back and judge its impact. But nurses must stand back and judge.

The process should begin with an examination of how technology shapes the broader society within which nursing functions. Franklin (1990, Chapter 1) provides a useful analogy, comparing technology to a house that is always being extended and remodelled. Everyone lives in the house, she says, and hardly any human activity takes place beyond its walls. All are affected by the house's design.

The shifting design includes everything from computerized workplaces that alter the way people relate to one another, to time-saving kitchen gadgetry, to sophisticated media imagery that turns everything (including human misery) into a product for consumption. By variously altering perceptions of time, space, and reality, technology's design thus includes ways of knowing the world. And once a particular way of knowing is embodied in a set of tools and systems, cautions Menzies (1989, p. 44), it tends to foreclose on other avenues of knowing and doing. Nowhere is this more true than in nursing.

TECHNOLOGY'S EFFECT ON NURSING PRACTICE

Nurses tend to value human interaction more than quantifiable efficiency measures; collaborative decision making more than hierarchical lines of command; and a holistic view more than a reductionist one (Adamson, Briskin, and McPhail, 1988). As will become clear, however, technology challenges these values, giving nurses reason for concern as well as optimism. Optimism focuses on how new products and procedures might extend nurses' knowledge and skills (Campbell, 1990, p. i). A point of continuing concern, however, is whether the quickly changing world of high technology health care will result in the end of nursing as a holistic, caregiving profession (Campbell, 1990, p. 11) (see box).

According to Pillar, Jacox, and Redman (1990), technology's effect on nursing is felt in two ways: through the changing nature and intensity of patient care and

Preparing Nurses for Technological Environments

Technology's advance has sparked demands for relevant training and education. The following are suggested to help nurses cope, now and in the future:

- The right to adequate training for safe practice
- Collective agreements and manufacturer sales contracts that define training needs
- Planned staff education that is fully supported by management and includes the best-qualified teachers, including engineers (Clochesy, 1987); compensation should be provided (ONA, 1989)
- User-friendly orientations, practice, and feedback until mastery has been accomplished
- 24-hour resource centers in clinical agencies for independent learning (Gothler, 1989)
- Paid professional development days (ONA, 1989)
- Nursing research courses that include content relative to technology assessment (Abbey, 1989)
- Courses that strengthen nurses' grasp of physics, ethics, and technology's effects on worklife (Campbell, 1990)
- A stronger theory base for nurses working in increasingly technologized settings (Campbell, 1990)
- Conferences that bring together nurses, industry, and governments
- Increased and improved training provided by manufacturers
- Realistic scheduling that encompasses staff nurses' dual responsibilities of caring for patients and teaching less-experienced staff (ONA, 1989)

through the impact on the quality of nurses' work life. For example, as life expectancy increases, so does the complexity of care for multiproblem older adults (CNA, 1990, January). Meanwhile, advances in technology and the treatment of illnesses have increased the number of Canadians with chronic illness in all age groups (CNA, 1990, January). Increased patient acuity, coupled with shortened stays, means hospital-based nurses must carry rapidly changing caseloads of acutely ill patients (Shaver, 1986). All these factors contribute to an increased demand for nursing care hours (CNA, 1990, January).

As well as adjust to the changing nature and intensity of patient care, nurses must deal with the increasingly rapid growth of new health care knowledge, equipment, and procedures—growth that not only increases workloads and thus stress (Campbell, 1990, p. 58) but also demands complex decision making and a wider range of nursing skills. Intensive care units and operating rooms are still the bastions of hospital-based technology. General medical-surgical units display an increasing array of hardware and software: infusion pumps, fax machines, fetal-heart monitors, and computer-aided patient teaching systems are commonplace; bedside computers for data entry and retrieval increasingly so. Meanwhile, technologies such as ventilators, dialysis equipment, and apnea monitors in the home care setting, changing both home and hospital environments and placing new learning demands on nurses in the community.

Despite such demands in all settings, nurses often must fill gaps in training, service, and resources, teaching themselves how to operate and maintain new equipment (ONA, 1989). They must also gain an understanding of when each new technology should or should not be used to help patients understand the purpose, operation, hazards, and limitations of new treatment modalities (Reed, 1989). Meanwhile, the process of reducing patient anxiety grows more complex as the technological environment becomes more sophisticated (Pillar et al., 1990). High noise levels, more people at the bedside for monitoring, and devices that flash or sound alarms, all heighten the anxiety of hospitalized patients and their families and call for sensitive care and support (Pillar et al., 1990). The life-saving marvels of technology notwithstanding, it is useful to remember Benner's (1989) assertion that "Cure cannot be understood or accomplished without a background of care and caring practices" (p. 8).

For nurses who feel anxious in technological environments, providing background of care and caring practices can be difficult. Campbell (1990) states: "There are prevailing concerns about nurses losing sight of the patient due to their involvement with technology. Yet the literature suggests that nurses nurse machines [only] when they are insecure about their knowledge and ability to operate those machines" (Campbell, 1990, p. 47).

According to Pillar and Jacox (1991), technology can engender such feelings of nervousness and dread that a nurse may avoid, or try to avoid, working with it. These authors claim, however, that technology anxiety *is* amenable to education and experience. A large-scale study examining factors related to technology anxiety among hospital nurses found that, overall, nurses working in surgical and adult intensive care units (ICUs) were least anxious about technology, whereas those working on psychiatric units were most anxious (Kjerulff et al., 1989). In reviewing the results of this study, Pillar and Jacox (1991) note that the nurses most anxious about technology "also felt more stressed by their work, reported less job satisfaction, had less-positive attitudes toward the physicians with whom they worked, and were generally older" (p. 51). An assessment of personality characteristics reveals that the nurses most comfortable working with technology showed more autonomy and adaptability. Indeed, if continuing change is a way of life for nurses, adaptability to change is a desirable professional trait. This is as true for nurse managers as for staff nurses.

Technology both complicates and eases the job of nurse managers. On one hand, they must consider factors such as the cost of technology, need for relevant staff training, and loss of staffing flexibility for high technology units (Pillar et al., 1990). On the other hand, says Campbell (1990), sophisticated management information systems allow them to "collect objective data to support their ideas, the authority and apparent neutrality of these data overcoming gender bias and nurses' traditional professional subordination" (p. 72). This has helped nurses move into positions of greater power in their organizations (Campbell, 1990).

However, in a financially stretched health care system, nurse managers are caught between increasing demands for cost efficiency based on objective information and the real but often invisible human factors affecting nurses' clinical decisions. In Campbell's (1990) words:

> It seems true that computerized information about nursing designed primarily to help nurse managers become more effective in their jobs is articulating nursing practice more and more securely to the framework of cost-efficiency being advanced by Canadian health care funders. . . . Staff nurses, who might in the past speak from the standpoint of care, are increasingly bound to act in ways that are inconsistent with their caretaking role image. They are urged to accept a different ideal image—that of information provider and receiver. Their sanctioned behaviour is underwritten by the standpoint of cost-efficiency carried in the information systems they use. (p. 72)

Indeed, Menzies (1989) asserts that the patient care information system transforms nursing work from a social process involving personal judgment into a technical process characterized by the execution of preset "patient care tasks" or orders. As such, nurses' thinking and decision making focus less on human beings in the wards and increasingly on how the computer system sees the human beings: "as composites of standardized patient-task requirements" (p. 88).

All this introduces the question: Is technology coming between nurses and their patients? Campbell's comprehensive literature search suggests that it is and cites various explanations for decreased humanity in nurse-client interactions. Explanations include those underlined by Menzies, as well as the intensification and increased pace of work. Says Campbell (1990):

> Technology is part of the problem. Machines must be tended, maintained, moved, stored, and their output monitored. Nurses must learn to do all those things *and* relate to patients as well. Using objective data reinforces nurses' value orientation towards objectivity and against experiential knowledge. There is a cumulative effect on interpersonal behaviour which affects both patients and nurses. (p. 58)

Yet there is experiential knowledge so strong that machines apparently have no power to overshadow it. Degner's and Beaton's (1990) 4-year study on life-death decisions and their effect on nurses indicates that such knowledge often grows out of technological environments. For instance, the researchers describe how nurses in neonatal ICUs become attached to infants for whom they care over long periods of time: "Nurses talk directly to the infants and question them about their health status, worries, frustrations and problems. . . . It is emotionally difficult for the nurses if one of these infants dies" (p. 22). But whether caring for infants or adults, nurses emphasize how physicians' "waffling" and unclear decisions leave nurses in the difficult ethical position of making treatment decisions for the physician. Assuming such responsibility is especially upsetting when nurses have to decide whether to resuscitate a patient who suffers a cardiac arrest. Nurses consistently spoke of the unfairness of being placed in this position. And yet it is a position nurses could be placed in more and more. "People don't die anymore," critical care nurse Mary Ellen Gurnham told registrants at the 1990 conference of the Canadian University Nursing

Students Association. "They arrest." She suggested that when nurses do not agree with physicians' treatment decisions, they must communicate how they feel. They must say: "When this happens, this is the situation I'm left in. . . ."

WHY PERPETUATION OF TECHNOLOGY?

The perpetuation of health care technology ensures that nurses will continue to face complex ethical dilemmas. In *Technology and Health Policy,* a paper prepared for the Canadian Hospital Association, Taylor (1989) notes that technology is a central driving force in the structure and organization of hospitals. The source of this push, says the author, is multinational corporations that are in part drawn by health care's large and captive market. Technology's accelerated advance is fueled by industry marketing efforts that encourage the public and medical establishment to demand the latest and most sophisticated technology and that lead hospitals to believe that without that technology they will be unable to attract quality physicians and staff. Physicians and nurses have come to regard technology as a source of prestige, and hierarchies flourish in each profession: the more technology, the more status, and with status comes power. Technology's advance is also fueled by medical specialization and the technological imperative: physicians, bound by social contract to provide the best possible care, feel pressed to intervene when technology allows them to do so (Taylor, 1989).

Furthermore, the media are quick to jump on the high technology bandwagon, grateful for attention-grabbing stories such as "baby receives baboon heart." But the predominance of such stories only skews reality to shape an ideal world in which anything seems possible. Therefore although the public is well informed about high technology such as xenotransplants, computerized axial tomography (CAT) scans, and in vitro fertilization, it receives little information about low technology cost-saving advancements, such as products and services for use in the home environment or improved nutritional techniques (Taylor, 1989). As well, says Taylor, universal hospital insurance insulates consumers from the true costs of health care. Governments, however, are not insulated from health care's costs. Indeed, in the last decade a number of provincial health commissions and task forces recommended more controlled introduction of high-cost medical technology (Senate, 1990, p. 9).

In an attempt to slow technology's rapid and costly advance nurses can:
- Conduct public education campaigns stressing that resources for health care are limited and choices must be made (Taylor, 1989)
- Lobby federal and provincial governments for policies to address the rapid diffusion and increasing cost of technology in health care (Taylor, 1989)
- Advocate incentives for the introduction of cost-saving technologies and alternative approaches to the delivery of health care (Taylor, 1989; Senate, 1990)

NEED FOR TECHNOLOGY ASSESSMENT

Concern about the accelerated introduction and expense of high technology health care is coupled with growing demands for systematic technology assessment, a process Pillar, Jacox, and Redman (1990) call evaluation with the objective of providing information for decision makers. That decision makers need information about technology is clear. Studies indicate that 10% to 20% of procedures performed in the health care system are unnecessary and inappropriate (Senate, 1990). For example, the *Report of the Commission on Selected Health Care Programs* (New Brunswick, 1989) states: "Too much attention has been given to providing the resources for health services, such as personnel, buildings and equipment, with not enough going to outcomes and results" (p. 44). Rachlis and Kushner (1989) argue that indiscriminate use of technologies, without controlled studies to demonstrate their effectiveness, is primarily to blame for Canada's financial difficulty in the health care sector.

A comprehensive technology assessment must examine not only effectiveness, but efficacy, safety, and cost versus benefits (Pillar et al., 1990). Ripple effects such as lost production in other sectors, the effect on institutional and home care staffing, work stress, pain and discomfort to clients, and added anxiety for families are also important considerations.

Still, critics of technology assessment argue that technologies represent moving targets with increasingly short half-lives (Carter and Abramson, 1986). Thus conclusions with respect to a specific technology may not be applicable to the technology that quickly replaces it. To be relevant, then, technology management must address speed of diffusion as well as assessment (see box) (Taylor, 1989).

Current Technology Concerns

- High technology perpetuates an illness-focused system at the expense of adequately funded health promotion services (Taylor, 1989)
- Many technologies are used indiscriminately, without controlled studies to demonstrate their effectiveness (Rachlis and Kushner, 1989)
- Innovation and change are progressing at a greater pace than evaluation (Taylor, 1989)
- Technologies are changing so rapidly that ensuring timely and relevant education in their use is difficult (Reed, 1989); this raises safety concerns for patients and places nurses at increased risk of liability
- Nurses are not adequately involved in acquisition decisions and in the design and critical assessment of technologies they use
- Patient care information systems transform nursing work from a social process involving personal judgment into a technical process characterized by the execution of preset "patient care tasks" or orders (Menzies, 1989)
- There is a danger that machine-generated information will be viewed as superior to information gained through direct experience (Campbell, 1990)
- Nursing's values could change in response to fiscal restrictions that are becoming the predominant preoccupation of nurse managers (Campbell, 1990)
- The complexity of ethical dilemmas increases as high technology becomes more pervasive

To date, technology assessment is fragmented and uncoordinated, with most evaluation conducted as independent research (Taylor, 1989). In a 1990 submission to the Senate of Canada Standing Committee of Social Affairs, Science, and Technology, the Canadian Nurses Association (CNA) challenged the federal government to take a leadership role in establishing processes for the assessment of new technologies and in developing appropriate guidelines for use (CNA, 1990, January).

In the last few years, recognition that governments have an important role to play in technology assessment is reflected in the establishment of health technology assessment bodies in Quebec and British Columbia and in the release of a task force report recommending the formation of such a body in Ontario. As well, the Ottawa-based Canadian Coordinating Office for Health Technology Assessment (CCOHTA), a private, nonprofit corporation, was established in 1990. Funded by the federal, provincial, and territorial governments until December 1993, its stated purpose is:

> To facilitate information exchange, resource pooling and coordination of the assessment of health care technologies in accordance with priorities of the Conference of Federal-Provincial-Territorial Deputy Ministers of Health. The technologies of concern include all procedures, devices, equipment and drugs used in the maintenance, restoration and promotion of health. (Senate, 1990, Appendix III)

CCOHTA is administered by a 12-member board of directors, representative of all provinces and territories. Because members are appointed by their respective deputy minister of health, a nurse could be invited to sit on the board. Beyond this possibility, CCOHTA sometimes refers to nurses' expert opinions during the preparation and review of documents it produces. Nurses can also request that CCOHTA study specific technologies. For instance, in a September 1990 brief to the Royal Commission on New Reproductive Technologies, CNA recommended that these technologies become an immediate priority of CCOHTA (CNA, 1990, September).

Indeed, the controversy over the use of new reproductive technologies underlines Jennett's (1986, p. 275) point that there are no good or bad technologies. Rather, each technology has benefits and burdens when used in various circumstances; the challenge for society is to discover the balance between the two. Since nurses see the human costs and benefits of technology use, they are in a good position to contribute to this balancing process. For example, the CNA brief to the Senate Committee stresses that the high cost of new reproductive technologies that benefit a relatively small number of clients must be weighed against the potential improvement in reproductive health for large numbers of people should an equivalent amount be invested in health promotion and prevention of infertility. The association also notes that, since many new reproductive technologies are still in the developmental stages, women may become experimental subjects. Thus the CNA asks not only for the assessment of new reproductive technologies but for their appropriate use, a point central to both technology management and primary health care. Fundamental to such use are principles of accessibility, universality, and public participation.

If nurses can contribute to debates on technology's use, they must also ensure that they are key participants in the acquisition, design, and critical assessment of technologies with which they work. Nurses must see themselves as decision makers regarding technology rather than passive implementors of the decisions of others (Lindeman, 1989). By changing their attitudes, nurses—most of whom are women—can help change the commonly held misconception that women are inept users of technology. Indeed, from household machinery to cars to office and industrial machines, women have a long tradition of mastering technologies of the day.

To enhance their profile as decision makers in regard to technology, nurses can promptly report medical device failures or problems to the proper authorities. They can also lobby to participate on ethics or technology committees in their places of work. If such committees do not exist, nursing can instigate them. In her 1988 article "Harnessing Technology," Joachim envisioned in-hospital technology committees composed of a nurse, a physician, an administrator, a data programmer, and, perhaps, a representative from industry. The committee would promote new ideas and solve problems with the use or development of technology.

According to Taylor (1989), innovation depends not only on demand but also on a foundation of knowledge provided by basic research. Nurse researchers have already contributed to this foundation and to increasing understanding of current technology use. For example, a systematic investigation by Pierson and Funk (1989) illustrates how a common procedure can be both unnecessary and harmful. The researchers found that fluid management data provided by pulmonary artery catheters left in situ for 18 or more hours after coronary artery bypass grafting were not used as a basis for decision making. Thus the catheters could have been removed much earlier, minimizing the possibility of side effects such as dysrhythmias, infections, and patient discomfort.

Questions remain about how much support should be diverted to developing nursing research into the design, development, and use of technology (Abbey, 1989). There are also concerns regarding whether device research belongs within the province of nursing and nurses.

INTO THE FUTURE

"There is a world to be lost and a world to be gained," says Zuboff (1988, p. 5) of technology. What is lost and what is gained will grow from decisions made now. One of the most important decisions nursing must make is how to divide its attention and resources between preparing nurses for practice in technological environments and refocusing the overburdened illness care system toward a better balance of illness care, rehabilitation, prevention, and promotion (CNA, 1990, January).

Whatever the decision, nursing will not become less technologically intensive (Pillar and Jacox, 1991). This means a future marked by rapid change, increasing diversity, new knowledge, and new horizons (Rogers, 1988). As in the rest of society, communications, analytic abilities, and computer skills will be essential, says Foot (cited in Stoffman, 1991). So will resilience.

"How do you prepare yourself for tomorrow's working world?" asked a September 1991 article in *Report on Business Magazine*. "You never stop," replied its author, Daniel Stoffman. "The truism about education being a lifelong affair has never been truer" (p. 41). In the same article, University of Waterloo president Douglas Wright predicted: "The people who are not too narrowly educated and who have an attitude that allows them to change with the changes in the world around them are the ones who will do well" (p. 41).

In the future, nurse recruiters will promote the image of nurse as knowledge worker (Lindeman, 1989) and emphasize the profession's intellectually stimulating aspects—high technology education and practice. However, in a world in which people interact more and more with machines (at home, school, and in places of business) nursing's particular appeal will remain its human, caring dimension.

Hannah (cited in Estrin, 1989) projects that as nurses become more involved with high technology they will humanize health care by having more time to spend with patients. Yet, registrants at a 1988 conference on nursing and technology, held in Annapolis, Maryland, learned that high technology could affect nursing in another, less positive way. Norman Estrin (1989), vice president of science and technology with the Washington-based Health Industry Manufacturers Association, told registrants:

> The technologies could become so sophisticated that only lesser-trained nurses will be necessary. If nurses do not meet these challenges, a new kind of medical technician could emerge who would be responsible for insertion of a device and monitoring data. (p. 18)

In Canada, as in the United States, nursing's professional and labor organizations must be prepared to take a stand on this issue.

Milio (1986) raises another concern: that heavy nursing involvement with computers and information technologies could weaken collegial ties and shrink the collaborative skills nurses need to collectively define problems and find workable solutions. She warns that these individual and group skills are especially needed during periods of rapid change and in relationships with the many services and groups that more and more nurses will encounter as they move outside of hospitals. In Milio's words:

> This major shift, if it is to be health effective, requires nurses to have breadth in perspective and range of skills rather than narrowness; to integrate, not subdivide; to have flexibility and wide scope of judgment and action, not rigidity. (1986, p. 46)

As technology becomes more pervasive, nurses must openly debate how to maintain a healthy balance of human-to-human and human-to-machine interaction. National, local, and workplace conferences are excellent vehicles for such debate and encourage human contact.

Despite the potentially negative effect of high technology on nursing, it seems clear that technology can help advance nursing's agenda. Computer-based knowledge, including artificial intelligence, will enhance nurses' ability to make expert clinical judgments. Also, the widespread use of information technologies within a shift to nonhospital services will allow many care, coordination, information, and education services to be organized, managed, and performed by nurses (Milio, 1986). Whatever the setting, touch-sensitive screens and voice-activated programs will allow nurses and patients to interact with computers in ways that encourage more familiarity and immediacy (Zuboff, 1988). Technophobia among nursing staff will decrease as a new generation, raised on high technology, moves into practice. Other trends include:

- The pervasiveness of information technologies in nursing workplaces will change the nature of labor relations (Milio, 1986). Nurses will want guarantees that computer-generated information will not be used against them. According to Milio, whether or to what extent nurses will be manipulated by corporate information technologies or be co-opted and become the computer-base manipulators of their peers will depend on the unity they can forge and the safeguards they can negotiate. To use information technologies to their advantage, says the author, nurses must effectively organize and analyze relevant data.
- There will be increased demand for certification of nursing specialties, as nursing and the public look for assurances of competence. Meanwhile, specialty groups will call for increased education in their fields. Since both certification and specialty education are costly endeavors, new funding will need to be sought.
- Major health technologies will be required to undergo rigorous testing for clinical effectiveness and safety (Feeney et al., 1986). Such testing will include randomized trials that compare the therapeutic effectiveness of different treatment modalities and population-based studies that demonstrate the magnitude of the effect on communities. Nurses will contribute research expertise to these efforts.
- Advances in biomedical technology will continue to challenge nurses with profound ethical decisions, particularly surrounding life-sustaining technologies. Relevant standards and guidelines will need to be developed. Milio (1986) describes a future in which computer-applied standards could entirely eliminate many of today's ethical dilemmas.
- Perhaps as a reaction to, or in spite of, the technological age, alternative health care practitioners who rely minimally on technologies will gain increasing credibility and acceptance. These practitioners include midwives, massage therapists, chiropractors, osteopaths, and native and spiritual healers. Likewise, the holistic nursing movement will gain momentum.
- The pressure to ensure that alternative care choices are safe, tested through research, universally accessible, and governed by professional standards will be strong, and may alter their nature.
- As high-cost medical technology and an aging population increase stress on health care budgets, an enlightened media and public will become more questioning of technology and of how health care is organized. This will make it easier for nursing to advance its vision of a less costly, more client centered, and community based system of care.

CONCLUSION

In many ways, the future is already here for nurses. They experience the pressures of the constantly changing workplace, struggle to sort out new ethical dilemmas, and feel the excitement of being on the cutting edge of advances in treatment and care (Campbell, 1990). Aware that technology is changing their practice, they know they must act now to ensure that change moves in a positive direction. Such change will be complicated by scarce resources and vested interests that fuel technology's advance. Greater participation in policymaking and in setting the agenda for technological change should be nursing's goal. At stake are the values that characterize nursing as a caring, people-oriented profession.

REFERENCES

Abbey, J. (1989). The key issues in device use as they relate to nursing education [Panel presentation]. In *Proceedings of Nursing and Technology: Moving Into the 21st Century* (pp. 29-31). Rockville, MD: U.S. Department of Health and Human Services.

Adamson, N., Briskin, L., & McPhail, M. (1988). *Feminist organizing for change.* Toronto: Oxford University Press.

Benner, P. (1989). *The primacy of caring.* Menlo Park, CA: Addison-Wesley.

Campbell, M. (1990). *Technology and nursing: A review and analysis of selected literature.* Ottawa: Canadian Nurses Association.

Canadian Nurses Association. (1990, January). *Accessibility to acute care hospital services* [A brief to The Senate of Canada Standing Committee on Social Affairs, Science and Technology]. Ottawa: Author.

Canadian Nurses Association. (1990, September). *New reproductive technologies: Accessible, appropriate, participative* [A brief to The Royal Commission on New Reproductive Technologies]. Ottawa: Author.

Carter, E.D., & Abramson, J.H. (1986). Health technology assessment. *Israel Journal of Medical Sciences, 22,* 167.

Clochesy, J.M. (1987). Introducing new technology: Biomedical engineers and staff nurse involvement. *Critical Care Nursing Quarterly, 9*(4), 64-69.

Degner, L.F., & Beaton, J.I. (1990). Life and death decisions: The impact on nurses. *The Canadian Nurse/L'infirmière canadienne, 86*(3), 18-22.

Estrin, N.F. (1989). The technological, regulatory, and legal factors that impinge on the nursing environment [Panel presentation]. In *Proceedings of Nursing and Technology: Moving Into the 21st Century* (pp. 17-19). Rockville, MD: U.S. Department of Health and Human Services.

Feeney, D., Guyatt, G., & Tugwell, P. (Eds.). (1986). *Health care technology: Effectiveness, efficiency, and public policy.* Montreal: Institute for Research on Public Policy.

Franklin, U. (1990). *The real world of technology.* Toronto: CBC Enterprises.

Gothler, A.M. (1989). The key issues in device use as they relate to nursing education [Panel presentation]. In *Proceedings of Nursing and Technology: Moving Into the 21st Century* (pp. 32-33). Rockville, MD: U.S. Department of Health and Human Services.

Jennett, B. (1986). *High technology medicine.* Oxford: Oxford University Press.

Joachim, G. (1988). Harnessing technology. *The Canadian Nurse/L'infirmière canadienne, 84*(10), 14-16.

Kjerulff, K.H., Pillar, B., Mills, M.E., & Lanigan, J. (1989). *Technology anxiety in the hospital setting.* Paper presented at the Fifth Annual Meeting of the International Society for Technology Assessment in Health Care, London, England.

Lindeman, C.A. (1989). Nursing and technology: Moving into the 21st keynote address. In *Proceedings of nursing and technology: Moving into the 21st century* (pp. 7-15). Rockville, MD: U.S. Department of Health and Human Services.

Menzies, H. (1989). *Fast forward and out of control: How technology is changing your life.* Toronto: Macmillan of Canada.

Milio, N. (1986). Telematics in the future of health care delivery: Implications for nursing. *Journal of Professional Nursing, 2*(1), 39-50.

New Brunswick. (1989). *Report of the Commission on Selected Health Care Programs.* Fredericton: Author.

Noble, D.F. (1977). *America by design: Science, technology, and the rise of corporate capitalism.* New York: Alfred A. Knopf.

Ontario Nurses Association. (1989). *The impact of technology in the nursing context* [Prepared for Labour Canada's Technology Impact Program]. Toronto: Author.

Pierson, M.G., & Funk, M. (1989). Technology versus clinical evaluation for fluid management decisions in CABG patients. *Image, 21*(4), 192-195.

Pillar, B. & Jacox, A. (1991). The introduction of new technology on the nursing unit. *Nursing Economics, 9*(1), 50-51, 63.

Pillar, B., Jacox, A.K., & Redman, B.K. (1990). Technology, its assessment, and nursing. *Nursing Outlook, 38*(1), 16-19.

Rachlis, M., & Kushner, C. (1989). *Second opinion: What's wrong with Canada's health care system and how to fix it.* Toronto: Collins.

Reed, R.R. (1989). Response to a challenge. In *Proceedings of nursing and technology: Moving into the 21st century* (pp. 3-4). Rockville, MD: U.S. Department of Health and Human Services.

Rogers, M. (1988, August). Keynote address to the Third International Intensive Care Nursing Conference, Montreal, Canada.

The Senate of Canada Standing Committee on Social Affairs, Science and Technology. (1990). *Accessibility to hospital services - Is there a crisis?* Ottawa: Author.

Shaver, J. (1986). High touch nursing in a high tech world. *The Canadian Nurse/L'infirmière canadienne, 82*(5), 16-19.

Stoffman, D. (1991, September). Brave new work. *Report on Business Magazine,* pp. 33-41.

Taylor, B. R. (1989). *Technology and health policy* [An executive brief prepared for the Canadian Hospital Association]. Ottawa: CHA.

Zuboff, S. (1988). *In the age of the smart machine: The future of work and power.* New York: Basic Books.

Among the career scientists in nursing gathered at the National Nursing Research Conference in Kingston, Ontario, in June 1991 were: Ada Sue Hinshaw, director, National Center for Nursing Research, Maryland, U.S.A.; Betty Davies, associate professor, School of Nursing, University of British Columbia, and nurse investigator, British Columbia Children's Hospital; Sharon Ogden Burke, professor, School of Nursing, and core researcher, Better Beginnings Research Coordination Unit, Queen's University; Janice Morse, professor, Faculty of Nursing, University of Alberta, and National Health Research Development Program (NHRDP) Scholar; and Barbara Kisilevsky, Ontario Ministry of Health Career Scientist, and assistant professor, School of Nursing, Queen's University. (Photograph courtesy of *The Canadian Nurse*. Used with permission.)

CHAPTER SIXTEEN

Research Issues

JUDITH ANNE RITCHIE, RN, PhD

Judith Anne Ritchie, RN, BN (New Brunswick), MN, PhD (Pittsburgh), holds a joint appointment as Professor in the School of Nursing and Faculty of Graduate Studies, Dalhousie University, and as Director of Nursing Research, Izaak Walton Killam Hospital for Children, in Halifax. She has experience as a staff nurse, camp nurse, clinical nurse specialist, university educator, and nurse researcher. Her current research areas involve study of how hospitalized children cope with painful procedures and long, repeated, hospital stays and family centered care. Author of several research and clinical papers, she also serves as a reviewer for several journals and funding agencies. She has served at various times as member and chair of the Canadian Nurses Association's Committee on Nursing Research, as CNA Member-at-Large for Nursing Research, and is a former president of CNA.

The continuing search for knowledge is a responsibility of any profession committed to provision of services. As the Canadian Nurses Association has acknowledged: "Nursing research is central to the development of theories for nursing practice. It stimulates growth of the body of knowledge upon which the practice of nursing is built" (1990a, p.2). However, although most nurse researchers profess that nursing research deals with problems that arise in the practice of nursing, many nurses do not see research as a priority for, or even relevant to, their practice.

The three main areas of discussion in this chapter are: historical issues central to the development of research for nursing practice in Canada; current issues and pressure points that can affect the continued development of research in nursing; and the directions that might be taken if the research base of nursing practice is to flourish. In this chapter, nursing research is defined as the systematic collection and analysis of data about how individuals and families function in health and illness situations and the strategies that nurses use to meet their goals (Canadian Nurses Association, 1981). The discussion is based, however, on the assumptions that research-based knowledge is not the only knowledge required to provide quality nursing care (Benner, 1984), and that scientific research is not "the sole source of, and means to, nursing knowledge" (Kikuchi and Simmons, 1986, p. 31).

In a recent position statement on nursing research, the Registered Nurses Association of British Columbia (1990) notes that nursing research generates a broad spectrum of knowledge related to the following:
1. Health and health promotion of individuals, families, and groups
2. The influence of social and physical environments on health and illness
3. Care of individuals who are acutely or chronically ill, disabled or dying, as well as their families
4. Nursing interventions that promote and maintain health and prevent illness or minimize its negative effects
5. Policies and systems that aim to deliver nursing care that is effective, efficient, and ethical
6. The nursing profession and its development
7. Systems that prepare nurses to fulfill the profession's current and future social mandate

But if this is where nursing research is today, how did nursing research in Canada get started?

PATH TO CURRENT STATE OF NURSING RESEARCH

In Canada, nursing involvement in research began in the early twentieth century (Cahoon, 1985). The early research was in areas relevant to nursing education (Allen, 1986), with the first major study of nursing education in Canada being commissioned in 1932 by a joint committee of the Canadian Nurses Association and the Canadian Medical Association (Allemang and Cahoon, 1986; Weir, 1932). Subsequent studies in nursing, until the mid-1960s, tended to focus on those areas in which nurses were prepared at the graduate level—education, administration, or community health. As master's programs in nursing began to change, researchers began to study nurses' roles, patients' responses to situations and treatment, and other aspects of nursing practice (Griffin, 1971; Imai, 1971).

Funding for nursing research continues to be a major problem area for nursing research in Canada. Early researchers relied on personal, institutional, or private sources, such as the Kellogg Foundation, for funds. In the 1970s, the National Health Research and Development Program (NHRDP) became the major source of federal funding for nursing research in Canada. Since 1979, nursing has been eligible for funding from the Medical Research Council (MRC). However, only in recent years, following changes in nursing representation on committees with MRC, have nurses begun to receive more than one or two grants a year from that body.

TABLE 16-1 Types of Nursing Projects Funded by Major National or Provincial Agencies

Type of project	1983/ 1984	1984/ 1985	1988/ 1989	1989/ 1990
Descriptive clinical	9	14	44	50
Clinical intervention	7	8	22	22
Other (e.g., education, administration)	2	2	12	18
TOTAL	18	24	78	90
Total Funding	$549,128	$640,846	$1,155,844	$1,437,276
Mean	$30,507	$26,702	$14,819	$15,970

Compiled by the author from the Medical Research Council *Reference list of health science research in Canada* for the years 1984 to 1989.

A major shift in the availability of funds for nursing research developed when some provincial governments began to meet their responsibilities for the development of knowledge for society by establishing provincial health research granting councils, and nursing became eligible to apply for their grants. Alberta, however, is the only province with a provincially-funded research foundation for nursing.

The actual state of funding of nursing research is extremely difficult to establish. A review of the lists of research in health sciences in Canada (Medical Research Council, 1984 to 1990) reveals relatively uneven levels of funding for research projects done by nurses or teams that include nurses. The titles of the research studies indicate that the funded projects were predominantly clinical research (see Table 16-1). Table 16-1 also shows that the average grant per project has decreased, even though the costs of doing research have steadily increased over those years.

National agencies now account for a relatively small proportion of research funding in nursing. In 1986 to 1987, 67% of the funds were granted by the Ontario Ministry of Health and 14% by the Alberta Foundation for Nursing Research (AFNR). In 1989/ 1990 the NHRDP provided 26.3% of the total and AFNR, 17.8%. Such shifts in the sources is evidence of the instability of funding for nursing. The need to rely on NHRDP for national funding is particularly problematic given that agency's vulnerability to government budget cuts.

The MRC listings of funding do not include such sources as the provincial nurses' foundations, internal university or agency funds, American sources, corporations, or local agencies or donors. Table 16-2 (see p. 310) provides an incomplete sketch of the potential sources of funds for research. The Canadian Nurses Association also publishes a directory, which is regularly updated, of sources of funds.

TABLE 16-2 **Potential Sources of Funds for Nursing Research**

Level	Government	Nursing associations	Private agency or foundation
National	Medical Research Council	Canadian Nurses Foundation	National Cancer Institute
	NHRDP*	Some nursing specialty groups (e.g., Canadian Nurses Respiratory Society)	Hospital foundations (e.g., Hospital for Sick Children Foundation)
	SSHRC†		
	NSERC‡		Canadian illness-related foundations (e.g., Heart and Stroke, Lung, Kidney foundations)
			Canadian Geriatric Foundation
Provincial	Health Care Research Councils (all provinces except Atlantic)	Professional nursing associations or foundations sponsored by associations (in 6 provinces)	Private nursing research and development funds
	Alberta Foundation for Nursing Research (AFNR)		Private foundations
Local	None known	Varies	University research and development funds
			Health care agency foundations

Compiled by the author.
*NHRDP, National Health Research Development Program.
†SSHRC, Social Sciences and Humanities Research Council.
‡NSERC, National Science and Engineering Research Council.

DEVELOPMENT OF RESEARCHERS

Development and implementation of research requires special preparation and training. There are three areas of particular concern in consideration of the development of researchers: establishment and support of programs to develop researchers, support of individuals to pursue graduate education and research careers, and availability of positions that permit the conduct of research.

Programs for Researchers

The development of researchers must begin early in the educational process. In nursing, baccalaureate programs should, as their major thrust, prepare nurses to access and use research. Development of graduate programs in Canada and the availability of funding for students enrolled in such programs has been a slow process. Chapter 22 shows the current status of Canadian master's and doctoral programs in nursing. The most recent published statistics (Lamb and Stinson, 1990) reveal that in 1989 there were only 257 nurses in Canada with doctoral degrees and that only 23% of those had that preparation in nursing. There is no change in that percentage since the 1986 survey and the rate of change likely will continue to be slow. In 1989/1990, just nine nurses (six of them studying in nursing) were awarded Health and Welfare or Medical Research Council scholarships for doctoral study (MRC, 1989, 1990). Although nursing benefits in many ways from the richness of having scholars with preparation in varied disciplines, the difficulty with this pattern is that a nurse with preparation in another discipline has to spend time getting back into nursing and that many are uncomfortable, at least in the initial years following completion of their doctoral studies, doing research that is clinical nursing research (Krueger, Nelson, and Wolanin, 1978).

Funds for Researchers

The second major issue related to development of researchers is availability of funds for support during their studies and following completion of study so that they can establish a research career. The Canadian Nurses Foundation (CNF), established in 1962, was the first national source of scholarship funds for nurses studying at advanced levels. In 1972, following successful lobbying by CNA and nurse researchers and following appointment of Dorothy Kergin to the Medical Research Council, nurses studying at the doctoral level became eligible for the renewable studentships awarded by MRC and Canada Council. With the establishment of the NHRDP funds, that agency became the major source of significant financial support for nurses studying at the doctoral level.

To develop fully a body of nurses prepared to do research following completion of their doctoral programs, newly prepared nurses need opportunities to conduct a number of studies and to establish programs of research. A few nurse researchers have had the opportunity to pursue such activities through programs that provide funds to pursue investigative careers. Canadian nursing has benefitted from the naming as NHRDP Scholars of such nurse researchers as Shirley Stinson (Alberta), Jacqueline Chapman (Toronto), Gina Browne (McMaster), Janice Morse (Alberta), Sharon Ogden-Burke (Queen's), and Joan Anderson (UBC).

In 1989, MRC and NHRDP established a new joint program to offer School of Nursing Development Grants. The results of this program are disappointing overall because of the relatively small number of scholars and the failure to fund any programs of research. However, by mid-1990 this program had expanded the number of nationally-funded nursing career investigators to six from a previous high of three. In 1990, the NHRDP/MRC scholars were: Celeste Johnston (McGill), Janice Morse (Alberta), Hiliary Llewellyn-Thomas (Toronto), Annette O'Connor (Ottawa), and Louise Levesque (Montreal); Joan Anderson (British Columbia) was an NHRDP scholar. "Career scientist" awards from the Ontario Ministry of Health and the Research Division of the British Columbia Children's Hospital are held by six other Canadian nurses. These programs permit "immersion" in research by requiring that 75% of the scholar's time is devoted to research and scholarly activity and prevent time and energy being absorbed by teaching and administrative responsibilities that traditionally drain researchers away from the research effort.

Positions to Encourage Research

The establishment of positions that expect and permit research is the third major factor important to the development of a strong research base. University faculty members are expected to be productive researchers, but they often find it difficult to devote time to projects because of teaching duties. The ultimate in providing "protected time" for research at universities is through the establishment of a "research chair." This position is usually funded through an endowment to the university and permits the professor to spend all his or her time in research. To early 1991, only one Canadian nurse, Margaret Cahoon at the University of Toronto, has had the honor of appointment to a nursing research chair.

The most exciting development in the 1980s was the growth of research positions in service agencies. Rosemary Prince Coombs held the first such position at the Ottawa Civic Hospital in 1976. The Victorian Order of Nurses, in 1982, appointed Dorothy Pringle to a full-time position as nurse researcher. Many Canadian teaching hospitals have appointed nurse researchers to their staffs, and several have established departments of nursing research. Degner (1990) estimates that there are now 30 to 40 nurses directing such departments. As well, there are increasing expectations for nurses employed as clinical nurse specialists to increase the research components of their roles. The models used in these initiatives vary (Pepler, 1988). Some researchers and clinical nurse specialists hold full-time positions in the agency. Increasingly, researchers in clinical agencies hold joint appointments with university nursing faculties, and faculty members are using clinical agencies as their work bases. The volume and quality of clinical studies being conducted in agency research departments, as described in recent studies (Tenove, Thurston, and Church, 1986; Thurston, Tenove, and Church, 1990; Thurston, Tenove, Church, and Bach-Peterson, 1989), demonstrate the great impact of such models.

RESEARCH: BASIC TO THE DISCIPLINE

Although many issues are basic to development of a "nursing research reality" (CNA, 1990b), critical ones relate to the communication of research findings, the structure available to advocate for and support the research effort, and the use of research findings in nursing practice.

Why is it that so many nurses do not know about many research findings or do not use them in their practice? One of the major historical contributors to this state has been the manner in which research has been communicated. In many cases, the language and format of research articles or presentations is difficult for clinicians.

Although Griffin (1971) and Stinson (1986) suggest that, by the 1970s, most ongoing research in Canada was focused on clinical problems, published research reports did not follow the same pattern. During the first 10 years publication of *The Canadian Journal of Nursing Research* (formerly *Nursing Papers*), the majority of articles were related to education (Ritchie, 1979). By the late 1980s that pattern had changed to a balance of topics with clinical research comprising nearly 50% of the articles.

The language ("researchese") in which most published research reports are written poses further difficulty for the majority of nurses, who have little background in research. The editor of *Nursing Research* has decried the notion that research articles are written for an "elite" group of nurses (Downs, 1986). However, if nurses will not read such reports because they feel unprepared to understand them, then research will not be available for use in practice.

Canadian nurses have extremely limited Canadian sources of published research findings. *The Canadian Nurse/L'infirmière canadienne* and several provincial/territorial association newsletters sometimes publish research abstracts or reports. *The Canadian Journal of Nursing Research*, the only Canadian nursing journal that regularly publishes research papers, has a small circulation and only recently received any stability in its funding (Jeans, 1988a). New research journals are emerging, such as *Qualitative Health Research*, which had its first issue in early 1991, and *Clinical Nursing Research*, which was scheduled to appear in February 1992. Journals in specialty areas, such as the *Canadian Journal of Cardiovascular Nursing*, present Canadian nursing research within particular practice areas. However, there is some concern about the viability of these journals given the rising costs of publication and small potential circulation size.

A major source of information about current research is the national nursing research conference. These conferences have been held on an irregular basis since 1971. Although approximately 380 nurses attended the first conference, registration at the next five conferences was restricted. This practice was to allow senior researchers to communicate and discuss issues and problems in detail. However, the limited registration and the focus of discussion on methods of research lent an air of mysticism to the research endeavor and, for some, indicated that research was a matter only for a select few—most of whom were not involved in direct patient care. The emphasis at conferences from 1980 to 1985 was on research for nursing practice (Allen, 1986). Since 1987, national research conferences have been organized by the Canadian Association of University Schools of Nursing; unfortunately, attendance has decreased and is dominated by university faculty. The 1990s may see such conferences organized by the Canadian Nursing Research Group because there is considerable feeling that this more broadly based group would attract more researchers, as well as nurses, from a wider variety of settings.

A review of the proceedings or programs of the most recent national and international nursing research conferences held in Canada reveals that the majority of research is on clinical practice issues (see, for example, King, Prodrich, and Bauer, 1986; Stinson, Kerr, Giovanetti, Field, and MacPhail, 1986). Agency-sponsored research conferences are characterized by presentations of research findings to an audience of clinicians and managers with the focus of discussion on the implications of the findings for practice. Such opportunities serve to help nurses speak the same language, to demystify research, and to make clear what kinds of research are available to form a base for practice.

There are many activities and structures that might lead to increased awareness and use of research by nurses in direct care positions. Conferences are one way, but budget and staffing restrictions increasingly limit attendance at such conferences. Therefore other strategies, such as publishing review articles to provide "user-friendly" research in clinical journals, research interest groups in agencies, research presentations at conferences of provincial associations, and readers' discussion groups at the unit level, are needed to allow nurses to become comfortable in assessing research reports and considering their usefulness for practice.

Development of research positions or departments within agencies has several benefits. On-site, regular-staff researchers increase the awareness of research among all nurses and other disciplines within the agency. In many cases, nursing staff are more comfortable in seeking assistance or consultation from a fellow staff member than from a nurse researcher employed in another setting. Another major asset in such positions is the proximity to clinical realities. The interest and enthusiasm of staff nurses and nurse managers in using nursing research to seek solutions to clinical problems is infectious and adds elements to the design of applied research that are difficult to capture without such rich clinical contacts.

The pattern of structural support for nursing research by professional or specialty nursing associations is uneven. Both the Canadian Nurses Association and the Canadian Association of University Schools of Nursing have long-standing commitments to the development of research. The CNA Member-at-Large for Nursing Research is a member of the Executive Committee and the Board of Directors, and chairs the standing committee on research. CAUSN's first vice-president carries the research portfolio.

The patterns within provinces are greatly varied and change rapidly. In 1990, two provincial associations (Nova Scotia and Ontario) had Research Member-at-Large positions; two others (Alberta and Manitoba) had standing committees on research. Two associations (British Columbia and Saskatchewan) had research consultants on staff, although only one of those (Registered Nurses Association of British Columbia) had full-time responsibility for consultation and development of research.

Other models have been developed in the western provinces. The Saskatchewan Nursing Research Unit (NRU), established in 1983 under Director Norma Stewart, was jointly sponsored in its early years by the College of Nursing at the University of Saskatchewan, the Saskatchewan Registered Nurses Association, and the Saskatchewan Union of Nurses. Now funded by the University, the unit's services are available on a fee-for-service basis. Major activities include: providing consultation, providing information on resources for research and education in nursing research methods, creating liaison with research committees and groups, and developing collaborative projects. A similar model was initiated in Manitoba with the appointment, in 1985, of Lesley Degner to the Manitoba Nursing Research Institute (MNRI). The Manitoba Association of Registered Nurses and the School of Nursing at the University of Manitoba jointly support the Institute to provide Manitoba nurses with leadership and support services in the development of nursing research. Although the specific objectives and activities of Saskatchewan and Manitoba institutes vary, each resource increases the availability of research consultation for nurses throughout the province. A Nursing Research Unit now exists as well at the University of British Columbia. In 1988, the University of Alberta established the Institute for Philosophical Nursing Research.

The Registered Nurses Association of British Columbia's research consultation service was established in 1987 following a membership resolution to approve funding; Heather Clarke is RNABC's first research consultant. Such structures provide clear messages to nurses, and to the public, that the research base for practice is growing and is a vital and valued part of the discipline. Perhaps their greatest contribution is that they provide clear and easily accessible resources to nurses who are interested in locating research-based information for practice or who are developing projects in their own setting.

One national, two provincial, and several local agency "interest groups" provide additional resources for both researchers and those interested in research. The development of the national group was debated for many years (Stinson, 1986; Stinson, Lamb, and Thibaudeau, 1990). The 1986 launching of the Canadian National Nursing Research Group provided a national group for nurses interested in a forum for the promotion and discussion of nursing research and research issues (Bulbrook, 1986). In 1990, this group boasted a membership of more than 250 nurses in eight provinces and became a Special Interest Group of the Canadian Nurses Association.

The numbers of studies investigating issues of relevance to clinical practice have increased steadily during the last 20 years. However, there is a lack of awareness of and use of research findings in clinical practice (Barnard, 1984). Even well-established, research-based findings are not widely used (Brett, 1987; Coyle and Sokup, 1990). The results of the "CURN Project"—Current Utilization of Research in Nursing (Horsley, Crane, Crabtree, and Haller, 1983)—provided practitioners with a model for ascertaining whether there is a sufficient basis for implementing a specific research-based approach in a particular practice setting. A different model of research use in nursing is advocated by Stetler (1984), who suggests that, following a positive evaluation of the adequacy of the research and the suitability for the setting, nurses are faced with two choices: "action application" where the proposed change in practice would be implemented on a specific unit or units or in a protocol and evaluated, or "cognitive application" where the nurse adds the information in the research report to his or her knowledge base and "uses" the information in assessments and problem solving. In both models, the nurse who is considering application of research in practice must be able to read and evaluate research reports. For that reason, preparation in research at the baccalaureate level must lead to the development of wise consumers of research. In addition, agencies must increase activities that enhance those skills in their nursing staff.

CONTRIBUTIONS TO NURSING RESEARCH

It is impossible to credit all those who have contributed to the development of research in Canada. The current state of nursing research could not have been achieved without the creative efforts of many individuals who worked behind the scenes to foster research development. Early pioneers such as Katherine MacLaggan and Helen Mussallem did not always have a high profile for their research development endeavors. Deans, professors, and leaders in professional associations inspired and fostered the career development of students, facilitated the pursuit of graduate education for faculty, and permitted emerging researchers to pursue their research-related activities. These pioneering individuals include those who, with tremendous foresight, founded the Canadian Nurses Foundation to promote education and research in the nursing profession. The founding members (Helen Carpenter, Ella M. Howard, Electa MacLennan, Alice Girard, Mary L. Richmond, Katherine MacLaggan, Lillian E. Pettigrew, Corinne E. Laflamme, and M.P. "Penny" Stiver) must surely be regarded as midwives at the birth of support for nursing research in this country. During its first 28 years (until 1990), CNF awarded more than $1.2 million in scholarships to 480 nurses. By 1990, the sixth year of its small-grants program, CNF had awarded more than $66,500 for 26 research projects.

The nurses usually considered to have led the development of nursing research in Canada represent many regions and areas of practice in nursing. Verna Huffman Splane, as Principal Nursing Officer, and Pamela Poole, as Nursing Consultant, with Health and Welfare Canada, were active and articulate spokespersons for the need for research and the need for careful and valid research designs throughout the late 1960s and 1970s. Moyra Allen, now retired from McGill University, is referred to by some as the "dean" of nursing research in Canada. Dr. Allen was one of the prime faculty members responsible for the development of clinical graduate programs and thesis research on issues in clinical practice. She established Canada's first nursing research center at McGill University in 1971 and was the first nurse to be named as an NHRDP Senior Scientist. Dr. Allen promoted the research endeavor on many avenues in CNA and CAUSN and lobbied for support of research through federal and private granting agencies.

Varied and quite different levels of activity in support of the development of nursing research are noted in the work of Shirley Stinson from the University of Alberta. For more than 20 years, Dr. Stinson worked behind the scenes and at the forefront of nursing on provincial, national, and international levels. Her contributions and leadership led to the establishment of the research focus of the graduate program at the University of Alberta, the Alberta Foundation for Nursing Research, the CNA's committee on nursing research, collaboration between CAUSN and CNA in such research development activities as the national conference on doctoral programs in nursing in 1979, and the International Nursing Research Conference in Edmonton in 1986. In the 1990s, Dr. Stinson continues to take pro-active and vigorous steps to influence positively the state of funding for nursing research in Canada.

Many others have made significant contributions, and their place in the history of nursing research deserves to be documented. Floris King, a faculty member at the University of British Columbia, was chief organizer and chair of the first National Nursing Research Conference in Canada in 1971. Amy Zelmer founded and created CORN—the computerized Canadian Clearinghouse Of Research in Nursing, which served as the only source of information on ongoing research and completed master's theses in the country until the late 1980s. Margaret Cahoon's strong research programs and many contributions to the development of research culminated in the historical event of her being named as the Rosenstadt Professor in Health Care

Research at the University of Toronto from 1980 to 1982. Marie-France Thibaudeau (Université de Montréal) has been influential in establishing a climate of understanding of nursing research in such venues as the Advisory Committee of the NHRDP and in increasing nurses' knowledge of the process and skills of "grantmanship" (the art of writing successful research grant applications) (Thibaudeau, 1985). She has had a marked effect on Canadian nurse researchers through her teaching and enthusiasm at conferences and in published form.

In the 1990s, the number of nurses serving as advocates for and facilitators of the development of nursing research has expanded to the point where it is impossible to name them. Nurses such as Denise Alcock (1990-1992 CNA Research Member-at-Large), Phillis Giovanetti (1990 president of the Canadian Nursing Research Group), and Leslie Hardy (CAUSN vice-president, responsible for nursing research) are only three of the nurse researchers who are working to ensure that research is accessible to nurses who provide direct care, and to ensure an adequate, stable funding base for nursing research. They, and many others, are striving to develop a solid base of knowledge for practice. This last decade of the twentieth century will have several research leaders whose programs of research are now yielding a rich base of theory that is grounded in research.

Various nursing associations at the national, provincial, and local levels have been vigorous in their contributions to the development of research. CAUSN supports the efforts of university faculty members through the work of its committee on research and through national surveys to determine funding levels of university researchers. CAUSN and its members have worked actively and collaboratively with the CNA and provincial associations on many activities related to the development of research. CNA has an extremely active role in development of research through such activities as lobbying for changes in granting councils and for funding for research and doctoral programs, publication of the *Index of Canadian Nursing Research*, funding for the collection of statistics on nurses prepared at the doctoral level, and production of several publications relating to issues in research. CNA's recent submission to the Royal Society of Canada University Research Committee (CNA, 1990b, 1990c) has led to discussions with the Royal Society on the most appropriate funding structures and amounts for nursing research.

CURRENT ISSUES AND PRESSURE POINTS

Many of the issues that led to the current picture continue to be relevant to the maturation of nursing research in Canada. The prime issues facing nursing research today vary, depending on an individual perspective. From the perspective of increasing the knowledge base for practice, the priority issues are: use of research in practice, development of research methods and research programs, ethical issues related to research, and funding for research and researchers.

Utilization

One major criterion for the appropriate application of research findings is that there should be a sufficient number of scientifically valid and replicated studies (Horsley et al., 1983). Although many areas of nursing study meet this criterion, many clinically relevant projects have not been replicated or have an insufficient base of support. One of the major pressure points, therefore, is the need to replicate useful clinical projects and to develop projects that build on previous research. A further issue is that some clinical projects may not be viewed by clinicians as relevant to today's practice (Degner, 1988). This may be because clinicians often see other practice issues as being more important than those that have been studied. Some research results that are reported by researchers as statistically significant are not viewed by clinicians as being practically significant. Only when there is a sufficient volume of clinically relevant research will a large number of practitioners take seriously the plea to examine and change their practice on the basis of research findings.

A further prerequisite to that goal is the availability of the research findings to the practitioner. The related pressure point is how to provide the practitioner with current research-based knowledge. Should researchers publish reports both in research journals that include details on the research methods and analysis and in clinical journals with a greater focus on the findings and their implications for practice, or, as Downs (1986, 1990) suggests, should basic and continuing nursing education programs give priority on how to read research reports? The use of research in practice also depends on the availability of consultation on the ways and means of using such research. Until greater numbers of nurses know how to access, assess, and use the research base, such consultation must be available on a wide scale. Several issues exist in this area: Is it the responsibility of nurse managers to ensure that access to such consultation is available through, for example, a staff nursing research consultant? Is it the responsibility of professional nursing associations to provide such consultation, as in the models provided in Manitoba or British Columbia? The resolution of these issues will shape the development of research in nursing into the next century.

Development

The full development of a strong research base on which nursing care can build requires a range of new investigative techniques. At the beginning of the 1990s, investigators were using a balance of qualitative and quantitative research designs. Formal experimental methods may be the only way to answer some questions but, as Jacox (1984) suggests, may not provide adequate answers to other important nursing questions. Practitioners and nurse managers must support the conduct of research with varied designs. For example, nurse managers must ensure that their agencies provide a valid scientific and ethical review of proposed research by reviewers well acquainted with the research method being proposed. Some medical reviewers, for instance, are not familiar with qualitative research methodologies, but it is inappropriate for approval of a study to be withheld merely on the basis of the type of research method.

The strength of the research base is improving as more nurses and university nursing departments pursue programs of research (a series of studies in a specific area) and become involved in research being conducted simultaneously in multiple cities or agencies. In Canada, such programs are evident, for example, in the areas of pain, decision making, care of persons with cancer, nursing workload and worklife, and coping with chronic illness.

All of these developments are marked by varied views over the "best" means of achieving a research base for nursing practice. Such debate should be regarded as a sign of health in the system as researchers and other nurses become better prepared for and involved in research.

Ethics

Nurse researchers face ethical responsibilities common to any research; these include the assurance of the scientific validity of the research and the rights of research subjects to freedom to consent, protection from harm, and assurance of confidentiality. In addition, researchers in service settings have ethical responsibilities to follow agency policies, to adhere to the stated research plan, to protect staff time, and to communicate fully to the agency staff both the research plans and results.

Agencies also have ethical responsibilities in relation to research, such as facilitating conduct of research, providing a valid system for ethical review and monitoring of projects, and using research results in practice. Agencies must be certain that staff nurses are aware of the rights of the research subjects and must ensure nursing's cooperation as nurse researchers recruit subjects. Procedures for research approval must not be more cumbersome for the nurse researcher than for researchers from other disciplines. A major, and increasing, issue in this country is the question, "who controls access to the patient?" Should there be policies that state that the attending physician's approval and consent must be obtained before any patient is enrolled as a subject in a nursing study? Will such differences in the policies in relation to nursing studies increase the threats to the validity of the study?

Funding

The question of how to provide an adequate funding base for research projects and for development of researchers is not one that most nurses consider to be primary to their practice. However, development of an adequate base of research for nursing practice is dependent on increased access to the funding provided for health and illness care research. Therefore nurses in all positions need to be acutely aware of the state of funding for nursing research.

The Canadian level of support for any research and development is far below the level of other industrialized countries. Nevertheless, review of various assessments of funding policies and practices in relation to research in nursing in Canada (Kerr, 1986; Wilmot, 1986; MRC, 1985b) indicate major deficits in the support of research in Canada and in the support of nursing research. In 1988, only 0.06% of the nearly $120 million Medical Research Council's research funds was awarded to nursing research projects (CNA, 1990c). Following Ginette Rodger's 1986 appointment to the MRC, the guidelines have changed to clarify that MRC can appropriately fund nursing research, and the programs for which nursing is eligible have increased. The peer review committees now include more nurses, and a nurse chairs one committee. Nevertheless, the total MRC funding for nursing projects in 1989 dropped even below the 1988 figure (MRC, 1989). Some of the major issues of funding of research remain: Which federal granting councils are the most appropriate for the funding of research in nursing? Will nursing be forced to demand a separate Nursing Research

Council? How can nursing ensure that the "peer review" committees have sufficient numbers of nurses to enable realistic review of the relevance of the research questions and the appropriateness of the methods? How do nurses obtain real development funding to enable the needed advancement in methods and researchers?

FUTURE FOR NURSING RESEARCH

As Canadian nursing moves toward the twenty-first century, the effort to establish the scientific foundation of nursing practice often seems not to be progressing quickly enough—nurses needed the knowledge yesterday! Much progress was made toward achieving the strategies outlined in the CNA plan for the development of research (CNA, 1984), but nurses now must act vigorously and collaboratively to achieve the goals of the new 5-year plan (CNA 1990a). In so doing, the profession must consider the roles of various types of nurses and nursing organizations in the research effort; the linkages between research, theory, and practice; and the focus needed in the research projects.

Educators must plan ways to "groom" students for research careers and to be alert to the potential of research for the improvement of their practice. Such "research-mindedness" also requires inspirational teaching by and collaborating with nurses actively involved in clinical research. Nurse managers and nurse educators must plan strategies for motivating young nurses to include graduate education and research preparation in their career plans. One mechanism to stimulate such interest is the active involvement of students in faculty members' research. Another is to involve staff nurses in some of the many roles in research: asking questions, reading research literature, joining research interest groups or journal clubs, collaborating on projects, ensuring that patients' rights in research are protected, working with researchers to apply and/or test research findings in their own settings, and facilitating the research process. Job descriptions for nursing staff now include specification of their research role; the mechanisms to support that role must also be provided.

For senior nurse administrators, the roles may vary in emphasis but not in essence. Nursing managers have roles in ensuring appropriate application of findings in the setting, developing nursing knowledge through protection of the researcher and facilitation of research, and protecting the subjects of research. Nursing educators must ensure that new research findings are incorporated as the basis for the content presented to students and must foster in students the ability to question practices, to read to discover answers to those questions, and to value the contribution that research can make to the quality of patient care. Regardless of the nursing position held, there is a research role for every nurse.

The means of achieving the base of clinical research is the establishment of strong practice-research-theory links. These links can be built only if nurses whose primary responsibility is giving care can talk regularly with nurses whose primary responsibility is research. Research departments, research units, joint appointments, nursing research groups, and conferences and "research roundtables" (Janken, Dufault, and Yeaw, 1988) provide opportunities for nurses to discuss the care they give, to explore ideas about clinical puzzles, and to identify the outcomes that should be used to assess the effectiveness of nursing interventions. The process is an unending spiral: the problems to be investigated must come from practice (often in the form of questions or collections of observed patterns of occurrences); the research studies must examine and test variables that are observed, manipulated, or controlled by nursing; the studies must be replicated and those in practice must test the results in their settings; and, finally, the suggested solution to the problem can be implemented in practice (Figure 16-1). As the care proceeds, there is no doubt that the questioning practitioner will at that point raise another question that will begin the next turn of the spiral!

There are clear trends toward the increasing relevance of nursing research projects for clinical practice and the development of thematic or programmatic research. In addition, many more nurse researchers are asking important questions about nursing's practice and practice field: What is nursing practice? What is effective in what nurses do? How do nurses who are regarded as being "experts" differ in their practice from those who are not as advanced? Nurses can and must document their practice and the nature of the expert care they give (Benner, 1984). Nurse researchers must also increase their attention to the investigation of the most appropriate working environments to support nurses in giving that care.

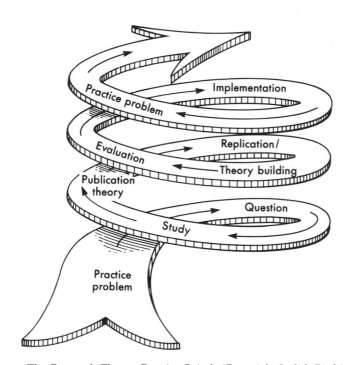

FIGURE 16-1 The Research-Theory-Practice Spiral. (Copyright Judith Ritchie, 1990.)

Another major direction that must emerge if the profession is to move more quickly to a "research-based practice" is the establishment of ongoing "utilization studies." Such projects have great potential for closing the current gap between the published literature and the actual practice of nursing.

Finally, the next decade will see the development of research-based nursing theory that provides guidance for practice. Several Canadian nurse researchers are now pursuing lines or programs of research. These endeavors will bear fruition in the emergence of relevant and empirically supported theories that provide direction, for example, in helping individuals reach decisions about their care, in establishing resources for caregivers, and in fostering optimal function in the face of chronic illness. The future also will bring careful documentation of the effects or outcomes of nursing practices. Perhaps most important, the future must bring together what Lindeman (1989) refers to as reality-oriented researchers and thoughtful, doing practitioners. Researchers and practitioners must be partners in the pursuit of truly relevant clinical studies, studies on nurses' worklife, and studies on the most effective use and mix of nursing staff (Pringle, 1989).

CONCLUSION

Major issues facing nursing research in Canada are those related to the use of nursing research in the practice setting. Several components are necessary to the development of a sufficient body of nursing research for "research-based practice": sufficient numbers of qualified researchers; funding for graduate education and for nursing research; sufficient numbers of well-designed studies investigating relevant practice problems; development of programs or lines of research; more replication of studies; and innovative means to help practitioners use research findings in their practice.

Until nurses in practice settings see research as relevant, can find ways to make it useful in their practice, and have working environments that allow them to think and plan more comprehensively, development of nursing research will be erratic. Nursing research needs a clear base of support from nurses and a demand from nursing and related disciplines for a strong, solid research base for nursing practice. Without these, agencies, universities, and clinical organizations will remain unmotivated and be unable to divert funds or provide support systems for nursing research.

Nurses need dedicated research—research needs dedicated nurses!

REFERENCES

Allemang, M.M., & Cahoon, M.C. (1986). Nursing education research in Canada. In H.H. Werley, J.J. Fitzpatrick, & R.L. Taunton (Eds), *Annual Review of Nursing Research* (Vol. 4) (pp. 261-278). New York: Springer Publishing.

Allen, M. (1986). The contribution of nursing to science in Canada. In K. King, E. Prodrick, & B. Bauer (Eds.), *Nursing research: Science for Quality Care*, Proceedings of the 10th national research conference (pp. 5-14). Toronto: Uiversity of Toronto.

Barnard, K. (1984). Knowledge development. *MCN: The American Journal of Maternal/Child Nursing, 9*, 175.

Benner, P.(1984). *From novice to expert: Excellence and power in clinical nursing practice*. Menlo Park, CA: Addison-Wesley.

Bulbrook, M.J.T. (1986). *Canadian National Nursing Research News Update* 1(1).

Brett, J.L. (1987). Use of nursing practice research findings. *Nursing Research, 36*, 344-349.

Cahoon, M.C. (1985). Development of the knowledge base. In M. Stewart, J. Innes, S. Searl, & C. Smillie (Eds.), *Community Health Nursing in Canada* (pp. 605-661). Toronto: Gage.

Canadian Nurses Association. (1981). *The development of nursing research in Canada: A background paper*. Ottawa: Author.

Canadian Nurses Association. (1983). *Ethical guidelines for nursing research involving human subjects*. Ottawa: Author.

Canadian Nurses Association. (1984). *The research imperative for nursing in Canada: A five-year plan towards the year 2000*. Ottawa: Author.

Canadian Nurses Association. (1985). *A statement on research in nursing*. Ottawa: Author.

Canadian Nurses Association. (1990a). *Research imperative for nursing in Canada: The next five years 1990-1995*. Ottawa: Author.

Canadian Nurses Association. (1990b). *Submission to the Royal Society of Canada University Research Committee*. Ottawa: Author.

Canadian Nurses Association. (1990c). *Supplementary paper to June 1990 Canadian Nurses Association submission to Royal Society of Canada University Research Committee*. Unpublished paper.

Coyle, L.A., & Sokup, A.G. (1990). Innovation adoption behavior among nurses. *Nursing Research, 39*, 176-180.

Degner, L.F. (1988). Nursing research: Impact for change inn practice. In L. Besel & R.G. Stock (Eds.), *Benchmarks 2: A sourcebook for Canadian nursing management* (pp. 98-105). Toronto: Carswell.

Degner, L.F. (1990). *The status of nursing research in Canada*. Paper presented to the ICN Task Force on International Nursing Research, Geneva, Switzerland.

Downs, F.S. (1986). Off with their heads! *Nursing Research, 35*, 195.

Downs, F. (1990). Accuracy counts, too. *Nursing Research, 39*, 131.

Griffin, A. (1971). Nursing research in Canadian universities. In *First national conference on research in nursing practice* (pp. 94-122). Vancouver: University of British Columbia School of Nursing.

Horsley, J.A., Crane, J., Crabtree, K., & Haller, K.B. (1983). *CURN Current utilization of research in nursing: A guide*. New York: Grune & Stratton.

Imai, H.R. (1971). Professional associations and research activities in nursing in Canada. In *First national conference on research in nursing practice* (pp. 89-93). Vancouver: University of British Columbia School of Nursing.

Janken, J.K., Dufault, M.A., & Yeaw, E.M.S. (1988). Research roundtables: Increasing student/staff nurse awareness of the relevancy of research to practice. *Journal of Professional Nursing, 4*, 186-191.

Jacox, A. (1984). Toward the development of a science of nursing. *Nursing Papers* (supplement), 15-25.

Jeans, M.E. (1988a). Did you see the editorial? *The Canadian Journal of Nursing Research, 20* (2), 1.

Jeans, M.E. (1988b). A drop in your bucket. *The Canadian Journal of Nursing Research, 20* (4), 1.

Kerr, J.C. (1986). Structure and funding of nursing research in Canada. In M.S. Stinson & J.C. Kerr (Eds.), *International issues in nursing research.* pp. 97-112. London: Croom Helm.

Kikuchi, J., & Simmons, H. (1986). Nursing: A science in jeopardy. In K. King, E. Prodrick, & B. Bauer (Eds.): *Nursing research science for quality care. Proceedings of the 10th national research conference* (pp. 28-31). Toronto: University of Toronto.

King, K., Prodrick, E., & Bauer, B. (1986). *Nursing research: Science for quality care. Proceedings of the 10th national research conference.* Toronto: University of Toronto.

Krueger, J.C., Nelson, A.H., & Wolanin, M.V. (1978). *Nursing research development, collaboration, and utilization.* Germantown, MD: Aspen.

Lamb, M., & Stinson, S.M. (1991). *Canadian nursing doctoral statistics: 1989 update.* Ottawa: Canadian Nurses Association.

Lindeman, C.A. (1989). Choices within challenges. *Communicating Nursing Research, 22,* 1-7.

Medical Research Council (1984 to 1990). *Reference list of health science research in Canada.* Ottawa: Author.

Pepler, C.J. (1988). The nurse researcher in the clinical setting. In L. Besel & R.G. Stock (Eds.), *Benchmarks 1: A sourcebook for Canadian nursing management* (pp. 214-225). Toronto: Carswell.

Pringle, D.M. (1989). Another twist on the double helix: Research and practice. *The Canadian Journal of Nursing Research, 21* (1), 47-60.

Registered Nurses Association of British Columbia (1990). *Position Statement: Nursing Research.* Vancouver: Author.

Ritchie, J.A. (1979). Does anyone out there practice? *Nursing Papers, 11,* 2-3.

Stetler, M.C. (1984) *Nursing research in a service setting.* Reston: Reston Publishing.

Stinson, M.S. (1986). Nursing research in Canada. In M.S. Stinson & J.C. Kerr (Eds.), *International issues in nursing research* (pp. 236-258). London: Croom Helm.

Stinson, M.S., & Kerr, J.C. (1986). *International issues in nursing research.* London: Croom Helm.

Stinson, M.S., Kerr, J.C., Giovanetti, P., Field, P. A., & MacPhail, J. (1986). *New Frontiers in nursing research: Proceedings of the International Nursing Research Conference.* Edmonton: University of Alberta.

Stinson, M.S., Lamb, M., & Thibaudeau, M.F. (1990). Nursing research: The Canadian scene. *International Journal of Nursing Studies, 27,* 105-122.

Tenove, S.C., Thurston, N., & Church, J. (1986). *Nursing research in Canadian teaching hospitals: A compendium.* Calgary: University of Calgary Faculty of Nursing and Foothills Hospital Department of Nursing.

Thibaudeau, M.F. (1985). Grantsmanship and funding. In M. Stewart, J. Innes, S. Searl, & C. Smillie (Eds.), *Community Health Nursing in Canada.* (pp. 726-737). Toronto: Gage.

Thurston, N., Tenvoe, S., Church, J., & Bach-Peterson, K. (1989). Nursing research in Canadian hospitals. *Canadian Journal of Nursing Administration, 2,* 8-10.

Thurston, N.E., Tenove, S., & Church, J. (1990). Hospital nursing research is alive and flourishing! *Nursing Management, 21* (5), 50-54.

Weir, G.M. (1932). *Survey of nursing education in Canada.* Toronto: University of Toronto.

Wilmot, V. (1986). Health science policy and health research funding in Canada. In M.S. Stinson & J.C. Kerr (Eds.), *International issues in nursing research.* (pp. 79-96). London: Croom Helm.

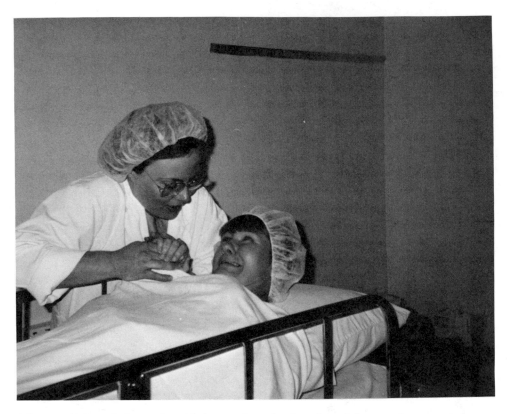

Advances in knowledge and rapid changes in technology in certain areas have created a demand for specialization in nursing practice. However, all nurses must still find ways to make even brief encounters meaningful. This photograph, one of a collection of more than 1000 photographs submitted by members to the Alberta Association of Registered Nurses for a commemorative book to celebrate its 75th Anniversary, shows two nurses role-playing the situation in which a nurse consoles a patient on the way to the operating room. The nurses are Lee Kelly and Donna Masson of the Grande Cache (Alberta) General Hospital. (The photographer was Carrie Rogalsky, RN. Photograph courtesy of the Alberta Association of Registered Nurses. Used with permission.)

CHAPTER SEVENTEEN

Specialization Issues

JOY D. CALKIN, RN, PhD

Joy D. Calkin, RN, BSN *(Toronto),* MS, PhD *(Wisconsin-Madison), was a staff nurse and then faculty member at the University of New Brunswick when she recognized the need for advanced preparation in pediatric nursing, which she completed in Wisconsin. She later turned her attention to the study of specialization of nursing knowledge in organizations and of administrative nursing. She is Professor and Vice-President (Academic) and Provost, The University of Calgary.*

D emands for "specialists" have arisen in many types of organizations, including those delivering health care. A look at advertisements for nurses indicates that almost as many employers ask specifically for nurses for positions in "specialty areas" such as critical care, operating room, psychiatry, gerontology, orthopedics, trauma nursing service, emergency, neurology/neurosurgery, maternal/child, pediatrics, specialty medical/surgical, or intensive care as ask for "general duty nurses." Some employers offer bonuses for work in specialty areas, especially if the nurse has had further study in the area. As well, specialization is often associated with credentialing in the form of certification. So what do these issues and trends really mean for nurses in the 1990s?

Specialization embodies a sense of precision in thinking and in acting. This precision arises from a balance of two general kinds of "knowing": (1) "knowing" is developed from structured knowledge available from the scientific discipline and relevant fields of study, and (2) "knowing" is developed from familiarity with recurrent phenomena or patterns that are observed and worked within a practice context. Both kinds of knowing may be the basis for specialization. They are believed to facilitate clinical judgments and to contribute to further development of knowledge. Perhaps most importantly, specialized knowledge in nursing is believed to enhance the care received by patients.

There tends to be confusion about the meaning of specialization within the field of nursing. Some of the confusion arises from the fact that the concept of specialization is old. Over time, ideas and meanings often change—and the changes lead to both clarification and confusion about meanings of words. DeWitt (1900) used the term *specialization* to describe nurses who had graduated from hospitals that were specialized in nature, such as those providing care for psychiatric patients. She indicated that private-duty nurses often chose to focus on one type of patient, such as women during childbearing. During the 1950s and 1960s the term was most frequently used in discussions of the "clinical nurse specialist." The designation "specialist" began to be associated with nurses who had advanced nursing preparation at the master's level. Therefore specialized knowledge became associated with formal educational programs that assisted nurses to develop knowledge and skill in working with particular populations, such as children or persons experiencing pain.

This chapter explores the need for nursing specialization, from the viewpoints of society, of policymakers and employers, and of the profession. Discussion of issues related to certification and to employment of specialists follows. The chapter concludes with a brief examination of how these issues might evolve in the future.

SOCIETAL NEEDS FOR SPECIALIZATION

Trends within Canada that have increased the degree of specialization in nursing are similar to those in other parts of the developed world. Rapid developments in both health and medical sciences have created a situation in which it is no longer possible for an individual to command the breadth of knowledge needed for precision in practice. For example, persons who had chronic renal disease resulting in the destruction of normal functioning of the kidney required relatively little nursing knowledge beyond comfort and hygiene measures in the 1950s because virtually all such persons died. Developments of medical technology, such as renal dialysis, led first to specialized hospital care requirements and then to specialized home care. In each instance the knowledge required of nurses increased exponentially. As a consequence, nurse clinicians with specialized knowledge in care of renal patients and clinical nurse specialists with advanced knowledge and skill are required. As well, physicians depend more on nurses for intelligent observation and informed action, and pressures have increased for nurses to gain physician-related knowledge and skills.

Parallel to the growth of knowledge in the medical sciences has been the development, refinement, and extension of knowledge related to health behaviors. Contributions from social psychology, education, exercise physiology, and nutritional science have increased the knowledge base from which nursing draws many of its assessments and interventions. In specific areas of practice such as the prevention and treatment of bedsores or the type of preoperative preparation that leads to reduction in discomfort and hospital length of stay for patients there is a burgeoning of the scientific basis on which to make clinical judgments.

Increasing public knowledge of health and medical services also encourages development of specialization. Many people understand more about their bodies and develop some interest in maintaining health through programs of exercise, dietary change, and so on. At least some parts of the population increasingly assert the expectation that they should be involved in decisions regarding their illness care and that they should have a clear understanding of what diagnostic and treatment interventions are being used and why. Parallel to these changes in self-care is the development of mutual help groups within families and communities. For example, the parents of diabetic children and diabetics have long had meetings and mutual support sessions that result in shared knowledge of this disease and its management.

If nurses are to be helpful to these better informed citizens, they must have knowledge and problem-solving skills that complement those of the population with which they are working. For example, a pregnant woman who had diabetes was referred to a high-risk pregnancy clinic for management of her care. She found, after several visits to the clinic, that the physicians and nurses in the clinic did not have her level of knowledge and skill about diabetes. Their lack of specialized knowledge and their failure to seek it through consultation led her to remove herself from care. This kind of situation will increasingly occur. The increase of chronic illness in our population is resulting in better informed people with sound self-help skills. Such people need providers with more focused expertise. If nurses fail to respond to this need for advanced or specialized knowledge then other providers will act to fill this gap.

In discussions on specialization of knowledge, restraining as well as driving forces must be considered. Some feminist writers point out that frequently there is considerable resistance in society against women developing expert levels of knowledge. To make bad matters worse, there are those who continue to suggest that educating nurses will result in reducing their compassion and ability to relate to patients. One belief is that it is not a "woman's place" to have a command of knowledge and authority beyond that of men.

POLICYMAKER AND EMPLOYER VIEWS

As early as 1972, a Canadian Nurses Association Task Force on Specialization noted that policymakers and employers perceived a need for specialized practice (Hall, Baumgart, and Stinson, 1973). Policy making, which facilitates various aspects of health care delivery, can exist at a broad level, such as the Canada Health Act initiated by Parliament or a decision of a provincial department of education to provide financial support for a new graduate program in nursing. The impact of employers is equally clear. Since the significant majority of nurses are employed by health and illness care delivery organizations, the perceived needs of employers have the most direct impact on advances in specialization in nursing—at least to the extent nurses wish to be reimbursed for services. Many other groups, while not policymakers or employers, may influence both of those sets of decision makers. In the illness care field, physicians and hospital administrators have been particularly dominant.

Policymakers and those who establish regulations can influence the range of providers of services required or permitted within programs. The absence of recognition of the need for specialization to deliver services would certainly slow its development in nursing. However, nurses can also influence policymakers. For example, it was through the action of nurses that Statistics Canada first collected data on the number of clinical nurse specialists in Canada.

Employers seem to be of two minds about the issue of specialization in nursing. One view is that "a nurse is a nurse is a nurse." This may serve the employers well under conditions in which they wish to "float" nurses from one type of service to another. That is, if there is no perceived need to provide specialized knowledge and skill for patient care by nurses working in different types of practice then it is far simpler to employ and to deploy nursing personnel. On the other hand, there is an increasing recognition by employers that nurses with specialized knowledge and skills are more efficient and provide safer care. A cursory review of the journal *Canadian Hospital* from the late 1970s until the present provides evidence that there is an increased concern on the part of administrators regarding the need for certain areas of specialization in nursing. The two most frequently cited needs are in intensive care nursing and administrative nursing in hospitals. To some extent, this increased attention is a function of shortages in each area. It also appears to be a reflection of concern regarding the need for increased competency in these and other areas of nursing practice. During the last nursing shortage in the United States a number of employers paid special bonuses to nurses in underserved fields of specialization. This shift in thinking on the part of employers of nurses lends credence to the recognition of specialization in nursing by those whose decisions are salient.

It appears with increasing frequency that employers and policymakers understand there is a need to develop and employ specialists within nursing. While the rationale behind these needs does not appear to be the same as that of the larger society, it at least tends to influence decision making in the same direction.

VIEW FROM WITHIN THE PROFESSION

One approach to dealing with the confusing issue of specialization is to clarify it by means of definitions or descriptions. For example, a nurse specialist is "a nurse prepared at any level to specialize in a particular area or branch of nursing practice" (ICN, 1984, p. 38). This International Council of Nurses document on the regulation of nursing then goes on to further define the nurse specialist:

> A first level nurse who is prepared through special post-basic experience and/or education to specialise in a particular area or branch of nursing practice; sometimes referred to as clinical specialist, nurse clinician, nurse practitioner, nurse mid-wife, health visitor, nurse anesthetist, nurse administrator, nurse education, nurse tutor, etc. (ICN, 1984, p. 38)

There is further discussion in the document identifying nurses in many countries who take basic programs in a particular area or branch of nursing practice rather then generalized basic programs; the registered psychiatric nurses prepared in several western provinces in Canada is an example. One can see immediately that someone intending to become a specialist or someone hiring a specialist may be unclear about the meaning of the term.

The Canadian Nurses Association (CNA) has been examining issues of clinical specialization and, more recently, certification since 1968. The need to reach a common understanding of specialization, specialists, and labels for specialty practice is reflected in CNA documents (Levesque, 1985). Within the profession, the view that specialization for the foreseeable future might be built on diploma, on baccalaureate, and on master's or doctoral degree preparation is widely held (Blais, 1980).

Hence while education is used in defining specialization by the ICN and CNA, it is not used in a manner that distinguishes the generalist from the specialist in terms of specialization of knowledge for practice. In contrast the American Nurses' Association policy is clear on this point:

> The specialist in nursing practice is a nurse who, through study and supervised practice at the graduate level (master's or doctorate), has become expert in a defined area of knowledge and practice in a selected clinical area of nursing. (ANA, 1980, p. 23).

There is a crispness and clarity in the statement that is useful in distinguishing the educational base for specialty from general practice. However, an examination of practice in the United States suggests the policy conveys more a sense of a preferred future than capturing "what is."

EDUCATION AND SPECIALIZATION

One way of thinking about specialty practice is to take the position that generalists in nursing are prepared in basic nursing education programs and that specialty practice is recognized and developed only through advanced nursing education at the graduate level. This approach parallels that of disciplines such as biology and some other professions such as law and pharmacy. The basic education program provides for "common practice skills" and "a general knowledge of nursing" in addition to the sciences and humanities, which contribute to an element of liberal education for professionals in nursing. Specialization is acquired through graduate programs, which focus on concepts and theories of nursing that are then applied to the particular phenomena in the student's population of study during clinical field study.

> Central to clinical field study . . . is skill in scholarly inquiry as well as in clinical decision-making. Skill in scholarly inquiry applied in a practice setting operates deliberately and systematically on already formulated knowledge as well as on clinical observation and interpretation of experience for the development of theory. (Pridham, 1990, p. 27)

For example, in preparing an advanced nurse practitioner in pediatrics, the general concept of anxiety may be specifically applied in the form of separation anxiety to help understand behavioral responses of young children to separation from their families and the impact on their illness or wellness states. This approach has a clear advantage of avoiding confusion about specialization by using undergraduate and graduate degrees as a mechanism for distinguishing levels of practice based on knowledge acquired through formal education programs.

An alternate perspective is the premise that there should be generalist and specialty knowledge at all levels of nursing education—baccalaureate, postbaccalaureate, and graduate (Bajnok, 1988). In the preceding paragraph the discussion was about basic (general) and advanced (specialty) education based on undergraduate and graduate *programs;* in this paragraph *knowledge* of general or speciality content may be in any educational program or be gained through practice. The failure to be aware of the differences in the thinking of authors may lead to unnecessary confusion about specialization (Janke, 1990).

The terms *generalist* or *specialist knowledge* frequently reflect a tension between educational activities and service needs. For example, baccalaureate education is generally perceived as providing knowledge basic to the understanding and treatment of problems arising from nursing phenomena. An understanding of comfort and the variety of approaches that can be taken to provide comfort, both physical and emotional, is an example of basic or generalist nursing knowledge. The use of knowledge of comfort under particular conditions such as in the care of the very young child, the renal dialysis patient, or the patient in the perioperative period can be considered specialty knowledge built on a generalist knowledge base. If one were discussing the particular conditions or settings for student learning in an undergraduate educational program one may be describing an area of "concentration," the provision of a "nursing minor" in the educational program, or simply the opportunity to focus on a particular area of practice. In many baccalaureate programs, this focus may take place in a senior nursing elective. Although this is neither advanced nursing nor specialty practice per se, such courses provide a basis for enhancing learning through developing a clinical focus.

While there is no inherent disagreement between the position that there should be generalist and specialist knowledge at all levels of nursing education and that the term *specialization* should be reserved for those who have advanced nursing education, there is frequently a semantic difficulty that seems problematic to overcome. The statement "I am a specialty practitioner in the care of children with diabetes" does not clarify the nature of the preparation or the level of the practice. For example, for almost two decades the term *clinical nurse specialist* has been used in the literature to refer to a master's-prepared practitioner. During the same period in Canadian practice settings the term *clinical nurse specialist* was held by some with a diploma and some with a master's degree in nursing. For more than a decade I have used the term *advanced nurse practitioner* to refer to the master's-prepared nurse in an attempt to avoid using the terms *clinical specialist* and *nurse practitioner* (Calkin, 1984) and to avoid confusion.

In discussing specialty knowledge it is helpful to determine whether one is addressing a branch of learning (theory and research base for practice) within a field of nursing or a particular aptitude or skill in performing an aspect of nursing. Although each is important to patient care, each does not require the same type or depth of education and experience. A 1989 publication by the Canadian Association of University Schools of Nursing attempts to create the background for a dialogue to sharpen our understandings of specialization and its subsets of advanced and speciality nursing practice (CAUSN, 1989).

EXPERIENCE AND SPECIALIZATION

In any field involving complex problems such as those presented by health-related responses in human beings, experience or time in practice are often viewed as highly salient to competence. Nursing is no exception. In any discussion of specialization someone is certain to raise the question: "How much experience is needed before one can be considered a specialist?" To phrase the problem differently: "How much experience does an experienced generalist need before being considered a specialist?"

In recent years this question is generally answered with the observation that both experience and formal educational preparation are required before one can be considered a specialist. The fact that the type of educational preparation is still broadly defined is evidenced by the Registered Nurses Association of Ontario (1984). Their position notes that specialization in nursing practice may be acquired through a variety of educational experiences, including staff development programs within particular agencies, workshops and conferences; formal specialty courses in colleges, universities, and self-directed learning; and other types of "education."

The real issue underlying the discussion of experience in the context of specialization needs to be clarified. Since there is no common agreement on how much experience or of what type, the question should be raised about the purpose of experience. As one reviews the variety of writing about the need for hiring experienced nurses—generalists or specialists—the underlying theme seems to be that experienced nurses can do something better than inexperienced nurses. Benner (1984) provides a rich description of the differences in behavior between novice and expert nurses. Tanner's (1987) research regarding clinical judgment shows that experienced nurses make decisions in a different way and use data differently than neophytes in nursing. Experienced nurses appear to be able to discern patterns of human responses that have meaning for clinical judgments. For example, an experienced nurse caring for a patient in labor may recognize a pattern that suggests a high probability for Caesarian delivery. This pattern recognition will lead to different actions than would be the case if the pattern was perceived to be that of a "normal labor." Hence, it is not experience as such but the effect of experience on judgments and actions that makes it an issue in discussions of specialization.

Experience alone is not the issue. When practitioners reflect on the things they experience in practice and/or when they build a large number of examples of patients' responses into their repertoire of understandings, they have learned in a way that enhances practice. To the extent that those teaching nursing are cognitively aware of patterns in practice, patterns can be analyzed and learned to some extent by basic and advanced students. However, there is a comfort, smoothness, and responsiveness of action needed in addition to that underlying understanding of practice, and these arise from experience.

Benner and Tanner (1987) suggest that intuitive judgment is an essential part of clinical judgment. They suggest that this essential part of expert practice is more likely to occur in the basis for actions of experienced nurses than in those who are less experienced. This kind of judgment has been described as making a difference in patient care outcomes (e.g., in "knowing" a patient is going to have a cardiac arrest before it occurs). Experience matters in developing both intuitive and analytic judgment.

Just how much experience is required to become an expert generalist or specialist is not known. We are often expert in some areas and novice in others. Given the current state of knowledge about practice decisions and actions it will no doubt remain conventional wisdom that experience needs to be included in any definition of a specialist.

CERTIFICATION FOR SPECIALTY PRACTICE

A few years ago, the word "certification" was usually associated with cardiopulmonary resuscitation or basic life support certification. In the 1990s, certification is most readily identifiable with discussions about specialty practice in nursing. Certification is a credentialing mechanism by which an individual presents evidence of having the commonly accepted level of competence within an area of specialty practice. Although one may discuss specialization without addressing the issue of certification, the converse is certainly not true. Certification is embedded in an understanding of specialty practice.

The most common form of credentialing for nurses in Canada is that of licensure through provincial statute. In many countries, licensure to practice is regulated at the national level (International Council of Nurses, 1984), and certification is a voluntary means of "recognizing nurses with preparation and expertise in an area of specialization" (p. 115). The ICN suggests that standards for certification should be determined by the professional association with appropriate consultation with interested groups, and the standards should be similar to those for specialists in other professions and should conform with universal definitions of specialty education and practice.

The ICN has been working to identify and define major branches of the field of nursing and to suggest appropriate educational standards for these branches of knowledge. To date, there is no international agreement about specialty fields in nursing. The CNA has mandated the proposal of speciality groups (Levesque, 1985). Others, for example Styles (American Nurses' Foundation, 1989), suggest options such as pediatrics, geriatrics, and community boards with specialty and subspecialty groups within each board(s) for categories of specialists such as clinical nurse specialist, nurse practitioners, and functional certifications.

In some countries, the nurse specialist is credentialed through a government regulatory body. The regulatory body sets the standards and methods whereby the specialist will be identified. In Canada, the position of the Canadian Nurses Association (1984, p. 7) is that credentialing primarily for the purpose of the protection of the public (licensure) is appropriately maintained by statute, whereas credentialing primarily for "other than public protection" is more appropriately managed through private regulation. Specifically, the Canadian Nurses Association and many specialty organizations maintain the view that, in Canada, certification should be provided through the joint work of the professional association and the appropriate specialty association.

In 1984, 106 occupational health nurses wrote the first certification examination, which was developed by the Canadian Council for Occupational Health Nurses with consultation and advice from the Canadian Nurses Association. This milestone in Canadian nursing history could help resolve one of the major issues in dealing with certification: what group or groups are to be involved in the certification process? The importance of this issue cannot be underestimated. In the United States, certification has little meaning. This problem occurred as a consequence of the many forms of certification and the standards for them that have been set by specialty organizations without any reference to a national standard or a process involving the national professional association (i.e., the American Nurses Association). As a consequence, standards, methods of testing, and the general use of the term *certification* have little shared meaning among nurses; care must be taken to avoid confusion about the terms and about the groups to set standards.

Having resolved the issue of the appropriate role of the national professional organization (the CNA) in certification, a second major issue looms. There are currently more than 120 national and provincial interest groups and specialty organizations for nurses in Canada. As Lane (1985) notes, the formation of the interest groups normally takes place before certification is developed. If even one half the specialty and interest groups were to seek certification the result would be problematic. The issue for nursing in Canada is to determine a limited and understandable group of nursing specialties. Should venipuncture, rehabilitation, and surgical specialties all be certified?

The current position of the Canadian Nurses Association is to use a set of guidelines whereby a specialty may be designated for certification (CNA, 1986) (see also Chapter 25). The first four guidelines focus on the knowledge criteria. Summarized, they state a specialty has a body of knowledge generated by and increased through research, which allows it to deal with recurrent phenomena that occur in a defined population or group of people receiving nursing care. This unique knowledge has a prerequisite basic nursing education. In addition, for CNA to recognize the specialty as one that may give certification, a group is expected to have written standards of practice and role descriptions. The guidelines have a pragmatic requirement in that the specialty group must have the human and financial resources to support the certification process. As a final guideline it is expected that the CNA Board of Directors will designate specialty groups for certification "within the context of current priorities and financial resources" (1986, p. 11). Although the information booklet is an attempt to create a screening process for designating specialty groups, it will not resolve the basic issue of how nursing will develop a consensus about specialty groups. As noted in the introduction of the booklet, "the development of certification policies in a program is an evolving process that calls for flexibility in adapting to future changes" (p. 1). The authors further note that, given the need to have the baccalaureate as the basis for entry to practice by the year 2000, it is likely that a master's degree in a specialty area will be required for certification in the future.

Current guidelines provide only a limited way of dealing with a long-term issue. What about the future? Baumgart (1985) suggests that "priority must be given to those fields in which there are clear benefits to substantial numbers of patients and where the breadth and depth of substantive knowledge are sufficient to provide a basis for specialized training" (p. 11). Nursing will have to develop some consensus about "clear benefits," "substantive knowledge," and other means of defining areas of specialized practice.

"Why would anybody want to be certified in a specialty?" Many nurses make sustained efforts to achieve certification and to maintain recertification in their specialty fields. These nurses describe the experience, educational programs, and preparation for rigorous certification examinations with a sense of pride in their competence, which they see reflected in having gained their certificate. Many of these nurses do not see their certification as having any effect on their career opportunities or the remuneration they receive. However, if one considers the effect of certification in other fields, it will not be long before specialty nurses with certification may begin to argue that there should be some external reward for their established level of competence.

Institutions of higher education will be increasingly challenged by developments in certification for specialty practice. Questions are already being raised about the extent to which universities will recognize certification "for credit" toward a baccalaureate or master's degree or will provide for certification within a degree program. This issue is unlikely to admit an easy resolution in nursing. Nurses who have undertaken rigors of certification will believe that universities should recognize this preparation and behave in ways that facilitate nurses' more rapid movement through their educational programs. Generally speaking, universities are not inclined to grant credit for experience in studies not undertaken within the aegis of the university. Further, areas of specialty practice do not necessarily fit within the curricular structure of university programs in such a way that it would make it easy to determine for which courses the certification might substitute. It may be, as CNA (1986) suggests, that this will be resolved when nurses entering practice hold a baccalaureate degree and certification is considered as part of advanced nursing practice through graduate education. Until then, the relationship between certification and credit for baccalaureate and graduate degrees will continue to be an issue for Canadian nurses (see CAUSN, 1989).

SPECIALTY PRACTICE IN ORGANIZATIONS

Finally, there is the issue of the relationship between specialization and organizational arrangements for practice. For example, will specialization and certification be required for a nurse to hold certain kinds of clinical positions?

In 1970, the first description of a practicing Canadian clinical nurse specialist entered the Canadian literature (Coombs, 1970). There had been some discussion about the need for specialization of practice in both hospitals and community health nursing, but before this the most common form of "specialization" was managerial or educational rather than clinical. Today, various forms of specialists and master's-prepared clinical nurse specialists are common.

In the field of management science, an underlying assumption is that specialization leads to increased productivity. Mintzberg (1979) summarizes much of the key research in this field. One form of specialization is referred to as "horizontal job specialization," a term used to describe the breadth or narrowness of work an employee undertakes. When specialization is narrow the worker is employed to perform repetitive and standardized tasks. In nursing, the term "functional" (task) specialization has been used to describe patient care tasks that are divided into clusters of activities. For example, a registered nurse might be responsible for giving medications to all patients on the unit while another nurse is responsible for changing dressings. A major problem of narrow horizontal or task specialization of this type is that there are high costs associated with coordinating work and communications among workers. Vertical specialization refers to the amount of control or authority that workers have to determine their work, to evaluate their performance, and to be self-directed or self-managed. Low levels of vertical specialization mean the workers have little control over decisions related to their work. Professionals are generally described as highly vertically specialized or as having a wide scope of practice with a job requirement of making complex decisions and selecting appropriate actions that require years of training. Management scientists generally note that close managerial control of professionals is neither productive nor efficient.

The first and most central issue for employers of nurses is how to implement specialty roles or how to fit expertise with the work required by the organization delivering health care. Calkin (1984) states that the level of expertise is different for the novice, the expert-by-experience, and the advanced nurse practitioner. The novice is most useful in providing patient care in relatively predictable areas of practice in which problems can be analyzed using basic knowledge. Experts-by-experience have, in addition to basic skills, knowledge of rather complex patient responses and a greater depth of intervention skills; such nurses may have strong intuitive skills related to practice but are not expected to be able to conceptualize issues arising from care nor necessarily to be able to explain to others the basis for decisions and interventions (Calkin, 1984). Advanced nurse practitioners have developed knowledge through formal education and experience and are prepared at the master's or doctoral levels for practice. As a result of their conceptual ability and preparation, they can communicate concepts and patterns as a basis for practice. Advanced nurse practitioners may be required to perform a wide variety of tasks such as facilitating the acquisition of knowledge by patients, staff, and students (education); consultation regarding care; research or use of research; program planning activities; or other related tasks in addition to functioning directly in the care of patients and families. These three levels of expertise should be used for their differing competencies in patient care. However, to understand the issues related to the use of specialists in clinical practice requires an understanding of management roles (see also Chapter 13).

If nursing's work is divided into narrow sets of nursing tasks (horizontal or task specialization) then the problems of coordination and communication fall largely to the manager. In a similar fashion, if nurses have limited control over clinical decisions and act largely under orders then, again, the manager must assume the major burden of coordination and decision making for nurses and communication with other health care providers. The larger or the more geographically differentiated the organization the harder this task of coordination becomes. It would seem sensible for health care organizations to employ nurses who have great breadth in their work and responsibility for decisions related to clinical practice. The net result, on the face of it, would be that the costs of coordination and communication through the manager would be decreased and more time and energy could be devoted to a different set of management tasks, such as staff allocation, budgeting, and program planning.

In all probability, movement of some nurses into more managerial functions should be balanced by development of specialty clinical practitioners. The issue for organizations delivering care to the different types of patients and in different settings is to develop position descriptions and establish personnel requirements consistent with agency or hospital needs. The general lack of understanding about the use of specialty nurses and advanced nurse practitioners is a major block to appropriately fitting differences in expertise with the work required in health care organizations.

A second issue for health care organizations and for nursing is the extent to which medical and paramedical professionals and technicians are narrowing their focus for practice. As early as 1965, MacLeod addressed the idea of specialized teams in institutional care. Employers "will almost surely see hospital nurses working more and more as members of teams of specialists. On these teams the nurse will of course continue to be the one who performs the unique functions of nursing" (MacLeod, 1965, p. 49). She outlined basic nursing functions and stated that nurses would further specialize according to medical teams in such areas as neurosurgery, cardiology, and other areas of medical treatment. In acute care hospitals, specialty practice in nursing is not infrequently driven by specialization of medical practice and/or the particular kind of unit in which patients receive care (e.g., intensive care units). To the extent that specialty nurses define their knowledge and experience in a way that is consistent with medically defined populations and problems, this does not present a major challenge to the organization. However, for nurses who specialize in mental health in a general acute care hospital or in pain management, it is difficult to determine how such personnel should be hired and how they should be "fit into" nursing services. Pick notes the need for specialized nursing skills "in virtually all clinical areas" in the acute care environment (1984, p. 23). It appears that specialization will be driven in part by the need for nurses who can communicate effectively and who can coordinate care for patients and families who enter the illness care system for medical interventions that in turn give rise to responses with which nurses must then deal. In less medically driven settings, the patient/client responses or commonalities are most likely to create nursing specializations.

A third issue for employers is that of job satisfaction. Mintzberg (1979) reports studies in which higher degrees of alienation are associated with jobs of narrow scope and little control. Although the findings are conflicting when one looks at all kinds of workers, studies of nurses in intensive care units (e.g., Kosmoski and Calkin, 1986) suggest that higher levels of preparation are often accompanied by more reports of dissatisfaction with work. Is this because of a poor "fit" between their education and employer expectations? A concern of employers is the creation of job enrichment and enlargement in a fashion that retains highly competent nurses in direct patient care. One response to this concern has been the implementation of clinical ladders or forms of advancement in responsibilities and remuneration through clinical practice rather than through a management ladder. Specialty practice and certification may be useful elements in developing such clinical ladders. That is, as graduates move from beginning practice through education and experience their increasing expertise is rewarded through promotion on a clinical basis. Development of clinical ladders has provided effectively for intrinsically motivated nurses in some settings. The attachment of adequate remuneration to levels on a clinical ladder currently is blocked largely by collective bargaining agents for nurses in a number of provinces. Barriers to adequate recognition of expertise, with its subset of expertise referred to as specialization, will not occur until collective bargaining associations, health care organization managers, and funding sources find an adequate resolution to this challenge.

The advanced nurse practitioner presents some special challenges to the current structure of health care delivery. Risk (1975) has pointed out the major limitations to the role development of the clinical nurse specialist in community health nursing. She identified the limitations as organizational, attitudinal, and legal in nature. Her own position, as is often the case with some clinical nurse specialist positions, was part of the administrative hierarchy rather than the clinical hierarchy, and she notes that this often placed her in a position of split loyalties between her clinical and administrative foci. The positive part of belonging to the administrative group was that it provided an excellent perspective on the functioning of the agency and its relationship to the community. She also notes that the administrative position provided her with power and status in an agency in which nurses were not recognized for their clinical expertise alone. Attitudinal problems include those she attributes to being a nurse and being female, which she points out are generally associated with a position of compliance. In addition to perceptions from groups external to nursing such as physicians, she also notes the issue of nurses not recognizing expertise through seeking consultation from their nursing colleagues. Although Risk's article was written in 1975 the issues she identifies are still salient and are equally true in settings other than community health.

At the beginning of this section, it was noted that management scientists see horizontal and vertical specialization as a means of achieving greater levels of productivity. The argument may be made that nursing should "prove" whether or not advanced nurse practitioners and specialty practitioners are more productive than nonspecialty practitioners (one might address the same question to theologians, physicians, teachers, lawyers . . .). Some comparative studies of nurse practitioners and physicians and of the differences in practice on units with and without a clinical nurse specialist (Georgopoulos and Jackson, 1970) have been done, but currently are not worth the high cost to develop extensively these kinds of studies. The important issue for the appropriate and productive use of nurses who specialize in certain areas of clinical practice is under what conditions they are most appropriately used in ways that will benefit patients. This is probably most fruitfully dealt with through the joint judgment of experienced managers and clinicians in nursing. If the development of specialty practice in health care organizations were to do nothing more than reduce turnover through increased satisfaction of workers it would be worth implementing.

The organizational perspective of specialty practice is perhaps the one, in the final analysis, that is most important. It is within these organizations that the majority of health and illness care is provided. Educational issues may be resolved, challenges of certification may be met, but patients' needs for highly knowledgeable care will not be effectively dealt with until organizational leaders come to grips with these and other organization-related issues influencing the use of these specialists.

A LOOK TO THE FUTURE

In the immediate future these and other issues will continue to be played out within the profession and the health care delivery system. The patterns around specialty practice have not yet emerged clearly enough for accurate predictions for the future.

One possible scenario is that specialty practice will become wholly aligned with medical specialties and with outcomes of care largely defined through the needs arising from illness states, their treatment, or their prevention. If this trend develops then the major focus and definition of specialty practice for nurses would occur in institutions where nurses are employed. Education for a specialty practice would therefore largely arise from institutionally derived needs and through continuing education and the development of expertise through practice in implementing this knowledge. In this scenario, nurses undertaking graduate education at the master's and doctoral level would focus their learning on patient responses that arise from medical treatment and the prevention of pathology. Trends in medical technology would become the most central issue in defining nursing problems and research regarding them.

A second scenario may be a logical extension of degree-granting educational programs as a mechanism for developing specialty practice. Nurses would certainly continue to operate as members of the health care team, but their focus would be unique within the team. In this picture of the future, although nurses may continue to develop considerable expertise based on their experience following their basic preparation, formal specialty practice preparation would be found within graduate preparation for specialty practice. In this case, specialty practice would not focus on knowledge necessarily associated with medical identification, treatment, and prevention of pathology but would come from patient and family responses to health-

and illness-related situations in which they find themselves. Nursing would focus on patterns in the responses of patients and research concerning those patterns. For example, family nursing specialists (Wright, Watson, and Duhamel, 1985) may focus on the dynamics that may disrupt a healthy family interaction as they respond to changes in the health behavior of a family member. In such a scenario there would be a great need for practicing faculty (Rankin, Stainton and Calkin, 1989). Clinically embedded faculty and students can bring their experiences to a shared exploration about the meanings of a range of patients' ways of being with their health or illness. The sensing and identifying of these patterns arises from practice-anchored conversations and are, I believe, a necessary complement to our traditional analytic and problem-solving approaches to teaching and learning.

A third scenario is that specialty practice will occur largely as an interaction of several factors, including social trends, demographic characteristics of the population served, health care approaches taken to deal with them, and the perspectives and power of the profession.

Some issues that will interact in this scenario include:
- Will government/employer pay schedules reflect specialist expertise?
- Will litigators in the courts expect assurance of expertise—and will certification of specialty practice meet these legal needs?
- Will nurse unionists continue to argue "a nurse is a nurse is a nurse" or will differences in competence and credentials be encouraged?
- Will the demographic shift to elder care provide an avenue for greater clarity about nursing practice as differentiated from medical/paramedical practice, or will current power and control issues continue?
- Will nurses develop certification through a nationally recognized process, or will Canadian groups create the same muddle as nurses in the United States?

These and other interacting issues will certainly create the context for recognized specialization and certification.

Actions regarding specialization and certification must be taken with a clear sense of a preferred picture. Nursing's knowledge and skill differences need to be understood and expressed for society in general and for those who need care in particular. These differences also need to be made clear in policy, employment, education, and organizational design and in the actions of the Canadian Nurses Association and of the specialty groups if nursing is to argue that what nurses know and how they know it affects the care provided for others.

REFERENCES

American Nurses Association (ANA). (1980). *Nursing: A social policy statement.* Kansas City: Author.

American Nurses' Foundation, Inc. (1989). *On specialization in nursing: Toward a new empowerment.* Kansas City: Author.

Bajnok, I. (1988). Specialization meets entry to practice. *The Canadian Nurse,* 88(6), 23-24.

Baumgart, A. J. (1985). The time is ripe. *The Canadian Nurse,* 81(6), 11.

Blais, M. (1980). Specialization in nursing. In G. Zilm (Ed.), *Back to Basics: The Nature of Nursing Education.* Ottawa: Canadian Nurses Association.

Benner, P. (1984). *From novice to expert: Excellence and power in clinical nursing practice.* Menlo Park, CA: Addison-Wesley.

Benner, P., & Tanner, C. (1987). Clinical judgment: How expert nurses use intuition. *American Journal of Nursing,* 87(1), 23-31.

Calkin, J. (1984). A model for advanced nursing practice. *Journal of Nursing Administration,* 14(1), 24-30.

Canadian Nurses Association (CNA). (1984). *The ad hoc committee report on credentialing.* Ottawa: Author.

Canadian Nurses Association (CNA). (1986). *CNA's certification program: An information booklet.* Ottawa: Author.

Canadian Association of University Schools of Nursing. (1989). *Specialization in Nursing and nursing education.* Ottawa, Canada: Author.

Coombs, R. (1970). Active-care hospital nurse expands her role. *The Canadian Nurse,* 66(10), 23-26.

DeWitt, K. (1900). Specialties in nursing. *American Journal of Nursing,* 1(1), 14-17.

Georgopoulos, B., & Jackson, M. (1970). Nursing kardex behavior in an experimental study of patient units with and without clinical nurse specialists. *Nursing Research,* 19(3), 196-218.

Hall, O., Baumgart, A. J., & Stinson, S. (1973). Specialization in nursing—where? when? how? *The Canadian Nurse,* 69(5), 35-38.

International Council of Nurses (ICN). (1984). *Project on the regulation of nursing.* Geneva: Author.

Janke, R. (1990). Letter to the editor on specialization. *RNABC News,* 22(1), 8.

Kosmoski, K., & Calkin, J. (1986). Critical care nurses' intent to stay in their positions. *Research in nursing and health,* 9(1), 3-10.

Lane, B. (1985). Specialization in nursing: Some Canadian issues. *The Canadian Nurse,* 81(6), 24-25.

Levesque, V. D. (1985). Specialization and certification: A review of CNA's activities. *The Canadian Nurse,* 81(6), 26-28.

MacLeod, I. (1965). Specialization for new nursing. *Canadian Hospitals,* 42(7), 49-51.

Mintzberg, H. (1979). *The structuring of organizations—A synthesis of research.* Englewood Cliffs, NJ: Prentice-Hall.

Pick, J. (1984). Specialization in nursing: Will we find a way to meet the need? *The Canadian Nurse,* 80(5), 22-23.

Pridham, K. (1990). Why clinical field study? *Nursing Outlook,* 38(1), 26-30.

Risk, M. (1975). The community clinical nurse specialist. *Nursing Clinics of North American,* 10(4), 761-769.

Registered Nurses Association of Ontario. (1984). Specialization. *RNAO News,* 8-11 +.

Stainton, M.E., Rankin, J.A., & Calkin, J.D. (1989). The development of a practising nursing faculty. *Journal of Advanced Nursing,* 14, 20-26.

Tanner, C. (1987). Teaching clinical judgment. In J. J. Fitzpatrick & R.L. Tanton (Eds.), *Annual Review of Nursing Research* (pp. 153-173) New York: Wiley & Sons.

Wright, L., Watson, W., & Duhamel, F. (1985). The family nursing unit: Clinical preparation at the master's level. *The Canadian Nurse,* 81(5), 26-29.

Career advancement usually must be planned; it does not just happen. Group meetings to stimulate discussion of career options can help. At this meeting, a group of registered nurses at the Hospital for Sick Children, Toronto, talk about goals and options. Left to right: Janice Waddell, Cory Murphy, Dawn Welstead, Krista Samson, and Roseanne Shin. (Photograph courtesy of the Visual Education Department, Hospital for Sick Children, Toronto.)

CHAPTER EIGHTEEN

Career Development and Mobility Issues

GAIL J. DONNER, RN, PhD

Gail J. Donner, RN, BSc (Pennsylvania), MA (New York), PhD (Toronto), *is Director of Nursing Education at the Hospital for Sick Children and Associate Professor (part-time) at the Faculty of Nursing, University of Toronto. She was Executive Director of the Registered Nurses' Association of Ontario from 1984 to 1989. She has worked in a variety of settings, including medical, surgical, psychiatric nursing, student health services, and community health clinics, in Canada and the United States. She is a former Chair of the Nursing Department at Ryerson Polytechnic Institute, Toronto.*

SPECIAL ACKNOWLEDGMENT

The author wishes to acknowledge the contributions of **Leslie K. Hardy**, RN, PhD, who was a co-author of the chapter for the first edition of the book. Dr. Hardy is a Professor and former Director of the School of Nursing, Memorial University, St. John's, Newfoundland.

The ways that people relate to work roles make fascinating study. In nursing, the ways that nurses relate to their work have implications for the individual nurse, for clients and their families, for those who work with nurses, for nursing as a profession, and for society itself.

How do nurses experience nursing work? Do they see it as a "job" or as a "career"? Do they enter nursing with some understanding that it is a profession? Do they intend to remain for some time and to progress into leadership positions? How does the organizational structure of the agency affect career development? What are the career opportunities for nurses who wish to remain at the bedside? Do nurses value their work and invest time and energy in improving or expanding their skills and knowledge? Do they see the work of nursing as affecting society and society's goals? Do they acknowledge the need for strong, positive leadership?

Before exploring some of these complex questions, it is important to differentiate between careers and jobs and to define what is meant by career development. Careers are usually seen as long-term commitments with intense personal involvement, whereas jobs are often seen as short-term and temporary with less involvement of the individual.

Hardy (1983) defines career development as a process that is:
- Characterized by decision making
- Dynamic
- Patterned and dependent on decisions made at critical points in one's life
- Capable of being guided
- Involving compromise between personal factors (values, aptitudes, abilities, perceptions), professional opportunities (both structural and psychological), and societal forces (e.g., nursing shortages, economic recessions)

Support from others enhances career progress. Lack of support in nursing workplaces has been linked to the classic concept of "reality shock" (Kramer, 1974, p. 1), which may occur when one enters the profession after a long educational period. Reality shock can result in high "wastage rates" because individuals become disillusioned and leave the profession (Kramer, 1974, p. 1). Lack of support also has been associated with job dissatisfaction and stress (Cohen, 1981; HCMT, 1985), with lack of clinical excellence (Benner, 1984), and with lack of leadership and unity in the profession (Brooten, Hayman, and Naylor, 1978; CNA and CHA, 1990; Desjean, 1975; Donovan, 1990).

This chapter discusses four aspects of career development that particularly affect individual nurses and their continued growth in the profession: professional socialization, types of career movement and how these are related to the structure of women's roles in our society, social support systems available to nurses, and structures of nursing workplaces. Issues and implications for the future of nursing are also presented. The chapter will further identify a model and process for assisting nurses at different stages of their careers with career planning and development.

PROFESSIONAL SOCIALIZATION

Students entering the profession of nursing have various attitudes, beliefs, and values about nurses and nursing. These attitudes often reflect society's view of the profession and have developed during the students' early lives through experience with parents, teachers, significant others, and media. Because the overwhelming majority of nurses in Canada are women (approximately 98%), societal views and values about women's work, appropriate roles for men and women, and opportunities provided or denied because of gender are particularly significant in shaping nurses' views about their profession.

Socialization may be defined as "the process through which individuals are inducted into their culture. It involves the acquisition of skills and behaviour patterns making up social roles established in the social structure" (Merton, Reader, and Kendall, 1957, p. 41). Professional socialization is the process of learning the culture of the occupation (Cotanch, 1981). Further discussion on this is in Chapter 4.

Professional socialization consists of three distinct dimensions: education, development of occupational orientation, and personal integration into the occupation (Cohen, 1981; Simpson, 1979).

Educational Socialization

As students proceed through their educational programs they gradually alter preconceived views of nurses and nursing and develop professional attitudes. These attitudes are developed by contact with other students, with teachers, with nurses in clinical and other settings, and with clients.

The nursing profession relies heavily on the educational experience to develop students into nurses and to transform them from people who "act like" nurses to people who "are" nurses. However, it is the internalization of the professional attitudes, skills, and values that enables individuals to contribute to the profession and society rather than just to respond to the needs and demands of others. The self-image of nurses must be formed by more than the reflected images of others.

The educational experience is also important in preparing nurses for advancement and for leadership roles. Recent interest and attention to issues of power, decision making, and policy determination reinforce the views that students must learn early in their careers to take an increased interest in these areas. Schools of nursing in Canada are providing increased opportunities for the study of women's issues, political processes, and health issues. Helping students to learn and to experience the application of these theoretical approaches in their daily practice remains a continuing challenge, however. Finding time and opportunity within curricula for more than the typical "change project" assignment is difficult and competes with time for the ever-increasing expansion of clinical knowledge. Educators must integrate raising consciousness about who the nurse is with what the nurse does.

Numerous studies examine the educational experience and its effect on socialization (Brown, Swift, and Oberman, 1974; Cohen, 1981; Cotanch, 1981; George, 1982; Meleis and Dagenais, 1981; Murray and Morris, 1982; Watson, 1982), but the research is almost exclusively American, is highly specific, and cannot be generalized. The American research describes and studies specific cohorts of students in specific schools in specific geographical areas. In Canada, no published studies examine the socialization process in educational settings, although a major study was begun in 1991 at the University of Alberta. Schools of nursing often conduct follow-up studies of their graduates, but the data from these are commonly used for curriculum revision and admission purposes rather than to identify trends and issues in professional socialization.

Research is needed on the ways attitudes about nursing and nurses are formed during professional education and on the factors that contribute to a positive professional self-image. As well, more knowledge on the image of the profession from the

Canadian perspective would make a significant contribution to the future of nursing in Canada. Specifically, such research could identify effects of clinical experience on attitude formation, the influence of content about the political process, and the role of the nurse on attitudes and on the future behavior of students as they become nurses. The variables that could be studied so that nursing can better understand how nurses' self-image is formed include the effect of clinical experience on attitude formation and the influence of knowledge about the political process and the role of the nurse in that process on future attitudes and behavior.

Follow-up studies are needed to document the careers of nurses and to link them to attitudes formed before they entered nursing school. As well, more research about specific educational experiences in nursing programs could assist educators in building programs that prepare the kind of nurses the profession requires for the future.

Occupational Orientation

Another critical period in the socialization process for nurses occurs when graduates leave formal educational programs and enter work settings (Hinshaw, 1977). In 1974, Kramer was the first to identify the "reality shock" that nurses experience when, in moving from student role to worker role, they confront the professional-bureaucratic conflict. In this orientation period, nurses must cope with incongruities between what they learned in the protected classroom and what exists in the "real world." How that conflict is resolved has a significant effect on a nurse's future functioning on the health care team and in the system, as well as on the profession and its future. Despite the concern Kramer emphasized so strongly (1974, 1981) and despite the attention "reality shock" attracted within the nursing community, not much change has resulted. New graduates continue to encounter unfamiliar and sometimes hostile work environments for which they feel ill prepared; this affects attitudes about practice and about the setting and is a potentially negative socializing agent that contributes to rapid turnover and, possibly, to nursing shortages (Anderson, 1989; Attridge and Callahan, 1990; HCMT, 1988; OHA, 1991; RNABC, 1989; Thomas, Bounds, and Brown, 1991).

With the demand for nurses likely to continue to increase in Canada and with a slower growth in supply also likely, employers must increasingly use recruitment and retention strategies that emphasize professional development rather than orientation and inservice education. Indeed, the trend seems to be swinging back from a decentralized model, in which inservice or continuing education is part of general staff development or human resources departments, to the more centralized model, in which nursing education is part of the nursing department. McMaster-Chedoke Hospital in Hamilton, Ontario, and the Sunnybrook Health Sciences Centre and Wellesley Hospital in Toronto are examples of the latter.

Cross-appointments (in which a nurse may work for an agency and a faculty of nursing) and other forms of improved communication between practice and education are becoming more common in Canada, and some innovative joint programs are beginning. However, the Canadian Nurses Association Joint Conference for Administrators and Educators held in 1986 concluded that there still is a long way to go to help novice practitioners adjust to the "real world." A number of studies conducted over the past few years document the changes required (Kasparin and

Young, 1985; McCloskey, 1990; OHA, 1991; RNABC, 1989). Recent initiatives in baccalaureate education in Alberta, British Columbia, Manitoba, and Newfoundland, where collaborative programs between hospital schools of nursing and universities are being developed and implemented, may also provide models for "post-education" collaboration between employers and educators. (See also Chapter 21.)

Personal Integration

The third dimension of professional socialization includes the way workers integrate into and eventually identify with an occupation. Donner (1986), in a study of staff nurses in Ontario, explored the influence of work setting and years of experience on the professional orientations of 501 nurses in hospital and community nursing settings. Although Donner did not find any changes in the nurses' professionalism at different stages of their careers, she did identify a difference between hospital nurses and community nurses. The community nurses had a higher degree of professionalism than did their hospital counterparts and, more specifically, the community nurses were more autonomous than the hospital nurses when the effects of education (diploma/degree), years of experience (0-5, 6-10, 11+), and hours of work (full-time/part-time) were controlled. Donner's sample was stratified and randomly selected so that inferences could be made to the population of staff nurses in Ontario.

Clearly, more research is needed to explore the professional socialization process beyond the early work experience. An understanding of more of the factors that influence nurses' growth as professionals would provide insight into how nurses integrate into their profession. Human resource issues in nursing have received more and more attention in the popular press and the professional journals within the past few years. Although most of the attention is directed to recruitment and retention, the solutions often involve strategies to help new recruits integrate into the work force, such as preceptorships, nurse advocates, small-group problem-solving, and participation in agency committees (AHA, 1989; Andersen, 1989; Barhyte, 1987; Grantham, 1989; Hospital Research and Educational Trust, 1989).

CAREER MOVEMENT AND THE ROLE OF WOMEN

In 1971, Mitchell reported on a study of 956 nurses in Alberta and revealed that professionalism and career expectations were rarely related to one another. Five significant findings were that:
1. In general, nurses were not interested in professional development activities, such as collegial relationships.
2. Nurses did not relate professional role expectations to professional association activities nor to further education.
3. Further education was considered a personal, not a professional, goal.
4. Planning for organized career development was nonexistent, and most career development occurred by chance.
5. Advancement to more responsible positions was related to stability rather than career development or professional concern

Qualitative research into careers of female nursing leaders in Canada (Larsen, 1984) and in Britain (Hardy, 1983) and informal reports from nursing leaders suggest that the scenario depicted in Mitchell's work continues.

Larsen (1984) explored career histories of 10 Canadian female nurses, aged 33 to 49 years, with earned doctorates. Her findings support the overall tenor of Mitchell's (1971) study and indicated a certain lack of commitment to the profession for much of one's early career. Larsen discovered that 7 of the 10 subjects entered nursing by default. Reasons such as financial constraints, wanting to be independent of parental bonds, academic failure, and assurance of a secure female occupation led the subjects into nursing. Singh (1979) labeled these motives as "undesirable" because they encourage more of a job mentality rather than a career plan. Larsen found that, even when they were ensconced into the rhythm and flow of nursing, many of the subjects' early career decisions were made without goal setting or consideration of implications. Larsen attributes this tentative, peer influenced decision making to a lack of adult role models and mentors. These young people were testing alternatives with little guidance and advice from experienced members of the profession. For many, their careers began only after their late twenties. Larsen remarks:

> The subjects pursued their lives in a manner fashioned more by events, opportunities and people, than by an overriding notion of where they were going, except that some of the subjects wanted to teach nursing. (p. 129)

Thus commitment to nursing occurred only when the subjects were between ages of 30 and 40, and most (7 of 10) of them decided only then to complete their educations, with four gaining their doctorates in those years.

Hardy's (1983) study of 36 influential female nurses in England and Scotland reveals similar findings. She explored the subjects' entire lives in an effort to identify factors that affected their life decisions. She found that the majority of the subjects, who ranged in age 39 to 71 years in 1981, came from middle-class families, had excelled in school, and were active in extracurricular and community work. One third of the subject group originally had other career goals but entered nursing for the same reasons given by Larsen's (1984) subjects. World War II also redirected several of the subjects into service for their country, namely nursing. As well, motivations for those wanting to enter nursing were vague and not career oriented.

Thus these British nurses embarked on careers that moved slowly for at least 10 years. Hardy proposes that career movement during the early career period constitutes a "lateral movement syndrome," in which there is little or no guidance to help young nurses make career decisions; they therefore make many lateral moves that keep them at a certain level in the profession. These moves were either educational or occupational. The subjects, as young nurses, changed jobs frequently or took short educational courses and always began again at the bottom of a new career ladder. On average, the women collected five qualifications each (not including the initial nursing qualification); most of these were nondegree nursing qualifications. Many of the subjects described their early careers as "drifting" or influenced by the advice of inexperienced peers. Hardy viewed her subjects' careers as being in two stages. In the second career stage, career stabilization and mobility were prime characteristics.

Hardy concludes that the influential nurses in her study could be grouped into the following five career patterns:

1. *Steady climbers* generally remained within a hospital setting in which a career ladder was visible. Progression was orderly and logical. Most did not experience the lateral movement syndrome because senior personnel provided guidance.
2. *Joiners* were lateral movers but broke the circle by entering teaching or administration and joining a career ladder.
3. *Fast movers*, a small group, moved from relatively junior positions into senior positions mainly by chance. The subjects themselves admitted there was little rational planning in these cases.
4. *Pioneers* were innovative despite the rigidity of the profession. Of the three who exemplify this pattern, creativity came late and arose out of necessity because the profession denied them influence in other spheres.
5. *Mavericks* broke all the unspoken rules and succeeded in unorthodox ways.

These career progression patterns indicate that career orientations for most began only with increasing age, generally around age 30. In both Larsen's (1984) and Hardy's (1983) research, subjects reported few helping relationships in the early part of their careers. It appears that the nursing profession was set on a course that encouraged only those who had "paid their dues" with long years of waiting.

Various authors comment on this tendency of female workers to "plan" the first decade of their working lives in a casual manner (Cohen, 1981; Dingwall and McIntosh, 1978; Hennig and Jardim, 1978; Pape, 1978). Current research in women's studies may help identify how society's changing attitudes about women and women's changing attitudes and expectations of themselves could affect nurses' work lives and commitments in the 1990s.

Vance, in a 1977 study of influential American nurses, asked her subjects to identify major disadvantages of belonging to a predominantly female profession. Five factors identified as more common to nurses are:

1. A self-image problem
2. Lack of career commitment
3. Lack of power and political know-how
4. Limited perspective
5. Family and personal responsibilities

The first four factors, in particular, may be generated during the relatively uneventful early career period of nurses. For example, an individual's self-esteem is reinforced by his or her experiences; if opportunities are not available, young nurses cannot grow and develop a sense of personal power and authority nor learn how to manipulate the political process through trial and error. These opportunities are especially important during the days of youth when the desire to try is greater than the desire for security. As a result, nursing loses many capable young people because they become frustrated with the system. An extended "weeding out" period may result in the loss of those who have a drive to attain and ambition to succeed— exactly the qualities needed for leadership and innovation in nursing.

As the average age of entrants to the profession increases and the average age of nurses in practice increases, nursing must identify how career movement affects career paths and career aspirations. To begin with, more data are needed to document what the work lives of "middle-aged" nurses encompass. For example, do employers recognize differences in physical stamina and complex lifestyle of the nurse in her twenties and the nurse in her fifties? Are there career opportunities that recognize age differences within the institution? Likewise, do schools of nursing adapt their programs to recognize the difference between the high school graduate and her needs and the mid-life individual entering nursing as a career for the first time? Attention to the nurse as an individual and to development of programs and policies that reflect this attention is imperative whether nursing is to be a lifelong career or a second career for individuals already in another occupation.

SOCIAL SUPPORT SYSTEMS

Since nurses work with others, the social supports they do or do not receive will affect how much they will accomplish within the profession. Two types of widely discussed social support in nursing are mentoring and networking.

Classic mentoring is described by Levinson and his colleagues (1978) as a relationship that benefits mentor and protege. The mentor is usually older by 8 to 15 years; has more experience and seniority; and teaches, sponsors, offers advice and support at critical stages, and welcomes the young protégé into the social, political, and cultural work scene. This crucial relationship helps the younger person negotiate barriers in the workplace. It may last a short or a long period of time. There is an intensity involved that is similar to a love relationship. Often, the impact of the relationship is recognized only after it has ended.

Various studies on female careers (Fogarty, Allen, Allen, and Walters, 1970; Gitterman, 1986; Hennig, 1970; Kanter, 1977; Phillips, 1977) identify mentoring as critical for advancement. In nursing, Vance (1977) explored mentor connections as an important career feature. In her sample of influential American nurses (99% female), 83% reported the presence of mentors with an average of two mentors per subject. Educators were prominent as mentors. Whether these mentors were inside nursing was not clearly distinguishable, although gender gave some indication; in the United States, females constitute approximately 97% of the nursing population, yet Vance's subjects report that 21% of mentors were male.

Larsen's (1984) study of Canadian nurses did not find mentoring to be a common experience. Only two of the ten subjects reported that they had been protégés before age 30. In the years between ages 30 and 40, four subjects had mentors—and two of the mentors were men outside of nursing. For most, the mentoring function was by female friends outside of the hierarchies in which the nurse was employed.

Mentoring proved to be of acknowledged importance to 60% of Hardy's (1983) British female nurse subjects. However, she found that less than half of the mentoring episodes occurred during the subjects' early years and that 36% of the experiences happened when the subjects were between 35 and 45 years of age; this would have been at a time when they should have been acting as mentors themselves. Nearly half of the mentors identified by Hardy's subjects were outside the profession, and 28% of the total number of reported mentors were males.

In her Canadian study of mentoring in a large tertiary care hospital, Gitterman (1986) interviewed 26 nurses who reported having mentors and identified the following as benefits:

- An increase in self-confidence
- Feedback about their strengths
- Help with career planning
- Access to challenging learning experiences
- Help with decision making

Gitterman's findings suggest that, for the nurses studied, mentor relationships help nurses cope with the frustrations common early in nursing careers. Twenty-three (88%) of Gitterman's subjects described their mentors as having more influence on them during their careers than friends, family, or spouses. "The successful relationship, built on warmth, trust, and understanding, was a powerful and central force in their professional lives" (p. 64).

The second type of social support system common in nursing is networking. Mentoring contributes to networking in that a circle of influential colleagues who can foster career development is created through contacts. However, formal networks such as professional associations and service clubs can be used and are said to accomplish various objectives, including support, communication, education, and social contact.

Two reports (Brockopp and Lee, 1985; Carr, 1982) suggest that networking does occur in the profession, both for social support and individual development. However, as with mentoring, the lack of a clear definition of its purposes has resulted in networking being related to a wide range of purposes. Thus studies link networking to better patient care (Meisenhelder, 1982), reduction of attrition rates (Anderson, Pierce, and Ringl, 1983), battling burnout (Francis, 1980), production of quality professional education (Presler and Bolte, 1982), and the effect on research development (Hunt et al., 1983). Career growth is considered a secondary or merely an unplanned by-product of networking. Two studies (Brockopp and Lee, 1985; Stern and Hirsch, 1984) explore networking with regard to career progress. Both are small, descriptive studies and compare Canadian and American nurses and their attempts to set up contacts; their reports indicate that networking was occurring.

Even an informal network (i.e., a group of individuals with similar professional interests) can be a helpful support. Many of these develop "naturally" from within a workplace and should be encouraged by nurse leaders as supports in career development. A combination of formal (a professional organization's interest groups are one such network) and informal networks can provide support and also direct assistance with the search for a new position or the problem solving associated with determining one's current job satisfaction. Networks therefore can range from annual reunions to monthly dinner clubs to regular meetings with formal agendas. All of these have as their primary function the support and informal education of their members.

Kanter (1977) notes that strategic alliances, of which mentoring and networking are examples, are empowering strategies. Without such strategies, there may not be sufficient scope for nurses to develop their careers. A "how-to" book for nurses by Puetz (1983) identifies the increasing popularity of these two social support processes.

A third form of social support—preceptorship—is being tested in nursing and has mentoring and networking functions (Greipp, 1989; Hitchings, 1989). A preceptor is often referred to as a "buddy" or a "practice partner," and is often a senior nurse assigned to a beginner to assist in easing the transition to a new workplace. The preceptor provides informal instruction about policies and procedures of the specific setting and generally provides support. Preceptorships are more and more visible in nursing workplaces as a means to combat reality shock and to aid in retention of nurses. McMaster-Chedoke Hospitals, Credit Valley Hospital, Women's College Hospital, and Hospital for Sick Children in Ontario and Greater Victoria Hospitals in British Columbia are a few examples of hospitals in which preceptorship is considered a viable and productive strategy. Within the next several years, evaluation of these programs could yield valuable data to add to the literature on social supports for nurses, as well as to the career path and career opportunity literature.

WORK SETTING

Work settings play an important part in the way individuals react to the work role and whether they will develop and expand and be retained within the profession. Nurses in Canada are, generally, employees of organizations. Knowledge about organizations, the workplace hierarchies, the roles nurses have in them, and the relationships between nurses and other workers is crucial to an understanding of how the collective nursing identity is developed. With this knowledge, individual nurses can participate in the development of policies that will help shape their futures.

In the mid-1970s, Kanter (1977) determined that the structure of organizations may be viewed along three dimensions: the structure of power, the structure of opportunity, and the proportional representation of different kinds of people. In hospitals, in which nearly three quarters of all nurses work, large numbers of nurses reside near the bottom of a hierarchical structure, and opportunities for career advancement are limited. The compartmentalization of hospitals into units of specialization further restricts opportunity for career advancement. Although some nurses work in nonhospital settings, these, with few exceptions, are also highly ordered, with the bulk of nurses at the bottom of the structure and with little opportunity for mobility within the workplace.

Further, opportunities for career development may be limited because authority (power) in most nursing agencies rests with a few individuals. Nurses usually do not occupy positions of ultimate authority, although in most hospitals nursing is the largest group and is responsible for the greater part of the hospital budget. In most work settings, nursing work is directed by others, primarily by hospital administrators or their agents and by physicians.

There is increasing interest in decentralization of nursing service as a strategy to deal with such power imbalances. Although decentralization can give individual professionals more power and move decision making closer to patients or clients, unless it is accompanied by changes to the structure to allow nurses to make and control decisions around the nursing care of patients, power will continue to remain with a few. Decentralization could mean that those providing care have a major role in decision making; alternatively it may merely be a "structural change that decreases the links in an organization's chain of command" (Wellington, 1986, p. 37). Most hospitals have some aspects of centralization and decentralization in their organization; more decentralization may provide more opportunities and power for the nurses at the bedside and more opportunity for creative and fresh ideas to emerge. However, it also can make coordination difficult and advancement less available (Wellington, 1986).

What is probably most important is that nurses be involved in determining the structure of the organization in which they work. At issue for nurses and nursing is control over nursing work. Work settings must be structured in such a way that opportunities for nursing control are maximized.

The "shared governance" model attracted considerable attention in recent years as a means of retaining experienced nurses, recruiting new nurses, and generally responding to the control over work issue. Shared governance is a way of enabling staff nurses to have more control of their work and practice and to ensure their centrality in the nursing department. The concept was made prominent by Porter-O'Grady and Finnigan (1984) and more recently was described in a Canadian context by Perry and Code (1991).

Self-scheduling is one of the results of shared governance models. This allows nurses on a unit or in an agency to plan and take responsibility for the schedule. This system gives nurses control of their work by giving them control over when they work. However, shared governance in and of itself implies a "way of doing business" and a value set, not merely an administrative activity (Belanger, Snell, and Fortier, 1991; Comack et al., 1991). Although self-scheduling is used in agencies primarily as a response to the retention issue, it might be better addressed from the career development perspective (i.e., conceptualized as a method to assist nurses in developing their potential as clinical leaders).

In a broader context, changes to the Public Hospitals Act in Ontario in 1989 provide for shared governance in the entire hospital. These changes require hospitals to develop bylaws that provide representation from staff and management nurses on decision-making committees (e.g., patient care and fiscal advisory committees). These kinds of changes, which seem to be happening throughout the country, provide opportunities for nurses to develop and grow professionally within the nursing role, particularly at the staff nurse level.

Staff nurses perform two roles in hospitals. They are agents of the institution and implementers of the cure/care process. They are therefore employees in a bureaucracy, as well as professionals. The conflict in these roles presents a central dilemma in career development. The nurse is hired as a professional practitioner with a particular set of skills but, if he or she is to advance up the administrative ladder, must develop and learn to use an additional set of general and administrative skills. The strategies needed by individuals and the needs of individuals are different at various points on the ladder. One result is that some nurses who achieve senior administrative positions are not secure and, as a result, are unable to assist staff nurses in their demands.

The importance of the structure of the work setting and its relationship to the professionalism and, more particularly, to the autonomy of the nurse also has a relationship to job satisfaction, to recruitment and retention of qualified professionals, and to career development and mobility. Spitzer (1981) suggests that "large numbers of our more talented, self-directed nurses have found hospitals too stifling an environment in which to work and have sought other alternatives, such as ambulatory care settings for the practice of nursing, or other alternatives outside of nursing entirely" (p. 241).

CAREER PLANNING AND DEVELOPMENT

Enrollment in schools of nursing in the United States declined in the 1980s and shows only a very small increase into recovery in the 1990s. In Canada, concern is increasing about the need to ensure that nursing remains an attractive career opportunity. Schools of nursing report fewer applicants in general and also fewer well-qualified applicants. It seems as if the potential pool of applicants shrinks as opportunities for the "traditional" nursing applicant grows. Demand for admission to nursing education also may weaken as other professions, with more perceived opportunity for autonomy, compete with nursing for applicants. It is crucial that work settings and work experiences remain attractive, challenging, and sensitive to nurses'—and to women's—needs if nursing is to recruit the "best and brightest" into its ranks. But once the nurse is recruited, the challenge for professional organizations and employers is to develop a partnering relationship with the nurse so that, through better career planning and development, progression throughout the individual's career life can be rewarding and productive.

Career planning may be defined as "a continuous process of self-assessment and goal setting" (Kleinknecht and Hefferin, 1982, p. 31). Although career planning was once considered an activity and a responsibility of the individual, during the 1980s critics began urging employers to assume a role in assisting employees with career planning (Hudek, 1990; Kleinknecht and Hefferin, 1982; Sovie, 1983). As Hudek (1990) notes: "Employers and professional associations need to combine forces so that nurses have access to career planning" (p. 19). Because nursing shortages likely will continue, recruitment and retention strategies will become more and more important to employers, and the concept of a partnership in development is likely to become more important. Employers can provide assistance with orientation and inservice education and also with career and professional development. In exchange, as it were, nurses will remain in the work force and continue to provide employers with their skill as experienced providers of patient care. Both parties contribute and both parties gain.

In a description of such a career planning model, Kleinknecht and Hefferin (1982) identify the nurse's responsibilities as career status evaluation, interest and skills assessment, and career action planning; the employer's responsibilities include status evaluation of the employee, needs assessment, action planning, and career counseling. Sovie (1982) describes a model for developing nursing careers in the hospital setting and identifies three phases in the nurse's professional development: professional identification, which includes orientation and helps nurses identify their practice role; professional maturation, which focuses on staff development for career advancement, professional recognition, and professional satisfaction. This model formed the basis for a "career ladder" or professional advancement model.

With professional advancement and career development models developing almost daily, it is timely to consider the entire process of career development within nurses' professional lives. Figure 18-1 identifies four phases within nurses' careers. This model can help nurses, educational programs, professional associations, and employers identify kinds of programs and activities that aid the individual in professional advancement, whether as a clinician, a researcher, an administrator, or an educator.

The model shows that all phases of career development exist on a continuum, and that, although there is movement from one phase to another, there is also overlap between the phases. Phase One, the entry phase, involves selection of the first workplace by the newly registered nurse. In this phase, the nurse may select a position based on a previous decision regarding the type of practice he or she wishes to do, or may assess all the positions available and then select the one that "looks best." Nurses must learn to ask certain questions that will assist them in assessing the proposed workplace as a career-oriented entry position (see box). Assistance with this phase should be the joint responsibility of the almost-nurse and the educational program.

Questions to Ask on Entry to the Nursing Work Force

What is the selection process (e.g., individual, committee)?
What is the agency's philosophy and mission? the nursing department's?
What is the nursing delivery system?
What is the organizational structure of the agency and the work unit?
Is there an orientation program and, if so, how long is it and what is the content?
Is there an ongoing professional development program and, if so, what is its content and approach?
What is the delivery system used for staff education and development (i.e., unit-based, department-based, organization-wide)?
What are the supports available for continuing education?
What are the educational preparations of the staff in the nursing department?
Are there Clinical Nurse Specialists?
Is there a preceptor program, a clinical advancement program, a career planning program?
Is there a union? a staff nurse association?
What are the salary and benefits?

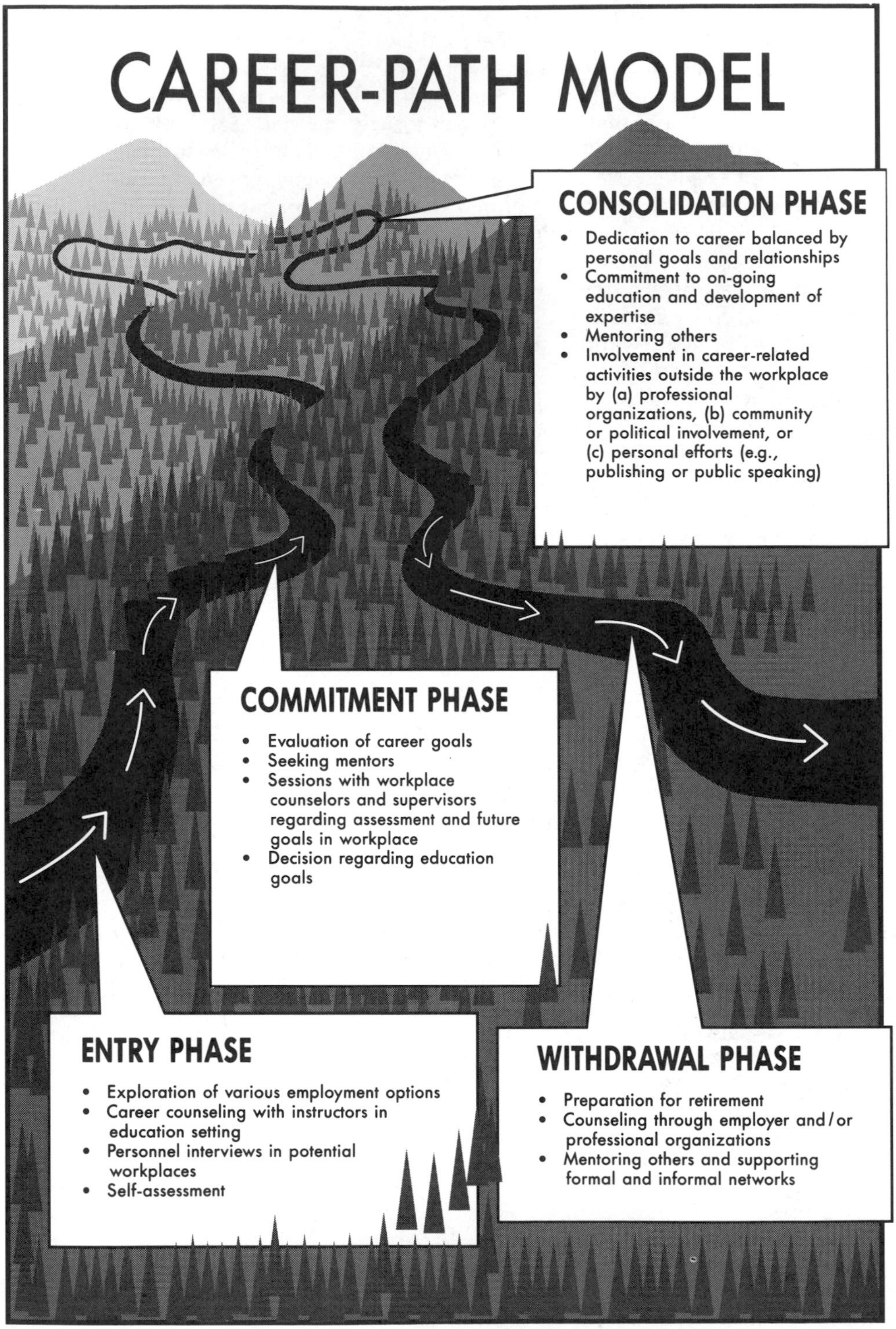

CAREER-PATH MODEL

CONSOLIDATION PHASE

- Dedication to career balanced by personal goals and relationships
- Commitment to on-going education and development of expertise
- Mentoring others
- Involvement in career-related activities outside the workplace by (a) professional organizations, (b) community or political involvement, or (c) personal efforts (e.g., publishing or public speaking)

COMMITMENT PHASE

- Evaluation of career goals
- Seeking mentors
- Sessions with workplace counselors and supervisors regarding assessment and future goals in workplace
- Decision regarding education goals

ENTRY PHASE

- Exploration of various employment options
- Career counseling with instructors in education setting
- Personnel interviews in potential workplaces
- Self-assessment

WITHDRAWAL PHASE

- Preparation for retirement
- Counseling through employer and/or professional organizations
- Mentoring others and supporting formal and informal networks

FIGURE 18-1 The four phases of career development.

Phase Two is the commitment phase. In this phase, nurses identify their likes and dislikes (e.g., clinical areas, geography, functional areas). This phase usually begins anywhere from the second to the fifth year of practice and ends with the nurse's commitment to a particular place and type of practice. This may be the time when nurses consider continuing their education, either to consolidate specialty knowledge with short courses and/or graduate work or to advance general nursing knowledge with baccalaureate preparation. This phase should involve cooperation between the individual nurse and the employing institution, with assistance from the professional organizations (including nursing associations and unions). Obviously, if employers were to take an active role in this phase, it could prove beneficial in terms of retention and in development of highly qualified and experienced staff.

Phase Three is the consolidation phase. The nurse becomes comfortable with the chosen career path, and work life, professional life, and personal life all fit together. At this stage, nurses often become active in their unions or professional associations, on workplace committees, or in community affairs. Negotiating this phase could be shared among the individual, the professional organizations, and the workplace.

Phase Four is the withdrawal phase. During this period, individuals prepare for retirement. The stresses, physical and emotional, of the job may need to be assessed and options found. Planning for financial security will be important. Experience in business organizations in Canada (e.g., Chrysler Canada and Bank of Montreal) may indicate that health care employers, professional organizations, and individual nurses can participate jointly in this endeavor.

Research to support this and other models of career development in nursing is virtually nonexistent. However, as career planning becomes something that both employers and employees value highly and see as a partnership activity with benefits accruing to both parties, perhaps it will also become an appropriate and interesting area of research.

ISSUES AND IMPLICATIONS

Lack of support for nursing as a career can have consequences in future decades. In a rapidly changing world, commitment to a profession cannot wait for 10 years. Nor can society invest in preparing individuals for careers only to have them leave without contributing to that career. Much valuable time and opportunities for innovations in health care will be lost. Three main areas particularly need to be addressed: individual nurses have false values and perceptions about their role in society; senior people in the profession do not acknowledge the need to promote others; and nursing workplaces have inflexible structures.

What can be done? In 1971 Stanley Mitchell noted:

> Nurses often move towards the fringes of nursing and out of nursing entirely because of the limitations of nursing. Our research suggests that nursing will be more balanced and less age decimated when the profession offers more rewards to the individuals who remain within it. (p. 267)

The "rewards," or incentives, for the career investment that Mitchell refers to can occur at individual, professional, or societal levels. Occasionally they may occur on all levels at the same time. An example of this is the need for a change in attitude about women having careers for their own satisfaction.

Earlier in the chapter it was noted that many nursing authors view mentoring and networking activities as solutions for various nursing problems. This may be a subtle denial of the needs and aspirations of individual nurses. The service ethic is so well bound to nursing that nurses feel guilty when they ask to meet their own needs, be it for decent wages and working conditions or for career ambitions. A balance between meeting nurses' needs and those of others must be established.

Some employing agencies are tackling this problem enthusiastically (Best, Burke, Walsh, and Mulchey, 1991; Perry and Code, 1991). They encourage innovation, support advanced education, and allow participation in decision making about one's own work. Such experiences must become widespread.

Plans for educational preparation should be rational in terms of the needs of society and of the individual, and flexible in that transferability, especially at the basic level, is possible. The reality in Canadian society today is that the population is highly mobile and that many women return to their careers after having a family if they do not continue during the years they bring up a family. Thus, mature students now constitute up to one third of university populations. These students have special needs, and these needs must be considered and met.

At present, the nursing profession is establishing its position among other health professions. The drive for recognition as an autonomous profession is emphasized in education at both the basic and continuing levels. However, educators must review how current programs may reinforce existing power and opportunity structures and discourage autonomous behavior. Are faculty members acceptable role models for independent, professional behavior, or are they merely supporting the status quo? Are clinical experiences chosen with attention to their socializing influences or just because of the clinical opportunities they provide?

Organizers of orientation, staff development, and continuing education programs must heed the ongoing socialization of the professional. Emphasis must be given in these programs to helping nurses understand the systems within which they work, the dynamics of relationships between and among health professionals, and the opportunities available for nurses to make significant changes in health care.

Employers of nurses (most often themselves nurses) must also explore the structure of the work setting and seek, with their employees, creative methods for recognizing and rewarding the work of nurses. Clinical excellence, leadership skills, and creativity should be identified, encouraged, and rewarded. Clinical ladders are one way in which these behaviors may be rewarded. Opportunities as preceptors to senior students and new graduates are other ways.

Senior professional nurses must evaluate their own roles in promoting younger nurses. Are they mentors? Do they provide opportunities for younger nurses to test reality? Do they know when to relinquish leadership positions and create space for new leaders? Some form of career counseling is needed; it should reflect the reality of women working in Canada today.

Larsen (1984) remarks: "Careful career planning would seem to be essential to ensure continued growth and productivity" (p. 309). Career development in nursing encourages satisfaction, achievement, and a sense of self that allows risk taking and innovation. All of these accomplishments reflect favorably on the profession and the work done for others.

REFERENCES

American Hospital Association (AHA). (1989). A model for hospital nurse retention: New findings. *Nursing Economics, 1*(6), 324-331.

Anderson, S.L. (1989). The nurse advocate project: A strategy to retain new graduates. *Journal of Nursing Administration, 19*(12), 22-26.

Anderson, R., Pierce, I., & Ringl, K. (1983). Networking: A method of retaining nursing staff. *Journal of Nursing Administration, 13*(9), 26-28.

Attridge, C., & Callahan, M. (1990). Nurses' perspectives of quality work environments. *Canadian Journal of Nursing Administration, 3*(3), 18-24.

Barhyte, D.Y. (1987). Levels of practice and retention of staff nurses. *Nursing Management, 18*(3), 70-72.

Belanger, D., Snell, C., & Fortier, W. (1991). Self-scheduling on trial. *Canadian Nurse, 87*(3), 17-19.

Benner, P. (1984). *From novice to expert:Excellence and power in clinical nursing practice.* Menlo Park, CA: Addison-Wesley.

Best, J.A., Burke, B.E., Walsh, R.G., & Mulchey, R.D. (1991). Healthy hospitals: Improving nursing worklife. *Dimensions in Health Sciences, 68*(4), 27-29.

Brockopp, D., & Lee, M. (1985). Women in academic nursing: Networking and mentoring. In *Nurses in academia - expecations, options, realities: Proceedings of the Annual Meeting of Western Region, Canadian Association of University Schools of Nursing* (pp. 67-82). Edmonton: University of Alberta.

Brooten, D.A., Hayman, L.L., & Naylor, M.D. (1979). *Leadership for change: A guide for the frustrated nurse.* New York: Lippincott.

Brown, J.S., Swift, Y.B., & Oberman, M.L. (1974). Baccalaureate students' images of nursing: A replication. *Nursing Research, 25,* 53-59.

Canadian Nurses Association & Canadian Hospital Association. (1990). *Nurse retention and quality of worklife: A national perspective.* Ottawa: Canadian Nurses Association.

Carr, E.M. (1982). Networking: A resource for change. *Nurse Practitioner, 7,* 32-34.

Cohen, H.A. (1981). *The nurses' quest for a professional identity.* Menlo Park, CA: Addison-Wesley.

Comack, M., Smith, S.D., Bowman, A., Gillow, K., Hunt, M., Snell, L., Thomsen, F., & Turner, D. (1991). Planning change in scheduling practises: A theoretical perspective. *Canadian Journal of Nursing Administration, 4*(1), 17-21.

Cotanch, P.H. (1981). Self-actualization and professional socialization of nursing students in the clinical laboratory experience. *Journal of Nursing Education, 20*(8), 4-14.

Desjean, G. (1975). *The problem of leadership in French Canadian nursing.* Unpublished doctoral dissertation, Wayne State University, Michigan.

Dingwall, R., & McIntosh, I. (1973). *Readings in the sociology of nursing.* London: Churchill Livingstone.

Donner, G.J. (1986). *Work setting and the professional socialization of nurses.* Unpublished doctoral dissertation, University of Toronto, Toronto, Ontario.

Donovan, M. (1990). What we need to change about nursing: Staff nurses share their ideas. *Journal of Nursing Administration, 20*(12), 38-42.

Fogarty, M., Allen, A.J., Allen I., & Walters, P. (1970). *Women in top jobs.* London: George Allen and Unwin.

Francis, B. (1980). A nursing network to battle burnout. *The Journal of Practical Nursing, 11,* 25-27.

George, T.B. (1982). Development of the self-concept of nursing in nursing students. *Research in Nursing and Health, 5*(19), 191-197.

Gitterman, G.E. (1986). *Mentors in nursing.* Unpublished Masters thesis, University of Toronto, Toronto, Ontario.

Grantham, M., et al. (1989). Recruiting and retaining competent clinical nurses. *Canadian Journal of Nursing Administration, 2*(2), 8-10.

Greipp, M.E. (1989). Nursing preceptors: Looking back, looking ahead. *Journal of Nursing Staff Development, 5,* 183-186.

Hardy, L.K. (1983). *An exploration of the career histories of leading female nurses in England and Scotland.* Unpublished doctoral dissertation, Edinburgh University, Edinburgh.

Hennig, M. (1970). *Career development for women executives.* Unpublished doctoral dissertation, Harvard University, Cambridge, MA.

Hennig, M., & Jardim, A. (1978). *The managerial women.* New York: Pocket Books.

Hinshaw, A.S. (1977). *Social and resocialization of nurses for professional nurse practice* (NLN Publication No. 15-1959). New York: National League for Nursing.

Hitchings, K.S. (1989). Preceptors promote competence and retention: Strategies to achieve success. *The Journal of Continuing Education in Nursing, 20*(6), 255-360.

Hospital Council of Metropolitan Toronto (HCMT). (1985). *Report of the HCMT Nursing Manpower Task Force*. Toronto: Author.

Hospital Research and Educational Trust. (1989). A model for hospital nurse retention: New findings. *Nursing Economics, 7*(6), 324-331.

Hudek, K. (1990). Nursing: Make it a career. *The Canadian Nurse, 86*(2), 18-19.

Hunt, V., Stark, J., Fisher, F., Hegedus, K., Joy, L., & Woldum, K. (1983). Networking: A managerial strategy for research development in a service setting. *Journal of Nursing Administration, 13*, 27-83.

Kanter, R.M. (1977). *Men and women of the corporation*. New York: Basic Books.

Kasparin, C., & Young, W. (1985). Nurse internship program reduces turnover, raises commitment. *Nursing and Health Care, 6*(3), 136-140.

Kleinknecht, M.K. & Hefferin, E.A. (1982). Assisting nurses toward professional growth: A career development model. *Journal of Nursing Administration, 12*(5), 30-36.

Kramer, M. (1974). *Reality shock: Why nurses leave nursing*. St. Louis: C.V. Mosby.

Kramer, M. (1981). Why does reality shock continue?In J. McClosky & H. Grace (Eds.), *Current issues in nursing* (pp. 644-653). Boston: Blackwell Scientific Publications.

Larsen, J.B. (1984). *A psychosocial study of the career development of selected nurses with earned doctoral degrees*. Unpublished doctoral dissertation, University of Alberta, Edmonton.

Levinson, D.J., Darrow, C.M., Klein, E.G., Levinson, M.J., & McKee, B. (1978). *The seasons of a man's life*. New York: Ballantine Books.

McCloskey, J. (1990). Two requirements for job contentment: Autonomy and social integration. *Image, 22*(3), 140-143.

Meisenhelder, J.B. (1982). Networking and nursing.*Image, 14*(3), 77-80.

Meleis, A.I., & Dagenais, F. (1981). Sex-role identity and perception of professional self. *Nursing Research, 30*, 162-167.

Merton, R., Reader, G., & Kendall, P. (1957). *The student physician*. Cambridge: Harvard University Press.

Mitchell, S. (1971). *A woman's profession...a man's research*. Calgary: University of Calgary.

Murray, L.M., & Morris, D.R. (1982). Professional autonomy among senior nursing students in diploma, associate degree, and baccalaureate nursing programs. *Nursing Research, 31*, 311-313.

Ontario Hospital Association (OHA). (1991). *Valued workplaces: Hospital snapshots*. Toronto: Author.

Pape, R. (1978). Touristry: A type of occupational mobility. In R. Dingwall & J. McIntosh (Eds.), *Readings in the sociology of nursing* (pp. 56-66). London: Churchill Livingstone.

Perry, F. & Code, S. (1991). Shared governance: A Canadian experience. *Canadian Journal of Nursing Administration*, 4(2), 27-28, 30.

Phillips, L.L. (1977). *Mentors and proteges: A study of the career development of women managers and executives in business and industry.* Unpublished doctoral dissertation, UCLA, Los Angeles.

Porter-O'Grady, T. (1989). Shared governance-Reality or sham? *American Journal of Nursing,* 89(3), 350-351.

Porter-O'Grady, T., & Finnigan, S. (1984). *Shared governance for nursing.* Rochville, MD: Aspen Systems Corporation.

Presler, E.P., & Bolte, I.M. (1982). Discovering resources for continuing education. *Nursing Outlook,* 30(3), 454-458.

Puetz, B.E. (1983). *Networking for nurses.* Rockville, MD: Aspen Systems Corp.

Registered Nurses' Association of British Columbia (RNABC). (1989). *Increasing nurse satisfaction: A guide to improving retention.* Vancouver: Author.

Simpson, I. (1979). *From student to nurse: A longitudinal study of socialization.* Cambridge: Cambridge University Press.

Singh, A. (1979). The student nurse on experimental courses. Attitudes towards nursing as a career. *International Journal of Nursing Studies,* 7, 201-224.

Sovie, M.D. (1982). Fostering professional nurse careers in hospitals: The role of staff development, Part 1. *Journal of Nursing Administration,* 12 (12), 5-10.

Sovie, M.D. (1983). Fostering professional nurse careers in hospitals: The role of staff development, Part 2. *Journal of Nursing Administration,* 13 (1), 30-33.

Spitzer, R. (1981). Alternatives in hospital nursing. In J.C. McClosky & H.K. Grace (Eds.), *Current issues in nursing* (pp. 241-250). Boston: Blackwell Scientific Publications.

Stern, P.M., & Hirsh, G.A. (1984, October). *Networking in nursing: A strategy for peer support.* Paper presented at the First International Congress on Women's Health Issues, Halifax.

Thomas, J.G., Bounds, W.T., & Brown, G. (1991). Helping nurses adjust: Who provides what job information? *Journal of Nursing Staff Development,* 7(3), 130-133.

Vance, C.M. (1977). *A group profile of contemporary influentials in American nursing.* Unpublished doctoral dissertation, Columbia University, New York.

Watson, A.B. (1982). Professional socialization of the Registered Nurse as measured by attitudes and problems identification skills. *Dissertation Abstracts International.* (University Microfilms No. 8304197).

Wellington, M. (1986). Decentralization: How it affects nurses. *Nursing Outlook, 34,* 36-39.

Regulation of health care professionals to ensure public safety will be under review during the 1990s. Regulation of nursing (registration, licensure) in most provinces is carried on by the professional nurses' associations. However, in Ontario, the regulatory function is the responsibility of the College of Nurses of Ontario. This photograph shows some of the members of the Council of the College of Nurses at its meeting in January 1992 *(from left):* President Pat Mandy, Executive Director Margaret Risk, and Executive Assistant Jenna Hofbauer. (Photograph is by Lynette Fortune, Print Production Coordinator and Writer for the College of Nurses of Ontario.)

CHAPTER NINETEEN

Regulatory Issues

MARGARET RISK, RN, MScN

Margaret Risk, RN, BScN, MScN (Toronto), has been Executive Director of the College of Nurses of Ontario since 1982. Previously she held positions in community health and education and in the Registered Nurses Association of Ontario. In her current position, she has worked closely with government and other professions in a comprehensive review of the health professions' legislation in Ontario.

Regulation may be defined as the forms and processes by which order, consistency, and control are brought to a practice or policy. In Canada, the public interest provides the basis for regulatory legislation and is strongly influenced by the views of specific groups in society. Nurses are subject to multiple regulatory controls in the workplace: legislation governing their profession (professional regulation), legislation governing their particular agency (e.g., public hospitals, nursing homes), legislation applicable to work settings (e.g., occupational health and safety), labor legislation (e.g., collective bargaining), and legislation for society as a whole (e.g., human rights/charter). This chapter focuses on professional regulation. The influences of professional regulation in the workplace, regardless of setting, are fundamental to the practice and practice relationships of nurses and the health professionals with whom they interact on a daily basis.

Professional regulation is based on the assumption of vulnerability, that patients or clients lack the knowledge necessary to protect their own interests in dealing with professional practitioners. Its basic purpose, therefore, is to protect the public's health, safety, and welfare. In Canada, the responsibility for the regulation and credentialing of health professions rests with the provincial governments.

Nursing has been granted, as have other health professions, the privilege of self-regulation and receives its authority under government statute. Self-regulation acknowledges the special knowledge of a profession and allows it to act as an agent of government in regulating its own members. When authority is delegated to a professional group, it is expected that this authority will be exercised in the public interest. Whereas there is a conflict between public and professional self-interest, governing bodies are expected to support the public interest. For example, in the event of job action by members of a health profession, the governing body's primary concern would be that the level of service does not decrease to the extent that it compromises the safety of the client.

Regulation of the health professions is one of a limited number of mechanisms available to government through which it directs the provincial health care system. Although other mechanisms such as allocation of financial resources and manpower planning are largely directed at influencing the nature of the services provided, professional regulation is directed at regulating both the nature and the quality of those services (Schwartz, 1989, p. 5).

Regulation of practitioners may be achieved through "licensure," which restricts practice to individuals who hold a license, or through "title control," which restricts the use of a particular title. "Registration" is the term commonly applied to title control. Physicians, for example, are licensed to practice medicine; anyone practicing without a license may be charged by the governing body in the particular jurisdiction. Nurses, on the other hand, traditionally have not been licensed, but the legislation protects use of such titles as "registered nurse," "registered nursing assistant," or "nurse"; anyone using these titles who is not currently registered may be charged with representing themselves as something they are not. "Certification," another regulatory term, usually applies to a nonstatutory, voluntary process (e.g., specialty certification).

NURSING LEGISLATION

Statutory regulation for nursing first appeared early in this century. Nova Scotia nurses were the first to secure such legislation, in 1910; this provided only for voluntary registration, and nonregistered graduates could also practice (Canadian Nurses Association, 1968). Historical debates on nursing governance contain recurring themes, particularly in relation to elements of statutory regulation. For example, governments and professional bodies have argued over such matters as the amount of government control necessary and/or desirable; whether its purpose is to protect the public, practitioners, or both; whether its powers should restrict the right to practice to qualified individuals (mandatory) or merely to confer titles (permissive); and how many levels or categories should be recognized (Styles, 1984, p. 19).

In 1983, the International Council of Nurses (ICN) adopted an official position on regulation and commissioned a project, directed by Dr. Margretta Styles of the University of California, San Francisco, to conduct a worldwide study on nursing regulatory systems. The overall findings revealed "that the structure of the profession is ill defined and diverse; educational requirements and legal definitions are generally inadequate for the complexity and expansion of the nursing role as it is emerging in response to health care needs; and the goals and standards of the profession world-

Twelve Principles of Professional Regulation (endorsed by ICN, 1985)

I. Purposefulness. Regulation should be directed toward a specific purpose.

II. Relevance. Regulation should be designed to achieve the stated purpose.

III. Definition. Regulatory standards should be based on clear definitions of professional scope and accountability.

IV. Professional ultimacy. Regulatory definitions and standards should promote the fullest development of the profession commensurate with its potential social contribution.

V. Multiple interests and responsibilities. Regulatory systems should recognize and properly incorporate the legitimate roles and responsibilities of interested parties—public, profession and its members, government, employers, other professions—in aspects of standard setting and administration.

VI. Representational balance. The design of the regulatory system should acknowledge and appropriately balance interdependent interests.

VII. Optimacy. Regulatory systems should provide and be limited to those controls and restrictions necessary to achieve their objectives.

VIII. Flexibility. Standards and processes of regulation should be sufficiently broad and flexible to achieve their objectives and at the same time permit freedom for innovation, growth, and change.

IX. Efficiency and congruence. Regulatory systems should operate in the most efficient manner, ensuring coherence and coordination among their parts.

X. Universality. Regulatory systems should promote universal standards of performance and foster professional identity and mobility to the fullest extent compatible with local needs and circumstances.

XI. Fairness. Regulatory processes should provide honest and just treatment for those parties regulated.

XII. Interprofessional equality and compatibility. In standards and processes, regulatory systems should recognize the equality and interdependence of professions.

From Styles MM: (1986). Credentialing in nursing: contemporary developments and trends, Kansas City: American Nurses Association. Used with permission.

wide are less apparent than 50 years ago" (Styles, 1986, p. 14). Consequently, in 1988, ICN initiated a follow-up project on regulation. This project was to assist national nurses' associations to develop and implement strategies and plans to establish regulatory systems that would assist the profession to reach its fullest potential in meeting present and future health needs. Representatives from nursing associations throughout the world have met to implement the project. Canada's specific aims in the project are to increase awareness and support of the 12 ICN Principles of Professional Regulation endorsed by ICN in 1985 (see box) and to secure endorsement of the guidelines for nurse specialist development with respect to title, scope of practice, regulation, standards, and methods.

NURSING LEGISLATION IN CANADA

In Canada, the approaches and forms of regulation vary between provinces and between professional groups in the same province. Statutory powers are designated under an Act passed by each provincial legislature, such as the *Nurses (Registered) Act* in British Columbia or the *Regulated Health Professions Act* and the *Nursing Act* in Ontario. Generally, there are similarities in the legislative authority (or power) granted to a regulatory body under legislation. The differences are in structure and in the specific mechanisms by which that authority is carried out. Some of these similarities and differences are described below.

Legislative authority usually includes responsibility for the following:
1. Entry to practice (new practitioners from basic educational programs and already credentialed practitioners from other provinces or countries)
2. Registration
3. Use of title
4. Scope of practice
5. Professional discipline
6. Establishing standards of practice
7. Monitoring competence and quality assurance
8. Accrediting educational programs

The provincial and territorial nursing legislation includes all or most of the responsibilities listed. An example of a difference in the legislative authority is that of Alberta or Ontario, where accreditation of nursing education programs is not included in the nursing legislation but is handled under a different body.

Structurally, there is more variation. With the exception of Ontario, the regulatory responsibility resides with the provincial or territorial professional associations. In most provinces, registered nurses and registered nursing assistants (also called certified nursing assistants, licensed nursing assistants, or licensed practical nurses, depending on the province) are regulated by separate organizations. In the four Western provinces, psychiatric nurses are regulated under separate legislation. In Ontario, where the regulatory function is separate from the professional function, both registered nurses and registered nursing assistants are regulated under one body.

The uniqueness in Ontario is based on the philosophical premise that there is an inherent conflict (real or perceived) between professional self-interest and public interest, and that regulatory decisions must be separate from profession advancement. Obviously, professional associations are genuinely concerned about public safety and quality practice. The debate, however, surfaces occasionally in the other provinces (most recently in British Columbia and Alberta). The controversy is whether an association that has as one of its goals the promotion of the profession can truly prevent maintenance of status and territorial protection from interfering with regulatory decision making. An example of this potential conflict, often cited in the current climate, is that of the position taken by professional associations on baccalaureate preparation as educational entry level for practice. The position, rightly or wrongly, is perceived by many in government, unions, and the public as a status issue rather than a public safety or quality effectiveness issue.

Regarding specific regulatory mechanisms, there are a number of differences between provinces. Strict comparison is difficult because legislative terminology differs and individual acts change. In nursing, mandatory registration and protection of title are the most common forms of regulatory credentials. All provinces protect the title "Registered Nurse"; some protect "Nurse." "Registered Nursing Assistant," "Certified Nursing Assistant," "Licensed Nursing Assistant," "Licensed Practical Nurse," and "Registered Psychiatric Nurse" are protected titles depending on the particular province. Requirements for reentry to practice after a period of absence vary considerably, and mechanisms to monitor ongoing competence are in differing stages of development. In Quebec, fluency in the French language is a requirement for practice; New Brunswick and Ontario require English or French; and the remaining provinces require English. Particularly in the area of entry to registration, the provinces are working toward removing unnecessary barriers to interprovincial mobility by standardizing entry requirements. Because of particular legislative requirements and varying provincial standards, however, reciprocal registration throughout the nation is not yet a reality.

TRENDS IN PROFESSIONAL REGULATION

Professional self-regulation can be traced to medieval guilds. The primary motivation underlying professional guilds even as late as the twentieth century was the desire to exercise monopoly power on behalf of members (Lieberman, 1976). As government was recognized as a central authority reflecting the public interest, professions sought government support and recognition of professional authority to protect the public from unqualified persons. Economic theorists postulate that, in a free market, competition provides the best mechanism for meeting consumer needs. In health care, however, it was believed that the consumer of health care is at a disadvantage in terms of knowledge and information and is not in a position to judge the quality of the service he or she needs or is receiving. As the following paragraphs will explain, this traditional belief is beginning to shift.

Since the early 1970s, the public, the media, and the bureaucrats displayed misgivings about professional self-regulation; reviews of existing professional regulation and requests for regulation by new groups operated in an environment characterized by this increasing distrust of professional self-regulation (Boase, 1986; Gaumer, 1984; Gross, 1984; Shimberg, 1982). Governing bodies increasingly are seen as protecting their members before protecting the public interest. Consumers are challenging the inaccessibility and paternalism of self-regulatory processes and the inability of governing bodies to ensure the competence of practitioners. Many of these attitudes toward professional self-regulation are related to broader social trends, such as challenges to traditional authority, democratization and increased public participation, increased educational level of consumers, and increased social and legal support for the protection of human and civil rights. There is evidence that there may be the beginning of a transition from protection based on the assumption of consumer vulnerability to regulation emphasizing consumer rights and needs. Consent and other rights issues are moving from the "soft" regulatory area of ethics to the "hard" regulatory area of protection mechanisms based on human rights legislation, values, and policies.

Health systems and health policy are moving toward decision making based on knowledge of what works (i.e., a transition from models based on consensus to research based models). Negotiation and consultation between different, sometimes competing, interests will continue to be central to the decision-making process. Evidence for the rationale of decisions, however, particularly as it relates to enhanced public protection and public accountability, will need to increase. This shift has implications for nursing regulation because of the strong tradition of consensus models within the profession. For example, most provincial nursing standards of practice have been structured around nursing processes rather than around outcomes measured in terms of safety and effectiveness for patients or clients. Criteria for evaluation of public protection mechanisms arising from this shift must be developed based on what is safe and effective, what the public needs, and what factors change behavior and practice.

The increased interest by many professional groups in case management, with its emphasis on client outcomes, may assist future regulation by integrating data bases of provider performance, utilization, and competence with organizational and outcome data bases. Also gaining support in most provinces is recognition of a need for consolidation of goals: goals of the jurisdiction for its population's health, of the provider organization or facility, of the profession or professions, and of the public for satisfactory outcomes. As a result, the future of regulation likely will be increasingly interdisciplinary; more integrated nationally, provincially, and locally; and more related to systemwide, population-based quality assessment and improvement.

CURRENT AND FUTURE ISSUES IN PROFESSIONAL REGULATION

Many issues in professional regulation for all health providers are being extensively debated and will have significant effects on the workplace because they will affect practice relationships and quality of care. Many of these issues relate to the trends described in the previous section and are also reflected in the section later in this chapter (see "Other legislation—interrelationships and influences"). Some of the more timely issues concern scope of practice, auxiliary personnel, quality assurance, professional discipline, public accountability, and barriers to entry to the profession. Each will be discussed in detail.

Scope of Practice

The way scope of practice is legislated is one of the critical elements of professional regulation. Regulation defines the practice and describes the boundaries within which a particular profession operates. Definitions of scope of practice may be broad, allowing the practitioner to act to the limit of his or her judgment and ability, or restrictive, relating to specific procedures. These boundaries are functionally, philosophically, and politically determined (Styles, 1986). Legislated definitions of scope of practice of nursing vary widely across the provinces. Examples of what is included in three recent pieces of legislation related to scope of practice are listed in the box.

Examples of Legislated Scope of Practice

Alberta

A registered nurse and a certified graduate nurse are entitled to apply professional nursing knowledge for the purpose of
(a) promoting, maintaining or restoring health;
(b) preventing illness, injury or disability;
(c) caring for the injured, disabled or incapacitated;
(d) assisting in childbirth;
(e) teaching nursing theory or practice;
(f) caring for the dying;
(g) co-ordinating health care;
(h) engaging in the administration, education, teaching or research required to implement or complement exclusive nursing practice or all or any of the matters referred to in clauses (a) to (g).

Nursing Profession Act (Alberta, 1987)

British Columbia

The "practice of nursing" means the performance for others of health care services that require the application of professional nursing knowledge and skills and includes
(a) promoting, maintaining or restoring the health of the general public,
(b) teaching nursing theory or practice,
(c) counselling persons in respect of health care,
(d) coordinating health care services, and
(e) engaging in administration, supervision, education, consultation, teaching or research for any of the foregoing.

Nurses (Registered) Act Rules, Part I
(British Columbia, 1988)

Quebec

Every act the object of which is to identify the health needs of persons, contribute to methods of diagnosis, provide and control the nursing care required for the promotion of health, prevention of illness, treatment and rehabilitation, and to provide care according to a medical prescription constitutes the profession of nursing.

Nurses Act RSQ, Chapter I (Quebec, 1989)

Quoted from Provincial Acts.

Traditionally, scope of practice was a means to maintain a monopoly over a particular area of practice. Professions have an interest in protecting and extending their scope of practice as far as possible, preferably to the exclusion of other practitioners. Although monopoly may be advantageous to the profession that wields it, Schwartz (1989) notes that it is difficult to justify any monopoly in terms of public interest. The trend in theory, if not in practice, is away from restricted forms of regulation, such as "licensure," which limit the right to practice to only those who are licensed. Although licensure may be warranted for certain occupation groups to protect the public and to ensure some degree of practitioner competency, the decision to license is increasingly being weighed against some of the negative effects.

In Ontario, a proposal for a unique legislated model for scope of practice is being viewed with interest by jurisdictions in Canada and the United States. The model is the same for all the regulated health professions and consists of a general statement (scope of practice) describing what the particular profession does and a series of controlled acts specific to that profession. The model, through the controlled acts, recognizes that some of the activities performed by health care providers pose a risk of harm if they are performed by unqualified persons. It also reflects the belief, however, that some health care services are not intrinsically hazardous, and that individuals should have freedom to choose the caregivers from whom they obtain these services; thus the general scope of practice statement is not licensed. The proposal reflects the belief that broad licensure is disadvantageous for four main reasons:

1. It necessitates hierarchical and unequal relationships between licensed and registered professions
2. It produces tensions between professions and may inhibit cooperation
3. It restricts evolution in the scope of practice of the unlicensed professions and inhibits the development of new professions
4. It inhibits innovation in how the various health professionals can be utilized, so that agencies have difficulty in using a combination of health professionals who will provide the best service at the lowest cost

The proposal continues to say that, whereas the current licensure model may have been appropriate in the past to regulate a relatively small number of health professions, such a model will not work with the larger number that exists today (Schwartz, 1989, p. 13-15). The recommendation in the Ontario proposal is that no profession be granted licensure, including those currently licensed.

Some questions regarding exclusive right to practice will be asked increasingly in the future: Does licensure impose higher costs of entry into a profession by limiting competition? Does licensure inflate fees for service? Does licensure preclude the provision of a particular service at a lower cost by prohibiting substitution? Does licensure contribute to fragmentation of service? Does licensure reduce geographic mobility and the evolvement of new roles? Most importantly, does licensure accomplish what it is intended to do, which is to ensure public safety?

Auxiliary Personnel

Auxiliary personnel are practitioners with less training than professionals who perform related functions under the supervision of a professional. Some examples of auxiliary personnel closely associated with the provision of nursing services are health care aides, attendants assisting the handicapped with activities of daily living, and community mental health workers. The question of whether or how these auxiliary groups should be regulated is one that is raised repeatedly, and one that is becoming more critical as health services move to community settings in which practice is less directly supervised.

With increased technology and an expanding aging population, the kinds and numbers of auxiliary workers are growing rapidly. In many cases, they are performing functions previously within the exclusive scope of practice of the professional. The client to whom they are providing care may or may not be competent to make decisions about his or her care. For example, many handicapped and elderly persons require assistance with activities of daily living but are capable of making decisions directing their care; others are dependent on the judgment of the caregiver.

Several options are available for regulating auxiliary personnel. One is to provide control by workplace legislation (e.g., public hospital or nursing home legislation would stipulate requirements for supervision by a professional); another is by delegation powers granted to the nurse under the nursing legislation (e.g., certain activities such as catheterization could be performed only if delegated and supervised by a nurse). Whichever approach or combination of approaches is used, public interest (including cost implications) must be the guiding consideration.

Quality Assurance

Principle components of quality assurance are the measurement of activity, comparison of activity to goals or objectives, and responses to changed activity. True quality assurance demands that effective and timely action be taken to improve matters that are done poorly. Standards of practice and conduct, programs to monitor continuing competence of professionals in practice, and disciplinary processes are three regulatory mechanisms that are intended to enhance practice and contribute to safe and effective care. The role of regulatory bodies in quality assurance is a timely issue, and one currently being discussed widely at the health policy level. Lomas (1989), in remarks to an International Conference on Quality Assurance and Effectiveness in Health Care, identified three reasons for the surge of interest in quality assurance. First, there is a growing body of evidence that the mere provision of health care services does not guarantee their appropriateness. Second, variations in practice patterns by health providers cannot always be explained by variations in patients' needs for service. Third, increasing possibilities in health care, which technology and more sophisticated approaches to health promotion offer, are conflicting with a limited fiscal capability.

Most nursing legislation grants the regulatory body the responsibility for establishing and maintaining standards of entry, qualification, practice, and ethics. Most provincial regulatory bodies have standards, guidelines, or "competencies" for practice. Most standards are implicit (i.e., they describe usual and customary practice), with the exception of Quebec and to a lesser extent Manitoba, which are explicit (e.g., they define specific criteria for care). Standards based on nursing processes are the common approach. However, there is increasing need for research-based, explicit standards to become part of an integrated quality assurance system that will lead to continuous improvement of the effectiveness and appropriateness of the practice of the majority of practitioners.

Current systems of ensuring professional competence are under scrutiny. In many instances, only a formal complaint against a practitioner to the appropriate regulatory body will bring shortcomings to light. If the complainant is a member of the public, he or she may or may not have sufficient expertise to evaluate practice. In other instances, the regulatory body may require examinations before re-licensing, mandatory continuing education, or other processes; however, these processes have not proven any more effective than the complaints process in terms of ensuring competence. In Canada, unlike the United States, there is less willingness to move to mandatory continuing education. Many provinces, however, require upgrading to return to practice after a specified period of absence.

Berwick (1989) submits that, in the future, there will be a move away from reliance on complaints and discipline, or the "bad apple" approach, to a "theory of continuous improvement." The theory of "bad apples" describes the belief that quality is best achieved by discovering bad apples and removing them from the lot. However, this leads to a tendency to blame the individual for deficiencies in the system (e.g., poor leadership, poor job design, unclear purpose). Berwick suggests that another way to focus on quality is the "theory of continuous improvement." This theory proposes that improvement will occur if people understand the connection between what they do and the outcome that is achieved, because they can then revise what they do on the basis of that awareness. This approach focuses on opportunities to improve quality throughout the system. Berwick acknowledges the need to maintain the current processes to weed out the "bad apples." The danger lies, however, in the naive belief that such things as programs to assess ongoing competence or publication of the names of health professionals who are found guilty of substandard practice or conduct will somehow induce otherwise indolent caregivers to improve their level of care and efficiency. Berwick believes that there is a role for regulatory bodies, in partnership with care providers (practitioners and agencies), in developing measurement tools and assembling data centrally to expand the scientific basis for rational and effective processes of care.

Professional Discipline

All provincial legislation in Canada delineates the requirements of the regulatory body pertaining to complaints and discipline processes. Specific processes and procedures vary among the provinces, but they are consistent in their purpose to limit or restrict from practice those practitioners whose practice, conduct, or health constitutes a danger to the public. Most legislation prescribes the procedural framework for investigative and hearing processes in some detail, stipulates the requirements for publishing decisions on individuals found guilty of an offence, and provides for an appeal process. An important principle is that members of the profession are judged by their peers, who understand the complex and specialized nature of nursing work.

Two issues related to professional discipline are in the areas of due process and in the integrity and openness of the processes. It is important that there are safe-guards to ensure that a nurse facing allegations of incompetence or unprofessional conduct has a full and fair opportunity to defend himself or herself against such allegations. Statutory committees or tribunals are composed of a professional's peers and, in most provinces, representatives of the public. The regulating body must be absolutely sure that any decisions made by the committee or tribunal are untainted by bias, actual and perceived. Appeal mechanisms should be in place for both complainant and defendant.

The move, in some provinces, toward public access to disciplinary hearings has caused debate about protection of the professional's integrity prior to a finding of guilt, as well as concern about confidentiality of client health information. Increasing articulation of public concern, however, about professions protecting their members and not making decisions in the public interest is having a strong influence on this trend. The challenge always has been to balance the individual and the public in-terest. This may shift as the administrative practice and the legislation on which it is constructed suggest that, in some matters, the public rights will take precedence over the rights of the individual ("Review of Ontario's Regulatory Agencies," 1989).

Public Accountability

A fundamental principle of the democratic political system is that those who make public policy decisions are accountable to those who are affected by the decision. Those who disagree with the decisions must have available avenues for redress. When government powers are delegated to regulatory bodies, the same principle applies (Trebilcock, Tuohy, and Wolfson, 1979).

Critics argue that professions use their specialized knowledge to protect and promote their own interests rather than the interests of the public, resulting in a dependence on government to institute greater public regulation of professional activity and to organize watchdog consumer groups (Schon, 1983). Paralleling this expression of concern is a public demand for more open and responsive processes. As a result, legislation is beginning to reflect this concern with requirements that processes and tribunals be more open and accessible to the public.

Public representation on the boards of regulatory bodies is a key component in meeting the expectation that public interest is truly served. In many provinces, public representation on governing boards or councils is a reality. The Registered Nurses Association of British Columbia was one of the first to appoint public (or "lay") members to its board. In Ontario, with the passage of new legislation scheduled for late 1991, the regulatory bodies for all health professions will be required to have just under half of the board made up of public, or lay, members. In most provinces, at least some of the public or lay members are appointed, by provincial cabinet, to bring the public's unique perspective to discussion and decision making. In future, regulatory bodies will be required to have close partnerships with consumers to clarify expectations of provider competence and to determine broad consumer per-spective on major issues.

Barriers to Entry

A primary obligation of regulatory bodies is to protect the public interest in respect to health, safety, and welfare. In fulfilling this obligation it is incumbent on a regulatory body not to construct barriers that unnecessarily restrict entry to practice for reasons that are more in the profession's interest than the public's. The duty to respect the individual's right to equality of opportunity and to equal treatment without unreasonable discrimination is fundamental to current societal values.

Cumming, Lee, and Oreopoulos (1989), in their report on access to professions and trades in Ontario, identify six barriers that could prevent individuals who have qualified elsewhere from entering a provincially-regulated profession:

1. Lack of information on how to become registered
2. Lack of reliable methods of evaluating foreign education and experience
3. Unavailability of retraining opportunities for people who have completed part of their training outside Canada
4. Relevance of a national examination to provincial needs
5. Level of language proficiency required
6. Inappropriateness of examinations currently used in assessing language proficiency

During nursing shortages, pressures come from numerous sources to relax the requirements for entry to practice to the profession, especially in relation to foreign-trained graduates. Few would argue that shortage is a reason to lower standards that affect quality of care. It is timely, however, to examine standards for entry, not only in light of shortages, but in the context of beliefs about basic human rights, and whether traditional criteria are outdated and over-restrictive in view of present values and practice requirements.

OTHER LEGISLATION—INTERRELATIONSHIPS AND INFLUENCES

Historically, nursing differs from other self-regulating professions in that most nurses work in an employee relationship. This is changing, however, as other health professionals increasingly move into salaried employment relationships. Self-regulation in an employment setting poses a particular set of problems not encountered by the professional in private practice. The potential for conflict between professional goals and institutional goals may surface in a number of areas. Examples of the wide range of legislation governing or affecting nurses in the workplace are described in the following section.

Institution or Agency Legislation

In all provinces there is specific legislation governing hospitals, nursing homes, mental health facilities, public health, and other community agencies. Most of this legislation includes a requirement to employ registered or licensed personnel. This can be a service to an employer in providing a "stamp of approval" in evaluating candidates for positions. In addition, if maintenance of competence is a regulatory requirement, the employer has some assurance that the nurse will perform competently. There may be some disadvantages, however, from the employer's view. The requirement to employ registered or licensed personnel may restrict the way in which work can be assigned (Trebilcock, Tuohy, and Wolfson, 1979).

A nurse, on occasion, may feel his or her professional status compromised if work orders contravene the professional code of ethics. By obeying the employer (or other professional), he or she may feel in jeopardy of disciplinary action by the regulatory body; alternatively, by following the professional code, employment may be jeopardized. This is more common in recent years because workloads are heavy, and nurses feel they are asked to assume more work than they can handle safely, or they are asked to perform specialized tasks for which they lack adequate knowledge or skill.

Occupational Health and Safety Legislation

The purpose of occupational health and safety legislation is to protect workers against environmental hazards in the workplace. "Safety" hazards include items such as slippery floors and improperly stored dangerous substances. "Health" hazards, which are often insidious and difficult to detect, contribute to or cause illness or disease. The best known example is asbestos poisoning.

Occupational health and safety, as it applies to the workplace, is provincial in scope. The comprehensiveness of the legislation throughout the country varies widely. Ideally, it provides employees the right to information regarding hazards in the working environment and the right to refuse unsafe work without reprisal.

Labor Legislation

Collective bargaining for nurses is well established throughout the country. Professional regulation can be a complicating or complementary factor in employer/employee labor relations. Regulatory bodies provide an external presence of a "professional code of ethics" and commitment to professional development. Employees can refer to this to reinforce their position in certain work-related disputes with their employers. They may also seek release time for professional development to maintain professional competence or to participate in certain professional activities. Nursing unions have been remarkably successful in this regard.

It is a matter of public policy in most provinces that the relationship between the regulatory body and the bargaining unit be distinct. The grounds for this policy lie in the necessity to distinguish between the regulatory body as a promoter of the public interest accountable to the public for its decisions and the bargaining unit as a promoter of group interests and accountable to its membership. There are areas of overlap, however, and these may conflict with or reinforce each other. "Professional clauses" (i.e., clauses that address such areas as ethics, appropriate workload for required patient care, or professional development) are easier to negotiate when a bargaining unit can refer to the existence of codes of ethics and continuing competence requirements of regulatory bodies. In disciplinary cases, on the other hand, a bargaining unit may provide support for an individual member in opposition to the regulatory tribunal, which has as its primary concern the public interest.

Human Rights and Other Broad Legislation

Other significant legislation includes the Canadian Charter of Rights and Freedoms and the provincial human rights codes, which encompass basic rights such as life, liberty, and security of person; the Canada Health Act, which addresses the right of access to care; and legislation governing privacy, confidentiality, and the right to informed consent and refusal of care (see Chapter 14). These types of legislation are sweeping and progressive. They influence and override other legislation and therefore have a major effect on the regulatory practices in this country.

CONCLUSION

Regulation in the workplace encompasses numerous legislative and nonlegislative controls. It can be as broad as the Canadian Charter of Rights and Freedoms or as specific as agency processes and procedures. The intent of regulatory legislation is to protect the public interest.

Nursing in Canada is granted self-regulation. Several trends in self-regulation will influence traditional approaches. One of the most significant trends, at least in theory if not in practice, is a move away from an exclusive monopoly over practice to legislative models that allow evolution of a more flexible, more cost-effective health care system and that respect the consumer's right to choose his or her provider from a variety of safe options. Public protection and public accountability are the bases of professional and other regulation, and these two important trends will gain in significance with pressures to ensure that regulatory mechanisms truly meet these criteria.

The surge of interest in quality assurance in the 1990s will also influence regulation in the workplace. Assessing the competence of individual practitioners, although important, will be less vital than assessing the health outcomes in the population. Effective regulation in the public interest has the same objective.

ACKNOWLEDGEMENT

The author acknowledges Dianne Patychuk, former policy planner for the College of Nurses of Ontario, for her assistance in compiling reference materials and reviewing the completed manuscript.

REFERENCES

Berwick, D. (1989). Continuous improvement as an ideal in health care. *New England Journal of Medicine, 320* (1), 53-56.

Boase, J.P. (1986). *Public policy and the regulation of the health disciplines: A historical and comparative perspective.* PhD thesis, Political Science, York University.

Canadian Nurses Association. (1968). *The leaf and the lamp.* Ottawa: Author.

Cohen, H., & Milke, L. (1974). Toward a more responsive system of professional licensure. *International Journal of Health Services, 4*(2), 265-272.

College of Nurses of Ontario. (1987). *Environmental scanning: Professional self regulation.* Toronto: Author.

College of Nurses of Ontario. (1989, November). *A proposed regulatory framework for the College of Nurses: Background paper prepared for Council.* Toronto: Author.

College of Nurses of Ontario. (1990, January). *Situational analysis for deciding the future of CNO standards of practice: Background paper prepared for Council.* Toronto: Author.

Cumming, P., Lee, E., & Oreopoulos, D. (1989). *Access!: Task force on access to professions and trades in Ontario.* Toronto: Queen's Printer.

Gaumer, G.L. (1984). Regulating health professionals: A review of the empirical literature. *Millbank Memorial Fund Quarterly/Health Society, 62*(3), 380-417.

Gross, S.J. (1984). *Of foxes and henhouses: Licensing and the health professions.* London: Quorum Books.

Lieberman, J. (1976). Some reflections on self-regulation. In P. Slayton & M. Trebilcock (Eds.), *The professions and public policy* (pp.89-97). Toronto: University of Toronto Press.

Lomas, J. (November, 1989) *Opening remarks.* Paper presented at The International Conference on Quality Assurance and Effectiveness in Health Care, Toronto, Ontario.

Sanford, B. (1989). *Strategies for maintaining competence: A manual for professional associations and faculties.* Toronto: Canadian Scholars' Press.

Schon, D. A. (1983). *The reflective practitioner: How professionals think in action.* New York: Basic Books.

Schwartz, A. (1989). *Striking a new balance: A blueprint for the regulation of Ontario's health professions: Recommendations of the health professions legislation review.* Toronto: Ontario Ministry of Health.

Shimberg, B. (1982). *Occupational licensing: A public perspective.* Princeton, NJ: Center for Occupational and Professional Assessment Educational Testing.

Styles, M.M. (1984). *Project on the regulation of nursing.* Geneva: International Council of Nurses.

Styles, M.M. (1986). *Credentialling in nursing: Contemporary Developments and Trends; U.S.A. within a world view.* Kansas City: American Nurses' Association.

Trebilcock, M., Tuohy, C., & Wolfson, A. (1979). *Professional Regulation. A staff study of accountancy, architecture, engineering and law in Ontario; prepared for the Professional Organizations' Committee.* Toronto: Ontario Ministry of the Attorney General.

SECTION IV

NURSING EDUCATION

Student nurses, such as this one walking across the campus at Queen's University, Kingston, Ontario, face enormous challenges as they begin their careers. Given the increasingly complex patterns of nursing practice, more students are taking their basic preparation in university nursing programs. (Photograph, 1987, by Annette Borger, supplied courtesy of Faculty of Nursing, Queen's University.)

CHAPTER TWENTY

Overview: Issues in Nursing Education

JENNIECE LARSEN, RN, PhD
ALICE J. BAUMGART, RN, PhD

To be effective, nurses who practice in the health care environments of the 1990s need both sound basic education and commitment to lifelong learning. These imperatives draw attention to basic, continuing, and graduate education programs as important resources to equip nurses to meet the daily challenges and to shape their changing roles. Through their basic educational programs, nurses acquire the foundation skills, theoretical knowledge, and values needed for practice. Continuing education creates opportunities for them to upgrade skills and qualifications through-out their careers. Graduate education prepares them for leadership roles and establishes the research skills necessary to expand knowledge and test new arrangements for organizing, delivering, and financing nursing services.

The nursing profession in Canada has made significant strides in building and strengthening these three levels of nursing education. However, society has a long history of low investment in education for nurses, which has made it difficult to develop a sufficiently capacious and coherent education system in step with con-temporary economic and health care needs. A major challenge for nursing in the 1990s is to awaken the public and the other members of the health care system to a recognition of the value of well-educated nurses.

This overview traces the evolution of nursing education in Canada from its for-mative years in the hospital training school, through the period of transition to higher education, and into the current era when nurses are accountable for a broader range of actions, when technology and research daily add new depth to care, and when consumers are more knowledgeable and demanding. In relation to each of the stages, characteristic features of curricula, students, faculty, and program funding are highlighted.

ERA OF THE HOSPITAL TRAINING SCHOOL

Patterns of education change as society changes. When hospital schools of nursing first opened their doors in Canada in the late nineteenth century, cultural attitudes toward education for women helped to define the workplace skills and attitudes taught to students, as well as the location of their education outside the formal system of public education. Women were not expected to seek higher education. Indeed, they were barred from most courses of university study. To contain women in their proper place, schools were attached to hospitals rather than educational institutions, and training emphasized development of personal qualities, such as altruism, womanly devotion, and dedication, rather than traditional educational objectives such as acquisition of knowledge or the ability to think and reason. According to the conventional wisdom of the day, paid work was a secondary and usually temporary facet of a woman's life. It was also commonly believed that a woman was biologically unsuited to the rigors of serious study. Thus, to educate her in a fashion similar to men would be wasteful and make her less womanly. What she needed was a brief, practical education in a carefully supervised environment where she learned by doing or "hands on" experience (Coburn, 1974; Gamarnikow, 1978; Gibbon and Mathewson, 1947). The remnants of this heritage are still evident in much of today's nursing education in the emphasis on closely supervised clinical training to perfect technical skills.

This ideology, which Gillett (1981) calls the "taboo on knowledge," facilitated the rapid growth of hospital training schools where student nurses were more coveted for the services they provided than for any deep concern for their education. Standards varied enormously from school to school, and the training often involved long, arduous hours of work in trying conditions. Classes, if offered at all, tended to be fitted in after hospital tours of duty were over. One report described this mode of training this way: "These were work study educational programs in the poorest sense of the term" (Southern Regional Education Board, 1982, p. 1).

The many problems characterizing nursing education in Canada in the period up to the Depression years of the 1930s were extensively documented in a landmark study popularly known as the Weir Report (1932). This report, commissioned by the Canadian Nurses Association with financial assistance from the Canadian Nurses Association with financial assistance from the Canadian Medical Association, was prepared by Dr. G. M. Weir, professor and head of the Department of Education, University of British Columbia. A succession of reports published over the next 30 years called for fundamental reforms in hospital-based nursing education. One of the most consistent recommendations made in these reports was that responsibility for basic nursing education should be transferred from hospitals to educational institutions so that learning experiences of students would be shaped by educational objectives rather than service needs of hospitals. However, because students were the mainstay of the hospital nursing work force, hospital schools remained the dominant method of preparing nurses until the 1960s, with more than 95% of Canadian nurses receiving their initial preparation in such programs.

These students were mostly 18 to 21 years old, fresh out of high school, and they lived in residence while in training. Their teachers often had limited preparation beyond a nursing diploma. A 1959 survey of instructors from 171 schools of nursing reveals that 31% had no special preparation for teaching, 42% had a certificate or a university diploma, 22% had a baccalaureate degree, and 3% had a master's degree (Keeler, 1960).

Despite this disappointing record of change, a good deal of educational planning and experimentation was undertaken to improve the quality of nursing education programs, especially after the end of World War II and continuing throughout the 1950s. Activities of note included development of educational standards, publication of curriculum guidelines and instructional materials, and a pilot project to evaluate Canadian nursing schools to assess their readiness for accreditation. In Chapter 21, Bajnok describes a number of demonstration schools and model programs that were established and evaluated for their effectiveness and efficiency in preparing graduates for the nursing work force. Much of this activity was stimulated by the Canadian Nurses Association, various provincial nursing organizations, and the Canadian Conference of University Schools of Nursing, later renamed the Canadian Association of University Schools of Nursing (CAUSN). These activities laid the foundation for major changes that took place in Canadian nursing education in the 1960s and 1970s.

Funds for innovations in nursing education during this early era came mainly from the increasing role of government in financing social services, including health care and postsecondary education. Severe shortages of medical, nursing, and other health care personnel had developed during World War II (1939-1945). After the War, provincial governments responded by increasing training programs. In nursing, much of this funding was directed to preparation of public health nurses, who were in particularly short supply, and to training of nursing assistants (Lang, 1974). A sharp rise in federal grants to provinces for hospital capital costs and technical and vocational education led to a boom in new hospitals and educational facilities, including new nursing schools. Improvements in hospital training programs were achieved as a result of the improved financial position of hospitals, which, in turn, is attributable in part to the rapid growth of privately sponsored and nonprofit hospital insurance plans (Lang, 1974).

ERA OF TRANSITION TO HIGHER EDUCATION

The 1960s saw the full emergence of a so-called "service state" in which governments were to provide far more social services than in the past (Lang, 1974). A major beneficiary of this development was postsecondary education. The federal program of direct grants to universities was replaced in 1967 by generous transfer payments to the provinces, aimed at meeting up to half the operating expenditures of post-secondary institutions (Leslie, 1980). This financial support fueled a major transformation in postsecondary education in most Canadian provinces. University operating budgets tripled, and several new universities were opened. A network of community colleges and technical and vocational training institutions was established to take over categories of basic education and training that did not fit the university pattern. This network was also seen as playing a major role in adult continuing education to help keep people abreast of rapid change and introduction of technology. These changes were accompanied by phenomenal increases in enrollment to keep pace with demands for postsecondary education and training from the "baby boom" generation.

The huge investment in postsecondary education led to equally impressive changes in nursing education. As the three chapters in this section of the book chronicle, the 1960s and the 1970s saw basic, graduate, and continuing education for registered nurses expand in scope, size, and resources. For example, before 1960, only one master's program in nursing existed in Canada (at the University of Western Ontario). By 1979, eight programs were underway and another three were added in the 1980s. The focus of the early programs was on teaching or administration, but, as Field, Stinson, and Thibaudeau record in Chapter 22, the orientation of most of the later programs was on specialization and advanced nursing practice.

An important part of the transition to higher education was implementation of new curriculum designs using nursing theories and concepts, rather than medical models, as organizing frameworks. In the clinical component of nursing education, preoccupation with procedures was gradually replaced by a concept of nursing practice as a patient-centered and theory-based activity (Chater, 1982).

Educational preparation for teachers of nursing also changed. Full-time nurse faculty members in diploma programs increasingly had baccalaureate-level preparation and a few had master's degrees. Substantial numbers of full-time nurse faculty members in university programs had master's-level preparation, usually in education or other non-nursing programs, and a few faculty had doctoral degrees.

Loree and Leckie's (1977) study of nursing students in New Brunswick provides insight into the nature of nursing students during this era. Ninety-five percent of students were 15 to 24 years of age; many came from farms or small towns with populations of less than 5000. Compared to diploma students, baccalaureate students came from families with higher incomes and educational attainment.

The most significant changes during this era occurred in preparation of registered nurses for entry to practice. Although both diploma and degree routes for initial qualifications were retained, the long-sought-after transfer of diploma programs from hospitals to educational institutions moved ahead rapidly. By the end of the 1960s, Saskatchewan, Quebec, and Ontario had closed all hospital schools and located diploma programs in their rapidly expanding community college systems. In British Columbia, Alberta, Manitoba, Nova Scotia, and Newfoundland, the transfer occurred piecemeal, but by 1989 only 21 hospital schools of nursing remained in operation in these provinces. In New Brunswick and Prince Edward Island, diploma nursing education became the responsibility of regional and independent schools.

With these changes, the number of diploma programs in Canada was reduced by 40%, from 186 in 1967 (CNA, 1968) to 110 by 1989 (Harris, Lobin, and Paddon, 1990). The same period saw the number of baccalaureate programs in Canadian universities offering initial preparation in nursing more than double, with 22 such programs offered by universities in all provinces but Prince Edward Island. However, this situation will change in the fall of 1992 with the closure of Prince Edward Island's only diploma school and the launching of a 4-year baccalaureate program in nursing at the University of Prince Edward Island. Prince Edward Island will become the only province in Canada to offer nursing education exclusively through the university route.

Despite school closures, the capacity of entry programs to supply new graduates increased markedly in the late 1960s and during the 1970s. Indeed, graduates of Canadian nursing programs have accounted for much of the recent growth in size of the Canadian nursing work force. The increased number of spaces available for students was made possible, in large measure, by increased government funding for postsecondary education and because more nurses with bachelor's and master's degrees were qualified for teaching posts.

Graduations from initial diploma and basic baccalaureate programs averaged more than 9500 per year in the peak years from 1973 to 1976, with an all-time high of 10,041 graduates in 1976. Of this number, close to 94% were from diploma programs with three quarters of these being from community college-based programs. In the late 1970s, graduations from initial diploma programs in hospitals and community colleges began to decline, reaching a low of 6478 in 1981 and slowly increasing to 7636 in 1989. Graduations from basic baccalaureate programs increased steadily from 613 in 1973 to fairly stable enrollment figures of just over 1200 throughout the 1980s. By 1989, close to 12% of all new graduates each year completed their initial preparation in a university program (Harris, Lobin, and Paddon, 1990).

Many of the changes in basic nursing education in Canada from the 1960s through the 1980s profoundly affected relationships between nursing education and nursing practice. Old dogmas about how to prepare nurses were challenged, and a new partnership between nursing educators and nursing employers had to be forged. This has been a slow process with a troubled history. To assist, the Canadian Nurses Association sponsored the National Forum on Nursing Education in November, 1979. The forum brought various sectors in nursing education together to debate the critical issues involved in preparing new practitioners for the 1980s. These issues included the need to examine the clinical component in entry programs, the need for increased communication between university and diploma nursing levels of education, the need for collaboration between nursing education and nursing practice, and the currency of clinical practice experiences of nursing instructors (Zilm, 1980). Another recurring concern is the "fit" between the kinds of nursing knowledge and skills major nursing employers and nursing educators perceive to be important and how these competencies should be acquired. In the 1970s, employers frequently claimed that the clinical experience students received in basic programs was inadequate. In turn, nursing educators often argued that employers held unrealistic expectations of new graduates. With the benefit of hindsight, one can see that neither analysis took into account the diversification of nursing roles and responsibilities occurring at the time. Nor was any account taken of the impact in the workplace of the changing ratio of experienced to inexperienced nursing staff, which had resulted from the heavy influx of novice nurses during the period of rapid growth.

ERA OF ACCOUNTABILITY AND CONSUMERISM

Just as the two preceding eras have been marked by social pressures and expectations, contemporary nursing education will be affected by the assumptions, attitudes, and ideals of the public and by the political and socioeconomic trends affecting the country. Increasingly, the public has come to expect a high quality of advanced health and sickness care and, in this information age, has become thoroughly knowledgeable about sickness and health. Nursing, like all health disciplines, has been affected by the explosion of knowledge, increased complexity of social structures, growth of consumer expectations, and implementation of advanced technologies. Many members of the public today know more about sickness and health than physicians were taught in medical schools in the early 1900s. Medical and nursing research is expanding health care horizons rapidly. In turn, this leads to a demand for well-educated, highly competent nurses with a broader range of skills and a thorough understanding of how to help people to help themselves. As well, nurses need to know how to keep abreast of the rapidly changing information that affects care.

Such changes also put pressure on those who teach nurses and on those who can carry out research to ensure that care is given in the best possible ways. At the university level, as reflected by advertisements for teaching positions, a doctoral degree is preferred, while a master's degree is required. Greater emphasis is being placed on faculty members' competence to teach, and questions are being raised about supervision of clinical practice. As well, there is an increasing thrust toward collaborative programming between universities and hospital schools/community colleges. To meet these needs for well-prepared nursing leaders, the profession had called for Canadian doctoral programs in nursing—the PhD (Nursing) degree— since the 1970s (Zilm, Larose, and Stinson, 1979). In the 1990s, these programs finally are becoming a reality. (See also Chapter 22.)

These changing expectations of nursing and of nurses for the 1990s and for the coming new century leads to the identification of several educational issues that are of vital importance. These include: recruitment and retention of student nurses; changes in entry level education; professional trends and demands; and educational equity for women. Many other issues related to curriculum planning, financial responsibility for education of nurses, graduate level education, research, and the increasingly global nature of the economy have major implications for the ways nurses will be educated in the 1990s. A brief discusson on these issues follows.

Recruitment and Retention

Recruitment into schools of nursing is arguably the most serious challenge confronting the nursing profession today. During the 1980s, the decline in the attractiveness of nursing as an occupational choice became a global phenomenon ("CNR delegates make . . . ," 1991). Recruitment prospects are also being affected by a decreasing number of young people in Canada's population because of a steady drop in birthrates since the mid-1960s. Other educational issues pale when the profession has difficulty replenishing its ranks with bright, capable men and women.

There has been a tremendous increase in university enrollment in the past 30 years. Remarkably, women were the primary beneficiaries as they entered occupations traditionally viewed as being nontraditional occupations, such as law, medicine, computer science, engineering, and, in the case of the health occupations, medicine and dentistry. Unfortunately, nursing programs at universities have not kept pace with other disciplines in this unprecedented expansion of opportunities for women in higher education. In the United States, schools of nursing experienced a 20% drop in enrollment between 1983 and 1986 (Aiken and Mullinix, 1987). This decline was a significant factor in the protracted nursing shortages in the United States during the 1980s (Prescott, 1988). More recent data suggest that applications to schools of nursing in the United States are slowly increasing.

Similar data concerning the applicant pool for Canadian schools of nursing are not available on a national basis. However, statistics from university nursing programs show a 23% drop (from 8629 to 6651) in applications between 1988 and 1990 (Pringle, 1991). These data need to be viewed with caution in that they represent applications, not individuals; individuals may have applied to more than one program. Similar data concerning applications to diploma schools of nursing in hospitals and community colleges are not available. However, anecdotal evidence from across the country suggests that diploma programs, especially in Ontario and Quebec, have experienced a similar decline and occasionally have been unable to fill their quota with suitable applicants. However, since most schools of nursing in Canada have an enrollment limit, admissions and graduations have remained relatively constant (Harris, Lobin, and Paddon, 1990; Richardson, 1991b).

Also of interest in relation to recruitment is the changing profile of the student population; nursing students are now older, frequently with previous education and work experience. Since the 1980s, fewer students enter nursing directly from high school. Many are mature students who have been out of school for some time. A number of these have had university courses and transferred into nursing. Some are embarking on nursing as a second career. Anecdotal evidence indicates that these students may have lower grade point averages than 5 years ago. Reporting on the American experience, Aiken and Mullinix (1987) note that the scholastic aptitude scores of high school students interested in nursing as a career were well below the national average for college-bound students and that the gap was widening over time.

To complicate a difficult situation, some of nursing's best undergraduate students transfer to other health disciplines before they graduate:

> These students tell us that they are not leaving nursing because they dislike it, in fact, they love the whole arena of caring for patients but they want more than nursing can allow them to do, and they want a health care career that will provide more scope and allow them more control over their practice. (Pringle, 1991, p. 71)

Since nursing is overwhelmingly female, potential candidates have traditionally been drawn from only 50% of the population, and, even in this 50%, members of visible minorities, including aboriginal people, are poorly represented. Canadian statistics indicate that females have increasingly entered previously male-dominated fields of study, but there has been no corresponding increase in males entering female professions such as nursing. Observers have expressed concern that the applicant pool may be affected by negative portrayals of nurses and nursing in the media. The policy that the baccalaureate degree will be the entry level for practice may further complicate an already problematic recruitment picture. There is no evidence that traditional diploma nursing students will choose to enter university programs when diploma programs are no longer available.

To maintain enrollment levels, and to prepare for changes in the way health care is offered in the 1990s, schools of nursing will need to intensify their recruitment efforts within the general population of students bound for universities and prepare for a different type of student in the future, for example, older adult students, part-time students, single parents, minority students, and males. Recruitment efforts alone will, however, not change this situation. The economic, social, and political status of nursing in the Canadian occupational structure will have to change to attract candidates who are now entering other health professions in which financial and social rewards are far greater. There may be a related need to examine both admission requirements for schools of nursing and losses from attrition. Few recent Canadian data exist on reasons students leave, although an attrition rate between 20% and 25% is the accepted norm for nursing programs. American studies suggest that the major reasons for attrition are personal problems, financial difficulties, illness, new career choices, and academic failure (Rosenfeld, 1988; Smith, 1990). As the number of applicants declines and the student population becomes more diverse, improvements are needed in the quality of support services available to nursing students (Cameron-Buccheri and Trygstad, 1989). Such services include orientation to and preparation for academic work and strategies to link students with each other and with faculty. Each school may need its own program to identify and help at-risk students (Campbell and Davis, 1990). The limited availability of scholarships and financial aid for nursing students needs intensive study. Many universities have programs to attract more women into science and engineering and special scholarships, available nationally, have been set aside so that women can enter engineering and scientific fields in greater numbers. However, similar programs do not exist to encourage students to enter nursing. Is society unconsciously suggesting that for women to enhance their status they must enter male-dominated fields? Ryten (1988) observes that considerable work must be done before intelligent women will feel comfortable again in female-dominated occupations, especially occupations, such as nursing, crucial to the well-being of the society.

Entry-Level Education

Entry-level education in nursing is designed to prepare a generalist practitioner. This model assumes that training for specialization will occur at the postbaccalaureate or postdiploma level. For the generalist model to be viable at the entry level, enhanced programming at the graduate level must be created in universities, and continuing education opportunities must be expanded. Much of the difficulty in offering specialty education at the master's level arises from the fact that nursing research to support highly specialized courses is in the early stages of development. The match (or mismatch) between the generalist model and the diversity and degree of specialization needed in today's workplaces needs to be examined. When new graduates enter a modern workplace, whether in a hospital or in the community, they require job-specific specialty skills and knowledge. Currently, most opportunities for education in highly specialized areas of nursing practice, such as adult, pediatric, or neonatal intensive care or operating room care, are offered as concentrated clinical training programs either in the nursing workplace or through nurses' interest groups (e.g., the Operating Room Nurses Association of Canada). (See also Chapter 17.)

In attending to concerns about specialization, it is important to keep in mind that new graduates of today will be working for approximately 40 years. Although it is tempting to dilute the generalist base on which entry-level programs are structured, intensive specialization at an early stage in education may prove costly in the long run. Durable careers require an adequate base of study to develop higher order analytical, problem-solving, and interpersonal skills; these are portable and can accommodate future changes in the work environment. (See also Chapter 18.)

Continuing education as a form of study and training is becoming more established within the comprehensive system of nursing education. As Attridge and Clark indicate in Chapter 23, continuing education has expanded beyond the notion of non-credit study to include study for credit and for both self-organized and self-directed learning. They explore timely issues of currency and career development, the controversy over mandatory versus voluntary continuing education, and issues related to accessibility and cost of continuing education.

Clinical nursing education, however, needs urgent attention. In most other health disciplines, students receive their clinical training from professional staff in the workplace, whereas nursing uses the "guest in the house" model of sending the faculty from academic institutions to supervise students (Glass, 1975). As the acuity of patients increases in highly specialized and technologically complex nursing units, the capability of faculty to supervise safely students caring for critically ill patients is severely compromised. The "guest in the house" model may have worked in the 1960s and the 1970s, but a new model required for the 1990s (Pringle, 1991). Hospitals, health care units, and nursing homes must become more intimately involved in clinical education.

Specialized and highly technical areas of hospital practice areas (e.g., operating rooms, emergency, intensive care units) usually are not included in basic undergraduate curriculums. This is a matter of considerable concern in face of the growing percentage of hospital beds devoted to these services. Rethinking the mission of entry-level education is urgently needed. This issue is also further complicated by differences between diploma education in community colleges and hospitals and baccalaureate education in universities.

Innovative programs, such as collaborative programs between universities, colleges, and hospitals, pose opportunities for integrating the diverse cultures of the university and college and other diploma settings. Recently, there has been an upsurge in development of these programs within Canada. Collaborative programs allow existing resources (financial, human, space, library, clinical) to be combined and used for a mutual, unified goal. These collaborative approaches also increases flexibility in terms of geographic access to nursing education. However, substantial upgrading of diploma school teachers to meet university standards for faculty is required. Particularly in the areas of research and scholarship.

Professional Issues and Demands

The Entry to Practice position taken by the Canadian Nurses Association in 1982 proposes that the baccalaureate degree in nursing be the preferred basic credential for entry to practice for all nurses educated in the year 2000 and beyond (CNA, 1982). In Chapter 21, Bajnok provides a perspective on the current debate concerning entry to practice. The entry to practice policy has had a divisive effect on the nursing profession in Canada. It has also diverted attention from other important educational issues, such as education for specialty practice, the need to increase opportunities for graduate education, and the development of a university-based research enterprise. As Pringle (1991) observed, much energy for the last dozen years has gone to figuring how to solve the question about where nurses should be educated rather than about how they should be educated.

The case in favor of increasing educational requirements for entry into nursing practice has generally been based on the competence or quality of care argument. The argument is that nurses need more basic education to cope with a changing world and to contribute in a thoughtful way to changing patterns of nursing practice. The professional skills and values that should be fostered are those that universities traditionally seek to develop. The case may also be made that the university credential would enhance nursing power. As the only major health occupation that has not standardized its entry qualifications and required a university degree for its basic preparation, nursing is in a disadvantaged position.

The two arguments just outlined center on the role of nursing education as a preparatory mechanism for entry into the workplace. As education has moved from being considered a privilege to a right, it has taken on the dual function of serving both the individual and society. For women, who have frequently faced economic disadvantages because of deficiencies in education, better educational options are important in achieving social justice and employment equity (Abella, 1985). In this light, the case for the baccalaureate degree as the entry qualification for nursing may also be built on arguments about social justice or equity and the need to give women the type of education that affirms their status as independent individuals who need the same long-term career interests and options as men.

The complex nature of entry to practice requires further research. Richardson (1988, 1991a) has proposed that research on prelicensure nursing education be directed at (1) exploring the knowledge, skills, attitudes, and costs associated with baccalaureate and diploma program graduates, (2) augmenting the historical research, (3) doing research on the selection, admission, and retention of baccalaureate students, and (4) conducting research on a thematic, rather than sporadic, issue-specific basis related to teaching and learning.

Women and Educational Equity

Feminist issues in education will be more important in nursing education in the 1990s. Women are under-represented in graduate studies programs and in teaching positions in universities, do not receive a proportional share of funds for teaching and research assistanceships, and need more travel support so that they are able to complete the "going-public process," which is considered essential in establishing an academic career profile (Gardner and Judge, 1989). The situation has so alarmed the Royal Society of Canada that members have proposed a plan for advancement of women in scholarship. This society represents research and scholarship in all disciplines and has, as its goal, equitable representation by gender for its membership (Royal Society of Canada, 1989).

Hall and Sandler (1985) have written about the chilly campus climate and its impact on the shaping of a woman's self-concept, thereby potentially affecting her ability to develop skills to meet future challenges, both academic and professional. This climate is created by male teachers' treatment of female students, which often reinforces the notion of the female as "second class" in the classroom. The "chill factors" include condescension, sexist comments, and insensitivity. Parr (1989) has extended the concept of chilly climate to include female faculty members. She suggests that all program cutbacks be evaluated to ensure that women are not disproportionately affected. Furthermore, she indicates the need for exit interviews with female candidates who are not hired, to evaluate whether they have been treated differently than their male counterparts. Wright (1991) found that college experiences related to teaching, learning, thinking, mental health, self-respect, and living need to be made more inviting for women.

Another issue related to education for women relates to skill training. Jackson (1987) takes issue with competency-based approaches widely used in programs for female-dominated white collar occupations, such as general nursing. She contends that competency forms of training, which emphasize disposable, short-term, limited-use careers, limit women's opportunities in the workplace.

Curriculum-Related Issues

The need to examine nursing programs to ensure these are relevant to immediate and long-term needs of the health care system and of students is an important issue for the 1990s. Changes in consumer expectations, in demographics, and in government financing will affect ways health care will be offered in the future, whether in hospitals or in homes, and will challenge nursing education to examine programs of study (e.g., for care of the elderly, for more intensive care units in hospital, for more home care, for more multicultural care). Two other immediate concerns, care for the mentally ill and mentally handicapped and midwifery, illustrate this need for change in nursing education.

With the thrust toward community-based care for psychiatric patients, the inadequacy of current nursing education for care of the mentally disabled becomes evident. The integration of psychiatric nursing content into the basic nursing curriculum does not seem to have resulted in practitioners who have sufficient psychiatric nursing expertise. Neither the diploma programs throughout Canada nor the psychiatric nursing programs offered in the four Western provinces impart the necessary skills and knowledge, particularly for the new, community-based care. Provincial governments in Western Canada continue to rely on graduates of psychiatric nursing programs because of shortages of psychiatrists outside metropolitan areas and because of a reluctance of registered nurses to practice in psychiatric settings. The government of Manitoba has already signaled its desire for a baccalaureate program in psychiatric nursing at Brandon University.

Nursing education is also facing a similar crisis because of the public's demands for midwifery services. Several provinces are studying ways to establish midwifery as part of the provincial health care system, and Ontario has passed legislation establishing midwifery as a separate health profession. Nurse educators need to mobilize efforts to develop relevant educational programs to ensure a supply of *nurse* midwives.

If nursing education does not take the initiative to ensure its programs meet public needs, it is conceivable that midwifery and psychiatric nursing—and perhaps other of nursing's holistic functions—may become independent of nursing and claimed by new groups. Considerable rethinking is required to ensure that registered nurses have sufficient basic and advanced education to meet changing patient care requirements, whether these are in institutions or in the community.

Accountability in nursing education was addressed at the National Nursing Symposium in Winnipeg in November 1990. Recommendations for nurse educators include a call for mechanisms to link nursing education with nursing practice more closely. Other specific recommendations included: the need to review nursing curriculums with employers of nurses; the need to provide education on use of computers and other electronic information systems; and the need to evaluate current teaching methods to ensure the environment rewards assertiveness, collaboration, independence, and critical thinking for both students and faculty.

Many other such issues are related to the day-to-day decisions over what is incorporated, or not incorporated, in nursing curriculums across the country. Increasingly, emphasis is placed on the importance of nursing education's accountability to students, to the profession, and to society. Undergraduate programs have always required approval from the provincial licensing bodies, but this allows programs and standards to vary across the country. The standards generally are set by the provincial nurses' associations, except in Ontario and Alberta, where other government-designated bodies approve the programs. Beginning in the 1970s, the Canadian Association of University Schools of Nursing took on the challenge of developing and implementing a voluntary, national accreditation process for its member schools and, since May 1987, has been the official accrediting body for its members. Approval is concerned primarily with protection of public interests by ensuring a program meets minimum standards set by a body designated in provincial legislation. Accreditation is voluntary and is carried out by an external, nongovernmental agency and is intended to provide the public not only with assurance of minimum standards but also with a measure of assurance about the quality of the program (see also Chapter 19). Between 1987 and early 1992, CAUSN reviewed 10 university programs. Use of the two review processes for nursing undergraduate programs will ensure that nurses will have the specialized knowledge and skills considered essential for delivery of professional services.

Financial Issues

Professional nursing education represents an economic investment and a cost to students, to the educational sector, and to health care agencies. It is associated with two tax-supported areas currently in great turmoil: health and education. Not a day goes by without some major governmental decision or report demanding health care reform or protesting the impact of government fiscal policy on universities or other institutions of higher education. The fiscal policies affecting both are essential, but often neglected, ingredients in any discussion of nursing education. Federal support to postsecondary education and to health care is declining steadily and is expected to continue to decline for the foreseeable future. The money to support nursing education programs is finite. Students pay tuition, but most other costs associated with nursing education are borne by the taxpayer.

Redman, Bednash, and Amos (1990) note that, for an individual with no previous educational preparation, the cost for a baccalaureate degree in nursing is higher than costs for a diploma or non-nursing degree. However, the total cost of first obtaining a nursing diploma and then returning to school for a baccalaureate may be higher than the initial cost of a generic baccalaureate. According to 1989 figures, the cost in Canada of education for a generic baccalaureate graduate was $45,000. This was not significantly different from the mean cost of an honors arts degree but was well below the mean for a comparable degree in science $59,000 (Roberts, 1989, cited in Redmond, Bednash and Amos, 1990).

Costs to nursing students include educational costs, such as tuition, student government fees, books, and equipment such as stethoscopes and uniforms. Living expenses, such as cost of transportation and costs associated with interest on loans, are other considerations.

Within these financial parameters, there are other issues that need to be addressed. For health care agencies, there are both costs and benefits, although generally the benefits of serving as a training site (e.g., recruitment savings) outweigh the costs (costs associated with coordination and scheduling of clinical rotations). Better data are needed for estimating costs and benefits of student learning experiences. As economic constraints affect all areas of the health care sector, health care agencies are beginning to demand payment for staff who act as preceptors for nursing students. This will place an additional strain on the budgets of the nursing education establishments from whence the students come.

The ways budgets are developed in educational institutions may inadvertently disadvantage nursing programs. Staffing policies do not adequately consider the clinical aspects of faculty activities; these policies may give equal weight to a lecture component (3 to 4 hours a week) and a clinical and laboratory component (3 to 12 hours a week).

Graduate Study and Research

Friesen (1990) contends that "in the absence of research, medical education would be a very different exercise. Its content and form would be relatively static" (p. 2). The same applies to nursing. Through research, new ideas and innovative practice are realized. The research endeavor depends on a synergy among faculty, students, those in the practice setting, and resources (money).

The slow growth of graduate programs has contributed directly to the current shortage of nurses with the necessary academic qualifications to teach at the graduate level. Nationally, only 1.1% of Canada's 256,145 registered nurses have a master's degree or higher (Richardson, 1991a). Furthermore, with insufficient numbers of doctorally-prepared faculty, graduate programs can provide high-quality research training to only a limited number of students. Thus nursing is faced with the dilemma of either compromising the quality of graduate education or continuing to prepare inadequate numbers of nurses with research training.

Ritchie has thoroughly discussed research issues in Chapter 16, but a few research issues that are tied closely to education also deserve brief mention here. For example, for student and faculty research efforts to thrive, a stable practice environment is essential. Practice environments where dissatisfaction abounds and quality of work-life is poor are unable to sustain research studies that involve nurses (Pringle, 1989).

Faculty involved in research often struggle to balance the demands of teaching with those for research, and a recent report on Canadian university education, conducted by the Association of Universities and Colleges of Canada (AUCC), identifies an imbalance between teaching and research. The report recommends that scholarship required for faculty promotion be defined beyond the narrow limits of publications, that teaching loads be increased and minimum teaching hours be established for all faculty, and that graduate students planning to pursue academic careers be required to demonstrate competence in teaching. Until the 1980s, university schools of nursing were concerned primarily with teaching, but efforts now are focused on creating a balance between the need for quality instruction and the need to expand research and scholarly activities.

A missing ingredient in the research enterprise is adequate funding. Only 1% of total health research money goes to nursing research (CAUSN, 1991b). In 1991, the Medical Research Council of Canada (MRC) and the National Health Research Development Program (NHRDP) began to evaluate their Joint Program for the Development of Nursing Research. In response, CAUSN and CNA submitted several recommendations for their consideration, including suggestions for a special competition for nursing research program development and an annual competition for postdoctoral funding for nurses (CAUSN, 1991b).

Nursing research development has been severely retarded by the growth of master's and doctoral programs in nursing. As Field, Stinson, and Thibaudeau point out in Chapter 22, the severe shortage of doctorally prepared faculty in Canada will not be solved quickly. Overall, only 24% of full-time nursing faculty in schools and faculties of nursing hold earned doctoral degrees (Richardson, 1991b). The recent introduction of doctoral programs in nursing in Canada will help. The doctoral nursing program at the University of Alberta first admitted students in 1989 and in 1991 had nine students. The University of British Columbia enrolled its first two doctoral nursing students in 1991 and there are also seven PhD (Nursing) special case students in the University of McGill/University of Montreal program.

Globalization of Education

The trend in Canada and other countries toward Free Trade, with a breaking down of barriers between nations for exchange of goods and services, indicates the world is moving toward an international economy. Not only is there a "growing interdependency of the global economy" (Naisbitt, 1990, p. 8), but also a growing emphasis on international educational ties. Nursing and other professions are feeling the effects of these moves.

The ties in nursing are being strengthened by provision of international courses in the curriculum, study opportunities for Canadian students abroad and for nursing students of other countries to study in Canada, and initiation of projects with appropriate foreign institutions. Currently, international projects between Canadian university schools of nursing and the international community include countries such as Botswana (Brandon University), Tanzania (Dalhousie), and China (University of Manitoba), for example. (See also Chapter 10.)

CONCLUSION

Nursing education in the past has been influenced by social trends of the times and has made changes—albeit slowly. Many of today's social and political trends are now in step with goals of nursing education that have been outlined during past eras. However, nursing education has some formidable challenges ahead as it grapples with the need to be responsive to current changes—locally, nationally, and internationally. This means changing public perceptions about nursing education and forging broad coalitions with consumers, policymakers, and allied health professionals. The reforming efforts will require dedicated leadership from faculty and administrators to redirect professionals skills and values and to experiment with new ways of organizing educational and research activity. Such reforms will not be accomplished easily, but new resources must be brought together to support the evolution of structures for lifelong learning. Two things are sure: society will demand greater accountability from health care practitioners, and nursing education can help shape the future nurses that will be needed.

REFERENCES

Abella, R. (1985, December). Equality at work and at home. *Policy Options*, pp. 27-42.

Aiken, L., & Mullinix, C. (1987). The nurse shortage: Myth or reality? *New England Journal of Medicine, 317*(10), 641-645.

Campbell, A.R., & Davis, S.M. (1990). Enrichment for academic success: Helping at-risk students. *Nurse Educator, 15*(6), 33-37.

Cameron-Buccheri, R., & Trygstad, L. (1989). Retaining freshmen nursing students. *Nursing and Health Care, 10*(7), 389-393.

Canadian Association of University Schools of Nursing. (1991a). *Evaluation of the accreditation process: The first five years of implementation 1986-1991: Report of the Committee on accreditation to CAUSN Council.* Ottawa: Author.

Canadian Association of University Schools of Nursing. (1991b). *Recommendations to federal research agencies for funding of nursing research.* Unpublished report, available from CAUSN, Ottawa.

Canadian Nurses Association. (1968). *Countdown 1968: Canadian nursing statistics.* Ottawa: Author.

Canadian Nurses Association. (1982). *Nursing in Canada, 1982,* Ottawa: Author.

Chater, S. (1982). The clinical component of nursing education: A conceptual approach. In Canadian Nurses Association, *Proceedings second national conference on nursing education* (Winnipeg, March 17-19, 1982), (pp. 13-20). Ottawa: Author.

CNR delegates make far-reaching decisions in Jamaica. (1991). *International Nursing Review, 38*(5), 138-144.

Coburn, J. (1974). I see and am silent: A short history of nursing in Ontario. In J. Acton, P.

Goldsmith, & B. Shepherd (Eds.), *Women at work: Ontario 1850-1930*, (pp. 127-163). Toronto: Canadian Women's Educational Press.

Friesen, H. (1990). Why not the best: The imperatives of education and scholarship. *ACMC Forum, 23*(3), 1-4.

Gamarnikow, E. (1978). Sexual division of labour: The case of nursing. In A. Kuhn & A.M. Wolpe (Eds.), *Feminism and materialism: Women and modes of production.* London: Routledge and Kegan Paul.

Gardner, J.S., & Judge, L. (1989). *Women in graduate studies at the University of Waterloo.* Unpublished paper, Department of Graduate Studies, University of Waterloo, Waterloo, Ontario.

Gibbon, J.M., & Mathewson, M.S. (1947). *Three centuries of Canadian nursing.* Toronto: Macmillan.

Gillett, M. (1981). *We walked very warily.* Montreal: Eden Press Women's Publications.

Glass, H. (1975). A guest in the house. In M. Davis, M. Kramer, & A. Strauss (Eds.), *Nurses in practice: A perspective on work environments* (pp. 178-189). St. Louis, MO: Mosby–Year Book, Inc.

Hall, R.M., & Sandler, B.R. (1985). A chilly climate in the classroom. In A.G. Sargent (Ed.), *Beyond sex roles* (pp. 503-510). St Paul: West Publishing.

Harris, J., Lobin, T., & Paddon, P. (1990). Profile of nursing education. *Health Reports, 2*(4), 379-381.

Jackson, N. (1987). Skill training in transition: Implications for women. In J. Gaskell & A. McLaren (Eds.), *Women and education: A Canadian perspective* (pp. 351-369). Calgary: Detselig Enterprises.

Keeler, H.B. (1960). Uncovering some facts. *Canadian Nurse, 56*(5), 403-404.

Lang, V. (1974). *The service state emerges in Ontario.* Toronto: The Ontario Economic Council.

Leslie, P.M. (1980). *Canadian universities 1980 and beyond: Enrollment, structural change and finance.* Ottawa: Association of Universities and Colleges of Canada.

Loree, D.J., & Leckie, I. (1977). Occupation and career perceptions of nursing students in New Brunswick. *Canadian Nurse, 73*(12), 30-33.

Naisbitt, J. (1990, Summer). Globalized education. *Inside Guide*, pp. 8-9.

Parr, J. (1989). Chilly climate: The systemic dilemma. *Forum (Ontario Confederation of University Faculty Associations), 6*(18), 1-2.

Prescott, P. (1988). Another round of nursing shortage. *Image: Journal of Nursing Scholarship, 20*(4), 204-209.

Pringle, D. (1989). Another twist on the double helix: Research and practice. *The Canadian Journal of Nursing Research, 21*(1), 47-60.

Pringle, D. (1991). Recruitment, education and retention of nurses. In the *National Nursing Symposium: Report to the Provincial and Territorial Ministers of Health* (J. Larsen, Chair) (pp.

69-83). Winnipeg: Manitoba National Nursing Symposium Steering Committee.

Redman, B.K., Bednash, G., & Amos, L.K. (1990). Policy perspectives on economic investment in professional nursing education. *Nursing economics, 8*(1), 27-35.

Richardson, S.L. (1988). *Baccalaureate entry into nursing practice in Alberta: An analysis of the articulation policy issue.* Edmonton: University of Alberta, Department of Educational Administration.

Richardson, S. (1991a). Research on prelicensure nursing education in Canada: Progress, promise, and problems. In P.A. Baj & G.M. Clayton (Eds.), *Review of research in nursing education* (Vol. 4) (pp. 141-169), New York: National League of Nursing.

Richardson, S. (1991b). *Student and faculty statistical summary of Canadian University Schools of Nursing 1984-1989: A research report.* Ottawa: Canadian Association of University Schools of Nursing.

Roberts, P.M. (1989). Estimates of the cost of educating a BN graduate and graduates of other disciplines at a Canadian university: A case study. *Journal of Nursing Education, 28*, 140-143.

Rosenfeld, P. (1988). Measuring student retention: A national analysis. *Nursing and Health Care, 9*(4), 199-202.

Royal Society of Canada. (1989). *Plan for advance-ment of women in scholarship.* Ottawa: Committee for Advancement of Women in Scholarship of the Royal Society of Canada.

Ryten, E. (1988, June). *Women as deliverers of health care* (The Marion Woodward Lecture). Vancouver: University of British Columbia School of Nursing.

Smith, V.A. (1990). Nursing student attrition and implications for pre-admission advisement. *Journal of Nursing Education, 29*(5), 215-218.

Southern Regional Education Board. (1982). Acclimating the novice nurses: Whose responsibility? In Southern Regional Education Board, *Pathways to practice: 4.* Atlanta, GA: Author.

Weir, G. (1932). *Survey of nursing education in Canada.* Toronto: University of Toronto Press.

Weston, J. (1991, December). New doctoral programs in nursing gain support. *University Affairs,* p. 20.

Wright, B. (1991). A thousand points of flight - Or why we need a kinder, gentler academy and how to get it. *Change, 23*(2), 8-10.

Zilm, G. (Ed.). *Back to basics: The nature of nursing education.* Ottawa: Canadian Nurses Association.

Zilm, G., Larose, O., & Stinson, S. (1979). *Ph.D. (Nursing): Proceedings of the Kellogg National Seminar on doctoral preparation for nurses.* Ottawa: Canadian Nurses Association.

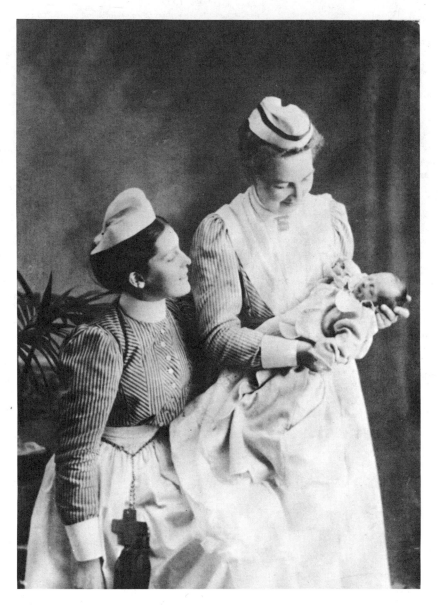

Education for nurses in the early part of the century was in hospital schools of nursing, but trends are changing in the latter part of the century. Student nurse, Jean Dick, observes as Rose Heise (class of 1901) demonstrates how to hold a baby. The two studied at the Mack Training School for Nurses, St. Catharine's, Ontario, the first school in Canada to be founded on the lines of the Nightingale Schools of England. (Photograph from the St. Catharine's Hospital Archives. Used with permission.)

CHAPTER TWENTY-ONE

Entry-level Educational Preparation for Nursing

IRMAJEAN BAJNOK, RN, MScN

Irmajean Bajnok, RN, BScN (Alberta), MScN (Western Ontario), is Education Advisor, Department of Nursing, Mount Sinai Hospital in Toronto. She is a former Director of the School of Nursing at Ryerson and was a member of the Task Force on Entry to Practice for the Registered Nurses Association of Ontario and Chair of the RNAO's Entry to Practice Monitoring Committee. She is completing her doctoral studies in epidemiology at the University of Western Ontario.

SPECIAL ACKNOWLEDGEMENT

The author wishes to acknowledge the contribution of Ria Rovers, RN, PhD, who was co-author of the chapter that appeared in the first edition of this book.

The minimum educational preparation for entry into the practice of nursing has been an issue throughout nursing's evolution as a profession. During the 1980s, the debate intensified as nursing knowledge expanded and society's needs for nursing care became more complex. As in many of the traditional professions, nursing has the autonomy to regulate its membership. Despite this, the nursing profession's efforts to keep educational requirements current with societal trends that affect nursing practice have been subject to various influences and wide controversy.

This chapter reviews past trends and current practices in nursing education for entry into the practice of nursing and presents a synopsis of factors that influence nursing practice and education in Canada today. A perspective on the current debate about future educational requirements for entry into the practice of nursing is also provided. Finally, the chapter will analyze and discuss some of the major changes in nursing education over the last 10 years. Planned changes for the future will be presented in the context of the health care environment and the entry to practice issue.

EVOLUTION OF NURSING EDUCATION IN CANADA

Systematic nursing education was not available in Canada until the first Canadian nursing school, The Mack Training School, opened in St. Catharines, Ontario, in 1874. Early nursing schools in Canada and the United States clearly were established to provide low-cost nursing services (Matejski, 1981; Mussallem, 1964). For decades, nursing education programs were based on an apprenticeship training model, with lectures considered as privileges when hospital duties allowed. Exploitation of student nurses was a concern in Canada well before the turn of the century and became a pervasive issue in nursing's attempt to set initial education standards (Mussallem, 1964).

As early as 1927, the inadequacies inherent in the "training of nurses" were highlighted sufficiently to prompt the Canadian Nurses Association (CNA) to strike a joint committee with the Canadian Medical Association to address the problems through a survey of nursing education headed by G.M. Weir, a professor of education at the University of British Columbia. As part of his report, Weir notes: "The field of nursing is bristling with problems that challenge solution and herein is offered a great opportunity for Canadian Universities to render a real public service" (Weir, 1932, p. 392). The report also suggests that "the modern nurse should be given an adequate liberal as well as technical education," and that "university training programs for nurses should, in the judgment of the survey, award degrees in nursing" (p. 393).

An initial response to recommendations for a school independent of hospital control was the establishment of the Metropolitan Demonstration School for Nursing in 1948 in Windsor, Ontario. Its purpose was to demonstrate that professional nurses could be prepared adequately in less than the traditional 3 years (Lord, 1952). Although the model proved successful, it was not until 1960 that a second independent school, the Nightingale School of Nursing in Toronto, was established, also offering a 2-year program (Nightingale School of Nursing, 1969).

The profession, in its zeal to separate nursing education from hospital control, did not have the foresight to continue to use the 3-year time frame to incorporate the rapidly expanding nursing science and health content that occurred during the 1960s. Hindsight suggests that it would have been appropriate to begin to move basic nursing education directly to the university setting at this time. The actions of organized nursing in this regard, especially since other professions were increasing program length, may have reinforced the view that nursing did not have an ever-expanding body of scientific knowledge. However, given the strong feelings regarding the nature and purpose of nursing education among hospital administrators and medical professionals (who wielded considerably more power in health care than the nursing profession), this "trade off" approach was no doubt the most feasible strategy at the time. These same dynamics mean that, more than a half-century later, many of the basic issues and controversies about the educational preparation for nurses outlined in the 1932 Weir report are still present and unresolved.

The first Canadian university-based nursing program was implemented in 1919 at the University of British Columbia. This initial baccalaureate degree in nursing has been described as a "sandwich" model of nursing education, and the university-to-hospital-to-university route became the prototype of subsequent university-level nursing programs in Canada until 1942 (King, 1970). Frequently cited criticism of this model is that universities took responsibility only for non-nursing academic courses, whereas affiliating hospitals maintained control over the nursing component of the educational program, with little if any integration between the two elements (Kergin, 1968; King, 1970).

Five universities—British Columbia, Toronto, McGill, Alberta, and Dalhousie—offered certificate courses in public health between 1920 and 1921. They were assisted financially by the Canadian Red Cross, which advocated the need for special training for public health nurses (King, 1970). This activity of the Canadian Red Cross was carried out in conjunction with the League of Red Cross Societies. The goals of this worldwide public health organization were to increase standards of physical and mental fitness through health promotion and disease prevention (Gibbon and Mathewson, 1947). Nurses were identified as potential leaders in these activities, and education focused on preparing nurses for major public health responsibilities. Concurrent with initiation of the public health nursing program at the University of Toronto, the director of that program, E. Kathleen Russell, launched a dynamic campaign for an integrated baccalaureate nursing education program. Russell's conviction that nurses needed a broad foundation in the humanities and sciences, as well as nursing, was evident in her proposals to obtain funding for the University of Toronto program and, in 1942, culminated with the first integrated basic baccalaureate nursing program in Canada. This meant that both nursing and non-nursing courses were offered by the university faculty and were integrated throughout all years of the program.

Russell is justly credited for providing visionary leadership for improvements in nursing education in Canada during the first half of this century (Carpenter, 1970, 1982; King, 1970), but her concept of integrated baccalaureate nursing education spread slowly to other nursing educational institutions. Concern about persistent problems in the educational preparation for nurses resulted in Mussallem's CNA-sponsored review of diploma nursing schools in Canada in the late 1950s. Her report, *Spotlight on Nursing Education* (Mussallem, 1960), concluded that a process of accreditation of nursing schools was essential if educational standards were to improve. Mussallem also recommended that the entire field of nursing education be re-examined before initiation of any program of accreditation, since only 16% of the schools reviewed in 1959 met established nursing education standards. Although many serious weaknesses were noted across schools, Mussallem concluded that the majority of the educational problems were a result of the continuing control over schools by institutions whose primary aim was nursing service (i.e., hospitals).

Within the decade, the issue of educational preparation for nurses was addressed again, this time by the Royal Commission on Health Services (1959-1963). The Royal Commission Report (Government of Canada, 1964) reflected the work of Weir (1932) and of Mussallem (1960; 1964), who had conducted a second review of nursing programs. Mussallem's 1964 review included a sample of diploma programs and all basic degree programs and introduced a new era for nursing education. Recommendations submitted to and arising from the Commission facilitated the expansion of nursing education in universities, movement away from nonintegrated nursing degree programs, and transfer of diploma schools from hospitals to postsecondary education settings.

The change in jurisdiction for diploma nursing education was initiated with the "Ryerson Project," when, in 1964, Ryerson Polytechnical Institute offered the first diploma nursing education program at a postsecondary institution in Canada. Perceived success of the project, which was promoted by the Registered Nurses Association of Ontario, stimulated development of various diploma nursing education programs outside the jurisdiction of hospitals. This change was most precipitous in Ontario, where in 1973 the government announced that all diploma schools would be under the aegis of the Colleges of Applied Arts and Technology. In Quebec, the same process occurred over a 5-year period from 1967 to 1972 when hospital schools closed and colleges (Colleges d'enseignement general et professionnel or "CEGEPs") began to offer nursing programs. The move was followed, entirely or in part, by several other provinces and eventually led to acceptance in Canada of divergent settings for nursing education.

The 1960s and 1970s were a period of rapid transformation in nursing education in terms of program content and context. Curricula in schools were revised to reflect the increasing scientific foundation of nursing practice and to eliminate the apprenticeship orientation of previous decades. This growth and change taxed the resources in Canadian nursing so much that many faculties were staffed with baccalaureate-prepared nurses, inexperienced in both the practice and teaching of nursing and ill prepared to meet the broader role expectations of academia. In some cases (primarily at the diploma level), schools were forced to hire nurses without preparation beyond diploma education to meet teaching obligations.

University nursing educators, now convinced that "full authority and responsibility for the teaching of nursing rested in the university" (King, 1970, p. 72), introduced integrated 4-year programs. The widespread acceptance of an integrated approach to university nursing education reflected a belief in the value of the intellectual component of nursing and linked the emerging profession of nursing to other, more established professions in the university (King, 1970). Although there was funding for education during this time, growth of nursing education was limited because there were insufficient numbers of prepared nurses available to expand the development of university nursing education and participate in the expected research and publication activities. Also, in Ontario, by far the most resource rich in terms of nursing education, considerable energy was expended in responding to negative reactions to the changes in the length and jurisdiction of the diploma nursing education programs.

HEALTH CARE TRENDS AFFECTING NURSING PRACTICE AND EDUCATION

Today, as in the past, major societal developments affect educational requirements for the nursing profession. Three developments are: changes in health status of Canadians; changes in the health care delivery system; and changes in the nature of nursing practice (CNA, 1982).

It is a well-established premise that the increasing proportion of elderly in our society will consume an ever greater portion of the health care dollar (Watson, 1985). Creative, knowledgeable health professionals will be required to examine how health care offered through different system entry points, from a different combination of professionals, in different settings, will affect cost effectiveness of care. The demographic trends suggest that future nurses will need more extensive theory and practice in geriatric nursing and in related community and family health nursing. Education in the application of nursing research, focused on specific interventions for age-related health conditions and broader system issues, is an integral part of nursing education for the future.

Numerous books and reports (Hall, 1980; Jackson, 1985; Norman, 1986; Rachlis and Kushner, 1989) since the Lalonde Report (1974) continue to document the relationship of health and life-style and environmental factors. Areas such as individual, community, and global health issues; policy development; lifestyle education; quality of life support; and self-care must occupy a greater portion of the education curriculum. As nurses accept a broader mandate for the achievement of health for all as a goal, the need for liberally educated professionals becomes increasingly evident. Indeed, the health care consumer today is demanding both knowledgeable and humane professionals as partners in care, and the health care system is becoming increasingly complex, costly, and cumbersome. Today, much more is possible in diagnosis and treatment, although issues of access and ethics abound as new norms are established in relation to settings of care, types of caregivers, payment for health care, and responsibilities of individuals for their own health. Such a system demands sophisticated professionals adept at identifying issues and creating solutions.

Nursing practice is changing; in all settings the acuity of the problems and the complexity of the situations are increasing. The knowledge base required by nurses and other professionals is necessarily more extensive. Diers (1986) professes that nursing's knowledge must incorporate three kinds of knowing: first, the knowing that includes art, history, philosophy, and other life studies and experiences that enable one to appreciate the human experience; second, the knowing that is based on physical, psychological, and sociological sciences; and third, the knowing that is nursing content and nursing knowledge.

Carper (1978) identifies four patterns or ways of knowing in nursing: ethics or moral knowledge in nursing; esthetics or the art of nursing; personal knowledge in nursing; and empirics or the science of nursing. Each pattern is equally important in the development of nursing science and equally necessary for clinical nursing. Nursing education since the 1950s focused on the empirical pattern of knowing based on traditional approaches to science and theory development (Chinn and Kramer, 1991). Currently, further work attempts to determine how one learns; demonstrates understanding; and creates ethical, esthetic, and personal knowledge in nursing. Nursing curricula in the future must move toward a balanced focus in all four patterns of knowing if the profession is to present adequately the totality of the discipline and the practice of nursing.

CURRENT NURSING EDUCATION PROGRAMS

As the countdown to the twenty-first century begins, diversity exists throughout Canada in academic jurisdiction over nursing education, and this affects content depth and breadth, role expectations, and skill levels. Although there is currently one category of practicing nurse registrant, the educational preparation for entry can be either a nursing degree or a diploma.

Diploma Nursing Programs

Diploma nursing education continues in hospital schools of nursing, independent nursing schools (called freestanding schools), technical institutions, and community and junior colleges. Program length varies from 20 to 36 months. In Canada, in 1989, the 27 hospital-based and independent schools graduated 1630 nurses; a further 6006 nurses completed diploma programs at the 83 college and technical schools, totalling 7636 diploma graduates. As of December 1989, in British Columbia, Ontario, Quebec, and Saskatchewan, all diploma nursing education was under the academic jurisdiction of a college or technical institution.

Tables 21-1 and 21-2 indicate that limited overall change occurred from 1985 to 1989 in number and type of schools, numbers of students admitted and enrolled,

TABLE 21-1 **Comparison, Number, and Type of Diploma Schools in Canada in 1985 and 1989**

Area	Hospital and independent 1985	Hospital and independent 1989	College 1985	College 1989	Total 1985	Total 1989
Canada	27	27	83	83	110	110
Newfoundland	4	4	—	—	4	4
Prince Edward Island	1	1	—	—	1	1
Nova Scotia	7	7	—	—	7	7
New Brunswick	5	5	—	—	5	5
Quebec	—	—	42	41	42	41
Ontario	—	—	23	23	23	23
Manitoba	5	5	1	1	6	6
Saskatchewan	—	—	2	2	2	2
Alberta	4	4	7	7	11	11
British Columbia	1	1	8	9	9	10

Compiled from information from the Research Department, Canadian Nurses Association, November 1990.

and numbers of graduates produced. A closer examination of the figures in Table 21-2 shows that admissions decreased over the 5-year period in Prince Edward Island, Nova Scotia, Quebec, Saskatchewan, and Alberta for a total decrease of 188 admissions. Furthermore, British Columbia decreased admissions by 178 from 1988 to 1989, largely because of the amalgamation of Vancouver General Hospital School of Nursing with the University of British Columbia's nursing degree program. (The 5-year decrease from 1985 to 1989 in British Columbia was 80.) However, substantial increases in admissions occurred in Ontario and Newfoundland, no doubt a response to the severe shortages of nurses in the later part of the 1980s, especially in Ontario. These increases brought the 1989 national total to 2% above the 1985 total. Similarly, the total number of enrollments in diploma schools increased over the 5-year period, as did the number of graduates produced in 1989. These figures seem to indicate a response to market forces rather than any rational plan to alter the mix of diploma and degree prepared nurses.

On the other hand, it is encouraging to note that the concern about declining enrollment expressed in 1987 and 1988 seems to have been alleviated in 1989. Reduced enrollment in 1987 and 1988 is believed to be related to factors such as a declining applicant pool because of wider career choices for women and/or a low perception of the status and value of nursing as a career in society, an increased attrition because of dissatisfaction of students with nursing, and an increasing rigor of nursing education as a science-based discipline. It may be that these issues no longer seemed important to students when they selected careers that might guarantee work in a time of recession and high unemployment. This, with the many provincial and local initiatives that were developed in response to severe shortages (such as salary increases, recruitment drives, education program developments, and a focus on the image of nursing) obviously had an effect.

TABLE 21-2 **Comparison of Admission Figures in all Diploma Schools of Nursing in Canada in 1985 and 1989**

Area	1985	1989
Canada	9982	10170
Newfoundland	286	340
Prince Edward Island	65	54
Nova Scotia	377	358
New Brunswick	375	374
Quebec	2975	2917
Ontario	3214	3509
Manitoba	517	624
Saskatchewan	383	310
Alberta	970	943
British Columbia	821	741

Compiled from information from the Research Department, Canadian Nurses Association, November 1990.

Examination of data on full-time faculty in diploma schools indicates a gradual increase in educational preparation of faculty over the 5-year period from 1985 to 1989 inclusive. During this period, a higher percentage of faculty reported graduate preparation and a lower percentage reported no degree preparation. Although over-all student enrollment increased marginally during this period, total numbers of full-time faculty decreased by 4%; total numbers of part-time faculty, however, increased by 10%. The proportion of full-time faculty with doctorate degrees remained virtually the same; the percentage of full-time faculty with master's degrees increased by 8%, and full-time faculty with baccalaureate degrees decreased by 6%. The percentage of faculty without degrees decreased, but this group still makes up 12% of full-time faculty, an unusually high number in any postsecondary academic setting. Also, in 1989, 26% (632) of faculty were part time (an increase of 3% from 1985) and, of those, 28% (149) had no degree preparation. Since part-time faculty are often in clinical teaching positions, this number of faculty with no degree preparation may well have a significant effect on the education process. In 1985, only 1% of faculty did not state their degree preparation; this figure increased to 4% in 1989.

Basic Degree Progams

Basic degree nursing education is less varied, in that there are programs in 22 universities or degree granting institutions in Canada, and they extend over 4 academic years. Perhaps because degree programs had to justify their existence in nursing in the past and also because the network of university deans and professors is relatively small and remarkably cohesive, there is a great deal of similarity in the programs in terms of non-nursing, as well as nursing, content.

Most basic degree programs have used a developmental model incorporating health and illness throughout the lifespan to guide the curriculum. Some have used nursing models to direct the sequence of nursing and related content and the nature and setting of the clinical experience. A few of the more recent degree programs use a pluralistic approach to inclusion of nursing theory, in which, as in the Ryerson School of Nursing Degree Program, each level of the program is based on a different nursing framework. Most of the nursing curricula incorporate study and application of nursing theory through use of one or more of the common nursing frameworks. The basic baccalaureate programs have maintained a substantial physical science base. There is a strong belief that content in the area of research, ethics, professional issues, and the health care system is important and necessary at the baccalaureate level. Most programs also emphasize basic social sciences and include sociology and psychology courses in the areas of developmental psychology, sociology of the family, and sociology of health. Other social science courses on health professions and certain demographic groups and/or cultural groups are often offered as electives.

The greatest difference in programs in the past has been in the number of clinical hours and in the presence or absence of a summer practicum. Clinical hours have been cut to a minimum as university faculty have had to come to grips with optimal practice time for students versus optimal research time for faculty and teaching limitations imposed by university budgetary constraints. There are, however, indications that there is a need to re-examine the issue of clinical internships or residencies as part of baccalaureate education. The complexities of the practice setting and the specialized nature of nursing practice are critical factors in regard to this issue.

Major changes over the years have been: strengthening of the theory base of the nursing courses and focusing on health promotion and the community as client; broadening the professional issues courses to focus on wider health care systems issues; and including health related social science courses such as psychology of dying, sociology of health, and sociology of aging. However, the most critical curriculum issues at the baccalaureate level remain the focus, length, and nature of clinical practice and how specialization will be addressed. Both these issues are being examined in curriculum revision activities because budget constraints, complexity of practice, and the specialized nature of nursing are forcing a review of the nursing practice component of the undergraduate curriculum.

One trend is closer affiliation with practice settings in the form of work/study cooperatives, being discussed, for example, in the University of Toronto and various teaching hospitals in Toronto. Another trend is a period of internship in an area of focus after the 4-year program; for example, the University of Manitoba approved an 8-week practicum at the end of the 4-year program, and Memorial University in Newfoundland is considering this option. The purpose of such revisions is to enhance the practice experience to reflect the complex and often specialized nature of nursing in the acute care setting. There will, of course, need to be a similar plan for student practice in community health settings and much more discussion pertaining to the meaning of work/study, remuneration, union issues, the preceptor role for clinical nurses, and the role of the university faculty.

Degree-Completion Programs

Degree-completion programs for diploma-prepared registered nurses (also called post-RN programs) are now offered at 28 Canadian university campuses. Twenty-four universities in Canada offer a post-diploma degree program, with one of the universities offering a program at each of its five campuses. These programs have considerable variation in time frame; they range from full-time programs of 2 or 3 years to part-time programs that could take up to 8 years, and programs are offered both on and off campus. A diploma-then-degree route for nurses in terms of full-time study can therefore range from 2-plus-2 years to 3-plus-3 years of educational experience with other variations in between.

Currently, most university schools of nursing with degree-completion programs offer some separate courses for the registered nurse and some courses in which registered nurse students and basic students are integrated. Nursing content includes areas similar to that of the basic degree programs, with variations in focus and nature of the clinical courses. Major time differences of degree-completion programs involve the number of electives, non-nursing courses, and clinical time required.

Table 21-3 shows minimal differences throughout Canada in enrollment and graduation numbers between 1985 and 1989 in the basic programs, with an overall enrollment increase of only 6% over the 5-year period and virtually no change in graduation numbers. In the degree-completion programs, however, there is a 36% increase in enrollments over the 5 years and a 46% increase in graduates in this same

TABLE 21-3 **Enrollment and Graduation Figures from Schools in Canada by Type of Program, Canada and Provinces in 1985 and 1989**

Area	Diploma			
	Enrollment		Graduation	
	1985	1989	1985	1989
Canada	23217	24024	7218	7636
Newfoundland	683	778	263	180
Prince Edward Island	161	138	50	48
Nova Scotia	703	627	361	271
New Brunswick	586	558	243	250
Quebec	7268	7833	1754	2174
Ontario	8051	8546	2525	2452
Manitoba	994	1086	409	473
Saskatchewan	790	624	315	302
Alberta	2028	2063	711	791
British Columbia	1953	1771	587	695

Compiled from information from the Research Department, Canadian Nurses Association, November 1990.

period. (In interpreting these statistics, however, it should be noted that the enrollment numbers in post-RN programs in 1985 represent the lowest figure in the period from 1984 to 1989.) All provinces contributed to the enrollment increase from 1985 to 1989, with the exception of Newfoundland, which had a 35% decrease, and Quebec, which had a minimal decrease. Substantial increases occurred in the other provinces: New Brunswick reported an increase in its enrollment by almost six times the 1985 figure of 74 students, and Ontario reported a record enrollment of 1342 students.

The challenge to the university system is in balancing basic and post-RN baccalaureate education, as well as graduate education, often within a relatively fixed set of full-time faculty resources. For example, during the period of 1985 to 1989, full-time faculty numbers in all university nursing programs increased by approximately 4%, whereas undergraduate student enrollment increased by 42%. The significant enrollment increases in degree-completion programs occurred with only a 17% increase in part-time faculty. In degree programs, as in diploma programs, the enrollment increases were accommodated largely with increases in the part-time faculty component.

Since 1985, according to Statistics Canada and the Canadian Nurses Association, virtually all nursing faculty who stated their level of education had degree preparation. In 1989, the number of faculty stating their level of education was 100%. The statistics show that the number of faculty with graduate preparation increased by 13% from 1985 to 1989, with 93% of full-time faculty prepared at the graduate level. Of these 600 faculty with graduate preparation, 25% (152) were prepared at the

| Basic baccalaureate | | | | Post-RN baccalaureate | | | |
| Enrollment | | Graduation | | Enrollment | | Graduation | |
1985	1989	1985	1989	1985	1989	1985	1989
5442	5793	1196	1202	3765	5136	761	1111
198	190	39	45	104	68	18	19
—	—	—	—	—	—	—	—
329	305	78	63	303	374	31	65
389	455	61	71	74	433	25	40
687	701	236	206	1299	1286	201	211
2311	2517	484	497	899	1342	137	307
318	398	55	66	95	307	19	61
301	292	60	61	67	80	32	26
567	583	97	131	496	615	180	207
342	352	86	62	428	631	118	175

doctoral level. Clearly, although numbers of full-time faculty increased only minimally over the 1985 to 1989 period, the educational preparation of faculty is gradually changing to become more congruent with university norms and requirements.

BACCALAUREATE MODEL OF NURSING EDUCATION

Although the 1980s were a time of turmoil within nursing, there is general agreement within the profession that education must reflect the more complex nature of clinical nursing judgments and interventions and that nurses need to understand and be more involved in health care decision making if the health care system is to survive (Growe, 1991). There is further agreement that the current diversified yet often conservative approaches to nursing education serve neither the profession nor society well.

The complexity of clinical judgments required for effective nursing practice in today's health care settings is not a temporary phenomenon. An accelerated rate of change in nursing practice is certain for the remainder of this century. An appropriate response of a profession to changing roles is to ensure that education requirements for entrance into the profession keep pace with changes in society and in the profession itself. The professional organizations, at national and provincial levels, support the view that a baccalaureate degree in nursing is the only logical entry level for nurses in the twenty-first century (CNA, 1986).

A baccalaureate nursing education model needs a careful blend of liberal and professional components. Hangartner (1965) provides one of the most relevant arguments for the need for a liberal-professional education for nurses. Hangartner notes that the hallmark of the liberally educated person is one who has developed tolerance and open-mindedness and who demonstrates responsibility and self-awareness. If nursing values holistic development of the person, then the value of patient or client, which has become central to the conceptualization of patient care, must also be central to the education of nurses themselves.

Baccalaureate education is directed toward the acquisition of skills and qualities that will serve the nurse as a person and as a professional. Baccalaureate education is the means by which one acquires the attributes associated with a profession in general and the nursing profession in particular (AACN, 1986). Professional nursing is based on the value system of the practitioner, on liberal and professional knowledge, and on clinical and cognitive skills.

Professional nursing requires a sound basis in nursing science, in other related sciences, and in the humanities. In addition, professional nursing requires communication skills in all forms of expression: written, verbal, and nonverbal. Problem solving, the development of an inquiring mind, and the need for accountability to oneself and to society are also integral goals of liberal-professional education for nurses. Critical thinking and problem-solving skills, in turn, must complement a deep and tolerant understanding of humanity if a nurse is to achieve one of nursing's most important roles: the therapeutic or helping relationship that can make an important difference in the health of the individual person or family.

RECURRENT ISSUES IN THE ENTRY TO PRACTICE DEBATE

The need to change minimum educational requirements for entry into the practice of nursing to a baccalaureate degree in nursing has been demonstrated repeatedly since a clear and logical rationale for the position was outlined by Kathleen Russell (cited in Carpenter, 1970) more than four decades ago. The Canadian Nurses Association supports the baccalaureate concept through various reports (Government of Canada, 1964; Mussallem, 1964; Weir, 1932). The official position that by the year 2000 the minimum educational requirement for entry into the practice of nursing should be successful completion of a baccalaureate in nursing was adopted by the CNA Board of Directors in 1982 (CNA, 1982). The unanimous endorsement by CNA resulted after extensive study of and wide response to the report of the National Task Force on Entry to Practice. The Canadian position means that the beginning practitioner in the profession of nursing, as of the year 2000, will require a baccalaureate degree in nursing. This position is a vision for Canadian nursing and as such holds no statutory power. However, over the 10-year period from 1979 to 1989 all provincial nursing associations, all but one (Ontario) of which do have statutory power over education, have taken the position that the baccalaureate will be the required educational preparation for entry to practice for those entering the profession as of the year 2000. The proposed change toward baccalaureate education as the requirement for entry into the professional practice of nursing is incorporated within the mandate of all of the provincial professional associations. Table 21-4 chronicles, by year, each provincal and territorial response to the issue.

TABLE 21-4 **Provincial Response to the Entry to Practice Issue: 1979-1989**

Year	Entry position accepted by statutory body	Entry position defeated by statutory body
1979	Alberta	
1980	Ontario (Professional Association only)	
1981		
1982	British Columbia	
	Quebec	
	Newfoundland	
	(CNA ACCEPTS POSITION)	
1983		
1984	Manitoba	
	Saskatchewan	
	Nova Scotia	
1985		
1986	Prince Edward Island	
	Northwest Territories	
1987		New Brunswick
1988	Yukon	
1989	New Brunswick	

In many cases, nurses' unions in the provinces have taken no public position related to entry to practice; Nova Scotia, Newfoundland, Northwest Territories, British Columbia, Alberta, and Prince Edward Island are in this category. On the other hand, nurses' unions in Saskatchewan and Ontario have taken a position against entry to practice, and the union in New Brunswick has taken a position in favor of entry to practice.

The nursing profession, in working toward the goal of baccalaureate preparation for entry to practice, engaged in considerable goal-directed activity, nationally and provincially throughout the 1980s. As a result, throughout Canada, provincial task forces were established to focus on the educational, political, economic, practice, and marketing aspects of the position over the next decade. Extensive analysis of current and future health care trends and nursing needs have been conducted. Explorations of innovations in nursing education and interprovincial and national networking among nurses characterize current efforts toward achievement of this goal.

However, the enormity of the task of reaching the entry to practice goal by the year 2000 can not be underestimated. Considering that through 1990 less than 20% of nurses graduated annually from baccalaureate nursing programs in Canada, the need for continued effort and unity is apparent.

Since the early 1980s, the achievement of the goal of entry to practice by the year 2000 has come to mean the need for increased accessibility to degree education for current and potential registered nurses. Increased accessibility has, therefore, become the mandate of professional associations, university and college faculty groups, nursing interest groups, and nursing unions. Indeed, the phenomenal progress in the growth and development of university nursing education programming and the many creative and collaborative efforts in nursing education have been fueled considerably by the entry to practice position.

The move toward higher education for all future nurses has not been without controversy. Winston Churchill is credited with observing that the further one looks back in history, the clearer one can see ahead. Certainly, the historical controversy over an appropriate educational preparation for entry into the practice of nursing provides a useful perspective on the current debate and demonstrates that nursing's efforts to have its educational base keep pace with practice realities, as well as further projections, have been and will continue to be influenced by many factors. Matejski (1981) warns that "where there is little insulation between an institution or professional organization and its environment, nonprofessional values can dominate it, resulting in a lessening of professional autonomy" (p. 19). In nursing, the influence of social forces related to the value of education for women, different perspectives on the role of nursing, and divergent views on the development of nursing as a unique scientific discipline affected the profession's progress throughout the century and must be acknowledged.

CHANGES IN NURSING EDUCATION

The 1990s may well be described as the decade of creative collaboration in nursing education programming, which follows a decade of "unfreezing" in university nursing education. New program initiatives include part-time educational opportunities, distance education, and transfer credits between universities. This is significant in that in the early 1980s part-time programs in nursing were almost unheard of, as were distance education opportunities and systematic programming between universities related to transfer of credit. In reference to the latter development, in Ontario, the University of Toronto, Ryerson, and McMaster University published a brochure for nursing students outlining similarities and differences in common degree courses and courses that are transferable among and between the three schools of nursing. This kind of university collaboration signals a new era of creative collaboration in nursing education, a welcome contrast from the rigid programming of the past.

There continues to be a focus on increased accessibility to degree education for diploma nurses, through part-time day and evening studies, employer-sponsored educational benefits, transfer credit systems between universities, and distance education delivery modes in all parts of the country. Two new degree programs for registered nurses have been developed in the last 3 years, one at the Athabasca University in Alberta and the Swampy Cree Project with the University of Manitoba.

Diploma programs, whether in hospitals or in colleges, are cooperating with each other and with universities to plan ways to increase access to degree education at both the basic and post-RN levels. For example, collaboration occurred between the university and long-standing nursing diploma programs in hospitals in British Columbia, Alberta, and Manitoba. In British Columbia, the University of British Columbia and Vancouver General Hospital School of Nursing collaborated to implement a new 4-year degree program, which began to accept students in the fall of 1989. In Alberta, the University of Alberta began major collaborative ventures with schools of nursing in the University of Alberta Hospital, the Royal Alexandra Hospital, and the Miseracordia Hospital, and these ventures culminated in approved programming (as of early 1991) that offers more accessibility to nursing degree education in the province. In Manitoba, the University of Manitoba began planning in 1990 for a joint degree program with schools of nursing in the Health Science Centre and St. Boniface Hospital. In Newfoundland, there is a five-way collaborative effort of Memorial University and the four hospital schools of nursing wherein all the non-nursing courses are taught by the university.

Community colleges and universities in many jurisdictions are working to alter programming to fit a collaborative university/college educational delivery model. For example, University of Alberta and Red Deer Community College now offer a collaborative program, implemented in the fall of 1989, in which the first 2 years of education are delivered at Red Deer College and the last 2 years of education are delivered at the University. Both a diploma and a degree exit are possible in this program. A similar type of offering has been approved as of 1991 between the University of Alberta and Grant MacEwan Community College. In Ontario, Cambrian College and Laurentian University have developed a proposal for a joint diploma/degree exit model of nursing education. In Calgary, a unique three-way collaborative effort for a basic degree program in the University of Calgary, Foothills Hospital, and Mount Royal College is undergoing internal and external review. The target date for implementation is fall 1993. In British Columbia, the University of Victoria is working with five community colleges on collaborative degree programming.

These collaborative efforts in nursing education are leading universities, colleges, and teaching health centers to re-examine policies and practices related to overall governance issues, curriculum development, and approval processes, and to jurisdictional issues related to faculty, students, type of programs offered, and type of awards offered to students on program completion. The common appreciation of the need for changes in nursing education in many sectors of nursing facilitates a remarkably smooth process of collaboration and change in nursing education.

There are also six new generic degree programs being planned in the universities of Prince Edward Island, Brandon, Victoria, Northern British Columbia, Quebec à Hull, and the University College of Cape Breton. It is anticipated that all these programs will be approved and will admit students by 1995. The degree program in Prince Edward Island will replace the freestanding diploma school of nursing, making Prince Edward Island the first province or territory in Canada to offer only degree education in nursing.

This increased demand for degree education in nursing, largely by practicing diploma nurses, coincides with the universities' changing agenda in many areas. The increased awareness of universities of the many barriers to advanced education for women, the focus on the adult student as a potential market, and the attention to enrollment in "hot" (popular) programs as a way of maximizing revenue in recessionary times have all affected developments in university nursing education.

Consequently, nursing has experienced an unprecedented period of growth in professional education programs in Canadian universities. These issues, plus the strong lobbying potential of the large pool of registered nurses wanting degrees and the changing view of nursing as a more valued profession (heightened recently with the contract settlement for Ontario nurses), will no doubt influence universities to continue to respond to the demands by nurses and the profession for increased opportunities for a broader education.

REGULATION ISSUES

Regulation of nursing education varies widely in Canada, and with the advent of changes to the entry level of education and development of new programs, such regulation has become a critical nursing issue. The professional associations in all but Alberta and Ontario play a key role in approval of schools of nursing in that the legislation regulating the profession of nursing specifies approval of schools of nursing by a committee that is established by part or all of the governing council or board of the nurses' association.

In Alberta, all programs leading to nursing registration are governed by the Universities Co-ordinating Council (Province of Alberta, 1987). The Council approves programs according to specific standards that it is responsible for developing. The regulations include specific procedures for approval of the establishment of new programs. In Ontario, the Regulations under the Health Disciplines Act (College of Nurses of Ontario, 1989) specify that the Ontario Region of the Canadian Association of University Schools of Nursing (OR-CAUSN) is responsible for approving basic degree programs leading to nurse registration. OR-CAUSN developed an approval process that includes standards of baccalaureate nursing education and procedures for the establishment of new programs. The Regulations under the Health Disciplines Act also specifies that approval of diploma nursing education is under the jurisdiction of the Ministry of Colleges and Universities, which is implemented under the Colleges of Applied Arts and Technology. The Colleges of Applied Arts and Technology have contracted with the College of Nurses of Ontario to provide an approval program based on standards developed within the profession.

Saskatchewan, with its most recent Standards for the Approval of Basic Nursing Education Programs and Nursing Re-Entry Programs (1989), delineated specific separate standards for diploma level and degree level education. Ontario and Saskatchewan are the only jurisdictions to have separate approval processes for diploma and degree nursing education. Saskatchewan also includes separate standards for approval of nursing re-entry or postdiploma programs, as well as procedures for new programs. Even though all professional organizations have taken a stand in favor of entry to practice by the year 2000, in the provinces where these same organizations are responsible for regulation no specific changes have yet been made in the regulations that reflect this new standard.

Within nursing at the undergraduate degree level, there is an established accreditation program developed by and implemented through the Canadian Association of University Schools of Nursing (CAUSN). (In 1972, CAUSN became the accrediting agency for baccalaureate programs in nursing in Canada, and in 1985 the Accreditation Program was fully established. Through this program, CAUSN provides recognition of programs that meet established standards and facilitate a high quality of professional nursing education (Accreditation Program, CAUSN, 1987). Several nursing programs have completed the accreditation process, and it is predicted that by 1995 approximately one half of the baccalaureate programs will have taken part in an accreditation review. In some jurisdictions such as Newfoundland, Nova Scotia, and Ontario there are plans by approval bodies to recognize an "accredited status" as evidence that basic standards of nursing education have been met.

CONCLUSION

Because nursing is predominantly a woman's profession, societal attitudes toward the education of women have been a significant external force in determining nursing's autonomy. Although it is unproductive to lament over events of the past, it is also naive to suggest that the traditional socialization of nurses as a predominantly female group has not affected nursing's progress toward university education (Bullough and Bullough, 1981; Growe, 1991; Matejski, 1981). Until recently, women have been conditioned to undervalue advanced education or careers that require full-time commitment. For example, Young (1984) concludes that a conflict between full-time career and marriage continues to be more serious for nurses than for women in the more established professions such as law and medicine. After decades of controversy, the organized nursing profession in Canada is finally unified on the value of and need for increased education for future nurses. That there continues to be caution about, if not active resistance to, degree programs for nurses from select groups in society should not be surprising when one considers the nature of the process of change in societal attitudes.

Although nursing's roles have changed progressively and significantly, in particular during the 1970s and 1980s, the profession's ability to portray the nature and value of its unique contribution to the health care system is problematic. In part, the problem rests within the profession. Historically, nursing has given a stellar performance in its service ideal. In fact, it may be argued that nursing's traditional socialization to the role of serving patients, the medical profession, and the institutional bureaucracies, simultaneously, serves the latter two groups very well but has done little to convince the public that nurses can address health, as well as illness related needs, in their practice.

Related to the public's limited view of the current and potential roles of nursing are the divergent views on nursing as a unique scientific discipline. Campbell (1984) warns that if nurses want to change their situations within health care settings, they must first take themselves and their knowledge more seriously. There is wide agreement that the competence of applied professions relies on their effective use of basic research in clinical practice (Matejski, 1981). Universities traditionally have been the main locus of scientific study. It follows therefore that advancements in nursing practice depends on knowledge most likely to be generated by nurses who are educated in a university setting.

In examining the present system of baccalaureate education, it must be remembered that every educational endeavor is a compromise that more or less approximates its ideal. Nursing education is no exception. Educational changes reflect societal changes—albeit reactively and belatedly—and the content, if not the model, of baccalaureate education appropriate for nurses in the next decade will certainly be different from the present one. Current baccalaureate programs are oriented toward the use of nursing theories and the study and practice of diagnostic reasoning and decision making. The focus is on clinical knowledge, as well as skills. The roles and responsibilities of the professional in the health care system also are important components in educational programs. Other essential elements of baccalaureate education have become more clearly defined through analysis of nursing practice trends in recent years, and this analysis will continue to direct curricula in schools of nursing in the future.

It is impossible to identify a finite educational requirement in the human service professions. After a specified higher educational level is attained, further research, knowledge, advances in practice, and specialization may indicate additional, or changed, educational requirements. The discussion in this chapter follows a historical analysis model. To reach a logical prediction for future nursing education requirements, one must study the patterns of the past, the facts of the present, and the projected systems of health care delivery in the future. When viewed in an evolutionary context, it is obvious that the achievement of continuing relevance in nursing education will require accurate monitoring of the health status of Canadians, of demographic trends, and of the effect of technology on nursing practice. Future educational trends will also depend on nursing's effectiveness in collaborating to shape the model of health care for the next century. Such a model must be oriented toward health promotion and illness prevention, be community based, and be fiscally accountable. Finally, continuing relevance in nursing education will require close collaboration of all facets of the nursing profession.

REFERENCES

American Association of Colleges of Nursing. (1986). *Essentials of college and university education for professional nursing*. Washington, DC: Author.

Bullough, B., & Bullough, V. (1981). Educational problems in a woman's profession. *Journal of Nursing Education, 20*(7), 6-16.

Campbell, M. (1984). Organizational settings define nursing: Let's change the definition. *The Canadian Nurse, 80*(8), 26-28.

Canadian Association of University Schools of Nursing. (1987). *Accreditation program*. Ottawa: Author.

Canadian Nurses Association. (1982). *Entry into the practice of nursing: A background paper*. Ottawa: Author.

Canadian Nurses Association. (1986). *Entry to Practice Newsletter, 2*(6).

Carper, B.A. (1978). Fundamental patterns of knowing in nursing. *Advances in Nursing Science, 1*(1), 13-23.

Carpenter, H.M. (1970). The University of Toronto School of Nursing: An agent for change. In M.Q. Innis (Ed.), *Nursing education in a changing society* (pp. 86-107). Toronto: University of Toronto Press.

Carpenter, H.M. (1982). *A divine discontent—Edith Kathleen Russell: Reforming educator* (History Monograph 1). Toronto: University of Toronto Faculty of Nursing.

Chinn, P.L., & Kramer, M. (1991). *Theory and nursing: A systematic approach* (3rd ed.). St. Louis: Mosby/Year Book.

College of Nurses of Ontario. (1989). *Health disciplines act and regulations nursing*. Toronto: Author.

Diers, D. (1986). To profess—to be a professional. *Journal of Nursing Administration*, 16(3), 25-30.

Gibbon, J.M., & Mathewson, M.S. (1947). *Three centuries of Canadian nursing*. Toronto: Macmillan.

Government of Canada. (1964). *Royal Commission on Health Services*. (E. Hall, Chairman). Ottawa: Queen's Printer.

Growe, S. (1991). *Who cares? The crisis in Canadian nursing*. Toronto: McClelland and Stewart.

Hall, E.M. (Chairman). (1980). *Canada's national-provincial health program for the 1980's: A commitment for renewal*. Ottawa: Department of National Health and Welfare.

Hangartner, C.A. (1965). The responsibilities of universities and colleges for the educational preparation of professional nurses. *Journal of Nursing Education*, 4(1), 19-27.

Jackson, R. (1985). *Issues in preventive health care*. Ottawa: Science Council of Canada.

Kergin, D.G. (1968). *An exploratory study of the professionalization of registered nurses in Ontario and the implications for the support of change in basic nursing educational programs*. Unpublished doctoral dissertation, University of Michigan, Ann Arbor.

King, K. (1970). The development of university education. In M.Q. Innis (Ed.), *Nursing education in a changing society* (pp. 46-63). Toronto: University of Toronto Press.

Lalonde, M. (1974). *A new perspective on the health of Canadians*. Ottawa: National Health and Welfare.

Lord, A.R. (1952). *Report of the evaluation of the Metropolitan School of Nursing, Windsor, Ontario*. Ottawa: Canadian Nurses Association.

Matejski, M.P. (1981). Nursing education, professionalism, and autonomy: Social constraints and the Goldmark report. *Advances in Nursing Science*, 3(3), 17-30.

Mussallem, H. (1960). *Spotlight on nursing education*. Ottawa: Canadian Nurses Association.

Mussallem, H.K. (1964). *A path to quality*. Ottawa: Canadian Nurses Association.

Nightingale School of Nursing. (1969). *Nursing Bulletin*. Toronto: Author.

Norman, R.M.G. (1986). *The nature and correlates of health behaviour* (Health Promotion Study Series No. 2). Ottawa: Health and Welfare Canada.

Province of Alberta. (1987). *Nursing Profession Act 1987*. Edmonton: Queen's Printer.

Rachlis, M., & Kushner, C. (1989). *Second opinion: What's wrong with Canada's health care system and how to fix it?* Toronto: Collins.

Saskatchewan Registered Nurses Association. (1989). *Standards for approval of basic nursing education programs and nursing re-entry programs*. Regina: Author.

Statistics Canada. (1990). *Nursing in Canada 1988*. Ottawa: Canadian Government Publishing Centre.

Watson, J. (Chair). (1985). *Health: A need for redirection* (Report of the Task Force on the Allocation of Health Care Resources). Ottawa: Print Action Ltd.

Weir, G.M. (1932). *Survey of nursing education in Canada*. Toronto: University of Toronto Press.

Young, K.J. (1984). Professional commitment of women in nursing. *Western Journal of Nursing Research*, 6(11), 11-26.

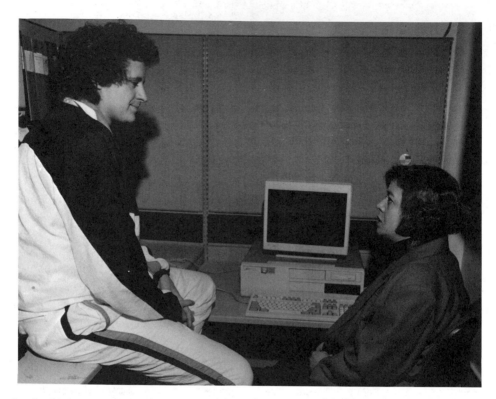

Sandra Kluka, graduate student in the School of Nursing, University of Manitoba, meets with Jeff Sloan, statistical consultant for the Manitoba Nursing Research Institute, to discuss statistical problems related to a master's-level paper. Cooperation and consultation between the School and the Institute allow students to take advantage of available expertise and resources. (Photograph by Bob Talbot, University of Manitoba Communication Systems, provided courtesy of the School of Nursing, University of Manitoba.)

CHAPTER TWENTY-TWO

Graduate Education in Nursing in Canada

PEGGY ANNE FIELD, RN, PhD

SHIRLEY M. STINSON, RN, EdD, LLD

MARIE-FRANCE THIBAUDEAU, RN, MScN

Peggy Anne Field, RN, BN (McGill), MN (Washington), PhD (Alberta), is a Professor, Faculty of Nursing, University of Alberta. She holds a cross-appointment in maternity nursing with University of Alberta Hospitals. Her research includes evaluation of graduates of the baccalaureate nursing programs, studies of client satisfaction in hospital and community, and validation of skills needed by beginning nurses in maternity settings. Well known as a clinician, Dr. Field's experience is in the areas of curriculum development, maternal-newborn nursing, and the use of nursing models as a base for practice. She was one of the original members of the CAUSN Committee that developed standards for accreditation.

Shirley M. Stinson, RN, BScN (Alberta), EdD (Columbia), LLD (Hon.Calgary), is a generalist, with experience in nursing practice, administration, teaching, and research. She holds a joint professorship in the Faculty of Nursing and the Department of Health Services Administration and Community Medicine. Professional offices held include: Past President of the Canadian Nurses Association (CNA), founding Chairman of the Alberta Foundation for Nursing Research, and Co-Chairman of the 1993 International Conference on Community Health Nursing Research. Author of more than 70 articles, chapters, books, and briefs, Stinson is an internationally recognized expert in the educational preparation of nurse administrators. Her honors and awards include: being the first woman to receive a

Senior National Health Scientist Award; the Sir Frederick Haultain Award in the Humanities; CNF's Ross Award for Nursing Leadership; and the CNA's Jeanne Mance Award, the highest nursing award in Canada.

Marie-France Thibaudeau, *RN, BN (McGill), MScN (Yale), is Doyenne, Faculté des sciences infirmières, l'Université de Montréal. She has an extensive background in nursing practice, research, education, and administration, and has taught graduate level research courses for seven years. She is well known for her demonstration and evaluative research projects conducted in community health centers, focused on the primary health care of families, particularly children, and including the care of patients suffering from chronic mental illness; for her work on committees of the National Health Research Development Program, including its Advisory Committee; and as a reviewer for several research funding bodies.*

T here has been progress in graduate education in nursing in Canada since the first program began in 1959. However there are still many pressing issues, problems, and priorities, at both the master's and the doctoral levels. This chapter provides a beginning overview, a *coup d'oeil*, of graduate education for nurses in Canada. Historical and current data are used to highlight origins and current characteristics.

BACKDROP

As a backdrop, attention is first directed to three major issues: What is graduate education in *nursing?* What is its relevance for nursing practice, education, and research? And what is "specialization" in graduate nursing education?

What is Graduate Education in Nursing?

Graduate education, or higher education as it is often termed, is education beyond the baccalaureate degree level, extending from the master's to the doctoral and postdoctoral levels. As reflected in Table 22-1, there are three interrelated major continua in the case of professional education: theory, research, and practice (Faculty of Nursing, University of Alberta, 1986). Taking theory of the art and science of nursing as an example, at the baccalaureate level the emphasis is on *knowing about* theory: acquiring it, retaining and reproducing it—and applying it. In contrast, at the master's level, the emphasis shifts to *exploring* theory. At the doctoral and post-doctoral levels the emphasis is on *developing and testing* theory, the terminal objective being that of becoming an authority on nursing theory.

Research emphases at the master's level include enunciating and judging nursing and preclinical knowledge (i.e., knowledge of disciplines that provide a foundation for nursing knowledge, including life sciences, arts, and humanities). The terminal objective is to function at a research "associate" level in nursing and interdisciplinary research. In contrast, at the doctoral and postdoctoral level, emphases are on advancement or perfection of knowledge and on learning to become an independent investigator who is also capable of co-investigation in nursing and interdisciplinary research (Faculty of Nursing, 1986).

The *raison d'être* of all professions—practice—is emphasized throughout all levels. Even at the baccalaureate level, "knowing about" theory is not enough; the student practitioner must also *apply* theory to practice. At the master's level, focus shifts to developing clinical expertise; testing selected practice interventions; integrating theory, research and practice; and implementing research findings into one's practice. What is distinctive about doctoral and postdoctoral programs in *nursing,* as compared to doctoral programs in other disciplines, is that nursing practice is a major emphasis. This emphasis includes identifying clinical phenomena for clinical investigation (e.g., preventing falls in elderly hospitalized patients or evaluating effects of nursing interventions on physiological status of neonates); scholarly practice (i.e., giving direct care and providing expert consultation to other nurses on the basis of comprehensive knowledge of nursing theory and research); designing nursing practice "systems" (e.g., primary nursing); and becoming an authority on nursing practice (i.e., being knowledgeable about all aspects of one or more dimensions of nursing practice such as helping people develop, maintain, and protect their health).

Table 22-1 illustrates that graduate education is not "higher skilling" (Muller, 1974) but higher *education,* which advances the professional nurse farther along the three continua of theory, research, and practice. It also provides a framework for nurses who intend to undertake a graduate degree, for it provides an analytical tool for comparing graduate programs in nursing.

Professional Relevance

What, then, is the relevance of graduate education in *nursing* to nursing practice, education, and research? Table 22-1 shows that graduate programs in other fields do not have *nursing* theory, research, and practice as their prime focus.

Knowledge from all "realms of meaning," including language, empirics, aesthetics, ethics, synnoetics (existential knowing), and synoptics (philosophy, history, and religion) (Phenix, 1964), is relevant to the art and science of nursing in the preclinical (foundational) sense. It is, however, *knowledge of the art and science of nursing* that makes the quintessential difference in nursing practice, education, and research.

If nurses undertake graduate education in other disciplines, they see phenomena through the "lens" of that discipline. Although nurses and nursing have been studied from many perspectives (including those of sociology, education, psychology, epidemiology, philosophy), it is the *nursing* "lens" acquired by undergraduate and graduate nursing programs and professional practice that makes the ultimate difference in the advancement and perfection of nursing knowledge—and the advancement and perfection of nursing practice, education, and research.

Specialization in Graduate Nursing Education

Historically, there was little specialization within graduate education in general, but this is no longer true. Indeed, Muller (1974, p. 153) maintains that "the fragmentation of knowledge involved in specialization has gone so far that the most advanced scholars in different fields have little academic substance to say to one another; they think and talk in mutually incomprehensible professional languages," resulting in "the academic Tower of Babel phenomenon." In the following section, the discussion is confined primarily to specialization in nursing master's programs. However, the principles apply to specialization at the doctoral level as well.

Prior to 1965 (see Table 22-2) graduate nursing programs stressed nursing education or administration (Allen, 1986). These programs often focused heavily on

---

TABLE 22-1 **Major Types of Theory, Research, and Practice Emphases, and Terminal Objectives at the Baccalaureate, Master's, and Doctoral/Postdoctoral Levels: A Continuum**

	BScN
Theory of the art and science of nursing	Knowledge about theory (acquire, retain, reproduce) Application of theory
Terminal objectives	Appreciation and application of nursing theory
Nursing research	Knowing about nursing and related research content Knowing about techniques and methods of research Acquiring knowledge
Terminal objectives	Research assistant in nursing research
Nursing practice	Introduction to applying theory to practice Under direction, apply selected nursing and related research to practice
Terminal objectives	Beginning practitioner

From *PhD in Nursing: a Proposal* (1986). Edmonton: Graduate Program and Policy Committee, Faculty of Nursing, University of Alberta, p. 13. Based on draft materials prepared in 1985 by Dr. Helen Simmons and Dr. June Kikuchi, (c) Faculty of Nursing, University of Alberta, revised by S. Stinson, December, 1986. Reprinted by permission.

education and administration as related to "hospital" nursing, primarily in terms of acute care. As such, it was not unusual for public health nurses to choose to undertake a master's degree in public health (MPH) per se.

By the 1970s, and evident in the master's programs described subsequently, there was a shift to clinical rather than functional specialization. In most programs, clinical specialties mirrored the specialties of medical practice, including psychiatry. However, as Allen observes (1986), the clinical foci are increasingly based on the *nursing* needs of clients and the milieu of practice, not on clients' "medical" diagnoses; also, the "boundaries" (p. 157) of clinical nursing specialties are becoming increasingly blurred.

Emphases	
MN	PhD nursing/post-PhD
Theory exploration	Theory development/construction Theory testing
Exploration of theory	Nursing theory authority
Enunciating and judging nursing and preclinical knowledge Assimilating nursing knowledge and knowledge prerequisite to it Interpreting research findings Designing and conducting required research project	Advancing or perfecting knowledge Developing knowledge Interpretation of knowledge Integration of knowledge Instrument construction Inventing methodologies Independent investigation
Association investigator in nursing and interdisciplinary research	Principal investigator, co-investigator and interdisciplinary researcher Nursing research authority
Development of clinical expertise	Identifying clinical phenomena for investigation
Testing selected practice interventions Integration of theory, research, and practice Implementation of research findings	Scholarly practice Designing nursing practice systems
Clinical expert in one or more practice areas	Nursing practice authority

There are plausible arguments why graduate nursing programs apparently are becoming less narrowly specialized. The central argument posited is that as the independent (substantive) knowledge base for nursing practice becomes increasingly developed and perfected, nurses are finally specializing in *nursing!* Put another way, if nursing practice is primarily a dependent type, one would expect graduate education "nursing" specialties to mirror the medical specialties, but this situation is changing. Indeed, the University of Alberta's proposed PhD in Nursing program is based on the idea that specialization *is* nursing. Students may choose a subfocus: on a particular phase of human development (e.g., preschool, midlife); on locus of practice (e.g., hospital, school, community clinic, prison, industry) and/or health

TABLE 22-2 **Phases of Graduate Education in Nursing in Canada, Pre-1965 to Post-1980: Teaching and Research Emphases**

Period	Graduate teaching	Research in nursing
Pre-1965	Master's programs for teachers and administrators	Problem solving Descriptive Evaluative
1965-1980	Master's programs with clinical specialization	Application of knowledge from other disciplines Descriptive Evaluative
Post-1980	Graduate programs oriented to nursing	Seeking knowledge from problems and situations that occur in [nursing] practice Scientific approach

From M Allen (1986). The relationship between graduate teaching and research in nursing. In SM Stinson and JC Kerr (Eds.): *International issues in nursing research* (p. 152), London: Croom Helm. Reprinted with permission.

promotion (generation, development, maintenance, protection, restoration, palliation), and/or on contexts of nursing practice (historical, current), including systems for providing nursing care.

The plethora of so-called nursing specialties in the United States is presenting profound problems in terms of credentialing, a situation that has profound consequences for graduate nursing education programs in that country. To date, the nursing profession in Canada has proceeded cautiously in the area of certification, at this point limited to one locus of practice: industrial settings. Neuroscience nursing was approved as a specialty for certification. In terms of the job market, there is a definite demand for evidence of specialized knowledge and skills. The question remains: In what ways should graduate programs approach the question of specialization? Allen (1986), a distinguished educator and researcher and one of the few people to write about graduate nursing education in Canada, sums up the situation:

> The study of nursing itself is becoming the target of our programs as the goals of nursing become more substantial and attain a degree of clarity and as theories of nursing delineate the nature of nursing and its constituent parts and relationships. This trend fosters a search for new approaches to the categorization of clinical specialties. It is as though previously the *context* for nursing was in relief and became the major focus of a program. . . . Now nursing is in relief and we are seeking ways to study it more intensively and in greater depth in the various locales in which nursing goes on. (pp. 157-158)

The following section provides an overview of the origins and selected characteristics of Canada's 11 nursing master's programs.

MASTER'S PROGRAMS IN NURSING

The first graduate program in nursing in Canada was established in 1959. By 1987, there were 11 nursing master's programs; the most recent was established in 1986.

Before 1959, Canadian nurses undertook master's degrees either in disciplines other than nursing or they took a nursing master's degree in the United States.

As evidenced by the review of nursing education research in Canada by Allemang and Cahoon (1986, pp. 241, 271-272), there is a paucity of literature on graduate nursing programs in Canada, a situation that merits greater attention by nursing scholars. The earliest research specific to Canadian graduate nursing education was Hart's (1962) survey of needs and resources, completed in 1962.

The following descriptions are based on two surveys (Field and Stinson, 1986, 1990) of Canada's 11 nursing master's programs to provide a brief overview of the origins and central characteristics. The descriptions are presented in terms of chronological development, beginning in 1959 with the University of Western Ontario (UWO) program and ending with the University of Saskatchewan program, established in 1986. Information on master's program emphases, length of program, and thesis requirements is presented in Table 22-3. Information on enrollment of master's students and master's student funding in the 1988-1989 academic year is presented in Table 22-4.

University of Western Ontario

The University of Western Ontario, London, had the first graduate program in nursing in Canada, established in 1959. Dean Edith McDowell initiated the program and was the first director. The program was two years in length leading to an MScN, the focus was nursing administration, and a thesis was required. The equivalent of a full-year course in research was required of all students. The program was established with a W. K. Kellogg Foundation grant of $142,000.

The current program is still two years in length, but a thesis is optional. A full year's course in research methods and proposal development is required, as well as a half-year graduate level course in statistics. The current focus of the program is administration and education. Students were awarded $59,241 in support in 1988-1989; of this, $51,291 was in the form of graduate assistantships. The only external source of funding was that of Ontario Graduate Scholarships, obtained from the Ontario Ministry of Colleges and Universities. In 1988-1989, there was a total of 52 students in the graduate program; of these, 23 were full-time and 29 part-time students.

McGill University

The master's degree program in nursing at McGill University, Montreal, began in 1961. Dr. Moyra Allen and Dr. Rae Chittick initiated the program, and Professor Mary Richmond was first program director. The degree offered an MSc(A), with a focus on nursing. The program was 2 years in length, and a thesis was not required initially. Research and statistics courses were offered and a research project (rather than a thesis) was a requirement. The program was funded by the W. K. Kellogg Foundation, which provided a grant of $195,000.

The programs currently offered are 2 years in length. Two degrees are given: MSc(A) or MSc (the latter involves a thesis). Students received $247,886 in bursaries and awards in 1988-1989, and $3500 in graduate assistantships. These funds were provided by McGill Graduate Fellowships, the Conseil formation de chercheurs et

TABLE 22-3 Selected Characteristics of Canadian Nursing Master's Programs, 1988-1989

University	Year established	Degree granted
University of Western Ontario	1959	MScN
McGill University	1961	MSc(A) or MSc
University of Montreal	1965	MSc
University of British Columbia	1968	MSN
University of Toronto	1970	MScN
University of Alberta	1975	MN
Dalhousie University	1975	MN
University of Manitoba	1979	MN
University of Calgary	1981	MN
Memorial University	1982	MN
University of Saskatchewan	1986	MN

*These "emphases" constitute "majors" within the various programs. However, a focus on other than "Research" does not imply that research is not of prime importance. For example, at the University of Alberta, all students take a minimum of four research courses, but the "major" is advanced nursing practice.

TABLE 22-4 Master's Nursing Student Enrollment, by Full-time and Part-time Status and Student Funding Support, 1988-1989

University	Enrollment			Graduates
	Full-time	Part-time	Total	1988-1989
Western Ontario	23	29	52	14
McGill	63	20	83	25
Montreal	66	52	118	57
British Columbia	28	65	93	21
Toronto	49	36	85	14
Alberta	40	13	53	22
Dalhousie	8	86	94	19
Manitoba	28	25	53	9
Calgary	34	27	61	19
Memorial	9	21	30	6
Saskatchewan	17	0	17	5
TOTAL	365	374	739	211

*Graduate Research Assistantships and/or Graduate Teaching Assistantships.
†Includes some full-time students on bursaries or on 75% salary (Dalhousie, 4; Memorial, 3).

Program emphases*	Thesis	Length of program (years)
Administration, Education	Optional	2
Advanced Nursing Practice, Nursing Research	Optional	2
Advanced Nursing Practice and Nursing Research, Administration	Optional	2
Administration, Education, Clinical Specialization	Optional	2
Research and Practice (which includes Clinical Practice and Nursing Administration)	Required	2
Advanced Nursing Practice, Minor in Midwifery, Minor in Administration	Required	2
Community/Public Health Nursing; Nursing of Adults; Maternal/Child (Obstetrics); Nursing of Sick Children; Mental Health Nursing	Required	2
Community Health, Restorative Nursing, Nursing Administration, Gerontological Nursing	Optional	2
Clinical Specialization	Not required	2
Advanced Nursing Practice and Leadership	Optional	2
Administration, Teaching, Clinical Specialization	Optional	2

Funding in Dollars		
Scholarships/awards	Assistantships*	Total
$ 7950	$ 51,291	$ 59,241
247,886	3500	251,386
100,556	57,830†	158,386*
10,700	15,497	26,197
191,020	71,271	262,291
175,460	81,996	257,456
173,000†	22,490	195,490
100,265	111,620	211,885
30,900	72,500	103,400
111,490†	544	112,034
80,000	35,838	115,838
$1,229,277	$524,377	$1,753,604

l'aide à la recherche, the Order of Nurses of Quebec, the School of Nursing Alumnae Funds, the Canadian Cancer Society, the Medical Research Council, the National Health Research and Development Program (NHRDP), the Canadian Heart Foundation, and the Corporation of Nurses, District of Montreal. As indicated, minimal monies are currently available for graduate research or teaching assistantships.

The School of Nursing offers a unique program for graduates of non-nursing undergraduate programs that enables them to obtain master's degrees in nursing within 3 years without the necessity of a baccalaureate in nursing. In 1988-1989 there were 83 students registered in McGill's MSc(A) and MSc programs: 63 full-time and 20 part-time.

University of Montreal

The master's degree in nursing program at the University of Montreal, offered in French, began in 1965. Dean Alice Girard and Professor Rita Dussault initiated the program with the latter becoming the first director. The program was 2 years in length leading to an MN. At first, the emphasis was on nursing administration, with nursing education offered as an alternative since 1966. In 1968, clinical options in psychiatry and mental health nursing were available as alternatives, and since that time other clinical specialties have been added. The initial program was 2 academic years in length and a thesis was required until 1977. The program was funded by special grants from the Ministry of Education with additional monies made available by the Ministry of Health for faculty development.

Program length is a minimum of four trimesters for either the clinical or the thesis option, with a maximum of three years allowed for completion of the degree. The degree now offered is an MSc. All students are required to take research and statistics course work. Students are encouraged to undertake a thesis in an area in which a professor is funded. Two current areas of particular research strength are nursing the aged and women's health. In 1988-1989, full-time students received $100,556 in scholarships, bursaries, and awards. Additionally, $57,830 was obtained through graduate assistantships and other financial assistance, reported by students. In 1988-1989, 118 students were enrolled: 66 full-time and 52 part-time.

University of British Columbia

The master's in nursing program at the University of British Columbia, Vancouver, began in 1968 and was initiated by Dr. Alice Baumgart and Dr. Margaret Campbell. The degree offered an MSN with emphasis on administration or education and a clinical option in either long-term illness or psychiatric/mental health nursing. The program was 2 years in length and initially a thesis was required of all students. One research course was required as part of the program. No external funding was acquired to begin the program.

Currently, students may elect to focus on one option from within administration, education, or a clinical specialty. The program is 2 years in length, with a thesis being optional. Student financial support totalled $26,197 in 1988-1989. Sources of funding were not identified. In contrast to 1985-1986, when there were no funds for graduate assistantships, $15,497 was available for graduate research assistantships in 1988-1989. There were 93 students enrolled in 1988-1989: 28 full-time and 65 part-time students.

University of Toronto

The master's degree in nursing program at the University of Toronto began in 1970. Professor Nellie Douglas Fidler and Dr. Helen Carpenter were the initiators, and Dr. Carpenter became the first program director. The degree offered an MSc(N), the program was 2 years in length, emphasis was on clinical specialization, and a thesis was required of all students. The program was initially funded by a grant from the W. K. Kellogg Foundation.

Program emphasis is now on research and practice, which includes clinical practice and nursing administration; program length and thesis requirement have not altered in the ensuing years. A research course is required as a part of each student's program.

Students obtained $191,020 in funding for scholarships and awards during 1988-1989 from University of Toronto Open Fellowships, Ontario Graduate Scholarships, Dean's Society Award, Special Fellowship Award, Florence Emory Award, Manuel and Anne Belle Pusitz Graduate Scholarship, Heart and Stroke Foundation Fellowship, Bloorview Children's Hospital Foundation, Ontario Nursing Home Award, Maurice Legault Award, Top-Up Award, Hospital for Sick Children Award, and Canadian Nurses' Foundation Award. Additionally, funding of $71,271 was received for graduate research assistantships. There were 85 students enrolled in 1988-1989: 49 full-time students and 36 part-time students.

University of Alberta

The master's in nursing program at the University of Alberta, Edmonton, began in 1975 under the leadership of Professor Ruth McClure and Dr. Shirley Stinson; the latter was the first director of the program. The degree offered an MN with emphasis on nursing acutely ill patients. The program was two years in length and a thesis was required. Two full-year courses in statistics and research design and a half-year course devoted to nursing research were a required part of every student's program. The program was funded internally by the University.

Currently the focus of the program is on advanced nursing practice in hospital, community, or educational settings. There is opportunity within the program for nursing practice, research, and concentrated study in relation to a selected client group in acute care and/or community settings. A combined MN degree and Certificate in Nurse-Midwifery is available. Also, beginning in September, 1990, an MN degree with a minor in nursing administration became available, an arrangement offered in collaboration with the Department of Health Services Administration and Community Medicine. Core coursework in every student's program includes content in relation to nursing philosophy, nursing practice, the nursing profession, and nursing research. The length of the program is 2 years, with a time limit of 4 years to complete. A thesis is required.

The support obtained by MN students in 1988-1989 for graduate research and teaching assistantships, bursaries and scholarships, and externally funded research grants totalled $257,456 (of this, $81,996 was for graduate assistantships). Sources include the University of Alberta Faculty of Graduate Studies and Research, the Faculty of Nursing, the National Health Research and Development Program, the Alberta Foundation for Nursing Research, Province of Alberta scholarship and bursaries fund, provincial nursing associations, the Canadian Nurses Foundation, and the Alberta Heritage Foundation for Medical Research. Fifty-three students were enrolled in 1988-1989: 40 full-time and 13 part-time.

Dalhousie University

The master's in nursing program at Dalhousie University, Halifax, (approved as a regional graduate program for the Maritimes) was first offered in 1974. It was initiated by Professors Florence King and Mona June Horrocks; the latter was appointed graduate coordinator in 1974, succeeded later in 1976 by Dr. Patricia Sullivan. The original program was 1 year in length, with clinical options in community health nursing and nursing of adults. A full-year course in nursing research and a research project was required; a thesis was an option chosen by a few students. No external funding was acquired to finance the program.

The program was changed in 1981 to a 2-year full-time or 6-year part-time, research-based degree with advanced clinical preparation. A thesis is required of all students, and clinical options include community health nursing, nursing of adults, nursing of young families, maternal-child nursing, nursing of sick children, and psychiatric/mental health nursing. Student funding obtained in 1988-1989 totalled $173,000, which included 75% salaries for four of the eight full-time students. Internal university student support was provided in the form of graduate student fellowships and monies from the Research and Development Fund for Humanistic and Social Sciences; external awards were from a variety of local, provincial, and national sources. Funds for graduate teaching assistantships amounted to a total of $22,490. In 1988-1989 there were 94 students enrolled in the program: 8 full-time and 86 part-time.

In 1982 the program began to fulfill its mandate as a Maritime regional program by offering classes on a distance learning basis. Transmission of selected courses by audio teleconferencing and faculty traveling to university sites in New Brunswick, Prince Edward Island, and Nova Scotia were undertaken, with students coming to the Dalhousie University campus only for short periods of time. At present approximately 40% of the 94 students are part-time distance students.

University of Manitoba

The master's degree in nursing (MN) program at the University of Manitoba, Winnipeg, began in 1979. Dr. Helen Glass initiated the program and was first director. Emphasis was on community health nursing. The program was 2 years in length; a thesis was optional. Completion of a nursing research seminar course was required of all students. No external funding was received to initiate the program.

The students may now select a thesis or a practicum option. The practicum involves the careful definition of a problem, application of appropriate knowledge and skills to the problem, and a reporting of results to an evaluating committee. Two additional research seminars were offered in 1989-1990: one designed for thesis students, the other for practicum students. Students were awarded a total of $211,885 in 1988-1989: $100,265 was from sources external to the University; $111,620 was for graduate assistantships. In 1988-1989 there were 53 students enrolled in the program: 28 were full-time and 25 were part-time.

University of Calgary

The University of Calgary's MN program was proposed by Dr. Janet Kerr in 1976 and was established under her direction in 1981. The program was developed under the deanship of Professor Marguerite Schumacher and brought to completion under the deanship of Dr. Margaret Scott Wright. The initial program was 2 years in length, and emphasis was on clinical specialization. It was a nonthesis program funded by a special grant from the Government of Alberta's Department of Advanced Education and Manpower.

The program is still two years in length with an emphasis on advanced nursing practice. It is a clinically focused, course-based, accredited degree program with opportunity for educational preparation in clinical practice, clinical management, and clinical education. Part-time students have up to 6 years to complete the program.

In 1988-1989 students received approximately $103,400 in funding, which included scholarship and bursary support from various sources, including Province of Alberta Graduate Scholarship Funds, Alberta Association of Registered Nurses, Alberta Government Social Services, Canadian Federation of University Women Nursing Students, the University, and several hospitals. Of this, $72,500 was allocated as graduate assistantships. In 1988-1989 there were 61 students enrolled in the program: 34 full-time and 27 part-time.

Memorial University

The graduate degree program in nursing at Memorial University, St. John's, Newfoundland, began in 1982, initiated by Professor Joyce Nevitt and Professor Margaret McLean. The first coordinator of the program was Dr. Mary Jo Bulbrook. The program was 2 academic years in length, leading to an MN, with a clinical specialization and an emphasis on nursing leadership. A thesis or a project was required of all students, with the thesis option encouraged. Two lecture courses in nursing research were required. No external funding was obtained for the program.

The degree, length, and research requirements of the Memorial program have not changed since its inception. Student funding in 1988-1989 totalled $112,034. Of that, $16,000 was from scholarships, $544 was for a graduate teaching assistantship, and the balance was from part-time salaries awarded to three full-time students. In 1988-1989, 30 students were enrolled: 9 full-time and 21 part-time.

University of Saskatchewan

The University of Saskatchewan graduate nursing degree (MN) program began in 1986, with an enrollment of six students. Between 1978-1985 four special case students had undertaken degree work with nursing as a major. Dean Hester Kernan and Professor Myrtle Crawford initiated the special case program. The special case students took research methods courses through the Department of Psychology, but theses were prepared under the supervision of faculty members of the College of Nursing. The degree offered was an MScN.

The MN program, which was established without additional external funding, is limited to a quota of six full-time students per admission period. The first coordinator was Dr. Anne Neufeld. The program is flexible, with options for a thesis or nonthesis; functional major in teaching, administration or clinical practice; and clinical focus, dependent on student's interest and faculty availability. Master in Nursing students received $115,838 of which $35,838 was for graduate assistantships. In 1988-1989 there were 17 full-time students and no part-time students.

Canadian Master's in Nursing Program Summary

As of September 1989 there were 11 Canadian graduate programs offering master's degrees in nursing. When nursing masters programs were first developed there was a tendency for the nursing major to be in administration or education; programs that developed between 1970 and 1980 more likely had a clinical focus. With one exception (Dalhousie) all programs were 2 years in length at inception; currently all programs entail a minimum of 2 years of study. It appears that enrollment numbers and the mix of full-time and part-time students have not changed dramatically since 1986. In 1985-1986, 708 students were enrolled: 384 full-time, 324 part-time; in 1988-1989, there was a total of 739 with 365 full-time, 374 part-time. There was an increasing enrollment of part-time students noted in 1986, when 45% of students were part-time. This trend continues. Currently 51% of students are part-time.

The number of nurses graduating with nursing master's degrees in the 1988-1989 academic year (Table 22-4) totalled 211, ranging from five from the newly established University of Saskatchewan program to 57 at the University of Montreal (Field and Stinson, 1990). Because this type of data was not included in the data reported by Field and Stinson in 1986, no comparisons are presented here.

Most programs initially required a thesis, but as the number of students increased, the thesis became optional in many programs. All programs require research courses, even when a thesis is not required. The University of Calgary is unique in that it is the only master's degree program in nursing in Canada in which a thesis cannot be taken. However, there is nevertheless provision for a thesis requirement on a special case basis; if so, the degree awarded is an MSc(N).

Three of the first five programs established in Canada (UWO, McGill, Toronto) were funded initially by the W.K. Kellogg Foundation. The University of Montreal and the University of Calgary received special government grants; the six other programs received no special funding external to their universities.

The ratio of full-time to part-time students varies greatly from one university to another, but the amount of student funding secured does not seem to be related to the ratios. In 1988-1989, scholarships and awards totalled $1,229,227 (ranging from $7950 to $247,886) compared to $773,443 in 1985-1986. Although at first glance this may seem a substantial increase, some Deans and Directors reported that these amounts include a few instances of full-time students with salaries of up to 75%. All 11 universities received monies for graduate teaching or graduate research assistantships in 1988-1989, compared to only eight in 1985-1986. The amount of funding for graduate assistantships in 1988-1989 ranged widely, from $544 to $111,620 per university; the total received was $524,377 compared to $234,769 in 1985-1986.

All universities had some students funded by both internal and external resources. Because there are no specific baseline data on funding support in these programs, the authors maintain that because all major awards and most other awards and assistantships required full-time enrollment, a feasible statistical technique for determining cross-program and cross-year comparisons is to divide the combined amount of internal and external funding by the number of full-time students. Using this approach, the 1985-1986 average support per full-time student was $2626 ($1,008,212 total funding divided by 384 full-time students); average support per full-time student in 1988-1989 was $4804 ($1,753,604 divided by 365), constituting a 55% increase within a 3-year time frame. The majority of the money was obtained through scholarships and awards; however it must be emphasized that total student funding also includes 75% *salaries* for at least 7 of the 365 full-time students, a factor that inflates the "average" support per full-time student. This amount of less than $5000 per student remains inadequate compared to the level of support for graduate students in the "hard" sciences, in which it is common for students to have support at $14,000 per year or higher. However the increased funding support of graduate nursing students is encouraging when compared to the 1985-1986 figures.

Other Master's Programs

By 1987, approximately 2000 of Canada's 211,000 actively registered nurses employed in nursing held master's degrees (Statistics Canada, 1987). Although a precise breakdown of master's degrees by type of discipline is not available, it is widely recognized that the majority were obtained outside of nursing. Some of the degrees represented are not health related, whereas others such as degrees in epidemiology, family studies, and health services administration are distinctly related. In the latter case, for example, there is provision for a nursing administration "minor" in the University of Alberta's Master's in Health Services Administration program; of more direct relevance to clinical nursing practice is McMaster University's interdisciplinary MHSc program, targeted for a wide range of health professionals, which has definitive provision for nurses to "major" in clinical nursing practice.

DOCTORAL PREPARATION FOR CANADIAN NURSES

Sister Denise Lefebvre, SQM, PhD, was the first Canadian nurse to obtain a doctoral degree *(Docteur de Pédagogie)*, which she earned from the University of Montreal in 1955. A survey in 1990 (Lamb and Stinson, 1990) indicates that 257 nurses in Canada held earned doctoral degrees. The types of degrees varied (e.g., PhD, DNSc, DPHN, EdD, DSc), as did the disciplines in which the programs were undertaken (e.g., education, nursing, epidemiology, medical science). Those whose doctoral degree focused on nursing are a minority: 122 of 257 (47%) (see Table 22-5). Eighty-five percent who reported their year of birth (n=187) were 40 or more years of age; and the median age at completion was 42 years. This indicates that

TABLE 22-5 **Disciplines Undertaken by Nurses in Canada with Earned Doctoral Degrees: 1989 Data**

Cluster	N	(%)
Education	122	(47)
Nursing*	59	(23)
Other Health Related	38	(15)
Social Sciences	30	(12)
Arts and Humanities	8	(3)
Physical Sciences	0	(0)
Unknown	1	(0)
TOTAL	258†	(100%)

Extracts from M Lamb and SM Stinson (1990). *Canadian nursing doctoral statistics: 1989 update,* Ottawa: Canadian Nurses Association.
*Nursing includes Nursing Education.
†One nurse holds two PhDs, one in Nursing, the other in Anthropology, thus N = 258 rather than 257.

nurses were considerably older at graduation than other women scientists with doctorates. Fifty-five percent obtained a doctoral degree from a Canadian university, 40% from an American university, and 3% from United Kingdom universities; 1% graduated from universities in France, Egypt, Portugal, and Poland.

It was further reported by Lamb and Stinson (1990) that, in 1989, 265 nurses were enrolled in some type of doctoral degree program in Canada (51%), the United States (23%), or abroad. The major disciplines involved were education (29%), nursing (24%), other health related disciplines (11%), and social sciences (10%); a few (1%) were enrolled in other disciplines and the disciplines of 65 (25%) were unreported (p. 33).

PhD in Nursing Programs in Canada

The need for PhD in Nursing programs was stressed by Symons as early as 1975, and emphasized by the Canadian Nurses Association (CNA) in 1976 and again in concert with the Canadian Association of University Schools of Nursing (CAUSN) and the Canadian Nurses Foundation (CNF) in 1978 (Zilm, Larose, and Stinson, 1979). By 1988, six nurses were enrolled as "Special Case PhD in Nursing" students: three at McGill University and three at the University of Alberta. The first Special Case to graduate was Francine Ducharme, from McGill in September 1990.

The PhD in Nursing program proposal developed by the University of Alberta (UA) Faculty of Nursing in concert with the University of Calgary (UC) Faculty of Nursing was approved by the Alberta Universities Coordinating Council in May 1986, "subject to appropriate funding." In December 1990, in response to the continued individual and group efforts of Alberta nurses, including the UA and UC graduate nursing students and Faculties of Nursing and the Alberta Association of Registered Nurses, financial support was finally obtained. The Alberta Department of Health is providing support for the first 3 years; funding will then be maintained by the Alberta Department of Advanced Education on the condition that there be an annual intake of no more than four students and a maximum enrollment of 16 (Lamb, Stinson, and Thibaudeau, in press). The program began in January 1991 with four students: with transfer of three Special Case students—Joan Bottorff, Joy Johnson, and Pauline Paul—and the direct admission of Ginette Rodger. Nine students were enrolled by September 1991. The degree offered is a research degree; the purpose is to prepare nurses for leadership positions in practice, research, education, and administration. Entrance requirements include the equivalent of the University of Alberta's MN degree program, which involves substantial research and relevant experience in nursing. The approach to program planning falls midway between the predominant patterns of PhD nursing programs in the United States and the United Kingdom: United States programs usually have extensive course work, with several courses mandatory; United Kingdom programs usually include relatively little course work, with few required courses.

In their article about the development of nursing research in Canada, Lamb and her colleagues emphasize that in addition to the University of Alberta's newly established PhD program, doctoral programs are proposed by four other universities:

> The conjoint PhD in Nursing program proposed by the Université de Montréal and McGill University has been reviewed by the Quebec Council of Universities and the Ministry of Higher Education and Sciences once and has, at the time of writing, been sent back for a second review. The conjoint committees of the Quebec Council of Universities and the Conference of University Principals have acknowledged the necessity of a PhD in Nursing. As McGill University has a clause in its regulations permitting *ad hoc* programs, three special case students have undertaken studies toward a PhD in Nursing. However, this avenue is limited as there are no program funds provided by the Ministry of Higher Education and Sciences. The University of Toronto (UT) and University of British Columbia (UBC) have both been engaged in planning PhD programs in Nursing. It is anticipated that the UBC program will be operational in 1991 . . . and the UT program in 1992 . . . . (In press).

The UBC program began in September 1991 with the admission of two students.

Lest Canadian nurses become discouraged at the arduous process of establishing doctoral programs, the literature (e.g., Grace, 1978; Murphy, 1981, 1985) indicates that American nurses, who now have over 40 such programs, also suffered many setbacks in attempts to establish doctoral programs in nursing *qua* nursing.

Postdoctoral Education

Education beyond the doctoral level is a rarity in Canadian nursing, although the value of postdoctoral study, which is the norm in so many disciplines, is recognized. The Field and Stinson survey (1986) indicates that there were no postdoctoral students in the 11 universities with graduate nursing programs. In 1988-1989, two were reported at the University of Alberta: one who is a nurse from New Zealand, and one from the United Kingdom. The authors of this chapter estimate that fewer than 10 Canadian nurses have had postdoctoral study. Several reasons why this type of education is underdeveloped follow:

1. The dearth of nurses prepared at the doctoral level results in immediate employment opportunities, and the norm is employment on a full-time basis

immediately after graduation from a doctoral program or even while studying for a doctoral degree

2. Inadequate funding throughout the doctoral program stage necessitates employment at full salary after graduation

3. Inadequate funding for postdoctoral study is often a deterrent because the awards are often less than one third of the salary potential candidates can obtain

4. There is a lack of adequate programs for nurses in Canada, including a lack of experienced or substantially funded nursing research teams with which postdoctoral students can be linked

As emphasized by Lamb, Stinson, and Thibaudeau (in press): "Over the next decade, attention must be given to development of postdoctoral programs and fellowships for nurses. In the latter respect, the one exception is that in 1990, the Alberta Foundation for Nursing Research established a postdoctorate [funding] category."

GRADUATE PROGRAM RESOURCES

Comprehensive literature on faculty resources for graduate education in Canada is nonexistent. What is evident from the sparse literature and from our knowledge of the national scene is that the faculty resource situation is in crisis in several respects, including lack of adequate numbers of faculty with expertise in nursing theory, research, and practice; general lack of substantial national, provincial, and local infrastructures for nursing research; and problems in funding and staffing graduate programs and providing financial support for students. Nevertheless, great strides have been made, particularly in the past decade. Attention is now directed to three resource factors: academic staff, research development, and research funding.

Academic Staff

Although CAUSN is currently obtaining statistics on academic staff in Canada's university schools/faculties of nursing, Stinson and Giovannetti (1985) discovered that (1) of the approximately 600 full-time faculty members, fewer than 80 (<13%) were qualified at the doctoral level; and (2) of the 305 faculty members holding major appointments in the then 10 universities with nursing master's programs, only 63 (19%) were prepared at the doctoral level.

By 1986, 115 of university nursing faculty members teaching in undergraduate and/or graduate nursing programs were qualified at the doctoral level. The greatest increase is occurring in universities with master's in nursing programs. For example, in 1982 there were only 50 such nurses in the 10 master's in nursing programs; in 1986, there were 73 in the 11 programs (Stinson, MacPhail, and Larsen, 1988). In 1986, 159 nurses with doctoral degrees were employed in university undergraduate and graduate nursing programs; of these, 101 (64%) were employed by universities offering nursing master's programs.

In 1988-1989, graduate nursing student enrollment in the 11 master's programs was 739 (see Table 22-4). It is emphasized here that even in schools that have graduate nursing programs not all faculty members with doctoral degrees are directly involved in teaching the graduate students, because the major responsibilities of several are in teaching undergraduate students and/or in administering programs. Also, many of these academics are extensively involved in professional and public service endeavors, which further dilutes resources in terms of graduate education and research. However, most of these faculty members are remarkably productive; further, some of their colleagues prepared only at the master's level and who teach graduate students are actively involved in research and/or are themselves undertaking doctoral degrees on a part-time basis. Nevertheless, since Stinson and Giovannetti's study (1985), the overall picture has not changed dramatically.

Attempts by the schools/faculties to upgrade academic qualifications of faculty members include the following:

1. Limiting continuing appointments to those qualified at the doctoral level and/or to those who make a commitment to undertake doctoral studies within 2 years from the date of their appointment
2. Limiting promotion to the associate and/or professor level to those with earned doctoral degrees
3. Confining use of sabbatical leave to doctoral study or to involvement in research
4. Requiring peer-reviewed research publication for promotion and tenure (rather than just requiring evidence of publication)
5. Providing assisted leave for doctoral studies for faculty members who do not qualify for sabbatical leave and/or release time for substantial research involvement
6. Providing a supportive faculty infrastructure (e.g., secretarial services, research assistants, research travel grants, space, equipment, computerized literature searches, seed monies) to enable faculty members to obtain major research support

Measures to improve and maintain faculty expertise in nursing practice include the following:

1. Scheduled time for "professional development," enabling faculty members to practice in health care agencies
2. Joint appointments involving "hands-on" nursing care
3. Travel grants for professionally related conferences

In summary, although the academic resource situation has improved, particularly in the past decade, it is still in crisis, considering the complex nursing needs of society, the explosion of nursing and related knowledge, the increased numbers of undergraduate and graduate students, the lack of adequate support for graduate education, and the fact that doctoral preparation in nursing is not readily accessible to Canadian nurses.

Research Development

Systematic description of research development in faculties and schools of nursing with graduate programs is lacking. However, several indicators of interest follow:

- Dr. Moyra Allen of McGill pioneered in establishing Canada's first nursing research unit in 1971, the Centre for Nursing and Health Research
- In 1976, Dr. Amy Zelmer of the University of Alberta Faculty of Nursing estab-

lished the Canadian Clearinghouse for Ongoing Research in Nursing, an online public file, later expanded by Dr. Janice Morse to include a file on ongoing and completed Canadian nursing master's theses (Stinson, 1986, p. 237)

- A clinical nursing research program was jointly initiated by the University of Toronto Faculty of Nursing and Sunnybrook Hospital in 1980
- A research unit was established by the University of Montreal Faculty of Nursing in 1981, beginning with a full-time secretary and later expanding to include a documentation center, data banks, and computer hardware and software facilities
- The University of Saskatchewan College of Nursing and the Saskatchewan Registered Nurses Association (SRNA) jointly developed and funded a Nursing Research Unit at the College, which was initiated in 1983
- In 1984 the University of Alberta Faculty of Nursing established a Research Facilitation Office as a research resource center for faculty members and students
- In 1985 the Manitoba Nursing Research Institute was founded, jointly planned, and funded by the University of Manitoba and the Manitoba Association of Registered Nurses (MARN)
- In 1985, the University of Calgary Faculty of Nursing established a Research Unit, beginning with its Learning Resources Centre and Family Nursing Unit
- In 1988, the University of Alberta Faculty of Nursing established the Institute for Philosophical Nursing Research, the first such institute worldwide

Of direct and indirect relevance to this list of specialized structures for nursing research are the nursing research development programs in health care agencies and agency based nursing research "units," (e.g., the Montreal Children's Hospital and the Victoria General Hospital in Halifax).

Several nursing faculties have associate or assistant deans whose position descriptions entail emphasis on research development, a trend that emerged in the past 10 years. Most of these people have other substantial administrative and/or teaching responsibilities, yet it appears that this structural provision gives much needed legitimacy, direction, and visibility to research, making research an explicit rather than tacit priority.

Other research development endeavors that make research manifest include faculty development programs; visiting scientist/lecturer programs; expansion of computer facilities; sponsorship of local, provincial, national, and/or international nursing conferences; collaborative research with nursing colleagues and graduate students; collaborative research with scientists in other disciplines; interinstitutional research; developing definitive promotion criteria to include research and scholarly endeavor; promoting scholarship in faculty development, not mere training in research technique; and establishing nursing research development committees and/or internal peer review committees; as well as the several measures, cited previously, designed to strengthen academic resources.

The nursing conferences include research conferences such as the 1986 International Nursing Research Conference, sponsored by the University of Alberta Faculty of Nursing, which was attended by some 800 nurses from 38 countries. Of all the initiatives mentioned here, the most central is faculty development, the pivotal factor.

Research Funding

Wilmot (1986) notes that, in Canada, "some $640 million is being spent annually on medical and health research and related scientific activities" (p. 90). Of this, $90 million is allotted by the federal government for medical research (p. 89). In contrast, the all-time high allotted for nursing research in Canada was $1.7 million in funding in 1979, with an annual average of less than $700,000 up to 1985 (Stinson, 1986, p. 240). In general, nursing research funding in Canada is a national disgrace.

The most relevant source of national level funding for nursing research is the National Health Research and Development Program; however, it must be emphasized that the federal government itself, the NHRDP, and the federal government's research-funding Councils do not "proactively" allocate funds for nursing research. With one exception, this situation applies also at the provincial level, in which there may be funding designated for "health" research but none assured for nursing research. Strong exceptions are that, in 1982, the Alberta Government authorized $1 million for nursing research for a 5-year period and established the Alberta Foundation for Nursing Research (AFNR). Then, in 1988, the government authorized a minimum of $1.2 million to continue funding AFNR for another 5 years.

Nationally, of special significance to the initial development of nursing research was the series of "Evaluation Seminars," sponsored by the NHRDP and initiated at McMaster University in 1970. In the past two decades, the several NHRDP research traineeships and research project grants awarded to Canadian nurses constituted the major form of support. In the former case, several of Canada's nurse researchers began "grantsmanship" and established their initial research networks through the Seminars; in the latter case, the NHRDP research traineeships have to date been the only national funding source of major consequence insofar as doctoral preparation for nurse researchers is concerned, albeit that only a minority of Canadian nurses enrolled in doctoral programs have ever had that level of financial support. It is estimated by Lamb, Stinson, and Thibaudeau (in press) that "only 1 in 13 nurses currently enrolled in a doctoral program holds a major research training award." In 1985 the Medical Research Council (MRC) made it explicit that it will accept research training and project funding applications from nurses (Medical Research Council, 1985). However as underlined by Lamb, Stinson, and Thibaudeau (1990), little has evolved in terms of "concrete results," although in 1989, MRC and NHRDP "established a Joint Program for the Development of Research in Nursing that was to begin in 1989."

Readers may refer to Kerr (1986), Wilmot (1986), and Stinson, Lamb, and Thibaudeau (1990) for more detailed analyses of Canadian nursing research funding. Kerr's chapter on the "Structure and Funding of Nursing Research in Canada" is especially informative in the specific sense. One of her conclusions is that "developments in [nursing research in Canada] have accompanied those in graduate education" (p. 110). Wilmot's chapter on "Science Policy, Health Research and Nursing Research Funding" provides a valuable description of the history and current context of nursing research funding in Canada. The analysis by Stinson, Lamb, and Thibaudeau of Canadian nursing research funding is testimony to the need for a comprehensive infrastructure for nursing research and the need for manifest support at the national Council level. Their analysis is also instructive in terms of the considerable variety of sources of nursing research funding in Canada, although the amount of funding available is grossly inadequate.

A brief commentary on the roles of Canada's professional nursing organizations in the development of graduate education—and their inextricable roles in the promotion and development of nursing research—follows.

Roles of Professional Nursing Associations

Each topic in this chapter deserves the attention of nursing scholars because there is so little literature on graduate nursing education available, and the roles of professional associations in Canada prove no exception. Again, only a few examples are described, but it is hoped they will illustrate that nationally and, with few exceptions, provincially much of the credit for the developments to date are due to the direct and indirect interventions of professional nursing associations. When such support was lacking, the leadership for graduate education came exclusively from within the ranks of nursing academia and university administrators.

Even a cursory look at historical and current accounts of the policies and activities of various nursing associations, including CNA, CAUSN, CNF, and the provincial professional nursing associations, indicates that they contributed extensively to the development of graduate nursing education. In the direct sense, they also used and are using their power and influence to press for graduate programs and nursing research and nursing program funding. In the indirect sense, without their constant collective endeavors to improve standards of nursing practice, education, and research, the working conditions of nurses and the development of graduate education would be very limited, at best.

Canadian graduate education has benefited too from the work of several professional associations in the United States (including the National League for Nursing's standards for graduate education) and those abroad (e.g., research endeavors of the Royal College of Nursing). At the national level, the champion of nursing master's programs in Canada is CAUSN, which in 1987 proposed a standing committee on graduate education and created an ad hoc committee on specialization in nursing. The CNF's primary role has been that of providing funding support for graduate education and establishing a "small" research grants program. The National Foundation for Nursing Unions has not been a force in graduate education. In contrast, several national clinical nursing specialty organizations have demonstrated financial and policy support for graduate education and research, primarily by providing research fellowships.

In 1976, CNA made a commitment to provide leadership for doctoral preparation for nurses and, in 1978, CNA, in concert with CNF and CAUSN, made a vital contribution by organizing the W.K. Kellogg National Seminar on Doctoral Preparation for Canadian Nurses. The National Seminar was part of CNA's "Operation

Bootstrap," a concerted effort to promote nursing research and doctoral preparation. Further, since 1971 the CNA's Nursing Research Committee contributed extensively to systematic planning for the development of nursing research in Canada, within and outside academia, as is evident in the Report of the MRC Working Group on Nursing Research (1985) and the MRC's *Grants and Awards Guide* (1986). It was through the combined efforts of CNA and CAUSN that the MRC began taking some initiative in developing joint funding arrangements with the NHRDP.

From these examples of the roles and influence of national nursing associations, we turn now to the provincial level, a dichotomy that is misleading because activity at the national level often is a function of developments at the provincial and local levels—and vice versa.

Most of the provincial professional nursing associations, which include professional bodies established by provincial or territorial legislation and province-wide clinical nursing interest groups, have taken initiatives to support baccalaureate education, graduate education, and/or research. They have used various interventions, including enunciating position and policy statements about baccalaureate and graduate education; holding direct discussions with ministries of health and education; establishing graduate fellowships, bursaries, and/or student loan programs; establishing small research grants programs; providing some financial support for nursing research units; contributing staff time and financial support to national and international nursing research conferences held in their provinces; preparing "blueprints" for the development of nursing research; and giving publicity to graduate education and research developments in their professional publications.

Additionally, the collective achievements of the provincial nurses' unions throughout Canada have done much to improve salaries and working conditions of nurses, particularly at the staff nurse and first-line manager levels, which in turn have produced higher salaries for nurses with advanced preparation.

Nationally and provincially, the extent of collaboration and support is impressive. It is hoped that nursing scholars will begin to describe and analyze these ventures in detail and link them with key contributions made to graduate education and research by other bodies such as the NHRDP, the Canadian Red Cross, and the W.K. Kellogg Foundation, to name only a few.

At the local level, many clinical agencies perform key roles in graduate nursing education. The development of graduate nursing education is a process that extends far beyond the parameters of any one university; it constitutes a complex systems problem, requiring national, regional, provincial, and local systems involvement and support. And, as the "global village" becomes a reality, the problems in—and solutions to—graduate nursing education will increasingly depend on factors, events, and policies external to graduate nursing programs themselves. The future of graduate education in Canadian nursing is promising, for much has already been accomplished in a remarkably short time, with few resources.

REFERENCES

Allemang, M.M., & Cahoon, M.C. (1986). Nursing education research in Canada. In H.H. Werley & J.J. Fitzpatrick (Eds.), *Annual review of nursing research, Vol. 4* (pp. 261-278). New York: Springer Publishing.

Allen, M. (1986). The relationship between graduate teaching and research in nursing. In S.M. Stinson & J.C. Kerr (Eds.), *International issues in nursing research* (pp. 151-167). London: Croom Helm.

Faculty of Nursing, University of Alberta. (1986). *Ph.D. in nursing: A proposal*. Edmonton: Author.

Field, P.A., & Stinson, S.M. (1986). *A beginning survey of selected characteristics of Canadian graduate nursing masters' programs*. Unpublished manuscript, Faculty of Nursing, University of Alberta, Edmonton.

Field, P.A., & Stinson, S.M. (1990). *Selected characteristics of Canadian graduate nursing programs: 1988-1989 update*. Unpublished manuscript, Faculty of Nursing, University of Alberta, Edmonton.

Grace, H. (1978). The development of doctoral education in nursing: A historical perspective. In N.L. Chaska (Ed.), *The nursing profession* (pp. 112-122). New York: McGraw-Hill.

Hart, M.E. (1962). *Needs and resources for graduate education in nursing in Canada*. Unpublished doctoral dissertation, Columbia University, New York.

Kerr, J.C.R. (1978). *Financing university nursing education in Canada: 1919-1976*. Unpublished doctoral dissertation. University of Michigan, Ann Arbor.

Kerr, J.C. (1986). Structure and funding of nursing research in Canada. In S.M. Stinson & J.C. Kerr (Eds.), *International issues in nursing research* (pp. 97-112). London: Croom Helm.

Lamb, M., & Stinson, S.M. (1990). *Canadian nursing doctoral statistics: 1989 update*. Ottawa: Canadian Nurses Association.

Lamb, M., Stinson, S.M., & Thibaudeau, M.F. (in press). Nursing development in Canada. In E. Levine, P. Leatt, K. Poultin, & P. Overton (Eds.), *Comparative Nursing Practice in the UK, USA and North America*. London: Chapman and Hall.

Medical Research Council. (1985). *Report of the MRC working group on nursing research*. Ottawa: Author.

Medical Research Council. (1986). *MRC grants and awards guide: 1986-87*. Ottawa: Author.

Muller, S. (1974). Higher education or higher skilling? *Daedalus, 103*(4), 148-158.

Murphy, J. (1981). Doctoral education in, of, and for nursing: An historical analysis. *Nursing Outlook, 29*(11), 645-649.

Murphy, J. (1985). Doctoral education of nurses: Historical development, programs, and graduates. In H.H. Werley & J.J. Fitzpatrick (Eds.), *Annual review of nursing research (Vol. 3)* (pp. 171-179). New York: Springer Publishing.

Phenix, P.H. (1964). *Realms of meaning.* New York: McGraw-Hill.

Statistics Canada. (1987). *Revised registered nurses data series.* Ottawa: Author.

Stinson, S.M. (1986). Nursing research in Canada. In S.M. Stinson & J.C. Kerr (Eds.), *International issues in nursing research* (pp. 236-258). London: Croom Helm.

Stinson, S.M., & Giovannetti, P. (1985). *Selected statistics on faculty members and graduate students in Canadian universities with graduate nursing programs, Fall, 1984.* Unpublished report, Faculty of Nursing, University of Alberta, Edmonton.

Stinson, S.M., & Kerr, J.C. (1986). *International issues in nursing research.* London: Croom Helm.

Stinson, S.M., MacPhail, J., & Larsen, J. (1988). *Canadian nursing doctoral statistics: 1986 update.* Ottawa: Canadian Nurses Association.

Stinson, S.M., Lamb, M., & Thibaudeau, M.F. (1990). Nursing research: The Canadian scene. *International Journal of Nursing Studies, 27*(2), 105-122.

Symons, T.H.B. (1975). *To know ourselves: The report of the Commission on Canadian Studies* (Vol. 1). Ottawa: Publication Office, Association of Universities and Colleges of Canada.

Wilmot, V. (1986). Health science policy and health research funding in Canada. In S.M. Stinson & J.C. Kerr (Eds.), *International issues in nursing research* (pp. 76-96). London: Croom Helm.

Zilm, G.N., Larose, O., & Stinson, S.M. (1979). *Ph.D. (Nursing).* Ottawa: Canadian Nurses Association.

Registered nurses who live outside Canada's major metropolitan centers appreciate and use the rapidly growing distance education programs that involve correspondence, teleconferences, television, and, sometimes, on-site visits by campus instructors or local preceptors. This photo shows a student telephone conference with Lynda Anderson, RN, MSN, a tutor in N406, the Nursing Management course offered through the BSN Outreach Program at the University of British Columbia School of Nursing. (Photograph courtesy Learning Centre, University of British Columbia School of Nursing.)

CHAPTER TWENTY-THREE

Continuing Education in Nursing Practice

CAROLYN B. ATTRIDGE, RN, PhD
KATHLEEN M. CLARK, RN, PhD

Carolyn B. Attridge, RN, BScN (McMaster), MN (Washington), PhD (Toronto), is an Associate Professor in the School of Nursing, University of Victoria. Her major areas of interest include the nature of nursing work and work environments, women's issues as they pertain to nursing, curriculum development and evaluation, impact of educational approaches on professional socialization, and distance education approaches as a vehicle for continuing education in the professions. She has conducted research and evaluation studies in most of these areas and has written articles and papers on these topics.

Kathleen M. Clark RN, BScN (Toronto), MA (British Columbia), PhD (Toronto), is the Research Coordinator (McMaster) with the Quality of Nursing Worklife Research Unit at McMaster University's School of Nursing and the Faculty of Nursing, University of Toronto. She has held continuing education positions in the hospital, college, university, and professional association sectors in British Columbia and Ontario. She was the founder and newsletter editor of the Self-Directed Learning Network. Her current research interests include nursing resources supply and demand, career choice, as well as public and professional policy.

SPECIAL ACKNOWLEDGEMENT

The authors wish to acknowledge the contribution of Gail Gitterman, RN, BA, MA who co-authored this chapter for the first edition. Gail Gitterman is currently the Director of Complaints and Discipline at the College of Nurses of Ontario.

S everal factors lead to the emergence of continuing education as a major area of concern of nursing. First, the nature of nursing work is continually changing. The increasing complexity of the clients of nursing—individuals, families, groups, and communities—results in a corresponding increase in the complexity of knowledge nurses are required to bring to client situations. Patients admitted to every kind of institutional setting are more acutely ill. They are increasingly older, reflecting the "age boom." For example, by the year 2031, individuals age 65 or older will account for 60% of hospital days (Abelson, Paddon, and Strohmenger, 1983; Epp, 1986). Chronicity is increasing. The incidence of life-style-related disease is growing. The sociocultural and economic diversity of clients is escalating. In any setting, nurses are likely to be confronted with highly variable and complex client situations and needs to which they must respond in relevant and competent ways.

At the same time the nursing workplace itself is changing. Numbers and variety of settings in which nurses practice are increasing. Every setting, including the home, is characterized by more complex technology that nurses must manage. Different ways of organizing and monitoring nursing are appearing. The multidisciplinary team has become a reality in most health care settings. However, even though the complexity of nursing work grows, the resource base for nursing, including continuing education resources, shrinks as concern about health care costs permeates the system. Nurses, who are the largest group of health professionals, feel much of the burden of economic restraint.

Second, the "shelf life" of specific nursing and health care knowledge and skills is short. No longer can nurses assume that a fixed body of knowledge, once mastered, will serve for life. Specialization is increasingly a fact of professional life as professionals realize the depth of knowledge they must possess to operate effectively. Also, individuals now can change careers several times in a lifetime. With the constant and rapid changes the world undergoes, conceptually as well as technologically, education must be a continuous process if nurses are to survive and effectively serve public needs (Granger, 1986; Naisbitt, 1982). Employers, the organized profession, unions, and the public are increasingly concerned with the maintenance of nursing competence and the assurance of quality care.

A third set of factors involves nurses themselves. Reflecting the position of women in society in general, more and more nurses see themselves as participating fully in the work force and developing a career rather than working at a job. As the professional goal of the baccalaureate degree for entry to practice becomes a reality, this is increasingly likely to be the case. Nurses will increasingly demand a variety of learning opportunities to assist them in their career aspirations. Society's emphasis on the importance of lifelong learning to enable personal and work-related growth and fulfillment fosters this perspective further.

This chapter provides a brief definition of continuing education as it is used in Canadian nursing today. It summarizes the history and development and the "infrastructure" of continuing nursing education in Canada. The chapter identifies several of the major current issues, including the emergence of new distance education approaches to help improve accessibility of programs, and concludes with a list of some of the questions that must be addressed if continuing education is to meet the challenges of the 1990s and beyond.

DEFINITION OF CONTINUING NURSING EDUCATION

The definition of Continuing Nursing Education in this chapter is designed to reflect the current situation in nursing. This definition accommodates the rich diversity of programs, consumers, and providers that has emerged and recognizes that continuing education occurs in many different settings (including the home) for many different purposes. In addition, the definition breaks with the more traditional view that continuing education is noncredit education only.

Continuing Nursing Education is any planned learning experience that is intended to build on first level nursing preparation and practice experience. It may take place under the auspices of an educational institution or other educational provider, or be self-organized and self-directed. It may be credit or noncredit. It is intended to contribute to the enhancement of nursing practice, education, administration, research, and policy and to the fulfillment of an individual nurse's professional goals.

According to this definition, consumers of continuing nursing education are diploma and generic baccalaureate graduates whatever their experience and additional qualifications might be. Although there are no studies that document actual national participation, the potential learner pool is the approximately 250,000 registered nurses in Canada today. The providers are all those who offer programs. They include hospitals and community agencies, colleges, universities, professional associations, unions, private entrepreneurs, and nurses themselves. The array of continuing education opportunities includes a wide range of activities, such as participation in a 2-day workshop to develop creative thinking, attending a convention examining the image of nursing, taking a refresher course, setting out individually to upgrade one's intravenous skills, enrolling in a post-diploma baccalaureate program to obtain a degree, learning on the job to read an electrocardiogram, or completing a college post-basic course in intensive care nursing. All qualify as examples of continuing education, although the time involved, the settings, the purposes, and the sponsors vary.

This definition differs from other definitions in several ways. It includes self-organized and self-directed learning, increasingly a feature of society in all fields and at all levels (Clark, 1986). It includes education obtained for academic credit, including post-basic baccalaureate and graduate level education. The perception of continuing education as noncredit study only is based in the early realities in Canada in which efforts were primarily confined to the requirements of particular jobs. This limited focus no longer represents the reality of continuing nursing education today. The definition excludes education to achieve personal goals not related to nursing in some respect. Although nurses often embark on educational opportunities to learn things other than nursing, and indeed should be applauded for doing so, these activities do not legitimately qualify as continuing nursing education. Finally, the definition confronts the contentious issue of education building on other educational opportunities and experience; this suggests a coherent, interrelated approach that in actuality is not often present.

HISTORY AND DEVELOPMENT OF CONTINUING EDUCATION

Continuing education is not a new phenomenon. Nurses always have taken advantage of formal and informal opportunities to improve their knowledge and skills. These opportunities initially were provided by alumni associations of schools of nursing, since graduates in early years seldom moved from the communities in which their schools were located and alumni groups made both social and educational activities available (Jensen, 1969). In the 1930s a new dimension of continuing education developed. The phenomenon of staff development, or inservice education as it later became known, emerged, with its goal to develop educational programs to equip nurse workers with specific job related skills (Schor, 1981).

Developments in continuing nursing education paralleled those in general education, particularly in adult education, which entered its boom period at the end of World War II. At that time, millions of dollars were made available to provide educational opportunities for returning veterans who were highly motivated, experienced, self-directed, and eager to pursue their educations. They also brought family and work responsibilities that could not easily be shelved to permit them to obtain schooling in traditional ways. Characteristics such as these led to the emergence of a different view of learners (Knowles, 1985) and different ways of delivering education. Nurse adult learners shared these characteristics, and they too sought additional opportunities to continue their professional growth, such as part-time study, self-directed learning, night school, and correspondence programs.

In the 1950s, 1960s, and 1970s, continuing education opportunities for nurses proliferated, predominantly noncredit in nature and job-related in focus. As nursing programs moved from hospitals to community colleges and the number of university programs increased, additional and more varied opportunities became available, including some that provided academic credit toward university degrees. Courses grew in numbers and the field became increasingly competitive as new providers, including private entrepreneurs, realized that nurses were a profitable target group. Throughout this period of continuing education expansion, inservice and continuing educators attempted to form interest groups at the local, provincial, and national level. Similar to any nursing interest group, they wanted to connect with professional colleagues to share information, give and receive support, and engage in professional development. Local initiatives have been successful and groups of inservice educators can be found in many communities throughout the country, although networking at the provincial and national levels represents a much greater challenge for all Canadian nurses, not just continuing educators.

In 1979, the first national forum on continuing education in Canada was held in Winnipeg. Individuals from all provinces and the Northwest Territories met to examine the problems and issues of the day (Niskala and Clark, 1980). A second conference was held the next year in Vancouver in conjunction with the Canadian Nurses Association Biennial Convention. The difficulty was finding a sponsor to help organize a national meeting of continuing educators on a regular basis. It was hoped that the Canadian Nurses Association (CNA) would be that sponsor. CNA did host two additional conferences in 1984 and 1986, but the conferences were designed for nursing administrators and basic nursing educators, as well as nurses interested in inservice and continuing education. CNA argued that resources did not permit separate conferences for independent groups and that there was much to be gained from encouraging administrative and educational groups to meet together.

Since then, the CNA has sponsored regional conferences on primary health care, AIDS, and nursing work-life issues. National meetings of nursing administrators also have been hosted by CNA in keeping with a priority concern for nursing administration. Limited resources and competing priorities have been deterrents to CNA sponsorship for continuing education. These same factors also account, in part, for the lack of a CNA policy statement on continuing nursing education. Only in 1990 was a discussion paper (CNA, 1990) circulated for comment and reaction.

A Canadian Nurse Educators Interest Group was formed in 1988 at the CNA Biennial Meeting in Charlottetown to provide an open forum for nurse educators, including baccalaureate, diploma, and hospital-based educators, clinical specialists, continuing education personnel, clinical educators, and hospital inservice educators.

At the provincial level, most professional nursing associations have published their positions on continuing education, and nursing education interest groups are being developed. For example, Ontario has a Provincial Nurse Educators' Interest Group, and in 1990 a Nurse Educators Professional Practice Group was established in British Columbia. These groups convene educators teaching in basic and graduate programs, as well as those teaching continuing education and inservice programs.

Although the goal of integrating all educators is rational and desirable, unfortunately the interests and concerns of those involved in continuing education or inservice education programs are often overshadowed by the agenda of the more numerous basic educators. For this reason, many continuing and inservice educators choose not to participate; instead, they continue to seek separate associations. For example, since an invitational conference hosted by Ryerson and the Registered Nurses Association of Ontario in May 1990, a group of Ontario nurses representing various continuing education interests continues to meet. Their initial project is the development of a nursing education recognition system that acknowledges different levels of nursing education, including continuing education. The energy, enthusiasm, and initiative of this group is reminiscent of the spirit of those who, in 1979, struggled without success to establish a national interest group.

Such national and international networking is not impossible, but it is certainly not easy. In 1982, Kathleen Clark established the Self-Directed Learning Network (SDL Network) to connect nurses, adult educators, and other health professionals interested in self-directed learning as an effective, efficient, and economic approach to professional development. The SDL Network had members in Canada, the United

States, Britain, New Zealand, and Australia. They communicated largely through a quarterly newsletter, but when, after 6 years, no one could assume responsibility for the publication of the newsletter, the Network regrettably shut down.

CURRENT ISSUES

Issues and concerns surrounding continuing nursing education in the early 1990s vary, depending on one's perspective. Nurses have such questions as:
- Why should I do it? (issues of currency and career development)
- Do I have to do it? (issues of voluntary versus mandatory continuing education)
- How do I do it? (issues of accessibility, cost, and support systems)
- What do I get out of it? (issues of rewards and recognition)

Others share concerns about these issues but focus on additional questions. Providers ask: Who takes continuing education programs and why? (issues of purpose and motivation). Professional nursing associations and employers ask: Does continuing education make a difference? (issues of quality, evaluation, and research). Funding agencies and taxpayers ask: How can a more rational, coherent continuing education system be developed? (issues of duplication, collaboration, and competition). This section explores each of these issues in more detail.

Currency and Career Development

Although there are nurses who believe that this should not be the case, first-level nursing education programs, whether diploma or baccalaureate, cannot and do not prepare nurses to meet all the changes that will occur in practice and in the workplace as society's health needs and our ways of meeting them evolve. There should be no question that nurses' accumulated experience contributes to their knowledge and skill, but there is also no doubt that sound educational programs, building on what nurses contribute to them, can cut the time involved in gaining necessary experience and augment the effect of experience on learning. Moreover, if nurses wish to specialize, if they wish to increase their alternatives and advance their careers, or if they wish to gain specific knowledge and credentials, it is increasingly likely that some form of additional educational preparation will be necessary.

Mandatory or Voluntary

The question, Do I have to do it? reflects a recurrent issue in Canadian continuing nursing education. Mandatory continuing education removes the option of whether to engage in continuing education activities or not. Under this approach, some continuing education becomes compulsory if nurses are to renew their registration, licensure, or other qualification. Mandatory continuing education is a mechanism intended to ensure practitioner competence and therefore public safety (Rockhill, 1983) and is based on a view of the practitioner as one who, having completed initial preparation, believes there is no more to learn (or if there is, does not want to learn it) and who therefore would not voluntarily participate in continuing education programs. Presumably every profession has some members whose skills have deteriorated and who may not wish to remedy their situation (Houle, 1981).

Proponents of mandatory continuing education argue that the assurance of competence for practice is its most significant advantage, and nurses need external incentives to accomplish this. Opponents argue the following seven main points:

1. There is no empirical evidence to support the view that continuing education maintains competency
2. It cannot be assumed that mere attendance at programs results in learning (Rockhill, 1983; Shimberg, 1980)
3. Continuing education programs are not universally available to all nurses, resulting in undue pressure for some who would need to access them
4. Accreditation and approval mechanisms are complex to design and expensive to implement
5. Tools to assess effectiveness are lacking
6. Records of accomplishment are difficult and costly to maintain (Cooper, 1974, 1980; Gaston and Pucci, 1982; Rizzuto, 1982)
7. Mandatory continuing education violates adult learning principals, which view the adult as self-directed and self-motivated, and as one whose learning cannot and should not be dictated by external forces (Rockhill, 1983)

Mandatory continuing education for nurses was introduced in the United States in the 1970s as a result of actions by state legislatures and professional organizations, and, by 1990, 21 states required some form of regular continuing education for relicensure or certification (Woods, 1990). The experience engendered some disillusionment, for the reasons mentioned, and mandatory continuing education is now being viewed as only one of several mechanisms available for measuring competence. In Canada, there is a difference. Because of the problems, none of the provinces or territories has mandated continuing education despite the advantages that might accrue to some vested interest groups by doing so. For example, unions (which could negotiate for paid educational leave in contracts), professional associations (which could have captive learners, a renewed raison d'etre, and some additional income), and providers (who clearly have strong vested interests) could benefit. Instead the nursing profession in Canada has chosen a voluntary approach, remaining true to an adult learner oriented philosophy and examining alternative ways of enticing nurses who may be reluctant to engage in continuing educational activities. In this regard, incentives take various forms, including increasing the array of programs available, offering certificates of attendance that can be used to enhance nurses' portfolios, or giving various financial benefits.

Effective ways of ensuring practitioner competence remains an issue, however. All provinces except Ontario require some minimum amount of time spent practicing nursing in some form. None has as yet devised mechanisms to measure competence per se. In Ontario, where the College of Nurses of Ontario (CNO) is awaiting changes to the health professions legislation, the self-regulating body for registered nurses and registered nursing assistants has studied several methods by which competence might be appraised: peer review (e.g., chart audits and performance appraisals), examinations, education and workplace accreditation, self-assessment tools, and multiple competency assessment systems (CNO, 1987). As a result of the change in the Ontario government in the fall 1990, the legislation was delayed. With its passing will come the obligation that regulatory bodies in Ontario establish programs of quality assurance. The challenge of defining and implementing quality assurance in the context of professional self-regulation will be the responsibility of the regulatory bodies.

Anticipating that some form of continuing competency requirements for nurses will be introduced, the Ontario Nurses' Association (the union representing 55,000 registered nurses) began awarding Continuing Education Units (CEUs) for all of its educational programs as of January 1991. ONA believes that ultimately all continuing education programs for nurses in Ontario will also give CEUs for completion (ONA, 1990, p.3).

Purposes and Motivation

Two issues for providers, professional organizations, and employers concerned with maintenance of nurse competence are: Who chooses to participate in continuing education? and Why? Answers may suggest strategies to encourage and enable increased nurse participation, an important outcome if participation is to remain voluntary yet competence be maintained. Houle's (1963) research indicates that adults participate in education programs because of relief from routine, compliance with authority, acquisition of credentials, professional advancement and improvement in professional knowledge, social relations, and welfare skills. Many of these factors operate in nursing. For example, recent studies of participation in continuing nursing education indicate that the strongest motivation factors are to obtain an increase in professional knowledge (O'Connor, 1979, 1982; Thomas, 1986) and professional advancement (O'Connor, 1982; Thomas, 1986). Motivational factors, however, apparently do not discriminate among those who are likely to take educational programs and those who are not (Scanlan and Darkenwald, 1984).

Some studies tried to link learner characteristics such as educational background to participation, but initial preparation (diploma or baccalaureate) has not clearly shown a relationship to participation, although evidence is conflicting (Parochka, 1985; Puetz, 1980; Trammell, 1986). Nurses with formal graduate level preparation are more likely to participate in continuing education (Millonig, 1985); this finding supports research in adult education that indicates past level of education is the most reliable predictor of participation (Cross, 1981).

Accessibility and Cost

In Canada, accessibility is one of the most critical issues of continuing education. The following factors affect accessibility:
- Canada is characterized by certain geographic, demographic, and socioeconomic features: large rural areas, diversity of terrain, population concentrations in relatively small pockets; health care, educational institutions, and the resources they provide tend to duplicate this distribution; there are major regional socioeconomic differences
- Nursing is predominantly a women's profession, and women are often locked into their locations by family responsibilities or husband's job commitments and have limited free time (Parochka, 1985; Richardson and Sherwood, 1985; Scanlan and Darkenwald, 1984)

- Economic restraint, health care cutbacks, and rising unemployment further compound these difficulties, resulting in nurses being reluctant to take leaves (even if available) from work; this is especially true when courses are of a longer duration, such as post-RN baccalaureate programs and post-basic certificate specialty programs

Many major barriers to accessibility arise from the workplace. Employer support in the form of administrative encouragement, time off with or without pay, permission to alter schedules of work/days off, and financial assistance with registration fees is often lacking, especially for programs located outside the employer's workplace (Parochka, 1985; Richardson and Sherwood, 1985; Scanlan and Darkenwald, 1984). Conditions of work (e.g., fatigue, burnout, shift work) hinder participation (Richardson and Sherwood, 1985). Lack of recognition for increased knowledge and skills or, more subtly, lack of opportunity to use increased knowledge and skills also serve as deterrents to participation (Blais, Duquett, and Painchaud, 1989; Friedberg and Harrison, 1983). Employer support varies with type of employer and category of practitioner. In Ontario, community and occupational health employers were more likely to give time off with salary and reimbursement of registration fees and travel costs than were hospital employers (Registered Nurses Association of Ontario, 1983, 1986). Hospitals display a rather dismal record of support for continuing education for their employees, particularly for programs offered outside the hospital or agency. A 1982 Saskatchewan study reports that only 16% of chief executive officers of Saskatchewan hospitals granted leave with pay to their nurse employees. More disturbingly, only 50% granted leave without pay, which suggests that half the province's nurses were not given any opportunity for post-basic training even if they were willing to forego their salary and receive only part of their expenses (Saskatchewan Health Care Association, 1982).

A few groups receive some support. A common view is that nurse administrators in hospitals, college/university educators, and critical care nurses are more likely to receive salaried time off than other groups of nurses. A survey was conducted in 1989 by Carol Wong, Victoria Hospital Corporation, to determine the factors involved in the allocation of nursing staff education funding in acute care teaching hospitals in Canada, but final results of this study, which was done for the Academy of Chief Executive Nurses, are not yet available. Teaching hospitals invest heavily in the professional development of their nursing staff. However, hospitals do not maintain cost accounting for what they spend on staff education, so the extent to which hospitals support staff development and how they compare to other health agencies and other industries in the public and private sectors has not been measured.

Professional nurses' associations and nurses' unions are increasing pressure on employers to provide educational leaves and some financial support for continuing education. For example, the 1988-1991 central collective agreement between the Ontario Nurses' Association and the Ontario Hospital Association included a prepaid leave plan that became effective on April 1, 1989. The plan, funded solely by the nurses, allows nurses to spread four years' salary over a 5-year period to enable them to take a 1-year leave of absence after the 4 years of salary deferral. ONA does not have statistics on the number of nurses enrolled in these plans. The chronic shortage of qualified nurses in specialized areas of practice, especially critical care units in large, urban, teaching hospitals has also put pressure on the hospitals to increase their support to nurses enrolled in post-basic specialty certificate programs in return for a commitment of service (Clark, 1990).

Even when workplace and cost factors are not barriers, geography and social factors such as family commitments continue to block accessibility to continuing education for many nurses, especially in nonurban areas. This induces providers to seek innovative ways to increase the accessibility of their programming. Several of these program initiatives are best described by the term *distance education.*

Emergence of Distance Education

Knowles' (1985) working definition of distance education contains two components: (1) physical separation of learner and teacher and (2) use of various technological media to carry educational content. Keegan (1982) delineates several characteristics of distance education. His list includes the following:

- Teacher and learner are separated (i.e., no or very little face to face interaction occurs)
- Programming is offered under the auspices of an educational organization of some kind (the institution's sole purpose may not be education, however), which distinguishes it from private study
- Technological media, almost always print but often other media, carry educational content and unite teacher and learner
- Some form of two-way interaction allows dialogue between teacher and learner
- Occasional meetings between teacher (or teacher surrogate) and learner may be provided for both didactic and socialization purposes
- Certain "industrial" features are usually present, such as planning, rationalizing procedures, division of labor, or mass production

In Canada, most of these features are present in programs purporting to use distance approaches. Generally, interaction between teacher and student varies with course type, purpose, and content, in addition to the degree to which factors such as physical proximity, numbers of students, and cost make contact feasible.

Nursing, in fact, is a relative latecomer to the field of distance education. Formal general education programs using distance methods existed at the technical and vocational levels for 130 years and at the higher education levels for 100 years. The inception of the United Kingdom Open University in 1969 was a critical event in distance education. It began admitting distance adult learners in 1971 and has an impeccable record of course quality at both undergraduate and graduate levels.

Distance education for Canadian nurses probably began with the development of the Nursing Unit Administration course, a noncredit course conceived by the Canadian Nurses Association and the Canadian Hospital Association as an inservice program to assist nurse managers and others in middle management positions to better handle their increasingly complex and demanding administrative responsibilities. The course was first offered in 1960-1961 and consisted of 12 home study sessions (in the jargon of the day, a correspondence course). In the mid-1980s the course was renamed the Introduction to Nursing Management Program, and the admission criteria were revised to accept staff nurses who wished to prepare for administrative positions. Throughout its first 30 years, the program graduated more than 19,000 students, including nurses from several countries in addition to Canada. In September 1990, there were 657 enrolled in the program; 42% were staff nurses and 9% were baccalaureate graduates. A short (3-month) module on budgeting was first offered in 1988 and is now available twice a year. Like the parent 10-month program, it is print-based distance education with regular telephone and some face-to-face contact between students and their educational consultants. Other modules are being considered as part of the program's strategic plan for the future.

Questions have arisen as to whether the Nursing Management Program deters nurses from going to university for baccalaureate or masters preparation in administration. For some, the program serves as an incentive and facilitates the gradual re-entry to formal education. Another controversy continues to center on whether program graduates receive credit. Some universities evaluated the program and grant credit toward an elective or required course.

Since the 1960s, many distance education developments have occurred, particularly in the western provinces. For example, in British Columbia, a province with large rural areas and difficult terrain, the establishment of two provincial organizations dedicated to distance education facilitated the development and delivery of distance programming for nurses. These were the Open Learning Institute (OLI), established in 1978 and dedicated to distance education of various kinds, including degree preparation; and the Knowledge Network (1980), an electronic delivery system of educational programming. The two are now integrated, and the Open Learning Agency (OLA) has a broader mandate to include an open university with degree-granting status, an open college, and the Knowledge Network. The University of Victoria, the University of British Columbia, and the British Columbia Institute of Technology (BCIT) are leaders in the development of nurse-directed distance programming through the Knowledge Network. Noncredit nursing refresher courses are also offered by OLA and by BCIT and, again, are delivered in many locations. Various progressional development courses are available for specific audiences and include a range of topics (e.g., gerontology, physical assessment, and osteoporosis). Satellite and cable television have a major role in distance delivery.

Alberta developed various distance options for nurses, including the Alberta Hospital Association hospital teleconference network, which links all 275 Alberta hospitals and enables a variety of inservice education opportunities using distance technology. A major influence in this province includes Grant MacEwan Community College, which as early as 1978 offered an Occupational Health certificate program delivered off campus. By 1986 this program was available in self-learning modules that could be studied in the home (Bailey, 1987). All the universities, including Athabasca University (a single purpose distance education institution that offers a baccalaureate degree in nursing) have key roles in nurse distance education, as have many community colleges.

As with the Management Program, acceptance of some of the newer distance education programs and some of their courses results in controversy. Some university nursing programs recognize and accept some or all distance offerings for credit in their basic and/or graduate programs; other nursing degree programs are adamantly opposed to some or all of these courses. Nursing students are frequently caught in the middle of the controversy, take courses anticipating that they will receive credit if and when they apply to a university, and are disappointed and frustrated when they discover that such credit is not given. The final decisions rest with the individual schools and are closely tied to the reputation of the individual programs. At issue are questions of standardization of degree programs and accreditation. At present, prospective students should be aware of the controversy and check on course acceptability before they take courses.

Baccalaureate Education and Distance Learning

One of the notable developments in the last 10 years in nursing education has been the increasing demand by registered nurses for opportunities to obtain their baccalaureate degrees. University schools of nursing responded by accepting larger enrollments in available post-RN baccalaureate programs and by developing new programs when possible. Whereas in 1980, only 937 post-RN students were reported enrolled in 12 of 23 university schools of nursing, in 1989 these numbers escalated to 5136 students in 28 of 31 schools. The most dramatic growth occurred in the part-time student group, which increased from 163 students in 1980 to 3176 students in 1989 (Canadian Association of University Schools of Nursing, 1980, 1989). Despite these increases, pressures on university schools continue to mount, particularly in areas of scarcity, because universities are unable to meet the present demand for post-RN baccalaureate education, let alone the future demand expected to occur as the year 2000 approaches. Not only are spaces unavailable in campus programs; there remain large numbers of nurses who, for the reasons already mentioned, cannot access campuses even if space were available. They are seeking ways to increase their formal education without leaving home and work situations.

In response to these problems, universities examined less traditional ways to offer programming off campus. At first responses were alterations of course schedules to make courses available in the evenings and on weekends and movement of faculty off campus to deliver courses in other locations. These are probably better labeled outreach rather than distance approaches. As demand increased, technology improved, and faculties became more venturesome, individual university schools developed courses in a more truly distance mode (as distance is characterized in the preceding paragraphs). In 1977, in central Canada, Laurentian University (Sudbury, Ontario) became involved in distance credit nursing education in an attempt to make baccalaureate education available to nurses in isolated areas of Northern Ontario. The program was initially offered in two off-campus locations using print, video, other audiovisual materials, telephone, and face-to-face contact in which university faculty traveled to delivery sites (Kutschke, 1986).

In 1987 and 1989, Laurentian University admitted two groups of distance students to its nursing program. Each course is taught using various media. The clinical courses are taught by a university-based course professor and an onsite clinical teacher. The students in these two groups (approximately 140) have progressed in their nursing studies so that in 1992 the university will be offering the fourth year level of their curriculum, which includes courses in nursing research, nursing theory, and leadership, each with a clinical component. The program is now available in eight communities: Barrie, Elliott Lake, Kapuskasing, North Bay, Orillia, Parry Sound, Sault Ste. Marie, and Timmins. A satisfaction study conducted with the 1987 students produced positive results; students were particularly satisfied with the course manual and the work of the clinical teachers. The small numbers of students in various communities make the program very costly from an administrative perspective.

A leader in Western Canada is the University of Victoria, which in 1980-1981 developed its first credit nursing course using print, interactive cable TV, and telephone tutorial to reach its students located throughout British Columbia (Attridge, 1982; Attridge, Gallagher, and Collins, 1985). Courses more closely parallel the true distance style, since little face-to-face contact with university faculty occurs, although preceptors are hired in regions to supervise clinical courses. Since then, the entire baccalaureate program is available to British Columbia nurses, and the university is examining the feasibility of reaching outside its provincial boundaries to meet the needs of nurses in other areas of scarcity.

In 1983-1984, the University of Ottawa offered credit courses to nurses using teleconference as a core distance format and has now made courses available to locations as far away as New Brunswick and collaborates with other universities to complement their course offerings (DuGas and Casey, 1986). In the East, Memorial University in Newfoundland and the Maritime universities have developed distance education programs for nurses. For example, the University of New Brunswick and St. Francis Xavier University make baccalaureate nursing education accessible not only to the nurses in New Brunswick and Nova Scotia but also to nurses on Prince Edward Island.

Distance education methods now need to move to more creative methods of increasing teacher-learner interaction and to encourage and enable reflective thinking and professional socialization. This will mean smaller student groups and more faculty development, which will increase costs. As well, research on effective methods and learning outcomes must be performed.

Rewards and Recognition

Of particular importance to nurses is the return, or more accurately the lack of return, for participation in continuing education. The prevailing pattern of nurse participation is toward accumulation of various locally available courses. Few courses reward participants with credentials that receive other than local recognition. Generally financial return in the form of increased wages is not forthcoming. This phenomenon leads to "educational ghettoization," or second class status, of many nurses who follow this pattern. It is alarming therefore that this type of continuing education participation appears to be increasing. The exception is baccalaureate education, which at least provides a universally recognized academic degree. Even baccalaureate preparation results in only limited or no financial gains in many workplaces. The baccalaureate degree does, however, increase career alternatives open to nurses and increasingly is required for advancement in the profession.

Development of post-basic specialty courses, which have some recognized mechanism certifying success in the program, has in some instances resulted in financial remuneration. This is more likely when courses are longer, are offered by educational institutions with recognized certificate granting privileges, and have approval from a professional body. For example, in British Columbia, nurses who complete a post-basic specialty course of 6-months duration or longer, recognized by the Registered Nurses' Association of British Columbia, receive some wage differential. To receive the differential, they must be employed in the area in which they received the additional preparation and must have participated in the course no more than 4 years previously.

A recent study of the use of economic incentives in Toronto teaching hospitals for the purposes of recruiting nurses to intensive care units clearly demonstrates the inadequacy of existing salary differentials (educational bonuses) in specialty areas such as intensive care (Clark, 1990). The $15 a month differential, paid by four of the eight study hospitals to graduates of approved post-basic certificate programs, has not increased in the past 10 years (see also Chapter 17).

There are, of course, other than monetary awards. One of the strongest concerns expressed by consumers and many providers is the lack of academic credit, particularly credit toward degree education, granted for many lengthy and apparently high-quality post-basic specialty courses (National Federation of Nurses' Unions, 1987; Richardson and Sherwood, 1985). Until recently universities have been slow to respond to the building pressure in this regard, citing reasons such as the absence of quality appraisal mechanisms, overfull programs, inflexibility of curricula, and the belief that specialization should take place at the master's level. This reluctance on the part of the universities is frustrating to nurses who devote considerable time, energy, and often personal expense to participate in continuing education opportunities.

However, there is an indication that this is changing. Throughout the country, institutions of higher learning have begun to acknowledge specialty preparation with academic credit. The University of Alberta, the University of Manitoba, and Ryerson Polytechnical Institute in Ontario collaborate with hospitals in the development of critical care courses.

Another collaborative project involving Newfoundland and the Maritime provinces is exploring a cost-effective way of providing specialty preparation with university credit on a regional basis. The Maritimes Higher Education Commission and the Association of Atlantic Universities are funding a pilot project to explore the feasibility of a regional, collaborative approach to the design and delivery of distance education clinical courses. Beginning with the greatest assessed need for critical care nursing education, the project steering committee hopes to produce a blueprint for regional, baccalaureate level specialty nursing programs throughout Atlantic Canada.

In addition, the University of Victoria and Dalhousie University developed sets of criteria by which specialty courses can be assessed for their acceptability for university credit. Mechanisms such as these increase the potential for credit reward and create opportunities for influencing the level and content of specialty programs.

Quality, Evaluation, and Research

For continuing education to be an important concern of the profession, it must change nursing practice for the better. To do so it must affect the knowledge, skills, attitudes, values, norms, or other beliefs that influence nurse behavior. The process by which nurses learn these and come to internalize them is often called professional socialization.

Unfortunately, the effectiveness of continuing education in accomplishing such changes in practice has yet to be proven. There are few research and evaluation studies in this field, and those that are available have been plagued with methodological, conceptual, and practical difficulties (Abrahamson, 1968; Watson, 1986) and an apparent lack of agreement about what should be studied.

Cervero (1985) proposes three sets of variables believed to affect whether behavior change will occur: program characteristics, learner characteristics, and the social system in which the professional operates. Programs that supply individual learning approaches and performance feedback appear to have more success (Manning et al., 1986); learners who are motivated and who want to change their behavior (a key aspect of the process of professional socialization) are more likely to do so; a workplace social system that supports and does not block implementation of innovative practice approaches is less likely to frustrate practitioners who are trying to put into practice what they have learned (Friedberg and Harrison, 1983).

Cervero's variables are similar to those proposed by some social scientists (Bucher and Stelling, 1977; Cohen, 1981) and some nurse educators (Attridge, 1981; 1983) as affecting professional socialization and therefore practice. These variables include such features as learner characteristics. For example, older learners with previously established beliefs and values may prove more resistant to a program's messages about the "right" way to nurse. Visibility of nurses in the program whom learners will choose as role models appears to be important, but their characteristics should be consistent with the program's views about nursing and nurses if such views are to be internalized by learners. Length and depth of exposure are also factors. For example, the clearer a program's messages are about desired behaviors and beliefs and the longer learners are exposed to them, the more likely it is that program views will be internalized. Peer interactions are important. For example, peer support for program views about nursing can influence learners to accept them. The nature of the clinical practice environments for learning and practice after completing the program are factors. If there is workplace support for what learners have learned, intended socialization is more likely to occur. Although it is likely that a program of any substance will have some effect on participant socialization whatever program designers do about factors such as these, that effect may not be the desired one. If programs are to influence learners in the directions that they themselves value, that they believe to be important to better nursing practice, providers must attend carefully to the manifestation of some of these features when planning their programs.

Knowledge about professional socialization suggests program characteristics that might make continuing education more effective. It also suggests approaches and criteria that can be used to assess their effectiveness.

In sum, when one examines what is known about the quality and effect of nursing continuing education, one finds little research to guide decisions in the field. In areas such as distance education, hardly anything is available. Perhaps this reflects a less than central position in the eyes of the Canadian nursing profession. Much more needs to be done in this area if nurses are to be assured of the quality of continuing education.

Collaboration Versus Duplication and Competition

A vital issue in continuing education is the duplication of programs at some cost to providers and, with this, the danger of competition in a field that can ill afford it. This is particularly of concern in distance education, in which program development most often involves considerable outlay of funds primarily obtained from taxpayers.

In Canada, much of the development in universities and other institutions, whether in nursing faculties or elsewhere, occurs independent of or, in isolated cases, in direct competition with other similar initiatives. There are several reasons for this. First, Canada is a country characterized by diverse cultural perspectives; strong geographic, population, economic, resource, and other differences; and a political structure that places control of most matters, including education and health, in provincial hands. Relationships among provinces, territories, and federal governing structures have often been stormy and competitive as each region strives to serve its own constituency. In this context, it is not difficult to understand why those involved in the development of educational programs may not look beyond provincial borders to learn what is already available and of use. Second, the field of distance education is new, particularly in nursing education, but is growing rapidly. Many involved in the field are busy "doing it" rather than writing or talking about it. Consequently, it is difficult to be informed of the many initiatives. Third, underfunding causes some institutions to jealously guard their enrollments and seek ways to entice students to their programs rather than to look for ways to collaborate with others to best serve prospective learners. Duplication of effort may occur, and competition or, at least, lack of cooperation can result. At a time when the profession is striving to obtain the entry to practice goal and thousands of nurses may wish to obtain baccalaureate credentials, competition and duplication of effort are counterproductive.

There are many positive signs. The University of Ottawa participated in collaborative arrangements with Queen's University and University of Western Ontario. The University of Victoria is exploring ways to extend collaboration beyond provincial borders in an effort to offer baccalaureate education to those residing in areas of scarce education resources. The British Columbia Institute of Technology is collaborating with the Open University to develop a Bachelor of Health Sciences Nursing Program. Although these initiatives are encouraging, many more are needed in both credit and noncredit continuing education.

THE CHALLENGE

Much of the impetus for continuing education is a result of change: demographic change, technological change, organizational change, professional change, and personal change. The state of the Canadian economy and the demand for greater efficiency and productivity throughout the health care system clearly indicate the need for radical reform. Health care reform suggests changes in policies, delivery systems, personnel roles and functions, regulation, and preparation. These changes will certainly affect nursing. Continuing education is the primary means by which nurses learn to anticipate, influence, respond, and adjust to change.

This chapter examines the issues arising out of the past and present state of continuing nursing education. Several questions pose major challenges to the nursing profession for the future. When will a model of nursing education and professional growth be developed that successfully integrates continuing education as a fully recognized and valued partner with diploma, baccalaureate, master's, and doctoral preparation? Can nursing find the ways and means to develop continuing education at the same time as it revises and refines the systems of basic nursing education? If nursing continues along a linear path in the development of nursing education, the preoccupation with undergraduate and graduate education will mean that continuing education will never get the attention it deserves.

Preparation of nurses to work in specialized areas is a major focus of continuing education. What is the level of care required by patients and clients in specialized areas? What is the appropriate preparation for nurses caring for these people? Nursing must develop programs that conform to standards acceptable to the public and the profession, and nursing must recognize and reward nurses who successfully complete these programs.

When will professional, institutional, and public policies provide the legislative, financial, and organizational support for continuing education that already exists for primary, secondary, and postsecondary education? Most of the recent nursing association position statements on continuing nursing education reiterate the principle of shared responsibility. This has been the rhetoric for years. Are nurses, employers, providers, the profession, and governments fulfilling their responsibilities with respect to continuing education? These are only some of many questions that need to be carefully researched and properly answered. Problems in continuing education warrant priority on the nursing research agenda.

Colleges are the educational institutions providing most of post-diploma continuing nursing education; what about the universities? Nurses need and want credit and noncredit post-diploma, post-baccalaureate, post-master's and post-doctoral learning opportunities. Employers are another major source of inservice and continuing education. How much do hospital and community agencies support continuing education for nurses? How do the levels of support in health care compare with those of employers in other public and private sector industries? Until nursing discloses the current level of support, makes it visible, and defends it, nursing will not justify the importance of lifelong learning in the workplace. Nor will it have the resources to invest in the development of innovative methods of continuing education for nurses.

Finally, the lack of incentives, rewards, and support systems has been a problem in the past and remains a problem in the present. What can be done to ensure that the problem is solved in the future? Mandatory participation is not the answer. Nurses need carrots, not sticks, to encourage them to engage in lifelong learning. Most of all, nurses must remove barriers that impede nurses who want to continue their education.

ACKNOWLEDGEMENTS

The authors express their appreciation to those who provided current information for the revised chapter: Irmajean Bajnok, Mount Sinai Hospital; Jeanette Bouchard, Canadian Association of University Schools of Nursing; Kathleen Connors, National Federation of Nurses Unions; Gail Donner, Hospital for Sick Children; Barbara Greenlaw, Registered Nurses Association of British Columbia; Linda Hamilton, Registered Nurses Association of Nova Scotia; Nora Hammell, Canadian Nurses Association; Mary Hearn Hendala, Nursing Management Program; Myrtle Kutschke, Laurentian University; Bonnie Lendrum, Chedoke-McMaster Medical Centre; Frances Pym, University of New Brunswick; Glenna Cole Slattery, Ontario Nurses Association; Colleen vanBerkel, Hamilton-Wentworth Department of Public Health Services; Sue Williams, Ryerson Polytechnical Institute.

REFERENCES

Abelson, J., Paddon, P., & Strohmenger, C. (1983). *Perspectives on health*. Ottawa: Statistics Canada (#4-2303-566).

Abrahamson, S. (1968). Evaluation in continuing medical education. *Journal of the American Medical Association, 206*, 625-628.

Attridge, C.B. (1981). *Factors confounding the teaching and learning of innovative professional roles*. Paper presented at the American Educational Research Association, Los Angeles.

Attridge, C.B. (1982). Distance learners and distance education: Implications for professional nursing programs. *Proceedings: Canadian Association of University Schools of Nursing, Western Region*. Vancouver: UBC School of Nursing.

Attridge, C.B. (1983). *Curriculum evaluation: A measure of program socialization*. Paper presented at the Society for Research in Nursing Education Conference, San Francisco.

Attridge, C.B. (1986). Curriculum iatrogenesis. In *Theoretical pluralism in nursing science*. Ottawa: University of Ottawa Press.

Attridge, C.B., Gallagher, E., & Collins, F. (1985). Distance education for B.C. nurses, the University of Victoria experience. *Proceedings of the Canadian Association of University Schools of Nursing (National)*. Ottawa: CAUSN.

Bailey, C. (1987). Nursing education in Alberta (Part 2): A preliminary history. *AARN Newsletter, 43*(2), 15-17.

Blais, J-G., Duquette, A., & Painchaud, G. (1989). Deterrents to women's participation in work-related educational activities. *Adult Education Quarterly, 39*(4), 224-234.

Bucher, R., & Stelling, J. (1977). *Becoming professional*. Beverly Hills, CA: Sage Publications.

Calkin, J., Fitch, M., & Larsen, J. (1989). *Specialization in nursing and nursing education*. Ottawa: Canadian Association of University Schools of Nursing.

Canadian Association of University Schools of Nursing. (1980, 1989). Student/Faculty Statistics. Ottawa: Author.

Canadian Nurses Association. (1990). *Continuing nursing education. A discussion paper*. Ottawa: Author.

Cervero, R.M. (1985). Continuing professional education and behavioral change: A model for research and evaluation. *Journal of Continuing Education, 16*, 85-88.

Clark, K.M. (1986). Recent developments in self-directed learning. *The Journal of Continuing Education in Nursing, 17*, 76-80.

Clark, K.M. (1987). *The regulation of advanced nursing practice: A briefing paper for the Council of the College of Nurses of Ontario.* Toronto: College of Nurses of Ontario.

Clark, K.M. (1990). *Specialized nursing resources: The occupational choice of intensive care nurses.* Unpublished doctoral dissertation, University of Toronto, Toronto.

Cohen, H. (1981). *The nurses's quest for a professional identity.* Don Mills, ON: Addison-Wesley.

College of Nurses of Ontario. (1987). *Report of the Ad Hoc Committee on Competence.* Toronto: Author.

Cooper, S.S. (1974). Continuing education—the voluntary approach. In P.E. McGriff & S.S. Cooper: *Accountability to the consumer through continuing education in nursing* (Pub. No. 1401507, pp. 9-16). New York: National League for Nursing.

Cooper, S.S. (1980). Mandatory vs. voluntary continuing education. *Occupational Health Nursing, 28*(11), 9-12.

Cross, K.P. (1981). *Adults as learners: Increasing participation facilitating learning.* San Francisco: Jossey-Bass.

DuGas, B.W., & Casey, A.M. (1986). *Teleconferencing—possibilities and realities.* Paper presented at the First National Conference on Distance Education in Nursing. June 1986.

Epp, J. (1986). *Achieving health for all: A framework for health promotion.* Ottawa: Health Promotion Directorate, Health & Welfare Canada.

Friedberg, E., & Harrison, M. (1983). *Job satisfaction, continuing education and nurses.* Unpublished master's thesis, University of Ottawa, Ottawa, Ontario.

Gaston, S., & Pucci, J. (1982). Mandatory continuing education in Kansas—three years later. *Journal of Continuing Education in Nursing, 13*(2), 15-17.

Granger, D. (1986). Distant education: A new pedagogy encourages a new view of content. Paper presented at *The Distance Education Conference,* May 27, Vancouver, B.C.

Gosnell, D.J. (1984). A conceptual model: Evaluating continuing nursing education, *Journal of Continuing Education in Nursing, 15,* 9-11.

Houle, C.O. (1963). *The inquiring mind.* Madison, WI: University of Wisconsin Pres.

Houle, C. (1981). *Continuing learning in the professions.* San Francisco: Jossey-Bass.

Jensen, D. (1969). *History and trends of professional nursing.* Saint Louis: Mosby.

Keegan, D. (1982). From New Delhi to Vancouver: Trends in distance education. In J. Daniel et al. (Eds.), *Learning at a distance: A world perspective* (pp. 40-43). Edmonton: Athabasca University, ICCE.

Knowles, A.F. (1985). Distance education, new technologies, delivery methods: A review of recent publications, articles and documents. *Report prepared for the Ontario Ministry of Education, Ministry of Colleges and Universities, Continuing Education Review Project.* Etobicoke, ON: Humber College of Applied Arts and Technology.

Kristjanson, L.J., & Scanlan, J.M. (1989). Assessment of continuing nursing education needs: A literature review. *The Journal of Continuing Education in Nursing, 20*(3), 118-123.

Kutschke, M. (1986). *The BScN programme at a distance: what we have learned—our future plans.* Paper presented at the First National Conference on Distance Education in Nursing, June 1986.

Manning, P.R., Lee, P.V., Clintworth, W.A., Denson, T.A., Oppenheimer, P.R., & Gilman, N.J. (1986). Changing prescribing practices through individual continuing education. *Journal of the American Medical Association, 256,* 230-232.

Millonig, V.L. (1985). Nurses' educational backgrounds, position levels and participation in continuing education. *Journal of Continuing Education in Nursing, 16,* 70-72.

Naisbitt, J. (1982). *Megatrends.* New York: Warner Books.

National Federation of Nurses' Unions. (1987). *A presentation to the National Forum on Post Secondary Education.* Ottawa: Author.

Niskala, H., & Clark, K. (Eds.). (1980). *Proceedings of the First National Conference on Continuing Education in Nursing.* Vancouver: Author.

Nurses Association of New Brunswick Special Continuing Education Committee. (1989). *Final report to the Board.* Fredericton: Author.

O'Connor, A.B. (1979). Reasons nurses participate in continuing education. *Nursing Research, 28,* 354-359.

O'Connor, A.B. (1982). Reasons nurses participate in self-study continuing education programs. *Nursing Research, 31,* 371-374.

Ontario Nurses' Association. (1990). *The continuing education unit information*. Toronto: Author.

Parochka, J.N. (1985). Beliefs and intentions to participate in continuing professional education: A study of nonparticipant nurses in Rockford, IL: *Journal of Continuing Education in Nursing, 16*, 33-35.

Puetz, B.E. (1980). Differences between Indiana registered nurse attenders and nonattenders in continuing education in nursing activities. *Journal of Continuing Education in Nursing, 11*(2), 19-26.

Registered Nurses' Association of Ontario. (1983). *Market survey report*. Toronto: Author.

Registered Nurses' Association of Ontario. (1986). *RNAO membership study*. Toronto: Author.

Richardson, S., & Sherwood, J. (1985). Non-degree continuing nursing education need of Alberta's registered nurses. *Nursing Papers, 17*(1), 80-98.

Rizzuto, C. (1982). Mandatory continuing education: Cost versus benefit. *Journal of Continuing Education in Nursing, 13*(3), 37-43.

Rockhill, K. (1983). Mandatory continuing education for professionals: Trends and issues. *Adult Education, 33*, 106-116.

Saskatchewan Health Care Association. (1982). *Report of the Advisory Committee on Nursing Supply, Employment and Education*. Regina: Author.

Saskatchewan Registered Nurses' Association. (1986). *Position paper: Continuing education for registered nurses in Saskatchewan*. Regina: Author.

Scanlan, C.S., & Darkenwald, G.G. (1984). Identifying deterrents to participation in continuing education. *Adult Education Quarterly, 34*, 155-166.

Schor, I. (1981). The continuing nursing education and adult education movement in the U.S. *Nursing Forum, 20*(1):87.

Shimberg, B. (1980). *Occupational licensing: A public perspective*. Princeton, NJ: Educational Testing Service.

Thomas, C. (1986). Motivational orientations of Kansas nurses participating in continuing education in a mandatory state for relicensure. *Journal of Continuing Education in Nursing 17*(6), 198-202.

Trammell, D.B. (1986). Educational preparation: Its effects on selection and degree of involvement in continuing education activities. *Journal of Continuing Education in Nursing, 15*, 223-226.

van Reenen, J. (1990). Technology for health care education. *The Canadian Nurse, 86*(10), 24-26.

Watson, A.B. (1986). Professional socialization of the registered nurse. *Review of Research in Nursing Education, Volume 1*. New York: National League for Nursing.

Woods, L. (1990). Continuing education units: The Ontario Nurses' Association Continuing Nursing Education Unit Program. *ONA News, 17*(10), 8.

Young, L.J., & Willie, R. (1984). Effectiveness of continuing education for health professionals: A literature review. *Journal of Allied Health, 13*, 113-123.

NURSING POWER

Nurses can use their power to make essential changes in the way health care is offered. The University of Manitoba School of Nursing had to work closely with provincial, federal, and native leaders to achieve a special nursing program that could be offered in The Pas, in northern Manitoba. This photograph, taken at the announcement of the program, shows Dr. Jenniece Larsen, director of the school, with Oscar Lathlin *(left)*, chief of The Pas band and member of the Manitoba Legislature, and Manitoba Premier Gary Filmon *(center)*.

CHAPTER TWENTY-FOUR

Overview: Shaping Public Policy

JENNIECE LARSEN, RN, PhD

ALICE J. BAUMGART, RN, PhD

In the 1990s, people around the world are demanding fundamental change in the political processes of their countries. In Canada, the search for constitutional accord, with demands for reform in Quebec and the West and determined efforts by aboriginal peoples for inclusion, provides abundant evidence of the need to refurbish Canada's democratic processes. These changes in "political world pictures" (Dyson, 1980, p. 50) reverberate into other sectors of Canadian life, altering expectations about the conduct of political decision making. Like many other Canadians, nurses expect to be involved in shaping public and organizational policies to reflect their goals and values. And, like leaders in the broader political community, leaders of organized nursing groups are being challenged to find new ways to meet members' expectations for involvement.

In the 1980s, nurses discovered that they must use power to make essential changes in organizations and in the broader community. The time has come to take the further step of using nursing power to achieve a more central role in shaping public policy. The nursing profession is one of the largest nationally organized groups in Canadian society. This size and stable organizational structure, coupled with the level of education of members and the profession's well-known commitment to comprehensive health care for Canadians, provides a strong base for a more influential role in public policy. However, shaping public policy requires visible efforts to persuade politicians, government officials, and, often, the general public of the "correctness" of nursing views on policy issues.

The chapters in this section of the book analyze nursing's activities to shape public policy. This overview briefly describes key aspects of public policymaking and the role organized groups such as nursing unions and professional associations can play in this process. The discussion in the overview draws primarily on Canadian political science literature. A related purpose is to examine the evolving role of women in Canadian politics and the politicization of nurses. A final purpose, which occurs throughout the chapter, is to highlight prominent features of the chapters that follow.

MAKING PUBLIC POLICY IN CANADA

Policymaking is not simply a matter of problem solving or taking some common goal and seeking the best solution. Public policymaking is a matter of choice in which the resources are limited and in which the goals and objectives differ and cannot easily be weighed against each other. Since few "public goods" are available equally to all Canadians, public policymaking involves negotiation and compromise, and often, conflict. Most "public goods" distributed by governments confer differential benefits. Some people receive more than others; some pay more than others. Lasswell (1936) states, the most important question to ask in understanding public policymaking is "Who gets what, when, and how—and what difference does it make?"

In this chapter, public policy is defined as whatever governments choose to do or choose not to do, the values espoused, and the initiatives funded (Dye, 1976). Dye emphasizes that both decisions and nondecisions represent public policy. A decision of a government to ignore an issue is a policy decision, if only because the status quo is perpetuated. Public policies represent ways governments of the day respond to the manifold challenges confronting them and to the demands emanating from groups in the society.

Doern and Phidd (1983), two of Canada's leading experts in the field of public policymaking, point out that public policy develops from the interplay of *structures, processes,* and *ideas* within the society. These features are unique in every country and, in federations such as Canada, in each province. *Structures* are organizations and institutions from the public sector, as well as the private sector; they include federal, provincial, and, often, municipal levels of government. The combination of structures involved in public policy debates is shaped by the issues, by the particular context in which the debate occurs, and by the distribution of power within the government. Most nongovernmental agencies, (e.g., professional nursing associations or voluntary agencies such as the Victorian Order of Nurses) usually adopt organizational arrangements compatible with those of the federal and provincial governments. The individuals who head these structures are the elected and the appointed leaders of Canadian society. During public policy debates, leaders engage in the process of ranking, balancing, and allocating scarce resources of money, expertise, energy, and time. As the debate evolves and the focus shifts, different constellations of leaders participate.

The *processes* of public policymaking refer to the changing dynamics that occur when these leaders attempt to sort out the uncertainty created by the limits of knowledge, the lack of causality, and the political calculation of public and private reaction to policy initiatives. The often frenetic events associated with the failure to achieve ratification of the Meech Lake Constitutional Accord in 1990 were a stark example of the risks, uncertainties, and constantly changing contextual factors that are integral to the making of public policy. These are not negotiations for the faint of heart nor the weak of spirit, and it is in these negotiations that nursing leaders must attempt to put nursing's stamp on public policies.

Structures and processes are imbued with ideologies and dominant ideas and paradigms unique to the political culture of Canada (Doern and Phidd, 1983). These *ideas* are central elements of public policymaking, representing fundamental values of Canadian society. Involvement in shaping public policy necessitates a broad appreciation of the values embedded in democratic decisions beyond the limited objectives that a specific bill attempts to achieve. Three major ideologies—liberalism, conservatism, and socialism—are dominant in Canadian political life. Ideologies help to screen policy approaches that are unacceptable or that would be considered only as a last resort. For example, policies of a conservative government usually encompass the preservation of valued traditions and advocate market-oriented solutions that minimize government intervention in the life of citizens; socialism offers a collective view of society with a de-emphasis on individualism, favoring government intervention, particularly to achieve redistribution of wealth and power. Yet when the policies of Canada's political parties are viewed over time, a crazy quilt emerges, reflecting regional and economic as much as ideological factors. For example, all Canadian parties support the national health care program and certain elements of Canada's social "safety net," differing only on how to finance these "public goods."

Most public policy in Canada is developed within a second level of normative content composed of dominant ideas and paradigms. Dominant ideas in Canada include concerns for efficiency, individual freedom, equity, stability, redistribution and equality, regional sensitivity, and national identity and unity (Doern and Phidd, 1983). These ideas influence public policy debates and the evaluation of public policy alternatives regardless of the particular preference outlined in ministerial speeches or stated in the legislation. Regardless of the policy sector, these dominant ideas are often partially or even totally contradictory—and yet are considered desirable. The need to balance, order, and allocate scarce resources to a set of contradictory ideas within the same policy initiative is an enduring feature of public policymaking in Canada.

In addition to dominant ideas, policymaking often occurs within an accepted paradigm in each sector or policy field. A paradigm provides a series of assumptions that guide decision making and suggest solutions within a given field. Paradigms become entrenched and thus change slowly, often because they are tied to the education and socialization of experts and, at times, of the general public. An obvious example of such a paradigm is Keynesian economic theory in the field of financial policy. Since the 1970s, monetarism has emerged to challenge but not replace Keynesian theory, at least not in Canada. Similarly, health care policy is dominated by a medically-oriented curative approach, whereas the alternative paradigm espousing prevention of illness and promotion of health gains only marginal political support.

Organized nursing groups have supported a more preventive approach to health care in numerous briefs to provincial and federal governments and health services review commissions since the early 1970s. The chapters that follow present examples of these briefs and presentations. In 1984, the Canadian Nurses Association orchestrated an intensive and successful lobby to amend the Canada Health Care Act of 1984 to permit qualified health care practitioners to offer insured services. Discussion of the events surrounding this lobby were described by Adaskin (1988) in the first edition of this book. Although this amendment opened a legislative door at the federal level, the question of alternative health care delivery paradigms was not fully addressed, and no real initiatives have occurred in the provinces to implement the amendment. In fact, nurse-midwives and nurse practitioners who provide alternative but noninsured health care services to the public still risk charges of illegal practice of medicine. Supporting reform of the health care system is easy; the next and far more difficult policy negotiation is to ensure that nurses are full partners in a reformed health care system.

PUBLIC POLICYMAKING COMMUNITIES

Public policy is seldom a product of general public discussion. There are simply too many issues with which the public has to deal. Public policymaking has been described as being organized in policy communities. These policy communities include various levels of government officials and bureaucrats, both elected and appointed, representatives of organized societal groups, and influential individuals who interact to shape policy in a given sector over time (Coleman and Skogstad, 1990). Additionally, the health care policy community includes service agencies, such as hospitals and public health agencies, and voluntary organizations, such as the Victorian Order of Nurses, the Red Cross Society, and the Canadian Cancer Society. The ascendancy of the policy community is a relatively new phenomenon in Canada, emerging from the decline of bureaucratic power. Senior bureaucrats must now generate support from the policy community to achieve their objectives. As a consequence, these officials foster constant contact with various groups and individuals in the policy community. Government departments are usually at the center of these community networks; the groups representing dominant societal interests in the sector are in more proximal positions. Policy communities exist in most sectors of Canadian society. Contemporary policy communities bear the brunt of yesterday's decisions and must function in an economic situation of global interdependence. In addition, policymakers must consider a diverse spectrum of views in a Canadian society that has increasingly permeable boundaries. Over time, complex reciprocal relationships develop, binding the groups in the community together.

Although health care is primarily within provincial jurisdiction, the federal department of health and welfare has occupied a central role in the health care policy community for many years. However, with the continual reduction of federal dollars to finance health care, provinces are assuming a more prominent role. As the center of the policy community shifts, there is increased impetus for health care groups such as nursing unions and professional associations in the policy community to organize at the provincial, as well as the federal, level.

Influence in the policy community is a function of complex factors, including the degree of policy sophistication of the organized groups in the community. Coleman and Skogstad's (1990) study of public policy communities reveals that the relative influence of organized groups in these policy communities, whether provincial or national, is a function of the capacity of the group to take a longer term perspective on policy development and to have the resources to undertake independent policy analysis. Policy analysis by organized nursing groups in health care or education requires access to a range of expertise from diverse fields of study such as health care economics, law, higher education, epidemiology, and organizational design, as well as nursing, to mention but a few areas.

Organized nursing groups currently have limited capacity to undertake policy analysis and must rely heavily on the time and talents of volunteers who participate on boards and in committees. The often meager professional staff in provincial nursing organizations are primarily committed to regulatory and contractual obligations (e.g., registration, grievances, negotiations, and discipline). Greater influence in the health care policy community (or other policy communities) may depend on allocating more of nursing's scarce resources to make involvement a reality. Resources could be used to contract with university departments to provide the required research or to establish nursing policy units in professional associations and nursing unions, whose mandates would be to undertake the research necessary to support nursing's policy initiatives. The College of Nurses of Ontario established a policy analysis and development unit in 1987 with a mandate to provide policy advice on issues concerning regulation in nursing. Influence in the policy community also means seeking membership on national and provincial policymaking boards, including panels and commissions reviewing aspects of the health care delivery system. If nursing groups fail to achieve representation, the expertise of a nursing policy unit could be used to prepare an independent report to publicize a nursing perspective on issues.

However, the purpose of public policy analysis is not just knowing the correct policy but ensuring that policies nursing supports will be chosen and implemented. Under favorable conditions, policy analysis can have an independent effect on public policy decisions, but nursing ideas will have a greater chance of success if they are promoted by organized nursing groups that are active in the public policy process. In fact, Majone (1989) declares that policymaking consists of two thirds politics and one third analysis. As such, the tools of the policymaker must include rhetorical and persuasive skills in addition to analytical skills.

Translating nursing policy ideas into action depends in large measure on the language used to communicate with the intended audience and the debating skills of nursing's spokespersons. No matter how sophisticated the research, the communication of policy ideas to broad audiences demands clear, jargon-free language. Like other leaders, nursing leaders require rigorous academic and political training to be effective when articulating nursing values and goals in public debates (Mechanic, 1990). Mussallem, in Chapter 25, and Meilicke and Larsen, in Chapter 26, stress the historical emphasis placed on access to higher education to enable nurses to develop the skills needed to participate in policy debates.

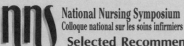

National Nursing Symposium
Colloque national sur les soins infirmiers

Selected Recommendations from the Report to the Provincial and Territorial Ministers of Health, 1991

- That the Ministers of Health support objective programs to recognize nursing excellence and support the establishment of rewards to pay tribute to the service of nurses who choose clinical practice as the focus of their careers
- That the Ministers of Health as a matter of policy establish a national nursing data base dealing with the supply and demand for nurses, as well as any other issues related to workforce planning as it affects nurses and nursing
- That the Ministers of Health support initiatives to revise nursing education programs and that Ministers of Health cooperate with Ministers of Education to provide adequate resources for entry, continuing, and specialized education with a particular focus on distance delivery
- That the Ministers of Health support an expansion of the role of nurses so that they can provide health care services as professionals in their own right
- That the Ministers of Health support broad policies to re-evaluate the work traditionally performed by women in the health care system and follow through with strategies designed to achieve equity in the workplace
- That the Ministers of Health provide financial support for educational programs and postsecondary institutions, as well as in the work places, so nurses can develop leadership and management skills
- That the Ministers of Health create a national nursing innovations fund and that the budget appropriation for the national nursing innovations fund be $5 million per year for a five-year period
- That the Ministers of Health create nursing policy advisory committees in each of their jurisdictions and that these committees report directly to the Ministers of Health
- That the Ministers of Health appoint senior nurse consultants as assistant deputy ministers to provide ongoing direction for issues that affect nursing
- That the Ministers of Health review existing legislation governing health care facilities so that nurses are represented on institutional boards of directors in a manner equivalent to physicians
- That the Ministers of Health actively support professional nursing associations as they establish formal and equitable mechanisms to resolve issues regarding role differentiation in nursing
- That the Ministers of Health establish policies to ensure that nurses are represented on committees that design health care facilities and assess health care technology

Those who initiate health care policy rarely consider the effect of policy alternatives on the practice of nursing. The difficulties nursing leaders experience in attempting to place nursing issues on the public policy agenda reflect the measure of nursing's current influence in the health care policy community. Nevertheless, nursing issues were raised to national level when the ministers of health for the provinces and territories sponsored a National Nursing Symposium with a mandate to explore cooperative and creative solutions to various nursing issues, including nursing's role in the health care delivery system and quality of work-life issues. The 3-day Symposium, held in Winnipeg in November 1990, was attended by 300 invited delegates from throughout Canada, representing major stakeholders concerned with nursing and health care. The final report contains over 100 recommendations addressed to ministers and other stakeholders (Larsen, 1991). Selected recommendations are in the box.

ROLE OF ORGANIZED GROUPS IN THE POLICY COMMUNITY

Coleman and Skogstad (1990) identify two main roles for organized groups in a policy community. The first is policy advocacy. Advocacy groups approach governments as lobbyists from outside decision-making networks and seek to influence the nature and content of a particular public policy. Success in advocacy usually depends on the organized group's capacity to develop a sound knowledge of the policy-making process, to generate information about policy alternatives, to mobilize support for its policy ideas, and to maintain internal group cohesion. In Chapter 30, Pringle and Roe discuss the role of one voluntary organization in advocating for and in mounting new and innovative programs for a particular interest community.

The second role for organized groups is policy participation, which requires that organized groups develop the same capacities as in the policy advocacy role, as well as exhibit stable organizational arrangements and the ability to cultivate a distinct identity within the policy community. Effective policy participation requires the capacity to coordinate complex information from which distinct positions are developed on sophisticated policy issues. Organized groups that are effective in the policy participation role must rise above the special interests of their group and have a long-term perspective on the policy issue. A second important requirement for effective policy participation is the need for financial autonomy from the government. Organized groups who receive a large measure of their financial resources from government (e.g., aboriginal groups, women's groups) are in a more precarious position in the policy community than groups such as nursing professional associations and nursing unions, which have stable, independent income from members' fees. Dependence on government funding necessitates closer attention to the preferences and approaches of the current government.

In policy communities, organized groups are important instruments of political communication. They give elected officials timely responses to policy initiatives and relay government concerns back to the members of the group. Governments rely on the endorsement of powerful organized groups when new policy initiatives are announced. Support from a group assists government to achieve general acceptance of the policy. Alternatively, organized groups may mount organized campaigns to resist government initiatives. Whether groups in the policy community provide widespread acceptance or organized resistance, government officials receive valuable information about the parameters of acceptable policy. As well, organized groups indirectly help governmental agencies disseminate information by publishing explanations of government policy in their journals (Pross, 1986). Additional roles of

organized groups include administration and regulation of programs such as regulation of nursing practice by professional nursing associations or grievance handling
by nursing unions.

Although there is little systematic study of the political activities of organized
nursing groups, the common wisdom is that nursing groups are slow to realize an
important role in generating public policy options and in responding to policy initiatives of governments or other societal groups. Although organized nursing groups
may have been slower than other health care groups (e.g., the Canadian Medical
Association) to participate actively in shaping public policy, this is now changing.
As documented in the chapters that follow, nursing activities to shape public policy
have accelerated in recent years.

However, in organized groups such as nursing unions and professional associations, involvement in policy advocacy and policy participation is usually secondary
to the primary purpose of the group. Although the main mission of nursing unions
is to negotiate fair collective agreements, advocating for increased federal funding
for the health care system is a secondary but closely linked means for achieving this
mission. Similarly, professional nursing associations have, as part of their mandate,
the monitoring and the improvement of nursing care. Political actions to influence
governmental policies that affect nursing practice appear basic to achieving this
mandate.

Using the Victorian Order of Nurses as an example, Pringle and Roe, in Chapter
30, describe the unique contribution voluntary charitable organizations make to the
Canadian health care system. Like professional associations and nursing unions, the
VON uses political involvement to draw attention to issues. Organizations such as
the Victorian Order of Nurses work to establish and maintain a presence in the policy
community. Their unique features—the involvement of volunteers to serve on
boards and to deliver certain services—increase their credibility and their responsiveness to community need.

BECOMING A PRESSURE GROUP: THE MOBILIZATION PROCESS

Sustained involvement is essential if nursing is to affect the policy community.
Pross (1986, p. 46) states that "to have a say, you need a voice." In nursing, professional associations and nursing unions are the major voices. In the political science
literature, organized groups active in shaping public policy are frequently referred
to as pressure groups. Pressure groups are "organizations whose members act together to influence public policy in order to promote their common interest" (Pross,
1986, p. 3). Members of the group are bound together by a common interest. In
nursing, the common interest is nursing practice.

Pross (1986) identifies a three-stage process by which interest groups evolve into
pressure groups. The first stage is the association of individuals who have common
interests, but who have no desire to act collectively. Subsequently, these loose associations may form groups in which members informally support one another and
have a degree of political awareness but have no established formal association to

engage in overt political action. Finally, a formal pressure group emerges when collective actions are used to promote common interests for political ends.

The progress of nurses' associations and unions through these three stages is illustrated in Chapter 25 by Mussallem, in Chapter 27 by Jensen, and in Chapter 29 by Goodwill. Mussallem describes how, in the early 1900s, groups of nurses throughout Canada met to discuss common concerns. These associations of nurses became more formalized in 1908, when the Canadian National Association of Trained Nurses was established and launched a campaign to encourage provincial groups of nurses to seek legislation to regulate the practice of nursing in their respective provinces. For many of the succeeding years, the activities of the professional nurses' associations focused on internal group objectives. The most notable expectations were during the years of the first and second World Wars when the energies of the associations were directed toward supporting the war efforts. However, by the 1970s the focus on professional association activities turned outward to national and provincial political events and issues.

In Chapter 29, Goodwill discusses the mobilization of a unique group of Canadian nurses, the Indian and Inuit Nurses of Canada. Recognizing a need for collective action, these nurses fought to establish a formal organization despite opposition from national Indian political groups, governmental agencies, and even the Canadian Nurses Association. Against this resistance, the group elected officers, established goals, and secured federal funding. Goodwill describes the success of the group in its efforts to influence public policy in the area of native health.

The formation of nursing unions, documented in Chapter 27 by Jensen, has been a long and often difficult struggle filled with organizational, legal, and ideological obstacles. The early roots of unionization are found in Quebec, where a group of nurses from Quebec City negotiated the first voluntary collective agreement with their employer in 1939, and in Montreal, where a group of nurses joined a large trade union as health care workers in 1945.

The growth of specialized groups represents a trend toward diversification in Canadian nursing. To acknowledge the diversity of nursing practice concerns and to ensure mechanisms for maintaining a unified voice, the Canadian Nurses Association established an advisory council of national nursing specialty groups in 1986. The Advisory Council provides the Board of the Canadian Nurses Association with valuable information about desirable policy directions. For example, the effect of technology on health care and nursing was the topic of the 1991 meeting of the Advisory Council.

CHARACTERISTICS OF PRESSURE GROUPS

Pross (1986) outlined four criteria for analyzing the structure of pressure groups. The chief characteristic is that they seek to influence, not to govern. Influence takes many forms—reasoned argument, arousal of public opinion, withdrawal from joint activities, or threatened economic sanctions. Influence requires organization, the second major characteristic of pressure groups. Organizational capacity permits the development of extensive knowledge of the substantive issues and policy processes, as well as the financial resources to communicate with the general public and other members of the policy community. Third, pressure groups have formal mechanisms and constitutional procedures to enable group members to identify demands they wish to make on governments and to sort out the inevitable conflicts that arise when the objectives of some members clash with those of others. Internal debate may lead to disagreement but, when well managed, results in agreement of the initiatives among members of the group. Fourth, pressure groups are composed exclusively of members committed to common goals and willing to work together to achieve these goals.

Analysis of the structure of provincial professional nurses' associations using these criteria leads quickly to the conclusion that they resemble pressure groups. Each provincial nurses' association has legislation, including regulations and bylaws that govern the manner in which the association is organized for the purpose of creating consensus about objectives. One of these objectives is usually to influence governmental choices in the fields of health care and higher education. All members of professional nurses' associations have a common interest in the delivery of nursing care. Provincial legislatures have authorized the autonomy in the association and outlined a broad mandate. Revenues are derived almost exclusively from membership dues and related activities, rendering the association financially independent. All this suggests that professional nurses' associations are structured to perform the roles of pressure groups in provincial policy communities.

A review of the activities reported in provincial nurses' association newsletters reveals accelerated involvement in the political life of provinces in the last few years. For example, the Registered Nurses Association of British Columbia launched a program in 1989, New Directions for Health Care, which focuses on policy development in the 1990s. Policy ideas related to primary care, allocation of health care resources, and special contributions to be made by nurses have been developed (RNABC, 1991).

Until recently, the Canadian Nurses Association (CNA) was nursing's only nationally organized group and is still the major national nursing voice advocating policy positions on issues such as the Meech Lake Accord, financial support to the health care system, and reproductive technology. In 1981, the National Federation of Nurses' Unions (NFNU) established an Ottawa office and is visible in debates concerning health care and nursing labor issues. For example, NFNU released a discussion paper on financial compensation issues in nursing (NFNU, 1991). Although the Canadian Association of University Schools of Nursing (CAUSN) has had a national office since 1985, the lack of full-time professional staff and a limited mandate constrain an active policy role. Of late, CAUSN is more visible, presenting briefs and lobbying on issues concerning higher education and research funding, often in collaboration with the CNA.

Provincial nursing unions have emerged as powerful nursing pressure groups since the mid-1980s. The unions' willingness to take tough and often highly visible stands on provincial health care, labor, and nursing issues solidified their credibility with their members and earned the respect of other members of the policy community. Members of the public media now routinely seek the views of provincial nursing unions on a broad range of issues. Provincial nursing associations are less visible in the media, often to the chagrin of their members.

POLITICAL RESOURCES OF ORGANIZED GROUPS IN THE POLICY COMMUNITY

Success in shaping public policy is contingent on numerous factors; among the most important are the resources available to the group. In fact, Presthus (1973) maintains that political activism and effectiveness are essentially a function of resources. A political resource, according to Dahl (1961), is "anything which may be used to sway the choices of another individual" (p. 226).

Presthus (1973, p. 121) identifies two main categories of political resources: socioeconomic and psychopolitical. The main resources in each category are listed in the box.

An important socioeconomic resource is the size of a group's budget, which professional nurses' associations and nursing unions generally obtain through membership dues. Money buys other valued political resources. Funds are essential to hire professional and support staff, to devise campaigns, and to send delegations to talk with governmental officials and other authorities about policy initiatives. Although the 1991 operating budget of the CNA is nearly $6 million, involvement in public policy is only one of many functions. A major portion of the CNA budget is allocated for membership services such as publication of a monthly journal, the certification process for specialty practice, and national conferences on significant nursing issues. The CNA Board determines allocation of the financial resources in accordance with its priorities. In establishing priorities, CNA considers long-term objectives of the Association and resolutions approved by membership. Some nurses

Political Resources of Organized Groups

Socioeconomic

- Budget
- Occupation
- Higher education
- Size of group
- Access to policymakers
- Legal authority
- Professional employees
- Experience
- Organizational cohesiveness

Psychopolitical

- Political efficacy
- Monopoly of expertise
- Prestige of group
- Political expertise
- Legitimacy
- Collaborative attitude
- Commitment of members

Modified from R. Presthus (1991). *Elite accommodation in Canadian politics*, p. 121. Toronto: Macmillan.

complain about having to pay professional association membership fees as well as union dues, but without adequate financial support, professional nurses' associations are unable to articulate policy positions and engage in political actions that benefit the nursing profession as a whole.

A second major socioeconomic resource is the "quality" of members (Presthus, 1973). By quality, Presthus refers to level of education, occupation, financial resources, and prestige of the members of the group. Higher education tends to increase political interest and knowledge and develops the conceptual skills required for political negotiation and debate. In this respect, professional nurses' associations are disadvantaged in comparison to the members of organized medical or legal societies. However, when compared to many other organized groups, particularly women's groups, professional nurses' associations and nurses' unions have well-educated members.

Van Loon and Whittington (1976) argue that size of the group is not a political resource. However with nearly 230,000 nurses in Canada, the potential impact of a group of this size cannot be denied. If a group of this size were mobilized around a policy initiative, the strength of its collective voice would force a governmental response.

Notwithstanding the weight of numbers, organizational cohesiveness is a political resource of considerable importance. Variables that contribute to organizational cohesiveness are formal organizational structure, membership participation, frequent personal interaction among members, and absence of conflicting loyalties (Pross, 1986). CNA's voice in the national health care policy community is compromised by the withdrawal of Quebec from membership in the association and by the fact that only a small fraction of Ontario nurses belong to their provincial professional association, and consequently to CNA. Similarly, NFNU represents nurses from only five provinces. Furthermore, organized nursing groups often are lacking when examination is made of variables such as interaction, participation, and absence of conflicting loyalties. Professional commitments for many women conflict directly with family obligations, resulting in less time and energy for professional activities.

A vital socioeconomic resource is access by the leaders of the group to elected governmental officials or senior members of the bureaucracy (Presthus, 1973). The executives of provincial professional associations and unions meet regularly with senior officials in the provincial ministry of health. When required, the Executive Director obtains a meeting with the Minister of Health to discuss issues of concern. Presthus' (1973) research indicates that direct intervention by the group's leaders is an effective strategy in influencing governmental policymakers. Access to the policymakers is said to be the *sine qua non* of group influence on public policy (Van Loon and Whittington, 1976).

Legal authority granted to groups by legislation is another crucial political resource (Simeon, 1972). As discussed by Mussallem in Chapter 25, provincial professional nurses' associations have legal authority for self-regulation, which includes registration of members, establishment of education and practice standards, and discipline of members. The legal authority of nursing unions to represent their members and negotiate contracts is derived from the labor laws of each province and is described in Chapter 27 by Jensen. Legal authority provides a powerful mandate. Conversely, legal authority also constrains the group to act within the limits of the mandate. For example, professional nurses' associations have no express powers to deal with employment concerns; these are the special concerns of nursing unions. This division of responsibilities occasionally creates difficulties for professional nurses' associations because they are seen by the members as not speaking out adequately on labor and employment issues.

The second category of resources is psychopolitical. Perhaps the most important psychopolitical resource of a pressure group is a sense of political efficacy. Van Loon and Whittington (1976) define efficacy as "an individual's feeling that he [sic] has a meaningful role in politics and a confidence that the system will respond to him" (p. 111). Having a high level of political efficacy becomes a self-fulfilling prophecy. Believing one can create change serves to increase self-esteem and political involvement. Recognition of the nursing profession's potential to influence public policy and success in the political arena has stimulated the collective efficacy of nurses to higher levels of political participation than in the past.

Another significant psychopolitical resource is the prestige or status of the group. Van Loon and Whittington (1976) argue that governmental decision makers may be impressed by a group's ideas in direct proportion to how impressed they are by the members as individuals. Traditionally nurses are viewed as having less prestige than physicians and lawyers. Stereotypical beliefs about women are significant factors influencing the prestige of nurses' groups.

All political resources are tenuous and are usually bound to a specific issue and social context and to perceptions of the policymakers. Political resources are distributed unevenly in any political system (Dahl, 1970). Differences in the effectiveness of a pressure group may be determined by the skill with which different groups use their political resources and by the extent to which different groups use resources for political purposes.

ENSURING SUCCESS IN THE POLICY COMMUNITY

Discourse and coercion are major tools used by organized groups to sway policy decisions: briefs are presented at royal commissions, testimony given at tribunals, legal arguments developed, demonstrations organized, private meetings attended, advertisements placed in prominent newspapers, and speeches given at business and professional meetings. Whatever the form, promises and threats are an implicit part of public debate and, when pushed, organized groups use whatever tools they have to advance a cause or protect a valued position. Even illegal means cannot always be discounted. As Hibberd notes in Chapter 28, nursing unions in Alberta and Quebec organized illegal strikes to assert their right to unrestricted collective bargaining with an employer and to ensure the availability of adequate nursing services to the general public.

Tools selected to sway policy decisions and how these tools are used depends on the strength and legitimacy of the group's mandate, the availability and use of political resources, and the conditions that prevail at each step in the policy debate. Pross (1986) states, the essence of an organized group's influence is the sense in the minds of governmental officials and other members of the policy community that the group speaks for a significant part of the public, a part that can be mobilized into political action if the group's interests are not reasonably accommodated in the policy process.

Groups strive to include as members everyone in the relevant community. Inclusive groups such as provincial professional nursing associations derive a large part of their authority from the fact that they can realize this aspiration. In all but one Canadian province, all registered nurses must, by provincial legislation, be members of the professional association. (The exception is Ontario, where registered nurses must be members of the College of Nurses of Ontario and not the Registered Nurses Association of Ontario.) The inclusive nature of the membership in nursing professional associations creates considerable legitimacy for professional organizations when they speak on nursing issues. Nursing unions are in the same fortunate position in many Canadian provinces in which the majority of nurses within each province are members of a major nursing union. Unions demonstrate that their members are willing to back leaders' demands for withdrawals of services or take other highly visible forms of public discourse and coercion. To be considered legitimate, the group must show that it speaks for an entire interest community or that it can elicit support from a significant part of the community. The ability to mobilize the membership to some form of action is an important aspect of this claim. A group that is known to speak for its community is heeded by governments regardless of the quality of advice tendered (Pross, 1986).

Success on a major policy initiative requires the support or the absence of active opposition from within the group's members and from members of the broader policy community. Professional nursing associations present policy recommendations to governments as a collective opinion of the members of the association. Professional nursing associations and nursing unions are often challenged by nurses and members of the general public to adopt positions on controversial issues not clearly related to the group's primary mandate, such as a woman's right to an abortion or Canada's involvement in the Gulf War. Although professional associations or nursing unions can comment about safe nursing practice during an abortion, or the need for adequate nursing care in a field hospital during a war, making statements on controversial issues in broadly based groups is extremely difficult because members of the group hold differing views as a function of other important affiliations, such as membership in religious organizations.

A major policy initiative supported by the Canadian Nurses Association and all provincial nursing associations is the baccalaureate degree in nursing as the entry qualification to the practice of nursing. Although significant progress is being made toward achievement of this goal, lack of support from the nursing community and from major organized groups in the policy community have been major obstacles. Nurses' unions are concerned about the effect of the policy on registered nurses who currently practice but lack a baccalaureate degree. Government officials and employers express concern about the increased costs that may result. Organized medicine identifies functional overlap as a matter of concern. The lack of internal unity and the external opposition within the policy community creates tremendous obstacles for this policy position. The situation is complicated by the limited available research to respond to questions raised. When an organized group is weakened by internal opposition, its effectiveness to achieve a positive outcome on a particular policy initiative is severely constrained.

To influence the policy community, organized nursing groups must be prepared to lobby in four different directions, and each direction must be approached differently (Pross, 1986). The most important target is the cabinet and other central agencies of the government. The government department at the center of the policy community is the second significant target of the lobby. Other organized groups and agencies in the policy community are routinely consulted in the formation of new public policy initiative, representing a third focus. And, occasionally, the group must address the fourth target: the entire policy community, including the general public. Groups with professional staff who are familiar with the workings of the governmental agencies and who have established good relations with prominent members of the policy community will have a considerable advantage in the group's efforts to lobby these four constituencies.

Experienced groups in the policy community prefer not to make direct demands of cabinet initially. To do so would be an admission of failure to obtain agreement within the policy community. Usually, the policy community seeks to clarify issues and avoid cabinet interference. Cabinet ministers are usually drawn into policy debates only as a last resort or at the end stage of a successful negotiation for the signing of a formal agreement. However, consultations by leaders of the policy community with cabinet ministers occur frequently. Organized nursing groups in Canada, at the provincial and national levels, routinely meet with various cabinet members offering nursing's perspective on various issues. Detailed policy work is normally undertaken by the professional staff or elected officials and government bureaucrats, but well out of the glare of the political or public spotlight. Symbolic appearances of cabinet members at official openings and to deliver after-dinner speeches are important and numerous, not because of what is said in public but because acquaintanceships are sustained. These brief encounters remind ministers of the group's work, influence, and interest.

Ongoing work in the policy community is primarily focused on the government department responsible for the policy area of immediate concern to the group; in health care policy this is the federal and provincial departments of health. To accomplish this work, groups organize in a similar fashion to that of the department and, to some extent, abide by the norms of consultation preferred by the department. To be effective the group must become familiar with the organization of the department and know who in the department deals with what issue and how much weight that individual's advice carries. The group must develop an intimate knowledge of the programs administered by the department and a thorough understanding of how this work takes place. Furthermore, the group must understand how the department conceptualizes issues. To accomplish these activities, groups usually employ professional staff members who familiarize themselves with the structure of policy development within the department and the paradigm applied by the department to the policy field. These professional staff members must maintain continued liaison with the sections of the department whose work is vital to the group. As well, groups usually establish committees to evaluate information derived from monitoring departmental activities and to formulate responses to initiatives from the department and other groups in the policy community. Frequently, groups must establish relationships with more than one government department. For example, the department responsible for health care may not be responsible for professional nursing legislation. In addition to working with the department of health, nursing unions must establish close ties to the department of labor.

Effectiveness in the policy community depends in large measure on the ability of the professional staff of organized nursing groups to establish and maintain relationships external to nursing, as well as having intimate knowledge of the issues and groups internal to the nursing community. Serious attention must be given to employing professional staff who are knowledgeable about the policy process and are able to work effectively within the broader policy community, especially with governmental departments. One of the primary responsibilities must be to build solid relationships with both nursing and non-nursing officials inside the bureaucracy. Thus professional staff need to establish a presence in the policy networks and act in a reconnaissance role to discover at early stages any governmental plans for new policy initiatives. This would enable professional associations and nursing unions to be in a proactive rather than a reactive policy position.

For many years, nurses have been employed at more junior levels of provincial departments of health as consultants to undertake assigned tasks that arise out of the departmental mandate. Although these nursing consultants do not have an independent role in the policy process, their advice may have considerable influence on nursing practice. Close liaison between the department's nursing consultants and professional staff of organized nursing groups and major health agencies in the policy community is essential.

In the last 5 years, some provincial governments (Alberta, British Columbia, Ontario, and Saskatchewan) established more senior provincial nursing consultant positions. These provincial nursing consultants frequently report to the deputy minister and have responsibility for initiatives important to the nursing profession. They often act as liaison for nursing within the government bureaucracy and between the government and organized nursing groups. Their access to deputy ministers and, often, to ministers provides them with unique opportunities to influence policies of concern to the nursing profession. However, most do not have direct responsibility for other nurses within the department of health and have no clear role in programmatic decisions. As a result, they may not normally be involved in departmental debates around standard setting for agency funding, staff mix, or other issues of critical importance to the practice of nursing. Because these positions are reasonably new, an evaluation of their effectiveness is premature. Nevertheless, the need for nurses at senior levels of the bureaucracy to shape operational policy must be addressed.

Although provincial ministries of health are now establishing senior provincial nursing consultants' positions and related policy advisory mechanisms, the organizational position of the principal nursing officer at Health and Welfare Canada is steadily declining in importance. This senior position was formally established in 1968 when Verna Huffman Splane was appointed principal nursing officer. Her forerunner, Dorothy Percy, was Chief Nursing Consultant in the Department of National Health from 1953 to 1967. Until the mid-1980s, the principal nursing officer reported to the Deputy Minister of Health and was active in senior departmental policy discussions. As the result of organizational changes in the federal department during the 1980s, the principal nursing officer reports through an assistant deputy minister on the nonoperational side of the federal department. The CNA and CAUSN are actively lobbying to have this situation reversed.

The important policy role nurses have in ministries of health, particularly at the national level, is the subject of an ongoing study by Splane and Splane (1990). These researchers interviewed chief nursing officers worldwide, examining factors associated with the establishment of chief nursing officer positions, their reporting relationship in national ministries of health, and the nature and extent of the chief nursing officer's participation in macro-planning policy and in administration of the ministry.

In addition to promotion of group ideas with the government departments, two other factors are paramount in the group's relations with the policy community. The first is position, and the second is cooperation (Pross, 1986). Recognition and position are essential to being consulted (Faulkner, 1982). Securing a recognized position in the policy community is the first priority for any group planning to exert continuing influence on the policy process. This involves continual struggle and often competition, especially for nursing groups, which, until recently, may not have sought a prominent position in the policy community or were excluded from the policy community due to various factors, including gender and social class. After groups become established in the policy community, they tend to become less vocal and seek less public means to resolve issues. As Pross (1986) observes, problems of legitimacy change to problems of communication: "Instead of clamouring to be consulted, they are hounded for advice" (p. 146). When governments decide that a specific group legitimately speaks for a significant part of the community, that group is consulted frequently (often on issues far afield from its immediate concerns) and requested to sit on advisory committees. Active participation in response to these requests is required to maintain the group's position as an integral part of the policy community, to tap into the information networks, and to guarantee consultation on issues of major concern to the group.

Monitoring is an important aspect of any established group's relationship with its policy community, particularly with central government departments. Being part of the information flow and establishing friendly contact with representatives from other groups helps the group keep abreast of changing opinion in the policy community, enabling the group to anticipate proposals for policy change and to prepare to react or adapt to them.

The preoccupation with keeping issues out of the political arena results from the tendency of members of the policy community to cooperate, the second major feature of relations between groups in the policy community (Pross, 1986). Cooperation promotes stable relations, ensures support, and provides credibility for the group. Most members of the policy community are aware that they will have to live with one another after debate on the current issue ends, and that tomorrow they may need allies on the new issue. Therefore there is incentive for reaching an accommodation and for exercising restraint and civility in the process (Pross, 1986). A current example of cooperation in the national health care policy community is the Health Action Lobby (HEAL), which is composed of seven national health organizations that have agreed to work together in an effort to preserve adequate federal funding for Canada's health care system. Prominent members of the lobby include the Canadian Nurses Association, Canadian Hospital Association, Canadian Medical Association, and Canadian Public Health Association.

Cooperation is not always possible. Since 1988 there have been province-wide strikes by nurses in Manitoba, Saskatchewan, Alberta, British Columbia, and Quebec. The longest was the 31-day strike in Manitoba in January of 1991 that involved nearly 10,000 nurses. In Chapter 28, Hibberd views nursing strikes as a power struggle between employees and employers. Hibberd's analysis of nurses' strikes reveals a determination by nurses to improve working conditions that jeopardize patient care and, as well, concern for salary and benefits. The concern for patient care is a powerful weapon for drawing attention to the socioeconomic needs of nurses. Hibberd describes the current trends in nurses' strikes—the level of public and professional support, failure by members to ratify negotiated agreements, defiance of the law, and type of issues being bargained—and discusses the outcomes and consequences of these current trends.

POLITICIZATION OF WOMEN AND NURSES

Heightened sensitivity to the importance of active involvement in political events by nurses closely parallels the politicization of Canadian women. Although women have long worked in back rooms, writing letters and answering telephones, involvement in political decision making was, until recently, believed to be unladylike. Even the right to vote came only after a political battle by women all across the country.

The organized women's movement in Canada began in the late 1800s when women began working together to obtain the right to vote. At that time only women who owned property could vote in some municipal elections. Wider suffrage was resisted by the male establishment who viewed women as unsuitable to vote or to hold elected office. In 1889, the Dominion Women's Enfranchisement Association was formed to advocate for voting rights. This association was supported in demanding women's enfranchisement by several other groups, including the Women's Christian Temperance Union, the National Council of Women, and the National Union of Women's Suffragette Societies.

An important breakthrough occurred in 1916 when Nellie McClung led a campaign that resulted in Manitoba becoming the first province to grant women the right to vote and to hold office. By 1918, Saskatchewan, Alberta, British Columbia, Ontario, and Nova Scotia granted the same rights. Although women in these provinces had the right to vote provincially, they still could not vote in federal elections. Lobby groups stressed the incongruence of women serving their country as nurses and ambulance drivers and working in essential industries during World War I but not being able to vote. Their views were recognized when the federal government granted female members of the Armed Forces and female relatives of soldiers the right to vote in the federal election of 1917. Federal legislation was passed in 1920 granting all women the right to vote in federal elections. Women also became eligible to sit in the House of Commons.

New Brunswick granted women the right to vote in provincial elections in 1919, but the corresponding right to hold office was not granted until 1934. Prince Edward Island enacted legislation allowing women to vote and hold office in 1922. In 1925, Newfoundland extended voting and office-holding rights to its female citizens. Only Quebec, with its conservative traditions, resisted, until a concerted campaign led by Therese Casgrain, in 1940, finally won the women of Quebec the right to vote and to hold office. However, the political experience gained in securing the right to vote and to hold public office was not translated by most women into recognition of their political power. Tragically, political parties quickly realized that they would not be held accountable if women's views and concerns were not addressed. This is now slowly changing.

Louise McKinney and Roberta MacAdams, who won seats in the Alberta Legislature in 1917, were the first Canadian women and the first women anywhere in the Commonwealth to hold such an office. MacAdams, a nutritionist serving overseas with the Army Medical Corps in World War I, held one of two extra, temporary "soldiers' seats" created under the wartime Elections Act. In 1921, Agnes McPhail became the first Canadian woman elected to the House of Commons. Only nine women sat in provincial legislatures before 1940, all of them in the four Western provinces. The continued dominance of electoral politics by men led suffragists to demand that women be allowed in public office by appointment. Alberta was first, by naming Emily Murphy and Alice Jamieson as police magistrates in 1916. Helen Gregory MacGill became a judge in the juvenile court of British Columbia in 1917.

Lawyers repeatedly challenged the right of these women to hold judicial office because they were not "persons" as defined by the British North America Act. However, the campaign by women's groups to have a woman appointed to the Senate initiated the celebrated Persons Case (Thompson and Seager, 1985). Emily Murphy and four other prominent Alberta women (Irene Parlby, Henrietta Muir Edwards, Louise McKinney, and Nellie McClung) petitioned the Supreme Court of Canada to rule on this matter. In 1928, the Supreme Court provided an unanimous judgment that women were not persons in the legal sense. The Alberta women then appealed to the Judicial Committee of the Privy Council of Great Britain, which overturned the decision of the Supreme Court of Canada in 1929, holding that women were indeed persons and were qualified to hold office. This decision led to the appointment by Prime Minister Mackenzie King in 1931 of Canada's first woman Senator, Clairine Wilson from Ontario.

There have been many milestones for Canadian women's involvement in politics since the 1920s. Therese Casgrain was the first woman to lead a political party, the

Cooperative Commonwealth Federation of Quebec, from 1951 to 1973. Ellen Fairclough became Canada's first female Cabinet Minister in 1957. In 1982, Iona Campagnolo became the first woman president of a federal political party (the Liberals). Jeanne Sauvé was the first female Speaker of the House of Commons before being appointed Canada's first female Governor General in 1984. In 1990, Audrey McLaughlin became the first female leader of a national political party (New Democratic Party), and in 1991, Rita Johnson became the first female premier of a province (British Columbia).

Notwithstanding these achievements, the number of women who have held elected office is small. Brodie and Vickers (1982) report that between 1919 and 1979 there were 134 federal and provincial elections with 6845 legislators elected, of which only 67 were women. In the 1988 federal election, 39 women were elected to the House of Commons, more than in any previous election but representing only 13% of all the members of Parliament. Further progress was made in the 1990 election in Ontario, in which 19 of the 73 members elected for the winning New Democratic Party were females and, of these, 10 received Cabinet posts. A few nurses sought and won elected office: Sheila Embury represented Calgary North West in the Alberta Legislature from 1979 to 1986; Marion Dewar was a popular mayor of Ottawa from 1978 to 1985; and Bonnie Mitchelson has been a cabinet minister in Manitoba since 1988.

While women fought for political equity they also struggled for educational rights and equality in the workplace. The first woman graduated from a Canadian university, Mount Allison, in 1875, and other universities slowly accepted enrollment of women students over the next 20 years. By the end of the 1920s, about 25% of university students were women. Today, women comprise nearly 50% of university enrollment. Access to university education gradually resulted in access to occupations previously reserved solely for men. However, access to university education for women in female-dominant occupations has been a slower and more difficult struggle.

Several factors have given rise to the growing demand by Canadian women to be treated as equal partners in our society. Urbanization, immigration, industrialization, and paid employment are key features. Changing socioeconomic conditions such as the increase in single parent families and family poverty triggered an influx of women in the workplace in the 1960s. Additionally, the declining birthrate and the delay in first births enable women to seek new roles. Increased education, human rights legislation, and a heightening sense of awareness of workplace inequity between men and women are also factors that mobilize women to demand equal participation in decisions at work and in the political arena. Since 1950, the number of working women has increased dramatically, so that females now make up more than 40% of Canada's work force. In spite of these rising numbers, women still are paid less than men. In 1990 the average female wage was 66% of that paid to the average male worker. Today, the National Action Committee on the Status of Women and many other contemporary women's groups still campaign for pay equity and equal pay for work of equal value.

Women's groups have successfully pushed women's issues onto the political agenda, such as during the constitutional debates of 1981 when a spontaneous and indignant gathering of women in Ottawa triggered change in the proposed new Constitution for Canada. Women's groups secured the near impossible by having equality rights entrenched in Section 15 of the Canadian Charter of Rights and Freedoms. These same groups expressed concern that the failed Meech Lake Accord had the potential to override the Charter's equality rights provisions. Notwithstanding this achievement, more recent efforts by women's groups have met with much less success, such as issues on child care and pay equity. Various explanations are offered: groups concerned with women's issues are now more numerous and offer diverse policy advice, government funding to groups to support concentrated lobbying is declining, and women's groups have organizational difficulties and problems mobilizing group members. In this context, governments find it easier to refuse to act, on the grounds that the women's lobby is divided (Burt, 1990).

Historical and current events undoubtedly influence the politicization of nurses. Although most professional nurses' associations at the provincial level received legislative mandates before 1920, the importance of political activities to shape public policy is primarily a phenomenon that began in the 1970s and accelerated in the 1980s. Before this time, governments, both federally and provincially, knew little, and one might believe cared less, about the silent thousands of nurses in Canada. Silence and inaction are not characteristic of organized nurses' groups today. The growing political visibility of professional nurses' associations and nurses' unions has contributed to the political maturation of nurses as individuals. Canadian nursing leaders now take bolder positions, urging political action by nurses individually and collectively on many issues. Aspects of the politicization of nurses are described in all of the following chapters. For example, in Chapter 25, Mussallem describes various roles of CNA in response to federal and international political events, and in Chapter 26 (about the presidents of CNA) Meilicke and Larsen document the role of these nursing leaders in mobilizing nurses to increased political involvement. In Chapter 30, Pringle and Roe describe the important contribution of the Victorian Order of Nurses (VON) in creating opportunities for nurses to offer innovative services to the public. Often the services piloted by VON have become an integral part of the health care system. A good example is visiting nurse services, which VON initiated 70 years before governments became involved.

The increasing politicization of nurses is also apparent in the activities of Canada's nurses' unions. By the 1960s nurses were demanding redress of inequalities in the workplace. While other women were entering other workplaces, nurses were unionizing to achieve some measure of social and economic justice. As documented by Jensen in Chapter 27, nurses' unions evolved from being employment-relations committees of professional nurses' associations to independent unions throughout the country. The employment relations committees gave advice on salary schedules and other conditions of employment to employers. At times this advice was accepted; most of the time it was not. Jensen discusses the separation of nurses' unions from professional associations, creating independent organizations. The issue of the overlapping membership between professional nurses' associations and nurses' unions, as well as the functions of each group and the potential for conflict that can and at times does result, is also discussed.

By the mid-1970s, nurses' unions realized that visible public action to support their demands at the bargaining table was required. As Jensen points out, every province had separate nursing bargaining groups by the middle 1970s and nearly every nurses' union had the right to job action, but the ultimate weapon, strike action, was rarely used until the 1980s. Although it is still common that nurses, both unionized and nonunionized, reject unionism and any form of job action as being unprofessional, unionization in nursing is a remarkable case study of the political socialization of a group of Canadian women.

LEADERSHIP OF ORGANIZED NURSING GROUPS

The leaders of organized nursing groups exist at the center of a communications network in the nursing community and in the policy community. In this network are members of the organized group, relevant officials from government departments, and other groups and individuals in the policy community and from the public at large. An important role of the leaders of organized nurses' groups involves representing viewpoints and transmitting concerns and demands of the nursing profession to members of governments and other relevant groups, as well as to the general public, and bringing back information to members of the profession. This communication role requires constant attention to changes in the policy environment that are important to the nursing profession. It also requires visible, articulate, and persuasive leaders to attract government and, when required, media attention.

Another critical ingredient in the effectiveness of organized nursing groups is the knowledge, skill, and political acumen of the leaders, especially of the executive directors and presidents. Executive directors require skills to manage the group and expertise about policy issues. Presidents need a complementary set of skills that enable them to respond to the aspirations and needs of the membership. The analysis by Meilicke and Larsen in Chapter 26 offers insights to the strategies used by leaders to communicate nursing values to the public and to members of the policy community.

The importance of the role of executive director is often misunderstood. Although executive directors are appointed and subject to the will of the board, they have a much longer tenure than elected officials. Presidents and board members are usually elected at annual meetings for 2-year terms, and these elected officers often rely heavily on the expertise of the executive director and professional staff. The Canadian Nurses Association has been fortunate in securing leaders of quality for this position (see box).

In many respects the relationship between the executive director and elected officers is similar to that of public servants to cabinet ministers. Public servants have considerable latitude in shaping policy initiatives of government and implementing decisions of elected officials. Similarly, the executive director of an association can be instrumental in shaping the policies considered by a board of directors. Executive directors also have a critical role in gathering information about the ongoing activities of government and other pressure groups. This environmental scanning function is important in devising effective political strategies and anticipating and responding

Chief Executive Officers of the Canadian Nurses Association*

Term	Name
1923-1943	Jean Scantlion Wilson†
1943-1944	Kathleen W. Ellis†
1944-1952	Gertrude M. Hall†
1952-1963	M. Pearl (Penny) Stiver†
1963-1981	Dr. Helen K. Mussallem
1981-1989	Ginette Rodger
1989-	Judith Oulton

From the Canadian Nurses Association (1968): *The leaf and the lamp*, p. 79, Ottawa: Author, CNA Library files.
*The Association was named the Canadian National Association of Trained Nurses from its formation in 1908 until 1924. The chief administrative officer was originally called the Executive Secretary, a title later changed to General Secretary (1944), then to Executive Director (1962).
†Deceased.

to changes in public policy. Most executive directors are highly educated and fairly well paid, factors that add to their political credibility and stature in relation to other groups. However, the disparity in levels of education, income, and social status between the executive director and the rank-and-file members of the nursing profession may create conflict.

Other typical functions of the leaders of organized groups include serving on government committees, consulting and negotiating with government officials, presenting and preparing briefs to legislatures and government committees, outlining policy positions in response to current government policy, performing and sponsoring research in an area of interest, and providing technical information and other types of services to members.

Executive directors and professional staff are involved in frequent interaction at various bureaucratic levels of government agencies, especially interaction to change administrative regulations. This kind of highly focused lobbying is undertaken by professional staff of a nursing association because of the network of contacts and the expertise staff members have gained as the linkage persons in the communications process. Presthus (1973, p. 245) concludes that the frequency of interaction between government decision makers and organized groups is also related to the development of trust and to the legitimacy of the group as perceived by government officials. Legitimacy and trust are clearly important determinants of the effectiveness of organized groups within the policy community.

Conclusion

The leaders of organized nursing groups are increasingly involved in public policy debates and provide evidence of nursing's increasing politicization. To assume a more central role in public policy in the field of health care, sophisticated skills in the art of political debate and action must be nurtured in a broader segment of the membership of nursing's groups, and organized nursing groups require enhanced capacity to undertake independent policy analysis.

REFERENCES

Adaskin, E. (1988). Organized political action: Lobbying by nurses' associations. In A. Baumgart & J. Larsen (Eds.), *Canadian nursing faces the future: Development and change* (pp. 475-487). Toronto: C. V. Mosby.

Brodie, M. J., & Vickers, J. M. (1982). *Canadian women in politics: An overview*. Ottawa: Canadian Research Institute for the Advancement of Women.

Burt, S. (1990). Organized women's groups and the state. In W. Coleman & G. Skogstad (Eds.), *Policy communities and public policy in Canada* (pp. 191-211). Mississauga, ON: Copp Clark Pitman.

Canadian Nurses Association. (1968). *The leaf and the lamp*. Ottawa: Author.

Coleman, W., & Skogstad, G. (1990). *Policy communities and public policy in Canada*. Mississauga, ON: Copp Clark Pitman.

Dahl, R. A. (1961). *Who governs? Democracy and power in the American city*. Newhaven, CT: Prentice Hall.

Dahl, R. A. (1970). *Modern political analysis*. Englewood Cliffs, NJ: Prentice Hall.

Doern, G. B., & Phidd, R. W. (1983). *Canadian public policy: Ideas, structure, process*. Toronto: Methuen.

Dyson, K. (1980). *The state tradition in Western Europe*. Oxford: Basic Blackwell.

Dye, T. (1976). *Policy analysis: What governments do, why they do it and what difference it makes*. University, AL: The University of Alabama Press.

Eckstein, H. (1960). *Pressure group politics: The case of the British Medical Association*. London: Allen and Unwin.

Faulkner, H. (1982). Pressuring the executive. *Canadian Public Administration, 25*(2), 240-253.

Larsen, J. (Chair). (1991, July). *Report to Provincial and Territories Ministers of Health*. Winnipeg, MB: National Nursing Symposium Steering Committee.

Lasswell, H. (1936). *Politics: Who gets what, when and how*. New York: McGraw-Hill.

Majone, G. (1989). *Evidence, argument and persuasion in the policy process*. New Haven, CT: Yale University Press.

Mechanic, D. (1990) Improving health status through health policy: An agenda for nursing leaders. In C. M. Fagin (Ed.), *Nursing leadership: Global strategies* (pp. 181-189) (Pub. No. 41-2349). New York: National League for Nursing.

National Federation of Nurses Unions. (1991). The implications of incremental salary structures in nursing: A discussion paper. Ottawa: Author.

Presthus, R. (1973). *Elite accommodation in Canadian politics*. Toronto: Macmillan.

Pross, A. P. (1986). *Group politics and public policy*. Toronto: Oxford University Press.

Registered Nurses Association of British Columbia. (1991). *Mental health: A priority for nurses* (Annual Report 1990). Vancouver: Author.

Simeon, R. (1972). *Federal/provincial diplomacy*. Toronto: University of Toronto Press.

Splane, V., & Splane, R. (1990, September). *Senior nurses in national ministries of health*. Paper presented at the 5th Biennial (Open) Conference of the Work Group of European Nurse Researchers, Budapest, Hungary.

Thompson, J., & Seager, A. (1985). *Canada 1929-1939: Decade of discord*. Toronto: McClelland and Stewart.

Van Loon, R. J., & Whittington, M. S. (1976). *The Canadian political system*. Toronto: McGraw-Hill Ryerson.

Since 1966, Canadian nurses have had a headquarters in Ottawa so they may meet easily and regularly with national politicians and with leaders of other national health care groups. CNA House, at 50 The Driveway, also is home to the Helen K. Mussallem Library and offices of *The Canadian Nurse/L'infirmière canadienne*. (Photograph from CNA Library archival files. Used with permission.)

CHAPTER TWENTY-FIVE

Professional Nurses' Associations

HELEN K. MUSSALLEM, OC, RN, EdD

Helen K. Mussallem, Officer, Order of Canada, BN (McGill), MA, EdD (Columbia), LLD (New Brunswick, Queen's, McMaster), DSc (Memorial), DStJ, FRCN, is special advisor to national and international health-related organizations. A noted author and internationally respected nursing leader, Dr. Mussallem carried out the Pilot Project for the Evaluation of Schools of Nursing in Canada from 1957 to 1959 and became Executive Director of the Canadian Nurses Association in 1963. She retired from CNA in 1981 and has continued to act as advisor and to carry out projects for such agencies as the World Health Organization, the Commonwealth Foundation, and the International Council of Nurses. She was elected President of the Victorian Order of Nurses for Canada in 1989.

Power of the professional nurses' associations in Canada is relatively strong compared with that in most other countries in the world. Our history, our traditions, and, especially, our leaders developed this organizational power, which grew and changed over the years. Because powerful organizations can help individuals achieve goals, every nurse needs to understand how organizations work and know their strengths and limitations so that organizational power can be used wisely and effectively.

The pattern of social, political, and economic trends and issues affects health care systems and nursing services. Nursing issues and structures also influence social, political, and economic systems. One of the main ways that nurses can have an effect on these external systems is through their national and their provincial or territorial professional nurses' associations. Within these organizations, nurses can affect local, provincial, national, and international trends and issues.

Most individual nurses in Canada belong to a provincial or territorial professional nurses' association. These nurses' associations work with provincial or territorial governments, other health-related professions, other groups, and the public to influence policy changes. For example, nurses' associations lobbied governments for better health care laws and other legislation such as that to introduce seat belts or to develop clean air policy.

The provincial nurses' associations, with the exception of Quebec, belong to the national professional body, the Canadian Nurses Association (CNA), which has the numbers and the power to speak authoritatively for the nursing profession at the national level. As well, through its link to the world federation of national nurses' associations, the International Council of Nurses (ICN), CNA can work with international associations and organizations and affect international policy.

Nurses' associations in Canada have some unique powers. Because of its history, Canada is the only confederated country in the world in which the provincial and territorial nurses' associations, except in Ontario, actually administer the statutes (acts) governing the profession. (See Chapter 19.) This combination of regulatory (licensure or registration) and other statutory powers plus the power of membership in a professional association is an important responsibility.

Although this chapter discusses statutory roles, its primary focus is on the professional roles, functions, structures, and resources of the national and provincial/territorial nurses' associations. (Chapter 19 provides further discussion of regulatory and disciplinary roles.) Because of the enormity of the changes in professional nursing, only an overview is presented. However, the chapter identifies trends and issues of concern to nurses, using an historical perspective. It also identifies the important role nurses' associations take in influencing health policy, promoting high quality of nursing services, setting standards for nursing, and providing means for communication in nursing.

EARLY ASSOCIATIONS

Although the practice of nursing is as old as the human race, and although nursing in Canada dates from the 1600s, no movements toward formal organization of nurses were made until the late 1890s. At that time, working conditions in hospitals in Canada, as in England and the United States, reached a crisis point and organization was viewed by nurses as one way of achieving minimum standards of education and practice. The greatest concern of nursing leaders was qualifications—or lack of them—of some individuals who were calling themselves nurses. Thus in 1887, Ethel G. Bedford Fenwick of England began pressing for registration and licensure of nurses—a concept, incidentally, that was opposed by Florence Nightingale (Styles, 1986). The British Nurses' Association was formed in 1888—the first professional nurses' association in the world. Its twofold purpose was to improve the education and status of nurses and to protect the public by legislation requiring the registration of nurses (Donahue, 1985, p. 360).

The first training school in Canada opened in St. Catharines, Ontario, in 1874. Graduates of training schools usually formed alumnae associations as social and supportive bodies, but there were no national associations in Canada or the United States. In 1893, Fenwick began urging North American nurses to form national associations to support nursing goals. Her speech at the Chicago World's Fair led to a meeting of a small group of training school directors from Canada and the United States and then to formation of the American Society of Superintendents of Training Schools. This became, in effect, an accrediting agency that approved nursing schools in Canada and the United States (Stewart and Austin, 1962).

This society worked for 2 years to develop a national association for graduate nurses. By 1896, the Society proposed that all alumnae associations be the route of entry to a new organization, one to which all nurses could belong. Its primary objective was to secure legislation that differentiated between "trained" and "un-trained" nurses. To obtain this objective, the new-formed Nurses' Association Alumnae of the United States and Canada sought incorporation. However, because New York law prohibited foreign membership, the Canadian group had to withdraw. A further consideration was the single-nation concept for eligibility for membership in the International Council of Nurses, which was formed under Fenwick's aegis in 1899.

Although a few provincial or local associations of trained nurses were formed (the Graduate Nurses' Association of Ontario or the Calgary Association of Graduate Nurses, both formed in 1904), Canadian nurses remained without a formal national or international affiliation until 1907. In that year, Mary Agnes Snively of the Toronto General Hospital sparked formation of the Canadian Society of Superintendents of Training Schools. Then in 1908, representatives of 16 organized nursing bodies met in Ottawa to form the Canadian National Association of Trained Nurses, which immediately applied for membership in ICN (Gibbon and Mathewson, 1947).

Because, under the British North American Act of 1867, health and educational matters remained the jurisdiction of provincial governments, the national association could only recommend standards in these areas. Nursing associations had to be formed in each province to work toward specific standards and regulations under provincial legislation. The Graduate Nurses' Association of Nova Scotia (GNANS) was the first to achieve legislation governing nurses; in 1910, the Nova Scotia government passed an act incorporating the nurses' organization and forming a type of voluntary registration for nurses to be administered by GNANS.

NATIONAL OBJECTIVES

At its formation in 1908, the primary objective of the Canadian National Association of Trained Nurses (CNATN) was to encourage mutual understanding and unity among nurses in Canada. As well, CNATN was concerned with elevation of standards of education and promotion of a high standard of professional honor. The other original three objectives concerned international coordination and cooperation. The changing role of the CNA, in response to needs of nurses and the profession and to social pressures from outside the profession, can be seen by examining the various changes and revisions of the objectives throughout the years.

In 1924, the CNATN constitution was amended to allow a name change to the Canadian Nurses' Association (the apostrophe was dropped later from the official name) and, although the objectives were revised as well, the primary one remained the promotion of national unity. In 1947, CNA was incorporated under the Statutes of Canada as a federation of provincial registered nurses' associations. The objectives of that era reiterated the emphasis on standards of nursing service and education, but new objectives on "ethics" and "public welfare" were added. In 1964, at the urging of provincial associations, CNA formed a social and economic welfare committee, again a reflection of a response to a changing need. When further amendments to the constitution were made in 1970, an objective on social and economic matters was also included. In 1982, additional objectives stated CNA's concerns for promotion of nursing research and for high standards of nursing administration. The objectives (or "objects," as they are now termed at CNA) approved at the 1986 annual meeting are listed in the box, with comments on the historical development in parentheses.

Objects of the CNA (1986)*

1. To speak for Canadian nurses and represent Canadian nursing to other organizations on national and international levels. (This objective, always a priority, was given greater prominence than in the last 78 years.)
2. To develop a national perspective on nursing and health-related issues. (This is the first time the word "issues" appeared and it suggests that greater emphasis and a proactive role will be taken by the national organization.)
3. To influence national health policy. (This new objective further indicates a reactive and proactive role.)
4. To promote high standards of nursing practice, education, research, and administration in order to achieve quality nursing care for the people of Canada. (This amalgamates previous objectives going back to 1910 for education, 1947 for "services" or practice, and 1982 for research and administration. It recognizes the concern for standards to protect the public, which go back to the original objectives, but also recognizes that, in Canadian law, health and education are under provincial jurisdiction.)
5. To provide leadership in issues related to the working lives of nurses. (As a result of increasing pressures from provincial members, CNA formed a social and economic welfare committee in 1964. The related objective was introduced in 1970 and in 1986 was enlarged to include all aspects of the "working life" of nurses.)

*These objectives were approved by members at the 1986 annual meeting of the Canadian Nurses Association. The comments in parentheses indicate the historical significance. (Canadian Nurses Association (1986): *Reports of biennial meetings 1981-1986*, Ottawa: Author.) Reprinted with permission from the Canadian Nurses Association.

PROVINCIAL REGULATORY ROLES

The national and provincial/territorial associations have many similar functions and deal with similar issues. As well, provincial associations provide considerable direct member services that support nursing practice. Most provide nursing practice consultation services and education programs for members. Some also provide bursaries, career information, and library services.

Primary functions of the provincial and territorial associations, however, are registration and licensing, setting and maintaining standards for nursing education and practice, and discipline of members who do not meet standards. Regulation/licensure is discussed in detail in Chapter 19, but a brief overview of these statutory roles provides further evidence of the dynamic nature of the professional associations.

The major reason for development of the provincial associations was to establish educational and practice standards for nursing and thereby protect the public from unsafe practitioners (CNA, 1968, p. 35). At the beginning of the twentieth century, almost any hospital could establish a "training school," and the main purpose of many such programs was to ensure a supply of cheap labor for the wards. Nurses who received a prescribed course of training found themselves competing for status and pay with nurses who received little or no education. Because there was no legislation, there was little opportunity to establish standards of nursing service.

In 1910, nurses in Nova Scotia were the first to secure nursing legislation. This legislation provided a voluntary Register (or approved list) to be maintained by the Graduate Nurses Association of Nova Scotia, which could set standards for those who were listed or registered. Voluntary registration meant that those who had not received an approved training or passed an examination could still practice nursing, but this was a beginning toward legislation for standards for nursing. In 1913, the Manitoba Association of Graduate Nurses was incorporated by a provincial Act, which also allowed the association to set standards for nursing schools and make provisions for registration and discipline. By 1914, all provinces except Prince Edward Island had provincial nurses' associations, but it was not until 1922 that all nine provinces (Newfoundland had not yet joined Canada) had some form of nurse registration legislation.

The purpose of registration is to protect the public from unsafe practitioners, but under early legislation not all nurses had to be registered; graduates could still practice, but could not call themselves "Registered Nurses" or use the initials RN after their names. In recent years, most provinces enacted mandatory registration, meaning that all nurses must be currently registered with a provincial body before they can provide nursing care or use the title "nurse." As well, many provinces now require practicing nurses to show evidence that they have kept their nursing skills up-to-date, usually by regular practice or refresher courses. In most provinces, the acts also regulate standards of nursing education and nursing practice and provide for the setting of educational requirements for admission to schools of nursing.

In most provinces and territories (the exceptions are Ontario and the Yukon), governments entrust administration of this legislation to the nurses' associations. The regulatory and professional functions are linked, and only one membership fee is paid. Such self-government is one of the criteria used to identify a true profession (see Chapter 1). The fact that this authority remains with most professional associations over the years attests to the governments' satisfaction with this method of administration. Occasionally, provincial governments question self-governing authority for the professions, but in such instances they usually withdraw objections when they examine the ways that nurses' associations perform their responsibilities for public safety. In addition, the governments recognize that the financial burdens for registration and for establishing and maintaining standards are borne by the associations.

One provincial nurses' association, the Registered Nurses Association of Ontario (RNAO), does not have this regulatory authority. Instead, these functions are the responsibility of the College of Nurses of Ontario (CNO), which is an organization of registered nurses and registered nursing assistants created by provincial legislation for self-regulatory purposes. RNAO performs nonregulatory professional functions similar to those of the national body. Registration with the College for practicing nurses is required for those wishing to use the title "Registered Nurse." Membership in RNAO is voluntary, and only about 15% of registered nurses in Ontario belong. This percentage is similar to that of the American Nurses Association in the United States, in which there is also separation between the regulatory and professional functions (see Chapter 19.)

Although registration is a provincial/territorial responsibility, CNA has a coordinating role. CNA board meetings offer the provinces and territories opportunities to discuss, compare, and debate issues related to regulation and standards. Throughout the years, CNA urged nation-wide registration standards that would allow nurses to move freely from one province to another. In 1934, a full-scale attempt was made to set up national registration, but it was not passed by Parliament. Reciprocity is established between some provincial associations, but each provincial association sets its own standards, and these still vary in a few minor respects.

Provincial associations at first developed their own tests for registration. Then, beginning in 1949, eight provinces made agreements with the National League for Nursing (NLN) in the United States to use its state board examinations. (Ontario developed its own tests and New Brunswick used the Ontario tests. French-language schools in Quebec also used a separate test.) When notice was given that, beginning in 1969, use of NLN tests would be restricted to the United States, these provinces then asked CNA to establish a national testing service to provide tests, in English and French, for registration purposes for all Canadian nurses. This was a complicated, expensive, work-intensive project, and unique for a national voluntary association. However, quality examinations were developed and form the basis for national standards. The CNA Testing Service (CNATS, usually referred to as C-NATS), contributes to the goal of reciprocity of registration between provinces because all provincial and territorial associations are using the same basic examination.

Table 25-1 provides a brief overview of the provincial professional associations and identifies some of the important issues and trends throughout their history.

TABLE 25-1 Provincial and Territorial Nurses' Associations

Association	Special note	Current issues (1990)
Graduate Nurses Association of British Columbia (GNABC), formed 1912 Registered Nurses Association of British Columbia (RNABC), legislation enacted 1918	Registration is mandatory Requirements for registration renewal Emphasis on member services that support professional nursing practice	Nursing shortages Attaining basic baccalaureate programs to prepare for year 2000 Promotion of primary health care as basis for provincial health care system
Alberta Association of Graduate Nurses (AAGN); formed, legislation enacted, 1916 Alberta Association of Registered Nurses (AARN), name change 1920	Registration is mandatory Does not monitor nursing education Administers Educational Trust Fund as a legislative responsibility	Monitoring several government initiatives that will impose greater control on professional associations, including specific means to fund acute care facilities and demands for greater cooperation among health care system stakeholders Lobbying for appointment of a provincial nursing consultant in the Ministry of Health at the Assistant Deputy Minister level
Saskatchewan Graduate Nurses Association (SGNA), formed 1914 Saskatchewan Registered Nurses Association (SRNA); name changed, legislation enacted 1917	Specific requirements for registration renewal Registration is mandatory	Working on Primary Health Care and role of the RN Increasing visibility of the Association Implementing new Act Working on educational issues • baccalaureate as entry to profession • collaborative models to move toward entry • availability of students in basic degree, post-RN degree, and master's programs • availability of distance education

From personal communications with provincial and territorial associations, June-August 1990; CNA, 1968; Gibbon and Mathewson, 1947.

Continued.

TABLE 25-1 Provincial and Territorial Nurses' Associations—cont'd

Association	Special note	Current issues (1990)
Manitoba Association of Graduate Nurses (MAGN); formed 1905, legislation enacted 1913 Manitoba Association of Registered Nurses (MARN), name changed 1930	First province to have comprehensive nursing legislation Registration is not mandatory	Working on standards for special interest groups (e.g., perioperative nursing care) Attaining basic baccalaureate programs to prepare for proposed entry levels by the year 2000 Examining roles of the nurse midwife in the health care system Developing protocols and systems to address issues related to "Nurse Abuse"
Graduate Nurses Association of Ontario (GNAO), formed 1904 Registered Nurses Association of Ontario (RNAO); name changed, legislation enacted 1925	Is a voluntary association of RNs Differs from all other Canadian provinces and territories; similar to USA, UK, and other Commonwealth countries	Addressing the impact of nursing on the health of Ontarians Positioning nursing prominently in the health system

In 1961, Ontario government established the College of Nurses of Ontario (CNO) to administer registration and statutory functions for practice and education. In 1974, under the Health Disciplines Act, the College relinquished educational functions to the government.

| Graduate Nurses Association of Province of Quebec, formed 1917 Registered Nurses Association of Province of Quebec; name changed, legislation enacted 1930 Association of Nurses of Province of Quebec (ANPQ), name change 1946 | Registration is mandatory Is not a member of CNA, withdrew in 1985 citing a multiplicity of factors, including dissatisfaction with membership costs, services, and representation | |

TABLE 25-1 **Provincial and Territorial Nurses' Associations—cont'd**

Association	Special note	Current issues (1990)
Association des infir-miéres et infirmiers de la province de Quebec (AIIPQ), name change 1969 Ordre des infirmiéres et infirmiers du Quebec (OIIQ), name change 1973		
New Brunswick Association of Graduate Nurses (NBAGN); formed, legislation enacted 1916 New Brunswick Association of Registered Nurses (NBARN), name change 1924 Nurses Association of New Brunswick (NANB), name change 1984	Early role especially concerned with social issues First association to include subscription of *The Canadian Nurse* as part of fee Registration is mandatory	Working on accessibility of continuing education Working on major initiatives for health care reform Working on Quality of Worklife for Nurses Focusing on relationship between individual nurses and the professional association (i.e., communication and image of nurses and nursing)
Graduate Nurses Association of Nova Scotia (GNANS); formed 1909, legislation enacted 1910 Registered Nurses Association of Nova Scotia (RNANS), name change 1931	First province to gain legislation to register nurses and so protect public, in 1910 Registration is mandatory	Ethical, legal concerns Continuing education for members Home care needs Insured health services: nurse as entry point to the health care system Funding for nursing education Continuing education for members
Graduate Nurses Association of Prince Edward Island; formed 1911, legislation enacted 1922 Association of Nurses of Prince Edward Island (ANPEI), name change 1950	Registration is not mandatory Has adopted the baccalaureate degree as the basis for entry to practice	Primary health care Levels of caregivers and scope of practice Image of nursing Family violence

Continued.

TABLE 25-1 Provincial and Territorial Nurses' Associations—cont'd

Association	Special note	Current issues (1990)
Newfoundland Graduate Nurses' Association (NGNA), formed 1913 Association of Registered Nurses of Newfoundland (ARNN); name change, legislation enacted 1953	Newfoundland did not become a province in Canada until 1949, but there was affinity of nursing interests since 1910 NGNA followed the registration and regulatory pattern of the Commonwealth until 1953 ARNN joined CNA in 1954 Registration is mandatory	Coordinating development of, funding for, and testing of the project "Primary Health Care: A Nursing Model" Implementing plans for baccalaureate as entry level Working with government and other groups on nursing workforce issues Working on issues related to proliferation of auxiliary health care workers
Northwest Territories Registered Nurses Association (NWTRNA); formed, legislation enacted 1975	Registration is mandatory Joined CNA in 1976	Promoting development of a basic baccalaureate program Working on revisions to the Nurses Act and Bylaws Revising guidelines for medical nursing responsibilities Developing discussion paper on maternal/infant care
Yukon Nurses Society (YNS), formed 1979	Does not have authority to register nurses Joined CNA in 1982	Has legislation committee working on a Nursing Profession Act for registration and other statutory powers

CURRENT ISSUES

Over the years, new objectives and roles have been accepted by the professional associations in response to the changing needs of society and the nursing profession. Almost any issue that affects nurses, the nursing profession, or health care generally will be introduced at meetings of the professional associations, which can then decide on action as a group. Issues that have national significance will be presented by the provincial executive to a board meeting of the national association for discussion, and perhaps action, there as well. The following sections identify some of the important trends and current issues in which nurses' associations have been and are deeply involved and shows how the associations influence change.

Educational Issues

Although the responsibility for education is under provincial jurisdiction and although the provincial nurses' associations have some variation in their standards, the role of the national association in promoting educational standards is significant. The earliest national nurses' organizations pressed for the preparation of nurses to be an educational experience rather than the mere apprenticeship or "learning on the job" method that was common in the late 1800s and early 1900s. As early as 1914, a special committee of the national association recommended that nursing schools or colleges be established under the education system of each province rather than in hospitals and that "the raison d'être . . . be the education of the nurse, not, as it is under the present system, the lessening of the cost of nursing in hospitals" (CNA, 1968, p. 84).

In 1927, CNA and the Canadian Medical Association sponsored a major study into nursing education in Canada. The report of this survey, which was conducted by G.M. Weir, an education professor from the University of British Columbia, was published in 1932. Among its more than 150 recommendations, two of the most vital and far-seeing were that nursing should be within the general education system (Weir, 1932, p. 197) and that, eventually, all education of nurses should be under university auspices (p. 195).

Throughout the next three decades (1930-1960), CNA's concern for reform in nursing education did not diminish. In 1936, CNA published and promoted *A Proposed Curriculum for Schools of Nursing in Canada*, written by Marion Lindeburgh, which was widely used by nursing schools. In 1940, CNA provided a supplement titled *Improvement of Nursing Education in the Clinical Field*. In 1946, CNA, with the Canadian Red Cross Society and the Ontario Department of Health, established a two-year nursing education program in Windsor, Ontario, known as the Metropolitan Demonstration School of Nursing. The purpose of this progressive project was to determine if a clinical nurse could be prepared in 2 years when the school, rather than the hospital, controlled the program. An evaluation in 1952 confirmed this to be true (Lord, 1952). This experiment was observed by leading educators in the United States and influenced the movement to 2-year associate degree programs for nurses in colleges in that country (Brick, 1964). It was also the prototype for the development of the 2-year community college programs in Canada.

Another significant CNA project, conducted from 1957 to 1959, was the pilot project for the evaluation of schools of nursing, directed by Helen K. Mussallem. The purpose of the study was to determine if Canadian nursing programs were ready for a national accreditation program so that standards would be similar from province to province. Data collected from schools across the country attested to an unsatisfactory state of nursing education, and this received wide publicity within the profession and in public, private, and government circles. Mussallem's report (1960) made four recommendations, which required an enlarged and changed role for CNA. Three of these were implemented immediately, and CNA appointed a director of special studies to oversee their initiation. As well, this new director was to be a liaison member with the Canadian Conference of University Schools of

Nursing. This organization, which changed its name later to the Canadian Association of University Schools of Nursing (CAUSN), was formed in 1942 by eight university schools of nursing to determine and support development of desirable standards for university programs for nurses. The appointment of the CNA liaison
member was the first major move to link CNA with issues related to a move to a
higher basic education for nurses (CNA, 1968, p. 93).

In 1960, CNA also tried to encourage funding from government to provide financial support for nurses seeking graduate education; it was unsuccessful but did
attain $150,000 from the W.K. Kellogg Foundation. Realizing that an enterprise could
function more effectively if donors could contribute funds on a tax-exempt basis,
CNA launched the Canadian Nurses Foundation (CNF) in 1962 as a major source
of financial support for advanced education for nurses.

In recent years, the provincial nurses' associations have had an important role in
the development and control of nursing education. The influence of the provincial
associations in this area has therefore been far greater than that of CNA. Most provinces require a review and/or approval process for nursing education programs.
As a result, the provincial organizations are particularly active in this area (see
Chapter 21).

As health care changed and as related science and technology advanced, nurses
recognized that their educational programs must also change in response to needs.
A significant recent educational issue concerns the growing awareness that, for
nurses to meet the challenges of nursing today and in the twenty-first century, a
broad-based university type nursing education is needed. CNA has therefore coordinated the movement of provincial nurses' associations toward the need for the
baccalaureate degree as the basis for entry to practice by the year 2000.

Nursing Work Force Issues

The professional associations have always been closely involved with the issues
that affect supply of and demand for nurses. For example, during the years after
the 1914-1918 World War, CNA and the Canadian Red Cross believed there should
be a national roll of registered nurses prepared for emergency service in case of war
or disaster. CNA operated this plan from 1927 to the end of World War II in 1945.
The advent of World War II in 1939 had a profound effect on every segment of
Canadian society; in nursing, the greatest problem was a shortage of nurses. Because
of CNA's key role, the federal government provided the association with funds to
increase the nursing population with recruitment programs, grants to schools of
nursing, special wartime programs, bursaries, and so on.

A CNA survey at that time revealed that, to alleviate shortages, salaries and
working conditions needed to be comparable to other occupations requiring equivalent preparation. This led to another role for the national professional association.
Provincial associations, particularly that of British Columbia, had already pressed
for a national policy statement on nursing and trade unions. A policy committee
reported to the CNA general meeting in 1944 and, as a result, CNA became a national
resource on collective bargaining and labor relations for nurses.

In 1946, CNA, with the Canadian Hospital Association, formed a national committee to study the persistent problems of nursing shortages in hospitals. Later, the

committee included representatives from the Canadian Medical Association, the Canadian Public Health Association, and, for a short period, two federal government departments. In the early years, this joint committee focused only on nursing shortages and concerns related to nursing, but as CNA's influence grew, issues concerning any of the associations were discussed and recommendations sent back to the parent organizations. In the mid-1980s, a new model for liaison and regular communications for this committee was developed, using annual joint seminar sessions that focus on supply and demand for all health care personnel.

At times of shortages, provincial nurses' associations have a more major role: they collect statistics, work with the media and provincial governments, and develop and disseminate recruitment material. Some sponsor nurse retention projects. To help prevent peaks and valleys in supply of nurses, CNA began a national inventory of all currently registered nurses and published its first annual report, *Countdown*, in 1965. The current statistical studies on nurses are now compiled by Statistics Canada based on data collected by the provincial registering bodies. CNA coordinates the process.

Specialization Issues

Although CNA remains the dominant national association for nurses, other national professional organizations developed as nursing roles become increasingly diversified. In recent decades, the trend is the formation of special interest groups within nursing (see Chapter 17). Nurses working in a specific field (or specialty) often express a need to meet with their peers and to gain more education to further their competency in practice. In the late 1970s, for example, Ontario Occupational Health Nurses explored the feasibility of accreditation for members.

Aware of this trend, CNA acted to prevent the situation that occurred in the United States. There, many nurses used their professional and political energy in national organizations that were outside of and competed with the American Nurses Association. This weakened and divided the American national and state nurses' associations (Clay, 1987, p. 30) and limited membership, and therefore the political power, of the professional associations.

By 1985, CNA established an Advisory Council structure that brought special interest groups into its organizational structure. The Advisory Council is composed of members of the CNA board of directors and presidents (or their delegates) of special interest groups that meet criteria for CNA support. The president of CNA chairs an annual meeting of the Council to share information and to advise the CNA board on national nursing and health care issues relevant to the special interest groups, such as certification, continuing education, entry to practice, research funding, structures and processes for communication, and collaboration. In addition, the Advisory Council appoints one representative of the special interest groups to a 2-year term on the CNA board.

CNA provides many services to the interest groups and in return requests certain information be kept current and an annual fee paid. By the 1990 annual meeting of the Advisory Council, 12 special interest groups had gained CNA approval (see Table 25-2). Several other groups indicated interest in becoming members but had not met the criteria.

TABLE 25-2 **National Nursing Interest Group Members of Canadian Nurses Association Advisory Council (as of February 1991)**

Name	Acronym	Year*
Academy of Chief Executive Nurses	ACEN	1986
Canadian Association of Neuroscience Nurses	CANN	1986
Canadian Gerontological Nursing Association	CGNA	1986
Canadian Intravenous Nurses Association	CINA	1986
National Emergency Nurses Association	NENA	1986
Canadian Council of Cardiovascular Nurses	CCCN	1987
Canadian Nurses Respiratory Society	CNRS	1987
Operating Room Nurses Association of Canada	ORNAC	1987
Canadian Association of Nurses in Oncology	CANO	1988
Canadian Association of Critical Care Nurses	CACCN	1989
Canadian Holistic Nurses Association	CHNA	1989
Community Health Nurses Association of Canada	CHNAC	1989
Canadian Association of Nurses in Independent Practice	CANIP	1989
Canadian Nursing Research Group	CNRG	1990
Canadian Clinical Nurses Specialty Group	CCNSG	1990
Canadian Association for the History of Nursing	CAHN	1991
Canadian Association of Nurse Educators	CANE	1991

*Year Admitted to Advisory Council of CNA.

Most provincial associations provide an interest group structure as well. For example, in 1990 RNABC had 20 such groups. In many cases, provincial interest groups form a link horizontally with the provincial nurses' associations and vertically with a national interest group that in turn becomes an interest group of CNA. This forms a grid of national/provincial/clinical liaisons that offers Canadian nurses a powerful professional network.

With the development of a liaison structure for nursing interest groups, CNA also developed a certification program for nursing specialties. Certification does not necessarily require establishment of a special interest group. The nursing specialty designation applies to an area of nursing rather than to a group or an association, and the process may be initiated by any group of nurses who can provide evidence that a specific nursing area meets CNA's criteria for specialty designation. The designation process is initiated by a request to the CNA board of directors via the association's special committee on certification. The first three requests were initiated by nationally organized special interest groups.

Although the occupational health nurses were the first to examine the possibility of accreditation, in October 1987 neuroscience nursing was designated the first specialty for CNA certification. Under the guidance of CNA's Testing Service, a group of nurses, mainly from the neuroscience nursing group, began to develop a certification examination for 1991.

Professional Liability Issues

In the early 1980s, lawsuits and litigation became increasingly commonplace, and costs of professional liability insurance rose. Malpractice insurance premiums for nurses were no exception. In response to this crisis in the market, CNA and the provincial/territorial associations considered alternatives for the commerical insurance group plans that were purchased by most provincial associations for their members. In October 1987, after several years of researching the issue, CNA introduced a national fund to overcome the uncertainties facing nurses over the availability and cost of professional liability protection in an increasingly litigious environment. The Canadian Nurses Protective Society (CNPS) began in January 1988 as a separate nonprofit corporation to administer the fund and to look after the professional liability interests of Canadian nurses ("Professional liability . . . ," 1989).

CPNS is conducted by nurses for nurses. It is governed by its own board of directors, and its first manager is nurse-lawyer Pam McLean. By March 1990, nine provincial/territorial associations had joined CNPS (the exceptions were British Columbia, Quebec, and the Yukon). Nurses who are members in good standing of the associations supporting CNPS are eligible for professional liability protection in the event of a legal claim against them up to a limit of $1 million per occurrence per year. The protection available from CNPS includes advice, defence or settlement of claims, payment of court-awarded damages, and payment of legal costs. (British Columbia nurses have similar protection from an insurance corporation that is a wholly-owned subsidiary of the RNABC; this self-insurance approach is made possible by legislation unique to that province.)

As well, nurses report occurrences and lawsuits to CNPS, and such information is entered in a computerized database that will assist the profession to identify and address future liability issues. This data will become a valuable tool for nurses involved in research, education, quality assurance, and risk management.

LIAISON AND LOBBYING FUNCTIONS

Two main professional functions of the nurses' associations involve liaison with other groups, such as the national or provincial medical associations and hospital associations, and lobbying of government and other agencies to ensure that the public's and nursing's best interests are considered when new policy is formed. Much of these functions involve the day-to-day efforts of elected officers and full-time staff members.

When CNA was formed, its business was conducted by the elected officers from their homes. The first CNA office was located in Winnipeg in 1922, and in 1923 Jean Scantlion Wilson was appointed the first full-time chief administrative officer (then called the Executive Secretary). A graduate of the Lady Stanley Institute in Ottawa, Wilson had taken a course in administration from the School for Graduate Nurses at McGill and had nursing experience in four provinces (Gibbon and Mathewson, 1947).

In 1932, the national headquarters was moved to Montreal, and the staff grew as functions of the national body increased. At first, its main role was to coordinate efforts of its provincial members and to speak nationally on needs to improve standards in nursing education and practice and in the working lives of nurses. In 1954, CNA moved its headquarters to the nation's capital in Ottawa, the first of all the major health and health-related organizations to do so. Since 1960, CNA has intensified its program in all areas to provide consultant services to member associations and to other groups as requested and needed. Activity has intensified in work with the public, governments, allied professional groups, and other agencies, nationally and internationally. Three moves in Ottawa were necessary to accommodate the expanding work of the association, with a move in 1966 to CNA House, which was built for and is owned by the nurses of Canada. In 1970, when CNA developed the Testing Service, space for these offices had to be found outside CNA headquarters. In the mid-1970s, plans were approved for an expansion of CNA House so that all services could be under one roof, and this expansion was completed in 1988.

CNA activities are now grouped under the following four services:

- Administrative Services, which are the human and material resources, accounting and financial services, and information systems needed to support the day-to-day activities of CNA, the Canadian Nurses Foundation, and the Canadian Nurses Protective Society
- Corporate and Public Affairs, which includes the executive director as secretary to the corporation and, with the president, as spokesperson for the Association; national and international liaison activities; promotion of CNA policies and information related to nursing and health issues; and public relations, government relations, national nursing interest group support, publications, and marketing
- Professional Services, which includes the professional experts (e.g., the national nursing library services) who assist the board and committees in development of policies related to nursing and health; provide consultative services to the association, its members, and others in areas such as education, research, practice, and management; and who identify trends, monitor developments in health care that have implications for the nursing profession, and recommend action to the board and member associations
- Testing Services, which provides registration and certification examinations and the developmental, administrative, evaluative, consultative, and educational services in testing and measurement

Many indicators could be used to show the growth of the national professional association; one is a comparison of the briefs made by CNA to government over the years. In 1962, CNA presented a brief, entitled *Statement to the Royal Commission on Health Services* (CNA, 1962), to the federal government's Hall Commission. The brief contained 24 recommendations: 21 related directly to nursing and no recommendations were made about the overall organization of health services or their financing (CNA, 1962). By contrast, and to illustrate the changing roles of the national organization, in 1980, CNA presented its brief *Putting Health into Health Care* (CNA, 1980) to the federal government, which was once again reviewing health services. This brief contained eight strong recommendations focusing on the health care system in terms of legislation, federal-provincial relationships, health care research, and health education. In the report of this review, Commissioner Emmett Hall states that the CNA's brief was one of the best received by his commission and that it was worthy of the closest attention from all levels of government (Hall, 1980). Not only did this difference in approach represent an improved vision of the association's role but also an increased skill and sophistication in articulating nursing's positions on health and policy issues.

A few other briefs presented since 1970 will illustrate some of the main issues of concern the national association addressed on behalf of its members: taxation; poverty and health; unemployment insurance; employment opportunities; part-time work; pension reform; economic union; social affairs, science, and technology; and federal-provincial fiscal arrangements. In 1988, CNA presented briefs to the Senate and House of Commons on relationships between preventive care and health costs (again!) and emphasized the need to consider alternate delivery modes and enlarged community services in any health care reforms. A 1989 brief related to the Goods and Services Tax was to be introduced in 1991 and urged the government to consider the long range effects of this tax on health care. In 1990, briefs to the Senate and House of Commons focused on accessibility and human resources in the health care system. CNA used these opportunities to comment on patterns of service use and to suggest needed reforms, including greater use of nurses to help control health care costs.

One of the most effective lobbying efforts was that initiated by CNA in 1983-1984 to influence changes in the Canada Health Act when it was introduced by the federal government. When the Bill outlining the proposed new Act was introduced in Parliament in late 1983, nursing leaders noted that it did not provide opportunities for the best use of nurses, recommendations made by CNA and others in presentations to the Hall Commission and to government departments since 1980. As well, nursing leaders recognized that economic and social conditions, because of the rapidly escalating costs of health care, needed better use of nurses. The CNA board of directors therefore launched a lobbying campaign to introduce nurses' concerns to the public and the politicians. This necessitated the hiring of additional staff, public speeches, and all the other tools of an effective lobbying effort (Adaskin, 1988).

With the CNA board, which includes presidents of the provincial/territorial associations, nursing leaders focused on one key clause in the proposed Act. As written, the proposed Act specified only physicians as providers of insurable services. A change in this one clause to "physicians and other health care providers" would allow nurses and others to provide suitable services, often at a lesser cost, and would allow nurses to offer additional care suited to their educational preparation and backgrounds. One of the most important aspects of the campaign was development of a system of improved communications within nursing so that all nurses could participate through informed discussions and presentations to their local members of parliament, letters to newspapers, and so on. Individual nurses in all provinces and territories responded magnificently, and the nurses' associations learned that they could mobilize an effective campaign in a relatively short time. When the Canada Health Act was passed in 1984, this key clause was included—and the public and Canada's political leaders learned a great deal more about the possible services that today's nurses can offer within the health care system.

In addition to this and other lobbying efforts with the federal government, the national association gradually expanded its role in liaison with government departments with which it collaborates or communicates. Over the years, CNA developed and maintained strong links with Health and Welfare Canada, sometimes pressing for change, sometimes collaborating on issues. For example, for many years, CNA urged the federal government to establish a principal nursing officer post so that a nurse would have a key role at the policy-making level. As a result of this urging, in 1953 a nursing advisory service was formed and a nursing consultant appointed, and in 1967 the principal nursing officer position was finally established. Other federal agencies with which CNA works or consults include Employment and Immigration Canada, Ministry of Justice, Consumer and Corporate Affairs, Statistics Canada, Ministry of Transport, the Medical Research Council, and the Metric Commission (CNA, 1986, pp. 33-37).

The expanding and changing role of CNA also involves communications and activities with an ever-increasing number of national nongovernmental agencies, such as the Canadian Council on Health Facilities Accreditation, Canadian Hospital Association, Canadian Medical Association, Victorian Order of Nurses for Canada, Canadian Red Cross Society, St. John Ambulance, Association of Canadian Medical Colleges, Canadian Public Health Association, Canadian Cancer Society, Canadian College of Health Service Executives, and many, many more.

CNA's role in decision making and involvement in programs of the International Council of Nurses and other international agencies has increased significantly. For example, CNA hosted the 1969 ICN conference, which was attended by more than 10,000 nurses from 80 countries. At that time, CNA received monies from the Commonwealth Foundation in Britain to assist 40 nurses from developing countries to attend, but one of the requirements for receiving these funds was that CNA should help establish the Commonwealth Nurses Foundation. This was achieved in 1971, with CNA remaining closely involved in many Commonwealth projects.

CNA established an international affairs department in 1984 to manage its out-of-country projects. In 1990 CNA was involved in international projects in 14 countries: Zaire, Nepal, China, Mexico, Nicaragua, Tonga, El Salvador, Uganda, Bolivia, Thailand, Argentina, Peru, Belize, and Benin.

The provincial/territorial associations have become effective lobby groups in their own right. Using many of the approaches already identified (e.g., briefs to governments, position papers, advisory services, committee representation, liaison), they speak on health and social policy issues at the provincial level. These associations are also effective in advocating national messages within their jurisdictions. Using experience gained in lobbying for changes in the Canada Health Act and in provincial nursing statutes; they have, for example, each addressed various provincial and national issues. National unity, taxation (e.g., the Goods and Services Tax or GST), environmental issues, AIDS, care for the mentally ill, requirements for future nursing education, nursing shortages, and health services for the elderly are only a few of the many issues acted on by the provincial nurses' associations.

PROFESSIONAL ASSOCIATIONS AND COMMUNICATIONS

Communication with members, with governments and other agencies, and with the public is an important function of the professional nurses' associations. A public relations or information service officer in each of the associations helps coordinate activities related to the external communications, and many of the associations are especially concerned with how the image of the nurse is presented to the public. Most associations release specific documents outlining their services, and these are available at little or no charge.

The earliest, and still the most important, national communication medium within nursing in Canada is *The Canadian Nurse/L'infirmière canadienne*, published by the CNA. Due to an unusual set of circumstances, this national professional journal preceded the formation of the national association. In 1904, the Calgary Association of Graduate Nurses wrote to the Toronto Medical Society for advice about publishing a magazine for nurses. This inquiry was passed to the nursing alumnae association of the Toronto General Hospital, which formed a publications committee to explore the possibility of launching a journal (CNA, 1968). In 1905, the committee introduced the first issue of *The Canadian Nurse: A Quarterly Journal for the Nursing Profession in Canada*. Dr. Helen MacMurchy, a physician and supporter of nurses' causes, became its first editor on a part-time basis, having agreed to assume this responsibility provided a nurse-editor would be found before the end of the year. No one was found to take the job, however, and Dr. MacMurchy continued to edit the journal until 1911 (Gibbon and Mathewson, 1947).

The journal was intended to be self-supporting. The subscription rate for the first year was 50 cents, but the committee hoped to obtain $300 through advertising to cover costs of publication. By 1906, *The Canadian Nurse* was a monthly publication and the official means of communication for several graduate and alumnae associations, primarily in Ontario. In 1916, the national association bought the publication from the Toronto General alumnae for $2000, to cover outstanding costs and bills. An editorial proposal at that time stated that a subscription to the journal should be part of every nurse's fee to the provincial associations. It was not until 1950, however, that the New Brunswick association became the first to include a subscription rate as part of the annual membership fee.

By 1932 the increase in subscribers and the growth in the size of the journal resulted in appointment of a full-time editor/business manager. The first was Ethel Johns, a well-known nursing leader who held senior nursing positions in Manitoba, Ontario, and British Columbia before accepting international duties with the Rockefeller Foundation of New York.

In 1946, French-language assistant editors were hired, and the journal included some content in French, partly as a way to attract the provincial associations into including subscriptions as part of their annual fees. In 1959, a separate French-language journal, *L'infirmière canadienne*, was launched when the Quebec nurses' association supported mandatory subscriptions for its members. In 1965, each magazine had a full-time editor who functioned independently under the aegis of CNA's executive director. Then in 1985, when the Quebec association withdrew from CNA, it became necessary, for financial reasons, to again combine the two journals into one, now called *The Canadian Nurse/L'infirmière canadienne*.

The influence of professional journals on nurses and nursing is difficult to measure precisely, but a survey of magazines over the years reveals that this major communication link assists in promoting new directions and new achievements in nursing. Until the 1950s however, there was a dearth of Canadian nursing publications other than *The Canadian Nurse*. Since then, there has been a rapid increase in numbers and in quality. The most significant journals or newsletters are published by the provincial/territorial nurses' associations (see box). Today these are a substantial link in communications among members. As well, most special interest groups have newsletters or journals.

Important professional journals in Canada now include *The Canadian Journal of Nursing Research* (launched as *Nursing Papers* by McGill University in 1968); the *Canadian Journal of Nursing Administration*, initiated in 1988 through the efforts of a group of senior administrators within the Academy of Chief Nurse Executives; and publications of the various nurses' unions. These and other Canadian nursing publications continue to report and influence nursing trends and issues. In 1991, there were more than 500 periodicals received at CNA's Library, of which 67 were Canadian nursing periodicals. Foreign and international nursing journals (e.g., the *International Nursing Review*, published by the International Council of Nurses) also enhance and enrich the understanding of today's nurses. The "Suggested List of Periodicals for Nurses for the Canadian Health Sciences Library," a list published by CNA, recommends more than 60 journals; many are available in the libraries of the national and provincial nurses' associations.

Professional Nurses' Association: Addresses and Journals

Address	Journal
Canadian Nurses Association (CNA) 50 The Driveway Ottawa, Ontario K2P 1E2	*The Canadian Nurse/L'infirmiére canadienne* (11 ×/year) Established 1905 (bilingual)
Registered Nurses Association of British Columbia (RNABC) 2855 Arbutus Street Vancouver, BC V6J 3Y8	*Nursing BC* (6 x/year) Established 1968; name change 1991
Alberta Association of Registered Nurses (AARN) 11620—168 Street Edmonton, AB T5M 4A6	*AARN Newsletter* (11 x/year) Established 1944
Saskatchewan Association of Registered Nurses (SRNA) 2066 Retallack St. Regina, SK S4T 2K2	*ConceRN* (6 x/year) Established 1917
Manitoba Association of Registered Nurses (MARN) 647 Broadway Winnipeg, MN R3C 0X2	*Nurscene* (5 x/year) Established 1975

Professional Nurses' Association: Addresses and Journals—cont'd

Address	Journal
Registered Nurses Association of Ontario (RNAO) 33 Prince St. Toronto, ON M4W 1Z2	*Registered Nurse Magazine* (4 x/year) Established 1989 *The RNAO News Tabloid* (4 x/year) Established 1988
Ordre des infirmiéres et infirmiers du Quebec (OIIQ) 4200, boul. Dorchester ouest Montreal, PQ H3Z 1V4	*Nursing Québec* (6 x/year) Established 1980 (bilingual)
Nurses Association of New Brunswick (NANB) 231 Saunders St. Fredricton, NB E3B 1N6	*Info* (5 x/year) Established 1969 (bilingual)
Registered Nurses Association of Nova Scotia (RNANS) 6035 Coburg Road Halifax, NS B3H 1Y8	*Nurse to Nurse* (6 x/year) Established 1960; name change 1990
Association of Nurses of Prince Edward Island (ANPEI) P.O. Box 1838 17 Pownal St. Charlottetown, PEI C1A 7N5	*ANPEI Update* (irregular) Established 1960
Association of Registered Nurses of Newfoundland (ARNN) P.O. Box 6116 55 Military Road St. John's, NF A1C 5X8	*ARNN News, News, News* (4 x/year) Established 1980
Northwest Territories Registered Nurses Association (NWT RNA) Box 2757 Yellowknife, NWT X1A 2R1	*Newsletter* (4 x/year)
Yukon Nurses Society (YNS) P.O. Box 5371 Whitehorse, YT Y1A 4Z2	*Yukon Nurses Society Newsletter* (irregular)

From personal communications with provincial and territorial associations June-August 1990.

POSSIBLE FUTURES

To achieve goals, people must work together. In Canada, nurses historically have used professional associations as a way to achieve better health care, high quality in nursing practice and nursing education, and mutual support for one another in a demanding profession.

Economic pressures of the 1990s will lead to positive and negative changes in nurses' roles and in the ways that nurses must work together for the benefit of the public and their own interests. Despite changes in the Canada Health Act, provincial nurses' associations have made relatively little progress in attempting to remove the physician as the sole "gatekeeper" to the health care system and so allow nurses and other health practitioners to provide services more economically. Politicians are still ignorant about the kinds of contributions that nurses can make to the health care system; nurses, through their professional associations, still have a major "selling" job in this area.

On the other hand, economic pressures might encourage nurses to advocate for nursing-operated community health delivery systems (nursing focused rather than medically focused). Nurses may once again provide more care in homes and in the community through health promotion programs. These matters must be explored and, if feasible, nurses will need to work together to achieve them (Mussallem, 1988).

The federal government may be decreasing its role in social and health care areas, leading to differences in the kinds and quality of health care offered in the provincial arenas. Nurses may wish to assume a leading role, through their professional associations, in urging promotion of national health objectives and, possibly, the establishment of a Canada Health Council. CNA is keeping abreast of these and other issues on the national scene.

Although there is a move to specialty organizations and new associations, many are duplicating activities that can be performed better by larger and more established professional associations. National and provincial professional associations have to be responsive to the needs of new groups and to welcome new organizations in ways that ensure the best interests of both can be maintained. Does the present model have sufficient flexibility to remain viable in the decades to come? This also is an issue that will be explored during the 1990s.

Nurses' unions, relative newcomers among nursing organizations, often are speaking out more strongly on any and all nursing issues. The rise of nurses' unions, which promote nurses' interests, has caused changes in the roles of the professional associations. The professional associations also must act in the public's interests and for the promotion of a better health care system. Some nurses fail to understand these distinct roles, want the professional associations to work in support of nurses' interests (e.g., wages and salary issues), and are disillusioned when they do not. As Jensen describes in Chapter 26, nurses' unions and nurses' professional associations have separate and overlapping roles, and the two need liaison, cooperation, and collaboration.

In some areas, governments, too, are confused about roles, and some threaten to remove administration of the nursing practice acts from the nurses' professional associations, as was done in Ontario. Although (as with any issue) opposing viewpoints must be considered, loss of responsibility for professional practice is a major issue and one on which nurses must be clear. Nurses must weigh pros and cons of having a government-administered licensing authority perform regulatory functions, as well as one or more unions and one or more voluntary professional associations all trying to speak for and about nursing and health care.

The present model is that of provincial or territorial professional associations that have as members all nurses registered for practice (in all but Ontario). These provincial and territorial associations are members of one large national professional association, which also includes representation for special interest nurses' groups. This model empowers the professional associations to speak with authority for and about nursing and health and social issues.

New trends, new issues, and new concerns related to health care and nursing will arise in the future. In the past, professional nurses' associations responded, changed, and adapted to meet needs of the public and nursing. However, individual nurses must understand and appreciate the important roles nurses' associations can obtain and must continue to work together. This is the basis for the preferred future role of professional nurses' associations.

REFERENCES

Adaskin, E.J. (1988). Organized political action: Lobbying by nurses' associations (pp.475-487). In A.J. Baumgart & J. Larsen, *Canadian nursing faces the future: Development and change* (1st ed.). Toronto: Mosby–Year Book, Inc.

Brick, M. (1964). *Forum and focus for the Junior College movement: The American Association of Junior Colleges.* New York: Teachers College, Columbia University.

Canadian Nurses Association. (1962). *Statement to the Royal Commission on Health Services.* Ottawa: Author.

Canadian Nurses Association. (1968). *The leaf and the lamp.* Ottawa: Author.

Canadian Nurses Association. (1980). *Putting health into health care.* Ottawa: Author.

Canadian Nurses Association. (1990). *Reports of biennial meetings 1981-1990.* Ottawa: Author.

Clay, T. (1987). *Nurses: Power and politics.* London: Heinemann.

Donahue, M.P. (1985). *Nursing, the finest art: An illustrated history.* Toronto: Mosby–Year Book, Inc.

Gibbon, J.M., & Mathewson, M.S. (1947). *Three centuries of Canadian nursing.* Toronto: Macmillan.

Hall, E.M. (1980). *Canada's national-provincial health program for the 1980's: A commitment for renewal.* Ottawa: National Health and Welfare.

Lord, A.R. (1952). *Report of the evaluation of the Metropolitan School of Nursing.* Ottawa: Canadian Nurses Association.

Mussallem, H.K. (1960). *Spotlight on nursing education.* Ottawa: Canadian Nurses Association.

Mussallem, H.K. (1988). Prevention and patterns and of disease: Prospects and research directions in nursing for the future. *Recent Advances in Nursing, 22:* 147-162.

Parrott, E.G. (1989). The move to criterion-referenced testing. *The Canadian nurse/L'infirmière canadienne* 85(10), 25-26.

Professional liability: A successful year of self-protection for Canadian nurses. (1989). *The Canadian Nurse,* 85(5), 26-29.

Stewart, I., & Austin, A. (1962). *A history of nursing* (5th ed.). New York: G.P. Putnam's Sons.

Styles, M.M. (1986). *Report on "The regulation of nursing."* Geneva: International Council of Nurses.

The Canadian Nurse/L'infirmière canadienne. Vols. 1-86, 1905-1990. Ottawa: Canadian Nurses Association.

Weir, G.M. (1932). *Survey of nursing education in Canada.* Toronto: University of Toronto Press.

Leadership is a complex and elusive quality, but Canadian nurses have been fortunate in having strong leaders for their professional associations. This photograph shows leaders of the Canadian Nurses Association (CNA) and the Canadian Association of University Schools of Nursing (CAUSN) during a 1991 meeting to discuss joint concerns. Left to right: Jeannette Bouchard, CAUSN executive director, Fernande Harrison, CNA president-elect, Judith Oulton, CNA executive director, Jenniece Larsen, CAUSN president, and Alice Baumgart, CNA president.

CHAPTER TWENTY-SIX

Leadership and the Leaders of the Canadian Nurses Association

DOROTHY MEILICKE, RN, MEd
JENNIECE LARSEN, RN, PhD

Dorothy Meilicke, RN, DHSA, MEd (Alberta), is Manager, Operational Commissioning, Cross Cancer Institute, Edmonton, and Assistant Professor, Faculty of Nursing, University of Alberta. She has long been interested in the contributions of nursing leaders, and her pioneering work on the biographies of the early presidents of the Canadian Nurses Association is available through the CNA Library.

Jenniece Larsen, RN, BScN, MEd, PhD (Alberta), is Professor and Director, School of Nursing, University of Manitoba. Throughout her career she has held a variety of elected and appointed leadership positions, and leadership, especially of female-dominated groups, is a special scholarly interest. Recently, she chaired the Symposium Steering Committee for the National Nursing Symposium sponsored by the Council of Ministers of Health for the provinces and territories.

The presidents of the Canadian Nurses Association (CNA) are a unique group of Canadian nurses. Since the association was formed in 1908, these 36 elected leaders have made strong and timely contributions to nursing and to health care in Canada and, in many instances, throughout the world. An analysis of their contributions helps illuminate how social, political, and economic circumstances shape events and their consequences, and study of their lives and the issues they selected for attention will provide important insights about the qualities Canadian nurses sought when choosing elected leaders.

This chapter introduces these 36 nurses—of necessity, briefly. The opening part of the chapter offers a reflection on the current thinking about leadership and leaders. The remainder of the chapter identifies major nursing and health issues of the times as reflected in the inaugural addresses of these presidents of the Canadian Nurses Association.

LEADERSHIP AND LEADERS

There is no shortage of thinking about leadership, doing research in the field, writing articles and books on the topic, pontificating at symposiums of learned colleagues, or producing snippets of wisdom on network television business programs. There is no shortage of experts on leadership. There is no shortage of enthusiasts who have read every business best seller in the last decade and have the complete works of management experts Peter Drucker and Tom Peters in their personal libraries. However, there is a shortage of leadership in practice: leadership observed, leadership experienced, leadership felt. In probably no field does the old saw apply more appropriately: everybody talks about leadership and no one does anything about it. Leadership is likely the most commonly used word used in any organization, but its presence is indeed elusive.

This is not to imply that the study of leadership is without merit, but only to indicate that, in spite of the abundant work in the field, leadership is only partly understood. This accounts for the predominance of highly abstracted conclusions on leadership. For example, writers in scholarly journals (Burns, 1984; Helgesen, 1990) assert that leaders share many qualities, such as the abilities to create a vision, communicate this vision, be focused, and empower others. However, this may be no more instructive than being told that comprehensive and extensive research on ballet concludes that success as a prima ballerina appears to be a function of strength, coordination, and an affinity for music. Surely there must be more substance to the concept of leadership than this.

Furthermore, Minzberg (1989) argues that our understanding of leadership is sufficiently flawed that when someone is trained to be a leader, in a business program, for example, the result is usually not a leader but an organizational mechanic obsessed with numbers and formal planning systems. Others take similar positions. Kotter (1985) contends that organizations often promote those who excel in a technical role and then, to the surprise of those who made the decision, find that this person, so skilled technically, continues to focus on this aspect of the job and fails miserably in the more complex and ambiguous aspects of leadership.

What should be concluded from the foregoing is not that the study of leadership is useless, but only that understanding is partial, and that much remains to be learned. Thus the field of leadership is less like that of biology, for example, in which new developments occur almost daily, and more like that of archeology or astronomy, in which progress is slow and conclusions tentative. Moreover, leadership study is a field in which new concepts look suspiciously like established paradigms but carry new names.

Leadership is surely among the most complex and elusive of qualities. But elusive is not the same as unobtainable. Bennis (1989a), who has written extensively on the topic, argues that learning to lead is a lot easier than is usually thought because each person has the capacity for leadership. Bennis believes that the process of becoming a leader is the same process as becoming an integrated human being. In taking this position, Bennis is attempting to demystify leadership. Nevertheless, Bennis (1989b) also argues that an individual in a leadership role all too often learns that the trivial drives out the important. A person in a leadership position can be so inundated with detail and with the day-to-day demands of the job that she or he is unable to rise above the mundane and respond to the significant and the long-range and to forge the vision. Thus while creating the vision may be the defining image of the leader, it is first necessary to get beyond personally managing every detail, solving every problem, and resolving every crisis.

In the mid-1970s, Carlisle (1976) interviewed more than 100 executives to determine to what extent these executives actually used participative management techniques with their subordinates. Most of those interviewed claimed to be participative, but Carlisle saw little tangible evidence to support these contentions. However, the last person interviewed, a Canadian whom Carlisle called McGregor, developed a method to delegate that ensured that the trivial never drove out the important. McGregor always had the time and energy to do his job for the simple reason that he refused to get involved in decisions that subordinates were being paid to make. He would assist each new subordinate in developing a generic problem solving strategy, but from then on they were on their own. He met with each subordinate individually once a week for a performance review and also once a week with them as a group. The result of this system was that McGregor's subordinates developed more skills and were more likely to be promoted than comparable-level executives in other plants in the company. As for McGregor, this system of delegation ensured that he had time to think, plan, and do his own job.

Release from a smothering amount of detail is only the first step. The next step is articulating a vision. Vision is increasingly perceived as an outcome of an intuitive rather than rational process. Minzberg (1989) believes that formal planning systems are clearly inferior to intuition in making complex decisions. Other recent exponents of intuition as a higher level of decision making than rational systems are Agor (1989) and Etzioni (1989), who assert that the complexity of the processes, especially with fragmentary information, requires less structured cognitive approaches.

In a recently completed study entitled *The Charismatic Leader: Behind the mystique of exceptional leadership*, Conger (1989) postulates that charismatic leaders move through the following four stages:

1. Sensing opportunity and formulating a vision
2. Articulating the vision so that it satisfies higher and lower order needs
3. Building trust in the vision
4. Achieving the vision of a desirable future state

Leadership, if Conger is correct, requires the cognitive power to sense opportunity and formulate a vision; the rhetorical ability to use metaphor, anecdote, and repetition and rhythm; the human insight and skill to enroll others into the vision; and the organizational ability to bring the vision to fruition. That few have high-level cognitive power, rhetorical ability, human insight, and organizational ability is obvious. And yet some examples can be found.

Perhaps the best contemporary example of a charismatic female leader is former British Prime Minister Margaret Thatcher. Whatever one thinks of her politics or her style, there is no question of this woman's impact. Apply the four qualities of leadership articulated by Conger. Mrs. Thatcher certainly formulated her vision of a more market-oriented economy as a replacement for a government regulated and managed economy. She had sufficient power to win an unprecedented three majority governments. She probably faltered in the application of human insight to further her goals. However, the fourth quality, the ability to implement, was demonstrated at a high level, a function of Mrs. Thatcher's incredible will and purpose.

Conger believes that much of what makes a great charismatic leader can be taught. As previously stated, so does Bennis. Each of us, or at least many of us, can be taught to communicate more dynamically, to understand people more insightfully, and to implement more successfully. What remains is vision, the key concept.

If leadership were reduced to its fundamental core, what would emerge is vision. This observation is supported by recent studies on leadership such as *Leadership and Innovation* by Doig and Hargrove (1987), *Making a Leadership Change* by Gilmore (1988), and *Thriving on Chaos* by Peters (1987). Vision may be, despite Conger's belief, the one element that cannot be taught. Vision is a high-level cognitive activity that is not well understood and thus cannot be easily taught. However, vision can be observed, and what can be observed can be learned.

Vision is not a common commodity. The power of vision is achieved by only a few. For every Beethoven there are many Bellinis, Borodins, and Bizets, but, in every field, visionaries exist. And visionaries can be studied, firsthand if possible, but usually at a distance in time or space. Studies need to focus on what makes visionaries different, what makes them special, what makes them visionaries. Students of leadership should endeavor to learn everything possible: Where do leaders obtain ideas? How do they process information? How do they make decisions? How do they communicate ideas?

Little study of elected leaders of voluntary professional associations in Canada has been undertaken, yet these leaders have a crucial role in the Canadian political process, articulating the viewpoints of the members of their associations to elected officials, senior bureaucrats, and the public at large. In this political process, the presidents of the Canadian Nurses Association have the opportunity to shape the direction of public policy in various sectors, including health, higher education, and women's issues, as well as policy within the nursing professions. They are what Welsh (1979) describes as "political elites"—individuals who actively participate in or influence major policy decisions.

Knowledge about leaders shapes the image of what future leaders should be like. The nursing profession provides hundreds of extremely significant opportunities to hone leadership skills, as well as to function as leaders at the institutional, local, provincial, national, and international levels. However, there is no research about Canada's nursing elite similar to the studies of contemporary influentials in American nursing by Vance (1977, 1986) and Kinsey (1986). These studies reveal that the elite in American nursing were drawn primarily from academic settings, earned graduate degrees (usually a doctorate), and were active in research and scholarly activities. These nursing leaders had well-developed communication skills and often used these skills for political purposes such as letter writing, lobbying, and testifying at hearings concerning public policy issues. Since advocates of revisionist history submit severe critiques of the actions of earlier generations of nursing leaders, future research about Canada's nursing leaders must be grounded in social context, which would aid a better understanding of the prominent issues and the directions chosen by the leaders (Melosh, 1982; Reverby, 1987). Mansell's (1991) ongoing study of leadership patterns in Canadian nursing beween 1919 and 1949 is an example.

Limited study of female leaders, especially female leaders of female dominant groups, has been undertaken. The available research suggests that more similarities than differences exist in actual leadership behavior between male and female leaders. Where differences occur, they are a function of the work culture and tasks to be performed, the size of the organization, the self-confidence of the leader and the unequal ratio between the sexes in the workplace, not gender differences (Epstein, 1988; Eagly and Johnson, 1990). However, Vance (1986) argues that women leaders are often still regarded as deviants in that they do not conform to commonly accepted cultural images of women. A successful female leader usually must be a role breaker and is often an outsider within groups.

Among the traditional methods used to study leaders are analysis of biographical data (family histories and career patterns) and the analysis of the leaders' communications (speeches and papers). Social scientists consider communications to be an essential part of the leadership process.

The balance of this chapter is based on Meilicke's ongoing study of the roles and contributions of the 36 CNA presidents who held office up to and including 1990 to 1992. It provides analysis of their presidential addresses with regard to the major policy issues they identified and the central values that they espoused. In the conclusion, the question of their leadership is discussed.

PRESIDENTIAL ISSUES AND VALUES

In 1990, the Canadian Nurses Association elected its thirty-sixth president. The first was Mary Agnes Snively. She helped found the Canadian National Association for Trained Nurses (CNATN) in 1908, partly as a result of a letter from Ethel G. Bedford Fenwick, president of the National Council of Nurses of Great Britain and Ireland. Fenwick urged that Canadian nurses establish a national organization of nurses in Canada to affiliate with the International Council of Nurses (Snively, 1908, p. 527). The name of the organization was changed to the Canadian Nurses Association in 1924 (CNA, 1957, p. 4).

Annual general meetings of the Association were held from 1911 to 1922 (with the exception of 1915, because of demands of the First World War). Since 1922, biennial conventions have been held (CNA, 1968, p. 79); on alternate years, an annual meeting is held but with limited attendance. From 1911 to the present (with the exception of 1926, which was devoted to the unveiling of a War Memorial for nurses who served in the 1914-1918 World War), the incumbent president delivered a presidential address, and most were then published, in whole or in part, in *The Canadian Nurse*.

In 1969, Dr. Charlotte Whitton, former mayor of the City of Ottawa, donated a beautiful gold chain of office to the Association. It consists of a double chain, connected by gold bars, that is joined to a center medallion. Each gold bar is engraved with the name of a past president. The center medallion portrays the CNA logo on the front, and the names of three nurses are inscribed on the back: Jean Gunn, Gertrude M. Bennett, and Agnes M. McLeod (Charbonneau, 1983). These three nurses were personal friends of Dr. Whitton, and their contributions to the nursing profession had earned great respect. The passing of the CNA chain of office from the outgoing president to the incoming president has become a symbolic ceremony at the inaugural proceedings of the biennial general meetings.

Who were these 36 past presidents? What issues concerned them? The major source of data to answer these questions is in the complete volumes of *The Canadian Nurse*, the official journal of the CNA. Unfortunately, the full text of every address has not been recorded, and a few were extensively edited. Helen H. Carpenter's 1962 presidential address, for example, was not published and limited coverage was provided of several addresses in the late 1970s and early 1980s. Similar difficulties were encountered in collecting biographical information. The available information is often fragmentary and occasionally contradictory. Several volumes of *The Canadian Who's Who* and *Who's Who in Canada* provide valuable data about some presidents. Additional information was obtained from the CNA archives, as well as from various provincial nurses associations, hospitals, and individual nurses.

The themes of the presidential address fall rather naturally into five eras, which are characterized by distinct professional issues and social, economic, and political developments in Canada. These eras span the time periods from 1908 to 1928, from 1928 to 1946, from 1946 to 1970, from 1970 to 1988, and the current era, which began in 1988.

The first era, 1908 to 1928, was characterized by issues related to the development of a national association within the context of events associated with World War I. The second era, 1928 to 1946, emphasized issues related to the development of national standards for nursing education within the constraints imposed by the Great Depression and, later, World War II. The third era, 1946 to 1970, was distinguished by issues related to the re-examination of nursing as a profession within the context of extensive developments in the scope of provincial and national social programs. The fourth era, 1970 to 1988, focused on issues related to the improvement of standards for professional nursing practice, as well as developing a proactive role for the Canadian Nurses Association in stimulating nursing research and shaping the health care system within the context of a strong economy and major advances in the complexity of medical technology. In the new era, beginning in 1988, issues related to the reformation of nurses' working environments within a broader social climate of concern about women's issues and the global environment are being addressed.

For each of these eras, a content analysis of the presidential addresses was undertaken. Dominant issues and values contained in the addresses were identified, and representative samples are discussed in this chapter. Following Emerson's observation that "there is properly no history; only biography," each era is accompanied by a table containing a thumbnail sketch of each president and a summary of the predominant issues expressed in her address (see Table 26-1).

THE FIRST ERA: 1908 TO 1928

Events of the first era related primarily to development of a national professional association, standardization of nursing education, and the struggle to meet the demands placed on the nursing profession by the First World War (1914-1918).

One of the major issues discussed by Mary Agnes Snively in her presidential address to the first meeting of the Canadian National Association of Trained Nurses in 1911, and referred to by Mary Ardcronie MacKenzie in her 1913 address, was the need to ensure that all graduate nurses were registered provincially and affiliated with the national nursing association. The national association worked with provincial nursing groups to obtain the required legislation. Snively observed in 1911:

> Given unity among nurses, and a thoroughly intelligent understanding on their part of all that registration involves, together with the sympathy and co-operation of an enlightened public, and the cause of registration cannot fail of accomplishment in the near future in our fair Dominion. (p. 397)

Another early issue was the establishment of formal affiliation with the International Council of Nurses and amalgamation of linkages with many nursing groups in Canada such as the Canadian Superintendents Society, District and Public Health Nurses, and Social Service Workers (MacKenzie, 1913).

Sharley Bryce-Brown was president when *The Canadian Nurse* journal was purchased for $2000 in 1916. Individual yearly subscriptions to the journal were $2.00. Bryce-Brown believed this journal could provide a much-needed means of communication to achieve unity of purpose, unity of understanding, and unity of effort. It is poignant that what now seems to be a modest sum of money was a matter of major concern regarding this extremely important move. Bryce-Brown noted in her 1916 presidential address:

> Two thousand dollars may seem an exorbitant price, but you must remember that we could not start a magazine for that sum. I think it is well worth $2,000.00 to us. (p. 516)

In 1914, Mary Ardcronie MacKenzie urged nurses to publicly promote the development of hospitals financed by municipalities, especially in Western Canada. In 1918, Jean Gunn urged the development of a national public health policy and advocated that nurses should be trained for roles in the prevention of illness. Edith MacPherson Dickson, in her 1922 presidential address, promoted a book on home nursing and on the organization of private duty nurses. As early as 1921, Edith

Dickson urged members to review the potential effect of a proposed state medicine plan.

The presidents in this era strove to improve the standards for nursing education, stressing the need for a balanced education for nurses. In 1913 and again in 1914, Mary Ardcronie MacKenzie strongly suggested that teachers of nurses be adequately trained. She observed that Canadian nursing needed to:

> Forget the past mistakes and start a system of nursing education on proper educative lines, establish schools, the "raison d'être" of which will be the education of the nurse in all branches of nursing. . . . Let us have the teachers of our nurses trained in the teaching of nurses, and let us desist from compelling nurse students to cut themselves off from all of the ordinary means of culture while they are training. This will cost more money, and it is time it did, but in the end it will be more economical, because it will make for more efficient service and for better satisfied workers. (MacKenzie, 1914, p. 562)

Further, as a result of municipal funding schemes, which began in Saskatchewan in 1916 (Meilicke and Storch, 1980), an increased number of hospitals were built, and many, including even very small hospitals, attempted to train nurses. Many students gave more in service than they received in training, and this led to variations in the qualifications of graduates. Presidents continued to express concerns about educational standards.

The dominant event of the time, World War I, prompted a concern about the health of Canadians. This was translated by Sharley Bryce-Brown (1914-1917) and Jean Gunn (1917-1920) into a concern for raising money to help support soldiers and nurses overseas during the War. Work for the Red Cross during the war years was given a higher priority than other Association objectives, and Jean Browne (who became president in 1922) became known to thousands of school children as the "Red Cross Lady" through her war-time work with the Junior Red Cross.

With the war over, attention turned to other matters, and Jean Gunn, in 1919, focused on the need for nurses at home, because of the War and the recent flu epidemic:

> I think one drawback to the progress of nursing in Canada, and every other country, is the indifference on the part of the public. When they have illness they want a nurse. They have never been particularly interested as to where that nurse came from, how she was trained, or what her living conditions were, etc. Now the whole attention has been turned to nursing conditions of our country, and the public begins to realize that we need a great many reforms. (p. 1920)

Developing an adequate response to the demand for nurses was complicated by the absence of a national registry of nurses for emergency services. Jean Gunn (1920) questioned whether enrollment for emergency services should be federal or provincial, and during Edith Dickson's 1920 to 1922 presidency, the need for "dominion registration" was also first raised.

The first era concluded with a national association firmly in place and improvements in nursing education under way. Affiliation in the International Council of Nurses was accomplished, legislation for registration of nurses was in effect in most provinces, the official journal of the association was operational, and membership in the CNA had significantly increased. The survey on nursing education, first proposed by MacKenzie in 1913 but not initiated until 1927 during Mabel Gray's term of office, was progressing (the "Weir Report"). This was eventually to provide challenge and direction for future presidents. While pursuing the resolution of these pressing issues, the presidents also endeavored to inspire the members by stressing the importance of self-sacrifice, vision, and loyalty to duty. MacKenzie's comments in 1914 are representative of the values that were espoused:

> Have vision, have faith in the vision, and others will see and believe. Never before were we so much in need of high ideals, never before was there so pressing a call for well-trained, well-poised workers in the field of nursing. What shall we do with that need? What with that call? From you must come the answer, followed by action. (pp. 562-563)

TABLE 26-1 Canadian National Association for Trained Nurses
Canadian Nurses Association: Presidents 1908-1928

President and term of office	Position at time of office	Birth/death	Education
Mary Agnes Snively 1908-1912	Lady Superintendent, Toronto General Hospital	Born: St. Catharines, Ontario, November 12, 1847, to Martin and Susan Snively Died: September 26, 1933	1884: Graduate, Bellevue Training School, New York

Issues: • Affiliation with International Council of Nurses • Unity among nurses • Registration of nurses • Health teaching (principles of right living to Canadians) • Archives • Reference library • Role of nurses in developing social service organizations

Mary Ardcronie MacKenzie 1912-1914	Chief Superintendent, Victorian Order of Nurses (VON), Ottawa	Born: Toronto, Ontario Died: Victoria, British Columbia, April 6, 1948	1892: BA, Toronto 1901: Graduate, Massachusetts General Hospital Training School of Nurses, Boston

Issues: • Registration of nurses • Unity among nurses • Organ of the Nursing Profession • Formation of committee to study nurse-training • Amalgamation of Canadian Superintendents Society with CNATN • Amalgamation of District, Public Health Nurses, and Social Service Workers with CNATN • Involvement in social issues • Review of hospital systems • Nurses trained to teach • Nurse education on proper educational basis • Preparation of nurses for the broad preventive campaign • Involvement in current social issues • Hospitals financed by municipalities • Hospitals managed by an elected Board • Funds for Florence Nightingale Memorial

---

Adapted from Meilicke, D.T. (1981). *CNA Presidents, 1908-1980: Beginning biographies and presidential themes.* Unpublished manuscript. (Available from CNA Library, Canadian Nurses Association, Ottawa.) *Continued.*

TABLE 26-1 Canadian National Association for Trained Nurses
Canadian Nurses Association: Presidents 1908-1928—cont'd

President and term of office	Position at time of office	Birth/death	Education
Sharley P. (Wright) Bryce-Brown 1914-1917	Charge of School of Nursing, New Westminster Hospital, British Columbia	Born: Toronto, Ontario, 1878 Died: New Westminster, British Columbia, 1944	1904: Graduate, Farrand Training School of Nurses, Harper Hospital, Detroit

Issues: • Purchase of *The Canadian Nurse* • Incorporation of CNATN • Affiliation with Canadian National Council of Women • Funds for soldiers • Promotion of CNATN membership • Priority of war demands • Priority of Red Cross work • Proper salary for editor of *The Canadian Nurse*

Jean I. Gunn 1917-1920	Superintendent of Nurses, Toronto General Hospital	Born: Belleville, Ontario, February 11, 1882 Died: Toronto, Ontario, June 28, 1941	1905: Graduate, Presbyterian Hospital School of Nursing, New York

Issues: • Demand for nurses overseas • Increasing nursing supply without lowering professional standards • Solicit government assistance to meet nursing crisis • Future preparedness of CNATN to meet war demands • Participation in women's organizations • A plan for future national emergencies • Teaching citizenship to foreign population • Input into national policy on public health • Increase supply of nurses to accommodate national welfare plan • 8-hour day for nurses • Support for scholarship in Training School Administration • Special education for administration

Edith MacPherson Dickson 1920-1922	Lady Superintendent of Nurses, Hospital for Consumptives, Weston, Ontario	Born: Belleville, Ontario Died: Ontario, 1967	1905: Graduate, Toronto General Training School

Issues: • CNATN and the BNA Act • Effective nursing service to all people • Review provincial plans for state medicine • CNATN nursing education committee • Decline of nursing ethics • War memorial • Promotion of private duty nurses group • Participation at conventions • Sponsorship of book on Home Nursing

TABLE 26-1 **Canadian National Association for Trained Nurses**
Canadian Nurses Association: Presidents 1908-1928—cont'd

President and term of office	Position at time of office	Birth/death	Education
Jean E. Browne (Thomson) 1922-1926	National Director, Junior Red Cross Society, Toronto Editor, *Canadian Red Cross Junior*	Born: Parkhill, Ontario, May, 1885 Died: Regina, Saskatchewan, October 7, 1973	Toronto Normal School 1911: Graduate, Toronto General Hospital 1920-1921: Postgraduate, King's College for Women, U. of London, England

Issues: • Amalgamation of Canadian Association of Nursing Education with CNATN • Narrow versus broad professionalism • Outside consultants

President and term of office	Position at time of office	Birth/death	Education
Flora Madeline Shaw 1926-1927	Director, School for Graduate Nurses, McGill University, Montreal	Born: Perth, Ontario, January 15, 1864 Died: Liverpool, England, August 17, 1927	1896: Graduate, Training School for Nurses, Montreal General Hospital 1906: Diploma (Teaching), Teachers College, Columbia

Issues: • (No presidential address, deceased in office in 1927)

President and term of office	Position at time of office	Birth/death	Education
Mabel Gray (Acting) 1927-1928	Assistant Professor of Nursing, Department of Nursing and Health, UBC, Vancouver	Born: Brampton, Ontario, 1880 Died: August, 1976	1907: Graduate, Winnipeg General Hospital 1920: PHN, Simmons College, Boston 1927: Studies with Teachers College, Columbia

Issues: • Proposed study of Nursing • Enrollment of nurses under Red Cross • ICN Montreal, 1929 • CNA membership via provincial associations • Financial instability of *The Canadian Nurse*

THE SECOND ERA: 1928 TO 1946

Events of the second era concerned the oversupply of nurses at the beginning and a shortage at the end of the era, the recommendations of the Survey on Nursing Education, and the demands imposed on the profession by World War II (1939-1945) (see Table 26-2).

When the Canadian economy collapsed in the Great Depression of 1929 and the 1930s, the presidents of the Canadian Nurses Association sought ways to reduce the consequent unemployment of many nurses. In this context, Mabel Hersey (1930) advocated increasing the entrance requirement to schools of nursing:

> We should give thoughtful consideration to the demands that the practice of nursing makes today on education. One important national aim should be to encourage a uniform system of nursing education: at present there is no uniformity. Universities have practically the same entrance requirements and the same standards in their work; if we examine nursing education we find by our Provincial Registration Acts, one Province requires one year high school, another two. The entrance requirements to our schools of nursing should be the same; a uniformity that will raise, not lower, the standard of nursing. . . . High entrance requirements will not stop the most desirable class of women from entering the profession, but will encourage the best. (p. 464)

Another solution was proposed by Florence Emory in 1934 when she promoted the increased employment of graduate nurses in hospitals; student nurses were the main nursing work force at this time. The absence of meaningful progress toward medical insurance plans impelled Ruby Simpson, in 1936, to work for the establishment of community nursing service bureaux as a means of providing care to the large numbers of people who could not afford hospital care but required skilled nursing services. The bureaux would supply nurses for work in the home at varying times of the day.

While attempting to reduce the number of new graduates from hospital schools of nursing, the presidents also stressed the need for immediate action on the long-awaited recommendations of the Survey of Nursing Education in Canada (Weir, 1932). This report advocated that nursing education should be incorporated into the general education system of the country and should be paid for by government funds. Other recommendations were for an upgraded and uniform nursing curriculum, for increased entrance requirements, and for minimum standards established for hospitals accepting nursing students. These standards, as remarkable as they may seem today, included the requisite that any hospital offering a nursing training program should have a minimum of 75 beds, with an average occupancy of at least 50 patients, and should be "properly equipped" (Cameron, 1932, p. 401).

In 1936 and 1938, Ruby Simpson advanced a remarkably prescient series of ideas that included schools of nursing separate from hospitals, implementation and further study of the proposed new curriculum, and the concept of nursing research. In regard to research, she suggested CNA should have a seat on the National Research Council's committee to review medical research. She wrote:

> What of research in nursing? Should we have a place in the National Research Council under the Committee recently appointed for medical research work? What of our attitude to Schools of Nursing separate from hospitals? There is no question as to our interest, but what of our responsibility? (Simpson, 1938, p. 415)

In 1939, members of the Canadian Nurses Association once again prepared to respond to the impact of a world war. Grace Fairley was installed as president in 1938, and in 1940 she was appointed Matron-in-Chief of the nursing corps of the Royal Canadian Army. The Association was concerned about the increased demands for nurses in national service during 1938 and 1939. In her 1942 address responding to the demand for nurses at home and abroad during the war, Fairley stressed the need for active recruitment programs and for nursing refresher courses for inactive nurses. She also was concerned with the need to maintain stability and standards of nursing services during the war years. She noted that:

> The cry from each province is shortage of nurses and turnover of personnel which is threatening the very stability of the services we are endeavouring to maintain. From some quarters also, we hear of a falling off of recruits, and that naturally causes anxiety. Our responsibility lies further ahead than today or the duration of the war—it must give assurance of our share in the health programme of the Dominion three, five, ten years from now—hence our responsibility for recruitment. (Fairley, 1942, p. 612)

As well, she was concerned about the hardships experienced by nurses who participated in the war effort and especially those who had become prisoners of war. She reported that:

> Outstanding in the Association's efforts to meet its responsibilities and obligations was the establishment of a relief fund for British Civilian nurses. . . . we have contacted the Australian Nurses' Association requesting they let us know if there is any need of interned or imprisoned nurses on the Eastern front that is not being met. Also, through the Red Cross, parcels have been sent to Hong Kong and Singapore with the hope that they may reach some of our sisters there. (Fairley, 1942, p. 613)

The second era, which began with a surplus of nurses, closed with a national nursing shortage. Marion Lindeburgh, in 1944, and Fanny Munroe, in 1946, discussed the use of nonprofessional workers to fill the gap in the nursing shortage. Munroe also argued that attention must be paid to the conditions of nurse employment. She felt there was a need for portable pension plans, a new "attitude" about summer vacations, and a review of the hours nurses worked in the hospital each week. Lindeburgh, in 1944, was concerned about the supply side of the equation and noted that there was a shortage of well-prepared instructors for schools of nursing; she advocated seeking government grants to prepare nursing instructors and nursing administrators.

During this era, the presidents worked to strengthen the national association by ensuring the viability of the national journal and planning for national registration. The first full-time editor and business manager, Ethel Johns, was appointed in 1933. In 1934, Florence Emory stressed that *The Canadian Nurse* could and ought to become self-supporting through subscriptions, and Ruby Simpson, in 1936, actively promoted a growth in personal subscriptions to *The Canadian Nurse* by individual nurses. A plan for nation-wide registration of nurses, introduced by Edith Dickson in the early 1920s, was being studied (Simpson, 1938, p. 413).

A dominant value during this era was the importance of positive thinking to solve the terrible problems created by the Great Depression and World War II. Marion

Lindeburgh, in her presidential address of 1944, exemplified these values in her observation:

> The attitude of the defeatist has no place in the nursing world today. The positive approach towards accomplishments must characterize the functions of administration, teaching and supervision, if we are going to surmount the problems which at first sight appear to be too difficult to solve. (p. 614)

TABLE 26-2 Canadian Nurses Association: Presidents 1928-1946

President and term of office	Position at time of office	Birth/death	Education
Mabel F. Hersey 1928-1930	Superintendent of Nurses; Director, School of Nursing, Royal Victoria Hospital, Montreal	Born: Ontario, 1872 Died: December, 1943	1905: Graduate, Royal Victoria Hospital, Montreal

Issues: • Increased demand on hospitals • Overproduction of nurses • Unemployment of private duty nurses • Nursing entrance requirements • Additional funds for Survey of Nursing Education

Florence H. M. Emory 1930-1934	Assistant Director, School of Nursing, University of Toronto	Born: Niagara Falls, Ontario, April, 1889, to Reverend Vernon and Margaret Emory Died: October, 1987	1915: Graduate, Grace Hospital, Toronto 1933: Postgraduate Study, Simmons College, Massachusetts Institute of Technology

Issues: • Review of Survey Education Report • Challenges of the Survey • Compass for the future • Reduce number of nurses graduating • Increase graduate nurses in hospitals • Establish community nursing bureaux • Establish committee on Health Insurance and Nursing Service • Self-supporting *The Canadian Nurse* • Funds for Florence Nightingale Memorial

Ruby E. Simpson 1934-1938	Director, Public Health Nursing Service, Saskatchewan Department of Public Health, Regina	Born: Neepawa, Manitoba, 1888 Died: Victoria, August 5, 1977	Winnipeg Normal School 1919: Graduate, Winnipeg General Hospital

Adapted from Meilicke, D.T. (1981). *CNA Presidents, 1908-1980: Beginning biographies and presidential themes.* Unpublished manuscript. (Available from CNA Library, Canadian Nurses Association, Ottawa.)

TABLE 26-2 **Canadian Nurses Association: Presidents 1928-1946—cont'd**

President and term of office	Position at time of office	Birth/death	Education
Ruby E. Simpson—cont'd			1924: Summer Course, Columbia University 1928: Rockefeller Travel Fellowship in the United States

Issues: • Community service preparation for nurses • Organization of nursing service to serve community • Study new curriculum for schools of nursing • Promote *The Canadian Nurse* membership • Nursing autonomy • Dominion registration • Advanced nursing education • Research in nursing • Experiment with separate schools of nursing • Funds for Florence Nightingale Foundation • Curriculum trial review

President and term of office	Position at time of office	Birth/death	Education
Grace Mitchell Fairley 1938-1942	Director of Nursing; Principal, School of Nursing, Vancouver General Hospital	Born: Scotland, 1882 Died: British Columbia, 1969	1905: Graduate, School of Nursing, Swansea General Hospital 1908: Postgraduate Studies, Isolation Hospitals

Issues: • War demands • Matron-in-Chief of army nurses • Nursing Districts for isolated areas • Refresher courses • Curriculum implementation • Recruitment of nurses • Stability of nursing services during war years • Maintenance of nursing standards

President and term of office	Position at time of office	Birth/death	Education
Marion Lindeburgh 1942-1944	Director and Associate Professor, School for Graduate Nurses, McGill University, Montreal	Born: Keetwa, Saskatchewan, 1888 Died: March 19, 1955	Regina Normal School 1919: Graduate, St. Lukes' Hospital, New York 1932: BSc, Columbia 1934: MA, Columbia

Issues: • Shortage of prepared instructors • Preparedness for developing social security schemes • Preparedness for health education schemes • Importance of postgraduate study • Development of nonprofessional workers • Government grants to prepare teachers and administrators of nurses

Continued.

TABLE 26-2 **Canadian Nurses Association: Presidents 1928-1946**

President and term of office	Position at time of office	Birth/death	Education
Fanny C. Munroe 1944-1946	Superintendent of Nurses; Director, School of Nursing, Royal Victoria Hospital, Montreal	Born: Woodstock, Ontario, April 24, 1888 Died: October 17, 1954	Collegiate Institute, Woodstock, Ontario Graduate, School of Nursing, Royal Victoria Hospital, Montreal Teachers College, Columbia

Issues: • Preparation of nonprofessional workers • Demand for nursing services • Unrest of bedside nurses • Portable pension plans • "New" attitude re summer vacations • Imbalance between hospital hours and public health hours • Public's right to expect service • Nurses' right to comfortable living

THE THIRD ERA: 1946 TO 1970

The third era was marked by issues related to a continued nursing shortage, which was exacerbated by the introduction of extensive provincial and national social programs (see Table 26-3). Efforts to streamline the corporate structure of the Canadian Nurses Association and to re-evaluate the concept of nursing as a profession were other prominent features of this era.

The initiation of the first government social program, the National Health Grants program, increased existing concerns regarding the nursing work force shortages and the quality of nursing education. Rae Chittick, in her 1948 address, observed:

> Federal and provincial governments were making extensive plans to improve the health of our people, yet these plans did not seem to include steps to increase the number in the nursing profession, nor to alter the character of their education to meet the changing pattern of health needs. (p. 704)

She also advocated reforming nursing education by linking nursing education to the general education system and by studying the result of the demonstration project at the school of nursing in Windsor, Ontario. The success of the Windsor concept, which showed that a staff nurse could be prepared in two years if the school controlled the program, was one of the factors that led the Association during Ethel Cryderman's presidency in 1948 to 1950 to endorse shortening the length of nursing education programs.

Another proposed solution to the nursing shortage, first suggested at the end of the second era, was the development of the nonprofessional worker. In 1948 and 1950, Presidents Rae Chittick and Ethel Cryderman addressed the need for expansion of enrollment in schools for nursing aides. Both leaders argued that this nonprofessional worker would save time and energy of the professional nurse. Chittick (1948) observed that:

> The public needs to know that poor nursing is not so much the result of the scarcity of nurses as the lack of other workers. Nurses are so hard pressed with routine and non-nursing tasks that the pleasure is being removed from the job of nursing; they are missing the joy of fine workmanship which comes with the art of nursing. (p. 707)

Cryderman (1950) notes that nursing time at work was being spent on clerical, secretarial, and housekeeping duties:

> This usurpation of time from legitimate duties is also causing considerable dissatisfaction and creating unrest among graduate nurses. The dissipation of nursing skills, which is affecting profoundly the amount of available professional nursing service, should be one of the major concerns of all those responsible for the provision of nursing care. (p. 696)

Both Chittick and Cryderman promoted a comprehensive national study of nursing that was concerned with recruitment, selection, employment, and the ongoing issues in the education of nurses. The need for this comprehensive study was supported by the Canadian Hospital Council (later the Canadian Hospital Association) and the Canadian Medical Association, but funding was not secured. The Department of National Health and Welfare did undertake a survey of the functions and activities of head nurses in general hospitals, and other surveys were undertaken by various provincial health authorities.

The nursing shortage continued to be a part of presidential agendas for the next several years. Helen McArthur, in her presidential address of 1952, noted that, even though the membership of the Canadian Nurses Association was more than 30,000, there was an estimated shortage of 8000 nurses to meet the demands for nursing service in institutions and agencies. She observed further that there was an acute shortage of qualified instructors for schools of nursing and that there were numerous withdrawals by students from the schools of nursing because of failure in their studies and for health-related reasons. McArthur pointed out that a Canadian Commission on Nursing had recently been appointed to study ways and means of improving the nursing situation. (It was composed of representatives from the Canadian Hospital Council, Canadian Medical Association, and the Canadian Nurses Association.) In this context, she complained that progress to implement the Weir Report had been slow. The essence of McArthur's agenda was expressed in her presidential address of 1954:

> Our great concern is that there should be sufficient nursing care available to reach all the people of Canada. We are seeking ways and means of correcting the conditions that prevent Canadians from receiving their rightful amount and quality of nursing service when and where they need it. (p. 702)

During the early 1950s, presidents turned their attention to the internal efficiency of its corporate structure. Helen McArthur's presidential address in 1954 focused on the theme "Measuring Progress." She stated:

> During the past few years, we have spent much time with our own association affairs—mainly because we have needed to stabilize our treasury, review and produce new machinery to make our association function adequately, and find the essential professional staff to develop our plans. Now it is time to sponsor a program of action. (p. 702)

A key part of the new machinery was the delegation of work to committees of the association. The committees were usually composed of members of the association both elected and nonelected. In 1952, a study committee, chaired by an external consultant, Dr. Pauline Jewett, recommended a reorganization of the committee structure into five standing committees. Gladys Sharpe supported change in her 1956 presidential address when she stated:

> Our organization is too large, our distances too great, and our meetings too brief to do more than plan for the work to be done, outline general policies for doing it and make final decisions. The work itself must be delegated to committees and, in certain instances, to subcommittees. (p. 598)

Trenna Hunter, in her 1958 presidential address, extended the internal assessment of the CNA by recommending that the association examine its external responsibilities to the individual nurse, to society in general, and to the profession itself. She also believed that an important role of the CNA was to act in an advisory capacity to government.

Interest in broader concerns was fueled by the spread of hospital insurance programs throughout the country, and Alice Girard, in her 1960 address, observed that the magnitude of the government plans necessitated re-evaluation of the objectives and strategies of the national association related to the nature of nursing. Recognizing the urgency of finding timely answers, the CNA formed a Research Committee. Girard, in her 1960 presidential address, notes:

> Most of the more urgent projects directed to the Research Committee hinged on such fundamental questions as: What is nursing? Is what we call professional nursing truly professional and, if not, what do we want it to be? What system of nursing education should we favor, and based on the findings, what changes are needed in nursing service? (p. 690-691)

The burgeoning activities of the Association, which stimulated an internal review and the reassessment of the mission, inevitably created financial problems. These became another major issue in the third era. One of the problems of the newly formed Research Committee was a lack of sufficient funds to carry out its mandate. Funds were required for new offices, and in 1964 Electa MacLennan urged the member associations to consider the need "to raise the walls and roof" (p. 859) of the CNA house in planning their various fund-raising activities nationally, provincially, and locally.

In her presidential address of 1966, Isobel MacLeod reiterated the issue of streamlining CNA's structure that had been ongoing in the previous few years. Part of the streamlining included setting up smaller executive committees that would meet frequently with professional staff so that policy decisions could be "put into action without delay" (p. 22). Concurrently, perhaps to counter any mood of emerging fiscal conservatism, she stressed that the budget of the CNA reflect the important values held by members of the organization:

> The way we spend our money will show the measure of our conviction. Underlying all plans for action is the budget. For too long we have tended to applaud those who spend little. This may have made sense in an earlier economy of scarcity. But, in today's affluent society, those who spend little usually accomplish little. (MacLeod, 1966, p. 22)

She noted that budget appropriations that seemed astronomical yesterday were a matter of course today. She underscored the importance of nursing speaking in "a strong united voice to interpret the place of the nurse in today's health programs and to win public support for its educational and service programs" (p. 22). In this statement, she echoed a quote from Katherine MacLaggan: "We are 80,000 members bonded together . . . and we have never tapped our resources" (Editor, 1967, p. 3).

This era also saw a reawakened interest in the terms and conditions of work, an issue that first emerged in the early 1940s. As early as 1958, the Association supported financial compensation for nurses who had increased educational preparation and work responsibilities. In 1958, Trenna Hunter argued that pension plans should be portable. The economic welfare of nurses was an important part of the presidential address of Isobel MacLeod in 1966, and during her presidency the Association approved the use of modern methods of collective bargaining.

Another long-standing issue resurfaced in the presidential addresses of this era: the integral relationship between education and the professionalization of nursing. In 1960, Alice Girard supported the recommendations of the CNA-sponsored project on evaluation of schools of nursing. This pilot project was conducted by Dr. Helen Mussallem (who replaced Pearl Stiver when she retired in 1963 as Executive Director of the Association). The report expressed concerns about the quality of schools of nursing in Canada and supported the concept of preparing nurses in less than three years (a position that was dramatically reversed in 1980). Girard also supported establishment of a nursing unit administration course in collaboration with the Canadian Hospital Association. Most nurses in administrative roles had no educational preparation for management positions in hospitals. This situation has improved only slightly since then and received renewed attention by the CNA in the mid-1980s. Electa MacLennan focused her 1964 address on educational issues surrounding professional preparation and argued for an improved educational milieu for the student nurse. She observes:

> The development of a profession is dependent upon its educational foundation. The problem of financing nursing education in hospital schools, which is the predominant pattern in Canada, presents a dichotomy of purpose that affects nursing education. . . . Education of professional nurses should be placed on a true professional basis. This will only be accomplished when schools are placed under the jurisdiction of institutions where both professional and cultural instruction are provided. (MacLennan, 1964, p. 860)

The main themes of the presidential addresses during this era were the calls for re-examination and introspection to improve the quality of nursing service. This is exemplified by Helen McArthur's observations in her 1952 presidential address:

> If we are to improve our service, we must periodically make an appraisal of our activities—both our achievements and our failures. . . . We must not walk backward into the future looking still at the way things were done in the past. (p. 543)

As the era ended, many nursing leaders felt that the period of introspection and re-examination, though valuable, ought to end. Verna Huffman, the keynote speaker at the 1970 convention, urged members to focus their attention "outward rather than inward, and to act on important national issues" ("Convention report," 1970, p. 24).

TABLE 26-3 **Canadian Nurses Association: Presidents 1946-1970**

President and term of office	Position at time of office	Birth/death	Education
Rae Chittick 1946-1948	Associate Professor of Education, University of Alberta, Calgary	Born: Burgoyne, Ontario, 1898 Died: Vancouver, January 27, 1992	Normal School 1922: Graduate, Johns Hopkins Hospital BSc, Columbia University, New York 1942: MA, Leland Stanford University, Palo Alta, California 1951: MPH, Harvard

Issues: • Nursing shortage • Nursing education geared to health nursing—not only nursing the sick • Appeals to federal government for assistance • Reform of nursing education system • Promote Director of Nursing position, Department of Health and Welfare • Facilitate nurses nursing • Study demonstration school in Windsor, Ontario • Expansion of nursing aide schools • Promotion of nursing education linked to general education • Promote national survey on recruitment, education, and employment

Ethel M. Cryderman 1948-1950	Director, Toronto Branch, Victorian Order of Nurses, Toronto	Born: Walkerton, Bruce County, Ontario, 1892 Died: October 17, 1963	1916: Graduate, Toronto General Hospital 1921: Certificate, PH Nursing, Toronto 1925: Midwifery Courses, Radcliffe Infirmary, Oxford, England

Issues: • Promotion of Windsor concept • State subsidization for independent schools • Expansion of Nursing Aide schools • Conservation of the professional nurse • Promote national survey • Influence government

Helen Griffith McArthur 1950-1954	National Director, Nursing Services, Canadian Red Cross Societies, Toronto	Born: Stettler, Alberta, July 30, 1911 Died: Guelph, Ontario, December, 1974	1934: BSc, Nursing, Alberta 1940: MA, Teachers College, Columbia

Adapted from Meilicke, D.T. (1981). *CNA Presidents, 1908-1980: Beginning biographies and presidential themes.* Unpublished manuscript. (Available from CNA Library, Canadian Nurses Association, Ottawa.)

TABLE 26-3 Canadian Nurses Association: Presidents 1946-1970—cont'd

President and term of office	Position at time of office	Birth/death	Education
Helen Griffith McArthur—cont'd			

Issues: • Shortage of well-qualified instructors • Plans for the future • Recommendations of Canadian Commission on Nursing • Provision of adequate nursing services from joint efforts • New approaches to service • CNA professional staff • Incorporation of nursing into total health care scheme • Nursing shortage

Gladys J. Sharpe 1954-1956	Director of Nursing; Principal, School of Nursing, Toronto Western Hospital	Born: Toronto, Ontario, September 30, 1902 Died: Ontario, 1975	1925: Graduate, School of Nursing, Toronto Western Hospital 1928: Certificate, McGill School for Graduate Nurses 1936: Certificate, Bedford College, London, England 1946: BSc, Teachers College, Columbia

Issues: • Review CNA organization and purpose • Promote public's best interests • Promote nursing's best interests

Trenna Grace Hunter 1956-1958	Director, Public Health Nursing, Metropolitan Health Committee, Vancouver	Born: Brandon, Manitoba, March, 1906	Brandon Normal School 1939: Graduate, Vancouver General Hospital 1940: Certificate in Public Health Nursing, UBC 1941: Bachelor of Applied Science (Nursing), UBC

Issues: • CNA's responsibility to individual, profession, and society • Additional studies and research • Promote growth of specialized knowledge • Promote CNA's advisory role to government • CNA support of Code of Ethics • CNA support of employment relations committee

Continued.

TABLE 26-3 Canadian Nurses Association: Presidents 1946-1970—cont'd

President and term of office	Position at time of office	Birth/death	Education
Alice M. Girard 1958-1960	Director of Nursing; Assistant Administrator, Saint-Luc Hospital, Montreal	Born: Waterbury, Connecticut, November 11, 1907	1931: Graduate, L'Hôpital St. Vincent de Paul, Sherbrooke, Quebec 1939: Diploma, Public Hygiene, Toronto 1942: BScN, Catholic University of America, Washington 1944: MNEd, Columbia 1954: Administration Course in Hospital Administration, Johns Hopkins

Issues: • Recommendations of Pilot Project on Schools of Nursing • Funds for Research Committee • What is nursing? • Is nursing professional? • Which system of education is best? • Nursing Unit Administration Course

President and term of office	Position at time of office	Birth/death	Education
Dr. Helen M. Carpenter 1960-1962	Professor; Director, School of Nursing, University of Toronto	Born: Montreal, Quebec, March 29, 1912	1933: Graduate Nursing Diploma, Combination Course, Toronto and Toronto General Hospital 1940: BSc, Teachers College, Columbia 1945: MPH, Johns Hopkins School of Hygiene 1965: EdD, Columbia

Issues: • Quality nursing service • Implementation of the recommendation of Pilot Project on Schools of Nursing • Study of quality of nursing service in student clinical areas

TABLE 26-3 Canadian Nurses Association: Presidents 1946-1970—cont'd

President and term of office	Position at time of office	Birth/death	Education
Edna Agnes Electa MacLennan 1962-1964	Director and Associate Professor, School of Nursing, Dalhousie University, Halifax	Born: Nova Scotia, March 31, 1907, to Robert Bryon and Annie (Johnson) Died: August, 1987	1929: BA, Dalhousie University 1932: Graduate, Royal Victoria Hospital, Montreal 1933: Certificate PHN, McGill University 1941: MA, Columbia

Issues: • Separate funding for nursing education • Economic conditions of nurses • Finances for CNA House • Education of nurses in educational facilities

A. Isobel (Black) MacLeod 1964-1966	Director of Nursing; Principal, School of Nursing, Montreal General Hospital	Born: Sturgeon Falls, Ontario, June 24, to Rev. A.E. and Isobel Black	1936: BScN, University of Alberta 1955: MA, Teachers College, Columbia

Issues: • Proactive rather than reactive • Clarify the nurse's role • Economic and social welfare of nurses • Recruitment of nursing candidates • Streamline organizational structure • Realistic CNA budget • Strong united voice to support education and social programs • CNA approval of modern bargaining methods

Dr. Katherine E. MacLaggan 1966-1967	Director, School of Nursing, University of New Brunswick, Fredericton	Born: Fredericton, 1913 Died: February, 1967	Teacher, General Education, Fredericton 1943: Graduate, Royal Victoria Hospital, Montreal 1947: BScN, McGill University 1957: MA, Teachers College, Columbia 1965: EdD, Teachers College, Columbia

Issues: • Need for public financial support of nursing education (Deceased during term of office in 1967)

THE FOURTH ERA: 1970 TO 1988

The fourth era began with a strong economy and national attention directed toward separatist activities in the province of Quebec. This era was characterized by the presidents of the CNA studying the role that the associations and individual nurses should play in shaping the Canadian health care system (see Table 26-4). Another major theme was the quality of professional nursing practice. The effect of the separatist movement in Quebec on nursing was also to be a big issue in the latter part of this era.

Sister Mary Felicitas, in her presidential address of 1970, echoed the call to action by Verna Huffman, the keynote speaker who concluded the third era and opened the fourth. The Reverend Sister urged members to make a decision about CNA's objectives, roles, and fee structures. She indicated that this would determine the future of the Association. She also urged members to make these decisions with an open mind and to weigh the evidence in reaching their conclusions. She noted: "There is no place for preconceived ideas in a matter of this importance" ("Convention report," 1970, p. 24).

Louise Miner, in 1972, reflecting her public health background, recognized the need for nurse leadership in health promotion and illness prevention. This was observed in federal government policies for health promotion in the 1980s. She advocated expanding community health services and giving high priority to health and prevention of illness. She observed:

> We constitute the largest group of members of the health team, and if we don't actively promote this, it will be unnecessarily delayed and we will lose a crucial opportunity to make a major impact on the health of the people of this country, which is supposed to be the reason for the existence of the Canadian Nurses' Association. ("CNA goes West," 1972, p. 26)

Miner's definition of objectives was followed by Huguette Labelle's proposal for proactive involvement of nurses in an even broader range of health care policy issues. In her 1976 presidential address, Labelle stressed that "nurses must become more directly involved in the planning and development of health care policy and services so that they are in a position to act rather than react" (p. 27). She further noted that the stable employment pattern of 1976 facilitated proactive response:

> We now have an outstanding opportunity to identify alternative services and to determine how and in what situations nurses can benefit the population. The question we must answer now is how we can increase our impact on the quality of Canadian life. (Labelle, 1976, p. 27)

With foresight, Labelle also urged that action be taken in forecasting nursing manpower requirements:

> Unless we develop better mechanisms for forecasting nursing manpower requirements more accurately, there could be another "shortage" within a few years, if natural attrition is not compensated by a new supply of nurses. (p. 27)

The proactive theme was re-emphasized when Helen Taylor, in her 1978 inaugural address, noted that the professional ought to press ahead with determination and become increasingly visible and involved in the planning and development of programs for health care. She observed that, as nurses:

> We must be prepared to voice our beliefs and then to defend our principles especially when, due to economic or other modern day pressures, we are admonished by others to forsake the principles. (Taylor, 1978, p. 57)

Again, reflecting the activist orientation of this era, outgoing President Taylor noted in 1980:

> Nurses of tomorrow must be steeped in the visions of the future . . . prepared for a burgeoning work world of science and technology. We will need to learn how to assess the need for specific services that directly affect health, and we will require the necessary skills to influence community and national leaders with the aim of promoting healthy environments. (p. 24)

In 1980, Dr. Shirley Stinson confirmed the scope of this vision when she stressed:

> The need for strong, relevant professional organization at the international, national, district and local levels. . . . I believe CNA can play a vital role at the national level and a vital role in strengthening professional organizations at all of the other levels. . . . Where CNA's role was primarily reactive in the past it is now becoming proactive, putting forth new ideas, being in the vanguard rather than the rear guard. (p. 25)

Concern for shaping the health care system culminated during Dr. Helen Glass's presidency (1982-1984) when she proposed that nursing speak out and clarify its position in support of a health-oriented health care system. Her presidency ended with CNA mounting an extensive and successful national lobby to obtain amendments to the new Canada Health Act. This concern for nurses to take an active and visible role in the development of public policy continues to the current day. Helen Evans, in her 1986 address, noted:

> I believe that CNA needs to become more visible to the public, to share with the public what nurses can and are doing and also to show that we are there to listen to them. (1986a, p. 19)

A second major theme in the presidential addresses of this era focused on the quality of nursing practice, beginning with Margaret Schumacher's 1974 presidential address proposing active involvement by the CNA in the national hospital accreditation program. Schumacher observed that acceptance of the Association, in March 1973, as a sponsor of the Canadian Council of Hospital Accreditation, was a major breakthrough after eight years of representation by the CNA ("Convention Report," 1974). Huguette Labelle, in 1976, pleaded for nurses not to lose sight of "the fundamental element of nursing—the care and support the profession provides for the people it serves" (p. 27). She expressed concern about the "trade off" that occurs when medical functions are transferred to nursing and warned "of the danger of losing sight of the fundamental care and support activities that are the basis of the nursing process" (p. 27).

Joan Gilchrist, in her 1978 farewell address, noted three areas in which nurses might have a more positive effect on quality of care. The first area is in the nurses' work environment, the second is in the area of professional and union environment, and the third is in the area of community environment. She stressed the need for risk taking and initiative in demonstrating new roles, for renewed efforts to prevent separation into management and nonmanagement groups, and for a more active leadership role in the development of innovative community services (p. 57).

With a downturn in the economy in the late 1970s and the associated cutbacks in health funding, Helen Taylor, in her outgoing presidential address of 1980, stressed that nursing standards, quality of nursing practice, accreditation of nursing education programs, and development of a code of ethics for nurses were the most significant priorities under review by CNA. She observed that "quality of care in practice settings should be our greatest concern both today and tomorrow" (p. 24). She reminded nurses that adoption of standards does not necessarily guarantee high quality care.

By 1982, Dr. Shirley Stinson and the CNA Directors warned that cutbacks in financial support by governments were eroding quality care within the health care system ("CNA directors meet," 1982). At the same time, Dr. Helen Glass (the incoming president) observed that economic constraints would inhibit funding for expansion and improvement of services and would exert increasing pressures on health professionals, including nurses, to be more innovative and creative.

Lorine Besel, in her 1984 address, outlined several areas in which improvements in the quality of care were needed. She expressed concern that the care for the elderly was too often placed in the hands of unskilled and unqualified workers. She felt that in large teaching hospitals nurses had "given into the 'too costly' pressure and allowed true care of the ill to be turned over to auxiliary personnel" (p. 8). She also suggested that nursing had "allowed the care of the sick to become low status in the eyes of the profession itself and then we wonder why those 'poor, downtrodden nurses' in the hospital don't participate in the profession" (p. 8).

Another significant initiative by several presidents to improve the quality of patient care was attention to the role of nursing administration. During the presidencies of Helen Glass (1982-1984) and Lorine Besel (1984-1986), the CNA developed standards for nursing administration. Lorine Besel emphasized the potential of nursing's role at the executive level of the health care organizations. Helen Evans, in her 1986 editorial to Canadian nurses, broadened the discussion with her challenge for strong nursing leadership within the profession. She urged "preparation of strong nursing leaders (that again dictates greater access to advanced education) so that our working environments will facilitate high quality care and professional development" (Evans, 1986b, p. 7).

The emphasis on nursing education issues was not as prominent in the presidential addresses of this era as in the past. Nonetheless, Helen Taylor, in 1980, discussed the need to develop the facilities and to obtain the resources required to prepare nurses at the doctoral level as one of the ingredients of quality care. During the presidency of Dr. Shirley Stinson (1980-1982) the Association accepted the baccalaureate in nursing as a minimum qualification for entry to the practice of nursing, and during Lorine Besel's presidency a priority was placed on developing policies for specialization and certification.

At the end of this era, Quebec nurses withdrew from membership in the CNA. Four major grievances were listed by Quebec in the preamble to the disaffiliation motion: an "unjustified" $6.00 increase in CNA's portion of each Quebec member's annual dues; a "lack of proportional representation" within the CNA Board of Directors; CNA's "lack of interest" in Quebec's special situation; and contention that CNA memberships amounted to "a duplication of services" for Quebec nurses ("CNA connection," 1985, p. 8).

These grievances were not new. They could be traced back over a period of 20 or 30 years. The concern about the level of fees, for example, was reported as early as the 1966 biennial meeting in Montreal ("Editorial," 1985, p. 9). Events that led to this withdrawal were evident early in the 1980s. For instance, during Dr. Stinson's term of office, a notice of intent to withdraw had been averted in 1981 (Rodger, 1981). After the withdrawal of the Quebec association in 1985, Helen Evans began a process of rebuilding with her presidential recommendation in 1986 for members to "reach out and touch our colleagues in Quebec and, in touching them, draw them back with us, so that we can once again be a unified voice for nursing in Canada" (1986a, p. 19).

Early in this era, the values expressed by the presidents in outlining the direction for the future were professional integrity, accountability, and responsibility in providing quality nursing care and acting proactively. Later in the era, the dominant values once again reflected recommendations for unity with the profession. Helen Evans (1986b) exemplified this value when she stated:

> We need to be in touch, so that we can speak and act for Canadian nurses and nursing in a single, unified voice. Together, we will achieve great ends and continue to be "proud to be a nurse." (p. 7)

The fourth era closed with a national commitment to a baccalaureate degree as the entry point to practice, the certification project in place, new directions for nursing in health care, and, last but not least, threats of major nursing shortage in the near future.

Unlike the cyclical nursing shortages of the past, which could be traced to natural ebbs and flow in demand, this shortage was linked to recruitment and retention problems and was primarily driven by the need for dramatic reform in the workplace of general duty nurses (Banning, 1987a; Kramer and Schmalenberg, 1988). A 1987 telephone survey conducted by Goldfarb, consultants for the CNA, reported that 72% of Canadian nurses work in hospitals (Banning, 1988a). Wilson's (1987) article "Why nurses leave nursing" struck a responsive cord among these practicing nurses throughout Canada. She showed that nurses were frustrated and angry with their working conditions. Morale was at an all-time low (Banning, 1987b). The degree of discontent and activism related to working conditions astounded even some of the unions (Banning, 1989). The direct relationship of good working conditions to quality nursing care resulted in the professional association addressing the problem and issues in the working environment of nurses and set the stage for the next era (Banning, 1988b; Ritchie, 1988.)

TABLE 26-4 **Canadian Nurses Association: Presidents 1970-1988**

President and term of office	Position at time of office	Birth/death	Education
Sister Mary Felicitas 1967-1970	Director, School of Nursing, St. Mary's Hospital, Montreal	Born: Fife, Saskatchewan, January 18, 1916 to Frank and Magdeline Wekel	1943: Graduate, Providence Hospital, Moose Jaw, Saskatchewan 1945: MSc, Ottawa 1953: MSc (Nursing Education), Catholic University of America, Washington

Issues: • CNA role and objectives • CNA fee structure • Unity and strength urgently needed • One voice on national issues • Open minds for decision making

| **E. Louise Miner** 1970-1972 | Director, Divison of Public Health Nursing, Department of Public Health, Saskatchewan | Born: Speers, Saskatchewan, July, 1915 | 1937: Graduate, Royal Alexandra Hospital, School of Nursing, Edmonton 1945: Diploma, PH Nursing, Toronto 1949: BN, McGill 1955: MPH, Michigan |

Issues: • Expand community health services • Priority to health and prevention of illness • Opportunity to be leaders in health promotion and prevention

| **Marguerite Schumacher** 1972-1974 | Chairman, Nursing Department, Red Deer College, Red Deer, Alberta | Born: Switzerland, June, 1920 | 1941: Graduate, Victoria Hospital, Winnipeg 1953: BScN, Case Western Reserve, Cleveland, Ohio 1954: MA and MEd, Columbia |

Issues: • Involvement in the profession • CNA and hospital accreditation • Potential dynamic role of CNA in future health care for Canadians

Adapted from Meilicke, D.T. (1981). *CNA Presidents, 1908-1980: Beginning biographies and presidential themes.* Unpublished manuscript. (Available from CNA Library, Canadian Nurses Association, Ottawa.)

TABLE 26-4 **Canadian Nurses Association: Presidents 1970-1988—cont'd**

President and term of office	Position at time of office	Birth/death	Education
Huguette Labelle 1974-1976	Principal Nursing Officer, Health and Welfare Canada, Ottawa	Born: Rockland, Ontario, 1939	1959: Diploma in Nursing; Ottawa General Hospital 1960: BA (Nursing), Ottawa 1968: MA (Education), Ottawa 1980: PhD (Education), Ottawa

Issues: • Mechanism for forecasting nursing manpower requirements • Study ways to reduce effect of unemployment • Pursue alternate service role opportunities • Affect quality of Canadian life • Proactive involvement in planning and developing health care planning • Nursing is "conscience" of the health care system

Joan M. Gilchrist 1976-1978	Director, School of Nursing, McGill University, Montreal	Born: Toronto, Ontario, June, 1928	1950: Graduate, Wellesley Hospital, Toronto 1958: BN and MSc (Applied), McGill

Issues: • Influence health care system • New roles and risk taking • Unity of nurse management and nurse practice groups • Involvement in community services

Helen D. Taylor 1978-1980	Director of Nursing, Jewish General Hospital, Montreal	Born: Quebec, March 18, 1932	1953: Graduate, Montreal General 1961: Diploma, Teaching and Supervision, McGill 1962: BN, McGill 1975: MSc (Applied), McGill

Issues: • CNA Code of Ethics • Standards for nursing education • Standards for nursing practice • Accreditation of nursing education programs • Assessment of special services • Development of skills to influence community/national leaders • Development of facilities and resources to prepare nurses at Doctorate level • Proposed national plan for continuing education • Quality nursing care

Continued.

TABLE 26-4 Canadian Nurses Association: Presidents 1970-1988—cont'd

President and term of office	Position at time of office	Birth/death	Education
Dr. Shirley Marie Stinson 1980-1982	Professor, Faculty of Nursing and Division of Health Services Administration, University of Alberta	Born: Arlee, Saskatchewan 1929 to Edwin and Mary Stinson	1953: BScN, Alberta 1958: MNA, Minnesota 1969: EdD, Columbia

Issues: • Need for strong, relevant, professional organization at the international, national, district, and local levels • Absence of linkages between CNA and specialty groups across Canada • Erosion of quality of care by cutbacks in health care

Dr. Helen P. Glass 1982-1984	Professor and Coordinator of Graduate Program in Nursing, University of Manitoba, School of Nursing, Winnipeg	Born: Regina, Saskatchewan, October 24, 1917	1939: Graduate, Royal Victoria School of Nursing, Montreal 1960: BS, Columbia 1961: MA, Columbia 1970: MEd, Columbia 1971: EdD, Columbia

Issues: • The contest between a social/community model and a medical model of health care • Economic constraints and their effects on entry to practice, research, acute care, etc.

Lorine Besel 1984-1986	Director of Nursing, Royal Victoria Hospital, Montreal	Born: Winnipeg, Manitoba, February 23, 1933	1954: Graduate, St. Boniface Hospital 1960: BN, McGill 1966: MSc, Boston

Issues: • Unqualified care of the elderly • Lack of initiative in family violence • Increased use of auxiliary workers in acute care • Worship of high-tech teaching hospitals • Union request for ICU premiums • Nursing executive's level in the organization • Declining status associated with caring for the sick

Helen Evans 1986-1988	Associate Executive Director–Nursing, Mount Sinai Hospital, Toronto	Born: Toronto, 1931	1952: Graduate, Toronto General Hospital

TABLE 26-4 **Canadian Nurses Association: Presidents 1970-1988—cont'd**

President and term of office	Position at time of office	Birth/death	Education
Helen Evans—cont'd			1960: Diploma, Nursing Administration, Western Ontario 1962: BScN, Western Ontario 1968: MS, Boston

Issues: • Need for CNA to be more visible to the public • Need for CNA to listen to its members • Need to be in touch with colleagues in other professions • Promote goals of health care for all, baccalaureate education, health care system reforms, strong nursing leaderships, theory-based practice, increased funds for research, and complete unified Canadian voice for nursing

THE NEW ERA: 1988-

Never before in the history of the CNA had presidents placed a major focus on the working conditions of nurses, except perhaps for Fanny Munroe (1944-1946) who identified the need to improve the socioeconomic conditions of nurses. In the past, working conditions were either ignored or seen as the domain of the unions. In the late 1980s, the link between working conditions and quality patient care was obvious to nursing unions and professional associations (see Table 26-5). The need for unions, management, and professional associations to work together to reform the workplace was the raison d'être for closer collaboration between these previously divided groups.

Dr. Judith Ritchie, in her 1988 inaugural address, declared the need to focus on nursing practice issues and working conditions; she dedicated the efforts of the CNA to this mission. She stressed: We must examine and find solutions for the issues that lead to nurses leaving nursing, especially those issues related to assuring working conditions that permit the delivery of quality nursing care, and make nursing an attractive career. (p. 31)

The CNA subsequently sponsored several well-attended national conferences on "Work-life Issues: Caring for practice," which were targeted for staff nurses and encouraged sharing creative ideas about reforming the workplace. Implementation of decentralized decision-making structures, flexible hours of work and self-scheduling, participative management, enhanced leadership skills, clearer definitions of policy and procedures, professional practice models, career ladders, continuing education, adequate support staff, and appropriate compensation for clinical experts were a few of the necessary changes identified. A professional consultant position at CNA, eliminated in 1985, was re-established to concentrate on work-life issues. Staff were to review collective agreements and to collect data on the working environments of nurses (CNA Connection, 1989). Initial data confirmed that the quality of a nurse's working life was a recurring theme, as was the need for adequate compensation for clinical nursing practice (Kubasiecwicz, 1989).

In 1990, Dr. Ritchie noted that things were changing:

> Individual nurses are working with their own agencies to change their working environ-ments. Nurse managers are implementing creative approaches that enable nursing care to be a challenge rather than a threat, and involve nurses in policy decisions in a way that matches the complexity of today's practice. Unions and associations are exploring ways to collaborate or approach issues differently. (Ritchie, 1990, p. 3)

Within a historical perspective, the activism and change occurring within nursing were viewed as establishing nurses at the vanguard of change for working women. Quoting a Toronto sociologist, Banning (1989) contended that:

> In the late 90s, society will look back at 1989 and say: "This is when it all started, when women began rebelling against their working conditions, and nurses will be seen as having led the way." (p. 3)

The irony is that nursing's role in advocating for change in women's work experience is rarely acknowledged, nor is it frequently cited in current women's literature. She predicts:

> Surely 1989 will go down in Canadian nursing history as the year that dissatisfaction with working conditions permeated nursing's ranks to a degree that even caught some unions off guard. The challenge to nurses and women, in general, to capitalize on such a positive force has never been greater. (Banning, 1989, p. 3)

Although work-life issues had a dominant role early in this new era, other issues were not neglected. In fact, significant strides were taken on many other important topics. The Canadian Nurses Protective Fund was introduced in February 1988; a certification program for neuroscience nursing became a reality; and nurse educators were taking major strides toward entry to practice, with innovative changes such as the collaborative baccalaureate programs in Alberta, British Columbia, and Manitoba. The CNA adopted a position statement on primary health care in June, 1989, and published a position statement on Nurses and the Environment in May, 1990. Nursing care of the elderly, people with AIDS, and organ transplantation patients also received attention. Finally, the need remained to restore Quebec membership.

Incoming president Dr. Alice Baumgart, in her 1990 nomination address, pledged to encourage and sustain the initiatives under way and also:

> To expand and strengthen opportunities for Canadian nurses to exercise leadership and creativity in designing the health care system of tomorrow, and to create new networks to link together nurses in various speciality groups, professional organizations and unions so that the nursing profession will not be hostage to vested interests wishing to keep nurses divided and thus controlled. (p. 35)

Change continues in this era of reformation in the workplace amid a climate of concern about women's issues and the global environment. To assist in shaping the future, the new CNA mission statement will serve nursing well:

> The mission of the Canadian Nurses Association is to foster excellence in nursing prac-tice, education, research and management, to promote high quality health care in Can-ada and internationally, and to speak on behalf of Canadian nurses on nursing and health-related issues. ("CNA Connection," 1990, p. 3)

TABLE 26-5 **Canadian Nurses Association: Presidents 1988-**

President and term of office	Position at time of office	Birth/death	Education
Dr. Judith Anne Ritchie 1988-1990	Professor, School of Nursing, Dalhousie University, and Director of Nursing Research, IWK Children's Hospital, Halifax	Born: June 13, 1943, Saint John, New Brunswick, to Lewis and Mary Ritchie	1965: BN, New Brunswick 1969: MN, Pittsburgh 1975: PhD (Nursing), Pittsburgh

Issues: • Improvements in nurses' working conditions • Need to increase information on issues affecting nursing practice • Improvement in continuing education programs • Better articulation of nursing to external publics • Development of national liability insurance • National conferences on Work-life Issues and Caring for Practice • Care of elderly, AIDS patients, and organ transplants

Dr. Alice J. Baumgart 1990-1992	Professor and Vice Principal, Human Services, Queen's University, Kingston	Born: Edmonton, Alberta, February 7, 1936 to George and Amanda Baumgart	1958: BSN, British Columbia 1964: MSc (Applied), McGill 1983: PhD, Toronto

Issues: • Restore Quebec membership • Sustain professional vitality and inventiveness to solve work-life issues • Create networks to link together nurses in specialty groups, unions, and professional organizations

CONCLUSION

Similar to leaders in other sectors of society, the presidents of the Canadian Nurses Association held senior positions in the profession at the time they were in office. These presidents were from various agencies, including hospitals, public health organizations, educational institutions, and government. A majority were directors of nursing service in hospitals or heads of schools of nursing. At the time of their presidencies, these leaders lived predominantly in large urban centers in Ontario and Quebec. In the early years, the presidents were graduates of hospital diploma schools of nursing, often with diplomas in more advanced studies, usually from American colleges or universities. By the mid-1940s, the presidents had baccalaureate degrees in nursing, and many had masters degrees. Since the 1970s, doctoral degrees have been evident. These educational achievements were more advanced than the educational levels of typical Association members.

Also similar to leaders in other fields, the presidents of the CNA presented their messages to members using symbols and metaphors to show how issues of the day were to be viewed—with vision, with courage, with integrity, and with unity. The repeated calls for unity by the presidents over the last decades may reflect the numerous cleavages that have appeared within the nursing profession in Canada, but without comparative data it is difficult to know whether this is unique to Canadian nursing.

The analysis of the issues addressed by the presidents reveal other recurring themes, including emphasis on the role and structure of the Association, issues associated with nursing education, cyclical shortages and oversupply of general duty nurses, and concern for quality nursing care. Apparent, as well, are effects of national emergencies, depressions, and wars on the problems addressed by the presidents.

Collectively, regardless of their positions and education or the circumstances during their terms of office, the presidents demonstrated all the leadership characteristics referred to in the introduction of this chapter. They were creative and dynamic, they understood complex problems facing the nursing profession, and they were sensitive to the circumstances and needs of the nurses to whom they were ultimately responsible. They sensed opportunity and built trust while negotiating issues and building coalitions. A few of them were clearly visionary—creating new ideas, new processes, new structures; in so doing, they increased the level of their own and their followers' motivations and aspirations, enabling nurses to accomplish more than was imagined possible.

Today's changing society will make new demands on future presidents of CNA and on the leaders of other professional nursing associations in Canada. A heterogeneous membership that is demanding a louder voice in decisions, a shifting political climate, a puzzling economy, and a turbulent social environment pressure nursing leaders to lead in new ways. Future nursing leaders must create environments and design new structures that encourage other nurses to discover their own strengths and talents. Nursing leaders of the future must serve as inspirational symbols who share leadership tasks and build coalitions. This review of a select group of Canadian nursing leaders may help guide and inspire nurses who now and in the future will be asked to play a leadership role in the profession and the community at large—those who will assume the responsibilities of the "political elite."

The 36 women described in this chapter represent the best of Canadian nursing. They warrant more study. But, even with this brief review, it is clear that they warrant emulation. Perhaps the essence of their legacy was best expressed by Mary Ardcronie MacKenzie in 1914: "Have vision, have faith in the vision. . . . From you must come the answer, followed by action" (pp. 562-563).

REFERENCES

Agor, W. (1989). *Intuition in organizations: Leading and managing productivity*. Newbury Park, CA: Sage.

Banning, J. A. (1987a). Nursing for a lifetime? *The Canadian Nurse, 83*(3), 3.

Banning, J.A. (1987b). Pie in the sky? *The Canadian Nurse, 84*(5), 5.

Banning, J.A. (l988a). A unique and important consumer group. *The Canadian Nurse, 84*(4), 3.

Banning, J.A. (1988b). Solidarity. *The Canadian Nurse. 84*(3), 3.

Banning, J.A. (1989). At the vanguard of working women. *The Canadian Nurse, 95*(9), 3.

Baumgart, A. (1990). President. *The Canadian Nurse, 86*(5), 35.

Bennis, W. (1989a). *On becoming a leader*. Reading, MA: Addison-Wesley.

Bennis, W. (1989b). *Why leaders can't lead: The unconscious conspiracy continues*. San Francisco: Jossey Bass.

Besel, L. (1984). Passion and conviction. *The Canadian Nurse, 80*(8), 8.

Browne, J.E. (1924). President's address. *The Canadian Nurse, 20*(8), 471-475.

Browne, J.E. (1933). In Memoriam. *The Canadian Nurse, 29*, 567-570.

Bryce-Brown, R. (1916). Canadian National Association of Trained Nurses. *The Canadian Nurse, 12*(7), 514-517.

Bryce-Brown, R. (1917). The sixth annual convention. *The Canadian Nurse, 13*(8), 406-407.

Burns, J. M. (1984). *The power to lead: The crisis of the American Presidency*. New York: Simon and Schuster.

Cameron, S.G. (1932). The medical and nursing professions and the survey report. *The Canadian Nurse, 28*(9), 399-410.

Canadian Nurses' Association (CNA). (1957). *CNA: The first fifty years*. Ottawa: Author.

Canadian Nurses' Association (CNA) (1968). *The leaf and the lamp*. Ottawa: Author.

Carlisle, A. (1976). McGregor. *Organizational dynamics. 5*(1), 50-62.

Carpenter, H.M. (1962). Note. *The Canadian Nurse, 58*(9), 786.

Charbonneau, L. (1983). A word from the past presidents. *The Canadian Nurse, 79*(9), 49.

Chittick, R. (1948). Let us take pride in our craft. *The Canadian Nurse, 44*(9), 705-709.

CNA connection. (1985). *The Canadian Nurse, 81*(3), 8.

CNA connection (1989). Work-life affairs position reaffirmed. *The Canadian Nurse, 85*(1), 8.

CNA connection. (1990). New mission statement. *The Canadian Nurse, 86*(5), 10.

CNA directors meet. (1982). *The Canadian Nurse, 78*(8), 12.

CNA goes West. (1972). *The Canadian Nurse, 68*(9), 26.

Conger, J. (1989). *The charismatic leader: Behind the mystique of exceptional leadership*. San Francisco: Jossey-Bass.

Convention report. (1970). *The Canadian Nurse, 66*(8), 24-25.

Convention report. (1974). *The Canadian Nurse, 70*(8), 20.

Cryderman, E.M. (1950). The immediate task. *The Canadian Nurse, 46*(9), 693-698.

Dickson, E.M. (1921). President's address. *The Canadian Nurse, 17*(7), 419-426.

Dickson, E.M. (1922). President's address. *The Canadian Nurse, 18*(8), 473-474.

Doig, J., & Hargrove, E. (1987). *Leadership and innovation*. Baltimore: Johns Hopkins Press.

Eagly, A., & Johnson, B. (1990). Gender and leadership style: A meta-analysis. *Psychological Bulletin, 108*(2), 233-256.

Editor. (1967). A tribute-Katherine E. Mac-Laggan. *The Canadian Nurse, 63*(3), 3.

Editorial: Disaffiliation of the OIIQ. (1985). *The Canadian Nurse, 81*(9), 9.

Emory, F. H. M. (1932). Whither? Presidential address. *The Canadian Nurse, 28*(9), 467-469.

Emory, F. H. M. (1934). Yesterday and tomorrow. *The Canadian Nurse, 30*(8), 349-353.

Epp, J. (1986). *Achieving health for all: A framework for health promotion*. Ottawa: Health & Welfare Canada.

Epstein, C. (1988). *Deceptive distinctions*. New Haven: Yale University Press.

Etzioni, A. (1989). Humble decision-making. *Harvard Business Review, 67*(4), 122-126.

Evans, H. (1986a). Inaugural address: Nursing in motion, nursing in touch. *The Canadian Nurse, 82*(8), 19.

Evans, H. (1986b). To Canadian Nurses. *The Canadian Nurse, 82*(8), 7.

Fairley, G. M. (1940). The president's address. *The Canadian Nurse, 36*(9), 537-538.

Fairley, G. M. (1942). The president's address. *The Canadian Nurse, 38*(9), 612-613.

Gilchrist, J. (1978). Farewell address. *The Canadian Nurse, 74*(7/8), 57.

Gilmore, T. (1988). *Making a leadership change*. San Francisco: Jossey-Bass.

Girard, A. (1960). Faith and beginning. *The Canadian Nurse, 56*(8), 689-692.

Glass H. (1982). The sleeping giant. *The Canadian Nurse, 78*(8), 6-7.

Gray, M. (1928). Address, acting president. *The Canadian Nurse, 24*(8), 396-398.

Gunn, J. (1918). Canadian National Association of Trained Nurses' Convention, 1918. *The Canadian Nurse, 14*(8),1210-1213. (microfilm).

Gunn, J. (1919), President's address, CNATN convention. *The Canadian Nurse, 15*(8), 1919-1924.

Gunn, J. (1920). President's address. *The Canadian Nurse, 16*(9), 519.

Helgesen, S. (1990). *The female advantage: Women's ways of leadership*. New York: Doubleday.

Hersey, M. F. (1930). President's address. *The Canadian Nurse, 26*(9), 462-465.

Hunter, T. G. (1958). Our professional association. *The Canadian Nurse, 54*(9), 807-809.

Kinsey, D. (1986). The new nurse influentials. *Nursing Outlook, 34*(5), 238-240.

Kotter, J. (1985). Why business has so few leaders. *New York Times*, October 20, #3, 2.

Kramer, M., & Schmalenberg, C. (1988). Magnet hospitals; Part l-institutions of excellence. *The Journal of Nursing Administration, 18*(1), 13.

Kubasiewicz, M. K. (1989). Work-life issues. *The Canadian Nurse, 85*(6), 10.

Labelle, H. (1976). A retrospective assessment. *The Canadian Nurse, 72*(8), 27.

Lindeburgh, M. (1944). The president's address. *The Canadian Nurse, 40*(9), 613-616.

McArthur, H. G. (1952). Open a better way. *The Canadian Nurse, 48*(7), 543-546.

McArthur, H. G. (1954). Measuring progress. *The Canadian Nurse, 50*(9), 701-702.

MacKenzie, M. A. (1913). President's address. *The Canadian Nurse, 9*(5), 588-590.

MacKenzie, M. A. (1914). President's address. *The Canadian Nurse, 11*(10), 561-563.

MacLennan, E. A. E. (1962). Courage. *The Canadian Nurse, 58*(9), 783-784.

MacLennan, E. A. E. (1964). A legacy of purpose. *The Canadian Nurse, 60*(9), 859-861.

MacLeod, A. I. (1966). President's address; CNA 33rd general meeting. *The Canadian Nurse*, *62*(8), 19-22.

Mansell, D. (1991). Leadership patterns in the history of nursing: Canada 1919-1949. A preliminary discussion. Unpublished manuscript, Faculty of Nursing, University of Calgary.

Meilicke, C. A., & Storch, J. L. (1980). *Perspectives on Canadian health and social services policy: History and emerging trends*. Ann Arbor, MI: Health Administration Press.

Meilicke, D. T. (1981). CNA Presidents 1908-1980. *Beginning biographies and Presidential themes*. (Unpublished manuscript).

Melosh, B. (1982). *The physician's hand*. Philadelphia: Temple University Press.

Minzberg, H. (1989). *Minzberg on management*. New York: Free Press.

Munroe, F. (1946). The presidential address. *The Canadian Nurse*, *42*(9), 734-737.

O'Rourke, T. (1928). Group nursing from standpoint of the nurse. *The Canadian Nurse*, *24*(9), 494-495.

Peters, T. (1987). *Thriving on chaos*. New York: Knopf.

Reverby, S. (1987). *Ordered to care: The dilemma of American Nursing 1850-1945*. Cambridge: Cambridge University Press.

Ritchie, J. A. (1988). Nursing: Accept the challenge. *The Canadian Nurse*, *84*(8), 30-35.

Ritchie, J. A. (1990). Feeling empowered. *The Canadian Nurse*, *86*(1), 3.

Rodger, G. (1981), Before it's too late (Editorial). *The Canadian Nurse*, *77*(7), 5.

Sharpe, G. J. (1956). Tomorrow's pattern. *The Canadian Nurse*, *52*(8), 597-600.

Simpson, R. M. (1936). Forward. *The Canadian Nurse*, *32*(8), 345-348.

Simpson, R. M. (1938). Thirty years of growth. *The Canadian Nurse*, *34*(8), 411-416.

Snively, M. A. (1908). President's address. *The Canadian Nurse*, *4*(2), 524-528.

Snively, M. A. (1911). Address of the president, Miss Mary A. Snively. *The Canadian Nurse*, *7*(8), 395-397.

Stinson, S. (1980). Incoming president. *The Canadian Nurse*, *76*(8), 24-25.

Taylor, H. (1978). President's remarks. *The Canadian Nurse*, *74*(7), 57.

Taylor, H. (1980). Outgoing president. *The Canadian Nurse*, *76*(8), 24.

The Canadian Who's Who (Vols. 1-13, 1935-1975.). Toronto: Who's Who Canadian Publication.

Vance, C. (1977). *A group profile of contemporary influentials in American nursing*. Unpublished doctoral dissertation, Teachers College, Columbia University.

Vance, C. N. (1986). Women leaders: Modern-day heroines and societal deviants. In E. Hein & M. J. Nicholson (Eds.), *Contemporary leadership behavior: Selected readings* (pp. 49-56), Boston: Little, Brown.

Weir, G. M. (1932). *Survey of nursing education in Canada*. Toronto: University of Toronto Press.

Welsh, W. A. (1979). *Leaders and elites*. Toronto: Holt, Rinehart & Winston.

Who's Who in Canada (Vol. 5 1966-68). Toronto: International Press.

Wilson, J. (1987). Why nurses leave nursing. *The Canadian Nurse*, *83*(3), 21.

Members of the British Columbia Nurses' Union received strong public support as they walked picket lines during their 1989 strike. This photograph shows nurses gathered outside the Vancouver General Hospital. Photograph by Aaron Bushkowsky for *BCNU Reports* (July/October 1989, p. 11). (Photograph supplied courtesy of the British Columbia Nurses' Union. Used with permission.)

CHAPTER TWENTY-SEVEN

The Changing Role of Nurses' Unions

PHYLLIS MARIE JENSEN, RN, PhD

Phyllis Marie Jensen, RN (Alberta), BA, MA (Western Ontario), PhD (Toronto), has worked in pediatrics, open heart surgery, and intensive care areas in Canada, and in industrial nursing in England. Pursuing interests in the social sciences and in research, she completed her doctorate in the sociology of health in 1984. She was an Associate on the Badgley Commission on Sexual Offences Against Children, the Principal Researcher on a federal study of spousal abuse, and an Associate on a provincial study of Pay Equity. She does consultant research work in health and justice areas and has a private practice in Toronto called Smokefree, which specializes in teaching women how to quit smoking and offers post-addiction counselling.

D espite a history of strong negotiations between the Nightingale Fund and directors of hospitals and evidence of many heated bargaining sessions between Florence Nightingale and the British Parliament (Woodham-Smith, 1977), the surviving image of the nurse is a romantic one of a self-sacrificing handmaiden. As a result, assertive actions by nurses today are thought to be inappropriate for professionals and damaging to the memory of Florence Nightingale and the Nightingale nurses. In fact, the first recorded labor dispute of nurses in Canada occurred in 1878 when a group of Nightingale nurses threatened to withdraw their services and return to England unless the conditions of their contract were met by the Board of the Montreal General Hospital (Seymer, 1960, p. 82).

Other labor disputes involving nurses occurred in Canada long before unionization. Except for a threatened strike in 1931 by Newfoundland nurses over a cut in pay to balance hospital budgets (Nevitt, 1978) and a walk-out by Comox, British Columbia, nurses in 1939 over demands for an 8-hour day (O'Brien, 1987), few of these early labor actions have been recorded. Like family chroniclers concerned with presenting a good public image, early nursing historians benignly neglected to document what they believed were rebellious acts that discredited the profession.

Learning to "fight for their rights" is not easy for nurses, most of whom are women trained from infancy to be nurturant toward others and nonassertive for themselves. Even today, many nurses equate labor unrest with unionization, believing that things were fine before unions. In fact, nurses' unions developed to resolve labor problems that have plagued the profession throughout its history. Paradoxically, under labor law, the process of coming to agreement is structured as adversarial and promotes conflict rather than resolution. By law, unions must take the initiative in the process and, as a result, tend to be blamed when the two parties fail to come to agreement.

This chapter reviews the historical roots of collective bargaining of nurses in Canada; discusses reasons why collective bargaining was sought; shows how current structures of collective bargaining evolved; and looks at the ongoing debate between the professional associations and the nurses' unions.

THE NEED FOR COLLECTIVE BARGAINING

In 1902, from prompting of the newly established International Council of Nurses, alumnae groups of nurses in Canada began to amalgamate, with the goal of creating a professional body to begin collective bargaining for nurses. Their purposes were numerous:

> to establish and maintain a code of ethics; to elevate the standard of nursing education; and to promote the usefulness and honor of the profession as well as financial and other interests of the members. (Canadian Nurses Association, 1958, p. 35)

Attainment of these goals was imperative: the primary purpose of schools of nursing at the time was to supply cheap labor for hospitals. Little importance was put on the quality of the educational programs, and no importance was given to the training of graduate nurses for future employment. Almost the entire staff of the hospitals was made up of students. Graduates who could find private employment usually worked around the clock, catching sleep in a chair in the sickroom. Wages and standards of practice were variable and working conditions wholly dependent on the benevolence of the employer. There was no sick leave, no paid holiday time, and no pension for nurses. There was discrimination in employment based on age, physical attractiveness, and ethnicity.

Around 1904 discussions began about the type of organization that would best represent the interests of nurses. There were two possibilities: (1) a professional association similar to that of the physicians, who like nurses were in private practice; or (2) a labor union. However, both organizations represented unique difficulties for nurses. Establishing a professional association required enactment of special legislation at a time when it was considered presumptuous and unfeminine for women to be involved in worldly matters. Organizing a labor union was equally problematic, since hospitals were staffed by students, not employees, and graduate nurses in private duty did not have a common employer with which to bargain. A further obstacle for nurses intent on raising the status of their occupation was their difficulty in identifying with the male-dominated, working-class, labor union movement.

Although the professional association was not the complete answer, it was selected to represent nurses' interests. By 1924, nurses in all provinces had secured legislation to enable them to form professional associations. This gave them professional status and some rights and powers over the educational curriculum of schools of nursing, but it did not give them the power to improve their wages or working conditions.

The continual supply into the community of graduates from the schools of nursing resulted in high unemployment. This was exacerbated by the Great Depression of the 1930s when few families could afford private nursing care. The federal government responded to the health care crisis by providing funds so the sick could be sent to hospitals and graduate nurses could be hired to care for them. Remarkably, the influx of experienced graduate nurses into hospitals did little to change the structure of authority in these institutions, and graduates were treated as students. The Weir Report (1932) documents the poor working and living conditions of graduate nurses and the exploitation of the students.

This situation existed until the Second World War (1939-1945) when many graduate nurses joined the armed forces as officers, resulting in a labor shortage in the hospitals. Women who had been forced to leave nursing employment when they married were asked to return to the hospitals. Because of the demands of home and family for married nurses, hospital authorities could no longer require all nurses to live within the hospital premises. Many single women took advantage of this opportunity to move out of the restrictive life of the nurses' residences.

Living outside the hospital, they found their costs higher than their salaries. They demanded higher wages. They also argued for a reduction in their work day so they could manage family responsibilities. However, hospital administrators rejected demands for the 8-hour shift, a standard promoted by labor unions, and, according to a news item in *The Canadian Nurse*, accused the professional associations of "leading their high calling toward a maelstrom of labour unions" (Coburn, 1974, p. 14). These accusations were not entirely unfounded because many nurses had begun to think once more about the need for unionization. It is not surprising that the two most pro-labor provinces, Quebec and British Columbia, were the first to establish nurses' unions.

Quebec

The first Quebec nurses' organization, Ordre des infirmières du Québec, was founded in Montreal in 1920. Eight years later, in the then distant and rival center of Quebec City, another nurses' organization, l'Association gardes malades du Québec, was formed under the leadership of two Catholic Sisters, Andrienne Bernier and Maria Beaumier. The goals of their organization were to change provincial statutes dealing with the profession, to provide continuing education for nurses, and to do volunteer work with the parish poor hit hard by the economic depression.

Quebec nurses joked that in anglophone Montreal the nurses worked for money and in francophone Quebec City they worked for God. The discrepancy in salaries between the two cities led the Quebec City nurses' organization in 1939 to negotiate the first voluntary collective agreement (outside the Labour Relations Act) of Canadian nurses with their employer.

In 1946 the Montreal organization won official recognition as the Nurses' Association of the Province of Quebec. Its role did not include collective bargaining for its members because this action did not fit the cherished ideals of its leaders. Denied assistance by their professional association, francophone Montreal nurses turned to the Quebec Labour Association to establish the first true nurses' union in the country, l'Alliance des infirmières de Montréal. Other hospital-based nurses' unions formed under their guidance and in the next two decades became la Fédération québécoise des infirmières et infirmiers (FQII).

The early assistance from organized labor to Quebec nurses and the shared ideological perspectives explains why nurses in that province have stronger ties with organized labor than nurses in other provinces (l'Alliance des infirmières de Montréal, 1971).

With official recognition of the Montreal professional association, the Quebec City nurses reluctantly halted many previous activities and concentrated their efforts on collective bargaining. They formed the second federation of nurses' unions in the province, Fédération des syndicats professionels d'infirmières et infirmiers du Québec (FSPIIQ).

Not until 1965 was an anglophone nurses' union organized, the United Nurses, in Montreal. This occurred under the leadership of Joan Gilchrist with the assistance of the professional association, which by then had changed its stance on collective bargaining. Soon this new union became a bilingual organization, eventually forming the third nurses' federation in the province, Fédération des infirmières et infirmiers unis, Inc. (FIIU).

In 1987 the three nurses' federations (FIIU, FQII, and FSPIIQ) retained some membership responsibilities but invested their collective bargaining power in the newly formed province-wide Fédération des infirmières et infirmiers du Québec (FIIQ). Three factors prompted this regroupment:

1. The need for nurses to work together, to become a cohesive voice in the province
2. Bureaucratic centralization by the provincial government, which attempted to simplify the collective bargaining process and produce standard, province-wide agreements for each occupation
3. The threat of raids on the nurses' unions by other professional federations

Nurses in Quebec have begun to move away from a three-tiered union membership (involving local, regional, and provincial federations) to direct membership of autonomous unions in the provincial body. In adopting a two-tiered system, nurses came closer to the collective bargaining structure of other labor organizations in Quebec. In 1991, about 90 autonomous nurses' local and regional federations belonged to the FIIQ.

British Columbia

In the early 1940s, labor unions in British Columbia, as in other parts of the country, began to organize municipal and hospital employees. However, nurses did not fully trust these unions to represent their interests. They appealed to their professional associations to make special requests to provincial labor relations boards to exclude nurses from these bargaining units. (Bargaining units are defined by law as the most appropriate group of employees to negotiate together and allow for many different combinations of occupations.)

In 1943, Alice Wright, the executive director of the Registered Nurses' Association of British Columbia, formed a local committee to investigate the matter. Three years later, the British Columbia professional nurses' association accepted the responsibility for collective bargaining on behalf of its members. Evelyn Hood, a British Columbia nurse, was hired in 1951 by the newly created Labour Relations Committee to help nurses at hospitals and other work-sites to form local staff associations. Each of these, with Hood's assistance, bargained for a collective agreement with their respective employers.

During the next 10 years the following 10 major gains (Hood, 1956, p. 584) were made for nurses through unionization:

1. Salaries doubled
2. Communication and understanding increased between nurses and their employers
3. Feelings of job security for nurses increased
4. Nurses obtained a voice in the quality of their working conditions
5. A grievance procedure was established (an agreed method for processing problems and complaints)
6. Vacation time was increased
7. Yearly pay increments for service were established
8. Hours of work were reduced to 40 a week
9. There was an end to discrimination against hiring married women
10. Previous nursing experience and postgraduate experience were given full recognition in salary differentials

In 1959 nurses and the hospital association moved to province-wide bargaining, which meant all eligible nurses in the bargaining unit were covered by one collective agreement.

Other Provinces

After some study, the Canadian Nurses Association (CNA) went on record in 1944 as approving collective bargaining for nurses. There was one condition: that the bargaining agent or formal body representing nurses should be the provincial professional association. "Collective bargaining for nurses by nurses" became the rallying slogan for many years.

Although nurses in Quebec and British Columbia continued with unionization, nurses in other provinces hesitated for several reasons. They were concerned that management nurses would not be protected because, under existing labor relations legislation, only staff nurses could be part of a bargaining unit. The professional associations feared this would split the profession into two camps. An attempt was made to obtain special legislation to allow staff and management nurses in the same bargaining unit. As CNA's Labour Relations Consultant Glenna Rowsell later pointed out, "The problem of deciding at what level a nurse becomes management (within the meaning of the labor act) has plagued employers and provincial labor boards" (Rowsell, 1982, p. 42). The issue still is not fully resolved.

Despite these attempts, many nurses continued to reject unionization. They believed the aggressive bargaining stance required for successful negotiations was unladylike and unprofessional. They feared unionization would lead to nurses' strikes. At the 1946 annual meeting, members of the CNA expressed these sentiments by introducing an antistrike policy, (which was later rescinded).

Many nurses truly believed there were ways other than unionization to improve wages and working conditions, and they wanted an opportunity to try them. Thus the first step taken by provincial professional associations was establishment of employment relations committees (also called labor relations committees). These committees prepared recommended salary schedules, and standardized plans for work hours were circulated to all employers of nurses. Even this action was difficult for many nurses who had been trained in the ideology of "lady nurse" and believed it was crude, inappropriate, and unprofessional to discuss money. The prevailing attitude was if nurses did good work it would be recognized and rewarded.

Although a few employers adhered to the recommended salary schedules—many of which had been prepared with reference to hospital yearly budgets—the number who did so quickly diminished. This rejection was coupled with three other factors that led, finally, to unionization:

1. Nurses were unable to obtain special legislation to include all levels of nursing employment in one bargaining unit
2. There was a wave of expansion in unionization as other professionals and white collar workers organized and new unions "courted" nurses as potential members
3. Nurses were concerned that without improvement in wages and working conditions the profession would not attract quality recruits or retain experienced graduates in the field

Clearly there was little choice but to unionize.

Because nurses were already "organized"—they had professional organizations, an established system of communication, and a membership interested in unionization—within a few years nursing became one of the most completely unionized occupations in Canada. Nevertheless, this was not easily accomplished, and nurses experienced a number of "growing pains" in the process.

During the 6-year period from 1964 to 1970, nurses in the eight provinces other than Quebec and British Columbia began to unionize: Alberta nurses began in 1964; Manitoba and Ontario nurses in 1965; New Brunswick nurses in 1967; Nova Scotia, Prince Edward Island, and Saskatchewan nurses in 1968; and Newfoundland and Labrador nurses in 1970.

Collective bargaining is in essence a group action, but several nurses accepted leadership roles in the early period and are remembered fondly as the "mothers" of collective bargaining. These include Evelyn Hood and her successor, Nora Paton, in British Columbia; Joyce Gleason in Manitoba; Anne Gribben in Ontario; and especially Glenna Rowsell, the Labour Relations Consultant at the CNA. As CNA's consultant, Glenna Rowsell traveled from province to province during 1966 to 1969 helping nurses' professional associations prepare the needed social and legal structures to allow staff nurses to begin collective bargaining. Rowsell then spent the next 10 years as chief executive officer for the New Brunswick Nurses' Union and returned to CNA in 1979 as the director of the Labor Relations Department, a position she held until 1985.

After forming a staff nurses' association the next step was securing an agreement with the employer. When employers were willing, voluntary agreements were quickly written because management personnel found these simplified their work. When management resisted negotiations, nurses sought certification or full legal status as a union to increase their rights and their power to secure a collective agreement.

Recognition has always been the crux of collective bargaining; negotiations can not begin without it. Conciliation, the assistance of a third party to open talks between employer and union, is often needed. When employers refused to negotiate with nurses and conciliation failed, some staff nurse associations bound by provincial essential service legislation (which does not allow nurses to strike) tried mass resignations. Others resorted to their legal right to strike to gain recognition for negotiations to begin and to secure a first contract.

No one likes a strike and it is never easy for nurses to strike. In Canada, nurses always ensure emergency coverage. The typical nurses' strike lasted 10 days and involved approximately 2000 nurses. Injunctions preventing strikes or mandatory legislation requiring nurses to return to work exist, but they are the exception (Jensen, 1984).

In some provinces the right to strike is replaced with a system of compulsory arbitration in which one person (or more), nominated by the union and the employer, is hired to draft new terms for items under dispute. Prior to the drafting, the union and employer agree to honor the new terms of the collective agreement. Both methods of dispute settlement—arbitration and strikes—have advantages and disadvantages.

With the advent of unionization, nurses had a voice in the quality of their working conditions. Wages improved considerably and relatively unknown fringe benefits (e.g., paid holiday time, overtime pay, pensions, and dental plans) appeared. Another result of unionization and collective agreements is the grievance procedure, a method for addressing individual work-site problems and enforcing the collective agreement. In Canada, grievance procedures have not been well-used in the past; many nurses do not fully appreciate their value. As nurses become more aware of their rights and less fearful of being labeled as troublemakers or of losing their jobs, they are more willing to enforce the collective agreement by filing grievances.

Not all nurses protected by collective agreements concur ideologically with unionization, but when the Rand formula is part of their agreement, they must pay union dues. This formula is named for Justice Ivan Rand, who, in handing down a Canadian Supreme Court legislative decision in 1947, argued that unions must be protected— at least financially—because collective bargaining benefits all employees, even those who work in non-unionized facilities. Employers of non-union workplaces copy the terms of local collective agreements to recruit and retain staff, but neither they nor their staff bear the financial cost of collective bargaining.

Although unionization improved wages and working conditions and established grievance procedures for staff nurses, those outside of the bargaining unit (i.e., management nurses) remain unprotected. Because of the exclusion of management nurses from bargaining units, a recent tactic of some employers is to redefine the job descriptions of nurses to include minor management roles. This has the effect of removing these nurses from the bargaining unit and from the protection of the collective agreement. In Quebec and British Columbia there have been attempts to establish collective bargaining for management nurses, who are in the difficult position of being employees with employer's duties.

The development of new corporate structures in health care institutions, in many instances, has taken senior nurses out of the top management levels. The result is that chief executive nurses do not have an effective voice at the corporate policy level. In British Columbia in the 1980s, union nurses combined with management nurses in a "new found militancy" to fight for a nursing presence at the top administrative level (O'Brien, 1987).

UNION AUTONOMY: THE SASKATCHEWAN RULING

In the late 1960s and early 1970s, collective bargaining by Saskatchewan nurses was on an individual worksite basis, with local staff associations negotiating voluntary agreements with employers. The bargaining agent was the newly created labor relations committee of the Saskatchewan Registered Nurses Association. There had been talk about an independent nurses' union composed of all the staff nurses' associations and about regional bargaining to obtain collective agreements between nurses and all employers in a specific geographic region. The plan was to move, eventually, to province-wide bargaining.

Before this was accomplished, a change in Saskatchewan labor legislation altered everything. The legal exclusion of professionals from other workers' bargaining units was withdrawn. This meant any union could attempt to organize and represent nurses. When the Canadian wing of the United States based-Service Employees International Union (SEIU) and the Saskatchewan Registered Nurses Association each tried to assist hospital employees in Nipawin to unionize, SEIU contested the right of the professional association to represent nurses in collective bargaining, and the provincial labor relations board ruled against the professional association.

Upset with the ruling, the professional association appealed and the matter ended in the Supreme Court of Canada, which ruled that the professional association could not act as the bargaining agent because it was management dominated.

This decision shocked the profession because the main bargaining agent for most nurses in every province except Quebec was a special committee within the professional association. There had been discussions in most provinces about a separate collective bargaining entity, but professional associations were reluctant to give up the powerful new "baby" for fear it was not ready to stand on its own. The reality of expensive and time-consuming court actions, such as those in Saskatchewan, spurred the separation of the unions from their parent bodies, the professional associations.

In Ontario, the nurses' union separated in 1973; in Newfoundland in 1974; in Manitoba in 1975; in Nova Scotia in 1976; in Alberta in 1977; in New Brunswick in 1978; and in British Columbia in 1981. In Prince Edward Island, the need for legislative changes did not allow the separation to be formally completed until 1988.

UNION MERGERS

After separation of the union from the professional association, small local staff nurses' associations began to merge into a single large provincial nurses' union. This made province-wide bargaining with the newly created hospital associations a strong possibility. However, a few small independent unions still existed, primarily unions of public health nurses. Nurses who were direct government employees continued to belong to provincial or federal public service unions.

During the late 1960s, when the nurses' union movement was gaining momentum across the country, executive members often turned to cohorts in other provinces for information and advice. In these exchanges, they began to recognize interprovincial effects of negotiations and settlements. Many union executives believed contract goals and priorities should be addressed at a national level and in 1981 an organization was created for this purpose, the National Federation of Nurses' Unions (NFNU). Six provincial nurses' unions, represented by their presidents, were part of NFNU's founding convention: Jill Jones, Saskatchewan; Sonny Arrajado, Manitoba; Mary Arsenault, New Brunswick; Lois Hall, Nova Scotia; Mary Macaulay, Prince Edward Island; and June Petten, Newfoundland and Labrador. Five years later two other nurses' unions joined, represented by their presidents: Louise Rogers, Staff Nurses Association of Alberta; and Pat McLeod, Professional Institute of the Public Service of Canada (PIPSC). This latter union represents federally employed nurses in the provinces and territories.

Not all provincial nurses' unions feel the need for the national body. In British Columbia, Alberta, and Ontario, nurses continue to discuss the issue; in Quebec, they believe the enormous task of setting up a provincial federation and making it work is a pressing priority.

Table 27-1 lists the major nurses' unions in the 10 provinces, showing the year collective bargaining activity began and, if it had been organized through the professional association, the year it separated. The union newsletters are listed and membership figures are given for 1990.

TABLE 27-1 **Major Nurses' Unions by Province, 1990**

Major Nurses' Union	Year Formed	Year of Autonomy
British Columbia Nurses' Union (BCNU)	1946	1981
United Nurses of Alberta (UNA)	1964	1977
Saskatchewan Union of Nurses (SUN)	1968	1973
Manitoba Organization of Nurses' Associations (MONA)	1965	1975
Ontario Nurses' Association (ONA)	1965	1973
Fédération des infirmieres et infirmièrs du Québec (FIIQ)	1987	
New Brunswick Nurses' Union (NBNU)	1967	1978
Nova Scotia Nurses' Union (NSNU)	1968	1976
Prince Edward Island Nurses' Union (PEINU)	1968	1988
Newfoundland and Labrador Nurses' Union (NLNU)	1970	1974
(Federally-employed nurses)		

Publication	Membership	Other Unions in Province Representing Nurses
BCNU Reports 6/year	20,500 RNs	Union of Psychiatric Nurses (UPN)
UNA News Bulletin 6/year	12,500 RNs	Staff Nurse Association of Alberta (SNAA) Alberta Union of Provincial Employees (AUPE) Several Public Health Nurses Unions and a few Staff Nurses Associations with voluntary recognition
Sunspots 9/year	6000 RNs	Saskatchewan Government Employees' Association (SGEA)
MONA Pulse 6/year	10,000 RNs, LPNs, ORTs	Manitoba Government Employees Association (MGEA)
ONA News 12/year	52,000 RNs	Ontario Public Service Employees' Union (OP-SEU)
Le pouls 4/year	44,000 RNs	Negotiation rights are invested in the provincial FIIQ. Three nurses' federations retain some membership responsibilities: Fédération des syndicats professionels d'infirmières et d'infirmiers du Québec (FSPIIQ) formed in 1939, Fédération québecoise des infirmières et infirmiers (FQII) formed in 1946, and Fédération des infirmieres et infirmiers unis inc. (FIIU) formed in 1965 A few nurses are members of trade unions
The Parasol 4/year	4800 RNs, CNAs	
NSNU Newsletter 4/year	3300 RNs, CNAs	Nova Scotia Government Employees Union (NSGEU), 2200 RNs
Concerns 4/year	680 RNs	Prince Edward Island Public Service Association (PEIPSA)
In Touch 4/year	3575 RNs	
	1600 RNs	Nursing Group, Professional Institute of the Public Service of Canada (PIPSC)

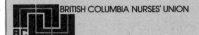

BRITISH COLUMBIA NURSES' UNION

Objectives of the British Columbia Nurses' Union

* The advancement of the social, economic and general welfare of nurses and other allied personnel.
* To regulate relations between nurses and other allied personnel and their employers through collective bargaining and negotiation of written contracts with employers implementing progressively better conditions of employment.
* The promotion of effective communication with employers.
* The promotion of knowledge of nurses and other allied personnel in all matters related to their social and economic welfare through education and research.
* The promotion of the highest standards of health care for all.
* To continue to offer and develop programs of professional development, financial and other programs of assistance for nurses and other allied personnel.
* To establish, organize, administer or participate in an assurance, benefit or protection plan, or subsidiary services, for the welfare of its members.
* Promotion of unity with the nursing profession and other allied fields through co-operation and support of organizations sharing these objectives, in particular, with the Board of Directors of the Registered Nurses' Association of British Columbia.

From British Columbia Nurses' Union. (1990). Article 2-Objectives. *British Columbia Nurses' Union Constitution and Bylaws* (As amended by voting delegates to the BCNU annual convention on October 23, 1990) (p. 3). Vancouver: Author. Reprinted with permission.

UNION OBJECTIVES

During the 1960s and 1970s when nurses' unions were drafting their constitutions, they collaborated on their objectives. As a result, the constitutions of the nurses' unions have similarities and, in many cases, identical wording. The constitution of the British Columbia Nurses' Union is shown in the box.

Several provincial nurses' union constitutions are worded to allow membership to other health care workers. Currently, only three (Manitoba, New Brunswick, and Nova Scotia) have expanded in this direction and include certified (licensed) nursing assistants and operating room technicians. The recent experience in Manitoba of having a certified nursing assistant as president of the nurses' union forced members to examine their prejudices and elitist attitudes fostered by the quasi-militaristic organization of work in the health care system. However, blurring status distinctions between health care workers is worrisome to a few nurses who see this as an overt rejection of the long struggle to become a distinct profession.

In provinces such as Alberta, which lack an industrial base and strong industrial labor movement and where the civil service unions are bound by essential service legislation forbidding strikes, the nurses' unions are forced into a leadership role in the labor movement. This new political responsibility of nurses' unions concerns many who strongly identify with the "lady professional" image.

CLIMATE OF CONFLICT

In each province, the nurses' union or unions and the professional association have overlapping, but not identical, memberships. By law, the union membership is confined to nonmanagement nurses (although some bargaining units include head nurses). In contrast, membership in the professional association is open to all nurses. In Ontario, where the College of Nurses has the legal responsibility for registering and licensing nurses and the professional association has a more "associative" function, not all nurses belong to the latter organization. In other provinces, where the statutory and associative functions are combined, nurses must be members of the professional association to practice, although they often are not active participants in the organization.

It is in leadership circles that the differences between the two nursing bodies are most often expressed. Leaders in the professional associations are often nursing administrators and educators, whereas union leaders are drawn from the staff nurse membership. Critics of the unions view staff nurses in leadership roles as a contradiction in status—subordinates who won political power without earning it through advanced education, positions of great responsibility, or years of service "paying their dues" and "learning how to handle power." Critics of professional associations view nursing administrators and educators in leadership positions as too aligned with management, "out of touch" with the bedside, and having "lost sight" of the real needs of nurses.

There is an awareness in unions and professional associations of each other's mandates and, following from these, of their separate roles and functions (see box, p. 570). However, it is in the interpretation and fulfilling of these roles that territorial and ideological disputes arise.

The mandate of the professional association is to promote the profession of nursing and to protect the public interest. This is accomplished by examination of graduates, registration and licensing of nurses, and disciplining of members. Related to these are the secondary functions: setting of educational standards; defining standards of nursing practice; carrying out research; and representing the profession to the public and to governments on professional matters and health issues.

The mandate of the unions is to protect and advance the social, economic, and general welfare of nurses. This is accomplished by collective bargaining and negotiations for wages, benefits, hours of work, and better conditions of employment. Related functions include monitoring standards in the workplace, enforcing the collective agreement through processing grievances, labor education, and research.

The grey areas, those in which the activities of the unions and professional associations often overlap and conflict, include ethics of the profession, standards of

Perceived Roles of the Professional Associations and Nurses' Unions

Professional Associations	Nurses' Unions

Mandates

To promote the profession of nursing and to protect the public interest	To advance social, economic and general welfare of nurses

Primary roles

• Registration of members • Licensing of nurses • Examination of graduates • Discipline of members	• Negotiations for wages, benefits, hours of work, and standards of employment

Secondary functions

• Establish educational standards • Establish standards of practice • Professional research • Representations to government	• Enforcing the collective agreement through processing grievances • Labor education • Labor research • Standards in the workplace

Grey areas
• Ethics
• Standards of practice
• Quality of care
• Political issues

practice, quality of care, and larger political issues. These are areas that must be addressed in the 1990s. For example, ethical concerns arose when the CNA introduced a new code of ethics in the late 1970s. This code contained a clause many unions interpreted as antistrike in nature. Such a statement, protested union executives, was a form of public chastisement, as well as a rejection of the rules and legal rights under which unions operate.

One major conflict in the grey area involves the range of items recently brought into contract negotiations by the unions—especially those on standards of practice. The main problem is one of definition. The associations, on one hand, view standards of practice as pertaining to the work of the individual nurse. Thus maintaining standards involves enhancing the knowledge and competence of nurses and disciplining them when this is warranted. The unions, on the other hand, view standards of practice as pertaining to the working environment. They accept the competence of the nurse. Good working conditions, they argue, mean nurses can give quality

care. Conversely, poor working conditions such as insufficient staff or badly organized working schedules result in poorer patient care.

To deal with poor working conditions, many unions negotiate for a professional
responsibility clause in the collective agreement. This clause outlines a special grievance procedure to address problems in the workplace related to quality of care. Some
members of professional associations argue that matters concerning the organization
of work are management issues and are beyond the mandate of the unions. The
unions, however, believe that all matters that affect the work of the nurse and the
ability to give good patient care are negotiable.

Some leaders in professional associations are jealous of a perceived preference
and loyalty by the staff nurses for the unions, which occurs because union representatives work with regular members in a relationship of equality. This allows more
effective communication between nurses and the union than between staff nurses
and the professional association. Since the professional association may also be
perceived as being management dominated and authoritarian, some staff nurses are
not comfortable with the professional association and believe association leaders do
not understand their problems. As a result, staff nurses usually complain to the
union, although this may not be the most appropriate body to handle the matter.

When good relations exist between unions and the professional association, there
is an active system of referrals. When hostility exists, the referral system breaks
down. The result is that both union and professional associations may ignore an
issue as outside its mandate or that both may take on the issue separately. Such
actions can generate feelings of territorial encroachment and result in anger between
the two executive bodies.

When they work together, the two organizations can be a powerful agent of
change, especially in the larger political arena where the game of divide and conquer
is skillfully played by other vested interests, such as politicians and physicians.

It is generally agreed that one of the tasks of the professional association is to
introduce new theoretical perspectives for the profession. Often, however, the association does not have the political power or "clout" to institute these ideals.
Through the process of collective bargaining, the unions do have this power, and
the professional status of the members often gives the nurses' unions greater credibility than those of other occupations at the bargaining table.

Matters in the grey area that will demand attention during the 1990s include:
- Pay equity for nursing, which addresses the classic problem of how women's
  work has been historically undervalued and underpaid
- Threats to the national medical and hospital insurance programs
- Environmental issues

In these areas, as citizens and professionals, nurses need to have a strong, united
voice.

Alice Baumgart, now president of the Canadian Nurses Association, stated in
1982: "The real issue [for professional associations *and* unions] . . . is how to assure
that each has enough power to exercise effective influence" (p. 23).

In several provinces, the unions and professional associations have liaison officers
whose role is to promote productive communications between their respective or-

ganizations and to foster cooperative efforts. With communication channels open, the resources of unions and professional associations can be combined to create a stronger profession and to work toward common goals, such as better patient care. With a continuation of prejudicial attitudes, petty personal competition, and a lack of understanding of the changing roles of each other, both organizations suffer. Nursing itself is weakened; its advocacy role for patients is diminished. Both organizations must demonstrate an openness and willingness to set aside old hostilities, to admit to each other's strengths and weaknesses, and to avoid unrealistic expectations of each other. Such actions will lead to more mature nursing organizations representing the profession and promoting quality health care in Canada.

ACKNOWLEDGEMENT

Special thanks are extended to Kathleen Connors, president, National Federation of Nurses' Unions, for information used in the tables, and to Doreen Whitehead, executive director of Fédération des infirmières et infirmiers unis, Inc., for recent information on Quebec.

REFERENCES

Baumgart, A. (1982). Nursing for a new century—a future framework. *Journal of Advanced Nursing, 7,* 19-23.

Botterhill-Conroy, D. (1980). *Labour relations, collective bargaining and nursing.* Unpublished Master's Degree Major Paper, University of Alberta.

Canadian Nurses Association (1958). *The first fifty years: An historical outline.* Ottawa: Author.

Coburn, J. (1974). "I see and am silent": A short history of nursing in Ontario. *Women at work in Ontario, 1850-1930* (pp. 127-163). Toronto: Canadian Women's Educational Press.

Hood, E. (1956). Economic security in British Columbia. *American Journal of Nursing, 56,* 583-585.

Jensen, P. (1984). *Collective bargaining of nurses in Canada.* Unpublished doctoral dissertation, University of Toronto.

l'Alliance des infirmières de Montréal. (1971). *Si Florence revenait au Québec.* Montreal: Author.

Nevitt, J. (1978). *White caps and black bands.* St. John's, Nfld: Jesperson Printing.

O'Brien, V. (1987). An introspective look at the history of RNABC. *RNABC News, 19*(1), 10-12.

Rowsell, G. (1982). Changing trends in labor relations: Effects on collective bargaining for nurses. *International Nursing Review, 29*(5), 141-145.

Seymer, L. (1960). *Florence Nightingale's nurses.* London: Pitman Medical Publishing.

Weir, G.M. (1932). *Survey of nursing education in Canada.* Toronto: University of Toronto Press.

Woodham-Smith, C. (1977). *Florence Nightingale.* (Original work published 1950.) Glasgow: William Collins & Sons.

During the January 1991 strike by Manitoba nurses, the longest-ever strike by Canadian nurses, a march to the Legislature was organized in Winnipeg so that nurses could make their positions known to members of the Legislative Assembly. (Photograph supplied courtesy of the Manitoba Nurses' Union. Used with permission.)

CHAPTER TWENTY-EIGHT

Strikes by Nurses

JUDITH M. HIBBERD, RN, PhD

Judith M. Hibberd, RN, SCM, MHSA, PhD, is a graduate of St. Thomas' Hospital, London, England, and of the Universities of Toronto and Alberta. Her work experiences include teaching and nursing service administration, and a major academic interest is in labor relations in nursing. She has been active in professional associations and is currently an Associate Professor, Faculty of Nursing, University of Alberta.

Collective bargaining is widely endorsed by Canadian nurses but the possibility of having to withdraw their services to achieve socioeconomic goals remains a controversial issue. Strikes by nurses are no longer rare events, a fact that represents a sad commentary on the historical relations between nurses and their employers. Effective use of the strike has done much to advance the socioeconomic status of nurses, but it has done little to achieve consensus among them on the question of its appropriateness as a strategy for professionals engaged in health care.

As a form of social conflict, strikes tend to be newsworthy events that attract considerable media attention, but they are often misunderstood by the general public. At the heart of every strike is a power struggle between employees and employers, and when disputes such as health worker strikes occur in the public sector, the government is invariably drawn into the conflict because of its role in funding health care and in protecting public interests. The threat posed by a reduction in health services to the health and safety of the public constitutes an additional dimension to the phenomenon of strike, hence labor disputes in the health field often occupy a central position in the political arena.

Unions may capitalize on the political nature of public sector strikes by timing them to coincide with national or provincial events. Alberta's nurses staged their 1988 strike on the eve of the XV Winter Olympic Games in Calgary, and Quebec's nurses walked out in 1989 just before a provincial election. At such critical times unions use their bargaining power to put pressure on governments and health agency employers to settle the dispute expediently to avoid negative political fallout. Rarely, however, is a strike purely political. One significant example of a political strike is the 1962 doctors' strike in Saskatchewan, which protested the implementation of medical care insurance in that province. According to Badgley and Wolfe (1967), the doctors' strike represented an abuse of the democratic process because it was an attempt to "subvert legislation to which a duly elected government had been committed" (p. 172). Many health care workers in Canada are prohibited from striking and some groups withdraw their services during contract negotiations to protest not only lack of progress at the bargaining table but also the labor laws they regard as restrictive and unfair.

Nurses turned to unions in significant numbers as a means of addressing their frustrations that resulted from an era of cost constraint, inflation, and failure of administrators to address their work-life problems and concerns. The proportion of nurses unionized in Canada is approximately 75% compared to 20% in the United States (O'Connor and Gibson, 1990). The structure of bargaining, in particular its centralization in each of the provinces, gives nurses' unions significant power to secure improvements in their terms and conditions of employment. In general, the economic and noneconomic gains could not have been achieved without their willingness to resort to strike and threats of strike. Most of the nonmonetary gains, however, are on institutional problems that relate to the context of nursing practice, such as securing mechanisms to protest operational deficiencies. The potential is there, however, for nurses to effect radical changes in the organization and management of nursing services designed to promote the quality of nursing practice and to bring about reform in the health care system at large. As Badgley (1975) notes, radical reshaping of the health system has seldom been the objective of striking workers, but that where the rights and health of patients are preserved, "strikes can serve as an important catalyst in converting a rigid and conservative health system into a more flexible democratic organization for all its workers" (p. 15).

This chapter explores the nature of strikes, reviews selected theories and research, and examines the incidence of strikes by nurses. Ethical issues are discussed, and several contemporary trends are identified that emerged as a result of four recent province-wide strikes in Alberta, Saskatchewan, British Columbia, and Quebec. The chapter concludes with a note on the alternatives to strike action and prospects for the future.

NATURE OF STRIKES

A strike is a temporary and collective refusal to work by employees acting together to compel an employer to agree to their demands or to resolve their complaints. It is generally agreed that strikes are complex forms of social conflict or group tensions, each consisting of a unique set of circumstances (Gouldner, 1954). However, four common elements—group activity, mobilization, refusal to work, and agreement—can be found in all strikes.

Group activity. A strike is a group activity and it is from its collective nature that a strike derives its coercive force (Gubbels, 1968). A strike is often described as a strategy of last resort because it is intended to impose pressure and significant costs on employers to the extent that they will prefer to settle on the union's terms. A strike is intended to hurt the employer. It is thus an aggressive and powerful economic instrument often referred to in warlike metaphors (e.g., weapon, fight, battle).

Mobilization. The second element is that when individuals act in concert to achieve a common purpose, there must be communication mechanisms and organization to mobilize, and these processes require leaders to effect group activity. Leaders must articulate the goals and dissatisfactions of the group (Karsh, 1958).

Refusal to work. A third element is the cessation of work that creates disorder in an otherwise stable environment. Gouldner (1954) explains that there are technological consequences when workers refuse to obey because the authority relations of a social system are disrupted. When nurses withdraw their services, the consequences are such that hospitals cannot continue to operate without major reductions in service, primarily because of the central position occupied by nurses in the sociotechnical system. Almost all the parts of the hospital system depend on the continuing function of nurses, and the effect of their absence may have dire consequences for patients. These factors, with the observation that nurses often include issues in their negotiating demands that tend to be less amenable to settlement at the bargaining table (e.g., nurse-patient ratios), have led to the description of nurses' strikes as "a breed apart" (Metzger, Ferentino, and Kruger, 1984, p. 89).

Agreement. The final common element of strikes is the resolution, which normally requires an agreement between the parties. Agreement is an act of cooperation, however grudgingly made. The agreement represents a new basis for the employment relationship, establishing the rules for ensuring fairness and equity. In a much-quoted summary of the nature of strikes, Karsh says:

> The strike, or threat of strike, is the ultimate device whereby the competing interests of antagonistic parties are expediently resolved leading to a *modus operandi* which permits both sides to accommodate their differences and live with one another. (1958, p. 13)

TYPES OF STRIKES

The strike may have many tactical forms. Before the days of bargaining collectively within a legal framework, nurses typically staged demonstrations, resigned, or threatened to resign *en masse* to protest the terms and conditions of employment (Cormick, 1969; Miller and Dodson, 1977). Other so-called job actions included calling in sick, working to rule, and other disruptive activities such as refusing to work overtime or to perform non-nursing duties. There was no legal or institutional protection for these activities, and employers were under no obligation to listen to nurses' complaints. With the passage of labor legislation permitting public sector unionization, some jurisdictions allow strikes by health workers under certain prerequisite conditions. For instance, if there is an impasse in bargaining, the parties may be required to obtain the services of a mediator before resorting to a strike or lockout.

It is useful to categorize strikes into types so that when examining the results of research, comparisons are made between the same type of social action. One typology distinguishes between official and unofficial strikes, depending on whether the strike has authorization of union executives (Hyman, 1972; Knowles, 1952). Strikes can also be categorized according to the status of the contract: for example, the majority of strikes in Canada occur during the process of renewing collective agreements; strikes may also be staged to obtain a first agreement, usually known as recognition strikes; and the third category refers to strikes that occur during the term of an agreement. This latter type is often referred to as a wildcat strike and is illegal in Canada. However, strikes during the term of an agreement in Canada account for 11.8% of all strikes and lockouts during the years 1980 to 1985 (Anderson and Gunderson, 1989, p. 293). Wildcat strikes by Canadian nurses are virtually unknown or, if they occur, are too brief and inconsequential to be labeled as such.

The threat of strike can be a very effective bargaining tool, and there have been many of these in nursing. Voting to strike creates a dilemma for nurses, but often what is needed is a show of support for union negotiators. Consequently a nurse may vote for strike action hoping not to make good the threat. When the majority of union members vote in favor of strike, it strengthens the power and credibility of their representatives who can then return to the negotiating table well armed for what is often the final showdown before reaching a settlement. Thus a strike threat may produce just enough pressure to resolve an impasse without the cost and anguish of an all-out strike. On an historical note, Florence Nightingale used such threats against her employer. Evidently frustrated by administrative policies while working in Harley Street, she wrote: "If a repair is not done I will encamp with my twelve patients in the middle of Cavendish Square and let the police and the Committee come and rout me out as a vagrant" (cited in Verley, 1970, p. ix).

The strike is the union's economic weapon; the corresponding weapon available to employers is the lockout. Simply stated, the employer notifies the union that the agency will temporarily cease operating, literally locking out employees to compel them to agree to the terms offered. Hospital employers are reluctant to use this strategy because of their mandate to the public, but they may be forced to if, for example, a union employs rotating strikes. Community health agencies have used the lockout against public health nurses, sometimes avoiding a budgetary deficit in the process.

THEORY AND RESEARCH

Theories of strikes are as varied as the disciplines that study them. Economists demonstrate relationships between strike activity and the business cycle, unemployment, and inflation rates. Such aggregate studies often attempt to explain differences in the level of strike activity across countries, regions, and industries. Industrial sociologists, on the other hand, usually focus on work settings and group interaction, whereas behavioral scientists search for explanations of strikes at the institutional level of inquiry using bargaining and game theories (Kochan, 1980). One of the most influential theories is that of Chamberlain and Kuhn (1965) who define bargaining power in terms of an opponent's willingness (at the bargaining table) to agree to a party's terms (demands). That willingness depends in turn on the cost of disagreeing with those terms relative to the cost of agreeing with them. In other words, a nurses' union can be said to exercise effective bargaining power if the employer decides that the cost of conceding to its demands is preferable to the cost of refusing to concede, thereby incurring a strike. Cost, in this case, is defined broadly to include the direct incremental costs of the salary and fringe benefit demands and also nonmonetary costs such as patient safety, angry physicians, negative public reaction, and even the psychological cost of "saving face." An assumption underlying the theory is that the parties rationally calculate their costs before deciding whether to strike or lock out. The truth is that negotiators often behave irrationally; however, the theory underscores the fact that strikes result from decisions made on both sides of the bargaining table. Although the union is regarded as the aggressor in strike action, employers are also responsible for the decision to "take" a strike rather than concede to union demands.

Strike as an investment is another approach to calculating whether the costs outweigh the benefits of strike action (Fisher and Williams, 1989). According to this theory, a worker invests what might be lost in terms of salary and benefits during a strike to induce the employer to improve the final offer. For the individual nurse, this suggests that in terms of salary alone, one week of strike action must produce at least 2% increase in wages to recover that "investment" over one year. A strike can also be viewed as a longer term investment in the bargaining relationship, setting the stage for future sets of negotiations by reminding management that the workers' union is a serious opponent.

Identifying causes or determinants of strikes generates a great deal of research. Causes of strikes can be categorized according to economic and noneconomic factors. It is commonly assumed that money is the causal factor in disputes, but most of the time strikes are caused by multiple factors. Noneconomic factors often contribute to strikes and may include legal, political, and historical factors; characteristics of the various actors in the negotiating process; bargaining structure; and personal and interpersonal relationships (Anderson and Gunderson, 1989). In a study of a series of strikes by nurses, economic and sociopolitical factors were identified as primary causes, including militant union leadership, wage demands that exceed public funding guidelines, and structural and procedural constraints of bargaining in the public sector (Hibberd, 1988).

Studies of strikes by nurses for the most part have been case studies, although there were at least three surveys: one in Canada (Jensen, 1984) and two in the United States (Kalisch, Kalisch, and Young, 1983; Miller and Dodson, 1977). Many case studies provide rich, descriptive information about particular struggles of groups of nurses and their hospital employers (examples include Bloom, O'Reilly and Parlette, 1979; Eberle, 1982; Grand, 1971; Hibberd, 1987; Jacox, 1969; Levi, 1980; Manning, 1982; Zacur, 1982). Although these studies are unlikely to contribute to any comprehensive theory of strikes by nurses, they suggest that nurses have a powerful means of bringing attention to their socioeconomic needs. The studies also reveal common concerns among nurses and a determination to improve working conditions that jeopardize the care of patients.

Ethical Issues

One of the more troubling aspects of collective bargaining by nurses is the right to withdraw services and under what circumstances. Unions generally agree that the freedom to strike is a fundamental, inalienable right of workers, but the Supreme Court of Canada recently ruled otherwise. A majority of judges state that:

> the guarantee of freedom of association in S. 2(d) of the Canadian Charter of Rights and Freedoms does not include (in the case of a trade union) a guarantee of the right to bargain collectively and of the right to strike. (Re: Public Service Employee Relations Act, 1987, p. 161)

Thus apparently the provisions of the Charter may not be used by unions to prevent Canadian legislatures from limiting the freedom of employees when their refusal to work deprives the public of essential services. When such restrictions are placed on use of the strike, the definition of essential services remains a controversial issue. It is a moot point whether or not all nursing services are essential, but in any event the underlying dilemma in a nurses' strike is one of conflicting principles. The problem is clearly outlined in a question posed by Kluge (1982):

> [Are nurses] by virtue of [their] profession, ethically bound to subordinate control over the disposition of [their] services to the needs of the client/patient, or may [they] resort to withdrawal of services in order to resolve working conditions that violate justice? (p. 3)

Answers to this question require thoughtful consideration of many issues, including contractual and professional arguments, ethical principles of beneficence and justice, and obligations and duties of a nurse as an autonomous moral agent. It seems clear from professional arguments that nurses have a duty to work toward securing working conditions that permit the achievement of health care goals (Canadian Nurses Association, 1985). Nurses may be obligated to withdraw services when working conditions beyond their control are such that ethical integrity cannot be maintained. It is also clear from ethical arguments that withdrawing services to produce a future good, such as attracting more nurses into the profession, is not sufficient reason for ignoring immediate duties such as providing care to an accident victim (Connelly, Evans, Dahlen, and Wieker, 1979; Lauer, 1986; Muyskens, 1982). Muyskens (1982) explains, there can be no possible moral justification for launching a strike to improve conditions so that future lives can be saved while losing a patient's life here and now. Although the precise responsibility of health workers at such times is questioned (Brecher, 1985, 1986), most physicians and nurses would concur with Muyskens, as exemplified by their customary willingness to maintain essential or emergency services during their strikes, although this has not always been the case.

The initial refusal of professional nurses' associations to adopt strikes as a bargaining tool was undoubtedly motivated by the highest of service ideals, but it represented a rejection of power by the powerless. Experience with the realities of collective bargaining soon revealed that any assumption nurse leaders may have had that employers would respect their gesture of good faith and refrain from exploiting them proved false. The Canadian Nurses Association (CNA) rescinded its no-strike policy in 1972 under pressure from the provinces (Mussallem, 1977), but this policy reversal did not resolve the issue for nurses. Lack of consensus exists, as illustrated by the divergence of opinion in the United Kingdom among unions that represent nurses. The largest union, The Royal College of Nurses, retains its ban on strikes by nurses (Thompson, Melia, and Boyd, 1988), and according to a physician's article in the *British Medical Journal*, the salaries of nurses in that country are scandalous (Delamothe, 1988). He also observes that:

> In return for no strike agreements made in the late 1970s policemen and firemen en-joyed large salary increases and then subsequent index linking of their salaries. If such arrangements are good enough for policemen and firemen, then surely they are good enough for nurses. (p. 123)

This evidence suggests that gender is an influential element in bargaining power even when services are deemed essential to public welfare.

Despite lifting its ban on strikes, the CNA Board of Directors approved a *Code of Ethics* in 1980 that stated unequivocally: "When a nurse is working under conditions which violate justice, the withdrawal of needed services to patients as a means of resolving such injustices is unethical" (Roach, 1980). Section III of the code, in which this statement appeared, was later deleted. A subsequent *Code of Ethics* (CNA, 1985) puts less stringent duties on nurses, recognizing their right to choose job action, as well as the right of "clients whose safety requires ongoing or emergency nursing care . . . to have those needs satisfied throughout the duration of any job action" (p. 30). According to this *Code of Ethics*, nurses "participating in job actions have a duty of coordination and communication to take steps reasonably designed to ensure the safety of clients" (p. 30). Thus it seems from a professional perspective that nurses must determine within their unions and associations how their duty to ensure the safety of patients will be fulfilled in the event of a strike.

ESSENTIAL SERVICES

Governments generally restrict the right to strike of workers who provide essential services to the public and substitute mandatory post-impasse procedures (Christensen, 1980). Hospital-employed nurses are regarded as essential services in several Canadian provinces, although it could be argued that the withdrawal of certain ambulatory and hospital-based services would not create an immediate threat to public health and safety. Even though a strike by hospital nurses can be tolerated for a while, the magnitude of the threat to public health and safety is likely to increase in direct proportion to the duration of the strike. Governments sometimes choose to enact back-to-work legislation, temporarily curtailing nurses' right to strike in the interest of public health and safety, and requiring the parties to submit their disputes to arbitration.

In some jurisdictions, for example in Quebec and British Columbia, nurses have a legal right to strike providing certain designated essential services are maintained.

Unions and employers are sometimes required to agree on the type and extent of services to be designated as essential during a strike. Reaching agreement on the designation of essential services often entails as much haggling as the bargaining issues themselves, and failure to agree may draw third parties into the process to impose an arbitrary decision. Employers are often unwilling to reduce the level of hospital operation to the extent demanded by nurses' unions, or they may agree to the reductions and then continue to admit patients, which usually leads to greater friction between the parties.

There has been no requirement to designate essential workers during nurses' strikes in Alberta or Saskatchewan. The policy of the United Nurses of Alberta (UNA) during its 1982 strike was to delegate the decision with respect to essential services to local unions. Rather than designating nurses to maintain specific essential services, most locals established an emergency service to respond to critical situations. The policy is outlined in the box. Predictably, physicians were angered by this policy, claiming it was their responsibility to determine medical emergencies. The policy of the union was motivated partly by skepticism as to whether employers would attempt to increase the level of operation if nurses provided essential or emergency services; partly because it wanted to avoid any preemptive move by government to declare a state of emergency as had been the case in two previous strikes; and partly because union leaders believed that when on strike a nurse has no obligation to an employer and consequently no obligation to an employer's patients. Nevertheless, small groups of nurses chose to maintain essential services in critical care areas, often being subjected to the derision of their peers as they crossed picket lines (Hibberd, 1987).

The statutory requirement to designate a proportion of union members to provide essential services during a strike may lessen the effect of a total withdrawal of services. However, the disruption in hospital services of the withdrawal of approx-

Nurses' Emergency Service Policy

1. Decision to provide emergency services rests with the local union
2. Local strike committee establishes terms of reference
3. Employer sends requests for assistance to the strike committee or designated person
4. Nurse(s) enter(s) the hospital to assess the legitimacy of the request and need for service
5. Patient(s) stabilized as necessary
6. Nurse(s) withdraw(s) from the workplace

From Hibberd JM (1987): *The labour disputes of Alberta Nurses: 1972-1982.* Unpublished doctoral dissertation, University of Alberta, Edmonton. Used with permission.

imately 25% of nurses in British Columbia and 10% in Quebec was sufficient to achieve some, if not all, of their bargaining objectives. The willingness to maintain essential services undoubtedly keeps public support on the side of nurses and is more consistent with the spirit of the CNA *Code of Ethics* (1985) than the ad hoc emergency system devised by the UNA.

In Alberta and Quebec, heavy fines have been levied against unions, union leaders, and individual union members for engaging in illegal strikes or ignoring court injunctions. It is not clear whether a nurse would be disciplined by a licensing body for unprofessional conduct, and no doubt it would depend on the filing of a complaint against an individual nurse by a member of the public. On the question of the legal liability of unions for the consequences of strikes, a class-action suit is currently being brought by a Public Trustee against three Quebec unions on behalf of mentally incompetent hospital patients, alleging deprivation of regular care causing emotional distress and insecurity. The case, if successful, may set a precedent in determining a union's responsibility to patients during strikes (*Nursing Report*, 1989, 17:26).

INCIDENCE OF STRIKES BY NURSES

There were 32 strikes by nurses in Canada between 1966 and 1982, according to official records (Hibberd, 1987, p. 33). In 1988 to 1989 there were five strikes, four of which were major province-wide work stoppages, giving the impression that there is a growing propensity among nurses to take strike action. Figures on the incidence of strikes are not readily available because official statistics since 1986 only account for strikes involving more than 500 workers. Nurses' strikes may range from as few as 29 nurses to as many as 11,000 (see Table 28-1). Table 28-1 also contains an approximation of the overall strike activity of Canadian nurses by province from 1985 to 1989. The data were collected from various sources, and no attempt was made to include strikes (if any) by nurses represented by industry or government employee unions. In this 5-year period there were ten strikes, one lockout, six threatened strikes, and one threatened mass resignation. In addition to problems of accurate and inclusive strike data, there are other peculiarities to consider before deciding if strikes are on the increase among nurses.

Terms of the various collective agreements are not uniform throughout the country; therefore the opportunity to take strike action is uneven. For example, the 1989 strike by British Columbia nurses arose while renewing a 4-year contract that was ultimately replaced by a 2-year contract. There was only one opportunity to strike between 1986 and 1989, but there may be more than one opportunity in the next 4 years, depending on the length of subsequent agreements. Therefore it is important to remember the bargaining calendar when examining the frequency of strikes.

It is estimated that, in general, strikes or lockouts occur in about 10% to 15% of contract renewal negotiations in Canada (Craig, 1986). Canada held the dubious record of ranking second only to Italy in terms of days lost per worker due to strikes during the 1970s and 1980s (Anderson and Gunderson, 1989), a phenomenon thought to be due in part to longer strikes in Canada and the United States compared to other industrialized countries. Frequency of strikes is only one component of the

TABLE 28-1 Strikes, Threatened Strikes, and Lockouts of Canadian Nurses: 1985 - 1989

Jurisdiction	1985	1986
British Columbia	120 Long-term care RNs and graduate nurses 21-day strike	
Alberta	Community health RNs 10-month strike	
Saskatchewan		
Manitoba		
Ontario		
Quebec		
Federal Government		

From Labour Canada (1985): *Strikes and lockouts in Canada*, Ottawa: Minister of Supply and Services; *Collective bargaining review* (1986-1990): Ottawa: Minister of Supply and Services; *The Nursing Report* (1987-1989) (various issues), Toronto: Carswell.

phenomenon. Official figures usually reveal additional factors, including scope (number of workers involved), strike duration, and total days of work lost as a percentage of total days worked. Provincial legislation also influences the incidence of strikes; for example, in Ontario, hospital-employed nurses are not permitted to strike but community health nurses have that right. A more detailed analysis is required before drawing conclusions about trends in the strike activities of Canadian nurses.

1987	1988	1989
200 Long-term care RNs and graduate nurses Rotating strikes for five weeks		Approximately 8350 hospital RNs 17-day strike
	11,000 Hospital RNs 19-day illegal strike	
	5750 Hospital RNs 7-day strike	Strike threat in 27 special care homes
	Strike threats by 9300 hospital RNs and 139 nursing home RNs	Personal care home RNs 5-day strike
29 Public health RNs 7-week lockout 100 Public health RNs 2-week strike 88 Public health RNs 15-week strike Strike threat by public health RNs		Strike threat by Victorian Order of Nurses RNs
		21,777 hospital RNs 7-day illegal strike
		Threat of mass resignation by 34 RNs in nursing stations over food subsidies

CURRENT TRENDS

An examination of four recent major strikes by nurses will help identify current trends and issues with respect to labor disputes in nursing. Table 28-2 contains details of province-wide strikes by nurses in Alberta and Saskatchewan in 1988 and in British Columbia and Quebec in 1989. While this book was in preparation, nurses in Manitoba and Saskatchewan engaged in province-wide strikes in early 1991; these strikes are not part of the analysis that follows.

TABLE 28-2 **Profile of Four Province-Wide Strikes by Hospital Nurses: 1988-1989**

UNA
(1988)

Total membership: 11,400
19-day illegal strike by 11,000 RNs in 96 hospitals
Issues: wage rollbacks, definition or ward or unit, staffing, benefits
Essential services: determined by local union on ad hoc basis
Settled by negotiation; ratified by 65% of members
Criminal contempt charges laid against union, with fines totalling
 $450,000

SUN
(1988)

Total Membership: 6300
7-day strike of 5750 RNs in 95 hospitals
Issues: staffing shortages, work load, salaries, Nursing Advisory
 Committee, job security for part-time RNs, letter of appointment
 for part-time nurses
Essential Services: union determined level required
Settled by negotiation with mediator and conciliator

BCNU
(1989)

Total membership: 19,000
17-day strike by 8350 nurses in 69 hospitals
Issues: wages, weekend premiums, shorter term of contract,
 broader mandate for professional responsibility committee, responding to nurse shortage
Essential Services: designation required (90%)
Settled by mediation/arbitration after one failure to ratify

FIIQ/QFN
(1989)

Total Membership: 40,000
7-day illegal strike by 21,777 RNs in 300 hospitals
Issues: salaries up to 85% of other professionals in health care,
 responding to nurse shortage, reversing full-time/part-time
 ratio of RNs now at 3:2, broadening mandate of the Nursing
 Committee
Essential Services: legislated designation (90%)
Settled by negotiation after one failure to ratify
Penalties: fines (salary deduction, 2 days for every day of strike);
 loss of seniority; withholding of union dues

BCNU, British Columbia Nurses' Union.
UNA, United Nurses of Alberta.
SUN, Saskatchewan Union of Nurses.
FIIQ, Federation des infirmières et infirmiers de Quebec.

Examination of the four strikes in 1988 and 1989 shows that centralization of bargaining in all four provinces is primarily responsible for the broad scope of institutions hit by the strikes; these range from a low of 80 in British Columbia to as many as 300 in Quebec. When strikes are as broad-based as these, the remaining hospitals and health agencies throughout the health system feel the impact of such disputes, whether or not their employees are on strike. Patients are transferred between hospitals and other agencies to obtain necessary services, and physician referral and treatment practices are altered if not curtailed. Despite the legal requirement to designate essential services in British Columbia and Quebec, these strikes significantly disrupted hospital services—a risk employers and governments evidently accepted in resisting the demands of nurses. In British Columbia and Quebec, nurses engaged in job actions before their strikes by refusing to work overtime and refusing to undertake non-nursing duties. In Quebec, 2100 hospital beds were closed as a result of nurses' refusal to work overtime, revealing the extent to which the province's health system was relying on the good will of nurses. Historically, nurses were willing to perform non-nursing duties on behalf of patients, which Curtin (1988) refers to as their "fatal availability." But now nurses are less inclined to be so accommodating. When they engage in work-to-rule activities (i.e., restrict their activities to the practice of nursing) the efficiency of hospitals can be seriously undermined. As such, this tactic might be considered a more acceptable alternative to the complete withdrawal of services.

Bargaining issues. A characteristic of nurses' labor disputes is the complexity of economic and noneconomic demands they bring to the bargaining table. Economic issues were central to these strikes because, in general, nurses wanted their salaries to reflect the value of their service to the system and to be compensated at least as well as employees with similar responsibilities. In Quebec, nurses slipped so far below this standard that they demanded an increase to 85% of the salaries of physiotherapists, dietitians, and social workers. Differences in education (i.e., the fact that nurses are generally not prepared at the university level whereas other professionals are) was one of the arguments used by management negotiators to justify the existing salary discrepancies between these groups.

Salaries are almost always the most contentious issue in nurses' labor disputes. This is because they represent the single largest item in hospital budgets, and perhaps because they are one of the few hospital costs that are susceptible to administrative control when compared to costs generated by such things as medical decisions, new technology, and drugs. Also, it is difficult to convince administrators (who are usually male) that nurses (who are usually female) should be adequately compensated for the dimensions of the job that complicate the fulfillment of child care responsibilities and other social obligations. The failure of administrators, conciliators, and arbitrators to seriously consider demands of nurses contributed in the past to the propensity of nurses to take strike action (Hibberd, 1987). Indeed, the rise in militancy among nurses' unions is a symptom and an integral part of the rise in feminist consciousness in society at large.

Almost as important as the economic issues are work-life issues, and there is little doubt that the protest underlying these strikes was motivated by the nature of the

demands placed on nurses. Nurses' work settings are now characterized by intensification of patient care, acceleration of change in technology and treatment regimes,
shortages of nurses, rationalization of work, and severe cost-cutting measures. Moreover, nurses frequently experience feelings of powerlessness in the system, lack of
respect, verbal and physical abuse, unsatisfactory management practices, and insufficient continuing education benefits. The stresses and frustrations experienced
directly by each individual nurse are translated into bargaining demands, many of
which are designed to solve particular problems in particular institutions. Disap-
pointment occurs when the cumbersome structures of province-wide negotiations
cannot and do not address small-group or individual concerns. Professional responsibility committees (by whatever title) are designed to allow representatives of
nurses and management to address these specific patient care problems at the local
level. Early experience with the committees led to the perception that they lacked
clout because management was not obliged to act on any of the recommendations.
Nurses therefore sought to expand the range of issues to be discussed at union/
management committees and to secure a more effective dispute resolution mechanism by referring the problem either to hospital boards or to external review bodies.
From the employers' point of view, such demands undermine their common law
rights to manage the enterprise, and consequently there is a great deal of resistance
to them at the bargaining table.

Shortages of nurses and strategies for increasing recruitment and retention of
nurses featured in all four disputes. According to Eileen King, treasurer of the Quebec
union involved, the part-time/full-time ratio of nurses in Quebec is currently 3:2,
and so the union built into its demands strategies for reversing the ratio, as well as
responding to the problem of the shortages of nurses in general. Pat Savage, president of the British Columbia union, reported a similar trend. British Columbia nurses
were demanding terms and conditions of work that would increase the levels of
staffing by attracting nurses to the province. Ironically, British Columbia nurses also
sought to make it easier to leave nursing by demanding the lowering of the retirement
age to 55; this is an example of the problem faced by unions in representing competing
membership interests.

It has been suggested that after professionals secure the traditional economic
provisions in a collective agreement, they expand the scope of bargaining demands
to include items pertaining to the professional role and practice (Kleingartner, 1973).
This trend is occurring in nurses' unions, particularly in the United States where
nurses negotiated a code of ethics into a collective agreement and statements defining
the role of the nurse (Rothman, 1983). Work-life issues are likely to remain a significant item on the future bargaining agenda. Unless employers make major improvements in the workplace environments in which nurses practice, the nature of
union demands may become less palatable to employers and more complex to administer.

Defiance of the law. Canadian collective bargaining legislation severely restricts
the use of strikes and lockouts (Carter, 1989). Two of the four nurses' strikes were
illegal, one because of outright prohibition of strikes in the Alberta hospital industry,
and the other because prerequisite procedures had not been completed (Quebec).

The right to strike in many provinces is postponed until all interim steps are exhausted, for example, cooling-off periods, conciliation procedures, and strike votes and notices. Where public sector strikes are outlawed altogether, the parties are required to submit their disputes to a third party for arbitration.

The United Nurses of Alberta (UNA) refuses interest arbitration, arguing that the mechanism is merely an instrument of government. Alberta's public sector labor statute requires arbitrators to consider public fiscal policy and restricts the issues on which they may make decisions. UNA leaders and members were willing to accept the consequences of an illegal strike rather than submit to arbitration, and they incurred fines totalling $450,000. They also risked decertification of the union, which did not occur. The penalties for Quebec nurses were more severe and included the loss of seniority rights, fines of 2 days' pay for each day of strike, and the withholding of union dues. According to Eileen King, treasurer of the Quebec union, the union underwrote all individual fines and costs, and the total cost of the strike created a major financial crisis for the union.

Whether or not defiance of labor laws by nurses will become a trend is too early to predict. It is not uncommon for unions to engage in illegal strikes and to ignore court injunctions, as history of the labor movement attests. Nurses were willing to disobey the law for many of the same reasons that led to their decision to abandon their no-strike policy in the 1970s. They believed they were being unjustly treated and that they had no other recourse for bringing their case to public attention. They also believed that taking such action was necessary to ensure the adequacy of future nursing services to the public.

Failure to ratify. In two of the four strikes, union members failed to ratify tentative agreements reached by their respective negotiating teams. In British Columbia, a "no" splinter group campaigned among the locals of the union to prevent ratification of the memorandum of agreement. In Quebec, failure to ratify led to the resignation of the negotiating team and the election of a new one. There is at least one other recent case of failure to ratify, which in the past would have been regarded as an unusual event—but such events introduce very interesting questions. Are union members becoming more militant than their leaders? How effective are the union procedures for processing bargaining demands? How are negotiating priorities determined within the union and how involved is the general membership in the process? How effective are negotiators at communicating the progress of negotiations to members? To what extent are union leaders in touch with the problems, attitudes, and expectations of the membership? Such questions could just as readily be asked of employers' associations in province-wide bargaining, even though failure to ratify does not seem to be a current problem on the management side of the bargaining table. The process of making sure the goals and aspirations of the membership are aligned with those of negotiating representatives has been labeled "intra-organizational bargaining" by Walton and McKersie (1965). The process of intra-organizational bargaining is vital to effective bargaining outcomes and applies as much to unions as it does to employers' associations.

Walton and McKersie (1965) state that unions are political organizations whose leaders are elected to their offices. Their tenure in office thus depends on their ability to obtain agreements acceptable to the membership. Two points alluded to earlier are relevant. First, although nurses' unions are homogeneous in the sense that they represent only one occupational group whose members are predominantly female, there may be conflicting ideas about the nature and priority assigned to particular bargaining goals. Negotiators must be fully aware of membership expectations and priorities and maintain contact throughout the process of hammering out an acceptable deal. Intra-organizational bargaining attempts consensus building between members and their representatives to avoid nonconfidence votes in leaders and the weakening of bargaining power vis-à-vis employers. According to Metzger, Ferentino, and Kruger: "[The] inability of nurse union leadership to translate the real concerns of nurses into acceptable settlements has played a role in the proliferation of strikes by professional nurses" (1984, p. 100).

The second point is that the renewal of contracts occurs infrequently and much can change within the life of one agreement. Provincial economic fortunes fluctuate, as do the supply and demand for nurses. Nurses have said that they prefer not to withdraw their services because of the dilemma created by having to choose between loyalty to patients and loyalty to peers (Hibberd and Norris, 1990). Once the decision is made and services are withdrawn, solidarity is built up on picket lines and feelings of liberation and power otherwise rarely experienced by nurses contribute to militancy and rising expectations, nurses expect to see real progress in bargaining. The experience of walking a picket line may have a radicalizing effect on nurses, especially if the strike is successful in securing important bargaining objectives. The recommendation of union negotiators to strike is probably the most important decision in union affairs. Recent experiences among nurses suggest that recommendation for strike action must be based on a careful assessment of membership needs and mood, as well as on the possibility of making further gains acceptable to them. Failure to deliver a ratifiable agreement will likely be followed by a change in union leadership. Because of the relationships between successful bargaining outcomes and tenure of union leadership, union members have a responsibility to question whether their leaders release comprehensive and accurate information sufficient to make informed decisions on whether to ratify or to strike.

Public and professional support. In the event of an impasse, the parties may continue bargaining in the public domain. It has been suggested that media coverage of social protest can be viewed as a resource susceptible to cultivation (Kalisch, Kalisch, and Young, 1983). The parties may communicate to their own and their opponents' constituents in the media; for example, employers often make sure the press hears about nurses crossing picket lines in an attempt to undermine union solidarity. Gauging public support tends to be impressionistic and depends largely on radio talk shows, letters to newspapers, and editorial comment. Union leaders in each of the four strikes claimed they received the support of the public, including donations of food and money to the picket lines, as well as support from other labor organizations.

Systematic surveys of public opinion on whether nurses should be permitted to strike reveal a fairly even balance of responses. An Angus Reid Associates poll revealed 44% of those surveyed in Canada would permit nurses' strikes, 48% would not, and 8% were undecided (cited in *Nursing Report*, 1988, 1:25). In Alberta, where there have been four major strikes within 11 years, the Alberta Association of Registered Nurses (AARN) commissioned a public opinion survey. It was concluded that on an overall basis Albertans have a positive view toward nurses and the nursing profession. However, on the question of whether nurses should be permitted to strike, the public was divided. When asked if nurses should be permitted to strike to be compensated on a par with other professions, public opinion shifted in favor of nurses having the right to strike (AARN, 1989).

A more controversial question raised by unionized nurses is why their professional associations do not give them more support during strike activities. Licensing bodies such as the College of Nurses of Ontario have a single regulatory function and presumably no mandate for commenting on nurses' labor disputes. Professional associations that have both regulatory and professional development functions are unequivocal in supporting collective bargaining but are usually silent on the question of withdrawal of service. To the surprise and delight of Quebec nurses, the Order of Nurses of Quebec made public statements in support of striking nurses, and, according to Raymonde Bossé, vice-president of the Quebec union, testified at a public tribunal as to the absence of complaints against individual nurses. However, according to Eileen King, union treasurer, Quebec's nurses continued to provide 100% coverage of all critical care areas and emergency departments during the strike—more than required under Bill 160, which stipulates the designation of essential services. In the past, Quebec nurses used "anti-strike" tactics such as overstaffing of critical care areas as a means of emphasizing the seriousness of their demands (Wavroch, 1981).

Announcements that someone died as a result of hospital workers' strikes are fairly common. Such allegations are difficult to substantiate, but there is an increasing interest in measuring the effect on health outcomes of strikes by hospital workers. There may well be an increased interest in litigation against hospitals, unions, and individual professionals whose patients claim delays or irreversible damage as a result of strike action. One recent attempt against a hospital and surgeon ended in failure to prove its case (*Dineen* vs. *Queen Elizabeth Hospital*, 1988).

CONCLUSION

The recent wave of province-wide strikes signals a new stage in the maturation of nurses' unions. The strikes give nurses new confidence in determining their socioeconomic status and a sense of political efficacy seldom experienced in their professional associations and workplaces. Unionization allows nurses to confront the patriarchy and conservatism of health agency employers in legitimate and effective ways. By civil disobedience nurses protest against restrictive labor legislation and they force governments to hear and deal with their complaints.

It can be argued that strikes by nurses put the health and safety of the people they are committed to serve in jeopardy. This argument is intuitively attractive but not supported by objective evidence. There is evidence to suggest that nurses do not want to use the strike weapon and would prefer to find an alternative means of resolving their disputes (Hibberd and Norris, 1990). As Judith Ritchie, then president of the Canadian Nurses Association, noted in 1990:

> We need to think about our alternatives to strike action in order to achieve our goals. Strikes should be a last resort. Strikes do effectively demonstrate our needs to the public; for the most part media coverage is extremely positive when nurses explain why they feel compelled to go on strike. But strike action is only effective for a limited time, and we must think about other collective actions. (1990, p. 30)

Several reasonable alternatives to strikes are available, but none is without associated problems. These alternatives include mediation leading to arbitration, conventional arbitration, final offer selection, or any system the parties might voluntarily agree to, such as "locked-in" bargaining (i.e., establishing a mutually imposed deadline for reaching a settlement, with or without recourse to arbitration). Arbitration is a preferred dispute resolution mechanism of community health nurses because they have less power to disrupt services than their hospital-employed colleagues. In other words, strike is a less potent weapon to use against a community health employer, although this may change with the growth in home care services and the increase in severity of illnesses of people cared for at home.

Based on the experience of British Columbia and Quebec nurses, a less strident alternative to full-scale withdrawal of service is the work-to-rule type of job action. Refusal to perform anything but nursing duties or to work overtime can result in significant disruptions in hospital operation without violating the basic commitment to people in need of nursing care or creating friction between nurses who have opposing ethical views on strikes. Such job actions, however, are likely to prolong the process of achieving settlements with employers, and in some jurisdictions they may be regarded as actual strikes. They have the added disadvantage of requiring each nurse to engage in individual acts of protest while remaining on the job, potentially attracting disciplinary action from employers. Even if nurses abandon the strike weapon, they still have to decide their position in relation to respecting the picket lines and strikes of other health care workers (Thompson, Melia, and Boyd, 1988).

The outlook for improved labor relations appears to be good, although there will always be potential for conflict between nurses' unions and employers. There are positive signs of changing attitudes toward the role of nurses within the health care system (as exemplified by public policy initiatives in Alberta and Ontario) to appoint nurses to Boards of Trustees and to senior financial advisory committees of hospitals. These governments are also allocating funding for innovative projects to enhance the quality of nurses' work lives. Public support is strong, and professional nurses' associations and nurses' unions are finding it easier to collaborate on common projects and goals. More initiatives are needed to restructure decision making at the care and treatment level of individual health care agencies. This will require the strengthening of educational preparation of all levels of nursing management and changes in attitudes among administrators, boards, and government bureaucrats toward nurses as an investment in health care for Canadians rather than as an exploitable resource.

ACKNOWLEDGEMENTS

Appreciation is expressed for the contribution to this chapter of the following people: Kathleen Connors, President of the National Federation of Nurses' Unions; Pat Savage, President of the British Columbia Nurses' Union; Pat Stuart, President of the Saskatchewan Union of Nurses; Heather Smith, President of the United Nurses of Alberta; Eileen King, Treasurer, and Raymonde Bossé, Vice-President of the Fédération des Infirmières et Infirmiers et Québec; Shelly Ewart-Johnson, Director, Employee Relations, Alberta Hospital Association; Dianne Godkin for assistance in gathering strike data; and Larry Haiven, Associate Professor, University of Saskatchewan, for his critique of an earlier draft.

REFERENCES

Alberta Association of Registered Nurses. (1989). *Insight: The 1989 provincial public opinion study of nursing in Alberta*. Edmonton: Author.

Anderson, J.C., & Gunderson, M. (1989). Strikes and dispute resolution. In J.C. Anderson, M. Gunderson, & A. Ponak (Eds.), *Union-management relations in Canada* (2nd ed.) (pp. 287-316). Don Mills, ON: Addison-Wesley.

Badgley, R.F. (1975). Health worker strikes: Social and economic bases of conflict. *International Journal of Health Services, 5*(1), 9-17.

Badgley, R.F., & Wolfe, S. (1967). *Doctors' strike: Medical care and conflict in Saskatchewan*. Toronto: Macmillan of Canada.

Bloom, J.R., O'Reilly, C.A., & Parlette, N. (1979). Changing images of professionalism: The case of public health nurses. *American Journal of Public Health, 69*(1), 43-46.

Brecher, R. (1985). Striking responsibilities. *Journal of Medical Ethics, 11*, 66-69.

Brecher, R. (1986). Health workers' strikes: A rejoinder rejected. *Journal of Medical Ethics, 12*, 40-42.

Canadian Nurses Association. (1985). *Code of ethics for nursing*. Ottawa: Author.

Carter, D.C. (1989). Collective bargaining legislation in Canada. In J.C. Anderson, M. Gunderson, & A. Ponak (Eds.), *Union-management relations in Canada* (2nd ed.) (pp. 25-42). Don Mills, ON: Addison-Wesley.

Chamberlain, N.W., & Kuhn, J.W. (1965). *Collective bargaining* (2nd ed.). New York: McGraw-Hill.

Christensen, S. (1980). *Unions and the public interest: Collective bargaining in the government sector*. Vancouver: The Fraser Institute.

Connelly, C.E., Evans, L.K., Dahlen, R.M., & Wieker, N.A. (1979). To strike or not to strike. *Supervisor Nurse, 10*(1), 52-59.

Cormick, G.W. (1969). The collective bargaining experience of Canadian registered nurses. *Labor Law Journal, 20*(10), 667-682.

Craig, A.W.J. (1986). *The system of industrial relations in Canada* (2nd ed.). Scarborough, ON: Prentice-Hall.

Curtin, L.L. (1988). Editorial opinion: Fatal availability. *Nursing Management, 19*(12), 9-10.

Delamothe, T. (1988). Nursing grievances II: Pay. *British Medical Journal, 296*, 120-123.

Dineen v. Queen Elizabeth Hospital (1988). 11 ACWS ((30)D) 446 QUE CA McCarthy, LeBel, Meyer.

Eberle, P.A. (1982). *Strikes/work stoppages: differences between militant and nonmilitant nurses*. Unpublished PhD dissertation, University of Colorado, Boulder.

Fisher, E.G. and Williams, C.B. (1989). Negotiating the union-management agreement. In J.C. Anderson, M. Gunderson and A. Ponak (Eds.), *Union-management relations in Canada* (ed. 2) (pp. 185-234), Don Mills, ON: Addison-Wesley.

Gouldner, A.W. (1954). Wildcat strike, Yellow Springs, OH: The Antioch Publishing Co.

Grand, N. (1971). *The role of ideology in the unionization of nurses*. Unpublished doctoral dissertation, Case Western Reserve University, Cleveland, OH.

Gubbels, R. (1968). The strike: a sociological analysis. In B.C. Roberts (Ed.), *Industrial relations: contemporary issues* (pp. 67-80), London: Macmillan.

Hibberd, J.M. (1987). *The labour disputes of Alberta nurses: 1977-1982*. Unpublished doctoral dissertation, University of Alberta, Edmonton.

Hibberd, J.M. (1988). Structure as a causal factor in nurses' strikes, *Healthcare Management Forum 1*(4):16-21.

Hibberd, J.M., & Norris, J. (1990). *Experiences of nurses in a hospital under siege. Final Report.* Faculty of Nursing, University of Alberta, Edmonton.

Hyman, R. (1972). *Strikes.* London: Fontana.

Jacox, A.K. (1969). *The nurse's cap: A case study of administrator-nurse conflict.* Unpublished doctoral dissertation, Case Western Reserve University, Cleveland.

Jensen, P.M. (1984). *Collective bargaining of nurses in Canada.* Unpublished doctoral dissertation, University of Toronto.

Kalisch, B.J., Kalisch, P.A., & Young, R.L. (1983). Television news coverage of nurses' strikes: A resource management perspective. *Nursing Research, 32*(3), 175-180.

Karsh, B. (1958). *Diary of a strike.* Urbana, IL: University of Illinois.

Kleingartner, A. (1973). Collective bargaining between salaried professionals and public sector management. *Public Administration Review, 33*(2), 165-172.

Kluge, E-H.W. (1982). The profession of nursing and the right to strike. *Westminster Institute Review, 2*(1), 3-6.

Knowles, K.G.J.C. (1952). *Strikes: A study in industrial conflict.* Oxford: Basil Blackwell.

Kochan, T.A. (1980). *Collective bargaining and industrial relations: From theory to policy and practice.* Homewood, IL: Richard D. Irwin.

Labour Canada. (1985). *Strikes and lockouts in Canada.* Ottawa: Minister of Supply and Services.

Labour Canada. (1986-1989). *Collective bargaining review.* Ottawa: Minister of Supply and Services.

Lauer, E. (1986). *Human service strikes: A contemporary ethical dilemma.* St. Louis, MO: The Catholic Health Association of the United States.

Levi, M. (1980). Functional redundancy and the process of professionalization: The case of registered nurses in the United States. *Journal of Health, Politics, Policy and Law, 5*(2), 333-353.

Manning, B. (1982). *Nurses on strike: A case study.* Unpublished doctoral dissertation, University of Connecticut.

Metzger, N., Ferentino, J.M., & Kruger, K.F. (1984). *When health care employees strike: A guide for planning and action.* Rockville, MD: Aspen Systems.

Miller, M.H., & Dodson, L. (1977). Toward a theory of professional work stoppage: The case of nursing. In M.H. Miller & B.C. Flynn (Eds.), *Current perspectives in nursing: Social issues and trends* (pp. 131-142). St. Louis: C.V. Mosby.

Mussallem, H.K. (1977). Nurses and political action. In B. LaSor & M.R. Elliott (Eds.), *Issues in Canadian nursing* (pp. 154-181). Scarborough, ON: Prentice-Hall.

Muyskens, J.L. (1982). Nurses' collective responsibility and the strike weapon. *Journal of Medicine and Philosophy, 7*(1), 101-112.

The Nursing Report. (1987-1989). Toronto: Carswell.

O'Connor, K.S., & Gibson, J.F. (1990). Why are we seeing more unionization? In J.C. McCloskey & H.K. Grace (Eds.), *Current issues in nursing* (3rd ed.) (pp. 298-303). St. Louis: Mosby–Year Book, Inc.

Re: Public Service Employee Relations Act, Labour Relations Act and Police Officers Collective Bargaining Act. (1987). 38 D.L.R. (4th), 161-240.

Ritchie, J. (1990). A framework for caring practice. *Canadian Nurse, 86*(5), 28-31.

Roach, M.S. (1980). *Reflections on a code of ethics for nurses in Canada.* Ottawa: Canadian Nurses Association.

Rothman, W.A. (1983). *Strikes in health care organizations.* Owings Mills, MD: National Health Publishing.

Thompson, I.E., Melia, K.M., & Boyd, K.M. (1988). *Nursing ethics.* Edinburgh: Churchill Livingstone.

Verley, H. (1970). *Florence Nightingale at Harley Street.* London: J.M. Dent & Sons.

Walton, R.E., & McKersie, R.B. (1965). *A behavioral theory of labor negotiations: An analysis of a social interaction system.* New York: McGraw-Hill.

Wavroch, H. (1981). Inconvenience, importance or emergency—the problem of "essential services": Canada. In S. Quinn (Ed.), *What about me? Caring for the carers.* Geneva: International Council of Nurses.

Zacur, S.R. (1982). *Health care labor relations: The nursing perspective.* Ann Arbor, MI: UMI Research Press.

A growing number of native nurses are working through the Indian and Inuit Nurses of Canada (IINC) to develop culturally acceptable, scientifically sound health practices for native Canadians. The 1990-1991 executives of IIINC are (*left* to *right*): Dorothy Russell, secretary-treasurer, Madeleine Dion Stout, president, and Rozella Kinoshameg, vice president. (Photograph courtesy of IINC, Ottawa. Used with permission.)

CHAPTER TWENTY-NINE

Organized Political Action by a Group: Indian and Inuit Nurses of Canada

JEAN CUTHAND GOODWILL, OC RN, LLD (Hon)

Jean Cuthand Goodwill, RN, LLD (Queen's), was one of the founding members of the Indian and Inuit Nurses of Canada in 1974 and served as President from 1983 to 1990. A Plains Cree born on the Little Pine Reserve in Saskatchewan, she first worked as a nurse with Indian and Northern Health Services in northern Saskatchewan, then in a hospital in Bermuda. Since her return to Canada, she continued to nurse but became increasingly involved in the development of organizations to improve Indian health care. She has been employed in various capacities in government departments. In 1980, she was appointed "Special Advisor" to the Minister of National Health and Welfare. In 1986, she received an honorary Doctorate of Laws from Queen's University. The following year she accepted a 2-year assignment as Head of the Indian Health Careers Program, Saskatchewan Indian Federated College, University of Regina, while maintaining her position as President of IINC. In 1990, during the eighth International Congress for Circumpolar Health, she was elected President of the Canadian Society for Circumpolar Health for a 3-year term. In 1992, she was named an Officer of the Order of Canada.

The 1990s will be a crucial time for major changes in the health care delivery system for native people in Canada. The change in jurisdiction from federal to territorial government in the North and the proposed transfer of health services from Medical Services Branch, Health and Welfare Canada, to native communities south of the 60th parallel will have a great effect on the changes in approach to health programs and services for Indian and Inuit people.

This trend is already being felt by the association of Indian and Inuit Nurses of Canada (IINC) which will no doubt have a greater role in helping to make changes. Conceived in 1974, amid the preparation for International Women's Year, the group was originally named the Registered Nurses of Canadian Indian Ancestry and was the first native professional organization in Canada. From the beginning, these nurses had a deep concern for the health status of native people in Canada. As well, they were concerned with developing and maintaining a registry of Registered Nurses of native ancestry, attracting more native students into nursing and other health professions, and establishing a mechanism to work for and lobby on behalf of better health care in Indian and Inuit communities. Although these objectives have been refined and expanded (see box), they are still primary goals.

This chapter outlines some of the reasons for the establishment of this group, discusses the problems of becoming a group with some political force, describes how native nurses fit into the overall picture of health care in Canada in general and in native communities in particular, and suggests some of the current issues that must be faced.

BACKGROUND TO NATIVE HEALTH ISSUES

Since implementation of the Medical Health Insurance Plan in 1967-1968, the average Canadian enjoys and appreciates benefits envied by most developed and developing countries. Most Canadian citizens believe they have the right to the best available health care. To the Indian people of Canada, health care has always been a highly political issue, which is the result of treaties signed with the federal government in most areas of the country in the 1800s. In particular, the Indian people rely on a "Medicine Chest Clause" (Assembly of First Nations, 1979, p. 3) plus other promises concerning medical care. These were understood to mean, as part of the treaty agreements, that Medical Services would be provided to Indian people whenever they might need them. These services were to be provided to all Indian people and be appropriate for the type of medical care available at the time.

Canada's native groups believe that this Medicine Chest Clause should mean that a comprehensive health care plan, incorporating all aspects of present day health care, should be available. Such health care would include curative, mental health care, preventive and promotion services, essential medications, hospital care, ambulance services, diagnostic services, optometric and dental care, and medical appliances—the same kind of services available to other Canadians (Assembly of First Nations, 1979, p. 7). By the beginning of the twentieth century, Indian people were reduced to almost complete destitution and dependence. Today, nearly 100 years later, medical services to native peoples do not compare with those available to most

Objectives of the Indian and Inuit Nurses of Canada (IINC)

1. To act as an agent in promoting and striving for better health for the Indian and Inuit people, that is, a state of complete physical, mental, social and spiritual well-being.
2. To conduct studies and maintain reporting, compiling information and publishing of material on Indian and Inuit health, medicine and culture.
3. To offer assistance to government and private agencies in developing programs designed to improve health in Indian and Inuit communities.
4. To maintain a consultative mechanism whereby the association, bands, government, and other agencies concerned with Indian and Inuit health may utilize.
5. To develop and encourage courses in the educational system of nursing and health professions on Indian and Inuit health and cross-cultural nursing.
6. To develop general awareness of Native and non-Native communities of the special health needs of Indian and Inuit peoples.
7. To generally encourage and facilitate Native control of Indian and Inuit health involvement and decision making in Indian and Inuit health care.
8. To research cross-cultural medicine and develop and assemble material on Indian and Inuit health.
9. To actively develop a means of recruiting more people of Indian and Inuit ancestry into the medical field and health professions.
10. To generally develop and maintain on an on-going basis, a registry of Registered Nurses of Canadian Indian and Inuit ancestry.

From *Indian and Inuit Nurses of Canada: 10th Anniversary*, 1984. Used with permission.

other Canadians (Berger, 1980; Indian Affairs and Northern Development, 1980; Postl, 1986). (See also Chapter 9.)

Although the treaty clause is interpreted differently by legal experts, federal bureaucrats, and Indian and non-Indian politicians, the Indian people maintain their right to health care is based on a historic belief that the government has an inherent,

legal responsibility to provide health services in lieu of the land and resources sur-
rendered throughout this country. Interpretation of this clause remains a point of
serious political dispute that affects the administration of health care.

The Medical Services Branch of Health and Welfare Canada has been responsible
for administering to the medical needs of native peoples. In terms of conventional
diagnosis and treatments, the Medical Services Branch has achieved a notable measure of success. Many diseases that ravaged native communities in the past are
under control—although not completely; for example, tuberculosis is by no means
eradicated.

Native leaders, especially since the mid-1960s, have an increasingly active role in
trying to improve the status of their peoples. For example, most Indian reserves in
Canada have their own government structure with a chief, a council, and an administrator who conducts the business of a community. Regional tribal and district
councils advance common interests, in addition to an Ottawa-based national body,
the Assembly of First Nations. At the band level, health is only one aspect of a
variety of issues and is often not a priority. However, health issues can lead to crises
such as epidemics, violence related to alcohol or drug abuse, or medical emergencies,
and can quickly become a hot political issue.

These political realities and health care problems put those who work in native
health care in uniquely sensitive political positions not ordinarily experienced by
those who work in the general health care system. If nurses working in native
communities perform their duties with side blinders and do not look beyond their
daily routine of clinical care or community health, they will never appreciate why
the job so quickly becomes frustrating, is filled with misunderstandings, and leads
to quick "burnout."

ROLE OF INDIAN AND INUIT NURSES OF CANADA

These realities increase pressure on native nurses to take a more active role. Indian
and Inuit nurses experience the rigors of life on reserves or northern outposts, face
discrimination and lack of support in the Canadian educational and health care
systems, and can recognize problems associated with the need to meet increasingly
high standards in health care and in education. Some of these difficulties arise from
within the nursing profession itself, such as the emphasis on the baccalaureate to
gain entry and to practice. Many young native men and women, for various academic, economic, and social reasons, have difficulty in achieving high school education. For these reasons, native nurses seek the support of one another to help
resolve some of these difficulties.

Since the inception of IINC, members of the association are aware of and active
in all these and many other political areas: listening, watching, and working in
whatever capacity required within their profession, yet ever mindful of what is
happening to families, friends, and nursing colleagues. A vital role is the support
of young native men and women to gain entry to the health professions.

The Registered Nurses of Canadian Indian Ancestry (RNCIA) was initiated in
1974 by Jean Goodwill, a Plains Cree from the Little Pine Reserve in Saskatchewan,

and Jocelyn Bruyere, a baccaulareate-prepared public health nurse and Swampy Cree from The Pas reserve in northern Manitoba, and by several other nurses of Indian ancestry who wished to find potential members for a support group. The name was chosen deliberately so that the group would include status and nonstatus Indians, a matter that, at the time, involved considerable political dissension (Indian and Inuit Nurses of Canada, 1984).

Government officials did not support and some even actively discouraged the project. However, with the help of some non-native nurse colleagues, the founders eventually identified 80 potential members. In August 1975, a group of 40 nurses of Indian ancestry met in Montreal to form the association. The first chairman was Tom Dignan, a Mohawk who was in the United States Marines before becoming a nurse and later achieving a baccalaureate in nursing. The election of a male president during International Women's Year was questioned by feminists, but the native nurses persevered with the belief that he had the qualities the group wished in a leader.

Despite setbacks and skepticism from some colleagues, the association continued to stress the need to establish networks for native nurses on common grounds of education, cultural background, and mutual concerns. After a rocky start, the group became especially vulnerable in 1978. Financial backing was a major problem; a national Indian political group blocked one early federal funding initiative. Initial funding was obtained from the Native Women's Program, Native Citizens Directorate, and the Secretary of State—but then a program officer in one department objected to the inclusion of a male nurse (Tom Dignan had decided to attend medical school and to obtain his medical degree). However, the association continued to welcome male nurses and would not compromise its professional status to achieve funding.

The fledgling association was saved when the Manitoba Indian Nurses Association (MINA) was formed as a provincial body with some funding, and the late Grace Easter of MINA also accepted presidency of the national group. The Secretary of State's office continued to provide regular annual funding, enough for one board meeting and a national conference each year.

In the early 1980s, financial support was received from the Medical Services Branch of Health and Welfare Canada for special projects and later for administrative and staff costs. This support was provided with the understanding that IINC would seek other sources of funding and eventually be financially self-sufficient. Some attempts were made, with minimal success, in the mid-1980s with project proposals submitted to foundations and funding agencies. With the recent federal cutbacks to native groups, IINC is again faced with project funding as mutually agreed by Medical Services Branch, Health and Welfare Canada and by the association. Other major project proposals are being submitted to foundations and funding agencies and to date all responses have been negative.

Despite setbacks and opposition, however, the association continues to introduce ideas about better health and care for native peoples and to encourage native students to enter the nursing profession. The members repeatedly lobby government departments, using knowledge gained from experiences, to describe health conditions and to recommend new approaches to health care for native communities. In 1979, the federal government adopted a new Indian Health Policy by which it is committed to involve more native people in the planning, budgeting, and delivery of health care programs. These recommendations had been urged by the RNCIA. In 1980, the appointment of Jean Goodwill, one of the founders of RNCIA, as Special Advisor to the Minister of National Health and Welfare, created opportunities for further improvements in health services to native people. This new position also allowed for the appointment of a second native nurse, Carol Prince from Manitoba, to become Special Advisor on Native Affairs to the Assistant Deputy Minister of the Medical Services Branch, Health and Welfare Canada. In 1983, a third native nurse, Madeleine Dion Stout of Alberta, was appointed Special Advisor on Indian health to the Minister. For the first time in history, three native nurses were in prime positions at the Medical Services Branch in Ottawa.

In 1982, the Registered Nurses of Canadian Indian Ancestry moved its head office to Ottawa from its shared quarters with the Manitoba group in Winnipeg. In 1983, the membership accepted Inuit nurses and the name was changed to Indian and Inuit Nurses of Canada (IINC).

As IINC grew and established its reputation as a professional organization, support came first of all from other organizations of health professionals, such as the Canadian Nurses Association (CNA). CNA now grants IINC status as an affiliate group. The Canadian Association of University Schools of Nursing, the provincial nurses' associations, the Canadian Public Health Association, the Indian and Inuit Health Committee of the Canadian Pediatric Society, the Canadian Society for Circumpolar Health, and the Canadian Council for Multicultural Health have also provided support.

IINC IN 1990

The Indian and Inuit Nurses of Canada is governed by three elected executives (president, vice president, and secretary-treasurer) and a 13-member board (representatives from northern and southern Ontario and one from each of the other nine provinces and two territories). Elections are held every 2 years at an annual meeting, which also includes sessions on nursing education and on Indian and Inuit health issues. For the past 2 years, IINC concentrated on family violence, focusing on nursing approaches to wife abuse, child sexual abuse, and elder abuse. These meetings are held in a different center each year, preferably one near a native community.

Membership has grown to approximately 400, up from 276 in 1986. Associate membership, approved in 1986, allows participation by nurses and other health professionals not of Canadian Indian or Inuit ancestry but who support the objectives of the association; associate members cannot vote, however.

The association has an executive director and one other staff person in Ottawa to manage day-to-day affairs. Communication is accomplished by a newsletter, *The Native Nurse*, published twice a year since 1985, and by distribution of reports on special workshops held throughout the year. This keeps members informed about new educational programs for native nurses, community-based programs seeking native health care workers, and concerns related to health care for Canada's indigenous peoples.

Funding comes from membership fees and from grants and donations to the association. The Baxter Corporation of Canada provides two annual scholarships for native nursing students who wish to pursue a career in northern communities. Members also raise money for the organization with sales of promotional materials such as sweatshirts, T-shirts, and pins, and with raffles and other activities throughout the year. Only one province (Manitoba) has a provincial association, although meetings have been held in Saskatchewan, British Columbia, and Quebec. Most Board members of IINC recognize the advantage and the need for provincial associations. Lack of financial resources restricts travel to meetings, however, especially for Community Health Nurses based in remote areas.

Executive and board members frequently act as advisors and resource persons to other organizations and groups such as the Assembly of First Nations Health Commission and to bands on request. As well, members meet regularly with representatives of Health and Welfare Canada, such as the Professional Indian and Inuit Health Careers Program (to review bursaries, scholarships, and student financing) and the Nursing Directorate (on recruitment and retention of native nurses). The Association collaborates with the Saskatchewan Indian Federated College, Science Department, to support and encourage development of a comprehensive math and science program, especially for mature students. Members interact with the native student counseling services to direct more students into health-related careers. IINC also works closely with the Native Women and Inuit Women's associations on economic development for aboriginal women.

In particular, IINC collaborates with university and college nursing programs throughout Canada to help with entry of native students who are still under-represented in many institutions. As well, the association supports programs such as the National Native Access Program to Nursing at the University of Saskatchewan; the Native Nurses Entry Program, Lakehead University, Thunder Bay, Ontario; and the Northern Bachelor of Nursing Program, University of Manitoba at The Pas, Manitoba. IINC members are represented on advisory committees and sit on a selection board for nursing students. Some members teach cross cultural health care and other relevant courses on native health. These programs will continue to accept students from northern communities in the coming years, but among the many problems these students face is the fact that basic science education in federally funded reserve schools is often of poor quality. Members also continue to meet with representatives of educational institutions and band level education committees to discuss the poor quality of science and math education in schools and seek ways of providing additional programs in such communities (Jacobs, 1989). They also participate as role models at career fairs, providing added support and encouragement for native students aspiring to a nursing career (see box).

Because of their role as advocates for an improved health care system in native communities and for increased numbers of native professionals, IINC members must be aware of the political implications and keep informed of current issues. With the

We Need Native Nurses

The Indian and Inuit Nurses of Canada (IINC) works closely with colleges and universities to attract native students into nursing. One such program is the National Native Access Program to Nursing (NNAPN), a program sponsored by the University of Saskatchewan. NNAPN provides counseling and courses for students until they are admitted to university nursing programs. This short article describing the program is reprinted from the IINC newsletter.

The National Native Access Program to Nursing (NNAPN) addresses the need for native nurses by helping students of aboriginal ancestry to enter university nursing programs across Canada. Marilyn Sanderson is one such student. She is a graduate of the 1989 Spring Access Program and is now studying nursing at the University of Saskatchewan.

Marilyn grew up on the James Smith Reserve in Saskatchewan and always wanted to become a nurse. After leaving the reserve, she finished high school, went to business college, and worked as a secretary for a number of years. She still had the dream of becoming a nurse, so while she worked full-time she also went to high school to take the math and science courses needed for nursing.

Marilyn felt that the biggest obstacle to entering nursing was that she did not have the background she needed in maths and sciences. She stresses the importance of counseling for young people about the courses needed to get into health careers. Students who attend the Access Program must have the basic courses needed for university entrance. However, seats have been saved at university schools of nursing across Canada for successful graduates of the Access Program.

During the nine-week Spring Access Program in Saskatoon, Marilyn studied the major subjects that are taken in nursing programs and had the experience of taking classes at a university level. There were five other students in Marilyn's class and they became very close during the nine weeks that they spent together. The students came from different backgrounds. Marilyn and three others were from Saskatoon, one was from La Ronge, and one was from Fort Franklin, NWT. Several of the students were upgrading to meet university entrance requirements while others had taken previous university classes (in education, arts and sciences, and physical education). Five of the six students had children, ranging in age from toddlers to teenagers. Balancing activities and time while in the Spring Access Program was a challenge.

The Access Program has a strong cultural component, looking at native culture and traditional health beliefs and practices. This helps to strengthen cultural identity and demonstrate positive native role models. Marilyn's class had a special opportunity to attend a traditional native feast held in Prince Albert. For some, this was a first time experience, while others were familiar with the tradition and meaning of such an event

From *The Native Nurse*, December 1989, p. 5. With permission.

We Need Native Nurses—cont'd

and were able to share their knowledge and experience.

The Spring Program was a time for Marilyn to look at her goal of nursing and to evaluate herself for success in a university nursing program. Marilyn felt that the experience gave her further incentive to become a nurse. She also felt that studying the different subjects helped her to know what to expect in her first year university classes.

At the end of the Spring Program, Marilyn and two other students were recommended for direct entry into first year nursing at the University of Saskatchewan and one student was recommended to Arts and Sciences for a pre-nursing year. Another student was rec-

ommended to a pre-nursing year at the University of Alberta, and one moved out of province and will be looking into nursing programs there.

In the future, Marilyn hopes to nurse overseas for a year and then to work in a hospital with children or newborns. She agrees that there is a need for more native nurses and feels that it is important for native individuals to have someone of their own culture to relate to when they are in hospital. Nurses trained at a university level, like Marilyn, will be able to support the overall health and well-being of native communities through leadership and involvement in community health and development.

pending transfer of health services to native communities, the number of nurses employed directly by bands (rather than by Medical Services Branch) has increased from 30 in 1987 to 120 in 1991. IINC has held three workshops for these band-employed native and non-native nurses on such issues as liability and protection, ongoing educational opportunities, expanded duties resulting from greater expectations by the new employers, and the perpetual uncertainty of pending political changes at the Band level and funding resources from government departments.

The equal opportunity provision in the federal civil service hiring regulations, introduced in the late 1970s, increased the number of native workers hired by Medical Service Branch for positions primarily in administration, in headquarters and regions. A few senior native nurse positions are held by native people in some regions, but the one senior nurse position that should be available at headquarters is not yet filled.

Before this provision, a training program for Community Health Representatives provided several para-professional workers for native communities. Although many of these community health representatives provide a necessary and useful service, some are relegated to positions of translators for non-native nurses and have little hope of advancement or recognition for their services.

Efforts by IINC were at least partially responsible for the Indian and Inuit Health

Careers Program that was launched by the Medical Services Branch in 1984, and there are efforts to refocus the programs from para-professional to professional training. Some community health representatives now are entering health career programs, particularly nursing programs. However, this may create a new rift among front-line health care workers. In some communities, chiefs are asking whether Indian students in Health Career Programs are developing into an elite group who may not wish to return to their communities after experiencing a different life-style "outside." Although it was never presumed nor anticipated that all students in Health Careers Programs would return to their home reserves, there has always been a hope that many would do so in time. With the increase in band-employed nurses, native nurses are filling more of these positions as they become available.

There are also strained relations between professionals and para-professionals, between native and non-native practitioners, and between some professionals, especially between diploma-prepared and baccalaureate-prepared nurses. Native community health nurses with diploma preparation, hired because of their knowledge of cultural differences, have to cope with resentment from baccalaureate-prepared, non-native nurses. In some regions, Medical Services Branch personnel question IINC members about the number of extra meetings they attend; this suggests that non-native nurses see native nurses, who are often in less senior positions, as a threat. It should not be surprising that native nurses feel the need to take a close look at native health issues that, in some cases, have been neglected for so many decades.

As members become more visible and recognized for their abilities, the demand for their service and expertise increases dramatically. Although membership has grown steadily, the association cannot meet all the requests—from chiefs for their communities, from academic institutions, and from urban and rural health-care agencies for well-prepared native nurses. In particular, managers of health service delivery programs look for qualified personnel with the ability to cross cultural barriers that have always posed a major challenge to effective health care in native communities.

With this in mind, IINC made a conscious effort to focus on transcultural nursing in recent, ongoing educational efforts for members. At the 1986 annual assembly in Victoria, for example, a 1-day seminar based on the work of Madeleine Leininger was held. Leininger (1977) argues that the health status of Indian communities will never approach that of the non-native population unless transcultural concepts are incorporated in the delivery of health services, so that a community's cultural beliefs and values remains intact.

At every annual meeting and other workshops held by IINC, members try to incorporate the holistic concept of health care, a concept based on the Circle of Life and the importance of introducing elders as mentors and consultants.

With the work of transcultural nursing and continuing support for these ongoing activities across the country, IINC continues to demonstrate a strong commitment for an improved health system delivered by and for Indian and Inuit communities. What IINC members have not been willing to do is to take a political stand on issues such as the transfer of Indian health services to band administration. They are always aware of the need to support Indian governments and decisions of chiefs and councils, while maintaining their professionalism and a healthy working relationship with their colleagues and the clients they serve.

FUTURE FOR IINC

Today's nurses in Indian health services are confronted with serious issues. In recent years, Indian people have become increasingly aware of their right to effective, culturally appropriate health care, in line with a growing demand for meaningful political rights. There is an air of uncertainty prevailing in Indian communities as the federal government moves toward the transfer of Indian health services and programs into the administration of the bands. Regarding this transfer, IINC works closely with officials in the Medical Services Branch, at the same time giving support to native and non-native nurses employed by Band councils. With the cooperation of the Nursing Directorate of Medical Services Branch, IINC (1989) published a *Handbook on Nursing* as an information booklet for communities. It would be grossly unfair for all if Bands are left with an ambiguous health care situation and Medical Services Branch then declares that "it's out of the department's hands."

In this charged atmosphere, the previously mentioned divisions between professional and para-professional health workers has increased because of a complex series of misunderstandings. A speedy resolution to the situation is imperative, and it would certainly be a gross injustice if the job of finding some synthesis between the activities of professional and para-professional health workers were left solely in the hands of nurses. This may be alleviated because a national advisory committee of IINC members has been established to meet with senior nurses in Medical Services Branch Headquarters three times a year. This group discusses nursing issues that affect native health care and personal and educational concerns, and attempts to resolve misunderstandings as they arise. Plans to expand this to form similar committees in each region and the territories are being suggested.

IINC will continue to play a role in directing today's nursing students and para-professional trainees to a more open attitude toward integrated health service delivery in native and non-native communities and other health care institutions by promoting culturally specific health care for Indian and Inuit people.

Community education is also needed. Indian people often find it difficult to differentiate between a nurse and a community health representative and to distinguish their respective duties, responsibilities, and reporting relationships. This will become even more difficult with the emergence of alcohol and drug abuse workers and mental health para-professionals on reserves. Accredited courses for these new workers must be made mandatory. These developments suggest that it is time for a new generation of Indian student trainees to enter the health professions, bringing with them a commitment to gaining acceptance in native communities, rather than being perceived as a professionally trained elitist group. Moreover, these students must maintain a presence in their communities so that they do not emerge as strangers after years of study in an institution. Indian students need support, which includes peers, parents, and members of the communities, who in turn must be made to understand why it takes so long for the students to become nurses before they can return to the communities. IINC must continue this work with the students, with the nursing programs, and with the communities.

Increased recognition and appreciation for tradition and culture in the curricula of a number of newly established health career programs for native students is most gratifying. Native and non-native nurses also need to grasp the difference in values and customs of the many tribes and regions in North America. Traditional practices in the United States are not necessarily applicable in Canada, and beliefs and practices of the Iroquois and other tribes in eastern Canada may not correspond to those in the Prairies and West Coast. IINC must continue to gather and make available information on cultural beliefs and practices that affect health care, such as that in a recent report on traditional medicine in the Arctic by Fjola Hart Wasekeesikaw (1989), published in *The Native Nurse*.

CONCLUSION

Nursing today has many individuals who are separated but who share common goals in seeking to provide better nursing care. These individuals can work alone to achieve their goals, but they can also form into groups—such as IINC's small group of individuals in 1974. Today, IINC is a thriving and growing group working toward objectives.

IINC's immediate goal is to have an increasing number of graduate native health professionals fill the cultural gap and end the main causes of misunderstandings and difficulties native Canadians have with Western medical practices. IINC will also work to ensure that more culturally acceptable programs are devised and that the transfer of health services to band administration goes smoothly and in the best interest of good health care for patients and clients. IINC will also support a significant increase in the use of surviving native elders to develop culturally acceptable, scientifically sound health practices and life-styles. Native nurses can have the best of all possible worlds by combining the strengths of traditional and Western medicine.

REFERENCES

Assembly of First Nations. National Commission Inquiry on Indian Health. (1979). *Indian rights to health care*. Ottawa: Author.

Berger, T.R. (1980). *Report of advisory committee on Indian and Inuit health consultation*. Ottawa: Department of National Health and Welfare.

Indian Affairs and Northern Development. (1980). *Indian conditions: A survey*. Ottawa: Minister of Indian Affairs and Northern Development.

Indian and Inuit Nurses of Canada. (1984). *Indian and Inuit Nurses of Canada: 10th Anniversary*. Ottawa: Author.

Jacobs, R. (1989). To the editor [letter on reduced budgets for schools]. *The Native Nurse, 4*(2), 2.

Leininger, M. (1977). Cultural diversities of health and nursing. *Nursing Clinics of North America, 12*(1), 5-8.

Nursing Division, Indian and Northern Health Services, Health and Welfare Canada. (1989): *Handbook on nursing*. Ottawa: Author.

Postl, B. (1986). Native health: A continuing concern (Editorial). *Canadian Journal of Public Health, 77*(4), 253.

Wasekeesikaw, F.H. (1989). Arctic medical history and traditional medicine. *The Native Nurse, 4*(2), 6-7.

We need native nurses. (1989). *The Native Nurse, 4*(2), 5.

In an effort to promote the work of the newly-formed Victorian Order of Nurses, four nurses (Georgia Powell, Amy Scott, Rachel Hanna, and Margaret Payson) traveled to the remote Klondike gold fields to provide care during the gold rush of 1898. Traveling with them on their journey to the Klondike was Faith Fenton, a reporter for *The Globe (in the dark suit)*. (Photograph is from the VON Canada Collection. Copyright Victorian Order of Nurses for Canada. Used with permission.)

CHAPTER THIRTY

Voluntary Community Agencies: VON Canada as Example

DOROTHY M. PRINGLE, RN, PhD
DONNA J. ROE, RN, MScN

Dorothy Pringle, RN, BScN (McMaster), MS (Colorado), PhD (Illinois), is Professor and Dean, Faculty of Nursing, University of Toronto. From 1982 to 1988, she was Research Director of the Victorian Order of Nurses for Canada. Her educational background includes psychiatric/mental health nursing and nursing of older people in the community, and her career has included practice as a clinical specialist, teacher, and administrator.

Donna Roe, RN, BScN (Ottawa), MScN (Toronto), has worked as a head nurse, supervisor, and clinical nurse specialist in a large acute care hospital and as a teacher in schools of nursing. In 1981, she became District Director for the Victorian Order of Nurses in Hamilton-Wentworth. Since 1986, she has been National Executive Director of VON Canada in Ottawa.

O ne of Canada's distinctive characteristics is its insured system of health care—the provincial health care systems are publicly funded by tax dollars, and therefore private profit making in the course of provision of health care services is disallowed. This insured system has its roots in the voluntary sector. In the early days of health care in Canada, volunteers, members of religious orders, and organizations governed by volunteers provided care directly or developed organizations to deliver care. Profit has never been a strong component of the Canadian system.

This voluntary tradition continues, and one of the best and oldest examples of a voluntary organization in Canada is the Victorian Order of Nurses (VON). By exploration of its history and development and by examining forces that are operating on the organization today, it is possible to analyze the role of the voluntary sector's contribution to health care in the last century. This examination of the VON also illustrates the leadership role of nurses in designing and managing health services in Canada. By speculating on the future of the VON, it is possible to explore possible futures of the voluntary movement.

This chapter will:

- Discuss characteristics of voluntary nonprofit and charitable organizations and give examples
- Examine the history of the VON as an example of a voluntary charitable organization
- Review the contribution that VON has made to health care in Canada
- Analyze current challenges to the voluntary sector and the implications of various results of these challenges

CHARACTERISTICS OF VOLUNTARY NONPROFIT AND CHARITABLE ORGANIZATIONS

The terms *voluntary nonprofit organizations* and *voluntary charitable organizations* are sometimes used interchangeably, but they mean different things in Canada. For an organization to be considered a voluntary charitable organization by the federal government, it must have one of four purposes: relief of poverty, advancement of education, advancement of religion, or otherwise benefit the community. Organizations that meet one or more of these conditions may register with Revenue Canada and then may collect donations and issue receipts that donors may use for income tax purposes. Nonprofit organizations that do not meet these conditions are not required to register with Revenue Canada and they may not solicit donations (Revenue Canada, Taxation, 1990). Examples of these latter organizations are trade unions and housing corporations.

Voluntary charitable organizations are usually the product of the efforts of a few individuals who share a common concern or a common perspective on an issue. They band together with missionary zeal and concentrate their efforts on obtaining public attention and raising funds. The Alzheimer Society of Canada is a recent example of this. Family members of individuals with Alzheimer's disease joined to educate the public, raise public awareness about the disease, lobby for improved services for individuals with this disease and for themselves as caregivers, and raise funds for research. They were joined by professionals, and as a movement, the Alzheimer Society has been remarkably successful in securing improved funding for research, in initiating better community services in the way of adult day care and respite services, and in educating the public about the disease. Some voluntary organizations are small, concentrating on a local problem or need, such as a local organization that provides home assistance services for seniors in their community; others are large, complex, multiple branch organizations with national and international connections, such as the Red Cross Society of Canada and St. John Ambulance. Regardless of the size, voluntary organizations are distinguished by their focus on a particular cause or need.

Voluntary organizations may concentrate on advocacy for the issue that concerns them, they may become directly involved in the provision of services, or they may do both. Meals-on-Wheels, the delivery of low-cost hot nutritious meals to people at home, is a service organization only. Various community groups may assume responsibility for developing a Meals-on-Wheels service, and they recruit volunteers to deliver the meals. Funding comes from fees paid by the meal recipients and from contributions from municipal and provincial governments. In contrast, the Canadian Cancer Society focuses mainly on raising funds for cancer research, educating the public, and advocating for research and services for cancer patients, but it also provides support for cancer patients. For example, women who have experienced surgery for breast cancer will visit newly diagnosed breast cancer patients to provide information and moral support.

Voluntary organizations are always controlled by a board of governors composed of volunteers. These volunteers are selected because of their familiarity with the community or with the cause the organization is pledged to represent. The board sets policy for the organization but it may hire paid employees to implement the mandate of the organization. This is the case with the VON. The Board of each VON branch hires an executive director who, in turn, hires nurses to accomplish the provision of patient care. Board members are never paid; the staff are. Voluntary organizations are nonprofit; they may raise money and seek contracts with governments to cover the costs of providing services, but there are no shareholders. Neither board members nor staff, beyond receiving their salary, receive profits from the organization. Any remaining funds after costs of the service delivery are met (i.e., the "profit") are used to expand services or to reduce the cost of the service to the clients if there are fees involved. In for-profit organizations, profit is paid to shareholders or to owners of the business.

Voluntary organizations are frequently politically minded. They use the political process to achieve their goals of advocacy for their special interests. This may take the form of writing briefs to various government departments or commissions stating the needs of their clients, familiarizing themselves with particular members of government and seeking support to introduce special interests to cabinet or in the legislature, and keeping the bureaucratic levels of government informed of activities and needs of the organization. Unlike private, for-profit organizations, they do not make contributions to particular political parties or members of legislature, and they do not campaign on behalf of particular parties or individuals; rather, they use the processes of government to achieve their goals.

In summary, voluntary charitable organizations are distinguished from public and for-profit organizations by their boards composed of volunteers from the community, by their nonprofit status, by their use of the political processes (but not political parties or politicians) to bring attention to their causes, and, frequently, by the use of volunteers to deliver services, particularly if those providing the services do not require professional knowledge or licensure.

The Victorian Order of Nurses for Canada

MISSION:
VON Canada provides leadership across Canada in the development of health and social policy, the delivery of innovative community-based nursing, and other health care and support services, based on the principles of primary health care.

Approved by the VON Canada Board of Directors
January 1989

Local and Provincial Branches (1990)

British Columbia 1	Quebec 5
Alberta 6	New Brunswick 11
Saskatchewan 5	Nova Scotia 14
Manitoba 1	Newfoundland 3
Ontario 34	

National Executive Director: Donna J. Roe
National President: Helen K. Mussallem

VON Canada
5 Blackburn Ave.
Ottawa, Ontario
K1N 8A2

The Victorian Order of Nurses for Canada exemplifies a voluntary charitable organization that has provided unique services within the Canadian health care system for almost a century. The following section discusses how the VON developed within this voluntary tradition (see box).

HISTORY OF THE VON

In the late 1800s, there were no organized home nursing services in Canadian communities. Immigration to the cities in the eastern part of the country was high, and new settlements were beginning to spring up across the west. The immigrant families had no access to health services of any kind, and childbearing and communicable diseases took a terrible toll on the women and children.

District nursing was established in England in 1859 when William Rathbone arranged for trained nurses to visit poor families in Liverpool to assist them to care for the sick. Other communities followed this example. Queen Victoria gave this movement considerable impetus in 1887 when she contributed £70,000 to establish the Jubilee Institute of District Nurses. The money had been raised to honor her 50 years as a monarch, and the nurses trained by the Institute were known as the "Queen's Nurses."

In Canada, a new Governor-General was appointed in 1893. His wife, Lady Ishbel, Countess of Aberdeen (Lady Aberdeen), had just accepted the presidency of the recently established International Council of Women. She created a Canadian National Council of Women and local councils in many communities. Members of these local councils, generally well-to-do and community-minded women, informed Lady Aberdeen of the nursing needs of the poor in cities and the settlers in the West.

Lady Aberdeen was aware of the Queen's Institutes of Nurses in England. Because 1897 was the Diamond Jubilee of Queen Victoria's reign, she proposed establishing the Victorian Order of Home Helpers to honor the Queen and to provide a service of practical help. At first, Lady Aberdeen believed it would be impossible to recruit sufficient numbers of trained nurses to meet the needs and that nurses were too expensive for most poor and middle-class families to afford. Although organized nursing and many groups of physicians opposed using nontrained workers, this new Order was formally inaugurated in February, 1897, with the Governor-General and Prime Minister Wilfrid Laurier present. Among others, Nora G.E. Livingstone, Lady Superintendent of the Montreal General Hospital Training School, argued persuasively that only trained nurses could manage the responsibilities these women would be required to assume. By March 1897, Lady Aberdeen was convinced, and the Victorian Order of Nurses was substituted for the earlier title. All VON nurses would be fully trained nurses with additional preparation in midwifery and 6 months training in district nursing.

The establishment of VON was not without opposition, particularly from physicians. From Victoria, British Columbia, to Halifax, Nova Scotia, groups of physicians predicted dire consequences for the population who would receive care from VON nurses. The most organized and most vociferous attack came from the Ontario Medical Association (OMA). The OMA insisted the nurses would only be half-trained and, in the course of functioning as midwives, would increase the mortality rate as they had in Britain, a piece of well-placed misinformation. Even in 1897, the lobby and influence of the OMA was strong enough to force the government to retract its earlier promise to provide substantial financial aid to the new organization. The underlying fear of the physicians was that VON nurses would usurp their work and reduce their income. That VON nurses would practice midwifery was a particularly contentious issue. To stem the opposition, a policy was established that VON nurses would act as midwives only in emergency situations and only when a physician could not be obtained.

The efforts of a physician were required to halt the opposition. Lady Aberdeen recruited Dr. Alfred Worcester, the founder of the Waltham Training School for District Nurses, located near Boston. He was a Fellow of the Massachusetts Medical Society and had credibility in the medical community. Lady Aberdeen arranged for him to come to Canada and meet with physicians and medical societies throughout the East. His experience and persuasiveness prevailed and endorsements were received from all the societies that he met, including the OMA.

Victorian Order of Nurses Early Leaders

Three of the early leaders of the Victorian Order of Nurses essentially developed community-based nursing in Canada. These women were exceptional in many ways: they were well-educated; they were visionary about what nursing should be; they were risk-takers, opting to begin services even when resources to maintain them were not clearly available; and they were political, getting to know power-brokers and getting things done. Their names should be known and honored by nurses today.

Charlotte Macleod

Chief Lady Superintendent 1897-1903, was born in New Brunswick and received her early nursing education in Canada. She continued to study district nursing with the Queen's Institute in England before going to the United States as superintendent of the Waltham Training School for District Nursing in the Boston area. Lady Aberdeen asked her to return to Canada, where she translated Lady Aberdeen's vision of VON into reality. Since there were no training programs for visiting nurses in Canada, Macleod established schools, along with the branches, and staffed them with Waltham graduates. She helped arrange the Yukon expedition, and during her tenure more than 20 branches of nursing schools were established in Canada.

Mary Ardcronie MacKenzie

Chief Superintendent 1908-1919, was born in Toronto and received a teaching certificate, then a Bachelor of Arts, from the University of Toronto; she taught in high schools before entering nurses' training in Boston and New York. She practiced in several hospitals in various United States centers before working as a visiting nurse in Washington, D.C., and Chicago. She returned to Canada as Chief Superintendent of VON in 1908. MacKenzie recognized the need to expand the training programs in district nursing run by local VON branches. She stressed the necessity of incorporating principles of sanitation and prevention into nursing practice and believed the national organization should assume responsibility for operating and financing educational programs, although there was never enough money. When universities in Canada provided courses in public health nursing, the VON was among the first to offer scholarships to its nurses to enable them to take the university certificate courses and degrees in public health nursing. MacKenzie left the VON to become the first professor in public health nursing at the newly-opened nursing program at the University of British Columbia.

Elizabeth Smellie

Superintendent 1923-1947, trained at Johns Hopkins Hospital and, after distinguished service in the Canadian Army Medical Corps in the 1914-1918 World War, completed a course in public health nursing at Simmons' College in Boston. She oversaw a rapid expansion in the visiting nurse service in the 1920s while phasing out VON's involvement in cottage hospitals. The 1930s were difficult years: the Depression produced an increased demand for services while patients' abilities to pay diminished. Despite few resources, Beth Smellie guided the branches to meet the demands, and in 1938 the Canadian Nurses Association selected her for its highest honor, the Mary Agnes Snively Award. In 1939, she became the vice-president of the American Public Health Association. When the 1939-1945 World War began, she was recruited to become Matron-in-Chief of the Nursing Service of the Royal Canadian Medical Corps and was on leave of absence from VON for four years. During this time, she rose to the rank of Colonel, the first Canadian woman ever to receive this rank.

The Waltham Training School connection had an even more fortuitous result because Charlotte Macleod, a Canadian nurse who was the superintendent at Waltham, agreed to return to Canada to head the VON. She brought several Waltham graduates, all Canadians, to Ottawa with her (see box).

Early Developments in VON

Four VON branches were established in 1897—in Halifax, Montreal, Ottawa, and Toronto. Since VON was created as a voluntary charitable, not-for-profit organization, the process of establishing a branch followed a similar pattern in most communities. It usually began with the Council of Women or another group of women recognizing the need for a nursing service and convincing their husbands or other prominent businessmen to establish a board. The board would contact the national director (known as the Chief Lady Superintendent) for guidance in how to establish a service and raise funds to pay for a nurse in charge and for an office. In each of the first communities, VON rented a house, which served as the branch office and residence for the nurses. The boards determined what types of services the branch would offer, and nurses in these early branches had varied and challenging caseloads that included people ill with infectious diseases, the dying, women in childbirth and new babies, and young children. Cleaning up filthy houses, bringing and preparing food, feeding children, and teaching mothers the basics of hygiene and nutrition were part of the daily routine.

Regional training schools in district nursing were also established. These training schools were a critical element in VON's history because they were the only means for hospital-trained nurses to develop the skills needed to provide care in the community.

In 1898, Lady Aberdeen saw the Klondike Gold Rush as an opportunity to get needed visibility for VON. The federal government was sending troops to the Yukon to help maintain law and order and to assist with the building of a railway. Lady Aberdeen dispatched four VON nurses to travel with this field force to provide nursing care to men en route and to give VON care in Dawson and Bonanza Creek (Greenhous, 1987). The conditions were primitive. Scurvy, typhoid, malaria, and pneumonia claimed lives. Despite the circumstances, the nurses succeeded in providing care and won the respect of the Mounties, the gold seekers, and the few physicians who were available.

In the Klondike, the VON nurses worked in makeshift hospitals as opposed to making visits to the tents and shacks where the men lived. Although VON has always been associated with visiting nursing, in the early days when distance or circumstances precluded home visiting, boards established cottage hospitals or provided the nursing staff for hospitals in communities where they already existed. Consequently for many communities on the prairies, in the British Columbia interior, and in the North, VON meant hospital nursing and visiting nursing. At one time, VON branches operated 38 such hospitals. When the community was able to assume control of the hospital, the VON board turned over the hospital service, and the branch returned to its visiting role. The last cottage hospital was transferred in 1924.

Organized preventive services were rare in the early twentieth century in Canada. Public health units were just being developed, and few communities had public health nurses as we know them today. Consequently in its early years, VON branches were involved in prevention and the provision of nursing care to the ill. Prenatal classes, school health programs, immunization, milk banks to provide uncontaminated milk to babies, postnatal care, and well baby clinics were a larger component of the VON nurses' work than was the care of the sick. VON established impressive statistics in the area of maternal health. Although the overall Canadian maternal death rate in the 1920s was between five and six per thousand, where VON nurses provided care the death rate was from 2.5 per thousand in 1927 to 1.2 per thousand in 1930.

In 1931, the National Office of VON commissioned Dr. Grant Fleming, professor of Public Health and Preventive Medicine at McGill, to examine the field of community health and to recommend future directions for the Order as a whole. The boards of individual branches could consider these overall directions relative to their local circumstances and develop policy decisions for their branches. Dr. Fleming acknowledged the quality of the preventive work VON was doing, but noted that, increasingly, publicly funded health units were being established and would assume responsibility for these services. The provision of care to the sick at home was the reason VON came into existence and the need was still there and would continue in the future. He recommended VON concentrate on this area.

The Depression of the 1930s slowed the development of the official public health programs so that VON continued with a program of services much as it had in the first quarter of the century. The Second World War also disturbed the orderly evolution of publicly administered services. It was not until the late 1940s and into the 1950s that a shift in VON services occurred. Although half the visits made by VON nurses continued to be pre- and postnatal, the other half included post-hospital care of medical and surgical patients, care of those with chronic illnesses, and the elderly. The emergence of home care programs in the late 1950s and 1960s and the expansion of public health nursing increased this trend so that in the early 1990s more than 98% of VON visits are for care of the ill either following hospitalization or as a result of chronic illnesses.

In 1990-1991, more than 200,000 people received VON visiting nursing services. The statistics also reveal the extent of the care needs of an aging population. Sixty-three percent of those receiving VON care in 1990-1991 were age 65 or older, and this group received 72% of the 3,092,934 visits that were made. In fact, almost half of VON patients are over 85 years of age.

The dominance of care of the ill produces another trend: specialized programs within the visiting nurse service. Until the late 1970s, VON nurses epitomized the generalist nurse. They provided care to everyone in their districts regardless of the nature of their nursing needs. Increased specialization within hospitals, increased technology, and the rapidly expanding knowledge base have made the wholly generalist model increasingly difficult to maintain. Specialty programs in enterostomal therapy, palliative care, respiratory care, peritoneal and hemodialysis, parenteral nutrition, gerontology, and cardiac rehabilitation are common in branches throughout the country. This results in pressure to prepare staff for these specialized roles.

VON STRUCTURE

As a voluntary nonprofit organization, VON has the responsibility of identifying unmet needs within each of the communities it serves and for developing services to meet those needs. Since communities vary in their service requirements, VON developed a series of separately incorporated local branches, each directed by a volunteer board of community-minded citizens and administered by a nurse. These branches provide different service programs depending on local needs. For example, in some communities, VON continues to provide school nursing because the public health nurses cannot meet this need; in several areas, VON nurses provide the preventive services in senior citizen apartment buildings, whereas this is done by public health nurses in other communities; and in some remote communities in Newfoundland, VON nurses operate primary care clinics, the only health services available locally, referring patients to physicians and hospitals in other towns when this is needed. Each VON branch is responsible for its own financial viability.

At the national level, VON has a board composed of representatives of provincial branches and members-at-large who have expertise in various areas important to VON. This board sets policies and standards for the entire network of branches. The national board is assisted by a national executive director, who, throughout VON's history, has always been a nurse, and by a small staff with nursing, health care programming, and financial expertise. The implementation of national policies and standards is accomplished by a network of provincial staff who work with the nurses in local branches. Originally, the organization consisted of only the local and national levels. However, constitutionally, health is a provincial matter in Canada, and as the health insurance programs evolved in the 1950s and 1960s, the need for provincial organizations to deal with governments and financing of community services became apparent. Now, all provinces but Prince Edward Island have a provincial board consisting of representatives of local branch boards and a provincial nurse administrator to provide direction and liaise with government.

FINANCING OF VON SERVICES

The history of finance in VON parallels or, perhaps more accurately, mirrors how Canada has come to pay for its health services. In 1897, there were no government financed health services; individuals paid directly for physicians' services, for hospital care, and for private-duty nurses; those who could not pay managed without. Consequently, VON operated on a fee-for-service basis, but patients were required to pay only what they could afford. The nurses had the responsibility of determining the fee with the patient. Throughout the years, a significant portion of all visits was free or only partly covered by the patient's fee. Free visits reached a peak in 1934 when patients were unable to pay for 63% of the visits. Covering the costs of the free and partial-pay visits was always a struggle.

Until the 1920s, public fund-raising appeals were held on a regular basis under the sponsorship of the Governor-General's wife. The money raised was used to finance the national office and subsidize local branches. The Ontario government provided a small annual grant to support branches in that province, and every local branch used ingenious fund-raising schemes to cover nurses' salaries and operating costs. VON branches were usually founding members of United Way fund-raising organizations in their local communities. VON was typical of nonprofit, voluntary organizations' approaches to financing their operations and dealing with their clients. Unlike the for-profit sector, voluntary organizations had policies of never denying service to people because they could not pay.

In 1909, a breakthrough occurred when the Metropolitan Life Insurance Company incorporated payment for VON visits into its health insurance policies. This program began in Montreal but quickly spread to other cities and other insurance companies. This meant that branches could rely on full payment for their insured patients and thus could begin to predict revenue. Furthermore it forced them to develop an accounting system for calculating actual costs per visit so that transactions with insurance companies conformed to good business practices. This paid off when governments began to assume the costs of visits to various sectors of patients.

Insured home care programs have evolved throughout Canada since 1950. In these programs, various services, including nursing, homemaking, and the rehabilitation therapies, are arranged for and provided without a direct fee to patients. VON has been an integral part of these developments.

The first coordinated and funded home care program was initiated by the Reddy Memorial Hospital in Montreal in 1950. A federal grant allowed hospital staff to identify patients who required post-hospital care and the hospital purchased visiting nursing services from VON Montreal. Following this project, the Montreal branch initiated a nurse liaison service at the Montreal General Hospital in which a VON nurse was assigned to units to identify and refer patients who could be discharged if home nursing care was provided. It was extended to other hospitals in Montreal and throughout Quebec based on recommendations from an evaluation by the Canadian Nurses Association. The Winnipeg branch introduced a liaison service to the Winnipeg General Hospital in 1961. Many other branches followed. These liaison nurses evolved into home care coordinators when more services were added and governments increasingly undertook the funding of community services.

A responsibility of voluntary charitable organizations is to identify and initiate services they believe the community requires. Usually voluntary organizations are the first to recognize unmet needs. Most governments are reluctant to fund service programs out of their regular operating funds until they are convinced that the programs are absolutely necessary. Consequently, voluntary organizations must raise the funds or seek special program demonstration grants from a provincial or the national government to establish a program and evaluate it to convince governments of its worthiness for regular, ongoing funding.

In 1963, the Ottawa branch was the first of 13 branches in Ontario to initiate and administer coordinated home care programs for post-hospital care. Provincial funding paid for the coordination and all the services, including nursing care to patients who qualified. By 1970, Ontario public health departments administered home care programs in some communities, and a decision was made provincially to transfer the administration of all home care programs to these official agencies. This is a typical course of action in community services in Canada; voluntary agencies initiate and run services, then governments fund them and assume their administration. In four communities, it was determined mutually by VON and public health boards that VON would continue to administer the program, but nine other programs were transferred. In other provinces, district home care boards were established and VON branches transferred programs they administered to them. By 1986, only the four branches in Ontario and the Winnipeg branch actually administered home care programs.

The evolution of insured services brought financial security to branches and, at the same time, threatened their existence. When governments accepted responsibility for funding the majority of visits to patients, the autonomy the branches had when they did the fund-raising to pay for services came to an end. In British Columbia, where VON established home care programs in the 1960s, the government contracted for the coordination and the visiting nursing services until the 1970s when it made home care a government agency, operated in the same way as public health nursing. This move led to the closure of all branches but one serving Richmond-Vancouver. This branch administered the Meals-on-Wheels service and saw the need for adult day care services. Consequently, in 1978, it established a center with specialized programs for people with Parkinson's disease, young people with trauma-induced neurological disabilities, and older people with dementia. A second center was established in 1985.

In Quebec, the Castonguay-Nepveu Commission led to a total reorganization of community services in the early 1970s. Local community services centers (Centres locaux du service communitaires, or CLSCs) were established throughout Quebec and a broad range of home care services (nursing, homemaking, physiotherapy, home helpers), as well as primary medical care and adult day care, were made available. These CLSCs were official government agencies and totally funded by them. The nurses in the VON branch in Montreal, which in the early 1970s was the largest branch in the country, transferred to government service and the branch was left to identify unmet needs that required services not provided by the government. On a much reduced scale, the branch developed and operated a nurse counseling and support service for newly diagnosed cancer patients, and after this service had become well entrenched in three hospitals, it turned the service over to the hospitals. Then the branch established a respite service for families of individuals with Alzheimer's disease.

In Ontario, Manitoba, Saskatchewan, Alberta, New Brunswick, and Newfoundland, some branches negotiated contracts to provide nursing visits with local home care programs. Unlike the days before the provincially-administered home care programs, the government paid for visits but also determined how frequently and on what schedule the visits would be made. VON nurses reported to their own supervisors and to home care coordinators and negotiated with the latter the type of nursing care the patients would receive. This transition from full autonomy with the nurse and patient determining what the nurse would do, how frequently visits would occur, and how much the patient was able to pay, to one of negotiation with home care agencies and, at times, responding to directives from them was difficult. Government departments believed that, because they were paying for services, it was their prerogative to control these services. VON branches, on the other hand, saw themselves as the originators of visiting nursing and home care programs and the agencies that kept such services alive during the lean years before government funding. Consequently, if home care coordinators made decisions VON nurses felt were not in the best interests of patients, the nurses made their views known. As well, the difference between assessing patients for nursing care needs (the prerogative of the visiting nurse) versus home care eligibility needs (the responsibility of the home care coordinator) can become very fuzzy when both assessments are performed by nurses.

In several communities, local administrators of home care programs, all of which are governmental agencies, operate their own visiting nurse services on the basis that they can do it more efficiently (i.e., at lower cost) than VON. This has occurred in some cities in Alberta, Saskatchewan, and Manitoba. This is a difficult challenge for VON because VON branches calculate per visit costs, which include office expenses, rent, nurses' salaries, transportation and administration, whereas governmental agencies do not maintain this type of costing. It may be that they can provide the service at a lower cost, but, to date, no governmental agency has produced a public document that demonstrates these cost savings.

Insured home care services have revolutionized community care. Many patients now receive services that allow them to return home from hospital earlier than would be possible without home care, other patients can avoid hospitalization completely, and still others can avoid or delay long-term institutional care. The fact that home care services are now paid for by the government introduces a new element into the delivery scene in several provinces: commercial for-profit agencies, such as Paramed, Med + Care, and Upjohn. Such agencies offer visiting nursing, homemaking, and personal care and now compete for home care contracts with traditional voluntary, nonprofit organizations such as the VON, Red Cross, and St. Elizabeth's Visiting Nursing Services. This puts considerable pressure on the voluntary sector to keep costs down and quality up to be competitive in the marketplace. Detailed cost accounting and computerized planning and billing are now an integral feature of many VON branches.

These three developments—the introduction of insured services, the potential for government agencies to absorb visiting nursing into their program, and the emergence of for-profit agencies—have changed the roles of VON boards and their nursing administrators.

Executive directors of branches now administer budgets that range in the millions of dollars. They must master the politics of the community health arena, and get to know the local and provincial players, the relationship between the party in power and the bureaucrats who administer home care, and the strategies in place for cost control. Contracts must be developed and negotiated with purchasers of VON services, requiring detailed costing of those programs. Some branches have unionized staff that require internal contract negotiations. Staff supervision is a requirement in smaller branches. Quality management must be introduced and maintained. The executive director of the branch is required to run a business and market products, while working with a voluntary board of directors. This is a unique role for nurse administrators in Canada. Their counterparts in official health agencies and hospitals are responsible to medical officers of health and hospital administrators respectively who, in turn, deal with the boards of those organizations. Furthermore these are not skills taught in most nursing programs. A continuing debate concerns whether the most appropriate preparation for the position of branch executive director is a graduate degree in a clinical nursing specialty or in health/business administration. The former provides a good background in clinical program development, whereas the latter produces graduates with more management skills. A closely related question is whether the administrator, particularly of large branches, needs to be a nurse. To date, the answer has always been yes.

The twin threats of government absorption of visiting nurse services and competition for contracts from for-profit agencies force VON branches to examine other services that are needed in the community and that may be appropriate for the branch to develop. This not only makes good business sense, but it is a responsibility of a voluntary agency. Program development has become a major thrust of branches across the country.

As mentioned earlier, the Richmond-Vancouver branch opened an adult day care center for physically and cognitively disabled people. The objective of this center and others that followed include long-term rehabilitation or maintenance of functioning within a recreational and social setting. Nurses have a key role in assessing individuals for the center, determining appropriate objectives for participation, and monitoring overall health of participants. However, adult day care is multidisciplinary care, and nursing complements recreational, physical, and occupational therapy. Thirteen branches currently offer adult day care.

Several branches administer community services that are not nursing related, such as visiting homemaking, Meals-on-Wheels, sitter services for disabled adults, and friendly/volunteer visiting. All of these programs are directed to supporting individuals so that they may remain in their homes in the community. A significant feature of these programs is the reliance on unpaid volunteers to deliver the service. Thousands of volunteers now augment professionally-based services and the trend is for this to increase in the future.

From 1988 to 1991, VON Canada received funding from Health and Welfare Canada under the Seniors Independence Program initiative to mount two programs throughout the country. The first national program was PEP (Promoting Elders Participation), a community development program. It involved assisting older residents in small rural communities to determine the kind of services they required to remain independent in their homes and, then, to establish these services. The provision of these services was sometimes undertaken by the residents themselves, or the group developed the skills of grantmanship and pursued funding from various sources to hire others to provide the sevices. PEP embodied the concept of empowerment of individuals to determine their needs for themselves. VON provided a facilitator to assist them with the process. This individual, who was trained as a social worker and gerontologist, functioned as a resource to these seniors in terms of sources of funding, and she worked with them to develop the knowledge and skills they required to manipulate the system so their independence was facilitated. Various communities in Newfoundland, Nova Scotia, and Ontario developed information services, Wheels-to-Meals, monthly lunches to provide a social outlet for relatively isolated seniors, transportation services, and home assistance programs.

After a community developed services the the residents desired, the facilitator moved on to other communitites.

The second national federally funded program, Keeping Canadians on their Feet, was another grassroots development project that assisted local communities to establish foot care clinics by using extant community groups as sponsors of these clinics. A team of highly trained foot care nurses worked with hundreds of community groups in churches, service organizations, and senior clubs to establish these clinics. Many of the clinics hired VON nurses to provide the foot care, but in Prince Edward Island, the Northwest Territories, and British Columbia, where there are no VON nurses, nurses employed by other agencies were trained by VON to provide the service.

These two programs represent a departure for VON from its usual method of operating; however, both are highly consistent with a voluntary organization. They are nonprofit, dependent on volunteers, and responsive to community needs. VON went to the government to generate funds to begin the programs, but both programs became self-sustaining after they were established.

CURRENT CHALLENGES TO THE VOLUNTARY SECTOR

Health care systems in every province are under pressure. Most of this pressure is generated by the relentlessness of cost escalations throughout the system. However, there is also a growing perception that too much care is concentrated in the acute care system and a shift needs to occur to a more fully developed community based system. This pressure is changing how services are delivered. These changes are affecting the voluntary sector by creating opportunities for innovation in service development and delivery, particularly in the community, and by requiring more efficiency in how services are delivered.

The original tradition of the voluntary charitable sector was to identify a need for a service, advocate for this service, find ways to implement it, and demonstrate to government the need to fund it on a continuing basis because of the service's fundamental value. It was understood that an established service would then be delivered by government and the voluntary agency would go on to other causes. This cycle was more theoretical than real. Essentially all voluntary agencies became attached to the services they delivered and were reluctant and resistant to turn them over to a government agency after they were well established. The usual pattern is for the voluntary organization to negotiate to continue to receive secure government funding to deliver the service. VON is an example of this. It took most provincial governments about 70 years after VON was established to begin to pay for visiting nursing services. During those 70 years, local branches became attached to their programs and were highly resistant to turning them over to governments in British Columbia, Quebec, and in parts of Alberta and Saskatchewan, although this, theoretically, was a natural evolution.

When fiscal pressures on government health expenditures increased in the late 1980s and early 1990s, the challenge to voluntary agencies was to convince governments that the voluntary organizations actually were the best to deliver the services they had begun and that they should receive guaranteed funds with as few restrictions as possible. This challenge is shifting now and is being replaced with the threat of loss of funding or a reduction in funding and an expectation that the agency will make up the difference. Alternately, governments are allowing for-profit agencies to provide services on a contractual basis on the premise that the profit sector is more efficient than the voluntary sector. These changes create difficult circumstances for the voluntary sector. Many for-profit agencies are part of large organizations that can afford to provide some services at a loss to get contracts. Not-for-profit agencies do not have this financial capacity. Circumstances challenge not-for-profit organizations, including the VON, to examine their operations to gain efficiencies wherever possible; however, if quality must be sacrificed beyond acceptable levels to gain the level of efficiency necessary for financial viability, the agency may decide it is not worth it. The agency may then decide to shift the nature of services it offers and to begin the cycle of advocacy and program development again.

The other major challenge to voluntary agencies comes from the shift in community care that is occurring in most provinces. This shift might be expected to create wonderful opportunities for voluntary community agencies because of the expanded range and quantity of services that will need to be developed. However, expansion of services and guaranteed government funding frequently can lead governments to conclude that it is easier to coordinate and administer services themselves than to coordinate services offered by a spectrum of agencies. To maintain service delivery contracts, voluntary agencies are required to compromise some of their independence in the areas of quality assurance, recording methods, and communication and to participate in multi-agency systems.

CONCLUSION

The voluntary charitable sector has a long tradition of service to Canadians. Voluntary charitable organizations are responsible for creating most of the services that are now part of the insured health system that Canadians take for granted. The charitable organizations are an important source of employment for many professionals, including nurses, social workers, occupational therapists, and support workers such as homemakers and home health aides. Through VON and other smaller voluntary visiting nurse agencies, such as St. Elizabeth's in Ontario and the Martha Home Nursing Service in Nova Scotia, nurses initiate and administer important community services.

The 1990s will present many challenges to this sector as the health care system reshapes itself. By its very nature, however, the voluntary sector has proven to be resilient and innovative. It should do well.

REFERENCES

Gibbon, J.M. (1947). *Victorian Order of Nurses for Canada; Fiftieth anniversary 1897-1947*. Ottawa: VON Canada, 1947.

Gibbon, J.M., & Mathewson, M.S. (1947). *Three centuries of Canadian Nursing*. Toronto: Macmillan.

Greenhous, B. (Ed.) (1987). *Guarding the goldfields: The story of the Yukon field force*. Toronto: Dundurn Press.

Hampton, I.A. (Ed.) (1949). *Nursing of the sick, 1893: Papers and discussions of the International Congress of Charities, Correction and Philanthropy, Chicago, 1893* (Reissue). New York: McGraw-Hill Book Company.

Revenue Canada, Taxation. (1990). *Charities, Non-Profit Organizations and the Income Tax Act, 1990*. Ottawa: Author.

Shackleton, D. (1983). *Missioners of health: A history of the Victorian Order of Nurses for Canada*. Unpublished manuscript, VON Canada.

SECTION VI

FACING THE FUTURE

Nurses must be prepared to take action to help create the futures that they wish to see for health care for Canadians. This photograph shows Alice Baumgart, president, and Judith Oulton, executive director, Canadian Nurses Association, presenting a CNA brief to the Senate Committee studying effects of the Goods and Services Tax (GST). The CNA brief, presented in June 1990, warned of possible negative effects of the tax on health care services. (Photograph courtesy of *The Canadian Nurse*.)

CHAPTER THIRTY-ONE

Who Owns the Future?

JENNIECE LARSEN, RN, PhD
ALICE BAUMGART, RN, PhD

Jenniece Larsen, RN, BScN, MEd, PhD (Alberta), is Professor and Director, School of Nursing, University of Manitoba.

Alice Baumgart, RN, BSN (British Columbia), MSc (McGill), PhD (Toronto), is Vice-Principal, Human Services, Queen's University.
Both have experience in creating nursing futures. Dr. Larsen created new programs and projects in all her work settings. A recent example is the Northern Bachelor's of Nursing Program at the University of Manitoba, which was launched in 1990. For this she had to obtain new financial resources from the Government of Manitoba and Health and Welfare Canada, and work collaboratively with the Swampy Cree Tribal Council and Keewatin Community College. Dr. Baumgart has been instrumental in changing the ways that Canadian nurses think about themselves and others. For the past decade, for example, she has spent enormous time and energy in making Canadian nurses aware of the effects of gender on the nursing profession.

A ssuming we do not live in an oppressive society, each of us owns his or her body. Assuming a memory in good working order, each of us owns his or her thoughts and reflections. Assuming an inclination and capacity to formulate a code of behavior, each of us owns integrity and principles. Assuming the necessary resources, each of us can own worldly goods.

Given certain assumptions, there is much that we might argue that we own in the present. However, under what assumptions might we say we own the future? How can anyone own what has not yet happened? We know that a future, or more accurately, multiple and overlapping futures, will emerge, but where will ownership reside? The nature of the human condition is that we do not "live" just in the present. We may reside in the present and remember the past, but we also, apparently unlike our closest animal relatives and other highly intelligent species, anticipate the future. Presumably all humans think about what might happen in our personal lives: our health, prosperity, family, friends, work. Some of us may reach beyond our personal concerns and consider the prospects for people we do not know, the environment, the economy, and issues of war and peace. A few ethereal beings may even contemplate cosmic concerns such as the future of earth and our planetary system.

In what sense might we consider that we could own these issues? Can we claim to own our personal future? Certainly no one could own anything in the future in the way we own our lives in the present. But we can act today in certain ways in an attempt to influence the future. We do this with children. We do not own our children, at least in the sense that we own things, but we typically try to shape their thinking so that we may have some influence over their lives as adults. We anticipate that our children will reflect our values and secretly hope that they uphold these values more faithfully than we have. In this sense, we endeavor to own the future. Each of us attempts, within our apparent sphere of influence, and this usually extends no further than family, to shape a small part of the future.

But what of the larger dimensions of the future? Who owns these? Who owns the future of war and peace, health, education, and environment, to say nothing of values such as liberty, equality, and fraternity? To paraphrase an old idea, if history teaches us nothing else, it informs us that evil will prevail in the world when good women and good men do nothing.

Before the conditions of ownership can be decided, and the assumptions that would justify them, the realm of future thinking must be examined. The oldest and still most common type of futurism is making predictions. Predictions from the past that have or have not come true can be reviewed, as well as current predictions on the nature of some future world.

Predictions from the past usually seem quaint and often comical. Daniel Webster, for example, in an American Senate speech in 1848, issued this passionate declaration:

> I have not heard of anything, and cannot conceive of anything more ridiculous, more absurd, and more affrontive to all sober judgment than the cry that we are profiting by the acquisition of New Mexico and California. I hold that they are not worth a dollar. (Dickson, 1979, p. 36)

In 1939, Dr. Alfred Velpeau confidently stated:

> The abolishment of pain in surgery is a chimera. It is absurd to go on seeking it today. "Knife" and "pain" are two words in surgery that must forever be associated in the consciousness of the patient. To this compulsory combination we shall have to adjust ourselves. (Dickson, 1979, p. 36)

Whereas Daniel Webster's prediction is hilarious and Dr. Velpeau's is merely wrong, that made by Dr. Forbes Winslow in 1910 is debatable:

> We are gradually approaching, with the decadence of youth, a near proximity to a nation of madmen. By comparing the lunacy statistics of 1809 to those of 1909 . . . an insane world is looked forward to by me with a certainty in the not far distant future. (Dickson, 1979, p. 36)

Indeed, were one, for example, to transpose the last two numbers in the dates in the above statement so that 1809 was 1890 and 1909 was 1990, Dr. Winslow might be perceived by some as a provocative contemporary observer.

Sometimes predictions are uncannily accurate. In the nineteenth century, Jules Verne, for example, described a trip to the moon that was very like the actual Apollo landing in 1969 (Dickson, 1979, p. 36). His spacecraft size was within 17 inches of the length of the actual craft, his crew size of three was identical to that of Apollo, and his spacecraft was to leave from Florida, just as Apollo actually did many decades later. Of course, Verne was wrong about many other things. For those with an inclination to speculate on the future, two fundamental rules about making predictions apply: one, make many predictions to increase the chances of being right at least some of the time, and two, avoid providing dates when anything will happen so that you can never be proven wrong.

In the era of Jules Verne, or H.G. Wells, or Edward Bellamy, the preferred vehicle for the futurist was the novel. Today, fortified by the resources of a university, research institute, or think tank, the futurist engages in consultant work for corporations, advises on special projects for the military and other agencies of government, and writes articles and nonfiction books. One other difference is that the predictive insight of current futurists, unlike those in the past, cannot be assessed until after some years have passed.

What makes a good futurist? A study of futurists by Coates and Jarratt (1989) indicates that a good, well-rounded futurist must do three things well: characterize the society or situation being studied and recognize, outline, and account for the present conditions; generate, at a minimum, a coherent image or images of the future; and provide a road map or description of how to get there (Coates and Jarratt, 1989, p. 45). Coates and Jarratt describe good futurists as remarkably nonscientific: they do not use qualitative techniques, they have no grand theory of social change, and they rarely refer to each other or cite each other in their work. The futurists selected for evaluation in the study were all white males, from 42 to 76 years in age, with an average of 58 years. One woman was invited and declined; other women considered for inclusion were deemed not of the stature of the men selected or focused on women's issues only.

These futurists had areas of general agreement, as follows:

- Human systems and institutions are becoming more complex, and new tools will be needed to cope with this complexity
- Current institutional structures, such as governments, are not the answer to this increasing complexity
- Science and technology will drive change
- Energy, specifically the transition away from oil, will be a key feature of the next few decades
- World economic growth will slow
- Significant changes will take place with a framework of continuity
- Nuclear war is unlikely
- All continents will be increasingly interdependent
- The United States will gradually become less influential in world affairs
- Educational systems are in long-term decline and may lack the capacity to improve

- The information society will make greater demands on basic literacy and competence of citizens
- Aging of the population in the United States will lead to a more rigid society and to intergenerational conflict (Coates and Jarratt, 1989, pp. 20-22)

Perhaps because all these futurists were male, there was little attention to the future worldwide status of women, the role of minorities in society and related cultural conflicts, family life, housing issues, death and dying, crime, and religion (Coates and Jarratt, 1989). Are these issues of no concern, or were they eliminated or minimized as a result of having no women in the group of futurists under study? As indicated previously, several women futurists were considered for this study but were rejected because they were "narrowly focused or ideologically oriented towards women's issues only" (Coates and Jarratt, 1989, p. 10). Does this imply that details of day-to-day living, which consume most of the energy of so many women throughout the world, are excluded from "futurism" because they are of little interest to men? Further, does this suggest that more women must become futurists, or at least future oriented, to ensure that issues of primary concern to women are not ignored? Ultimately, what this presumably indicates is that women must press their concerns on the agenda of futurists, whether male or female.

The major focus of futurism is prediction, the attempt to determine what will happen next year or next decade or next century based on trends and developments today. Another focus of futurism might be initiation, the process of imagining a desired future and then working back to the present to determine what needs to be done today to increase the likelihood of achieving the desired state in the future. Whereas prediction at least pretends to be logical, rational, and objective, initiation is basically political, goal oriented, and, ultimately, passionate. Initiation is the conscious attempt to create a desired future. Achieving the desired future requires a three-stage process of articulated mental images: possible futures, probable futures, and preferable futures.

Possible futures are primarily prediction based on creativity and intuition rather than on any rules of science. Possible futures are constructed from everything that can evolve from the current state—trends, information about the world, all possible data. The obvious problem with possible futures is that no future, no matter how horrendous or how divine, is excluded. Everything is possible—from nuclear holocaust to heaven on earth; from starvation and degradation by millions in an environmentally impoverished planet to a world in which all are healthy, well fed, and active.

Probable futures are potential outcomes leavened by judgment, insight, bias, and all the glories and frailties of the human intellect. Few futurists believe that total nuclear holocaust is a probable future because, if so, at least in the near future, why would one write about it if we are all doomed anyway. Futurists consider the almost countless nuclear weapons around the world and ask: Is it not likely that someone will use one, which will lead to a second use and the inevitable descent into hell? Many current futurists conclude that, since a nuclear weapon has not been used in nearly half a century, they will not be used. We have been inoculated, they say, once in Hiroshima and again in Nagasaki, against the horrors of nuclear war.

This does not mean that futurists are optimists. For example, a consensus of the 17 futurists in the study is that Africa will be a "total disaster that will require vast amounts of resources" (Coates and Jarratt, 1989, p. 78). On the other hand, Canada is viewed as "linked to the future of the United States. Could grow rapidly if separatism does not cause crisis" (p. 77).

Probable futures are the most likely of possible futures and are the result of the application of some judgment to the information available. Preferable futures are possible futures that could lead to desirable outcomes for mankind, or a country or region, or an organization, association, or profession. Preferable futures are those for which the ideals and mission of the person or group involved are believed to be desirable. In the three-stage process of delineating the futures outlined here, it is only in the latter stage (that of preferable futures) that values become paramount. Possible futures and probable futures are primarily value-free predictions. In contrast, preferable futures are value-rich anticipations and, as such, are usually transformed into a deliberate endeavor to influence events in such a way as to make the preferable congruent with the probable.

After a preferable future is determined, this image of the future must then be tested with the following criteria: Is it feasible? Is it ethical? Is it affordable?

The feasibility of any preferable future must be assessed in two dimensions: technology and human nature. Does this preferable future depend on some advanced technology in electronics, computers, biotechnology, or other materials that are not yet available? If so, then this future may not be feasible. More fundamental is the human-nature test. If the feasibility of this preferred future depends on a basic change in human nature, then failure is almost certain because human nature appears highly stable and resistant to significant change. Most utopias founder because they assume that fundamental change in human nature is possible. When this change does not occur, the basic tenets of the utopia collapse. The disintegration of the Soviet bloc in 1989 to 1991 gives dramatic evidence of this.

The second criterion is ethical. A future preferable from the perspective of one group may be abhorrent to another. Any future based on the premise of exploitation of others is ethically dubious and is likely to be vigorously resisted for that reason. The extreme, a future preferable to one group but that tramples on the rights of others, will lead to war. History is replete with examples.

And, of course, no matter how preferable a future may seem, all things are limited by the third criterion: resources. The world has a finite amount of resources, and these resources are competed for by those with other visions of the future. The achievement of any preferred future must be accomplished within these financial limitations. Naturally, the more compelling the future vision, the more likely it will attract the resources necessary for implementation.

Ultimately, any preferable future depends on the human factor. Change is created by singular human beings, those whom Scharf describes as the "boldly bold" (1985, p. 9). Scharf suggests four archetypes based on predilection to change: the cautiously cautious, the boldly cautious, the cautiously bold, and the boldly bold.

The cautiously cautious are so timid and fearful of making mistakes that they are afraid to even advocate change, much less practice it. The boldly cautious would like to be bold, but their reticent nature ensures that they spend most of their time anticipating failure and planning their retreat. The cautiously bold can accept a few changes, but are continually "looking over their shoulder, as if they believe that someone is gaining on them." The boldly bold are those who make a difference, those with courage and convictions, "a fanciful few, each with his own piece of the sky" (Scharf, 1985, p. 9).

Scharf began his "Water Walking" article with an observation about American naturalist and philosopher Henry David Thoreau and Thoreau's beloved Walden Pond. He returned to this image in his conclusion:

> Walden Pond is as small in size as it is large in frame. With the right approach, one might be able to walk in it. The cautiously cautious would simply announce that, if it were possible to water walk, someone would already have done it. The boldly cautious would march presidentially up to the edge and then remember the meeting that they had to attend. The cautiously bold might actually try it but so tentatively that they would sink half way across. The boldly bold would hit the shore line with enough purposefulness that they would, more often than not, make it over in one big hop. The boldly bold had learned that water walking has less to do with how you move your feet than where you set your sight. (Scharf, 1985, p. 9)

CONCLUSION

This chapter began with the question of who owns the future. Of course no one in any literal sense could own the future. However, the future is amenable to influence, and generating this influence is a function of the clarity of the vision of the individual or group wishing to influence the future. Clarity of vision depends on the process of distillation of preferable futures from probable futures, which in turn are derived from possible futures.

The answer to who owns the future is thus clear. The future is owned by those who pay for it, not with money but with ideas and will, purposefulness and drive, ambition and insight, and convictions and intuition. The future is owned by those who want it most and those who are willing to pay the highest price to bring their vision to fruition.

ACKNOWLEDGEMENT

This chapter was compiled with the assistance of John S. Scharf, Kelsey Institute, Saskatoon.

REFERENCES

Coates, J., & Jarratt, J. (1989). *What futurists believe*. Mount Airy, MD: Lomond.

Dickson, P. (1989). "It'll never fly, Orville": Two centuries of embarrassing predictions, *Saturday Review, 12*(79), 36.

Scharf, J. (1985, December 1). Water walking in six easy lessons. *College Canada*, p. 9.

Index